EU law in the UK

SYLVIA de MARS

OXFORD
UNIVERSITY PRESS

Great Clarendon Street, Oxford, OX2 6DP,
United Kingdom

Oxford University Press is a department of the University of Oxford.
It furthers the University's objective of excellence in research, scholarship,
and education by publishing worldwide. Oxford is a registered trade mark of
Oxford University Press in the UK and in certain other countries

Impression: 1

Published in the United States of America by Oxford University Press
198 Madison Avenue, New York, NY 10016, United States of America

British Library Cataloguing in Publication Data

Data available

Library of Congress Control Number: 2020933575

ISBN 978–0–19–880592–2

Printed and bound in the UK by
TJ International Ltd

About the author

Dr Sylvia de Mars is a Senior Lecturer in Law at Newcastle University, where she specializes in EU law and public international law. Her most recent work has focused on the trade dimension of Brexit, and particularly how it affects Northern Ireland. Alongside her academic commitments, between 2018 and 2020, Sylvia worked as a Senior Researcher in EU and International Law and Policy for the House of Commons Library.

To Laura and Zoe, for their endless patience and support

Context for this chapter

Each chapter begins by setting out a hypothetical scenario, an extract from an official document or meeting record, or real-life quote, which provides context to the topics under discussion throughout the chapter.

> **Context for this chapter**
>
> Bristol, 14 March 2019
>
> Dear Ingrid,
>
> So—a lot has happened since I last emailed you! Sorr

Discussing the scenario, or Discussing the quote

'Discussing the Scenario/Discussing the Quote' questions are positioned throughout each chapter, and refer back to the 'Context: Scenario/Context: Quote' at the start of the chapter. You are asked to consider the legal implications of what you have learnt in the section of the chapter, within the context of the opening scenario or quote. At the end of the chapter, you are asked to consolidate your answers to these questions, and you can find guidance on how to approach these questions in the online resources.

> **Discussing the scenario**
>
> Think back to your answer to the (fictional) restriction
> think it violated Article 45 TFEU? Now consider if you
> to speak Spanish, even if they teach English, can be j
> *Gebhard* test? What would make such a requirement

Boxed extracts from cases, legislation, and articles

Boxed case extracts, articles, and legislation ease you in to being able to read and digest primary material, with additional support in the form of highlighting the key points in bold. The extracts are introduced to you where the language is more complicated, and the author discusses the subject's most influential cases in more depth in the main text.

> **European Union (Withdrawal Act) 2018, s**
>
> 4. The Charter of Fundamental Rights is **not part of**
> 5. Subsection 4 does not affect the retention in dom
> dance with this Act of **any fundamental rights o**
> **the Charter** (and references to the Charter in any
> purpose, to be read as if they were references to

Pause for reflection

'Pause for Reflection' boxes raise important points and pose questions that will help you to think carefully about the laws discussed, helping you to critically reflect on the law, appreciate its contested and continually evolving nature (particularly in light of Brexit), and form your own opinions.

> **Pause for reflection**
>
> Consider all of the forms of secondary legislation that
> 1. Which of these do you think the Member States p
> 2. Which do you think the EU prefers to use?
> 3. Is there a legislative form that seems to strike a 'c
> State desires?

EU law in practice

'EU Law in Practice' boxes contain real-life events and the impact these events have on EU law in the UK. These real-life situations bring home the relevance of EU law in the UK, and focus closely on what is happening in the real world as a result of the Brexit vote.

EU law in practice

The notion of the EU 'overreaching' into dome
erendum outcome, where the concept of 'tak
tions and the messages of 'Leave' campaigr
that the UK had engaged actively with just hc

Key points

Following the conclusion, the essential concepts of the chapter are summarized in bullet points to help you to remember the key points of law covered. Tables and diagrams are also used to consolidate your learning, and ensure fundamental concepts are easily-referable as you progress to more difficult topics, and come to revise.

Key points

- Under Article 49 TFEU, EU nationals and ber State, and to equal treatment with na refers to a stable and continuous presen
- Under 56 TFEU, EU nationals and comp

Assess your learning

These end-of-chapter questions fall into two categories: questions to test understanding, and questions to be used for exam practice. They are designed to help you to think about what you have learnt, track your progress, and go back to any sections you need to spend more time on, thanks to helpful prompts cross-referencing to relevant sections of the chapter.

Assess your learning

1. Did economically inactive EU national 13.2.)
2. In what ways did the movement rights 1992? (See Sections 13.3 and 13.5.2.)

Further reading

Suggestions for further reading (both books and websites) focus your reading as you widen and deepen your knowledge of EU law.

Further reading

Catherine Barnard, 'So Long, Farewell, Auf V mental Rights' (2019) 82(2) MLR 350.

Gráinne de Búrca, 'After the EU Charter of F rights adjudicator?' (2013) 20 Maastricht

Guide to the online resources

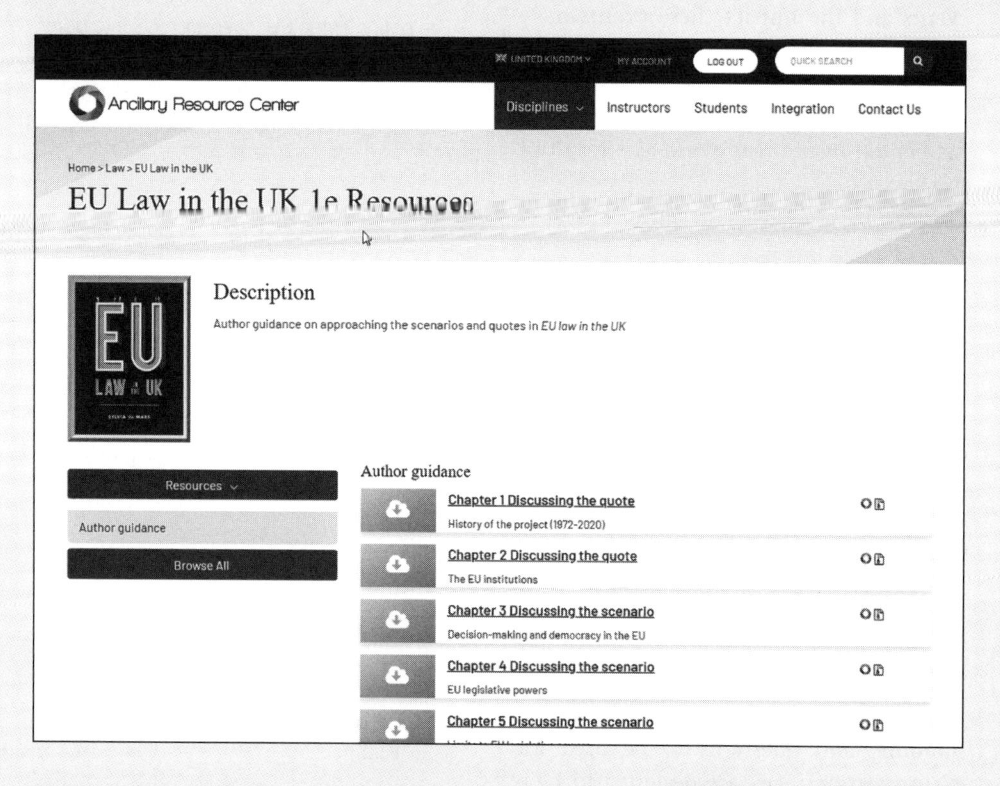

Sylvia de Mars has provided a suite of comprehensive guides to approaching the Discussing the Quote/Scenario questions in each chapter. These guides support the contextual approach of the book, and are designed to enhance your understanding of the topic of EU law. You can find these guides in the online resources. (www.oup.com/he/demars1e).

Acknowledgements

Extracts from EUR-Lex are reproduced with permission of the European Union, in accordance with Creative Commons Attribution 4.0 International: https://creativecommons.org/licenses/by/4.0/

Figure 4.1 reproduced with permission from: Woods, L., Watson, P., Steiner, J. and Costa, M., *Steiner & Woods EU Law* 13th ed (Oxford University Press, 2017)

Contents in brief

Detailed contents

Abbreviations

ACP	African, Caribbean and Pacific
AFSJ	Area of Freedom, Security and Justice
AG	Advocate General
AJCL	American Journal of Comparative Law
CAP	Common Agricultural Policy
CCP	Common Commercial Policy
CETA	Canada-EU Comprehensive Economic and Trade Agreement
CFP	Common Fisheries Policy
CFSP	Common Foreign and Security Policy
CJEU	Court of Justice of the European Union
CLJ	Cambridge Law Journal
CLPD	Competition Law and Policy Debate
CMA	UK Competition and Markets Authority
CMLRev	Common Market Law Review
DCFTA	Deep and Comprehensive Free Trade Agreement
DG	Directorate General
EBLR	European Business Law Review
EC	European Community
ECA 1972	European Communities Act 1972
ECHR	European Convention on Human Rights
ECLR	European Competition Law Review
ECSC	European Coal and Steel Community
ECtHR	European Court of Human Rights
EEA	European Economic Area
EEC	European Economic Community Treaty
EFTA	European Free Trade Association
EHRLR	European Human Rights Law Review
EJIL	European Journal of International Law
ELRev	European Law Review
EMU	Economic and Monetary Union
EPL	European Public Law
ERPL	European Review of Private Law
Eur Const Law Rev	European Constitutional Law Review
Eur Law J	European Law Journal
EWM	Early Warning Mechanism
FTA	free trade agreement
GATT	General Agreement on Tariffs and Trade
GCLR	Global Competition Litigation Review
Ger Law J	German Law Journal
ICLQ	International and Comparative Law Quarterly

I-CON	International Journal of Constitutional Law
IIC	International Review of Intellectual Property and Competition Law
ILJ	Industrial Law Journal
Int J Const Law	International Journal of Constitutional Law
Int J Law Context	International Journal of Law in Context
Int TLR	International Trade Law and Regulation
ISDS	investor-state dispute settlement
J Eur Integr	Journal of European Integration
JCMS	Journal of Common Market Studies
JEPP	Journal of European Public Policy
JHA	Justice and Home Affairs
JSEL	Harvard Journal of Sports and Entertainment Law
JWIT	Journal of World Investment and Trade
LIEI	Legal Issues of European Economic Integration
LQR	Law Quarterly Review
MEEs	measures having equivalent effect
MFN	most-favoured-nation
MLR	Modern Law Review
MSA 1988	Merchant Shipping Act 1988
NATO	North Atlantic Treaty Organization
NCA	National Competition Authority
NILQ	Northern Ireland Law Quarterly
OECD	Organisation for Economic Cooperation and Development
OJ	Official Journal
OJLS	Oxford Journal of Legal Studies
OLP	ordinary legislative procedure
OMT	Outright Monetary Transactions
Parliam Aff	Parliamentary Affairs
PJCC	Police and Judicial Co-operation in Criminal Manners
PL	Public Law
QMV	qualified majority voting
RCEEL	Review of Central and East European Law
REFIT	Regulatory Fitness and Performance Programme
SEA	Single European Act 1986
SLIM	Simple Legislation for the Internal Market
TEU	Treaty of European Union
TFEU	Treaty on the Functioning of the European Union
UKSC	United Kingdom Supreme Court
West Eur Polit	West European Politics
World TR	World Trade Review
WTO	World Trade Organization
YEL	Yearbook of European Law
YLJ	Yale Law Journal

List of figures and tables

Tables of cases

United Kingdom

European Union

Court of Justice and Court of First Instance/ General Court (alphabetical)

Court of Justice (numerical)

Court of First Instance/General Court (numerical)

Opinions

Commission Decisions

International

European Court of Human Rights

National

Germany

Tables of legislation

Statutes

Statutory Instruments

European Union

Treaties, Agreements and Declarations

Regulations

Directives

Decisions

International instruments

1

History of the project (1972–2020)

Context for this chapter

'The EU is a fundamentally different creature from the one on which we voted in 1975.'

Andrew Tyrie MP, European Union (Referendum) Bill, 5 July 2013, col 1171

1.1 Introduction

The UK and the EU have, since the EU's inception, had a relationship that can at best be described as *uncomfortable*. An examination of the history of the EU, and UK participation in the EU project at its key developmental moments, will make it clear that the referendum outcome on 23 June 2016 was perhaps a *shock*, but not a wholly unpredictable one. The EU's overall goals have never quite matched the UK's reasons for participating in the project, and without significant mutual compromises, the UK might have left the EU in just about every decade since it joined. This chapter will set out what goals the EU project has had over time, and how these have fitted with UK priorities and interests. It will look at each key revision of the EU's foundational Treaties in turn, and conclude with some thoughts on what will happen next in the now four-year-long Brexit saga.

The quote by Andrew Tyrie MP at the start of this chapter is one to be kept in mind while reading this chapter. Has the EU changed fundamentally over time—as many of those who have voted to leave the EU in the June 2016 referendum have argued—or are such changes overstated, and has it always been clear where the EU was going?

Before we get into this discussion, there are a few key concepts for you to understand. The first is that the EU's existence is rooted in **treaties**. Treaties are effectively contracts signed by different countries, governing their future relationships—they aim to provide clarity and legal certainty to countries when they engage in complicated international relations. The principle underpinning all treaties is that of **sovereignty**. In the UK we associate this term primarily with 'parliamentary sovereignty', or the supreme power of

Parliament over other UK governmental bodies. However, in more general terms, sovereignty simply means the ability to take fully free and independent decisions. Countries are sovereign, and what this means is that no country can be forced by another country to accept any laws. In the context of international relations, this means that signing up to any treaty is a *voluntary* act by a country. However, once a treaty is in force, countries are bound by the rules stated in that treaty. This limits their sovereignty while they are signed up to a treaty.

Ultimately, however, countries can also *withdraw* from treaties at any point in time—and so they retain the final sovereignty to determine what laws apply to them in their international actions. In the EU context, the UK willingly limited its sovereignty when it joined the EU in 1972 (in a process called 'accession'). It has now exercised its sovereignty again by withdrawing from the EU.

1.2 The early 1950s: origins of the project

1.2.1 The idea of a united Europe

The easiest way to conceptualize the European Union is perhaps as a grand experiment of cooperation. This may seem counter-intuitive, but in legal terms, the EU is still very much a baby. Consider the vast spans of time in which there was *no* cooperation on the European continent—instead, there were constant attempts by different sovereign territories to invade *other* sovereign territories. This marks the vast majority of European history: periods of calm in these ongoing wars signified that the conquering territory was particularly powerful, rather than that there was any legitimate *peace* in Europe. In a way, when we discuss Europe's history, what we are looking at is *an EU by force*: the Holy Roman Empire wanted a single, united Europe much in the way Napoleon and Hitler also attempted to create it.

The root of these 'earlier' versions of united Europes, however, lay in the dominance of a single nation. What marks the EU as being a break from that past is that it does not demand a single *dominant* member, but rather counts on *shared* membership in order to maintain both peace and stability in the region of Europe.

This idea did not emerge for the first time after World War II, though it did gain potency then. Indeed, the more costly the conflicts raging across Europe as a continent became, and the more lives they cost and nations they involved, the more philosophers in Europe slowly started thinking of *other* means of coexisting. Ideas of international cooperation have been around since the seventeenth century; William Penn, an English philosopher, published *An Essay Towards the Present and Future Peace of Europe* in 1693 which suggested that, to prevent wars, there should be a cross-European parliament of some sorts, populated by representatives from all European nations.[1]

The idea did not catch the attention of the heads of European states back then, nor did the more radical suggestion put forward by French philosopher Saint-Simon, who in 1814 argued strongly for the need of a single centralized political institute that would govern *over* nation states when it came to issues of common interest.[2] He did not propose the abolition of national parliaments, but rather wished for some sort of European

[1] William Penn, *The Political Writings of William Penn* (Liberty Fund, 2002).

[2] Henri de Saint-Simon, *On the Reorganisation of the European Society* (1814).

parliament to deal with these 'common interests'. His ideal European parliament would have two houses, representing civil society in a House of Commons and the noble classes in a House of Lords.

The Penns and Saint-Simons were not heeded by the ruling classes in Europe, however. Ideas such as theirs did not catch the attention of governments until European wars started becoming global. World War I was a turning point of sorts, in that it led—for the very first time—to the concession on the part of sovereign nations that they *needed* to create spaces in which they could deal with their disagreements as an alternative to going to war. This led to the establishment of the precursor of the United Nations: the League of Nations. However, the League of Nations had such limited powers that it was unlikely to actually *stop* wars. By the late 1920s, the French in particular noticed the political sentiment sweeping across Germany's post-war Weimar Republic, and the French Foreign Minister, Jacques Briand, wrote a memorandum in 1929 that proposed a European Federal Union: a bolstering of the League of Nations, actually *forcing* European nations to cooperate rather than merely giving them space in which to do so.[3]

None of the 26 European countries to which he sent his proposal was amenable to it at the time; subjugating sovereign nation states to some sort of all-powerful European centralized government was seen as too radical and unnecessary. World War II, however, would make this idea seem far less radical, and far more necessary.

1.2.2 The aftermath of World War II

The 1950s were the start of a new era of international relations in a lot of ways. Many European countries, formerly in charge of world-spanning empires, suddenly found themselves economically devastated. War was expensive, both in pure monetary terms and in terms of its overall impact on the available workforce, and these sovereign nations had to swallow significant pride for the sake of ongoing survival. More than that, however, World War II also made European countries much more willing to work together purely for the sake of *preventing* further wars. This combination of moral and economic drivers led to a slew of cooperation efforts, primarily in the form of international organizations being agreed to by many different countries. Such organizations spanned the entire world in cases such as the United Nations and the General Agreement on Tariffs and Trade (GATT), setting out common terms for trade between sovereign states;[4] or they focused on the European continent in cases such as the Council of Europe and the North Atlantic Treaty Organization (NATO). The treaties produced by these organizations required cooperation in distinct policy areas: in some, such as the Council of Europe's European Human Rights Convention, the concession on shared standards in different countries was a relatively smooth process, as there was a general will to achieve a shared standard of human rights. The GATT, as precursor to the World Trade Organization, on the other hand, required the sacrifice of a different and less *morally* necessary set of national powers, in that it limited the economic policy options of all member countries for the duration of membership. Not all countries, whether in Europe or elsewhere, were immediately 'on board' with the sacrifice of sovereignty in these economic fields.

[3] Jacques Briand, *Memorandum on the Organisation of a System of Federal European Union* (1929).

[4] The GATT itself was not formally an organization, but worked as one in practice until in 1994 the World Trade Organization was formally established.

The United States led the charge on economic cooperation at the expense of sovereignty, and it did so in two ways. First, it was the major proponent of the GATT internationally, encouraging free trade on a global scale for the benefit of all countries. Secondly, in 1947 it launched the European Recovery Plan (known as the Marshall Plan), giving both loans and grants to the war-ravaged western European economies in exchange for more open trade relationships with the United States. The Marshall Plan was tremendously successful in stimulating European economic recovery, but it was also tremendously expensive, and not intended to last beyond four years. So what was to become of Europe *after* the United States' financial support?

Could Europe be financially independent without a functioning German economy? Probably not; and this seems to have been understood by all parties negotiating a peace at the end of World War II. West Germany, after all, was going to be a Marshall Plan recipient, and was intended to regain control over its own industrial territories after a four-year period of international oversight. However, while the idea of Germany regaining control over the Ruhr made economic sense, on a political level it gave the French nightmares. With control over the Ruhr, West Germany would be in charge of a significant proportion of European steel production. And what would Germany do with steel? It could clearly be used in developing military-grade weaponry . . . which was an activity the French absolutely did not want to see the Germans engaging in again.

1.2.3 The Schuman Declaration

Much as the first idea of a 'European Federation' had come from a French politician, the birth of the EU project can be traced back to a French politician. The impending potential threat of West Germany's ability to rearm had the French thinking desperately about ways to counter this threat. Finally, an inventive solution was drafted by a French civil servant by the name of Jean Monnet, and delivered by the French Minister of Finance: Robert Schuman.[5]

The Schuman Declaration proposed something far simpler than European federalism. It merely suggested the pooling of French and German coal and steel production under a common, independent High Authority, which would make decisions that would bind France and Germany.

The Schuman Declaration 1950 (emphasis added)

Europe will not be made all at once, or according to a single plan. It will be built through **concrete achievements** which first create **a de facto solidarity**. The coming together of the nations of Europe requires **the elimination of the age-old opposition of France and Germany**. Any action taken must in the first place concern these two countries . . .

The solidarity in production thus established will make it plain that **any war between France and Germany becomes** not merely unthinkable, but **materially impossible** . . .

The pooling of coal and steel production should immediately provide **for the setting up of common foundations** for economic development as **a first step in the federation of Europe**.

[5] See http://europa.eu/european-union/about-eu/symbols/europe-day/schuman-declaration_en.

Germany was relieved at the proposal—as it permitted it to become a functioning economic actor again—and various other countries in Europe wished to participate in this coal-and-steel-sharing project as well. Consequently, in 1951, we see the birth of the European Coal and Steel Community (ECSC), joined by France, Germany, Italy, and the Benelux countries. The ECSC Treaty created the 'High Authority' that Robert Schuman had alluded to. It was composed of international civil servants, and wholly independent from the six member countries of the Community. It had unheard-of powers: it could set prices for the sale of coal and steel, as well as rules on how it was to be produced. However, demonstrating again that this was indeed a concession of sovereignty on the part of independent nations, the High Authority itself was supervised by an Assembly and a Council, which were composed of national parliament appointees and Member State government representatives, respectively. The oversight bodies of the decision-making body, in other words, were still controlled by the six countries that made up the ECSC. Finally, the ECSC Treaty also established its own dispute settlement body: the Court of Justice, made up of nine judges, and charged with interpreting the Treaty if there was disagreement between the Member States.

The UK was not one of the six original members. It was invited to participate by the French government, but it declined: the High Authority was deemed too powerful, and the UK did not care to surrender this kind of control over its coal and steel industries to an institution it could not fully control.[6] Indeed, even in these limited sectors, the UK had no interest in sacrificing its sovereignty in the 1950s, and so it did not participate in the start of the European project.

Discussing the quote

Look at the excerpts posted from the Schuman Declaration. Is its focus on peace? On economic cooperation? Or on something else? What does that suggest about the Andrew Tyrie quote at the start of the chapter?

1.3 The late 1950s: The Treaty of Rome

Following the ECSC Treaty, further economic cooperation proved to be a relatively easy sell to the ECSC Member States. The Member States were all experiencing tremendous economic growth in the 1950s, and consequently started trading with each other in a variety of other sectors. As Ian Ward has put it, 'the idea of sacrificing a bit of sovereignty for a lot of wealth seemed to be more and more attractive.'[7]

The next significant step in European cooperation was less like a 'big bang' that changed how European countries interrelated. Instead, it was the logical consequence of a lot of *incremental* cooperation between the six ECSC Member States. In the middle of the 1950s, it became apparent that it might be more *efficient* to simply sign a single *large*

[6] Sean Greenwood, *Britain and European Cooperation Since 1945* (Wiley, 1992) 34–6.

[7] Ian Ward, *A Critical Introduction to European Law*, 3rd edn (CUP, 2009) 11.

agreement covering *all* economic activity, than to keep signing existing trade agreements covering only particular economic sectors.

This kind of incremental cooperation between countries in Europe on economic matters is at the root of one of the theories of European integration (or, what caused the change from fully separate European countries in 1947 to the extensive cooperation and power-sharing in the EU that we have today). The theory of **neo-functionalism** suggests that where countries cooperate in one policy area, such as trade in coal and steel, they will start cooperating in similar policy areas. The institutions that oversee this cooperation, such as the High Authority, will eventually realize that in order to successfully cooperate in *trade*, cooperation in areas that are much more sensitive than trade (such as social policy, dealing with pensions and social security) is also necessary. This process is called **spill-over**, and the functionalist theory of European integration suggests that it accounts for what has happened in Europe: bodies like the High Authority will keep moving into more and more policy areas in order to carry out the functions they were given.

A detailed version of the idea of greater economic cooperation was found in a 1956 report prepared by the Belgian Prime Minister, Paul-Henri Spaak.[8] The Spaak Report suggested significant steps forward in areas that were purely economic, and advocated the creation of a common market. This common market would be run by something akin to the High Authority: an independent body that took decisions independent of the Member States. However, there was no appetite for this type of surrender of sovereignty in non-economic manners, even though it was agreed that countries could not open up markets for *trade* without also considering how to deal with related policy areas, such as budgetary, monetary, and social policies. In these far more sensitive policy areas, the Spaak Report suggested that only Member States would have decision-making powers, but for the sake of the common trade market, they should aim to coordinate their policies.

1.3.1 The EEC Treaty

The Spaak Report was positively received by the ECSC Member States, and it culminated in the signing of two new treaties in 1957 in Rome. The first of these was the Euratom Treaty, establishing the European Atomic Energy Community—a stand-alone Treaty signed by all ECSC Member States with the aim of establishing a nuclear energy market in Europe.[9] The second, and the more interesting one, was the European Economic Community Treaty (EEC). The EEC Treaty, also called the Treaty of Rome, was simultaneously very innovative and wide-ranging, and very conservative. Its innovation lay in its potential scope: it was *indefinite*, it covered *all trade in goods*, and aimed to eliminate all barriers that would make trade in goods more difficult. The drafters realized that in order for *goods* to travel freely between countries, it was also necessary for businesses, employees, and money to move between these countries—and so it also called for measures that would achieve 'free movement' of services, workers, and capital. These 'four freedoms', of which goods, workers, and services will be covered in detail in Chapters 11, 12 and 14, lay at the heart of the project, which was very much focused on *economic* cooperation and integration, and the establishment of the 'common market' of the European Economic Community.

[8] See http://aei.pitt.edu/995/1/Spaak_report.pdf.

[9] Euratom uses the same institutions as the EEC/EC/EU does, and has identical membership, but remains legally distinct to this day.

What about other policy matters? As noted, the Spaak Report suggested that the Member States of this new agreement would retain full control over 'more sensitive' policy areas. Indeed, the fact that the EEC Treaty was going to be about economics was in many ways obvious after failed efforts earlier in the 1950s to start ECSC-level cooperation in policy areas such as defence.[10] In the 1950s, the only 'sensitive' policy areas that were dealt with by the EEC Treaty Members were those that *had* to be covered, such as agricultural policy in the Member States. Agriculture in all six of the EEC signatory States was heavily subsidized by national governments, and these subsidies put up significant barriers to the *free movement of goods* that Article 2 of the EEC Treaty wished to achieve. However, French farmers were opposed to a 'common market' in agriculture, and so the solution that was crafted was a common *policy* rather than a common market. This is often presented as a compromise between France and Germany, with France declining to agree to free trade in industrial goods—which was of key importance to the German economy—unless the other EEC Treaty signatories agreed to help maintain agricultural subsidies and simply coordinated agricultural policy.[11]

The only way to ensure that agricultural subsidies did not disrupt the functioning of the EEC Treaty was to transfer the operation of these subsidies to the European Economic Community, so that they could be coordinated and harmonized under a Common Agricultural Policy (CAP). The CAP is hardly an example of *willing* cooperation in sensitive policy areas, showing that indeed, the EEC Treaty limited itself to economic ambitions.

Even looking beyond its pure economic focus, the EEC Treaty can be described as conservative. It was a very 'negative' treaty: it prohibited trade barriers, such as the charging of customs duties at borders between different Member States, but did not contain any provisions that would actually make trade otherwise more attractive. Simply saying that a Dutch maker of bicycles would no longer have to pay in order to get their bicycles across the border between the Netherlands and Germany might not have been enough to give that exporter the motivation to *start* selling in Germany: what if there were different safety standards for bicycles in Germany, for instance? And how could he persuade a German customer base that his bicycle was at least as good as the German bicycles they were used to already?

The combination of this minimalist approach to economic policy, and a lack of willingness to cooperate on more sensitive areas of policy, resulted in a Treaty that was difficult to associate with some of the more wide-ranging language used in the Schuman Declaration. The EEC did *not* look like a political project, however unique it was in setting up a variety of governing bodies that stood above and separate from its Member States.

What the EEC Treaty did create, by abolishing barriers to trade (such as charges at the border) between the different EEC Treaty Members, is known as a **free trade area**. Within a free trade area, there are no customs duties (or taxes) charged on products when they cross from one 'member' of the free trade area into the territory of another 'member'.

However, the EEC Treaty went further, and also set up a single policy covering trade between the EEC Treaty Members and *any other country* in the world. This setup, which regulates external borders and trade policy, is known as a **customs union**: it means that

[10] The European Defence Community Treaty was actually signed in 1952 by the ECSC Member States, but the French National Assembly refused to ratify it in 1954; the plans were subsequently tabled.

[11] Alan Milward, *The European Rescue of the Nation State*, 2nd edn (Routledge, 1999) chapter 5; Robert Ackrill, *Common Agricultural Policy* (Sheffield Academic Press, 2000) 39–41.

any product entering any of the EEC Member States from anywhere else in the world will experience the exact same treatment at every Member State's border. These concepts are considered in much more detail in Chapter 10.

1.3.2 **The EEC Treaty: Institutions**

The institutional setup of the EEC Treaty *was* truly revolutionary. You can see the structure of the EEC institutions in Figure 1.1. In order to successfully cooperate in these limited economic terms, the EEC Member States surrendered a significant amount of sovereignty. The ECSC's 'High Authority' was mirrored in the establishment of the European Commission, which would function as the executive of the EEC, as well as the proposer of legislation. Its members were drafted from the Member States, but they were to function independently of their home States, representing the EEC's interests when in office. The ECSC's Assembly was shared with the EEC, but a new Council was created for the EEC. The EEC Council had significantly more power than the ECSC Council did: it had the sole power of legislative *approval* in the EEC, and also had executive powers in international relations and the EEC budget. The EEC also shared the ECSC's Court of Justice. Nothing quite like the EEC's setup, granting power to institutions that were situated *above* the nation state (or 'supranational institutions'), existed elsewhere in the world in the 1950s—and though the powers of the individual institutions making up the EU have changed over time, their basic form has not changed since the signing of the EEC Treaty.

1.3.3 **The UK on the Treaty of Rome**

Given the UK's reluctance to participate in the ECSC project, it is unsurprising that it had no interest in joining the EEC when it was first created. The UK's primary objection was one of sovereignty; it saw the supranational institutions in the EEC as having far too much power. However, other objections were more cultural: it preferred a 'special relationship' with the USA and Commonwealth countries, and saw itself as quite separate from 'Europe' in a lot of ways. Comments from political leaders in the UK in the aftermath of World War II are illustrative: Ernest Bevin, the post-war government's Foreign Secretary, famously commented on European integration initiatives with, 'I don't like it. I don't like it. When you open a Pandora's Box, you'll find it full of Trojan Horses.'[12]

Subsequent UK governments were even less enthusiastic than the post-war government. Churchill, an advocate for European integration, was surrounded by the very first

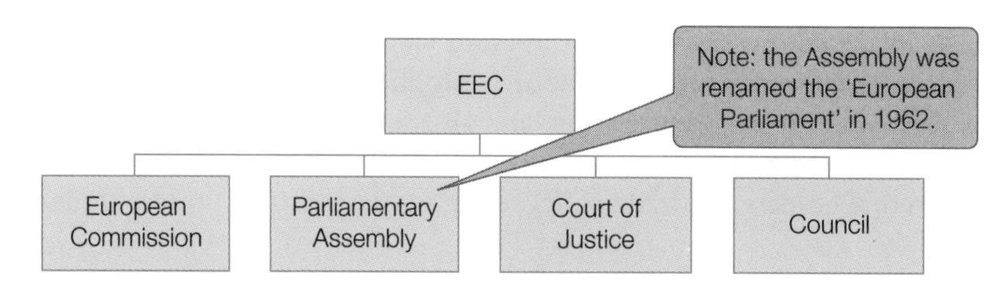

Figure 1.1 The EEC institutions

[12] Lord Strang, *At Home and Abroad* (Andre Deutsch, 1956) 290.

Eurosceptics when he succeeded Clement Attlee as Prime Minister; his Foreign Secretary, Anthony Eden, indicated that the UK knew that joining the EEC was 'something which we know in our bones we cannot do'.[13] Meanwhile, the Treasury was circulating memos that suggested that the EEC was part of a French plot to dominate the rest of Europe![14]

Harold Macmillan, the next UK Foreign Secretary, was a little more enthusiastic about what was happening on the continent, but was held back by others in the UK government who were wary of Europe. He reluctantly declined invitations to the conference that eventually produced the Spaak Report, and indeed went looking for an alternative to the EEC when it was created.[15] The EEC required too much of a sacrifice of sovereignty; the UK eventually, in 1960, set up an alternative that limited itself to aiming to remove many *internal* barriers to trade, but did not aim to regulate external trade policy like the EEC did. The European Free Trade Area, or EFTA, was immediately joined by six other countries who thought the EEC went 'too far'—and to this date, it continues to operate as a free trade area distinct from the European Union.

1.4 The 1970s: Accession of the UK

The 1960s and the 1970s were, in many ways, quiet times for European integration. There were a number of reasons why the goal of the 'common market' appeared to be stagnating, but the two most significant ones were economic on the one hand, and institutional on the other.

The 1950s were a decade marked by growth, and when economies are doing well under international collaboration, political leaders are happy to commit to more of it. In periods in which employment statistics, wages, and investments are all performing well, there is very little pressure from voters to *stop* looking towards the international community. But, and we saw this time and again in the twentieth century, when the economy starts to slow down, and incomes start to suffer, it becomes politically more difficult and undesirable to push for free trade. Trade, otherwise perceived as creating cheaper products and enabling consumer choice, suddenly starts being seen as helping *other* countries keep up their employment, at the expense of domestic employment.[16]

The 1960s were marked by a global recession. In a recession, the urge for political leaders to adopt 'protectionist' policies—ones that aim to safeguard domestic industries, rather than necessarily to get the best/cheapest products—becomes significantly greater. In the 1960s, the benefits of EEC membership were becoming less obvious, and the pressure to look inward was increasing. Consequently, there was not much of an *economic* driver to pursue greater trade.

The EEC's setup was also causing its own problems. For one thing, the CAP was ballooning in terms of cost, to the point where it took up 70 per cent of the EEC's budget

[13] Speech by Anthony Eden at Columbia University (New York, 11 January 1952), in Denise Folliot (ed), *Documents on International Affairs, 1952* (OUP, 1955) 43–4.

[14] Sean Greenwood, *Britain and European Cooperation Since 1945* (Wiley, 1992) 64–7.

[15] Roy Douglas, *Liquidation of Empire: the Decline of the British Empire* (Palgrave, 2002) 142; N J Crowson, *Britain and Europe: A Political History Since 1918* (Routledge, 2011) 71.

[16] For the classic account of why free trade benefits all nations, see Adam Smith, *The Wealth of Nations* (W Strahan and T Cadell, 1776).

by the 1970s.[17] The compromise struck to get France on board was starting to become increasingly unpalatable to some other Member States, among which the UK once it joined, but reform would prove to be almost impossible because of the institutional structure of the EEC. All legislative proposals in the EEC were drafted by the Commission, but had to be approved unanimously by the Member State representatives in the Council during the EEC's first years. The consequence of this was that not much legislation was adopted as a practical matter: every Member State had an effective veto.

At this time, the theories of EU integration were revisited by observers. **Neo-functionalism** explained how the Member States went from the ECSC to the EEC, but seemed to ignore a very significant factor: all cooperation at the EEC level required *consent from the Member States*. As the Member States started to feel as if the EEC was benefiting them less, they also proved to be less interested in expanding what the EEC could do—resulting in the legislative stalemate just described. The EEC's supranational institutions could do very little without agreement from the EEC's Member States. The 1960s and 1970s thus saw a competing theory to neo-functionalism arise: **intergovernmentalism** argues that European integration can only be explained by observing that as long as it benefited those in charge of national governments, they were keen to integrate further; when they were not keen to integrate, the EEC project went nowhere.

The 1960s saw clear hesitancy about further integration on the part of the Member States. In 1965, the Council's decision-making was meant to shift from *unanimity* to a form of **qualified majority voting** (QMV), which allocated a proportion of votes to each Member State representative on the basis of the population of the Member State. This proved too contentious for France, and, in 1965, the French representative walked out of a Council debate on the EEC's income streams when it was clear that he would be outvoted. From June 1965 to January 1966, France refused to attend any Council meetings, and in January 1966 it finally came back to the table only after the adoption of the so-called Luxembourg Accords. The Luxembourg Accords granted every Member State a veto over all EEC legislative proposals, regardless of how they were to be adopted, if they pertained to 'very important interests' of that Member State.[18]

Perhaps unsurprisingly, 'very important interests' turned out to be 'basically all interests'. The plan to make EEC legislation easier to adopt from 1965 onwards was consequently thwarted, and there was very little progress in the establishment of the 'common market' the EEC was meant to create, as the secondary legislation that would support the 'common market' was simply not getting passed.

One of the limited ways in which the EEC did progress was in terms of membership. Despite its staunch disinterest in joining the EEC in 1957, and its creation of the alternative EFTA, the global recession of the 1960s resulted in a rather pragmatic change of priorities for the UK government. Indeed, Harold Macmillan had compromised by establishing EFTA, but found himself applying to join the EEC as Prime Minister in 1963. The economic gains the organizations presented were simply too interesting, and the economic pressures that the UK was facing were enough to make earlier concerns about the EEC project less relevant.[19]

[17] Milward (n 11) 197.

[18] 'Final Communiqué of the Extraordinary Session of the Council' [1966] 3 *Bulletin of the European Communities* 5.

[19] Duncan Watts and Colin Pilkington, *Britain in the European Union Today*, 3rd edn (Manchester University Press, 2005) 27–8.

Both this application to join and a subsequent one in 1967 were vetoed by President Charles de Gaulle of France. In hindsight, his reasons for vetoing the UK's joining may seem prescient:

President Charles de Gaulle, Press Conference, 14 January 1963 (emphasis added)

England in effect is **insular**, she is maritime, she is **linked** through her exchanges, her markets, her supply lines to **the most diverse and often the most distant countries**; she pursues essentially **industrial and commercial activities**, and **only slight agricultural ones**. She has in all her doings **very marked and very original habits and traditions**.

A third application to join the EEC, made in 1970, was finally successful—and largely because de Gaulle was no longer President of France, though an EU-enthusiastic prime minister in the shape of Edward Heath also helped the UK's accession. However, accession in 1973 came with more strings attached than joining the project originally would have done. The original six Member States had significant budgetary demands that worked out particularly poorly for a country that had a very small agricultural sector, and thus would not benefit tremendously from the CAP.[20] An agreement was ultimately reached only to encounter substantial resistance in the UK House of Commons: the Treaty of Accession was passed by a majority of only 112 votes.[21] The Labour Party in particular remained very wary of the EEC project, and ran a political campaign in 1974 that promised a referendum on staying *in* the EEC a mere three years after formally joining.[22]

That referendum, at a time when economic progress was desperately needed, resulted in a 2:1 decision for *remain*. However, across the EEC Member States, popular support for the EEC appeared to be at an all-time low at the end of the 1970s. The CAP was expensive and unpopular, and apart from the CAP, the EEC appeared to not be doing much: the Council managed to put a halt to virtually all Commission legislative efforts. Attempts to make the EEC project more accessible to voters, such as making elections to the European Parliament *direct* in 1976, had no significant impact. The public was either disinterested in the EEC project, or outright did not like what it was doing, which also seemed to be 'nothing' a lot of the time. Where could the EEC go next?

1.5 The 1980s: The Single European Act

By the early 1980s, the EEC was steadily growing larger—with the UK, Ireland, and Denmark joining in 1973, Greece in 1981, and Spain and Portugal in 1986—but it still did not seem to be going anywhere. Indeed, in 1982, the President of the European

[20] Uwe Kitzinger, *Diplomacy and Persuasion: How Britain Joined the Common Market* (Thames and Hudson, 1973).

[21] Christopher Preston, *Enlargement and Integration in the European Union* (Routledge, 1997) 33–5.

[22] Watts and Pilkington (n 19) 29–31.

Parliament—as it had been renamed in 1962—declared that '[the] anniversary of the European Community does not seem to be an occasion for much celebration . . . [the] infant which held so much promise twenty five years ago has changed into a feeble cardiac patient.'[23]

The heads of EEC Member States were slowly coming to the conclusion that all efforts to improve the EEC in the eyes of the public were failing because the foundations underpinning the EEC were deeply flawed. In other words, it was the Treaty of Rome that was the problem, and it had to be revisited if the EEC project was ever going to achieve a true 'common market'.

Unity among the EEC Member States on a renewed willingness to work together and seek compromise was, ironically, in part brought about by the UK. Margaret Thatcher had come to power in the UK in 1979, and found that the membership 'deal' that the UK had been presented with in 1972 was simply not in the country's best interests. In particular, the UK's budgetary contributions were seen as so unfair by her government that she used the Luxembourg Accord vetoes almost constantly in an attempt to force through a revision of the budget. By 1984, the other EEC Heads of State had grown so tired of this that they actually abolished the veto!

A change in the guard in the UK was not the only driver for change, however; it was the new Heads of State in France and Germany who proved key in revitalizing the European project. François Mitterrand, the new French President, and Helmut Kohl, the new German Chancellor, not only found themselves broadly agreeing on the direction the EEC project should travel in, but also found themselves popular with the other Heads of State. Together with a new head of the European Commission, a Frenchman named Jacques Delors, they proved influential enough to attempt to heal the 'cardiac patient' they had inherited. Their focus was twofold: first, on making the EEC *achieve* new economic progress—and so stopping the legislative stalemates that had dominated the 60s, 70s, and early 80s—and second, on making the public *care* about the EEC. Discussions between Kohl, Mitterrand, and Delors eventually led to a 1983 Solemn Declaration by the EEC Heads of State, which promised 'further work' on the common market.[24] Over the course of the next year, this 'further work' culminated in the first genuine reform of the EEC Treaty.

1.5.1 The Single European Act 1986

The next section on EU integration requires a preliminary understanding of some of the EU institutions that we discuss in more detail in Chapter 2. Specifically, there are two bodies that have the word 'Council' in their name, but they have very distinct functions:

- The **Council of Ministers**, commonly simply called **the Council**, is the EEC/EU body where national government ministers meet to approve legislation in particular policy areas.
- The **European Council** is the EEC/EU body where heads of national governments meet to discuss 'big picture' matters like Treaty amendments, accessions, and the overall plans for the European project.

[23] Peter Dankert, 'The European Community: Past, Present and Future' (1982) 21 JCMS 3, 8–9.
[24] Available at: http://aei.pitt.edu/1788/1/stuttgart_declaration_1983.pdf.

(The EU maintains that these institution names were not chosen purely to confuse students . . .)

It is the role of the Council of Ministers (the Council) that proved key to further EU integration as of the reform of the Treaties in the 1980s. The Single European Act (SEA), drafted in 1984 and enacted in 1986, promised to take the EEC project from a period of stasis into a period of hyper-productivity. Its most significant promise in this regard was the so-called 1992 project, where the EEC promised to *complete* the 'common market' by the end of 1992. The 'common market' was to enable the *full* free movement of goods, services, capital, and workers—not merely stop protectionism, but actively *enable* the free trade the EEC was meant to accomplish.

How was this going to get done? By eliminating the possibility for Member States to block all legislative proposals that were coming from the Commission. Consequently, a new Article 100a EEC was adopted, which ensured that all decisions in the Council in relation to the internal market were to be taken by QMV. The Member States' votes would be calculated as a percentage of EEC population, giving Germany the largest share of the vote and Luxembourg the smallest. The heads of the Member States, meeting as the European Council, proved willing to give up a little more control for the promise of far more substantial benefits.

In anticipation of the completion of the 'common market', and in light of the increasing membership of the EEC, the SEA also made arrangements to introduce a further court, primarily to hear cases brought against the other EEC institutions. This second court, then known as the Court of First Instance, started operating in 1989; its establishment reduced the Court of Justice's increasing case load and resulted in quicker decisions, making the EEC function more smoothly.

In other ways, the SEA went further than simply promising to *finish* the project that had started the EEC. For the first time, a European Treaty was promising to look at policy areas that went beyond the purely trade-related. There were provisions in the SEA that dealt with coordination of *monetary policy*, which would enable the eventual introduction of a single European currency. The reasons for moving towards a single currency were pragmatic rather than necessarily ideological, however: the project was approved by the EEC Heads of State because a single currency would make cross-border trade both *easier* and *cheaper*, which would stimulate the 'common market' in ways that other legislative measures could not.

Beyond work on a common currency, there were also provisions in the SEA that encouraged deeper cooperation on other policy areas, such as social rights, research and technology, and environmental regulation. However, in these policy areas, unanimity in Council voting remained the norm—and the Member States consequently retained all control over progress.

Discussing the quote

Remember the Schuman Declaration and its mentions of a *federation of Europe*. How far do you think the SEA goes towards such a *federation*, or as Andrew Tyrie would call it, a 'fundamentally different creature'?

1.5.2 The UK and the SEA

Margaret Thatcher's relationship with the EEC project was an interesting one. She had campaigned to remain in the EEC in the 1975 UK referendum, and in the late 1970s had actually first suggested a European currency of sorts. However, none of this was rooted in any particular love for 'Europe': rather, it was the faltering sterling in the 1970s and 1980s, and the Conservative Party's economic plans for the UK, that made her interested in closer collaboration with the EEC.[25] The 1980s in the UK saw a massive transition from industrial manufacturing towards the services industry—and because the country was in many ways a pioneer in creating a services industry, *and* the EEC permitted the 'free movement of services' to other countries, there was significant money to be made for the UK in encouraging the completion of the 'common market'. Thatcher consequently signed the SEA for the UK with little hesitation—though she later referred to it as her 'greatest political mistake'.[26]

What caused this change of heart? The unwillingness of the other EEC members to adjust the 'bad hand' the UK had been dealt upon accession to the EEC was one part of it. The 1979 Conservative Party manifesto contained an explicit promise to correct the 'unfairness' of UK budget contributions; as discussed, Thatcher pressed this point in meetings with the other European Heads of State to a point where they willingly sacrificed their own vetoes in order to stop Thatcher from using hers. The budget wrangling carried on for four more years until a compromise was reached in 1984, resulting in the UK's rolling rebate, which restored approximately two-thirds of UK contributions to the EEC budget to the UK. The fact that it had taken five years, however, played a part in souring Thatcher's opinion of the EEC, and had not endeared her particularly to the other European leaders—they referred to the affair as BBQ, standing for 'British budgetary question' or 'bloody British question', depending on their mood.[27]

Her opinion of the EEC project when it proved that it wished to stretch *beyond* the 'common market' did not improve, and her own political party split between those who thought the EEC was beneficial to the country and those who mistrusted and disliked it. Thatcher's own opposition to the EEC grew so vocal that members of her own Cabinet resigned from her government; her Chancellor, Geoffrey Howe, mocked her comments on Europe publicly. His description of her viewing Europe as 'a continent that is positively teeming with ill-intentioned people, scheming, in her words, to extinguish democracy' proved to be the beginning of the end of her power within the Conservative Party.[28] UK membership of the EEC consequently, and somewhat reluctantly, continued into the 1990s.

1.6 The 1990s: The Maastricht Treaty

The SEA's 1992 deadline was as ambitious as it was overdue: the EEC was now going to try to achieve 'in seven years what the Community should have accomplished in the preceding thirty'.[29] The Commission headed by Jacques Delors did indeed have its work cut out.

[25] Philip Norton, '"The Lady's Not for Turning" But what about the Rest?—Margaret Thatcher and the Conservative Party 1979–1989' (1990) 43(1) Parliam Aff 41–59.

[26] Wilfried Martens, *Europe: I Struggle, I Overcome* (Springer, 2006) 93.

[27] Watts and Pilkington (n 19) 31–5.

[28] Geoffrey Howe (London, 13 November 1990), in Brian MacArthur (ed), *The Penguin Book of Modern Speeches*, 3rd edn (Penguin, 2012).

[29] Joseph Weiler, *The Constitution of Europe* (CUP, 1999) 64.

However, the political will for *big change* finally seemed to be present among the EEC Member States again. Work on the 'common market' project led to further meetings of the European Council, called **intergovernmental conferences**, at which the prospect of an 'economic and monetary union' and even a 'political union' was discussed. The desire for 'economic and monetary union' was perhaps less rooted in a desire for closer cooperation than a fear that the 'common market' simply would not function if exchange rates between different European currencies fluctuated all the time, but talk of a common currency led to talk of something *beyond* that—not least because both Kohl and Mitterrand were interested in seeing what *more* the European project could accomplish.

In 1989, the Delors Report concluded that a common currency was indeed desirable and achievable, but not without further Treaty amendment. Kohl and Mitterrand thought the establishment of a common currency would fail without further *political* collaboration—and that, too, would require changes to the SEA. Under the rules set out in the SEA, the EEC simply had not been given the power by its Members to establish a new currency or integrate further.

After 30 years of the EEC Treaty, then, we ended up with an SEA that would not make it past six years—simply because most Member States wanted *more* than an almost exclusively trade-oriented Treaty could accomplish.

1.6.1 The Treaty of Maastricht 1992

It was Maastricht, not the SEA, that proved a 'sea change' in the setup of the European project. For one thing, a lot of the changes introduced by the Maastricht Treaty in 1992 were of clear symbolic, political value. The Treaty of Maastricht formally established something called the *European Union*. Union, of course, sounds significantly closer than 'Community'—more like a marriage than a neighbourhood in which all European countries just happened to live. The new Treaty of European Union (TEU), which absorbed the earlier EEC Treaty, had a list of objectives in its Article 2 that explicitly referred to the creation of a political union and of the Economic and Monetary Union (EMU). This was *well* beyond anything Rome or the SEA had alluded to.

However, the Member States' willingness to compromise for the sake of further European cooperation remained distinctly limited. Maastricht was not an absolute surrender of sovereign power in all matters, even where those matters were going to be *discussed* at the European level in the future. The TEU dealt with the fact that the Member States were handing over different degrees of power in different policy areas to the EU by setting up a so-called 'pillar' structure, which you can see in Figure 1.2.

The first pillar absorbed the former EEC Treaty. It renamed it the European *Community* Treaty (EC, rather than EEC), to once more stress that the European project was moving beyond being a purely economic project. The EC pillar was the one where supranational decision-making was omnipresent. Here, the Commission proposed legislation; the Council voted to adopt it under QMV *without* veto powers; and for the first time, in certain policy areas, the European Parliament was granted 'co-decision' powers in adopting legislation. This meant that both the Council *and* the European Parliament had to approve Commission proposals in order for them to become binding EU law. The thought underpinning the expansion of this 'co-decision' procedure was linked strongly to making the EU more approachable and appreciated by the public: as they could *vote* for the European Parliament, they now had a further *indirect say* into what EU laws were being adopted, beyond the fact that the national governments they had already elected were represented in the Council.

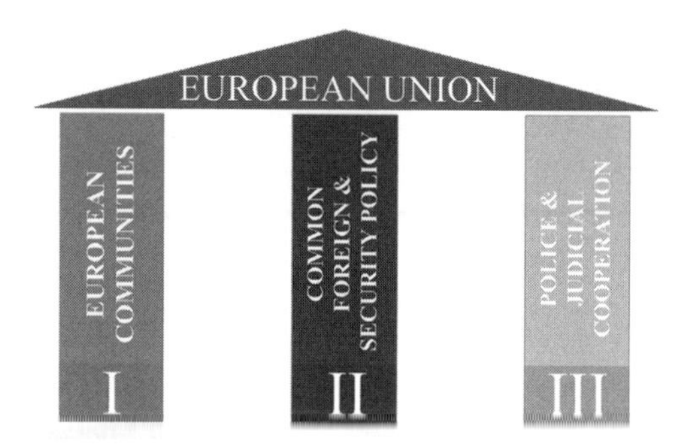

Figure 1.2 The 'Three Pillars' of the EU

The other two pillars of the EU were *less* accessible than the European Communities. In two areas named Common Foreign and Security Policy (CFSP) and Justice and Home Affairs (JHA), the Council would still vote on legislative proposals by unanimity. In other words, Pillars II and III of the EU were to remain fully intergovernmental, and only Pillar I would be fully supranational. Pillars II and III were also excluded from the scope of what the Court of Justice could rule on, and so the TEU presented the public with a very mixed result. On the one hand, it had a closer say in economic policy than it had had under previous Treaties; but on the other hand, the EU was making laws in new policy areas that were likely to directly affect European nationals in very serious ways, and there was very little democratic participation or judicial oversight in these areas.

There were other efforts to 'sell' the EU to European voters. The most interesting of these was the Maastricht introduction of a new status for all nationals of EU Member States: European citizenship. What the consequence of this status was to be was entirely unclear: as happens regularly when multiple sovereign countries have to agree to a single policy, the provisions in the TEU on citizenship were rather vague. Citizenship appeared to be a rebranding of the 'free movement of workers' that had already been a part of the EEC Treaty—no new rights were extended to Member State nationals who were *not* workers, and even for the workers, the Treaty made it clear this was a secondary status. Was this, then, merely an effort to dress up the EU as being *about the people*, in order to justify it becoming a 'Union' that was going to try to attain a single currency? Or was the creation of citizenship a starting point for a much closer relationship between the people living in Europe?

Discussing the quote

Think back to the Andrew Tyrie quote at the start of the chapter, as well as the Schuman Declaration. Do you think the creation of EU citizenship is significant in *changing* the EU, or not?

1.6.2 The UK and Maastricht

The UK's relationship with the European Union was significantly more fraught than it had been under the EEC Treaty. That Treaty could be brought back to the UK and explained as being *purely* about economic cooperation; even the SEA could be marketed in the same way. However, the Treaty on European Union of 1992 started with the following observation in its preamble:

TEU, Common Principles, Article A (emphasis added)

This Treaty marks a new stage in the process of creating an **ever closer union** among the peoples of Europe in which decisions are taken as closely as possible to the people.

An earlier draft of the Treaty, prepared by the Dutch Presidency of the European Council, had actually proposed the words 'federal union', which the UK outright rejected. There was no appetite in the UK for a 'federal' Europe. Instead, the UK delegation pushed for the phrasing '*ever closer union*': a vague enough objective that would satisfy those in the UK who wanted further European integration without frightening those who did not want federalism. With the benefit of hindsight, in light of the exemption from 'ever closer union' that David Cameron specifically sought to negotiate in 2016 so as to encourage a vote to remain in the EU, this seems more than a little ironic.

The UK delegation also pushed most strongly for the inclusion of Article F TEU, which stated that '[the] Union shall respect the national identities of its Member States . . .'.[30] These Treaty-based promises that the EU was not going to *get rid of the nation state* were thought necessary for the TEU to be ratified in the UK, and were consequently included. Even with these promises, however, ratifying the TEU in the House of Commons was touch and go: the required amendments to the European Communities Act 1972 were almost not passed. There was a factor of embarrassment at play here: the UK had attempted to *join* the EMU, as it would have reduced the cost of doing business across the continent, but the pound sterling crashed out of the EMU in 1992 when it simply could no longer meet the conditions for 'currency fixing' set out in the EMU. Attempts to stay in cost the UK tremendous amounts of money, and a failure to do so significantly increased hostility towards the EU.[31]

That said, in 1992 the UK successfully obtained promises that the project was not going federal, and an increasing number of opt-outs from new EU initiatives (such as the Economic and Monetary Union, but also a slew of social policy collectively known as the EU's 'Social Chapter', granting a variety of rights to employees). The Maastricht Treaty was consequently backed by Prime Minister John Major, but the concessions he gained did not prove as persuasive as he would have hoped. Euroscepticism in the Conservative Party remained rife, and the Conservative Party's relationship with the EU remained very conflicted.

1.7 The late' 90s and 2000s: Rapid revisions

Did the Maastricht Treaty result in a boost in popular acceptance of the EU project?

The answer to this question appeared to be *no*. The Maastricht Treaty made significant progress in terms of giving European people more *input into* the EU, and more benefits

[30] Treaty on European Union, together with the complete text of the Treaty establishing the European Community [1992] OJ C244/1.

[31] Alex May, *Britain and Europe Since 1945* (Routledge, 1999) 82–3.

from the EU. The European Parliament gained greater legislative power, and the Community was going to start extending both new statuses and rights to EU nationals in an increasing number of policy areas. However, the fact that the EU was doing more for voters in Europe was not necessarily *clear* to those voters—and regardless, there was still ample criticism of how Maastricht set up the EU.[32]

Three particular problems kept being raised by both politicians and academic commentators. The lack of power held by the European Parliament was one; 'co-decision' was an improvement, but only applied in limited areas, and the Council still held virtually all legislative adoption cards under the TEU. The European Parliament remained the 'weakest' institution in other ways: it was the most democratic institution, but also the only one that could not challenge another EU institution before the Court of Justice. The steps taken by the Maastricht Treaty when it came to democratic representation mattering in the EU were simply too small.

The second resurfacing criticism was of the empty nature of EU citizenship as a status; it appeared to some to be a PR exercise more than a legitimate improvement.[33] However, it is the final objection to the Maastricht Treaty that is perhaps most interesting to us as lawyers: it is the silence of the Treaty on the division of legislative power between the EU and the Member States. The EEC Treaty and the SEA had not explicitly set out in what areas the EEC had law-making powers, but that was less problematic—its power was all centred on the creation of the 'common market'. Maastricht, however, moved into far more sensitive policy areas—and did not clearly set out when the Member States could make law, or when the EU could.[34] This could lead to practical problems, but more than that, it proved politically toxic. In countries such as the UK, fearful of an EU that was making laws in ever more numerous areas, the lack of a clear limitation on the EU's law-making abilities was deemed very problematic.

These persistent criticisms did not go unheard by the European Council: Maastricht was accused of attempting too many things at once, and being legally unclear and unworkable as a consequence.[35] The next intergovernmental conference had been planned already at the time Maastricht was adopted—for 1996—and in response to the criticisms launched at Maastricht, it resulted in yet another new Treaty.

1.7.1 The Treaty of Amsterdam 1997

The Treaty of Amsterdam was primarily a cleaning-up of the Maastricht Treaty. To the delight of law students and EU lawyers everywhere, the Amsterdam amendments to the EEC Treaty both renamed and renumbered it—so, for example, the old Article 100a EEC, enabling 'common market' QMV in the Council, was now Article 95 EC.

Beyond that, Amsterdam made limited progress, by incorporating into the TEU some areas of law in which the Member States were already voluntarily cooperating with each other: environmental law and employment law thus officially became part of 'the European project'. Amsterdam also rebranded Pillar III 'Police and Judicial Co-operation in

[32] For a balanced but critical account, see Deirdre Curtin, 'The Constitutional Structure of the Union: A Europe of Bits and Pieces' (1993) 30 CMLRev 17, 67.

[33] Joseph Weiler, 'European Citizenship and Human Rights' in Jan Winter et al, *Reforming the Treaty on European Union* (TCM Asser, 1998) 68.

[34] See Chapter 4 for more detail. [35] Curtin (n 32).

Criminal Manners' (PJCC) and made a first explicit reference to the EU's commitment to 'human rights and fundamental freedoms' in Article 6 TEU. These measures were intended to tackle the public's lack of interest in the EU. Beyond that, the Council's QMV was extended to even more policy areas, and the European Parliament's co-decision procedure was also extended further. In short, tackling the EU's lacking democratic qualities and improving the legibility of the Treaty were the primary achievements of the Treaty of Amsterdam.

However, while generally unambitious, the Treaty of Amsterdam also marked a new schism in the European integration project. Some of the EU's most controversial accomplishments were introduced in Amsterdam, but they were not introduced to *all EU Member States*. Key here is the Schengen Agreement, which eliminated physical borders between all countries willing to sign up to the agreement. This was intended to be all EU Member States, but the UK, Ireland, and Denmark plainly refused to surrender border controls to the EU. Similar steps were being taken with the EMU and certain Member States' opt-outs from Justice and Home Affairs policies: where agreement could not be found between *all* Member States, or where not all Member States *qualified* for a given EU policy, the Treaty of Amsterdam enabled only *some* Member States to go ahead with these policies.

The Treaty described these types of opt-in policies with the title 'closer cooperation'. In reality, what we were seeing was a 'two-speed' Europe—to the satisfaction of John Major, who understood that this was the start of a process whereby the EU would go 'wider' without going 'deeper'.[36] Indeed, when Austria, Sweden, and Finland left EFTA and joined the EU in 1995, even more voices were being added to the table, and finding unanimous agreement would be almost impossible if the EU wished to extend into more policy areas. Two-speed Europe, in the eyes of the UK, was the best way to avoid federal Europe.

What about the balance of power between the different EU institutions that had been so consistently criticized? Clearly, institutional structure of the EU was an area where 'closer cooperation' between only *some* Member States would not be possible—and perhaps unsurprisingly, it consequently remained largely unaltered. Telling is the comment of Commission President Jacques Santer, on what the Treaty of Amsterdam had achieved: shortly after it was signed, he made clear that the EU had wanted something *more* than Amsterdam, but simply had not managed it.[37]

The only solution to fixing a disappointing Treaty was, of course, another Treaty.

1.7.2 The Treaty of Nice 2001

The next Treaty was both a consequence of the failures of Amsterdam and a political development on the European continent. Negotiations for former Soviet satellite states to join the (western) European project had been anticipated since the end of the Cold War in 1989, and had started in 1998. In 1999, the European Heads of State agreed at an intergovernmental conference that while the process of 'enlargement' east was desirable

[36] Alexander Stubb, *Negotiating Flexibility in the European Union: Amsterdam, Nice and Beyond* (Palgrave, 2002) 63–4.

[37] John Palmer, 'EU Fails to Decide how Best to Decide', *The Guardian*, 19 June 1997.

for both democratic and economic reasons, it did mean that previous arrangements on the composition and powers of the EU institutions had to be revisited. A further consequence of the addition of 10 further EU Member States to the 15 that existed prior to the 2000s was that 'two-speed Europe' was going nowhere: if agreement between 15 countries proved difficult, agreement between 25 countries looked impossible. The EU thus did what John Major desired: it spread wider, but did not manage to integrate more deeply.

The intergovernmental conference in Nice in 2000 produced a new Treaty and two further documents of interest: the Charter of Fundamental Rights of the European Union, and a document called the Declaration on the Future of the Union. The new Treaty, which entered into force in 2001, dealt primarily with the institutional consequences of enlargement. QMV had to be reconsidered: the voting ratios that had applied since the SEA would not work in a 25-member EU, and the older EU Member States would have to make space in some of the institutions for newer members. These negotiations dragged on for an unbelievable 90 hours, to the great unhappiness of the UK's Tony Blair, with France and Germany posturing back and forth. Their vote share was likely to decrease the most, as it had been the largest prior to 'enlargement', but neither wanted to lose the *largest* share of the vote. Germany protested many proposals because its population was greater; and France protested alternative proposals because it, unlike Germany, had nuclear capability and thus should have a larger vote share. This was apparently not intended as a threat, but did require an incredibly complex formula to establish the new version of 'qualified majority voting'.

As a sign of the difficulty in finding workable compromises between 15 different countries, let alone more, it is worth stressing that QMV was extended to even more policy areas, but not without caveats. There were, in the Nice Treaty, a total of *38* different legislative procedures requiring different voting arrangements, depending on the nature of the policy area in which the procedure was to be applied.[38] Even to lawyers, this proved completely incomprehensible; we can only imagine what those without legal training would have made of it!

As had been the case in Maastricht and Amsterdam, however, the Nice Treaty did make some effort to engage the European public. The Charter of Fundamental Rights is the prime example of these efforts, but much like Maastricht's citizenship, it did not prove persuasive. For one, the Charter appeared to copy out vast portions of the European Convention of Human Rights, to which all EU Member States had already acceded. It was unclear what added value was offered by this EU Charter—not least of all because the intergovernmental conference failed to agree on what legal status the Charter should have. Original proposals had been to make it legally binding, but this proved controversial in several Member States, and it was ultimately adopted as a mere 'declaration'. It was another EU initiative to make the project more accessible to voters that ended up looking very half-hearted in its final form.

1.7.3 The UK and the Nice Treaty

The period between the Amsterdam and Nice Treaties saw a significant change of leadership in the UK. After several decades of being away from power, the Labour Party—running on a broadly pro-European platform—won a majority in the 1997 UK general

[38] Wolfgang Wessels, 'The Millennium IGC in the EU's Evolution' (2001) 39 JCMS 197, 201.

election. The UK was one of the largest proponents of the 'enlargement' East that the EU engaged in: for both economic and security reasons, bringing these former Communist countries into the fold was a significant priority for the Labour government. Drafting the Nice Treaty might have been a tedious and wearying exercise, but ratifying the Treaty was a non-issue in the UK, for once.[39]

However, Labour shortly thereafter stumbled into an error of judgement that would haunt it in the decade to follow. In its EU enthusiasm, the Labour government was in principle in favour of letting the 10 new EU Member States that were going to join in 2004 benefit from free movement of people immediately. The Nice Treaty, however, permitted a gradual opening of Member State labour markets, where only limited numbers of Eastern European nationals could benefit from free movement for the first few years following accession. In response to the Treaty's flexibility, the Labour government commissioned research to investigate what the likelihood of mass migration would be. This research was produced on the assumption that *all* original EU Member States would operate fully open borders from the date of 'enlargement' onwards, and estimated that 5,000–13,000 Eastern European nationals would settle and seek work in the UK each year.[40] On that basis, the UK government declined any sort of transitional arrangements for 'enlargement'.

However, in the two months before the 2004 'enlargement' was meant to complete, all Member States except Ireland and Sweden changed their minds about their willingness to have fully open borders immediately—and consequently, the UK ended up being one of the only Member States that permitted free movement of EU nationals from these newly joined Eastern European countries. Rather than a maximum of 13,000 new settlers per year, the influx proved to be at least four times that—resulting in both mockery of the Labour party's approach, and slowly increasing resentment of the EU among the UK population.[41]

1.7.4 A Constitution for Europe?

What about the Declaration on the Future of the Union that came with Nice? Much like the Charter of Fundamental Rights, it did not have binding legal value—but it is nonetheless of interest. In many ways, this Declaration—which was redrafted in a 2002 intergovernmental conference in Laeken—served as an apology to the European people. The European leaders were acknowledging that the Treaties simply were not up to muster. Amsterdam had set out to fix what had gone wrong *in* Maastricht, and Nice made the institutions ready for enlargement, but by 2002, the Treaties remained difficult to read; the division of law-making powers between the EU and its Member States remained incredibly opaque; and democratic participation in the EU project remained minimal. If anything, the decade between Maastricht and Nice only accomplished one serious step towards the future: 'closer cooperation' was to be the way forward in such a large Union, and EU projects could now proceed with the agreement of as few as eight Member States.

[39] Simon Bulmer, 'New Labour, New European Policy? Blair, Brown and Utilitarian Supranationalism' (2008) 64(1) Parliam Aff 597.

[40] See http://www.ucl.ac.uk/~uctpb21/reports/HomeOffice25_03.pdf.

[41] See http://visual.ons.gov.uk/uk-perspectives-2016-international-migration-to-and-from-the-uk/.

Romano Prodi, President of the Commission in the early 2000s, decided that apologies would not get the EU very far; instead, something drastic was needed to revitalize the EU. He declared the noughties to be the 'decade of Europe': the EU's official shared currency, the Euro, was introduced from 2000 onwards, and this should be used as a launching pad for further initiatives.[42] What kind of initiatives? The Heads of State were willing to concede that what the EU needed was almost a clean slate: not just tinkering with the Treaties, but finally resolving a lot of the constitutional problems that the EU had been battling since its inception in 1957.

It was decided that this kind of 'fresh start' Treaty should be *called* a Constitution, not least of all because people reacted strongly to their national constitutions and this might therefore finally bring the European people on board with the EU project. The drafting of this new EU Constitution took place at a special intergovernmental conference entitled the Convention on the Future in 2003. And it did produce a draft Treaty, but far from being a 'fresh start', in many ways it made an already complex and unloved project even *more* difficult and distant.

The Constitutional Treaty was massive: it was longer than all the previous Treaties and so remained impossible to read, and where it introduced new, 'constitutional' elements, these were vague and meaningless. The setup of the Constitutional Treaty was that it would have three substantive parts: vague general principles underpinning the Union in Part 1; a binding Charter of Fundamental Rights as Part 2; and a revamped EC Treaty as Part 3.

Was this, then, the thing to *finally* bring the European people on board the European project? Did this create the 'European' identity that the Heads of State were hoping for? They agreed to an amended draft of the Constitutional Treaty in 2004—but the Treaty, when put to the European people it was written for, was rejected by both French and Dutch voters in 2005. Tony Blair, too, had promised a referendum on the Constitutional Treaty in the UK, given the significant symbolic change it represented—but did not need to follow through on that promise, as the rejection by the Netherlands and France meant that the Constitutional Treaty was, for all intents and purposes, dead.

1.8 The Lisbon Treaty

It would be easy to think that the rejection of the Constitution was the beginning of the end of the EU. However, the fact that the Constitutional Treaty was *not* ratified only meant that the EU project carried on under the Nice Treaty, as if a new Treaty had never been attempted. The Nice Treaty was uninspiring, perhaps, but ultimately functional enough.

The real problem with the rejection of the Constitution was that the European Heads of State had gambled on a massive step forward, and had clearly lost that bet. It appeared that their only choice was to retreat and carry on with small amendments to the Nice Treaty, changing a few provisions at a time. But that was not good enough: the Union was getting larger, it was getting more and more unmanageable, and it was alienating people *more* rather than *less* with each successive minor treaty change.

[42] See http://europa.eu/rapid/press-release_SPEECH-00-41_en.htm.

So: what next?

In a moment she undoubtedly would rather forget, German Chancellor Angela Merkel wrote a very honest memo in 2007—a memo that was unfortunately then leaked, and fired up anti-European sentiment in already Eurosceptic countries like the UK even further. The Merkel memo suggested that the way forward for the EU was to 'use different terminology without changing the legal substance' of the Constitutional Treaty.[43] It was not a pretty suggestion, but it proved to be one that the other EU Heads of State were happy to adopt, and so we arrive at the most recent EU Treaty.

1.8.1 The Treaty of Lisbon 2007

The 'different terminology' suggested by Merkel meant that the Lisbon Treaty was presented as simply 'another Treaty', of which the EU had produced quite a number already in the preceding 20 years; this was intended to make adoption of the Lisbon Treaty uncontroversial, and in some ways it worked. For one thing, the promised UK referendum on the Constitutional Treaty was abandoned when it was replaced with the Lisbon Treaty, which was treated by the Labour government as not being a *substantial* change from what had come before.

This was only partially correct. If Amsterdam was an attempt to 'clean up' Maastricht, Lisbon was a more substantial remodelling of Nice. While the institutional structure of the EU did not change under Lisbon, and indeed has looked broadly the same since the start of the project in 1957, the EU Treaties' structure was completely overhauled. Lisbon replaced one very bloated Constitutional Treaty, as was proposed, with two separate Treaties: one called the Treaty on European Union (TEU), dealing primarily with the principles and institutional arrangements underpinning the EU, and a replacement of the EC Treaty called the Treaty on the Functioning of the European Union (TFEU). Lisbon also got rid of the Maastricht 'pillars', and removed all mention of the 'European Community' from the Treaties; instead, the European Union was granted legal personality and would carry out all functions formally hosted in separate pillars. The current structure of the EU institutions is depicted in Figure 1.3.

The Charter of Fundamental Rights became a binding source of primary EU law under the Lisbon Treaty, though like most EU innovations, this required some wrangling and compromise: the UK and Poland demanded opt-outs from the application of the Charter, and for the sake of adoption of the Treaty as a whole, received them.[44] The EU, now with legal personality of its own, was also tasked with acceding to the

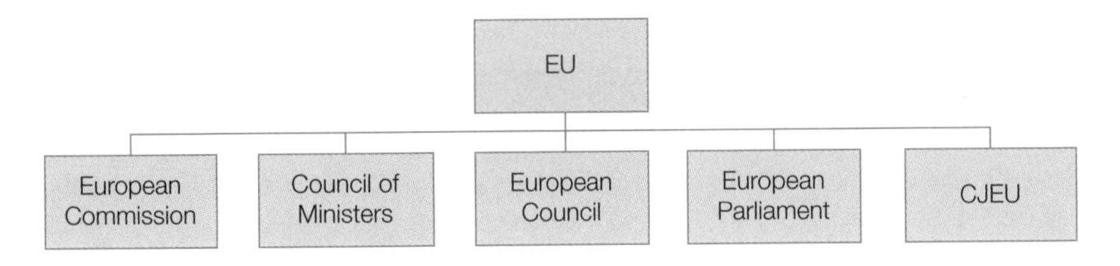

Figure 1.3 The current EU institutions

[43] Daniel Hannan, 'Merkel's Honesty not the Best Policy', *The Telegraph* (London, 27 April 2007).

[44] See Article 6(1) TEU and Protocol (No 30) on the Application of the Charter of Fundamental Rights of the EU to Poland and the United Kingdom, which will be discussed in Chapter 9.

ECHR, which would apply the ECHR to actions taken by the EU institutions.[45] The EU's commitment to human rights thus seemed significantly more persuasive with the adoption of Lisbon.

The other big changes introduced by the Lisbon Treaty were intended to tackle both Member State concerns *and* popular disenchantment with the EU. The primary innovation that Lisbon introduced in order to deal with nervous Member States was the now infamous Article 50 TEU, discussed in detail in Chapter 2, which sets out a process of withdrawal from the EU. It was obviously possible to leave the EU before—a sovereign nation can withdraw from any treaty it has ratified—but in setting out an express process on *how* to do it, the EU responded to concern from Member States like the UK, who were getting increasingly twitchy at notions of the promised 'ever closer union'.

Other efforts to address Member State concerns are of a more technical nature: a key one of these is a clear setting out of the EU's legislative powers and limitations thereof, alongside the limiting of legislative procedures to only *two* after Nice's nightmarish 38. Finally, it seems the EU Heads of State were tired of writing endless new Treaties every time change was required: Article 48(6) TEU permits simplified Treaty amendment at the European Council's initiative. This still requires constitutional approval *within* all the Member States, but forgoes the requirement for an intergovernmental conference specifically aimed at Treaty revision.

To address popular disinterest and wariness of the EU, the Lisbon Treaty proposes a variety of measures aimed at making the EU institutions more democratic, and enabling EU citizens to be more involved with EU processes. In terms of increasing voter involvement, the Lisbon Treaty introduced a European Citizens' Initiative, which enables EU nationals to suggest legislative action at the EU level to the Commission if they gather a million signatures from a number of Member States backing a given policy matter.

A variety of formally recognized posts in the EU institutions were introduced by the Lisbon Treaty; for instance, the President of the Council of Ministers is an official post now, and the Presidency of the European Council also is clearly set out in the Treaties, making it more obvious who is *in charge* of the various EU institutions at any time. The EU, along with its legal personality, also received its own 'foreign secretary' of sorts: the High Representative of the EU represents the EU in most diplomatic activities. These efforts are all geared at making the EU seem *more* like what voters are used to: something akin to a country, though without unwanted references to constitutions or a 'federal' Europe.

Discussing the quote

Consider what the Treaty of Rome aimed to achieve—and then look at what the Treaty of Lisbon has set out. Does Andrew Tyrie have a point when he declares the EU to be a 'fundamentally different creature'? How much is different, and how much has stayed the same, since that first Treaty?

[45] Article 6(2) TEU.

Did Lisbon's efforts to engage the public work? Ireland, under the Irish Constitution, has to hold a referendum whenever the EU Treaties are changed; and the first Irish referendum on the Lisbon Treaty resulted in a rejection in 2008. This time, however, a compromise was sought—and following guarantees to Ireland on its neutrality and a variety of other technical matters, the Irish people were asked for their opinion on the Lisbon Treaty again. The 2009 Irish referendum passed, and the Lisbon Treaty came into force on 1 December 2009.

In the UK, it was brought into force by Prime Minister Gordon Brown, whose Labour government failed to win the next general election. The Conservative Party regained power in a coalition with the Liberal Democrats in 2010, which caused specific tensions on the issue of Europe. Prime Minister David Cameron himself wished for the Conservatives to stop 'banging on about Europe', but Euroscepticism in the party ran deep, and he had to find a way to appeal to his party as a whole.[46] His government thus enacted a European Union Act in 2011 that would require a referendum on any further substantial Treaty change. With David Cameron, then, a UK referendum on the EU seemed to have become inevitable, unless the EU simply *never* rewrote the Treaties again.

We can wrap up this analysis of the EU's development over time by revising the theories of integration that scholars have developed to explain its path of integration. In the 1950s, **neo-functionalism** appeared to explain the EU. In the decades that followed, instead, **intergovernmentalism** seemed to dominate, either with the Council blocking all progress, or the Heads of State pushing hard for further integration. But do either of these accounts *fully* explain how we ended up with the Lisbon Treaty in 2009?

Recent theories on European integration have become more sophisticated: rather than assuming that *either* the supranational or intergovernmental institutions dominate the direction that the EU is travelling in, they argue that there is a whole range of actors who influence EU policy-making and European integration. Theories rooted in **(New) Institutionalism** focus not on one set of institutions versus the other, but rather argue that after several decades, each of the EU institutions developed distinct characteristics and practices, and that these internal practices explain what has happened in the EU better than looking purely at Member States or 'the EU' as actors. **Multi-level governance,** meanwhile, looks towards the roles played not only by the EU institutions but by a wide variety of national and regional actors, including interest groups, and how their interests and practices can shed light on the EU's initiatives.

The reality is that it is unlikely that one theory can *fully* explain the process of integration. As the EU has become a far grander and more complex project, all-inclusive accounts for its shape and policy initiatives have become less persuasive. Even so, there are merits to all these theories, and it is worth bearing them in mind as we consider different aspects of both constitutional and substantive EU law in the chapters that follow.

1.9 The 2016 UK referendum and the future

To their own surprise, the Conservative Party won an overall majority in the 2015 UK general election. This meant that David Cameron's 2015 government was elected with a manifesto commitment to plainly offer a referendum on UK membership of the EU before

[46] BBC, 'Cameron Places Focus on Optimism' (BBC, 1 October 2006).

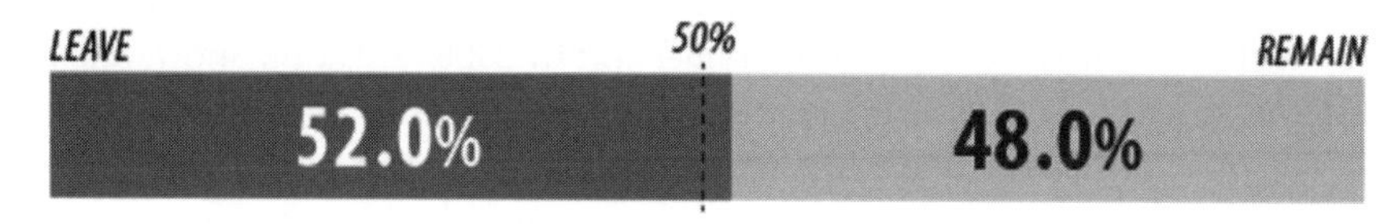

Figure 1.4 The EU referendum result

the end of 2017. Following a deeply flawed campaign, where both the 'Remain' and the 'Leave' sides misrepresented information about the consequences of EU membership and withdrawal from the EU, the question was put to eligible UK voters on 23 June 2016.

The result of the referendum revealed, more than anything, significant divisions within the UK. Scotland and Northern Ireland, on the whole, voted to remain in the European Union; England and Wales voted to leave. The overall majority for 'Leave' was 4 per cent of the vote—but there were no conditions placed on the referendum in order to make the result 'valid', and so the UK had voted to leave the EU. Figure 1.4 illustrates the dividing vote of 'Remain' and 'Leave'.

However, the referendum itself was not binding—merely advisory.[47] The next steps to take were consequently in the hands of the UK government. David Cameron resigned upon losing the referendum he had proposed. Following a leadership contest within the Conservative Party, reluctant 'Remainer' Theresa May became the new prime minister.[48] For most of the remainder of 2016, the only comment that came from the UK government on the referendum was that they would honour the result, and that 'Brexit' meant 'Brexit'. Details did not follow until 2017, when a speech by May promised that her government would invoke Article 50 by the end of March 2017, and that honouring the vote meant a full withdrawal; not a 'half-in, half-out' solution.[49]

1.9.1 What next for the UK?

It is, at the time of writing, more than three and a half years later—and yet we still have not fully 'Brexited': while we formally left the EU on 31 January 2020, also known as 'exit day', we are currently in a transition period that means that we are in most ways still treated as an EU Member State.

A look at Article 50 TEU will enable us to consider the progress that has been made:

[47] European Union Referendum Act 2015.

[48] See, eg, https://blogs.spectator.co.uk/2016/04/theresa-may-has-revealed-she-is-a-reluctant-member-of-the-in-campaign/.

[49] See https://www.gov.uk/government/speeches/the-governments-negotiating-objectives-for-exiting-the-eu-pm-speech.

Article 50 TEU (emphasis added)

1. Any Member State may **decide to withdraw from the Union in accordance with its own constitutional requirements**.
2. A Member State which decides to withdraw shall **notify the European Council of its intention**. In the light of the guidelines provided by the European Council, **the Union shall negotiate and conclude an agreement with that State**, setting out the **arrangements for its withdrawal**, taking account of **the framework for its future relationship** with the Union . . .
3. **The Treaties shall cease to apply to the State in question from the date of entry into force of the withdrawal agreement** or, failing that, **two years after the notification referred to in paragraph 2, unless the European Council, in agreement with the Member State concerned, unanimously decides to extend this period.**

Theresa May, after triggering Article 50 TEU in March 2017, negotiated a Withdrawal Agreement with the European Union in 2018 that was rejected by the UK Parliament on three separate occasions, not least because it was felt to reflect a 'half-in, half-out' solution by those adamant about leaving the EU. Following her resignation in 2019, the new Boris Johnson government negotiated some further changes to that Withdrawal Agreement in October 2019, particularly as it applied to Northern Ireland.[50] We have seen the Article 50 TEU negotiating period, set out in Article 50(3) TEU, extended not once but twice—in March 2019 and in October 2019, when the Johnson government also failed to quickly get its version of the Withdrawal Agreement through Parliament.

Only following a victory for Johnson's Conservative Party at the December 2019 general election was the October 2019 Withdrawal Agreement approved by Parliament.[51] As such, that Withdrawal Agreement (setting out the 'arrangements for withdrawal', per Article 50(2) TEU) entered into force at the end of January 2020. As of 31 January 2020, at 11pm UK time, the UK is no longer an EU Member State.

Under the Withdrawal Agreement, however, the UK is in a so-called 'transition period' until at least the end of December 2020. During 'transition', EU law will continue to apply to the UK as if it *were* still a Member State. This 'transition period' exists to buy time for the UK and the EU to negotiate their 'future relationship', without the legal system in the UK experiencing extreme upheaval. It is important to stress that the 'future relationship' negotiations will *not* take place under Article 50 TEU; as we will explore in detail in Chapter 16, these will be conducted between the EU and the UK with the UK as a *third country*, and so under separate EU 'international relations' procedures.

The 'future relationship' negotiations are guided by a non-binding Political Declaration on that future relationship, agreed by the UK and the EU as part of the Article 50 TEU process.[52] The EU published its negotiating directives—or the aims and limits that

[50] Agreement on the withdrawal of the United Kingdom of Great Britain and Northern Ireland from the European Union and the European Atomic Energy Community [2020] OJ L29/7 ('Withdrawal Agreement').

[51] In the form of the EU (Withdrawal Agreement) Act 2020.

[52] Political declaration setting out the framework for the future relationship between the European Union and the United Kingdom [2020] OJ C34/1 ('Political Declaration').

the Commission, as EU negotiator, will pursue—in February 2020, and the UK set out its general aims for the 'future relationship' in a written statement to Parliament at that time as well. The actual negotiations commenced in March 2020 and, to avoid the 'legal system upheaval' mentioned, need to be concluded by the end of the 'transition period'.

It is worth stressing that, according to the Withdrawal Agreement itself, the 'transition period' can be extended by one or two years if the UK and the EU agree to this; technically, therefore, there *is* more time available for negotiating the 'future relationship' desired.[53] However, the Johnson government was elected in December 2019 on a clear platform of getting Brexit and these future relationship negotiations done by the end of 2020, and as such, it will be difficult domestically for it to request an extension. The European Union (Withdrawal Agreement) Act 2020, implementing the Withdrawal Agreement in UK law, actually outright prohibits UK ministers from requesting an extension to the 'transition period'—though, if this proves desirable at any later point, Parliament can of course amend that Act as it can any other.[54]

Figure 1.5 sets out the 'Brexit' process as it has taken place to date.

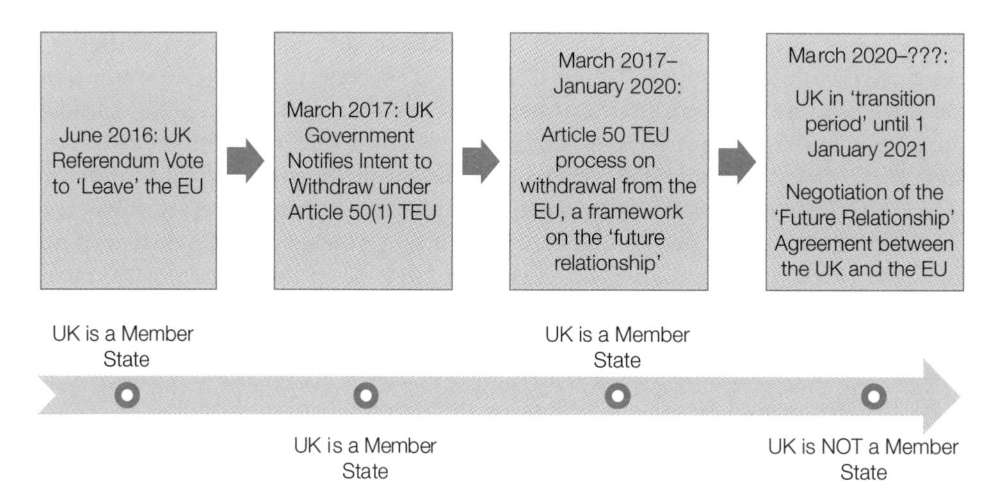

Figure 1.5 The 'Brexit' process

It may feel like not much has happened since 2016, but for lawyers, it has been a fascinating few years. Late 2016 and early 2017 marked some of the most in-depth analysis about the functioning of the UK's constitution in recent history, when the UK Supreme Court was asked to consider if the prime minister could invoke Article 50 TEU *without* approval from Parliament—or, if you will, what exactly the UK's 'constitutional requirements' as indicated in Article 50(1) TEU were.[55] The government argued that in approving the referendum, Parliament had granted the government the right to invoke Article 50, and that the government, regardless, could enter into and withdraw from treaties under the royal prerogative. The Supreme Court disagreed with this assessment, however, and

[53] Withdrawal Agreement, Articles 126 and 132.

[54] EU (Withdrawal Agreement) Act 2020, s 33.

[55] *R (on the application of Miller and another) v Secretary of State for Exiting the European Union* [2017] UKSC 5.

found that the EU Treaties were not like *other* international treaties. Indeed, triggering Article 50 proceedings would start the UK on an inevitable path of leaving the EU, and its departure would result in profound changes to *UK domestic law*. The Royal Prerogative could not, in the Supreme Court's majority judgment, result in changes to domestic law, and consequently invoking Article 50 TEU without the consent of Parliament would be unconstitutional.

What of the devolved regions? They, too, protested unilateral action by the UK government—but in a blow to the meaning of their semi-independence, the Supreme Court declined a constitutional obligation on the UK government to obtain the assent of the Scottish or Northern Ireland governments before invoking Article 50. Scottish, Welsh, and Northern Irish representatives in Westminster are, consequently, the only citizens of the devolved nations who are going to hold voting power over the next phase of the Brexit negotiating process.

The remainder of this textbook will shed light on what the next steps in the Brexit process will look like:

1. The UK and the EU successfully negotiate a 'future relationship' that closely resembles the Political Declaration, agreed by the UK and the EU under Article 50(2) TEU by the end of the 'transition period', as agreed under Article 50(2) TEU; or
2. The UK exits the 'transition period' with some sort of different 'future relationship' with the EU: perhaps a more minimal agreement than that set out in the Political Declaration, or no agreement at all, resulting in trade on World Trade Organization terms.

In either scenario, it is important to remember that the Withdrawal Agreement has entered into force, and so certain dimensions of UK–EU relations after Brexit are already legally binding: the ones we focus on over the course of this book is the provisions in the Withdrawal Agreement on Citizens' Rights (in Chapters 12 and 13), and the provisions that have been agreed to avoid a 'hard border' on the island of Ireland (at the end of every chapter).

The final section of each chapter of this book will consider how a particular aspect of the functioning of EU law in the UK will change as a result of Brexit, first under the Withdrawal Agreement, and second, under the 'future relationship', both if the aims set out in the Political Declaration are met by the end of the 'transition period', and if they are not.

1.9.2 What next for the EU?

'Brexit' has been but one of the big constitutional crises the EU has gone through since the ratifying of the Treaty of Lisbon. The first years under Lisbon marked a global financial crisis that put significant pressure on the EU's 'single currency' experiment: the northern Member States were effectively forced to lend money to the southern Member States, in exchange for the southern Member States becoming subject to stringent fiscal rules set by the EU and other international financial institutions. There was little democratic consent for either of these moves, and, as we will see in Chapter 3, they have raised significant questions about what the EU stands for, as well as the sustainability of the Euro without further fiscal integration.

More recent years have been marked by the largest humanitarian crisis since World War II, with the EU Heads of State struggling to agree a managed response to the influx of refugees from the Middle East and the African continent.[56] Equally worrying has been a developing 'rule of law' crisis in Poland and Hungary, where populist governments have enacted policies that appear wholly incompatible with the values of the EU, but the EU has struggled to respond to these challenges clearly.[57]

The EU project, in its significant changes between Rome and Lisbon, still has not found a golden solution to all the problems its Members may encounter. Difficult compromises between independent, sovereign nations remain necessary, and 'closer cooperation' has become the policy-making norm. As could have been said in the 1970s and early 1980s, the primary sign of progress in the EU seems to be growth of membership, with Croatia becoming the 28th EU Member State in 2013. However, even 'enlargement' is occasionally extremely politically complicated: Turkey's accession process has stagnated at an associate customs union state for decades because of Member State opposition, and, much more recently, France has indicated it does not want to open up accession talks with North Macedonia or Albania.

Many big questions about the EU as a project are by their very nature open-ended, and it is always worth remembering just how relatively 'new' the EU is as a project. Will the Euro prove sustainable? Will the EU Heads of State find a way to agree to a migration and refugee policy? Can the EU cope with elected Member State governments moving in a seemingly illiberal direction? And what will relations between the UK and the EU look like in the future—will the UK be treated more as a friendly neighbour, or as an 'ex-spouse' following an acrimonious divorce, deterring other Member States from engaging with Article 50 TEU in the process?

Again, we will simply have to wait and see.

1.10 In conclusion

A limited sacrifice of sovereignty in the 1950s, primarily geared at ensuring peace in Europe, led to the signing of a succession of Treaties between an increasing number of Member States, and has culminated in the Treaty of Lisbon of 2009. With each successive Treaty, the Member States have given more law-making and decision-making powers to the EU institutions, while simultaneously attempting to 'sell' the European public on the European project by trying to inject it with greater democratic qualities. These efforts have proven unsuccessful in the UK, and so, for over three and a half years now, the country has been on a mission to regain law-making powers in many policy areas that it has not controlled in several decades. The remainder of the EU, meanwhile, will have to continue to wrangle the Eurozone, refugee, and 'rule of law' crises that have plagued it for the last few years—and determine if the EU's future lies in greater integration, or a strategic retreat that will send significant legislative power back to the Member States.

[56] For analysis of EU legal responses, see Caterina Molinari, 'The EU and its Perilous Journey through the Migration Crisis: Informalization of the EU return policy and rule of law concerns' (2019) 44(6) ELRev 824.

[57] For analysis of EU legal responses, see Dimitry Kochenov and Laurent Pech, 'Better Late than Never? On the European Commission's Rule of Law Framework and its First Activation' (2016) 54(5) JCMS 1062.

Key points

Table 1.1 outlines the key dates in treaty history.

TABLE 1.1 Key dates in treaty history

Year	Treaty	Key Development
1951	European Coal and Steel Community (ECSC) (**foundational**)	Establishment of a common market in coal and steel (Section 1.1)
1957	European Economic Community (EEC) (**foundational**)	Establishment of a general common market (Section 1.2) for all trade in goods and services and free movement of workers and capital
1973	UK Accession Treaty (**amending**)	The UK joined the EEC
1986	Single European Act (SEA), establishing the EC Treaty (TEC) (**amending**)	A rebranding of the EEC as the 'European Community', and a restructuring of the voting rules within the EC institutions to permit more EC legislation to be adopted—and a promise to 'finish' the common market by 1992
1992	Maastricht (the TEU and the TEC) (**foundational**)	Establishment of the European Union (instead of the Community), and the start of a clearly more ambitious and political project (also involving citizenship and a currency for those Member States interested)
1997	Amsterdam (**amending**)	An attempt to clean up Maastricht, and the introduction of 'closer cooperation' to permit progress without *all* Member States' participation
2001	Nice (**amending**)	A restructuring of the voting rules in light of enlargement east, and a further attempt to clean up Maastricht
2004	Constitution of Europe (**foundational?**)	The failed Constitutional Treaty, rejected by referenda in the Netherlands and France
2009	Lisbon (the TEU and the TFEU) (**amending**)	A rebranded version of the Constitutional Treaty, culminating in two Treaties currently in force

Assess your learning

1. What were the original goals of the European project? How, and when, did they change? (See Sections 1.1–1.5.)
2. What (in *your* view) did the Constitutional Treaty *most* need to address regarding the setup and structure of the EU? Did it address this issue? (See Sections 1.2–1.6.)
3. How does the Lisbon Treaty differ from the Constitutional Treaty? (See Section 1.7.)
4. Where do you think the EU will go next, without the UK? Does Brexit mean the 'end' of further integration or not? What makes you think that? (See Section 1.8.)

Further reading

Matej Avbelj, 'Theory of European Union' (2011) 36(6) ELRev 818.

Paul Craig, *The Lisbon Treaty: Law, Politics and Treaty Reform*, rev edn (OUP, 2013) chapter 1.

Dora Kostakopoulou, 'What Fractures Political Unions? Failed Federations, Brexit and the Importance of Political Commitment' (2017) 42(3) ELRev 339.

Joseph Lacey, 'National Autonomy and Democratic Standardization: Should popular votes on European integration be regulated by the European Union?' (2017) 23(6) Eur Law J 523.

Dominik Lasok, 'Some Legal Aspects of Fundamental Renegotiations' (2015) 40(1) ELRev 3.

David Phinnemore, 'Crisis-ridden, Battered and Bruised: Time to give up on the EU?' (2015) 53(5) JCMS 61.

Jean-Claude Piris, *The Future of Europe: Towards a Two-Speed EU?* (CUP, 2012).

Robert Zbiral, 'Restoring Tasks from the European Union to Member States: A bumpy road to an unclear destination?' (2015) 52(1) CMLRev 51.

Issue 53(1) of the Journal of Common Market Studies

(This special issue examines UK political attitudes to various aspects of the EU and provides very interesting context to Brexit.)

Issue 41(4) of the European Law Review

(This special issue contains post-referendum reactions from leading EU law scholars on a variety of EU law issues.)

Online resources

Visit www.oup.com/he/demars1e for a sample approach to discussing the quote.

2

The EU institutions

Context for this chapter

'The European Union is ruled by an army of unelected bureaucrats who dream up new legislation and run day-to-day business.'

Sub-headline of a *Daily Express* article, 30 September 2016

2.1 Introduction

Much like learning about UK public law requires a good awareness of what institutions make up 'UK government', any investigation of the EU's impact on its Member States has to start with an investigation of the different institutions that make up the 'EU government'. The EU's institutional setup has the potential to be confusing: the different bodies that run the EU do not clearly map onto the expectations that we might have of what a 'government' looks like. This is, however, by design: remember, at all times, that it is the Member States who invented the EU's institutional design, and who allocated powers to the different institutions in the EU.

The fact that 'Brussels' is very distinct from 'Westminster' has made it relatively easy for Eurosceptics to take aim at the setup and functioning of the EU via exaggerated headlines like the one used as context for this chapter. The *Daily Express* is quoted at the start of this chapter to provoke a discussion about a common complaint launched about the EU in the UK press, which is that it is unrepresentative, undemocratic, and managed by some 'unelected civil servants' in Brussels that UK voters have no means of controlling. Are these complaints rooted in the reality of how the EU works?

Picking apart to what extent such accusations are on point requires, to start with, a detailed look at all the different institutions that make up 'the EU', their composition, and their respective powers. This chapter will provide that foundation and will examine the Article 50 TEU process on withdrawal from the EU as a topical case study that illustrates the roles of the EU institutions. Once we have this foundational knowledge,

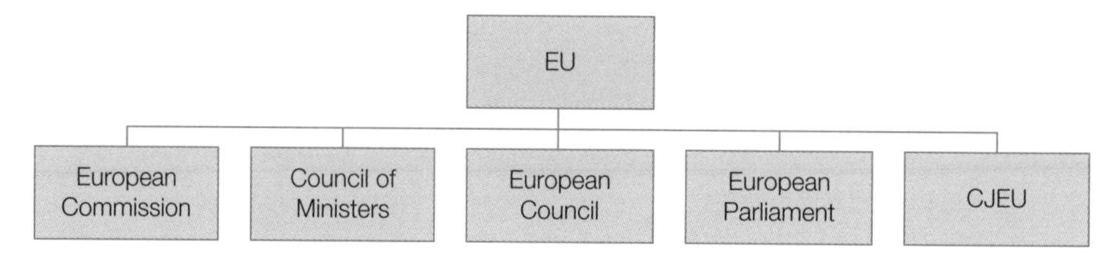

Figure 2.1 The EU's main institutions

Chapter 3 will allow us to dig into just how the EU takes decisions, and to what extent those decisions are consequently 'democratic'.

This chapter and Chapter 3 will also compare the EU's setup with that of the UK government, and will thus be drawing on a number of concepts from public law that it is important to keep in mind. The first of these concepts is separation of powers. Simply put, the separation of powers doctrine suggests that in order to prevent tyrannical government, it is important to ensure that no *one* part of government has too much power. The consequence of the doctrine has resulted in the idea of separate branches of government in most Western democracies: a legislature, where law is made; an executive, which determines the policy direction of the country and ensures laws are enacted by the government; and a judiciary, which resolves conflicts in interpretation of the law.

The second concept that we will keep referring to over the course of these two chapters is that of democracy. In its most basic sense, democracy refers to a system of governance whereby the people of a given territory have input into how they are governed. There are two forms of democracy that are commonly practised. Direct democracy means that the people *directly* decide on policy, as the UK population did in the 2016 referendum on EU membership. More commonly, countries are run via a representative democracy, where the people vote for *representatives* like MPs who then form a government that develops policy.

The EU's formal institutions (with legal capacity) are set out in Article 13 TEU. In Figure 2.1, you can see the five institutions that are of most interest to those studying law. There is no 'correct' way to order the different institutions that make up the EU; no one institution is technically superior to the others. For the sake of presenting a logical overview, this chapter discusses the institutions in the order in which they participate in the law-making process. We start with the body that is involved in the conclusion of the EU Treaties, and finish with the Court that interprets the law that all the other institutions together produce. There are two further EU institutions that will be briefly mentioned at the end of the chapter, but they do not participate in the EU's law-making function, and consequently are of less interest to law students.

2.2 The Article 50 TEU process

As mentioned in Chapter 1, one of the notable additions to the Lisbon Treaty is the Article 50 TEU process, which sets out how a Member State can leave the EU. Leaving the EU was possible prior to the Lisbon Treaty, but the specific *process* for withdrawal set out by Article 50 TEU is entirely new.

Two particular parts of Article 50 TEU are of interest in a chapter that examines institutional involvement:

Article 50 TEU (emphasis added)

2. A Member State which decides to withdraw shall **notify the European Council of its intention.** In the light of the guidelines provided by the European Council, **the Union shall negotiate and conclude an agreement with that State,** setting out the **arrangements for its withdrawal,** taking account of **the framework for its future relationship** with the Union. That agreement shall be negotiated in accordance **with Article 218(3) of the Treaty on the Functioning of the European Union. It shall be concluded on behalf of the Union by the Council, acting by a qualified majority, after obtaining the consent of the European Parliament.**

. . .

4. For the purposes of paragraphs 2 and 3, **the member of the European Council or of the Council representing the withdrawing Member State shall not participate in the discussions of the European Council or Council or in decisions concerning it.**

First, Article 50(2) TEU sets out what each of the EU institutions is responsible for when dealing with a Member State that wishes to withdraw from the EU. As we explore the EU institutions in turn in the remaining sections of this chapter, we will come back to those particular responsibilities.

The other key dimension of Article 50 TEU, for the purposes of this chapter, is its fourth paragraph, which makes it clear that the Member State intending to withdraw can still *generally* attend EU institutions—but not when those EU institutions are discussing its withdrawal process. While the UK thus remained a Member State throughout the Article 50 TEU process, from March 2017 onwards we already had to start speaking of meetings between the so-called EU27: the EU, but without the UK.

2.3 The European Council

If there *were* a hierarchy of EU institutions, it is arguable that the European Council would sit at its pinnacle, as it is most easily recognized as the 'Cabinet' of the EU. It was established formally in the Lisbon Treaty, but has been meeting as a matter of standing EU practice since 1975. Its core functions are set out in Article 15(1) TEU:

Article 15(1) TEU (emphasis added)

The European Council shall provide the Union with the necessary impetus for its development and shall define the **general political directions** and priorities thereof. **It shall not exercise legislative functions.**

Despite its stated exclusion from 'legislative functions', it engages in what is probably the most important law-related EU function of all: that of Treaty negotiation. Under the Treaty revision procedures set out in Article 48 TEU, the European Council both launches and concludes any attempts to revise the EU Treaties.

These types of high-level political functions are similar to what we would expect the Cabinet in the UK to carry out. Composition of the European Council, set out in Article 15(2), makes it clear that an analogy to the Cabinet is not inappropriate: members of the European Council are the Heads of State (or government) of the Member States, alongside the President of the European Council and the President of the Commission. A third EU-specific functionary, the High Representative of the Union for Foreign Affairs and Security Policy, shall 'take part in its work'.[1] The European Council is where the winners of national elections across Europe meet—much as a UK Cabinet is the product of a UK election.

However, in many other ways, the European Council is quite distinct from the Cabinet. For one thing, it does not actually deal with the day-to-day running of the European Union. Indeed, Article 15(3) makes it clear that the European Council only meets twice in a six-month period; it can arrange for a 'special' meeting outside of that cycle, but even then would not meet very regularly.

European Council meetings are chaired by the President of the European Council. Until the Lisbon Treaty, the 'presidency' of the European Council was an unofficial position, held on a rotating basis by heads of the Member State that concurrently held the Presidency of the *other* Council (which will be discussed in Section 2.5). The Lisbon Treaty changed this, opting instead for an elected President who did not hold a national office. This change was introduced to ensure that the President of the European Council could function as an independent party who would organize discussions between the Heads of State, all interested in their own domestic priorities first and foremost.[2] The President consequently cannot hold a national office, and instead is a full-time EU employee.

A look at the functioning of both of these EU Presidential elections introduces us to the two most common voting systems that exist within the EU: **consensus/unanimity voting** and **qualified majority voting (QMV)**. Consensus voting is another term for unanimity voting: it means that a proposal only passes when *all those with voting power* vote in favour of a given proposal. As outlined in Chapter 1, historically, all legislative adoption decisions in the EU were taken by consensus within the Council of Ministers. The larger the EU becomes, the more difficult it is to obtain this kind of consensus—but, the more sensitive the area of policy in which the EU is active, the more likely it is that Member States will wish to effectively keep a **veto**, by insisting on unanimity or consensus decision-making.

The alternative to consensus is what the EU calls **qualified majority voting (QMV)**. As you are not reading a maths textbook, we will gloss over the details of the formulae that underpin QMV—but rather explain its general functioning. A qualified majority is what it sounds like: not a *standard* majority, where 51 per cent of the vote for a proposal sees it enacted, but

[1] Article 15(2) TEU.

[2] This is set out in Article 15(6), where establishing 'cohesion' between the Member States is explicitly listed as one of the goals for the President to meet.

rather a majority that is *qualified* by some other criteria. Since the enactment of the Lisbon Treaty, this is normally the *population* of EU nationals represented by a given vote—so, for a proposal to pass, 55 per cent of the Member State representatives in an EU body have to vote in favour of it, *and* that majority of Member State representatives has to represent 65 per cent of the EU population. This prevents 15 of the smallest Member States being able effectively to 'outvote' a bigger Member State—but simultaneously, the large Member States cannot force policy onto the smaller Member States unless enough of their representatives also agree to a proposal. QMV represents a mitigated loss of control for the Member States: it provides less certainty than a veto, but much more certainty than a simple majority.

It is worth noting that only the Heads of State have voting power within the European Council. The President of the European Council is consequently decided by QMV amongst the Heads of State. In practice, the President of the European Council is normally agreed upon unanimously, though 2017's re-election of the former Polish Prime Minister, Donald Tusk, was opposed by Poland's Prime Minister and consequently approved through QMV.

2019 marked the end of Donald Tusk's second term as President of the European Council; each term can last two and a half years and is renewable once. Brexit was Tusk's final but probably most complicated job to navigate through as President: he formally represented the EU in all 'external' representation that dealt with Common Foreign and Security Policy, and also more generally spoke on behalf of the European Council, whose guidelines indicated the direction in which the EU wanted to push the Article 50 TEU negotiations. Following three days of negotiation amongst the European Council, Tusk's successor as of 1 December 2019 is former Belgian Prime Minister Charles Michel, who is similarly faced with Brexit as a priority.

When establishing policies or guidelines, like the Article 50 TEU negotiating guidelines, the European Council adopts policy by consensus unless the Treaties state otherwise. This means that the negotiating guidelines are indeed a document to which *all* of the EU's 27 non-UK Member States have agreed. It is consequently more than mere rhetoric to say that the EU approached the Brexit negotiations 'as one': the operating procedures of the European Council plainly require that, when acting on behalf of the EU, the Heads of State come to a *single, agreed position*.

Such a single, agreed position is also expected of the European Council when it comes to the drafting of new EU Treaties. The European Council is not the *only* party involved in this process, but it is the dominant and concluding player. As already noted, the Treaty revision procedure set out in Article 48 TEU is formally launched by the European Council, whether it concerns a rewrite of a single Treaty article or one of the big Treaty relaunches discussed in Chapter 1. When any interested party—a Member State, the Commission, or the European Parliament—proposes to revisit the Treaties, the European Council takes a majority vote examining that proposal, and then organizes a so-called '**convention**'. Such a convention brings together representatives from national parliaments, the Heads of State, Members of European Parliament, and delegates from the European Commission, who will all discuss the proposed changes. The final recommendations, adopted by consensus, then proceed to a formal **intergovernmental conference (IGC)** which is convened by the President of the European Council and consists of representatives of Member State governments, who negotiate a new Treaty. At the very end of an IGC, a new final proposed Treaty text is then considered by the European Council—who then unanimously approve the text, and send it off to national parliaments for ratification.

Discussing the quote

Think about the quote at the beginning of this chapter. Is the European Council composed of 'unelected bureaucrats'? Have they seized power from the Member States? Why or why not?

2.4 The European Commission ('Commission')

The European Commission, or the 'Commission', is the EU institution that is most commonly meant by UK press mentions of policies or rules coming from 'Brussels', or indeed when they accuse the EU of being run by 'unelected bureaucrats'. Unlike the European Council, it *is* responsible for most of the day-to-day running of the EU. However, calling it 'the EU's civil service' is a shorthand description that is not entirely accurate: as a hybrid legislative and executive organ, it is not directly comparable to any UK institution, and consequently requires looking at in some detail.

Its functions are broadly set out in Article 17(1) TEU, and consist of the following:

- Promoting 'the general interest of the Union';
- Ensuring 'the application of the Treaties, and of measures adopted by the institutions pursuant to [the Treaties]';
- Overseeing 'the application of Union law under the control of the Court of Justice of the European Union';
- Executing the EU budget and managing EU programmes;
- Representing the EU externally *except* in matters of Common Foreign and Security Policy.

The bulk of these descriptions are very general, and need a little more expanding on in order to clarify whether the Commission is a powerful institution. 'Ensuring the application of the Treaties' and 'overseeing the application of Union law' before the Court both hint at one of the Commission's key tasks, which is the **enforcement** of EU law.[3] Enforcement is an 'executive' style function, in that it is one of the tasks carried out to ensure that EU laws are being abided by (and so that EU goals are being met) by all EU Member States and bodies. Domestically, it will be the police forces that ensure that UK laws are abided by; but there is no such thing as 'law enforcement' by a police force at the EU level. After all, EU law is directed at *Member States*—and it is not possible to throw those in prison! Instead, there is an administrative enforcement process that the Commission administers—and so whenever the Commission feels that a Member State or an EU institution does not comply with the law as it is set out in the Treaties or in other binding EU legislation, it commences **infringement proceedings** under the Treaties. We will look at how these proceedings work in much more detail in Chapter 8, but it goes without saying that it is a very important function for the Commission to carry out.

[3] For much more about the enforcement of EU law, see Chapter 8.

Other 'executive' functions are the budgetary and programme management ones: here, and in foreign representation in most matters, is where the Commission most resembles a 'civil service' for the EU. It behaves as we would expect UK governmental departments to. However, its most interesting function for our purposes (beyond **enforcement** of EU law) is the one that is only hinted at by the first part of Article 17(1) TEU. The 'general interest of the Union' provision looks relatively toothless, but actually hints at a more explicit power that is set out clearly in Article 17(2) TEU:

Article 17(2) TEU (emphasis added)

Union legislative acts may **only** be adopted on the basis of a **Commission proposal**, except where the Treaties provide otherwise . . .

That is to say, the power of **legislative initiative** lies with the Commission. Only the Commission can write up proposals for new pieces of EU secondary legislation. This is a job that we would expect to be performed by the EU's Parliament, as it is clearly performed by the UK Parliament—but the EU has an institution called the European Parliament, and it does not hold the power of legislative initiative.

So then *who* actually proposes legislation in the EU? Who is on the Commission?

Per Article 17(3) TEU, members of the Commission—called 'Commissioners', who serve on the College of Commissioners—serve for five years and are chosen 'on the ground of their general competence and European commitment from persons whose independence is beyond doubt'. Probably the most important parts of that description are the 'European commitment' and 'independence'. The Commission is there to protect the interest of the EU, rather than the Member States, and consequently Commissioners must be committed to the EU, rather than to their own Member States. What this means in practice is that legislative initiative in the EU lies with people whose ultimate loyalty is to *the EU Treaties*, rather than to any one of the Member States.

The neutrality of Commissioners is emphasized repeatedly in Article 17 TEU, and is also implied in changes proposed in the Lisbon Treaty to the number of Commissioners who would serve at any point in time. Historically, and at present, however, there are as many Commissioners as there are Member States.[4] The larger the EU becomes, however, the less practical this is: each Commissioner has to be given a bespoke policy 'portfolio' that is their area of responsibility, and there are only as many policy portfolios as there are areas in which the EU can make law. This list is not infinite, as we will see in Chapter 4. Consequently, the Lisbon Treaty, in Article 17(5) TEU, promises as of November 2014 to reduce the size of the Commission (including its President and Vice President, whom we will look at shortly) to a number equal to two-thirds of the number of Member States. At current tally, that would mean between 16 and 18 Commissioners in total, who would hold Commission 'portfolios' on a rotating basis.

However, this provision has not yet come into force. It allows for an exception if unanimously agreed by the European Council, and such an exception was agreed following

[4] See Article 17(4); note also the role of the Commission President there, and the High Representative, who serves as Vice President of the Commission.

Ireland's first referendum on ratifying the Lisbon Treaty. As a concession to Ireland's demands to be consistently represented in the Commission, the European Council agreed that the Article 17(5) membership changes would not be revisited until 2019, and in 2019 they were again pushed back. The precise rationale for Ireland's request remains opaque: Ireland's Commissioner, after all, was not intended to be representing Ireland at all, but rather will represent the EU, as all Commissioners do.[5]

The 2019 Commission, however, does have one fewer Commissioner in the College . . . in light of Brexit. The UK government, anticipating (or hoping) that the Brexit process would come to completion before the new Commission took up its seats, did not propose a candidate. There are thus only 27 portfolios and places filled in the 2019–2024 College.

At the head of the College of Commissioners is the Commission's President. Historically, this was an appointed post: unanimously, the European Council would simply pick a candidate and appoint them. Lisbon has attempted to make this process more transparent and more democratic. Instead of a unanimous appointment by the European Council, Article 17(7) TEU now asks for the European Council to pick a candidate by QMV, and that candidate then needs to be confirmed by a majority of the European Parliament to take up office. They will normally be the candidate put forward by the European Party Grouping with the largest majority in the most recent EP elections.

The first Commission President appointed in this way was Jean-Claude Juncker, a former prime minister of Luxembourg. His nomination was *almost* unanimous despite the change in procedure; the only objector was David Cameron, then still Prime Minister of the UK, who thought Juncker to be far too pro-European a choice to run the body in charge of proposing EU legislation. Cameron was outvoted, however, and Juncker confirmed by the European Parliament without any further complications. Juncker's replacement is Ursula von der Leyen, who was most recently German Minister of Defence. She was confirmed by the European Parliament in July 2019.

The President's role is important, in that the President does set out the general operating guidelines for the College of Commissioners—but it is perhaps a less important role than Cameron's concerns made it out to be. There is very little the Commission President can do without consent from other EU bodies. This includes making up the remainder of the College of Commissioners: the President has to respond to suggestions made by the Member States and reach a 'common accord' with the Council of Ministers, which we will discuss in Section 2.5, in order to propose a list of Commissioners. The entire College of Commissioners is then subject to a 'vote of consent' before the European Parliament, which per the Treaties means that a simple majority must approve of their make-up.

In practice, each individual candidate is considered separately by the European Parliament via an interview process. The proposed Von der Leyen Commission ran into some stumbling blocks here, in that the French, Hungarian, and Romanian candidates she had put forward lost their European Parliament 'confirmation votes' in early October 2019. New candidates were confirmed by the European Parliament, however, and the Von der Leyen Commission took office on 1 December 2019.

Finally, once the European Parliament's consent has been obtained, the Commission will be formally approved by the European Council. In other words, while the President

[5] See OJ [2013] L165/98, Article 2.

gets to allocate the different 'portfolios' within the College of Commissioners under Article 17(6), the actual composition of the College of Commissioners is checked by virtually all other EU institutions.

Control over the actions of the Commission does not stop with its appointment. While individual Commissioners and the High Representative can be asked to resign by the Commission President under Article 17(6), Article 17(8) stresses that the Commission as a whole is responsible to the European Parliament. The European Parliament thus can pass a 'motion of censure' to disband the Commission if it is performing work that the European Parliament disapproves of, and it is worth noting that it has had this power—albeit at a high threshold, with two-thirds of the Parliament needing to vote in favour of the motion for it to succeed—since the Treaty of Rome. To date, such a motion has never been passed, although its use was threatened in 1999 against the Commission operating under President Santer, which resulted in an entire Commission resigning before it could be replaced.

Discussing the quote

How 'unelected' is the College of Commissioners under the Lisbon Treaty?

The one member of the College of Commissioners we have not yet discussed is its Vice President. The role of the High Representative of Foreign Affairs and Security Policy was formalized in the Lisbon Treaty in Article 18 TEU; the first holder of the 'new' post is Federica Mogherini, who, prior to taking up this role, was the Italian Foreign Minister. Her 2019 replacement is former European Parliament President Josep Borrell.

Whereas the Commission's President has a roving policy brief (much like the UK Prime Minister) and all other Commissioners are responsible for portfolios allocated to them by the Commission President, the High Representative is responsible for coordinating the Commission's external actions, including external trade, development cooperation, and humanitarian aid. This is perhaps not quite what you would assume the High Representative for *Foreign Affairs and Security Policy* would be in charge of—but that is because the High Representative's role takes place across the Commission and the Council of Ministers. External trade, development cooperation, and humanitarian aid are policy areas that the Member States have quite willingly transferred to the EU institutions; but other aspects of foreign affairs and particularly security policy are of so sensitive a political nature that the Member States have not wanted to relinquish 'control' over policy direction in the same way. Remember that, as a Commissioner, the High Representative will be representing *EU* interests, rather than Member State ones.

Finally, a word of caution: the word 'Commission' is normally used to refer to the College of Commissioners, or those at the head of specific policy portfolios. However, the actual European Commission has approximately 33,000 employees, and works very much like the civil service does: each 'portfolio' has a Ministry working behind it, called a 'Directorate-General' or 'DG'. The Commissioner in charge of a DG is the visible spokesperson, but significant work takes place behind the scenes; much like in the UK, where not all technical details of law are debated in Parliament, a lot of what the EU has termed 'delegated' or 'implementing' legislation is actually produced within the Commission's DGs rather than as part of the EU's ordinary legislative process. This has been very controversial; we will explore why in Chapter 3.

As the Commission's formal roles are primarily rooted in the introduction of secondary legislation, and the enforcement of EU law, the Commission as a *whole* is not one of the key players in the Article 50 TEU process. It is actually not mentioned at all in Article 50 TEU. However, noteworthy here is the wording in Article 50(2):

Article 50(2) TEU (emphasis added)

. . . **the Union shall negotiate** and conclude an agreement with that State, setting out the arrangements for its withdrawal, taking account of the framework for its future relationship with the Union. **That agreement shall be negotiated in accordance with Article 218(3) of the Treaty on the Functioning of the European Union** . . .

The reference to 'the Union' in Article 50(2) TEU is usually to the Commission. The mentioned Article 218(3) TFEU explains how it is involved:

Article 218(3) TFEU (emphasis added)

The Commission . . . shall submit recommendations to the Council, which shall **adopt a decision** authorising the opening of negotiations and, depending on the subject of the agreement envisaged, **nominating the Union negotiator** or the head of the Union's negotiating team.

President Juncker's proposal for the Brexit negotiations was Michel Barnier, a French politician who served as the European Commissioner for the Internal Market for five years under the previous Commission. He now heads up the negotiating team, called 'TF50' or 'Task Force 50', which conducted the 'withdrawal' negotiations on the basis of the European Council's guidelines and the European Parliament's resolution on the negotiations. The latter parties, as well as the Council of Ministers, all have to agree to what the Commission negotiates—so, in a way, its role in the Article 50 TEU process is a logical continuance of what its general legislative role is: it proposes, but it does not adopt.

Pause for reflection

Note that legislative initiative is only one part of 'law-making'—a proposed law only becomes an actual law once it has been adopted, and the power of **legislative adoption** is not mentioned in Article 17 TEU. Why do you think the job of 'law-making' has been split like this?

2.5 The Council of Ministers ('Council')

To the delight of all students of EU law, the EU is made up of two completely separate institutions that both have the words 'European' and 'Council' in them. We have already looked at the European Council—but now it is time to examine the Council of the European Union, which is a completely different body with completely different powers.

For the sake of making this *slightly* easier to remember, the European Council is **always** called the European Council; the Council of the European Union, on the other hand, is normally called either the 'Council of Ministers' or just the 'Council'.

It is perhaps best to think of the Council as the opposite of the European Council. We saw in Section 2.3 that the European Council can establish big policy ideas, but cannot actually adopt legislation; the Council, on the other hand, does not develop overarching EU policy, but instead has the primary power of **legislative adoption**. As set out in Article 16 TEU, the Council's role is to 'jointly with the European Parliament . . . exercise legislative and budgetary functions'.

In the original Treaty of Rome, the Council of Ministers had exclusive control over legislative adoption.[6] This was for a very simple reason: the mere joining of a project of international cooperation like the European Economic Community was a sea change for its Member States, and the idea of surrendering control over the type of law produced by such a project was untenable. What the drafters of the EEC Treaty consequently did was ensure that no legislation could be adopted without unanimous agreement from a body composed of government representatives. This was the Council of Ministers, which gained the 'of Ministers' branding because it is composed of a rotating set of government representatives at *ministerial* level.[7] The Finance Council consequently involves a meeting of national Ministers of Finance; and the Foreign Affairs Council, headed by the High Commissioner, involves the national Foreign Ministers.

A small sacrifice of sovereignty with retained control over all law produced by the European Economic Community was palatable to the Member States but, as we saw in Chapter 1, resulted in very little progress in the adoption of legislation that would achieve the Community's goals. In the 1970s and the 1980s in particular, virtually all Commission-proposed legislation worked *slightly* less well for one Member State than for others, and resulted in a failure to reach a unanimous position. Consequently, virtually no proposed legislation made it through the Council on account of the Council's practice of seeking consensus where possible *and* the creation of the Luxembourg Veto system discussed in Chapter 1, permitting a 'veto' of a Commission proposal by any Member State if they felt it threatened their 'very important national interests'. The Single European Act changed this forever: in 1984, the Member States agreed that Council voting could not remain unanimous if the single market was ever going to be 'completed'. Since then, and in an ever-increasing number of policy areas, the Council has voted by **QMV** unless the Treaties explicitly stipulate otherwise.[8]

As explained earlier, **QMV** in the Council requires at least 55 per cent of the Member State representatives to vote in favour of a Commission proposal, *and* that 55 per cent of the Member States must represent at least 65 per cent of the EU population. There is a small caveat to this surrendering of sovereignty, however, and it is that Article 16(4) enables something called a 'blocking minority'. While clearly not as extreme as the Luxembourg Veto, it remains a sign that, where Member States feel very strongly that the EU should not be producing a particular law, a small number of them can stop this from happening. The Council's role consequently remains of fundamental importance, and no EU law can be made without at least tacit approval from 23 out of 27 Member State representatives.

[6] See Chapter 1. [7] Article 16(2) TEU. [8] Article 16(3) TEU.

It is probably unsurprising that deliberations in the Council have been a mystery throughout the EU's existence; we do not necessarily demand transparency from discussions that take place in either the Cabinet or amongst the various ministers in charge of policy briefs within a given Whitehall department. The EU is a magnified version of that—but while it is logical that many 'senior' discussions about what laws to adopt and how to amend proposals for laws take place behind closed doors at both the national and the EU level, this was never deemed to be *acceptable* at the EU level in the same way as it is taken for granted domestically. As a compromise to long-standing complaints about the secrecy underpinning Council decision-making, Lisbon's Article 16(8) promises that the Council will 'meet in public when it deliberates and votes on a draft legislative act'. However, this does not mean that the entirety of Council meetings are now *public*; rather, it means that Council meetings are now split between 'deliberations on Union legislative acts' and 'non-legislative activities', the latter remaining as mysterious as they ever have been.

The Council, ultimately, ensures that the Member States retain significant control over the law coming out of the EU. Its administrative support body, known as the Committee of Permanent Representatives of the Governments of the Member States or COREPER, is also composed of national representatives, there primarily to ensure that their own governments are briefed on EU matters arising and how those will impact their particular governments. Given the nature of the Council's work, there is also no independent 'president'; instead, the Council presidency rotates on a six-monthly basis between the Member States as set out in Article 16(8) TEU. The exception to this, as mentioned, is the Foreign Affairs Council, of which the High Commissioner is the President.

Much as it has an ultimate 'adoption' role in the EU's normal legislative process, the role of the Council in the Article 50 TEU process is one that involves taking key decisions. Under Article 218(3) TFEU, as we saw in Section 2.4, it has the power to both open negotiations and nominate the actual negotiator. Article 50(2) TEU then also makes clear that the Council has the job of 'concluding' the agreement by a qualified majority vote, after it has obtained consent from the European Parliament. The concluding 'vote' to take place in the Article 50 TEU process was consequently the Council's in late January 2020: when it adopted the Withdrawal Agreement, it became formally binding on the EU.

Discussing the quote

In terms of law-making, which body do you think is more powerful: the Commission or the Council? Why? And how does your answer to the question reflect on the quote at the start of the chapter?

2.6 The European Parliament ('EP')

If you think back to the history of the European Union, very few things have changed in the appearance of its institutional setup. However, this is misleading, because at least *one* institution that has been around since 1958 has undergone very significant and expansive change between Rome and Lisbon. This is the European Parliament (EP): the final EU institution involved in the legislative process.

When established under the Treaty of Rome, it was called the European (Parliamentary) Assembly. It was composed of Member State representatives, but it was not directly voted for by EU citizens. Instead, it was composed of national parliamentarians who were sent as delegates to work in the European Assembly—and while it voted for its own President[9] and set up its own procedures, it had no actual legislative power. The body was there to be *consulted* by other EU institutions at most, but did not play a direct role in the EU's law-making processes.

An unelected parliament will sound strange to most of us—and indeed, under the Treaty of Rome, it was *intended* to be a body of directly elected representatives. However, the voting system that would result in these elections had to be determined by the Council of Ministers—and as we saw in Section 2.5, this was not the only area in which the Council failed to find agreement in the 1960s and 1970s. It was only when the EP itself threatened to start proceedings against the Council before the Court of Justice that the Council compromised and permitted direct elections to take place. The first direct elections to the EP took place in 1979, and have recurred every five years since then.

Even this directly elected EP, however, remained on the sidelines of the legislative process: it was composed of elected representatives who had very little power. The one area in which they managed to get some direct say in the 1970s was in the EC's budgets via hard-fought minor Treaty amendments; but by our understanding of what a parliament should look like and should have powers over, the EP remained extremely weak until the 1980s.

It was not until the Single European Act that we see a genuine shift in the relationship between the Council and the EP. As discussed in Section 2.5, the SEA marked a willingness on the part of the Member States to surrender slightly more control over the EU's law-making processes. This came paired with an increase in powers for the EP, as well as a few other changes. For example, we saw in Chapter 1 that it had been calling itself the Parliament since 1962, but it only had its new name approved in a Treaty in 1987. The Single European Act also introduced a new legislative process under which the EP not only had to be *consulted*, but its approval of a piece of legislation was actually required for it to be adopted by the Council. This new procedure, set out in then-Article 252 EC, was known as the 'cooperation procedure'. Under cooperation, if the EP rejected a legislative proposal, it could only be pushed through by the Council if the Council then unanimously voted to adopt it.

Cooperation was a compromise: what the EP had actually proposed in its work on what would end up becoming the SEA were *co-decision* powers. Under co-decision, approval of both the EP *and* the Council was required for a legislative proposal to be adopted. Where they did not agree on a draft proposal, the draft would be 'volleyed' back between the respective institutions until a compromise solution could be found, or the legislative proposal was abandoned. A shift to a process that would give the EP powers that were effectively *equal* to those of the Council, even in only a few policy areas, could not be agreed upon at the IGC that resulted in the SEA; cooperation was the compromise that the Member States arrived at.

However, by 1992, a concrete effort was made to give the EU project greater popular appeal. Part of this effort was an extension of power to the only directly elected

[9] The first President was none other than Robert Schuman.

EU institution. Maastricht consequently did successfully introduce co-decision, albeit in limited areas. Every subsequent Treaty until Lisbon continued to expand the policy areas in which co-decision was the normal legislative procedure, and so the EP's legislative powers continued to grow. As of the Lisbon Treaty, the co-decision procedure has been renamed the **'ordinary legislative procedure'**, and has expanded into a further 40 policy areas.[10]

What started out as a powerless, unelected body to which Member States simply sent some delegates has transformed into a body that has almost equivalent powers to the Council of Ministers, in nearly all policy areas. Paul Craig has described the EP as the 'winner' of the Lisbon Treaty on an institutional level,[11] in the sense that out of all the institutions it gained the most novel powers from the 2009 amendments—and it is hard to deny that all attempts to make the EU more appealing to European citizens seem to have resulted in a larger role for the Parliament in the EU's work. Has this worked?

Not necessarily—and not least because of a number of institutional 'quirks' that somewhat undermine the positive nature of the EP's legislative powers. The first of these is practical one: while most obviously a 'democratic' institution, in that European citizens vote for MEPs directly, significant compromises have had to be made in order to ensure that, with every accession, the size of the EP remained manageable.

The Nice Treaty was the first one to introduce a cap on the number of MEPs that could be elected—and since then, formulae have had to be devised in order to determine just how many MEPs each Member State would have. As discussed in Chapter 1, whenever these kinds of compromises on representation have to be struck simply for the sake of operational efficiency, the solution tends to be convoluted and have unexpected outcomes. The EP's compromise takes a form whereby the larger Member States *do* total more MEPs than the smaller ones—but the MEPs representing larger Member States represent significantly more inhabitants of that Member State.[12] This does not make MEPs feel particularly *close* to the people they are intended to represent—a concern we will revisit in Chapter 3.

A similarly practical 'quirk' that has haunted the reputation of the European Parliament is the manner in which its elections have been organized. The truly strange thing about having European elections like the parliamentary ones is that there are technically *no European political parties*. Instead, here in the UK, when we voted for MEPs, they represented domestic political parties like Labour, the Conservatives, or the Liberal Democrats. These parties are very clearly associated with *domestic* policies—and voters tend to follow their domestic policy preferences when electing MEPs. However, once an MEP is elected, they go off to work for the European Union, and all major domestic political parties in the EU are members of something called a **European Party Grouping**: a term for an alliance struck between these different domestic political parties along political lines. In other words, a vote for a Labour MEP then transformed into a vote for the European-level Progressive Alliance of Socialists & Democrats (known as S&D) . . . which is the body, composed of MEPs representing all Member States, that actually *has* European-level policies and adopts or rejects legislation produced by the EU on that basis. The 2020 European Parliament's make-up, in terms of seats held by European Party Groupings, is shown in Figure 2.2:

[10] Articles 289 and 294 TFEU.

[11] Paul Craig, *The Lisbon Treaty: Law, Politics, and Treaty Reform* (OUP, 2013) 36.

[12] Article 18(2) TEU.

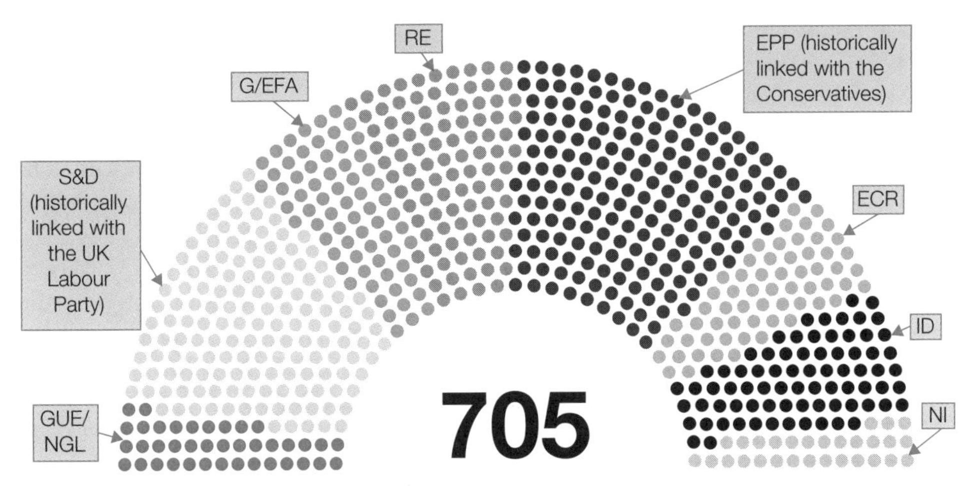

Figure 2.2 The European Parliament and its UK connections

Pause for reflection

How many UK voters, do you think, have ever heard of S&D? And what is the consequence of the fact that these European Party Groupings *are* unknown—does it make the work of the European Parliament less meaningful, or does it have no impact on how European citizens feel about the EU?

There are practical consequences to membership of a European Party Grouping. The two biggest party groupings—the aforementioned S&D, which the UK Labour Party belonged to, and the European People's Party (EPP), which the Conservatives belonged to until David Cameron withdrew the party in 2009—dominate two specific types of elections within the EU.

The first, and most obvious of these, is the election of the EP's President, who effectively acts as the speaker of the EP; the candidate for this role, set out in Article 18(4) TEU, is to be chosen from the ranks of elected MEPs in whatever way the Parliament itself wishes this to be done. In line with democratic traditions, the President is selected for their five-year term from the largest European Party Grouping in Parliament. As this historically has been either the centre-left S&D or centre-right EPP, these parties have developed a practice of 'role-sharing'. Consequently, within each parliamentary term of five years, for two and a half years the President will be the nominee of *one* of the two largest parties, and for the next two and a half years, the President will be the nominee of the other one. From 2014 until 2015, S&D's Martin Schultz was European Parliament President; and as of January 2017, the role fell to the EPP's Antonio Tajani. The current European Parliament President is David Sassoli of S&D, and he will likely be succeeded in January 2021 by an EPP nominee.

Lisbon has made EP elections interesting in a second way: after all, as set out in Article 14(1) TEU, the EP now also gets to 'elect' (or at the very least nominate) the Commission President, who will ordinarily be the candidate put forward by the European Party Grouping with the largest number of votes in EP elections. This process, known as the *Spitzenkandidat* process, resulted in the choice of Jean-Claude Juncker as the EPP's nominee in 2014, and Ursula von der Leyen as the 2019 nominee by the EPP. The prominence of the EPP in the selection of the Commission President under the *Spitzenkandidat* process is not uninteresting in light of David Cameron's decision to leave that grouping for a smaller, more Eurosceptic one upon becoming Prime Minister; his attempts to not have Juncker elected, discussed in Section 2.4, might have been more successful had he exercised pressure via Conservative MEPs in the EPP as opposed to as a Head of State in the European Council.

This discussion should demonstrate that EP elections function in a way that is likely to be opaque to a great many EU citizens; this, too, has done little to endear the EP to the European people. However, while its elections and internal organization might be justifiable in that it is not directly comparable to any domestic parliaments, there is one further source of constant criticism that the EP faces, and this one is harder to explain.

It sits in two different cities in Belgium and France, and, once a month, all MEPs and their staff travel from Brussels to Strasbourg. This fun exercise has been estimated to cost approximately £39 billion a year—and is maintained today largely because of French unwillingness to relinquish the Strasbourg sitting, as it serves as a fairly substantial tourist attraction there![13] The UK press has had a legitimate axe to grind with the EU over the bureaucratic waste that is the 'travelling Parliament' for many years now, but no change to the setup of old appears forthcoming.

These strange institutional quirks aside, however, it is very important not to underestimate the role that the EP *currently* plays in the EU's functioning. Not only is it co-legislator in nearly all policy areas as of the Lisbon Treaty, but it also holds significant oversight powers over the other institutions. As discussed in Section 2.4, Article 17(8) TEU sets out that where the European Parliament has lost faith in the Commission, it can pass a 'motion of censure' with a two-thirds majority vote that will result in the resignation of the entire Commission. The mere threat of this happening has been enough to cause at least one Commission to resign.

Beyond that, and of particular concern to the UK, the EP also holds a very significant power over the Brexit negotiations. Under Article 50(2) TEU, any withdrawal agreement the EU and the UK produced had to gain the 'consent' of the EP. This is a delicate way of saying that the EP could have vetoed the entirety of the negotiation in its final stage if it did not think that the deal struck between the EU and the UK appropriately served to benefit the EU citizens that the EP represents. As Martin Schultz said on 23 September 2016, 'the European Parliament will play a key role in setting the new relationship between the EU and the UK—not least because we must consent to any withdrawal treaty and subsequent treaty setting out the full relationship . . .'

Indeed, it is fair to generally conclude that the weak 1958 Assembly has transformed into a general 'key' EU legislative player over the last 60 years.

Discussing the quote

Consider the relationship between the Commission, the Council, and the EP. How much legislative power do the unelected bureaucrats have as of the Lisbon Treaty?

[13] Robert Mendick, 'The Farce of the EU Travelling Circus', *The Telegraph* (London, 11 January 2014).

2.7 The Court of Justice of the European Union ('CJEU')

The final EU institution of particular interest to law students is the Court of Justice of the European Union. The singular 'Court' in that name hides the fact that the Court of Justice of the European Union is actually the name for the court *system* in the EU, rather than just one court. You will see the EU court system referred to in a variety of ways in different reading you do on EU law: the most common abbreviations are the CJ, the CJEU, or the ECJ. The ECJ stands for the European Court of Justice, which is what one of the two EU Courts that make up the CJEU was called before the Lisbon Treaty renamed both of the Courts. CJEU consequently refers to *both* institutions that make up the 'Court'—the Court of Justice and the General Court—but, in practice, most people use the phrase CJEU to refer to the Court of Justice, the higher-level court. General advice to students here is to be current and consistent, so either CJ or CJEU will serve you best.

The CJEU, of course, is not part of the EU's *legislative process* in the way that the Commission, the Council, and the EP are. Article 19(1) TEU sets out that the role of the CJEU is to 'ensure that in the interpretation and application of the Treaties the law is observed', which is what we would expect from a court. However, as you will undoubtedly find out in other chapters of this book, the Treaties have been sparse to the point where the Court's interpretative function has become not too distant from law-making.[14]

Its day-to-day function is limited to interpreting and applying the Treaties and all secondary EU law. The make-up of both of the EU Courts is what law students would expect, with a minor Member State-oriented twist: both Courts have as many judges as there are Member States, so at current count that is 27.[15] The judges are chosen from 'persons whose independence is beyond doubt' with legal qualifications and who have held the 'highest judicial offices' in their home Member States.[16] They are chosen by consent of the Member States and serve six-year terms, but can be reappointed indefinitely if the Member States wish it.

The relationship between the two Courts that make up the CJEU is fairly straightforward. They each have a distinct jurisdiction and hear cases within that jurisdiction alone. Under Article 256 TFEU, however, a General Court judgment can be appealed to the Court of Justice. This is rare, not least because Article 256 TFEU also makes clear that only points of *law* can be appealed, whereas points of fact cannot. The Courts in the CJEU consequently do not mix much, but insofar as there is a hierarchy, the CJ is the more 'senior' court. As a student, most of the judgments that you will encounter will have come from the CJ.

So far, the CJEU does not sound dissimilar from UK courts. However, there are particular ways in which the CJEU is significantly different. One of these is the presence of Advocates-General (AGs) at the CJ. AGs are legal professionals whose job it is to offer 'opinions' on certain cases that are heard by the CJEU. In particular, where a case raises a new point of law, the AGs will offer neutral opinions on how *they* feel EU law applies to the scenario in the case before them. This is not binding on the CJ, but will usually have significant persuasive power.

[14] See, in particular, Chapters 6–9 and 11–14.

[15] Article 19(2) TEU.

[16] Article 253 TFEU.

2.7.1 Actions before the CJEU

The jurisdiction of the CJEU is set out in Article 19(3) TEU. It falls into three categories: the so-called 'action brought' category, preliminary rulings, and 'other cases provided for in the Treaties'. What these categories actually mean is set out in much more detail in the TFEU.

The CJEU's jurisdiction first of all covers a variety of actions that can be initiated by Member States, EU institutions, and, occasionally, other natural or legal persons. The 'actions' that Article 19 TEU refers to cover a variety of different processes that can be used to hold the Member States *or* the EU institutions to account. The first of these we will consider in detail in Chapter 8: it is the so-called **infringement proceedings** set out in Article 258 TFEU, wherein the Commission takes a Member State to the CJEU because it is not complying with EU law, and the CJEU is asked to 'enforce' EU law against that Member State.

The second 'action brought' category is the EU's version of judicial review, known as the 'annulment action'. This is set out in detail in Article 263 TFEU, and, if successful, can result in the CJEU declaring an EU measure void under Article 264 TFEU.

Article 263 TFEU (emphasis added)

The Court of Justice of the European Union shall **review the legality of legislative acts, of acts of the Council, of the Commission and of the European Central Bank**, other than recommendations and opinions, **and of acts of the European Parliament and of the European Council intended to produce legal effects vis-à-vis third parties.** It shall also review the legality of acts of bodies, offices or agencies of the Union intended to produce legal effects vis-à-vis third parties.

It shall for this purpose have jurisdiction in **actions brought by a Member State, the European Parliament, the Council or the Commission on grounds of lack of competence, infringement of an essential procedural requirement, infringement of the Treaties or of any rule of law relating to their application, or misuse of powers.**

The Court shall have jurisdiction under the same conditions in actions brought by the Court of Auditors, by the European Central Bank and by the Committee of the Regions for the purpose of protecting their prerogatives.

Any natural or legal person may, under the conditions laid down in the first and second paragraphs, institute proceedings against an act addressed to that person or **which is of direct and individual concern to them**, and **against a regulatory act which is of direct concern to them and does not entail implementing measures.**

Acts setting up bodies, offices and agencies of the Union may lay down specific conditions and arrangements concerning actions brought by natural or legal persons against acts of these bodies, offices or agencies intended to produce legal effects in relation to them.

The proceedings provided for in this Article shall be instituted within two months of the publication of the measure, or of its notification to the plaintiff, or, in the absence thereof, of the day on which it came to the knowledge of the latter, as the case may be.

Under Article 263 TFEU, any legally binding act produced by the EU can be reviewed.[17] In practice, the CJEU has taken a flexible approach to this concept of 'legally binding',

[17] This includes delegated and implementing acts, as they produce legally binding effects. For more on sources of EU law, see Chapter 4.

and will look to what the intention of the drafters of a measure was, as well as what the content of a particular measure is, to determine whether it produces the necessary legal effects for an Article 263 TFEU action. A key example of an action in which it did not find such 'legal effects' is in *IBM v Commission*, where the nature of a Commission document used in its competition law enforcement processes was considered.[18] The document in question set out for the company which was being pursued by the Commission for an infringement—IBM, in this case—what its preliminary findings were, so as to enable the company to prepare for a hearing before the Commission. The CJEU here determined that these preliminary findings did not produce 'legal effects', but at most informed a later Commission decision that *would* produce such effects, should it conclude after this hearing that an infringement had actually taken place.

Key to all actions under Article 263 TFEU is that they must be brought within two months of a measure being published, or the plaintiff finding out about that measure. The time limit is kept short deliberately, so as to make it clear as soon as possible whether or not an adopted EU measure is 'legal' or not. Any action brought outside of this two month period will be declared inadmissible.

Article 263 TFEU sets out that three different categories of actors have standing before the CJ in annulment actions. The first of these, known as **privileged** applicants, are the Member States, the European Parliament, the Council, and the Commission. Privileged applicants have automatic standing under Article 263 TFEU, and so where a Member State takes action against the Council or the EP (who, as legislative adopters, would act as 'the government' in annulment actions), the case can always be heard by the CJ.[19]

Other actors are also indicated. The category known as **semi-privileged** also has automatic standing, but only in situations where the Treaties directly carve out a role for them, and so they wish to 'protect their prerogatives'. The Court of Auditors, the European Central Bank, and the Committee of the Regions thus can bring an action under Article 263 TFEU if they were meant to participate in a given procedure under the Treaties but did not.[20]

The final category of actor with standing under Article 263 TFEU is the most complicated one. Article 263(4) TFEU raises the possibility that natural or legal persons can also take action against the EU institutions, but this is a significantly more limited right than what the Member States or the EU institutions have. Individuals are **non-privileged** applicants. As the term suggests, there are significant conditions attached to individual annulment actions. Article 263(4) says that any natural or legal person may bring an action for annulment when they are:

- explicitly addressed by an EU act; or
- where they are 'directly and individually' concerned by it; or
- as of the Lisbon Treaty, where they are bringing an action against a regulatory act that 'does not entail implementing measures' that they are 'directly concerned by'.

It is easy to determine if a private party is 'addressed' by an EU act. The other situations in which private parties have standing are significantly more complex and have resulted in a lot of case law before the GC, primarily because concepts like 'direct and individual

[18] Case 60/81 *IBM v Commission* ECLI:EU:C:1981:264; see Chapter 15 for more on competition law.
[19] Article 263(2) TFEU. [20] Article 263(3) TFEU.

concern', 'direct concern', 'regulatory act', and 'implementing measures' are not further explained in Article 263 TFEU.

The majority of this case law predates the Lisbon Treaty and relates to the concept of 'individual concern'. 'Direct concern' has been less controversial; the CJEU here examines whether there is a causal relationship between the EU act in question and the situation of the applicant, and this requirement is satisfied in all cases where a Member State or other domestic body does not have any discretion in *how* to apply the EU act.[21]

But when does a private party meet the 'individual concern' test? The seminal case here is *Plaumann*.[22] Plaumann, a German company, imported clementines into the EU. It challenged a Commission decision that refused a request from Germany (as a Member State) to partially suspend the application of EU customs duties to clementines. It is easy to see that Plaumann was in practice affected by the EU decision to maintain these customs duties: clearly its business was affected by the continued application of an import tariff. However, as the Commission decision was directed at a Member State, it could not contest the decision without demonstrating 'direct and individual concern'.

The CJ, in *Plaumann*, focused on individual concern, and defined it as meaning that a private party would demonstrate individual concern only where they were affected by an EU act 'by reason of certain attributes that are peculiar to them or by reason of circumstances in which they are differentiated from all other persons'.[23] This is a *very* narrow definition, which led to a finding that Plaumann was not individually affected because, at any point in time, any other German company could also start importing clementines. It thus concluded that Plaumann was in an 'open' category of people and seemed to imply that only those in a 'closed' category of people would have standing under the 'direct and individual concern' test. A category of people would be 'closed' only when nobody else could become part of that category after an act was adopted, as the CJ would confirm in later case law.[24] In practice, this meant that the distinction between addressed private parties and those not addressed but 'individually affected' became almost non-existent. Problematically, it seemed to make no difference how much a private party was actually *affected* by an EU act: if they were in a 'closed' class they had standing, but in an 'open' class, regardless of economic or other damage suffered, they would not.

The *Plaumann* test is one that can be criticized for how limited it is, but, more worrying for lawyers, it is no longer the *only* test applied by the CJEU, even if it is the main one. An example of a case that would have failed *Plaumann* but where the CJEU determined that a non-privileged applicant had standing anyway is *Les Verts*. Les Verts, a then-new political party, challenged a European Parliament decision to allocate funding to prepare for European Parliament elections only to parties already holding seats in the European Parliament. The *Plaumann* test would conclude they did not have 'individual concern' because they were in an 'open' category: new political parties could

[21] Joined Cases 41–44/70 *International Fruit Co v Commission* ECLI:EU:C:1971:53, paras 23–28; Case 294/83 *Les Verts v European Parliament* ECLI:EU:C:1986:166, para 31.

[22] Case 25/62 *Plaumann v Commission* ECLI:EU:C:1963:17.

[23] Ibid, para 107.

[24] See, eg, Case 62/70 *Bock v Commission* ECLI:EU:C:1971:108; Case C-209/94 P *Buralux v Council* ECLI:EU:C:1996:54; Case T-585/93 *Greenpeace International v Commission* ECLI:EU:T:1995:147; Case C-132/12 P *Stichting Woonpunt and Others v Commission* ECLI:EU:C:2014:100.

be established with ease. However, in *Les Verts,* the Court effectively ignored the *Plaumann* test altogether and ruled in favour of Les Verts because any other decision 'would give rise to inequality in the protection afforded by the Court to the various groups competing in the same elections'.[25] While it is easy to praise this as being a just outcome given how Les Verts were affected by the decision, it does make the case law on standing of private parties in annulment actions more uncertain, because it is wholly unclear what made the Court take notice of *this* situation but not any other ones where parties were clearly affected.[26]

Even more problematic is the key decision in *Extramet v Council,* where the Court expressly took notice of just how much economic damage a Council regulation inflicted on a private party in giving it standing.[27] Extramet was the largest importer of calcium metal into the EU, and the Council adopted a regulation that applied punitive tariffs to calcium metal as a trade defence mechanism. Extramet was found to meet the 'individual concern' test because it was the *largest* importer, and because it suffered serious economic harm from the regulation. The Court simply declared Extramet's situation to be 'exceptional', and did not apply a pure 'economic harm' test in subsequent cases on standing, reverting once again to the *Plaumann* test as the 'standard' test.

As the test for standing for non-privileged applicants appeared both very limited and not wholly consistently applied, it is not surprising that calls for reform to Article 263 TFEU were made. One notable critic was AG Jacobs in *UPA v Council*, who in his Opinion suggested that rather than declining standing for 'open' categories of applicants, the primary consideration the Court should make when deciding on the standing of private parties is whether an EU act 'has or is liable to have a substantial adverse effect on his interests'.[28] This would make *Extramet* the standard test, rather than an exception to the *Plaumann* test. The CJEU declined to follow AG Jacobs when deciding *UPA*, however, and made clear that any changes to its interpretation of Article 263 TFEU would result only from actual changes *to* Article 263 TFEU.

Pause for reflection

What do you think some of the benefits of the test proposed by AG Jacobs would be, when compared to *Plaumann*? Are there any obvious downsides?

It was thus that the Lisbon Treaty introduced the third situation in which a private party can bring an action for annulment: where a 'regulatory act' 'directly concerns' them, and does not involve 'implementing measures'. As the 'Lisbon test', as we will call it, removes

[25] *Les Verts*, para 36.

[26] See also Case C-309/89 *Cordoniu v Council* ECLI:EU:C:1994:197, where a manufacturer of sparkling wine who held a particular trademark that was affected by a Council regulation was considered to be in a 'closed' category *because* they held a trademark before that regulation was adopted. The connection between 'individual concern' and holding a trademark was not made explicit, but seems to be a separate test to the *Plaumann* test in determining individual concern.

[27] Case C-358/89 *Extramet v Council* ECLI:EU:C:1991:214.

[28] AG Opinion in Case C-50/00 *UPA* ECLI:EU:C:2002:197, paras 60, 103.

the test of 'individual concern', it is in *theory* an easier test to satisfy—but only if the concepts of 'regulatory act' and 'implementing measures' are defined relatively broadly by the CJEU in practice.

In *Inuit I*, the GC and CJ considered the notion of a 'regulatory act' for the first time, and defined it as 'an act of general application apart from legislative acts'.[29] This automatically limits the reach of the 'Lisbon test' significantly: it cannot be used to challenge any acts adopted using the legislative procedures set out in the Treaties, nor can it be used to challenge any acts that are addressed to specific parties. 'Legislative acts', meaning most legislation adopted by the EU institutions as described in this chapter, and 'specific acts' both remain subject to the *Plaumann* test.

Microban is a helpful demonstration of situations where the 'Lisbon test' can make a difference to non-privileged applicants.[30] Microban, an American manufacturer of antibacterial additives, challenged a Commission decision that was addressed to the Member States and that removed a substance called 'triclosan' from the list of additives that could be used in the manufacture of plastic food containers. The GC here found that the decision was an implementing act not involving legislative procedures (and so a regulatory act) and of a general nature (as 'all Member States' was considered a 'general' rather than a specific category). It further found that the act was of 'direct concern' to Microban because the Member States had no discretion in how to apply it, echoing the existing 'direct concern' definition; and finally found that the Commission's decision did not entail implementing measures as a ban on 'triclosan' did not require further domestic legislation to become effective.[31]

One issue left open by *Microban* is to what extent 'direct concern' and 'implementing measures' overlap in terms of what they examine. The CJEU has since clarified this in *Palirria Souliotis v Commission,* where it stressed that 'direct concern' examines whether the addressee of the EU act in question has *discretion* more than whether it *implements* a measure.[32] Imagine, for example, a Commission decision that applies a tax on soft drinks because of their sugar content. The tax itself is not discretionary—it has to be applied, to a set percentage—but it is likely that the Member States themselves will have to figure out how to *collect* the tax. Such a tax collection mechanism would need to be set up by domestic law—and so even though the Member States do not have 'discretion', there will be 'implementing measures', which means that the 'Lisbon test' could not be relied upon by a soft drink manufacturer to get standing for an action of annulment.

The reason for this focus on 'implementing measures' in the 'Lisbon test' is clear: where implementing measures exist, meaning domestic law or policy has been adopted to give effect to the EU act, it is possible for private parties to challenge that *domestic law* before a national court, and so standing before the EU courts is less necessary in these cases.[33] The 'Lisbon test' is thus less directed at fixing the issues with the *Plaumann* test, and more

[29] Case T-18/10 *Inuit I* ECLI:EU:T:2011:419, para 56; Case C-583/11 P *Inuit I* ECLI:EU:C:2013:625, paras 50–61.

[30] Case T-262/10 *Microban v Commission* ECLI:EU:T:2011:623.

[31] For more on implementing EU law, see Chapter 4 on the sources of EU law.

[32] Case T-380/11 *Palirria Souliotis v Commission* ECLI:EU:T:013:420.

[33] And, once a case is before a domestic court, that domestic court can involve the CJEU by asking it for a preliminary ruling on the interpretation of EU law under Article 267 TFEU. We cover this in Chapter 7.

aimed at compensating more generally for situations where challenges before national courts in light of EU acts are not possible. While this improves standing for private parties under Article 263 TFEU to an extent, it is clear that the Lisbon drafters went for a 'minimal' adjustment to the judicial protections offered to private parties by the CJEU, rather than the 'maximal' adjustment proposed by AG Jacobs in *UPA*.

Pause for reflection

Do you think the 'Lisbon test' does enough to give private parties standing to annul EU acts before the CJEU, or not? Should they have automatic standing, in your view?

A third category of action brought is set out in Article 265 TFEU and deals with actions against EU institutions where they have 'failed to act'. This is a corollary to the judicial review process set out in Article 263 TFEU; it means that EU institutions can be challenged both when they have acted *ultra vires, and* when they should have acted in response to an obligation set out in the Treaties but have not done so. Article 265 TFEU in setup and functioning is very similar to Article 263 TFEU: it also contains a specific rule for 'non-privileged applicants'. There are minor differences, however; the primary difference is that an EU institution, under Article 265 TFEU, first needs to be approached by a complainant, and has a two-month grace period to *take* action following that approach. There is no such grace period for *ultra vires* actions, meaning that the Treaties give the EU more scope for fixing *inaction* than *wrongful action*.

The CJEU can also hear claims for damages against the EU institutions. Articles 268 and 340 TFEU establish that 'in the case of non-contractual liability, the Union shall, in accordance with the general principles common to the laws of the Member States, make good any damage caused by its institutions or by its servants in the performance of their duties'. Private actors do have standing to bring claims for damages, provided they do so within five years of the relevant event that caused damage. As of the key case, *Bergaderm*, claims will succeed when a rule of law breached by an EU act was intended to confer rights on individuals, the breach was sufficiently serious, and there is a causal link between the breach and harm suffered by an applicant.[34] This applies the same test to non-contractual liability as the CJEU has applied to actions for state liability for breaches of EU law—and we consider the components of this test in detail when looking at the *Francovich* line of cases in Chapter 8.

Finally, as set out in Article 19(3)(b) TEU, the CJEU also has jurisdiction over something called the 'preliminary ruling' procedure. It is also called the 'preliminary reference' process, and refers to a situation where a national court *requests* an interpretation from the CJEU on a provision of EU law, as it needs that interpretation in order to resolve a domestic dispute. Article 267 TFEU sets out the 'preliminary reference' process in detail, and we will explore it in Chapter 7.

[34] Case C-352/98 P *Bergaderm v Commission* ECLI:EU:C:2000:361.

2.7.2 EU case law: a reading guide

As law students, you will find AG Opinions *very* helpful to read: one of the primary ways in which EU case law is very different from UK case law is in how brief and general CJEU judgments tend to be, whereas the AG Opinions will set out significantly more detail. The reason for the brevity and sparseness of EU case law is simple: there are also no visible *dissenting opinions* issued in EU cases. The Court writes as a 'whole'—which results in language of compromise and shorter judgments. Terms that are very specific to the common law—such as *ratio* and *obiter*—also do not apply to EU case law; if it is in the judgment, it is effectively a *ratio*, as the judgments are too short to contain any obiter statements.

The Court of Justice of the CJEU sits as either a Chamber (3–5 judges); a Grand Chamber (15 judges); or as a Full Court (all 27 judges). Depending on the importance of the legal question before them, the size of the court will increase. If you access a 'modern' EU case, or look at the official European Court Reports for the earlier cases, the type of chamber that decided a case is stated clearly at the start of the judgment.

Following a header that indicates the party names, the type of procedure at play, and the names of the judges and AGs involved in the case, the actual judgment will follow. The structure of how judgments are presented has changed over time but, as a general guide, the following applies:

1. The judgment begins with a legal context. This is the part of the judgment that sets out what provisions of EU law are being interpreted in a given case, and how they clash with domestic law (where appropriate). This is purely a list of excerpts of relevant legislation. It can be helpful to look at if you find that in reading the actual judgment, you don't understand a reference to a piece of national legislation—but it should not be the first thing you read when tackling an EU case!
2. Instead, start with the next section. This will be called something like 'the main proceedings' or 'the dispute in the main proceedings and the questions referred for a preliminary ruling'. Both describe a section of the judgment that sets out the *facts* that have led to a case being presented to the CJEU, and the specific questions that the CJEU has been asked to answer, which are at the end of this section.
3. Following this is the actual judgment; depending on the case at hand, this will be separated out per question asked, or all the questions will be answered together, because the CJEU believes they are best treated as a single whole. The Court will go through the questions *in the order presented*, so if you are only interested in the outcome of the second question asked, look for a subheading called 'the second question'.
4. The judgment then concludes with costs, which are not of interest to us (but will be to the parties, as the losing party usually pays), and with a number of bolded statements that form the actual ruling—the binding interpretation of the provisions of EU law that the CJEU had to consider in this case.
5. As you become more familiar with EU law, or as you are revising, rather than reading through the entire case again, you might find it helpful to very quickly look at the facts (second section of the case) and then look to the summary of the ratio of the case that is published at the very start of the judgment, above the party names.

An annotated version of a CJEU judgment is available as part of the online materials for Chapter 7, and you may find it helpful to have a look at in relation to this chapter as well.

2.8 The other institutions

Article 13 sets out two more 'formal' EU institutions that are of lesser interest to UK law students. In one case, the reason for that is very clear: the UK has not ever been in the Eurozone, and as a consequence has had very limited dealings with the European Central Bank.

The other EU institution that has a less obviously 'legal' role in the EU is the Ombudsman. Like all other ombudsmen, the role of the European Ombudsman is to hear complaints from persons who are seeking redress from a relevant institution but are not getting it via direct communication with that institution. In the case of the EU, the jurisdiction of the European Ombudsman is set out in Article 228 TFEU: their remit is all 'instances of maladministration in the activities of the Union institutions, bodies, offices or agencies, with the exception of the Court of Justice of the European Union acting in its judicial role'. The Ombudsman responds to those complaints, investigates them, and reports to the EP on their findings. Institutions or bodies that have had a complaint filed about them have three months to respond to the Ombudsman's findings before they are reported to the EP. The only type of complaint that the Ombudsman cannot respond to is one that is already being dealt with through legal routes.

The Ombudsman is appointed by the EP for the duration of their term, and can only be replaced in instances where the CJEU determines that the Ombudsman no longer meets the criteria of being 'completely independent' in the performance of their duties and not receiving instruction from or remuneration from any third party, *or* where they have displayed 'serious misconduct'.[35] Compliance with Ombudsman findings has historically been high, and complaining to the Ombudsman is seen as a worthwhile alternative to taking legal action against the EU: 81 per cent of the suggestions presented by the Ombudsman were adopted by the investigated EU institutions in 2017.[36] The current Ombudsman is Emily O'Reilly, who took office in 2013, and whose tenure was renewed in 2019.

2.9 Brexit and the EU institutions

Brexit remains, at the time of writing, ongoing—but one stage of it has now completed: the Article 50 TEU process is done, and so we can therefore offer some thoughts on how the roles of the EU institutions in the UK will change over the course of the next few years. In what follows, we consider both the Withdrawal Agreement and what happens after the so-called transition period.

2.9.1 Withdrawal Agreement

In October 2019, the UK government and the EU agreed on the means by which the UK and EU will separate. The Withdrawal Agreement primarily contains provisions on how to make that separation process work as smoothly as possible, and ensures the protection of the majority of rights currently held by EU nationals in the UK and UK nationals in the EU.[37]

[35] Article 228(3) TEU. [36] See https://www.ombudsman.europa.eu/en/annual/en/113728.
[37] See Chapter 13.

The main aspect of the Withdrawal Agreement itself that is of interest here is that it actually maintains the operation of all EU law, including the role played by the EU institutions, until the end of the transition period. However, during this period, the UK will have no formal representation in the EU institutions.[38] The UK will thus be expected to comply with EU laws and will have the Commission enforcing EU law in the UK, but will not actually play a role in *making* any laws.

2.9.2 The Protocol on Ireland/Northern Ireland

The avoidance of a physical border on the island of Ireland has proven to be one of the most complicated and contentious political aspects of the Brexit process to date. The agreed means of pursuing an open border between the EU and the UK are set out in detail in the Protocol on Ireland/Northern Ireland that is part of the Withdrawal Agreement, and its contents will be analysed at the end of every chapter of this book, as Northern Ireland will be subject to significantly different treatment than the rest of the UK in many ways.

Institutional representation, however, is *not* one of those ways. While the Protocol provides that a significant volume of EU law applies in Northern Ireland, there will be no Northern Ireland representatives in the Council, the European Council, or the Commission. We will discuss the democratic implications of and the conceived 'solution' to this problem further in Chapter 3. For now, we will turn to differences between the main Withdrawal Agreement and the Protocol.

One key difference is in the role of the Commission in enforcing EU law where it relates to Northern Ireland: whereas the Commission's general enforcement role ends with respect to the UK at the end of the transition period, Article 10 of the Protocol makes explicit that the Commission will continue to enforce certain aspects of EU law—namely, state aid—in the UK insofar as any subsidies given by the UK government to UK businesses affect trade between Northern Ireland and the EU.[39] Moreover, the Commission and CJEU will also have 'oversight' roles to play over the functioning of *other* aspects of the Protocol—and as a consequence, the UK and UK lawyers will be able to participate in cases concerning Northern Ireland as necessary.[40] Here, already, we can see that Northern Ireland is most definitely *not* leaving the EU in the same way that Great Britain is—an impression that will become stronger over the coming chapters.

2.9.3 The future relationship

With the exception of Northern Ireland, as discussed, after the transition period, the UK will not only no longer be represented *on* the EU institutions, but the EU institutions will also play no role in the UK (or Great Britain) any more, beyond the settling of ongoing cases before the CJEU and administrative processes before the other EU institutions.[41]

The Political Declaration agreed between the UK and the EU, sketching out the intentions for any future agreements concluded between the UK and the EU after Brexit, makes

[38] Withdrawal Agreement, Article 7.

[39] State aid is a specialist area of EU law and is not otherwise covered in this textbook; for a brief discussion of this aspect of the Protocol, see https://mlexmarketinsight.com/insights-center/editors-picks/brexit/europe/brexit-deals-state-aid-rules-might-have-long-reach.

[40] Protocol, Article 12(7).

[41] Withdrawal Agreement, Chapter 3, Title X.

it clear that the UK wishes to exclude CJEU involvement in those agreements. This, as a consequence, will mean that opting into areas of EU law becomes more difficult: with the application of EU law comes EU law oversight, and rejecting a role for the CJEU will mean a 'thinner' future agreement.

The non-judicial and non-enforcement branches of the EU are very unlikely to have any genuine role in the EU's future relationship with the UK as a whole regardless of its shape: they may send representatives to meet with UK representatives to discuss that relationship, but under any new agreements concluded, the UK and the EU's representatives will meet as equals in new bodies, such as 'Joint Committees' that oversee these new agreements and enforce them. It seems clear that the role of the European Council, Council, and European Parliament in general UK political and legal life will formally cease at the end of the transition period, regardless of what follows.

2.10 **In conclusion**

The EU's institutions, at first glance, look very alien: their setup is not directly comparable to the UK government's, and they appear to have a variety of overlapping roles, with some institutions seeming far more powerful than their closest UK equivalent—such as the Commission—and others seeming far weaker—like the European Parliament. By now, however, you should be starting to understand that direct comparisons between the UK and the EU are simply not the most helpful to make. The idea of 'unelected bureaucrat' running the EU is clearly an oversimplification of reality.

We will continue to explore EU decision-making and how democratic it is in the next chapter, now that you have been introduced to the main players in that decision-making process as well as the EU court system.

Key points

Table 2.1 outlines the EU institutions, their powers, and the roles of the individuals who make up the institutions.

TABLE 2.1 The institutions and their powers

Name	Powers	Composition
European Council	Setting out broad policy direction; approving make-up of Commission; initiating Treaty revision proceedings	Heads of Member State governments
European Commission	Legislative proposal (exclusively) and enforcement of EU law	Member State nationals who are **independent** and represent the EU's interests while in office

We consider existing 'Joint Committees' in EU international agreements in more detail in Chapter 16.

Name	Powers	Composition
Council of Ministers	Legislative adoption	Member State government representatives at ministerial level, meeting on a particular area of policy
European Parliament	Legislative adoption; nominating Commission President; 'censuring' entire Commission	Directly elected Member State nationals, representing their 'electorate' at the EU
Court of Justice of the European Union	Interpreting and applying EU law	Member State national judges (at the highest level), operating **independently**

Assess your learning

1. In your view, which institution plays the most important role in:
   a. The EU legislative process?
   b. The Article 50 'exit' process? (See Sections 2.2–2.6.)
2. How does the balance of power of the EU institutions compare to the balance of power between the executive, legislature, and judiciary in the UK? (See Sections 2.3–2.7.)

Further reading

Robert Bottner, 'The Size and Structure of the European Commission: Legal issues surrounding project teams and a (future) reduced college' (2018) 14(1) Eur Const Law Rev 37.

Michelle Cini, 'The Commission: An Unelected Legislator?' (2002) 8(4) J Legis Stud 14.

Alan Dashwood et al, *Wyatt and Dashwood's European Union Law*, 6th edn (Hart, 2011) chapters 6–7.

Gareth Davies, 'Legislative Control of the European Court of Justice' (2014) 51(6) CMLRev 1579.

Federico Fabbrini and Rebecca Schmidt, 'The Composition of the European Parliament in Brexit Times: Changes and challenges' (2019) 44(5) ELRev 711.

Marco Goldoni, 'Politicising EU Lawmaking? The *Spitzenkandidaten* Experiment as a Cautionary Tale' (2016) 22 Eur Law J 279.

Manfred Kohler, 'European Governance and the European Parliament: From talking shop to legislative powerhouse' (2014) 52(3) JCMS 600.

Stéphanie Novak, 'The Silence of Ministers: Consensus and Blame Avoidance in the Council of the European Union' (2013) 51(6) JCMS 1091.

John Peterson, 'Juncker's Political European Commission and an EU in Crisis' (2017) 55(2) JCMS 349.

Henri de Waele and Hansko Broeksteeg, 'The Semi-Permanent European Council Presidency: Some reflections on the law and early practice' (2012) 49 CMLRev 1039.

Online resources

Visit www.oup.com/he/demars1e for a sample approach to discussing the quote.

3

Decision-making and democracy in the EU

Context for this chapter

From: campaigns@remainalliance.uk
To: legal@remainalliance.uk
Date: 11 April 2016
Subject: latest quit.eu campaign video

Hi all,
I'm assuming you've all seen this by now, as it's been on bracketing the six o'clock news and has over 5 million views on YouTube. A short summary all the same:

quit.eu has brought out its latest video aimed at rejecting the settlement that the Prime Minister has come to with the EU, and it has come back to the idea that the EU is not, and will never be, a democratic entity; basically, voters are being told that they cannot vote for real change at the EU level and consequently staying in a close relationship with the EU in any way means that voters are, as quit.eu put it, 'giving up on living in a democracy'. As ever, the material is really vague and so we have no idea to what extent it is accurate: they repeatedly slam the 'powerless' European Parliament that nobody votes for anyway, and allude to secretive decision-making in the EU, before concluding that signing up to the negotiated deal means we will never stop being ruled by foreigners and bureaucrats in Brussels.

We really need to counter this with actual *facts* about how the EU works and what this means for British voters. The EU remains mystifying to most of them, but we've got to tackle this and tackle it hard.

Can you work something up for us? If the quit.eu video is just a bunch of nonsense, we should just point that out with as many facts as we can—but if it there is some truth there, we should work up counterarguments to mount a defence of the EU, if possible. Ideally we'd like something snappy and short, but I appreciate that nothing about the EU's setup and functioning *is* simple, so accuracy first. If we can launch a counter-campaign in the next few days, that would be ideal.

Many thanks,
Michael

Michael Jones
Campaign Director for the Remain Alliance
michael.jones@remainalliance.uk

3.1 Introduction

Chapter 2 commenced with a provocative statement on the nature of the EU, and explored how being in the EU could be viewed as eroding UK democracy. We've looked at the composition and duties of the EU institutions now, but in order to truly consider if the EU is as undemocratic as some Eurosceptics make it out to be, we need to go a step further, and consider a few additional questions.

This chapter will analyse what EU academics have termed the 'democratic deficit'[1] in the EU, and following that, investigate just how much 'democracy' exists in the EU decision-making processes. As with any long-standing legal debate, there are two sides to this argument: those who claim that the EU will never be democratic, and those who argue that the EU actually does not suffer from true shortcomings. This chapter will evaluate both of those claims, and consider how recent big events in the EU—such as the ratification of the Lisbon Treaty, and the so-called Eurozone financial crisis—impact upon the debate.

The scenario at the start of this chapter is fictional, but could have taken place in the lead-up to the 2016 UK referendum on EU membership. It sets out the main claims made in most arguments that the EU is not democratic enough. We will be referring to it throughout the remainder of the chapter, to enable you to decide if *you* think the EU is democratic enough or not.

3.2 Democracy

3.2.1 What is democracy?

Democracy is a concept that you might associate with politics rather than with law. However, it is the *legal institutions* that establish the functioning and setup of a government that determine how **democratic** it is—so **democracy** is of no less interest to constitutional lawyers than it is to political scientists.

Democracy does not have a single, 'quick' definition that you can memorize, and different authors will define it in different ways. For our purposes, we will use the word **democracy** to describe a form of government whereby the people are the ultimate decision-makers. Its root is the Greek word **dēmokratía**, which literally translates to 'rule of the people'. What we consequently expect to see in a government system that declares itself to be democratic is most of the following qualities:[2]

- Voters have law-making power—either **directly**, or more commonly, **indirectly**, via an elected legislature. This is the **input** dimension of a democratic system; where voters have indirect law-making power, the democracy in question is known as **representative democracy** (as the voters elect their representatives.) In the UK, it is ordinarily the **input** dimension of democracy that commentators focus on when discussing if a government or an institution is **legitimate**—because it represents the 'will of the people'.

[1] The term originated in the 1970s in academic and political literature; for an overview, see http://researchbriefings.files.parliament.uk/documents/RP14-25/RP14-25.pdf.

[2] For a detailed analysis of these qualities, see Vivien Schmidt, 'Democracy and Legitimacy in the European Union Revisited: Input, output and "throughput"' (2012) 61(1) Polit Stud 2.

- The function of the government is to achieve the goals the voters have expressed—by legislating in line with a governing manifesto that 'won' the election, for instance. This is the output dimension of a democratic system.
- In order to ensure that the people remain in ultimate control of law-making, all government institutions operate under a set of constraints commonly known as the separation of powers doctrine. This doctrine suggests that no one government institution holds more than one of the three key government functions (of executive, legislature, or judiciary). This prevents authoritarian rule, whereby one branch of government is so powerful that it can do what it likes, regardless of what the voters have expressed a preference for.
- And finally, the voters regularly evaluate the government's performance (or its output). At the next election, they decide if the government has delivered the policies they wanted. If so, they are likely to be re-elected. If not, a different government will take its place in the next round of input democracy.

A quick reminder of how democracy works in the UK will make this more concrete:

- Input: eligible citizens vote for political parties or politicians in a General Election, so as to populate the House of Commons.
- Output: the 'winning' political party then forms the executive, which promises to implement the manifesto that got it elected.
- Separation of powers: the government sets out a legislative platform in the Queen's Speech; the Houses of Parliament debate proposed laws and opt to implement them or not; and the UK courts hear disputes about the laws enacted by Parliament.
- The next election: the citizens evaluate whether the government performed as they wished them to—and vote accordingly. This restarts the cycle of democracy.

3.2.2 **Why do we *want* democracy?**

This is definitely more of a political science question than a legal one, but in order to understand the strength of debate about the democratic deficit, it will be helpful to briefly consider why it is that democracy is seen as necessary in the EU.

It is easier to explain why democracy is desirable by considering its alternatives, and why countries like the United States experienced civil wars in order to ensure that they had 'government of the people, by the people, for the people'.[3] In governance systems where the wishes of the people are not clearly respected, we see autocratic (or dictator-like) rulers who can impose *their* will on a population. While the exact connection between democracy and 'freedom' is heavily debated, it is difficult to argue strongly that anyone living under a dictatorship of any form has freedom in the way that those who can influence the shape of their government system do.[4] This, at least to some extent, explains why over the course of the last several centuries, most countries experienced outright

[3] Abraham Lincoln, 'The Gettysburg Address' (19 November 1863), as found in Roy P Basler (ed), *The Collected Works of Abraham Lincoln* (Rutgers University Press, 1955).

[4] See, eg, Jason Brennon, 'Democracy and Freedom' in David Schmidtz and Carmen E Pavel (eds), *The Oxford Handbook of Freedom* (OUP, 2018).

rebellion against ruler *kings* and demanded representative rule. It has also been argued by political philosophers that discussions which take place in representative institutions like parliaments are likely to result in improved decision-making (or better designed laws) and increased legitimacy and thus compliance with those laws.[5]

Wanting a governance system that is likely to result in more 'freedom' and equality and better laws is understandable at the domestic level, but those arguments do not quite explain why there is a desire for the EU to be democratic. It is not a demand voiced for many other international organisations. The explanation for the increased focus on the EU's democratic qualities lies in the transformation of the EU over time: while voters may be indifferent to being unable to influence the direction of travel of a coal and steel community, the modern EU takes on a number of tasks that either *used* to be carried out by its Member States, or in any event *restrict* what its Member States can do. The more 'political' the tasks that the EU takes on, or affects, in other words, the more desirable it is that it *itself* is democratic, and the less likely it will be that simply saying that Member States have taken a democratic decision to be *in* the EU is sufficient to satisfy those looking for population-influenced, legitimate law-making.

3.3 What is a 'democratic deficit'?

The words 'democratic deficit' simply refer to a *lack of democracy*. However, how such a 'deficit' is measured varies wildly, and so in different fields of study, different aspects of a government and its functioning may be flagged up and deemed short of democracy. In EU law, the concept of the 'democratic deficit' is used to classify the EU as a system that may hold *some* of the qualities of a democratic government, but is lacking others.

3.3.1 The EU on democracy

The Treaties make clear that the EU strives to operate as a democratic entity. The ways in which it seeks to be 'democratic' are set out in Article 10 TEU:

Article 10 TEU (emphasis added)

1. The functioning of the Union shall be founded on **representative democracy**.
2. Citizens are **directly represented** at Union level in the **European Parliament. Member States are represented in the European Council** by their **Heads of state or Government** and in the **Council by their governments**, themselves democratically accountable either to their national parliaments, or to their citizens.
3. Every citizen shall have the right to participate in the democratic life of the Union. Decisions shall be taken as **openly and as closely as possible** to the citizen.
4. **Political parties at European level** contribute to forming European political awareness and to expressing the will of citizens of the Union.

[5] See, eg, the 1861 work of John Stuart Mill, *Considerations on Representative Government* (Prometheus Books, 1991).

If we compare this to the key components of democracy set out in Section 3.2, we can already observe a few things. First, in terms of input, the EU promises direct representation only in the European Parliament. The rest of what Article 10(2) describes is a form of *indirect* representation, whereby politicians voted for *in domestic elections* then represent their Member States in the European Council and the Council of Ministers. The accountability, in their cases, remains at the domestic level. The theory here is that if domestic politicians misbehave in carrying out their EU-level functions, they can be punished for it in domestic elections.

Article 10(3) sets out a further interesting promise: all citizens can participate in the 'democratic life' of the Union, and decisions shall be taken 'as openly and as closely as possible'. The first sentence of the Article appears to merely reflect that all Member State nationals can vote in European Parliament elections. However, the second sentence already seems to indicate that the workings of the EU are not going to be entirely comparable to the workings of most Member States. The promise made here is not that all decisions will be taken *openly*, nor that they will be taken *close to the citizen*—but rather that they will be taken as *openly as possible*, and *as closely to the citizen as possible*. This leaves room for decisions to be taken in a more secretive fashion, and without direct input from voters, but with the explicit consent from all Member States—otherwise this would not be so explicitly stated in the Treaties.

This second sentence of Article 10(3) is a good example of the qualities of the EU that have caused much debate as to how democratic the EU is. Given that the Member States have agreed that not all decisions at the EU level can be public or have direct voter input, is Article 10(3) evidence that the EU is not democratic enough (as it restricts voter input and transparency, and thus the ability to see what the EU is doing, and respond to it with future voting behaviour) or perfectly democratic (as directly elected national leaders will have agreed to this)?

There is no simple answer to this question. Those who believe the EU suffers a democratic deficit would argue strongly that without input democracy, the EU can never be democratic; whereas those who believe the EU is perfectly democratic would argue that the input dimension is not always the most important dimension of a democracy. Either position is defensible in principle—hence why the democratic deficit debate is ongoing.

Discussing the scenario

Consider Article 10(3) in light of the scenario at the start of this chapter. Does its content help you engage with the quit.eu claim that the EU is completely undemocratic, because of its secretive decision-making that voters cannot affect?

For those of us interested in the EU from a constitutional law perspective, the implications of Article 10(3) are of paramount importance. If EU *decision-making* is undemocratic, critics will argue that that law made by the EU is not democratically legitimate, and it would be very difficult to see why any Member State would wish to follow EU rules. Consequently, we will need to dig a little deeper into the arguments that underpin the 'democratic deficit' accusation levelled at the EU, and consider to what extent these arguments are valid.

3.3.2 The pre-Lisbon 'democratic deficit' argument

As noted, there is no 'one' version of the democratic deficit—but there are *leading* accounts of it in the literature on EU law. One of the most regularly discussed analyses of the EU's problems with democracy was set out by Follesdal and Hix in 2006, and we can use it as a starting point for discussion.[6] Follesdal and Hix observed five specific aspects of how the EU was constitutionally set up and how it functioned under the Nice Treaty that meant that it was not, and could never be, democratic. Their five main points were that:

- EU decision-making is **unresponsive to democratic pressures**
- The EU suffers from **executive dominance**
- The EU legislative process **by-passes democracy**
- EU legislation suffers from the '**distance issue**'
- EU decision-making lacks **transparency** and is too **complex**.

The first and most significant problem that they see is that the EU is unresponsive to democratic pressures, meaning that when voters in Member States are wholly unsatisfied with what the EU is doing, they cannot actually vote *out* an 'EU government' of any sort. Remember the discussion of the EU legislative process in Chapter 2: there are three institutions involved in EU law-making, but only *one* of those three institutions is directly elected by voters. Consequently, even voting for different parties in European Parliament elections may not necessarily result in a substantial change in EU policy—it is not comparable to replacing a Conservative government with a Labour government.

A further problem with European Parliament representation is that it is spread across 27 countries—meaning that even where a given set of policy choices wins within one Member State (ie, one party 'wins' the European Parliament elections), this is unlikely to result in those policy choices becoming law at the EU level. Not only does this depend on the positioning of the Commission and the Council as well as the European Parliament, but the newly elected MEPs from any Member State do not form, by themselves, a substantial enough portion of the European Parliament, and so their views may not be the dominant ones. At that point, a vote for the European Parliament may be direct in technical terms, but it hardly has a direct impact on EU policy-making.

The second problem Follesdal and Hix observe is that the creation of the EU has stripped power *from* national parliaments, and instead has given it *to* national executives. In the UK, as in most parliamentary democracies, the most powerful institution on paper is the legislature; Parliament trumps the Cabinet in terms of decision-making ability. However, the transfer of power to the EU has resulted in the executive suddenly getting significant power at the level of government *above* the domestic level. The European Council is attended by the UK Prime Minister, and the Council of Ministers—with its legislative powers—is populated by Cabinet members. The European Parliament's direct democracy is not seen by Follesdal and Hix as compensating for this 'executive dominance', for the reasons already outlined. There is thus, in their view, a clear shift of decision-making power from Parliament to the government associated with EU membership, and the government is less representative than Parliament.

[6] Andreas Follesdal and Simon Hix, 'Why there is a Democratic Deficit in the EU: A response to Majone and Moravcsik' (2006) 44(3) JCMS 533.

Their view is echoed by Bartolini's empirical findings, which suggest that national political structures that attract loyalty from citizens are weakened by EU integration, and that loyalty is not recreated at the EU level, which leaves a potentially dangerous gap there—or a 'façade' of voter input.[7]

EU law in practice

In 2004, the Commission proposed the so-called Services Directive, which attempted to further open up the EU services market.[8] In EU law, 'services' describe activities where EU nationals temporarily conduct their business in a Member State other than the one they normally live in. The Services Directive aimed to get rid of 'red tape' surrounding service provision.

The most controversial aspect of the proposal was the 'country of origin' principle. This principle, which we will consider again in Chapter 14, requires that when, for instance, a Spanish company provides its services in the UK, the law applicable to how that company operates will be Spanish law rather than UK law. There were massive public protests against these proposals in France, Belgium, Sweden, and Denmark, and the unions in the UK also protested the Directive;[9] fears were that as a consequence of the 'country of origin' principle, Swedish companies, for instance, would become completely uncompetitive when compared to companies from Member States with lower standards of labour rights, because those companies would be able to provide services at a much lower cost than Swedish companies, regardless of *where* they provided these services. This would, consequently, trigger a 'race to the bottom' in all Member States: countries would get rid of all regulation in order to remain appealing to companies.

Led by France, a need for revision of the proposed Directive was agreed between the EU Heads of State on 22 March 2005, one day after a hundred thousand people marched in protest at the Directive in Brussels. However, such revision cannot be conducted by the European Council; instead, the Directive would have to be amended by either the European Parliament, the Council, or the Commission, as part of the EU's legislative processes.

Governments in the UK, the Netherlands, Spain, Poland, the Czech Republic, and Hungary strongly supported the original version of the Directive, and sent a letter of support to the Commission saying that they wished to see an 'ambitious' directive on services.[10] France and Germany were significantly more opposed to the Commission's initial proposal, and had been pushing for change since 2005.

The European Parliament removed the 'country of origin' principle in its first reading of the Services Directive proposal in February 2006. Their amended version of the Directive not only excludes 'export' of labour laws, but also excludes many sectors of service provision that were deemed nationally sensitive, such as healthcare, social services, and public transport. It also produced a

→

[7] Stefano Bartolini, *Restructuring Europe* (OUP, 2006) xv, 381.

[8] Proposal for a Directive of the European Parliament and of the Council on services in the internal market (2004) COM(2004) 0002 final.

[9] See http://www.ft.com/cms/s/0/2453f9b0-34fa-11da-9e12-00000e2511c8.html?ft_site=falcon&desktop=true#axzz4onZH8Fdp.

[10] See https://www.europarl.europa.eu/sides/getDoc.do?pubRef=-//EP//TEXT+IM-PRESS+20060418ST O07420+0+DOC+XML+V0//EN.

→

clear list of reasons why a country *could* introduce rules restricting foreign service provision, such as national security, public health, and environmental protection.

The European Commission produced a final version of the Services Directive in April 2006, which took the majority of the MEPs' amendments on board, and presented this to the Council of Ministers. The Council and the European Parliament approved this revised text in December 2006.[11]

How 'democratic' do you think the process of adopting the Services Directive was? Was this process dominated by executive actors, or not? And do you think that makes the adoption of the Services Directive more or less 'democratic'?

Follesdal and Hix's third criticism relates to how certain pieces of EU legislation are drafted and enacted. While they are critical of the democratic qualities of the EU's normal three-body legislative process, they have a much bigger problem with the categories of EU legislative activity known as '**delegated**' or '**implementing**' legislation.[12] Delegated legislation is what it sounds like: there are powers that the Treaties have delegated from the ordinary law-making institutions (the Council and the European Parliament) to the Commission, for reasons such as a need for rapid updating that the EU's normal legislative processes would not permit. Implementing legislation refers to rules produced at the EU level to ensure that all the Member States adopt EU legislation in *identical ways*. Under the Treaties in 2006, both implementing and delegated legislative powers lay with the Commission, and scrutiny of the Commission's exercise of these powers took place via a system known as '**comitology**'. In 'comitology', the Commission drafted delegated and implementing rules and then had these considered by committees of Member State representatives set up by the Council. These committees were headed by a member of the Commission, who required the committee's approval in order to adopt a piece of delegated or implementing legislation.

Follesdal and Hix are highly critical of 'comitology': they consider it a key example of legislation being produced in a way that is *not* open or close to the citizens. The composition of 'comitology' committees was a complete mystery, as were the committees' operating rules and debates surrounding the legislation they were tasked with producing. In practice, the operating rules themselves were often not followed—informal processes within the 'committees' appear to have been the norm.[13] In terms of oversight, in 2006 the 'comitology' committees were only subject to Council of Ministers control—thus resulting in further executive governance, with no clear role for directly elected institutions like the European Parliament or national parliaments. From 2006, the European Parliament gained an oversight function alongside the Council—but prior to the adoption of the Treaty of Lisbon, it still had very limited power to amend

[11] Directive 2006/123/EC of the European Parliament and of the Council of 12 December 2006 on services in the internal market [2006] OJ L376/36.

[12] For more on delegated and implementing legislation, see Chapter 4.

[13] Mark Rhinard, 'The Democratic Legitimacy of the European Union Committee System' (2002) 15(2) Governance 185, 198.

'comitology' practices. This meant that under 'comitology', a significant portion of secondary EU law was being produced effectively in secret by mysterious, unelected 'representatives' of Member States, with no particular voter input; a clear failure of democracy, per Follesdal and Hix.

Their fourth argument can be summarized as the 'distance issue'. This criticism addresses the other part of Article 10(3) TEU, which promises that decisions are taken as closely as *possible* to the citizen. This is, in practice, not very close; by its very design, the EU is always one extra level removed from the citizen than the nation state can be. However, that distance results in a number of practical problems: apathy about European Parliament elections and a general unawareness of the EU's activities are paramount among these. Follesdal and Hix ultimately ask a salient question: is it possible to ever have a functional democracy without a *demos* (or voting population) that is interested in participating? The fact that European Parliament elections are treated as 'second order' elections, where voters express their unhappiness with domestic political parties rather than their concerns about Europe, does not help with this: voters choose between national parties in these elections, which makes them additional 'national' elections rather than genuine 'European' elections.[14]

There is also a 'distance' dimension to the transfer of power *away* from national parliaments. Follesdal and Hix do not dwell on this, and we will revisit it in detail in Chapter 6, but it is worthwhile to flag up the EU's principle of supremacy now. This CJEU-developed principle, geared at ensuring that the EU's laws are not overridden by conflicting national-level legislation, means that *any* law produced by national parliaments has to be compatible with EU law—and where it is not, EU law has 'supremacy' over national law, and national law must then be set aside. The principle of supremacy receives criticism because of how it appears to curtail the powers of national parliaments *beyond* what the Treaties themselves set out—and this, of course, has implications for the extent of voter representation that the EU can offer. If national parliaments follow domestic voter preferences in legislation, but this legislation is made impossible by existing EU commitments, national parliaments *cannot* act on the input they are receiving from voters. If the EU's commitments are not themselves produced in democratically legitimate ways that respect voter input, as Follesdal and Hix question, this limitation on national parliaments then further limits democracy at the *national* level.

Finally, they raise a fifth issue that ties in to their issues with comitology and the 'distance issue', which is that the EU's functioning is far too opaque and complicated for the EU to ever be properly democratic. The opacity of course is a reference to 'comitology', but also reflects on *other* levels of EU decision-making. A key example here is that Council of Ministers deliberations are not ordinarily made public. Even where legislative materials are made available, there will be significant redacted information in the Council documentation. Beyond that, the EU's decision-making process was incomprehensibly complex at the time Follesdal and Hix were writing; as Chapter 1 mentioned, there were over *38* different ways of adopting EU legislation. It was an unrealistic challenge to expect EU law students to remember all of these and what areas of the Treaties they applied to—let alone members of the voting public. Follesdal and Hix stress, not without reason, that the immense

[14] See Joseph Weiler, Ulrich Haltern, and Franz Mayer, *European Democracy and its Critique: Five Uneasy Pieces* (EUI, 1995).

complexity and scope of the EU's different legislative processes worsened voters' apathy and mistrust of the EU as an institution, and consequently worsened the EU's democratic shortcomings.

In summary, Follesdal and Hix are highly critical of the setup and functioning of the EU as it was under the Nice Treaty in 2006. Their primary concerns were that voters *did not vote* in EP elections, and, when they did, this seemed to make little difference to the EU's policy output; that national executives had pushed national parliaments to the side without any democratic 'compensation' in the form of a very powerful European Parliament; and that most EU processes were neither 'open' nor 'close to the citizen'.

Discussing the scenario

Think back to how Michael Jones describes the quit.eu video, and consider the overlap between what quit.eu claim and what Follesdal and Hix argue. Can you try to put the quit.eu arguments in more legal terms after reading what Follesdal and Hix think about the EU?

3.3.3 Defending the EU's democratic qualities

There is nothing in what Follesdal and Hix set out that was simply *untrue* in 2006. However, this does not mean that the strength of their argument cannot be challenged—both generally and in light of changes that have taken place to the EU's constitutional setup since 2006.

Starting with a few general points, it must be noted that their argument focuses very heavily on the **input** dimension of democracy: the lack of voter control over what the EU does and the lack of voter insight into what the EU does. Not all commentators would agree, however, that the input dimension of democracy is *the most significant* one—even if it is the one that most of us would instinctively associate most closely with democracy.

For one, it can be questioned whether Follesdal and Hix's desired version of democracy, constantly responsive to voters who have all the information they need to express their views, is a realistic one. In the *ideal* democracy, a parliament is the most powerful actor, and it is directly or indirectly representative. There is then also clear separation of powers between governmental branches, and the government enacts the legislation that voters have voted for. But does this ideal actually exist *anywhere*? It would seem rather unfair to hold the EU to a standard that most nation states do not meet.

The UK represents an excellent case study of 'democracy in practice'. No one would deny that the UK is a democracy—but it does not meet the golden standard set out by Follesdal and Hix. For one thing, while Parliament in principle is the central actor of the UK government, there is significant overlap between the UK executive and the UK legislature—Cabinet members carry out roles in both branches of government. Beyond that, Parliament's conventions on manifesto legislation also mean that the executive ultimately dictates at least the *direction* of policy in Parliament, if not its literal content. Does this make UK law-making democratically illegitimate? Few would make that argument.

More generally, some of the concerns expressed about the level of representation the UK has in the EU—eg, having only a small number of MEPs—seem to be automatic consequences of any system of majoritarian democracy. After all, how many of their preferences does a voter for a losing political party see in the UK? 'First past the post' means that a substantial portion of the UK voting population is not represented by the government and thus does not get to see their policy choices enacted. Again, nobody would actually argue that the UK is undemocratic as a consequence of this—but the idea of getting 'outvoted' in the European Parliament or even in the Council of Ministers somehow is not seen as being very similar.

EU law in practice

In 2015, the European Parliament considered a recommendation that would require large companies to disclose their gender pay gap.[15] MEPs voted 344 to 156, with 68 abstentions, in favour of a resolution that urged the European Commission to put forward legislation that would close the gender pay gap, and to provide a more effective way to monitor gender pay gaps in the Member States.

All 14 Conservative MEPs present in the European Parliament voted against the part of the resolution that recommended mandatory pay audits for companies listed on stock exchanges throughout the EU.

The 2015 Conservative Party manifesto, however, pledged that companies with more than 250 employees would be made to disclose their gender pay gaps if the Conservatives were elected; and then-Prime Minister, David Cameron, promised to put legislation to this effect in place by the middle of 2016.

What do you make of these events? Can the EU be held responsible for what MEPs do, and how it corresponds to what voters want?

The representative nature of institutions is another area in which the EU faces constant accusation, but it is debatable whether all Member States are significantly more representative in how their governmental branches function. After all, the House of Lords is no more representative than the EU Commission; and one could argue that the Council of Ministers, at least indirectly, is actually more representative than the House of Lords. A similar point can be made about the transparency of secondary legislation being produced by the EU: implementing legislation may not be subject to much democratic scrutiny, but neither is delegated legislation (such as statutory instruments) in the UK.

We can thus see that ideals of democracy, especially on the input dimension, are not fully satisfied by the UK itself. At this point it becomes worth asking whether it is realistic that the EU is expected to meet these ideals. Even under the Lisbon Treaty, the EU remains a community *of* nations rather than a 'single nation'. It does not hold all the functions a 'nation' does, and consequently also cannot be evaluated in the same way that a 'nation' is. In other words, it can be argued that as the EU is not a nation, it cannot be expected to meet the democratic ideals set *for* nations.

[15] See http://www.europarl.europa.eu/news/en/press-room/20151002IPR95366/pay-gap-between-men-and-women-meps-call-for-binding-measures-to-close-it.

Discussing the scenario

Think back to the scenario at the start of the chapter. What are your views on the democratic nature of the EU at this point—do you agree that it 'is not, and will never be, a democratic entity'? Do you have any further ideas on how to counter some of the arguments made by quit.eu? Which arguments remain the most difficult to counter?

A further point worth making is that input is only one dimension of a successful democracy; a government made up of candidates that the public voted for, but which does not enact any of the policies the public wanted, is still not a democracy. Some academics argue that because the EU is *not* like a nation, in assessing whether it functions in a democratic way we have to consider what it was created for. Majone and Menon and Weatherill stress that the aim of the EU project is to establish a regulatory body that acts *above* the state, and that voters' expectations of such a regulatory body are very different than they would be of a 'government'.[16] They primarily expect the EU to achieve the goals that the Member States have set for it; providing it does this, it satisfies the output dimension of democracy. When writing about the deficit initially, Majone stressed the Member States' ultimate responsibility for the lack of input democracy in the EU: the reason there is no active political sphere at the EU level is *because* the Member States—out of concerns for their sovereignty—designed it to be a 'regulatory state', focused on limited and normally economic goals.[17]

By their reasoning, the fact that the Commission is unrepresentative of the voters is not a major issue. Its job is not to be representative, but rather to produce rules and regulations that achieve the goals that domestic democratic actors have set for the EU. In other words, as long as the Commission's legislative agenda matches the overall policy direction set by the European Council, the Commission's proposals for laws are democratically legitimate. This kind of thinking is also endorsed by Raz, who argues that what justifies institutions like the EU is not that they were legitimately established—but that they are justified by 'the results' they achieve, and how well those coincide with the aims of the people.[18]

This focus on output results in empirical findings that the EU actually does produce the policy that people want. Crombez thus found in 2003 that, in investigating the legislation being produced by what is now the ordinary legislative procedure, there is no significant difference between average voter preferences in the EU and what kind of policy the EU produces.[19] By that measure, the Lisbon Treaty's changes to the ordinary legislative procedure (as will be discussed in Section 3.4.1) are particularly significant and effective responses to accusations of a 'deficit'.

[16] Anand Menon and Stephen Weatherill, 'Democratic Politics in a Globalising World: Supranationalism and legitimacy in the European Union' (2007) 13/2007 LSE Law, Society and Economy Working Papers, http://ssrn.com/abstract=1021218.

[17] Giandomenico Majone, 'Europe's "Democratic Deficit": The question of standards' (1998) 4(1) Eur Law J 5.

[18] Joseph Raz, 'The Democratic Deficit' (2018) King's College London Dickson Poon School of Law Legal Studies Research Paper No 2018-07. Available at: https://scholarship.law.columbia.edu/faculty_scholarship/2082.

[19] Christopher Crombez, 'The Democratic Deficit in the European Union: Much ado about nothing?' (2003) 4 Eur Union Polit 101.

There are still further academics who think that the purpose of democracy is to give voice to the people, but primarily for the sake of preventing rule by an authoritarian government. Giving the people voting powers, again, is not very effective if their opinions can be easily ignored because a powerful branch of government simply does what it wants. This notion of **separation of powers** as being essential for a democracy combines the ideas of 'input' and 'output' dimensions of democracy, and argues that a governing system can only remain 'of the people' if the governmental functions are split amongst various separate branches. A particular version of the **separation of powers** doctrine comes from the US Constitution, where it is referred to as **checks and balances**—the idea being that the way to ensure that 'the people' have the ultimate say on how the US government works, is for each branch of government to control each other branch of government.

The US Constitution is, of course, very much distinct from the EU Treaties, but commentators like Andrew Moravcsik have persuasively argued that the qualities that make the US Constitution democratically legitimate also exist in the EU, which has very high quality **checks and balances** itself.[20] In 2002, writing before Follesdal and Hix, Moravcsik argued that the democratic deficit debate was much overstated. He wrote that (emphasis added) '[c]onstitutional checks and balances, indirect democratic control via national governments, and the increasing powers of the European Parliament are sufficient to ensure that **EU policy-making is, in nearly all cases, clean, transparent, effective and politically responsive** to the demands of European citizens'.[21]

His work here is what prompted Follesdal and Hix's account of the democratic deficit—so it is worth examining in further detail. After all, these are polar perspectives: Moravcsik seems to think there is *no* problem, whereas Follesdal and Hix argue there is an *unsolvable* problem.

First, on the notion that there is executive dominance in the EU, Moravcsik argues that there is actually *less executive dominance* in the EU than there is in most nation states. The Nice Treaty, in his view, contains very rigorous constraints on what the EU can do—legally, procedurally, administratively, in terms of scope, and in terms of budget—and thus constitutionally ensures that the EU does not actually go further than its Member States wanted it to.[22] How can a body that was created by democratically elected national representatives, and signed off on by national parliaments, lack democratic legitimacy when it acts? Indeed, it is the Member States who determine what policy areas the EU engages with—and those policy areas of particular voter concern, such as welfare, taxation, and education, were kept out of the Treaties. Consequently, what the EU offers is a *balance* between executive and legislative institutions, in which neither institution can accomplish goals without the other, and the Treaties themselves act as a constitutional boundary that prohibits the EU from acting in a tyrannical manner. To Moravcsik, this is a highly functional democracy.

Regarding distance from the voter, and an inability to control what policy the EU actually produces following a vote for the European Parliament, Moravcsik again argues that the problem of a lack of democracy is overstated: not because the EU institutions cannot

[20] Andrew Moravcsik, 'In Defence of the "Democratic Deficit": Reassessing legitimacy in the European Union' (2002) 40(4) JCMS 603.

[21] Ibid, 605. [22] Ibid, 607.

be criticized, but because the areas of policy in which the EU acts in are those that in most countries are *also* distant from the voter and not responsive to voter pressure. His examples here are 'central banking, constitutional adjudication, criminal and civil prosecution, technical administration and economic diplomacy'; his argument is consequently not dissimilar from that of Menon and Weatherill, who would also argue that the EU is tasked with producing output in very select areas, and by providing that and only that output, it is behaving democratically.[23]

Others defend EU decision-making on similar grounds. For example, Franchino's assessment of work that has been delegated via the 'comitology' process found that, in practice, delegated legislation still experienced significant Council oversight, even when EU law did not formally require it.[24] He furthermore found in 2004 that the majority of what was 'delegated' by the Council actually ended up in the control of national agencies, rather than the Commission—which would actually bring these decisions *closer* to the people, rather than further away.

Taking all of these views together, it becomes clear that, despite the fact that there is much merit to criticism of the EU's democratic qualities, it is important to not overstate the problem—and to consider it from all possible angles, both in terms of what the EU *is* and what it is *doing* before we can come to an overall conclusion on whether there is a 'deficit' at play.

Pause for reflection

We have seen, broadly, three different views on what 'makes' a democracy and, consequently, to what extent the EU is a democracy. What do you think is the most important measure of the EU's democratic nature—whether it satisfies the input dimension, the output dimension, or a clear separation of powers? Why?

3.4 Recent 'democracy' developments: Lisbon and the Eurozone crisis

Majone was writing in 1998, Moravcsik was writing in 2002, and Follesdal and Hix were writing in 2006. This means that none of their writing considers how the Lisbon Treaty has affected the EU's democratic qualities, whether in a positive or a negative sense. We can start by noting that the EU is not deaf to accusations that it is undemocratic: every Treaty revision has been accompanied by attempts, successful or otherwise, to amplify voter participation in the EU project. However, each EU Treaty has also come with a significant expansion of the EU's powers—which may undermine the view of Majone and Moravcsik that the EU only deals with *regulatory policy* and not policy of concrete interest to voters.

[23] Ibid, 613.

[24] Federico Franchino, 'Delegating Powers in the European Community' (2004) 34(2) BJPolS 449.

3.4.1 The Lisbon Treaty's democracy boosters

There are four clear ways in which the EU attempts to 'boost' democracy in the Lisbon Treaty:

- An expansion of powers to the European Parliament;
- An expansion of powers to national parliaments;
- A reworking of the comitology system;
- And, the introduction of a process by which EU citizens can try to influence EU law-making directly (called the Citizen's Initiative).

The first way in which the Lisbon Treaty increased the EU's democratic qualities was again to give greater power to the European Parliament. The EP is now co-legislator with the Council in an additional 40 areas of legislation, bringing the total to 85 set policy areas and covering the majority of the areas in which the EU can make law. Articles 289 and 294 TFEU set out that the newly named **ordinary legislative procedure** puts the European Parliament on an equal footing with the Council in all but the rarest policy areas, where something called the 'special' legislative procedure applies.

A brief reminder of history here is not misplaced. As discussed in Chapters 1 and 2, the Treaty of Rome gave no legislative powers to the European Parliament whatsoever; it has gained further legislative power, including in areas that were once deemed far too sensitive for the Member States to surrender the control they held in the Council, with each successive Treaty from the SEA onwards. We consider the working of the **ordinary legislative procedure** in more detail in Chapter 4, but it is worth remembering that increasing the role of the European Parliament and making it the Council's co-legislator has resulted, at least in theory, in successive increases in how democratically legitimate the EU's law-making is.

Some might argue that this was not the most obvious way to tackle the perception that the European Parliament seemed powerless compared to national parliaments, as it still does not have the power of legislative initiative—that remains principally with the Commission. However, it does demonstrate that the EU at the very least is trying to respond to the notion that there is not enough direct voter input into EU policy-making. Every increase in legislative power for the European Parliament chips away to an extent at arguments that the EU is executive-dominated and not responsive to voters' concerns.

The European Parliament is not the only parliament that gained an enhanced role in the Lisbon Treaty; indeed, Lisbon has made significant attempts to ensure that decisions *will* be taken as closely as possible to EU citizens, as Article 10 TEU promises. As such, national parliaments have for the first time been given explicit mention in the EU Treaties: Article 12 TEU defines the aim of 'inter-parliamentary cooperation' and indicates that the details of the role of national parliaments in the EU will be set out into two Protocols attached to the Treaties. These Protocols are primary law, meaning that Protocols 1 and 2 give enforceable rights to national parliaments.

Protocol 1 is geared at ensuring that national parliaments are *informed* of EU legislative and policy measures; this is aimed at boosting the transparency of the EU's activities. It obliges the EU institutions to now do the following to involve national parliaments in EU law-making:

- The Commission has to keep national parliaments up to date with its legislative activities—they have to be sent information on legislative proposals at the *same time* as the Council and the European Parliament.
- The Council has to send national parliaments agendas and documents that set out the outcomes of Council meetings.

Protocol 2 outlines arguably the most important power extended to national parliaments in the Lisbon Treaty: a process called the 'Early Warning Mechanism' (EWM), which we consider further in Chapters 4 and 5. Under the EWM, the Commission has to explain to national parliaments how every legislative proposal it introduces meets the requirements of Article 10 TEU. In other words, it has to justify why EU action is necessary, and why Member State action alone cannot satisfy a given policy goal. Protocol 2 demands that where a third of national parliaments object to the Commission's justifications for proposing legislation, the Commission reconsider its proposals.

While various practical aspects of how the EWM operates have been heavily criticized,[25] for our purposes the EWM is an example of the EU attempting to involve national parliaments in decisions that would have been taken exclusively by the EU executive in years past. If national parliaments are able to exercise the new power they are given, and if the Commission responds to these in good faith, a significant further dimension of democratic control 'close to the people' will have been introduced.

Pause for reflection

Which of these steps do you think has the most impact on how 'democratic' the EU is—more power to the European Parliament, or more power to national parliaments? Why?

Another step taken in the Lisbon Treaty to make the EU's processes more transparent is a technical one: it has reworked the comitology system in an attempt to make it more transparent and subject to oversight. This is not to say that the Commission has lost the implementing powers that it had under the Nice Treaty, but rather that the Lisbon Treaty has attempted to provide more substantial oversight of the comitology process by other EU institutions.[26] Article 290(1) TFEU consequently makes clear that when it comes to powers delegated to the Commission, the European Parliament and the Council have two key rights:

- The right of 'revocation', meaning they can cancel a delegation of power altogether;
- The right of 'opposition', meaning they can object to a specific delegated act, which as a consequence will not be adopted.

The adoption of implementing acts still involves committees of Member State government representatives, in conjunction with Commission staff, but the procedures under which the committees can adopt implementing acts are now set by the Council and the European Parliament.[27] This means that the 'committees' of comitology are now subject to oversight by both indirectly *and* directly representative EU institutions.[28] The European

[25] See Chapter 5. [26] See Chapter 4 for more detail. [27] It is detailed in Article 291 TFEU.

[28] These rules are set out in Regulation (EU) No 182/2011 of the European Parliament and of the Council of 16 February 2011 laying down the rules and general principles concerning mechanisms for control by Member States of the Commission's exercise of implementing powers [2011] OJ L55/13.

Parliament's increased involvement in scrutinizing 'comitology' improves democracy both from the perspective of transparency and reducing executive dominance, though of course much depends on the extent to which the EU legislature (and especially the European Parliament) actually carries out its oversight on Commission delegated acts.[29]

For those unconvinced by the EU's various ways of offering indirect representation to voters, the Lisbon Treaty offers one final innovation that bolsters direct representation in Article 11 TEU.

Article 11 TEU (emphasis added)

1. The institutions shall, by appropriate means, give **citizens and representative associations** the opportunity to **make known and publicly exchange their views** in all areas of Union action.
2. The institutions shall maintain an **open, transparent and regular dialogue with representative associations and civil society**.
3. The European Commission shall carry out **broad consultations with parties concerned in order to ensure that the Union's actions are coherent and transparent**.
4. Not less than one million citizens who are nationals of a significant number of Member States may take the initiative of **inviting the European Commission**, within the framework of its powers, to **submit any appropriate proposal** on matters where citizens consider that a legal act of the Union is required for the purpose of implementing the Treaties.

. . .

It first generally promises that the EU institutions will make themselves available to EU citizens, and that where legislation is drafted or policy developed, civil society will be broadly consulted. More interestingly, it creates something called the Citizens' Initiative in Article 11(4) TEU. Under the Citizens' Initiative, where the EU is either acting or *not* acting in a given policy area that the EU could be acting in, a million EU citizens from different Member States can sign a petition and send it to the Commission in order to stimulate legislation being produced. This is akin to the petitions that UK residents can send to Parliament for debate, and quite clearly is geared at resolving 'the distance issue'.

However, the wording of Article 11(4) TEU is very general, and while it forces the Commission to *consider* Citizens' Initiatives, it does not force them to *adopt* or *scrap* legislation in response to them. It is also unclear if Article 11, generally, is enforceable before the CJEU: if citizens feel unheard, or ignored, can they take the EU institutions to court over this?

Several challenges have been launched regarding Commission rejections of initiatives on account of their not falling within the framework of Commission legislative powers.[30]

[29] See, analysing the new system, Paolo Ponzano, 'The Reform of Comitology and Delegated Acts' in Carl Fredrik Bergström and Dominique Ritleng (eds), *Rulemaking by the European Commission: The New System for Delegation of Powers* (OUP, 2016); and critical of the take-up of the new system, Carlo Tovo, 'Delegation of Legislative Powers in the EU: How EU institutions have eluded the Lisbon reform' (2017) 42(5) ELRev 677.

[30] Case T-754/14 *Efler* ECLI:EU:T:2016:306, which was successful; Case T-361/14 *HB* ECLI:EU:T:2017:252, which was dismissed.

The EU's General Court confirmed in 2018 that complaints about the administration of the European Citizens' Initiative are in principle admissible—but simultaneously confirmed that the Commission is not actually *obliged* to make a proposal on the basis of an initiative reaching the submission threshold.[31]

To date, the Citizens' Initiative has not been a roaring success: only four petitions have, at the time of writing, made the 'one million votes' threshold and thus been heard by the Commission,[32] and only in one case did the Commission state it would undertake action—but without specifying *how,* specifically, it would respond to the Initiative. The EU has launched consultations to try to bolster how the Citizens' Initiative works in response to a lacklustre take-up in the first five years of its existence, so it is undoubtedly trying to make it a useful tool to bolster participatory democracy in the EU. However, for now, it can be very much questioned if it *is* making a difference to the voters.[33]

What we can take from this short summary of specific changes made in the Lisbon Treaty to tackle the 'democratic deficit' is that the EU is certainly trying to address some of the issues raised by Follesdal and Hix; and in the areas of greater legislative transparency, less distance, and more power to representative institutions, it has definitely made progress.

Discussing the scenario

Which quit.eu arguments are addressed by the Lisbon Treaty 'democracy boosters'? Does it address all of them?

Regrettably, certain post-Lisbon events in the EU have made it clear that questions about how democratic its decision-making processes are remain very relevant. As commentators have noted sharply, the idea that the EU was making progress in becoming more 'democratic' was delivered a significant blow by its handling of the 2007–2010 financial crisis when it hit countries that had adopted the Euro.[34]

[31] See Case T-561/14 *One of Us v Commission* ECLI:EU:T:2018:210, paras 111 and 112.

[32] See Commission, 'Communication on the European Citizens' Initiative "Ban glyphosate and protect people and the environment from toxic pesticides" COM(2017) 8414 final; Commission, 'Communication on the European Citizens' Initiative "One of Us"' COM(2014) 355 final; Commission, 'Communication on the European Citizens' Initiative "Water and sanitation are a human right! Water is a public good, not a commodity!"' COM(2014) 177 final; Commission, 'Communication on the European Citizens' Initiative "Stop Vivisection"' COM(2015) 3773 final. 'Water and sanitation are a human right!' is the only Initiative to have received a positive response from the Commission, albeit an unspecific one.

[33] See https://ec.europa.eu/info/consultations/public-consultation-european-citizens-initiative_en.

[34] See, for instance, Eduardo Chiti and Pedro Gustavo Teixeira, 'The Constitutional Implications of the European Responses to the Financial and Public Debt Crisis' (2013) 50 CMLRev 683; Fritz Scharpf, 'Legitimacy Intermediation in the Multilevel European Polity and Its Collapse in the Euro Crisis' (2012) 12/6 MPIfG, http://www.mpifg.de/pu/mpifg_dp/dp12-6.pdf.

3.4.2 The Eurozone crisis and democracy

Greece was, by 2008, on the verge of bankruptcy; this was for a wide variety of reasons, the most significant of which was its staggering amount of accumulated debt. It had hidden this debt from the rest of the Eurozone, but when the markets realized just how little money Greece actually had, and how much money Greece owed, a debt crisis broke out.

This was not simply a problem for Greece, however. In a country that is not part of a single currency like the Euro, the normal response to a debt crisis is to basically print off more of the national currency and use it to pay off that debt; this means the currency becomes worth less overall, but it prevents the country from defaulting on all of its loans. However, Greece does not have that ability: countries that have adopted the Euro have handed over their monetary policy, or control over the value of their currency, to the European Central Bank. And the European Central Bank cannot devalue the Euro in Greece without also driving down its value in *all other Member States* that have adopted the Euro. Given that not all Eurozone economies were experiencing a crisis like Greece, this was not a decision that the European Central Bank was willing to take.

Something *else* had to be done in order to save Greece, then, because Greece effectively going bankrupt would *also* harm the value of the Euro. However, the Member States could not agree if they wanted to help Greece by lending it money on an emergency basis; and the European Central Bank did not actually *have* the power to act as a lender to any of the Member States. To regain stability in Europe, finally, the Heads of State of the Member States, largely on a German initiative (as German banks made up a significant portion of the institutions from which Greece had borrowed money), set up two 'ad hoc' mechanisms to save the Greek economy. The first of these two so-called 'bail-out' funds was funded directly by the Member States; the other was funded by the EU, but as the EU itself operates on the basis of a budget that it collects from the Member States, in effect both funds were funded by the Member States.

Here we see a number of legal potholes. For one thing, there were no mechanisms in any of the EU Treaties to deal with the possibility of an EU Member State going bankrupt. The Eurozone Member States retained control over their own 'fiscal' or economic policy, but could not touch the value of the currency; conversely, the EU had no control over national economic policies in the Eurozone, but had to maintain the value of the currency for the sake of all Member States. Faced with this crisis, what the EU Heads of State ended up doing was moving *around* the EU Treaties in order to set up rescue funds as quickly as they could. The temporary bail-out facilities were eventually replaced with a formal, standing rescue fund called the European Stability Mechanism (ESM) and a new set of rules that commits Eurozone Members to new debt limits, called the European Fiscal Compact (EFC). Both the ESM and the EFC, however, were signed as separate Treaties: they were agreed by the EU Heads of State without the participation of the EU institutions and without the functioning of a normal **intergovernmental conference**, in large part to sidestep protests by non-Eurozone Member States (like the UK) and to ensure that quick responses could be taken at a time of crisis.[35]

[35] Chiti and Teixeira (n 34).

The European Parliament, consequently, did not have a say in the content or adoption of these Treaties; nor did the Commission. However, these new non-EU Treaties do require cooperation and participation from various EU institutions, both for oversight (the Commission) and enforcement (the CJEU), so they are hardly 'extra-EU' arrangements. This puts a dent in the efforts made in Lisbon to greatly increase the European Parliament's involvement in EU law-making and to ensure that national parliaments are consulted widely on EU policy and law; instead, new Treaties came into force primarily through executive action, further marginalizing the representative institutions.

A larger problem, however, is that even where voters within the Member State were given a voice on the EU's approach to resolving the Eurozone debt crisis, these voters were ignored entirely. Greece was going to be saved by bail-outs from the established rescue funds: but those bail-outs came with strings attached. In order to make it palatable to voters in Germany that their taxes would be used to rescue a 'foreign country', strict conditions on how Greece was to manage its economy were attached to the granting of these bail-out funds. As a consequence, Greek economic policy—which was a power never transferred to the EU—would be determined *by* the EU in order for these rescue funds to be available to it. The Greeks voted in a referendum to reject the loan settlement offered to them in 2015—but the Greek government felt it had no alternative but to take the money in order to stay in the Euro, regardless of the conditions attached to it, and so the Greek voters' wishes were ignored.[36]

Kratochvíl and Sychra summarize the ways in which the Eurozone crisis exacerbated the democratic deficit by noting that the EU executive has grown significantly in power, while the European Parliament has lost some of its power, and the national parliaments are once more sidelined, having to agree to proposed domestic budgets *after* these have been approved by the Commission, as is required by the European Fiscal Compact. They also point out that 'distance' between the EU and its citizens increased tremendously during the crisis, and policy drift from voter preferences was also exacerbated, even if only for a short time.[37] Not only did **input** suffer during the crisis and how it was handled by the EU, but **output** and **checks and balances** were also undermined, as the traditional EU institutions and their national equivalents were effectively at most an *influence* on how the EU Heads of State and their ministerial representatives in the Council tackled the crisis.

Indeed, the Eurozone crisis prompted Majone—an early defender of the EU—to conclude that the EU is no longer simply a regulatory entity that excludes citizen voice to an acceptable extent, but entire *Member States* are now being forced to accept solutions put forward by financial institutions, with the backing of the leaders of several Member States. He describes the minimization of the role that national parliaments and the Member States can play in determining their own fiscal policy because of the Fiscal Compact as potentially turning what is a democratic deficit into a 'democratic default'.[38]

[36] See https://www.theguardian.com/world/2015/jul/10/greeks-resigned-to-bailout-plan-despite-voting-against-austerity.

[37] Petr Kratochvíl and Zdeněk Sychra, 'The End of Democracy in the EU? The Eurozone Crisis and the EU's Democratic Deficit' (2019) 41(2) J Eur Integr 169.

[38] Giandomenico Majone, 'From Regulatory State to a Democratic Default' (2014) 52(6) JCMS 1216, 1221.

Pause for reflection

Can you think of more 'democratic' means by which the Eurozone crisis could have been resolved? Why were these not used, do you think?

The Eurozone crisis is, of course, an actual *crisis*—this is not the normal operation of the EU, and nor should it be used as a benchmark for how democratic EU decision-making generally operates. But it does remind us of a few of the qualities that Follesdal and Hix raised in 2006: occasionally, decisions taken at the EU level that have a massive impact on the voter are taken far away from the voter, may ignore voter input, and are largely taken by national executives, rather than national parliaments.[39] The Eurozone crisis tells us that, unfortunately, Treaty improvements are only one part of the EU's ongoing struggle with democracy: where the EU Heads of State manoeuvre around the rules they have written in order to bolster the EU's democratic qualities, it is nonetheless the EU that ends up appearing undemocratic. But is this genuine evidence of there being a persistent problem with the EU's democratic qualities—or is it just a reflection on how political decision-making, regardless of whether at the national level or the EU level, sometimes falls short of democratic ideals? There is, unfortunately, no clear, definitive answer to that question—and so the 'democratic deficit' debate about the EU continues.

3.5 Brexit and 'democracy'

It seems obvious that, whatever your feelings about the *extent* of the democratic deficit in the EU, leaving the EU project will restore 'democracy' to the UK: after all, decisions that were taken at the EU level will now in principle be taken by Parliament again, and Parliament is significantly 'closer' to the UK voter than the EU can be.

However, the form of Brexit has a significant impact on just *how much* input and oversight is restored to the UK voter: the closer the relationship between the UK and the EU, the less 'control' will be taken back. Looking at the likely differences between the nature of Brexit during the Withdrawal Agreement's transition period, and the 'future relationship', will help make this point clearer.

3.5.1 The Withdrawal Agreement

We discussed the EU institutions and what roles they will play during the transition period in Chapter 2, but it is worth stressing that under the Withdrawal Agreement, while EU law will continue to apply to the entirety of the UK, there will be no UK representation in any of the EU institutions.[40] The consequences of this on democracy are not ideal: even if you view the European Parliament as relatively powerless and the UK's influence on Council decision-making as too small, spending a possible three years in the

[39] Scharpf (n 34). [40] Withdrawal Agreement, Article 7.

Withdrawal Agreement's transition period presents a significant drop in the level of UK 'democratic' input into laws applicable to it.[41] However, it is very likely that the benefits of stability in terms of legal framework have been deemed by the UK negotiators to outweigh the 'loss' of democracy for an arrangement of expressly limited duration, like the transition period.

3.5.2 **The Protocol on Ireland/Northern Ireland**

Not all aspects of the Withdrawal Agreement are temporary, however. The Protocol on Ireland and Northern Ireland sets out a future in which Northern Ireland will be subject to a range of EU law, as well as a degree of oversight and enforcement by the Commission and the CJEU, but again without any representation *in* the EU bodies that make the laws that will apply there.[42]

Northern Ireland's 'voicelessness' after Brexit was one of the key reasons that the original Withdrawal Agreement, negotiated by Theresa May's government in 2017 and 2018, failed to be approved by UK Parliament. The October 2019 renegotiation, however, did not change this aspect of the Withdrawal Agreement, presumably signifying that the EU was adamant that a non-Member State could not sit and take decisions in EU institutions.

Nonetheless, for the sake of restoring 'democracy' to Northern Ireland and not just Great Britain, the UK government lobbied for a different novelty in the Protocol. Article 18 of the Protocol now calls for a process of 'democratic consent' in Northern Ireland. As the EU did not budge on Northern Ireland representation in its institutions, the UK government proposed a unilateral mechanism by which Northern Ireland can *reject* the further application of the Protocol, which would result in the provisions of the Protocol no longer applying to Northern Ireland.

The 'democratic consent mechanism' designed by the UK does not allow anyone in Northern Ireland to protest the adoption of particular EU laws, in the way that Member States can via the Council and the European Parliament, but rather enables the Northern Ireland Assembly to vote four years after the end of the transition period on whether it wishes to continue the arrangements in the Protocol (which are discussed in more detail in Chapters 10 and 11).[43] If there is a cross-community vote in favour, the follow-up vote will be eight years later; whereas if there is a simple majority vote, another vote on the Protocol will take place four years later. This 'voting to consent' process will continue indefinitely, unless the Northern Ireland Assembly votes *against* the application of the Protocol, in which case it will cease to apply after two years—during which period an alternative solution to maintaining an invisible border on the island of Ireland must be found by the UK and the EU.[44]

[41] On the possibility of extension, see Withdrawal Agreement, Articles 126 and 132; note that the EU (Withdrawal Agreement) Act 2020, s 33, prohibits UK representatives from asking for an extension as a matter of domestic law—though as is true for all Acts of Parliament, this can obviously be amended if an extension is desired after all.

[42] Article 7 of the Withdrawal Agreement also applies to the Protocol; on institutional roles in the Protocol, see Chapters 2 and 8.

[43] Protocol, Article 18(5). [44] Protocol, Article 18(4).

It is difficult to place this democratic consent mechanism on the 'democratic deficit' sliding scale. Clearly, allowing *a vote* is preferable to there being no democratic participation in the working of EU law in Northern Ireland at all, but it is still very far removed from being able to actually influence the nature of all the EU law that will apply to Northern Ireland under the Protocol. Whether Northern Ireland experiences democratic 'gains' after Brexit is thus very debatable.

3.5.3 The future relationship

The end of membership of the EU must represent 'peak' UK democracy, at least for Great Britain. But just how much democracy *is* that?

That largely depends on how the UK approaches its future relationship with the EU, as well as with other countries around the world. The bottom line of any international agreement is that it is built on mutual trust and cooperation, and the UK will always have to make compromises and agree on regulatory regimes in order to have a functional relationship with *any* country in the world. All countries will have their own demands in terms of concessions made by the UK: India, for instance, has made it very clear that it wishes for a looser visa regime in order to conclude a post-Brexit free trade agreement.[45]

The limited discussions in the Political Declaration on most non-economic aspects of a trade agreement reflect that the UK has already indicated it does not intend, for example, to continue an immigration regime which is as flexible as 'free movement of people' (discussed in Chapters 12 and 13).[46] The Political Declaration thereby implies a lot of independent choice for the UK—but only hints at the fact that this will come at a cost.

Generally, it can be observed that the global economy represents an inescapable compromise between sovereignty, democracy, and prosperity. A country can do whatever it wants to, and enact all of its voters' wishes—but it is unlikely to be able to build close relationships with *other* countries as a consequence. In practical terms, Brexit at best means that the UK will be able to take decisions on how to make that compromise with *each* of its trading partners—as opposed to having that choice made by the EU. In even more practical terms, it is likely to have to decide who its new closest economic partner is going to be: the EU, or the United States? If the former, the pressure will mount to comply with more EU rules and regulations; and if the latter, the UK will lose out on access to the EU market because it is instead complying with US rules and regulations.[47]

Certain aspects of what Follesdal and Hix and others have criticized about the EU's functioning apply equally to the UK outside of the EU. Withdrawal from the EU will not diminish executive dominance in UK decision-making. The EU (Withdrawal) Act 2018, setting out how leaving the EU will alter the domestic legal landscape, has given the executive extremely far-ranging powers to alter existing UK legislation so as to make it 'Brexit-proof', without detailed parliamentary oversight.[48] The reason given for these so-called

[45] See https://www.parliament.uk/business/committees/committees-a-z/commons-select/foreign-affairs-committee/news-parliament-2017/gobal-britain-and-india-report-published-17-19/.

[46] Political Declaration, Article 48.

[47] For more discussion on regulatory alignment, see Chapter 10.

[48] See EU (Withdrawal) Act 2018, s 8.

'Henry VIII'[49] powers is speed—Parliament cannot possibly cope with untangling the entirety of all EU law from all UK law in a reasonable amount of time. Regardless of motive, however, this quick sifting of legislation does not propose a transparent, democratic means of restoring power to the UK voter.[50]

Moreover, nothing in the EU (Withdrawal) Act 2018 or the EU (Withdrawal Agreement) Act 2020, implementing the Withdrawal Agreement, suggests that the devolved governments of the UK stand to gain power from Brexit.[51] In particular, the House of Lords has expressed significant concerns about the lack of involvement that the 2018 and 2020 Acts set out for the devolved regions in the development of any 'future relationship' with the EU—despite the fact that the devolved regions will be heavily affected by the shape of that future relationship, as they will be by Brexit.[52] It can be argued that not returning significant power to the devolved regions, or giving them a greater role in the future UK–EU relationship, is a missed opportunity to bolster democracy in the UK. After all, the voters in Scotland and Northern Ireland expressed significantly different policy preferences in the EU referendum than the voters in England and Wales did.[53]

The EU (Withdrawal Agreement) Act 2020 furthermore grants no power to Parliament in scrutinizing the 'future relationship' negotiations, beyond a vote on ratification at the end of the negotiations.[54] However, it is important to recognize that if those negotiations do not complete before the end of the transition period, the UK and the EU will experience significant legal upheaval in a number of areas on which they will have no agreed rules. Trade, although the area most frequently raised, is not one of these areas: trade in goods would take place on World Trade Organization terms in the absence of a 'future relationship' agreement, and so business has at least some ability to anticipate what those rules are—but there are many other policy areas raised in the Political Declaration (road and air transport, law enforcement and judicial cooperation, nuclear and other energy arrangements, and even UK participation in EU projects like the Erasmus student exchange) where it is not wholly clear what *would* replace the current EU law framework.

A lot of day-to-day life would, in other words, be heavily impacted, and even if the UK and the EU set up unilateral rules to very quickly ensure that—for example—trucks and

[49] See, for an explanation, http://blogs.lse.ac.uk/brexit/2016/11/30/rights-for-the-chop-how-a-henry-viii-clause-in-the-great-repeal-bill-will-undermine-democracy/.

[50] Delegated powers are also a prominent feature of the EU (Withdrawal Agreement) Act 2020, which implements the Withdrawal Agreement in the UK. See, eg, ss 18–21, 27, and para 39 of Schedule 2.

[51] See, eg, EU (Withdrawal) Act 2018, Schedule 2, part 3 and EU (Withdrawal Agreement) Act 2020, s 18.

[52] See the discussion in the Lords during the second reading of the EU (Withdrawal Agreement) Bill on 13 January 2020: https://hansard.parliament.uk/Lords/2020-01-13/debates/8EE15EAD-6927-4613-AC95-DA6B64711D28/EuropeanUnion(WithdrawalAgreement)Bill.

[53] It is worth noting that all three devolved governments refused legislative consent for the EU (Withdrawal Agreement) Act 2020, and that the UK government responded to these refusals only by noting that international relations were a reserved matter for the UK government. It has been argued that Brexit is putting the UK's existing devolution under considerable strain: see, eg, https://www.instituteforgovernment.org.uk/blog/sewel-convention-has-been-broken-brexit-reform-now-urgent; https://www.centreonconstitutionalchange.ac.uk/news-and-opinion/brexit-eroding-sewel-convention.

[54] The October 2019 version of the EU (Withdrawal Agreement) Bill gave Parliament these powers in clause 31, but that clause was gone when the Bill was reintroduced following the December 2019 election.

aeroplanes can still cross borders, the uncertainty generated by the absence of a 'future relationship' agreement would be very costly for businesses on both sides of the Channel. Whether Parliament is willing to risk such an outcome at the end of 2020 (or 2021, or 2022) by vetoing whatever the UK and the EU have negotiated by then is far from clear. Is this then a 'real' power to oversee the future UK–EU relationship, or one that in practice cannot reasonably be exercised?

Of course, these types of concerns stem from 'ideals' of democracy much in the same way as Follesdal and Hix's arguments do. No one can argue that Brexit means there is *no* policy control returning to the UK, and that this *can never* bring decision-making closer to the voter and thus amplify democracy. But a detailed look at democracy and how it works, both inside and outside of the EU, should caution us in signing up to overly optimistic versions of what 'taking back control' means. The measure of control regained, and how that control is exercised, is very much dependent on the outcome of negotiations and the UK's decisions on what compromises to strike with future trading partners. A return to an era where only Parliament's decisions impact on what policy exists in the UK is impossible. Instead, what Brexit can achieve is a greater ability for Parliament to consider whether it wishes to prioritize trade, or other values, in different scenarios—if the UK economy can afford *not* to prioritize trade, anyway.

3.6 In conclusion

In a perfect world, there would be a very straightforward answer to a question like, 'is the EU democratic enough'? In reality, however, it is a question that needs to be picked apart on a number of levels, by defining both what we look for in a **democracy** and what we mean by **enough**. The answer to the question, ultimately, will depend on how important voter *input* is to anyone looking at the EU, as well as how amenable they are to the argument that the EU is not a country and thus perhaps should not be held to the same standard that countries are.

One thing that is clear is that the EU is not wholly inured to complaints about its democratic shortcomings, and has made attempts to reorganize its legislative processes so as to provide for *more* input. Once again, however, there is great disagreement on the extent to which those attempts have been successful—just as there will continue to be significant disagreements on whether the trade-off between the benefits of EU membership and the relative democracy gains of Brexit will be worth it for the UK.

Discussing the scenario

Use the material in this chapter to write up a response to Michael Jones in light of what you now know about the EU and the 'democratic deficit' debate. Do the claims made in the quit.eu video have any merit?

If not, explain why you think they do not, and why you ultimately think the EU is 'democratic enough'. If yes, explain why the EU's efforts to become more democratic have not resolved the EU's 'democracy problem'.

A sample approach to a response can be found online.

Key points

The key points raised in the democratic deficit debate are summarized in Table 3.1.

TABLE 3.1 The democratic deficit debate

The Complaint	Counter-Arguments	Lisbon Comments
1 Decision-making in the EU is unresponsive to democratic pressure	**1a** The EU is not a nation; the EU is a regulatory project, acting in policy areas that are not usually subject to democratic pressure in most nations	**1a** EP has gained more power than ever before over legislative process **1b** However: EU has also gained legislative powers in increasingly sensitive policy areas
2 Executive dominance at the expense of parliamentary power	**2a** The executive is indirectly representative—national elections should produce accountability **2b** EP power has consistently increased	**2a** EP has gained more power than ever before over legislative process **2b** EP has also gained further oversight over the other institutions—see Chapter 2
3 Law-making in the EU bypasses democracy	**3a** Only in limited instances—comitology—and these are instances where democracy is bypassed in the UK as well—ie, delegated legislation	**3a** Neo-comitology comes with increased oversight from indirectly and directly representative institutions
4 EU legislation is 'distant' from voters	**4a** This is both by design—the Member States granted the EU powers in those areas where they did not *object* to voter distance, and do not want the EU to be a political union with its own political parties!—and inevitable in supranational cooperation	**4a** The Citizens' Initiative and increases in national parliamentary oversight bring legislation closer to the voter again
5 EU decision-making is opaque and too complex	**5a** The EU is a regulatory project, acting in policy areas that are not usually subject to democratic pressure in most nations (and so complexity and secrecy of decision-making somewhat irrelevant) **5b** The EU also does not promise absolute transparency (see Article 10(3) TEU)—nor does any government!	**5a** Simplification of legislative processes into only two procedures **5b** National parliaments more informed about EU activities EP also more informed about Council/Commission activities, which are now increasingly in public domain

Assess your learning

1. What *is* democracy? What makes decisions 'democratically legitimate'? (See Section 3.2.)
2. Do you think the EU suffers from a democratic deficit, even after the Lisbon Treaty? (See Section 3.3.)
3. What, in particular, about the EU's responses to the Eurozone crisis—from 2009 onward, and considering the summer of 2015—is democratically problematic? From what you know about how the EU works, do you think the EU could have responded in a different, more democratic manner? (See Section 3.4.)

Further reading

On the EU's democratic qualities

Deirdre Curtin, 'Challenging Executive Dominance in European Democracy' (2014) 77(1) MLR 1.

Dieter Grimm, 'The Democratic Costs of Constitutionalisation: The European case' (2015) 21(4) Eur Law J 460.

Anastasia Karatzia, 'The European Citizens' Initiative in Practice: Legal admissibility concerns' (2015) 40(4) ELRev 509.

Massimo La Torre, 'A Weberian Moment for Europe? Constitutionalism and the Crisis of European Integration' (2014) 20(3) EPL 421.

Anand Menon and Stephen Weatherill, 'Democratic Politics in a Globalising World: Supranationalism and legitimacy in the European Union' (2007) 13/2007 LSE Law, Society and Economy Working Papers, http://ssrn.com/abstract=1021218, accessed 27 August 2014.

Carlo Tovo, 'Delegation of Legislative Powers in the EU: How EU institutions have eluded the Lisbon reforms' (2017) 42(5) ELRev 677.

Wolfgang Weiss, 'The Future of EU Executive Rulemaking' (2019) 44(3) ELRev 337.

On the constitutional dimensions of the Eurozone crisis

Elisenda Casanas Adam et al, 'Democracy in Question? Direct Democracy in the European Union' (2018) 14(2) Eur Const Law Rev 261.

Moritz Hartmann and Floris de Witte (eds), 'Special Issue: Regeneration Europe' (2013) 14(5) Ger Law J 441.

Koen Lenaerts, 'EMU and the EU's Constitutional Framework' (2014) 39(6) ELRev 753.

Fritz Scharpf, 'After the Crash: A perspective on multilevel European democracy' (2015) 21(3) Eur Law J 384.

Bruno de Witte, 'Euro Crisis Responses and the EU Legal Order: Increased institutional variation or constitutional mutation?' (2015) 11(3) Eur Const Law Rev 434.

Online resources

Visit www.oup.com/he/demars1e for a sample approach to discussing the quote.

4

EU legislative powers

Context for this chapter

'In a speech to the European Parliament (EP) in July 1988, the then Commission President, Jacques Delors, predicted that within ten years (i.e. by 1998) 80% of economic legislation, and perhaps also fiscal and social legislation, would be of EU origin. Since this statement, the amount and impact of EU law has been the subject of considerable, often passionate and critical, debate, linked to issues such as the loss of national sovereignty and decision-making powers, the regulatory burden for business and industry, administrative mechanisms for agriculture and fisheries, and the effect on national culture and identity.'

Vaughne Miller, 'How Much Legislation Comes from Europe?'
(House of Commons Library Research Paper, 10/62)

'The Prime Minister claims, of course, that we have secured an "opt-out" from ever closer union, and thus from political union. . . . But this is little comfort, since we continue to be fully subject to present and future EU legislation, driven by the objective of full-blooded political union.'

Nigel Lawson, 'Lord Lawson's Chatham House speech—
The Case for Brexit' (24 February 2016)
http://www.voteleavetakecontrol.org/lord_lawson_s_chatham_house_speech_the_case_for_brexit

4.1 Introduction

Chapters 2 and 3 considered how decisions are made in the European Union, and to what extent those decision-making processes can be deemed 'democratic'. Chapters 4 and 5 consider what the *output* of European Union decisions is: the actual laws it makes, and the limits to its law-making powers.

The two quotes providing context to this chapter introduce a criticism of the EU that came to the fore in the 2016 referendum campaign, which is that it is creating more and more law, and that the end destination of all that legislation is to create a 'Federal Europe', at the expense of the identities and interests of the Member States.

In order to determine whether such concerns about the EU becoming an 'ever closer union' purely through its legislative processes are overstated or not, we need to consider what those legislative powers are, and what the Member States have built into the Treaties in order to prevent the EU *overreaching* when making law.

We can map the EU's legislative powers, and the limits placed on them in the Treaties, by asking two overarching questions:

- *When* can the EU make law? (Does it have the power to legislate, or do the Member States?)
- And, if the EU can act, *how* can it act? (Are there rules determining the *form* and *content* of legislation?)

We commence this chapter by considering aspects of *how* the EU can act, by assessing the EU's sources of law and the legislative processes that are used to adopt secondary legislation. Next, we assess *when* (or in what policy areas) the EU can make law by considering its competences.

Finally, we consider two mechanisms that aim to *prevent* the EU from extending its legislative power beyond what the Treaties have granted it. First, in those policy areas where both the EU and the Member States have legislative powers, the principle of subsidiarity aims to ensure that the EU only acts in those situations where it is necessary for the EU to act. Secondly, we consider the principle of proportionality, which aims to prevent overly *invasive* EU law from becoming binding on the Member States.

Once we are familiar with what the Treaties say about the EU's law-making powers, we can consider to what extent the limits set out by the Treaties are actually effective. This is what we do in Chapter 5: can the EU legislative process be 'stopped' by any particularly unhappy Member States? And if not, what does that say about the EU's legislative powers—have the Member States lost control of them?

4.2 Sources of EU law

Much as in any domestic jurisdiction, the legislative bodies in the EU have a set number of legislative forms that they can employ. EU law is separate from domestic law, but it has to be able to interact with domestic legal systems. Otherwise, we would end up with a lot of law being produced 'in Brussels' that simply never touches what happens in the Member States. This would make EU law extremely ineffective.

As with domestic law, there are two overarching categories of EU law: primary law and secondary law. We will investigate the specific legislative forms that make up EU law in each of these categories.

4.2.1 Primary law: the Treaties

The starting point for EU law is the EU Treaties. Though the Lisbon Treaty has dropped the 'Constitutional' title, the Treaties are *in effect* the 'constitution' for the European Union. All secondary legislation that the EU produces must have an origin in the Treaties.

Under Lisbon, two Treaties of equivalent legal value are in force:

- The Treaty on European Union (TEU)
- The Treaty on the Functioning of the European Union (TFEU).

The TEU covers the EU's 'mission statement' and basic setup. It sets out what the EU's policies and goals are, what the EU's institutions and their powers are, and sets out the general rules on some of the policy areas where non-standard EU procedures operate, such as external relations and Common Foreign and Security Policy.[1] However, the detailed rules on how the EU ordinarily functions, and in what policy areas it can undertake action, are all set out in the TFEU. This Treaty is much longer and more specific, and supplements the basic principles that are set out in the TEU. Whilst the TEU contains some key provisions of EU law (those on the institutions and, of particular interest in the UK, those on Treaty amendment and withdrawal from the European Union), most of the EU's *substantive* law finds its origins in the TFEU.

Additional binding primary sources of law appended to the Treaties are not of general interest, but may be of interest to specific Member States. For instance, there are a significant number of Protocols attached to the Lisbon Treaty that cover some of the opt-outs and special arrangements that various Member States have negotiated. For the UK, this included an opt-out from the Schengen Area (alongside Ireland) and the Euro, and most other Protocols contain a variety of arrangements struck with other Member States who have overseas territories that are not *quite* in the EU.[2]

Protocols need to be distinguished from Declarations, which are also found in Annexes to the Lisbon Treaty, but do not have binding legal value. They, instead, set out agreed-upon interpretations of certain Treaty provisions in significantly more detail. Many of these declarations confirm long-standing Court of Justice case law, which can be seen in Declaration 17 on Primacy.[3] Some other declarations contain statements by Member States on their specific understanding of how EU law will operate in their territory.

The EU being governed by two Treaties is not new—this has been the case since Maastricht—but Lisbon offers a novel source of primary law in that it made the Charter of Fundamental Rights binding, and of equivalent legal value to the EU Treaties. This means that not only has the EU now created its own 'human rights' regime, but its Member States have agreed that that 'human rights' regime is just as important as those agreements governing the EU's 'internal market' activities. We will explore the Charter in detail in Chapter 9.

4.2.2 Primary law: general principles of law

The written sources of EU primary law are limited and consequently easy to keep track of. However, they are not the only source of EU primary law.

Over time, the Court of Justice has developed a wide variety of criteria against which to check the appropriateness or validity of EU legislative action. These criteria are collectively known as the 'general principles of EU law', and their origin is the Court's case law. Opinions differ on whether this means that 'general principles' are evidence of the Court of Justice 'making up new rules'. The CJEU itself has argued that it has considered the rules that govern the validity of laws in non-EU legal systems, primarily those of the Member States, and chosen to apply them to EU law as well. Where such rules are not written into the Treaties themselves, the Court of Justice has frequently declared them

[1] See Chapter 16. [2] See, eg, Denmark and France.
[3] On the principle of supremacy, see Chapter 6.

to be 'general principles' of law, so as to ensure that EU legislation does not fall short of the expectations that we have of laws when they are produced by the Member States themselves.

In other words, general principles are used to evaluate both the *legality* and *appropriateness* of EU legal action. They constitute grounds for review that the Court will employ when considering Union actions, but also constitute grounds for review for what the Member States do when they are *implementing* EU law—or making it part of their domestic legal order—and when they are *derogating* from EU laws, by means of the limited number of derogations that exist. We will consider how general principles apply to the Member States when they are dealing with EU law in many other chapters; for now, as a means of introducing what general principles are and how they function, we will look at how the Court employs them when considering the validity of EU action.

We know that general principles form part of the Union's primary laws because the Court of Justice has declared them to have 'constitutional status'.[4] Confusingly for students, but unsurprisingly given that they stem from the Court's case law, there is no finite list of general principles. However, we can roughly categorize them into two separate groupings: *human rights-related* general principles of law, and *administrative* general principles of law. The *human-rights related* general principles have, by and large, been codified in the Charter of Fundamental Rights as of the Nice Treaty, and we will look at those in Chapter 9.

The *administrative* general principles of law, meanwhile, continue to primarily find their origins in domestic law and legal practice, and involve principles such as **proportionality**, **transparency**, **legal certainty**, and **legitimate expectations**. The purpose of these general principles is to provide a framework for how the CJEU will interpret EU law, as well as to establish the grounds of review of EU actions. Proportionality, transparency, and legitimate expectations reflect the overarching constitutional principle of the 'rule of law': they are employed by the CJEU as criteria against which to assess EU legislative action. Where an EU act or an action by an EU institution fails to respect one of these 'rule of law' principles, the CJEU will overturn that act or action.

Transparency is seen as essential for the legality of a governance system because without it, it is very difficult to hold either the legislature or the executive to account. The CJEU has, through its case law, stressed that documentary access and public information are key elements of complying with the 'rule of law'. In *Gottfried Heinrich*, it consequently disapplied an EU regulation that precluded the carrying of tennis rackets on aeroplanes in hand luggage because the annex to that regulation that listed the specific items that were prohibited had never been published in the *Official Journal* of the European Union.[5] The lack of transparency here, in failing to publish that annex, meant that the regulation in question could not be enforced—and Mr Heinrich should have been permitted to carry his racket onto his flight.

Legitimate expectations and legal certainty are similar but separate grounds for review of EU acts and actions. On legal certainty, the CJEU requires that the law is clear, precise, and foreseeable; and that individuals are able to see what their rights and duties are at any point in time.[6] The General Court, in reviewing the actions of EU institutions, has

[4] Case C-101/08 *Audiolux and Others* ECLI:EU:C:2009:626.
[5] See, eg, Case C-345/06 *Gottfried Heinrich* ECLI:EU:C:2009:140.
[6] See, eg, Case C-158/06 *ROM-projecten* ECLI:EU:C:2007:370.

thus overruled the institutions where they have applied inconsistent or contradictory rules to individuals, and where administrative processes have taken an unforeseeably long time.[7] With respect to legitimate expectations, the CJEU has forced the overturning of many EU administrative decisions because they ran contrary to the expectations reasonably held by affected individuals. A useful illustration is the *Di Lenardo* case, wherein two banana importers in Italy believed they were included in a 'quota' system for banana imports introduced by the EU—but found that they were not, according to Italian authorities which determined they had not imported sufficient bananas between 1994 and 1996, and thus did not qualify for a newly created EU status of 'primary importer'.[8] They challenged this finding, arguing that the Commission 'introduced new terms which are completely different to those previously used in the banana sector'—and so their legitimate expectations had been violated.[9] The CJEU disagreed, however, noting that 'if a prudent and circumspect trader could have foreseen that the adoption of an [EU] measure is likely to affect his interests', they could not rely on legitimate expectations.[10] As the CJEU found that the rules on banana imports had regularly changed since 1993, even if not in this specific way, the two importers could not reasonably have expected them not to change again—and so the EU measure did not violate the principle of legitimate expectations.

The most common ground for review of EU legal action, as well as Member State action, when engaged with EU law is proportionality, and we explore how it works in Section 4.6 of this chapter. Other 'general principles' arise in specific cases as the CJEU or the parties find them relevant.

It is important to keep in mind that 'general principles' remain an 'in progress' category of EU primary law, as the Court of Justice can 'discover' further common elements in Member State legal traditions, and apply those when considering the legality of EU action. This might make the 'general principles' seem more controversial than they actually are, however, as much of the Court's case law on the general principles has been codified as part of Treaty drafting. Consequently, as we will discuss in Section 4.5, we have Protocol 2 on Subsidiarity and Proportionality. Furthermore, 'good administration' rights reflecting on the rule of law—such as **the right to a fair hearing**—have been codified in the Charter of Fundamental Rights.[11] The Court has consequently filled 'gaps' in the Treaties with general principles, but seemingly has done so in a way that the Member States have not found objectionable.

Discussing the quote

What do you think Lord Lawson makes of the existence of 'general principles'? Do these suggest that the CJEU is 'making' law, beyond what the Treaties permit? Do you think this is problematic?

[7] See, eg, Case T-115/94 *Opel Austria v Council* ECLI:EU:T:1997:3, and Case T-347/03 *Branco v Commission* ECLI:EU:T:2005:265.

[8] Case C-37-38/02 *Di Lenardo* ECLI:EU:C:2004:443.

[9] Ibid, para 63.

[10] Ibid, para 70.

[11] For more detail, see Chapter 9.

4.2.3 **Secondary law: sources**

The forms that EU secondary law can take are set out in Article 288 TFEU.

Article 288 TFEU (emphasis added)

To exercise the Union's competences, the institutions shall adopt **regulations, directives, decisions, recommendations and opinions.**

A regulation shall have **general application**. It shall be **binding in its entirety** and **directly applicable** in all Member States.

A directive shall be **binding, as to the result to be achieved, upon each Member State** to which it is addressed, but shall leave to the **national authorities the choice of form and methods.**

A decision shall be **binding in its entirety**. A decision which specifies those to whom it is addressed shall be binding only on them.

Recommendations and opinions shall have **no binding force.**

This is not a finite list of legal forms—the EU institutions can adopt separate legal forms, particularly when it comes to internal management of the Union, and the Court has recognized these—but it is a list of the most common forms. There are significant differences between the forms specified in Article 288 TFEU, which we will now look at in detail.

4.2.4 **Secondary law: regulations**

The first form of secondary law listed in Article 288 TFEU is the **regulation**. Regulations, as described there, have a number of qualities:

- They have general application.
- They are binding in their entirety.
- They are 'directly applicable'.

The first two of those qualities are fairly easy to understand. First, regulations apply to *all Member States*—not to a specific Member State. Secondly, there is no 'picking and choosing' from a regulation—every word of an EU regulation is binding on the Member States.

It is the third quality that is more complicated, particularly in nations like the UK, which normally treats law from *outside* the UK (meaning international law) as not being immediately binding within the UK. International laws are only binding within the UK insofar as Parliament adopts legislation to *make* them binding in the UK. This form of legal system—clearly separating national law from international law, and making international law only binding at the point where it is translated into national law—is known as **dualist**.

Regulations are not meant to work only *once* they have been implemented in domestic legal systems. They are **directly applicable**, which means they are binding on the Member States as soon as they are adopted—and in the case of the UK, they represent an exception to the way it ordinarily treats international law.

The regulation is the strongest form of secondary legislation, as it does not allow for Member State discretion to any extent. Whatever the regulation says will be, from the date of its enactment, binding law in the Member States.

You might at this point wonder how this can be guaranteed, especially since regulations *do not* have to be translated into national law; what is to stop a Member State from just ignoring a regulation? The answer to this is a political commitment with legal force. When joining the EU, all the Member States sign up to a promise of '**sincere cooperation**' with the EU in achieving the EU's goals.

> **Article 4(3) TEU (emphasis added)**
>
> Pursuant to the principle of **sincere cooperation**, the Union and the Member States shall, in full mutual respect, **assist each other in carrying out tasks which flow from the Treaties.**
>
> The Member States shall take **any appropriate measure**, general or particular, **to ensure fulfilment of the obligations arising out of the Treaties** or resulting from the acts of the institutions of the Union.
>
> The Member States shall **facilitate the achievement of the Union's tasks** and **refrain from any measure which could jeopardise the attainment of the Union's objectives.**

The principle set out in Article 4(3) TEU is justiciable. This means that a Member State that fails to sincerely cooperate is not only unlikely to be on very good terms with the other EU Member States, but can be taken to the Court of Justice and fined for failing to comply with EU law.[12] In practice, therefore, regulations are by and large adhered to by the Member States, even without domestic law to reflect their content.

4.2.5 Secondary law: directives

The second form of legislation set out in Article 288 TFEU is the **directive**. The key features of directives are as follows:

- Directives are binding as to the result to be achieved.
- They are binding upon each Member State to which they are addressed.
- They leave to the national authorities choice of form and method.

Where a regulation is binding word for word, the directive offers significantly more flexibility to the Member States. What matters in a directive is the *legislative goal set out*—that is the 'result' that must be achieved by means of *national law*. This 'end result' is as binding as the regulation is as a whole, but the end impact on Member States is distinct: when a directive is enacted by the EU institutions, the Member States are then instructed to develop national law that will ensure that the objectives set out in that directive are met.

Article 288 TFEU further suggests that directives may only apply to *some* Member States—but in practice, most directives are again of general application. The exceptions are secondary laws set out in those areas of EU law that some Member States have opted out of (like, for instance, the Schengen passport area); any such laws will take the form of directives, as they cannot be 'generally applicable' the way regulations are.

[12] We will discuss this further in Chapter 8.

Finally, and importantly, regardless of what form or method national authorities choose to employ when giving effect to a directive, the directive will specify that this has to be done by a certain date. This is called the **transposition deadline**. It is normally set at two years after enactment—so a directive adopted in 2019 is meant to have been translated into national law by 2021.

Until the transposition deadline is met, the actual content of the directive is *not binding*. At that point, directives are to be treated as *instructions to Member States* to take further action domestically. Only when the period for implementing a directive into domestic law has passed does the content of the directive—and so, its 'result to be achieved'—become binding.

When are directives likely to be used, as opposed to regulations? It is usually in areas of law where the Member States are very likely to have widely varying domestic law in place already, and the EU recognizes that they will need to make adjustments *to* that domestic law in order to achieve an EU goal. The more straightforward a set of EU rules is, and the less they rely on some sort of action taken within the Member State by a domestic agency or part of the government, the more likely they are to take the form of a regulation; whereas complex areas of law that will require further domestic action to be taken and set out *broad* goals are likely to be set out in a directive.

Pause for reflection

Say the EU was interested in proposing legislation across the EU on the following issues. Which form of law do you think it would use—a regulation or a directive? Why?

- Rules setting out how elections to the European Parliament work.
- Rules aimed at the protection of endangered wildlife in each of the Member States.
- Rules establishing the right to have criminal proceedings in each Member State take place in the defendant's native language.
- Rules that eliminate roaming charges for mobile phone users across the EU.

4.2.6 Secondary law: decisions

Decisions are the third form of legislation listed in Article 288 TFEU. Their primary qualities again clearly separate them from regulations and directives, as they are:

- Binding in their entirety
- Upon each Member State to whom they are addressed.

Decisions thus offer the flexibility of directives, in that they can be addressed to a specific target audience (and, in this case, that audience can be both Member States and individuals, as Article 288 TFEU does not limit decisions as being directed *to* Member States), but also the rigour of regulations, in that they are literally and fully binding. In practice, many decisions actually apply to *all* Member States and consequently are not 'specifically addressed' to any Member State.

Most EU law students are unlikely to come across many decisions in the course of their studies. The one that is of most interest to students is a Council Decision made in 1987 that set up the Erasmus student exchange programme: this was an example of a 'non-addressed' decision that set up a programme that would operate in identical ways in all Member States.[13]

4.2.7 Secondary law: international agreements

One particular type of decision deserves a little more attention in light of the UK's departure from the EU. The EU directs most of its secondary legislation to its Member States and individuals living in those Member States. However, it is also an actor internationally, and can conclude agreements with *other* international actors, whether countries or international organizations like the World Trade Organization.

The Article 50 TEU process is now done, but the Withdrawal Agreement it produced only addresses the UK's *leaving* the EU. Once it has left, it will want to conclude a further agreement to cover trade and other relations between the UK and the EU *after* Brexit. That agreement will *not* be adopted under Article 50 TEU, but rather, will be adopted as the EU adopts *all* international agreements. In light of Brexit, the processes the EU follows when adopting international agreements have gone from being very specialist knowledge to something that will probably become a core UK concern for the next few years. As such, rather than summarize them here, Chapter 16 is devoted to considering how the UK and EU's future relationship will be concluded on the part of the EU.

We can make a few more general observations about the effects of international agreements here, however. If the content of a treaty ratified by the EU is clear and precise, it will (much like regulations and the Treaties), be directly applicable to the EU institutions and the Member States. On the other hand, where treaty provisions are ambiguous or set out general policy goals, the EU will have to adopt further secondary legislation to give effect to the international agreement. That secondary legislation will then be binding on the Member States as well.

As a general rule, all secondary law adopted by the EU institutions must also be compliant with international agreements to which the EU has signed up. The consequence of conflicting EU laws would be a breach of international law, for which a country could take legal action. For example, in the area of trade law, if the EU adopts legislation that conflicts with its promises at the World Trade Organization, any other WTO Member can start dispute settlement proceedings against the EU at the WTO.

4.2.8 Secondary law: 'soft law'

The final category of legislation specified in Article 288 TFEU is not actually what most of us would consider 'legislation'. 'Recommendations and opinions', as they are described, are legal documents issued by the EU that have 'no binding force'. In other words, they are a form of EU-issued 'soft law'—an expression of *intention* or *thought* by an EU institution, which does not come with justiciable rights or obligations.

Recommendations and opinions are not the only types of soft law that the EU issues; they are, in fact, not even the most generally *interesting* forms of soft law, for either law students or the Member States. Of significantly more interest to anyone paying attention

[13] Council Decision 87/327/EEC [1987] OJ L166/1.

to EU legislative activities generally are so-called Commission Communications. Any document titled a 'Communication' by the Commission is one of two things:

- A *proposal* for new secondary legislation in the form of a regulation or a directive; or
- A Commission *interpretation* of existing EU legislation.

If you think back to the roles that the Commission carries out within the EU, it is clear why these documents—despite not being binding—have significant persuasive power. First, any Commission proposal (in the form of a Communication) is the starting point of the EU law-making process. Indeed, it is a first clear sign for both the other EU institutions and the Member States whether the Commission is headed in a direction that they agree with. Secondly, even outside of the legislative process, Member States will care about what the Commission *thinks* EU law is. As discussed in Chapter 2, beyond being the proposer of EU legislation, it also acts as the enforcer of EU law. Therefore, when the Commission offers an interpretation of EU secondary legislation, the Member States are likely to pay attention because agreeing with the Commission's interpretation of the law is the easiest way to avoid being taken to the Court of Justice by the Commission for violating EU law.

More generally, and relating to all forms of soft law, in areas where full agreement between the EU institutions or the Member States cannot yet be achieved, we are likely to see something short of a 'binding' agreement but that nonetheless is a starting point for further negotiation. This will frequently take the form of soft law. A clear example of this is the Charter of Fundamental Rights. As mentioned in Chapter 1, by the time the Nice Treaty was adopted, there was no agreement amongst the EU Member States on just what the legal nature of the Charter should be, and so it was issued as a 'soft law' document without binding power alongside the rest of the Treaty amendments. However, by the time the debates about the Constitutional Treaty commenced, discussions about what to do with the Charter had advanced significantly, and it gained binding status in Lisbon.

Pause for reflection

Consider all of the forms of secondary legislation that have been set out in Section 4.2.

1. Which of these do you think the Member States prefer the EU to use, and why?
2. Which do you think the EU prefers to use?
3. Is there a legislative form that seems to strike a 'compromise' between EU and Member State desires?

4.3 The legislative process

How do the legal forms discussed in Section 4.2 come about? As mentioned in Chapter 1, one of the primary achievements of the Lisbon Treaty was a reduction in the number of EU legislative procedures from 38, spread across the Treaties, to a mere two. Now that we are looking at the EU's secondary legislative forms, it makes sense to discuss these two procedures in slightly more detail. They are introduced in Article 298 TFEU.

4.3.1 The ordinary legislative procedure

First, and predominant in EU legislative adoption, is the **ordinary legislative procedure (OLP)**, set out in Article 294 TFEU. This procedure, used in 85 policy fields of EU law in total, and covering approximately 80–90 per cent of EU legislation produced, is the 'standard' procedure by which law gets adopted.[14] Under the OLP, the Commission proposes legislation, and it then has to be approved by *both* the (relevant) Council of Ministers *and* the European Parliament. The Council must adopt the proposal using QMV, whereas the Parliament has to approve it by a simple majority.

If the Commission's proposal is acceptable to both the Council and to Parliament, the act will then be adopted. However, a more likely scenario is that either the Council or the Parliament, or even both institutions, will wish to suggest amendments to the Commission draft. In these situations, Figure 4.1 illustrates the order of events:

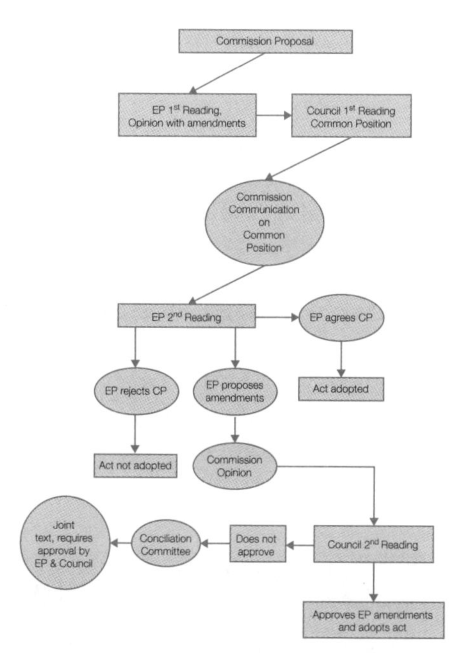

Figure 4.1 Procedure to suggest amendments to the Commission

In more detail, the steps are as follows (you might find it useful to read these alongside Figure 4.1):

- The Commission proposal will be sent to the Parliament, which will have a **first reading** of the proposal and offer an **opinion** on it with suggested amendments.
- The parliamentary opinion is then considered by the Commission, and it may amend its proposal in response to the suggested parliamentary amendments.
- The Council then has its **first reading** of the proposal—and for the sake of efficiency, this will usually be an amended version of the proposal, taking Parliament's comments into account.

[14] See https://www.ceps.eu/system/files/CEPS-Votewatch%20Special%20Report_0.pdf.

- If the Council agrees to the Parliament's amendments, as worked up by the Commission, the proposal can at this stage again be adopted by the Council, using QMV. If, on the other hand, the Council wishes to make further changes, or reject some of the Parliament's amendments, it adopts a position at the first reading, and sends this position to the Parliament for consideration.
- The Parliament will then have a second reading and can at this reading either accept or reject the Council's amendments; and it can propose further amendments itself.
- These amendments, including a Commission opinion on these amendments, are then presented to the Council for its second reading.
- If the Council accepts the amendments, the proposal is then adopted using QMV. If the Council does *not* accept the amended proposal, a so-called Conciliation Committee is formed to try to break the negotiating stalemate. A Conciliation Committee is made up of an equal number of Council members (or their representatives) and representatives of the Parliament.
- If the Conciliation Committee reaches a compromise, they will approve a joint text and this will be forwarded to the Council and Parliament for a third reading. To be adopted, both institutions will need to approve of this joint text. If this does not happen, the proposal will simply fail.

This is the formal process that results in legislative adoption. However, as with most political processes, there is significant negotiation that precedes *formal* proposals, particularly before the Commission redrafts a proposal in advance of the second reading. These informal negotiations are commonly called 'trilogues', as they involve representatives from all three EU legislators, in an attempt to speed up the legislative process.

The outline of the process, as set out in Figure 4.1, should make clear that even though significantly simplified since the Lisbon Treaty, the EU legislative process under OLP is still far from speedy—and there are portions of it that remain riddled with secrecy. This is not so much an accusation levelled at 'trilogues', as the outcomes of these informal meetings are always found in formal proposals that are still debated. However, the proceedings of a Conciliation Committee are not open to the public, resulting in lasting questions about the nature of the compromises that result in a 'joint text'.

4.3.2 The special legislative procedures

In comparison to what came before the OLP, definite improvements have been made—and this is perhaps best illustrated by a short discussion about what the alternative to OLP is, even under the Lisbon Treaty. The so-called special legislative procedures (SLPs) set out a different process, usually with minimized European Parliament involvement. The SLPs are used in policy areas where the Member States remain concerned about the involvement of the EU's supranational institutions in law-making. They tend to be more domestically sensitive policy areas, where expansions of EU power to act have been limited to date.

The two main SLPs are the consultation procedure and the assent procedure. The consultation procedure harks back to the days of the Treaty of Rome and Council dominance: it is a procedure that requires the Council to consult the European Parliament, but does not oblige it to actually heed Parliament's opinion to any effect. It continues to be used in relation to relatively sensitive policy issues: for example, in legislation relating to cross-border police operations as set out in Article 89 TFEU.

The assent procedure was introduced by the Single European Act and requires—as the name suggests—that European Parliament *assent* to a legislative proposal before the Council can adopt it. This is, in many ways, a prequel to the OLP: it involves Parliament in a binding, but very limited, way. Under the assent procedure, Parliament cannot propose amendments to the legislation, and can indeed only *reject* or *assent* to a legislative proposal. It is still used in relation to EU external relations law-making, as we will see in Chapter 16.

4.3.3 Other 'legislative' processes: delegated and implementing acts

Most EU secondary legislation is written up in quite general terms—it has to be usable in 27 different countries, after all. However, there are many instances where EU legislative objectives cannot be met if the Member States actually reacted to that legislation in 27 different ways. To prevent this happening, the Commission has an **implementing power**: it can develop rules that ensure that adoption of EU legislation is uniform in the Member States, and it can adopt those rules outside of the regular full legislative procedures.

As Chapter 3 discussed, the exercise of the Commission's implementing power has been carried out via a system called **'comitology'**. Chapter 3 also highlighted that 'comitology' was heavily criticized on the basis that it was secretive, opaque, undemocratic, and did not necessarily deal exclusively with very insignificant technical matters—referred to as 'non-essential matters' in EU terms.[15]

As of the Lisbon Treaty, committees of experts remain involved in the adoption of what are called **implementing acts**, but the European Parliament and the Council play a significantly greater role in terms of oversight of the 'neo-comitology' process.[16] Per Regulation 182/2011, implementing legislation can only be adopted by set procedures, of which the most important are the 'advisory procedure' and the 'examination procedure'. In each procedure, the Commission submits a draft implementing measure to a comitology committee. Under the 'advisory procedure', the committee then gives an opinion on that draft—which is to be taken into the 'utmost account' by the Commission before adopting the act. Should the Commission fail to take a committee opinion into account, that decision can be challenged before an Appeal Committee, if one is set up.

The 'examination procedure' is to be used primarily where the implementing acts are to have a more general scope, or are more (politically) contentious, according to Article 2 of the Regulation. Here, the committee will take a QMV vote on the draft submitted by the Commission. Article 5 explains that a positive QMV outcome results in adoption of the implementing act, whereas a negative opinion effectively scraps that version of the draft. Should an implementing act be necessary, the Commission has no choice but to redraft it, and send it to the same committee for a new vote. Where QMV does not result in either a 'yes' or a 'no' vote, because of abstentions or absences, the Commission can in principle adopt the implementing act.[17]

[15] See Section 3.3.

[16] Regulation 182/2011 of the European Parliament and of the Council of 16 February 2011 laying down the rules and general principles concerning mechanisms for control by Member States of the Commission's exercise of implementing powers [2011] OJ L55/13.

[17] Subject to the limited exceptions set out in Article 5 of Regulation 182/2011.

Secondary legislation itself will make clear if an Appeal Committee exists vis-à-vis implementing legislation, as well as under what terms which parties (the Commission or national governments) can refer implementing acts to it. Intended as a further control on Commission overreach, the Appeal Committee in practice can only overturn Commission decisions if a qualified majority of Member States vote against a Commission measure; this threshold is in practice rarely met. Further oversight is found through Article 11 of the Regulation, which allows the European Parliament and Council to argue that the Commission has acted *ultra vires* in a draft implementing act—but again, this only requires the Commission to explain to the European Parliament and Council whether it intends to change the act, and if not, why not.

Delegated acts are a new category of 'implementing legislation', and they operate somewhat differently: in any EU legislative act, the Council and/or the European Parliament can explicitly 'delegate' the power to adopt 'non-legislative acts of general application to supplement or amend certain non-essential elements of the legislative act'.[18] When delegating a legislative power, they must also make clear what the 'objectives, content, scope and duration' of that delegation entails. The number of restrictions in Article 290 TFEU, describing delegated powers, makes it clear that this is not intended to be a broad legal basis for the Commission. Instead, the EU legislators can transfer the power to *change* or *add to* (but not delete) aspects of existing legislation to the Commission, and can likewise revoke that power of delegation.

The reasons for having both implementing acts and delegated acts are not entirely clear. They are two different processes to arrive at similar types of rules, deemed to be dealing with 'non-essential' elements of legislation and thus not needing to involve the EU legislators in full. What do 'non-essential' and its corollary (that the legislators must be involved in setting out 'essential elements') actually mean? The CJEU has grappled with this question repeatedly, but has not yet come to a clear definition; the very vague 1970s *Köster* description of it being 'the basic elements of the matter to be dealt with'[19] has not been greatly clarified by later case law.[20]

4.3.4 Other 'legislative' processes: *passerelle* clauses and the emergency brake

Finally, while the Lisbon Treaty sets out two general legislative procedures to be followed, and includes a set of rules on how the Commission can exercise its implementing powers, it also introduces significantly more flexibility than previous Treaties have done, in that it permits EU bodies, via certain procedures, to either agree to legislate via a more flexible process than generally set out for a policy area, *or* to block the use of the ordinary legislative procedure if a Member State feels very strongly that adoption of a piece of legislation harms certain of its interests.

[18] Article 290 TFEU.

[19] Case 25/70 *Köster* ECLI:EU:C:1970:115, para 6.

[20] Case C-355/10 *European Parliament v Council* ECLI:EU:C:2012:516; see also Merijn Chamon, 'How the Concept of Essential Elements of a Legislative Act Continues to Elude the Court: *Parliament v. Council*' (2013) 50(3) CMLRev 849.

The first set of procedures, resulting in a lower threshold for legislative adoption, are known as the *passerelle* procedures. They come in two forms:

- In six parts of the Treaty, there are specific *passerelle* clauses to simplify legislating in a given policy area. For example, Article 153(2)(b) TFEU sets out a *passerelle* provision regarding social affairs that are ordinarily adopted by a special legislative procedure, but can, via that *passerelle* provision, be adopted by the ordinary legislative procedure.
- There is also a 'general *passerelle*' clause: Article 48(7) TEU permits switching from unanimity to QMV and from the use of the special legislative procedure to the ordinary legislative procedure in relation to all parts of the TFEU, and Title V (on Common Foreign and Security Policy) of the TEU. This requires unanimity in the European Council, after obtaining consent from the European Parliament, and after having notified national parliaments, which can also object to exercise of the general *passerelle*.

The general *passerelle* means that, effectively, the Treaties are being rewritten (albeit in a minor way), in order to enable easier decision-making in a given policy area than the Member States agreed to when the Lisbon Treaty was first drafted. It is clear why this provision was introduced: much like Article 48(6), which introduces a more general simplified Treaty revision process, the drafters of the Lisbon Treaty recognized that it would be preferable to avoid having to organize an intergovernmental conference for all minor changes desired to the Treaties.

However, there is a clear set of balancing provisions to these *passerelle* and revision clauses in the Lisbon Treaty. The Member States recognized in Lisbon that they might wish to enable quicker and less 'unanimous' decision-making on policy areas in future—but they also recognized that there are some policy areas where it should be possible to set aside a general commitment to QMV if a Member State experienced particular concerns about a legislative proposal.

These provisions are commonly referred to as 'brake' clauses, or the 'emergency brakes' of the Lisbon Treaty. They exist in areas that fall within the remit of Justice and Home Affairs—such as judicial cooperation in criminal matters, or EU action regarding rules for criminal offences[21]—and in EU action on social security legislation and coordination.

The latter was an 'emergency brake' insisted upon by the UK government during the Lisbon negotiations before it would agree to action in the field of social security for EU national workers being, in principle, covered by the ordinary legislative procedure. Article 48(2) TFEU now makes clear that where, in the opinion of a Member State, the EU is proposing legislation that negatively affects important aspects of its social security system, the Member State can bring their concerns to the European Council.

This 'referral' to the European Council effectively slows down the legislative process, though it does not necessarily stop it. The European Council *can* stop the legislative procedure permanently and request new legislation from the Commission, but it can also send the contested legislative proposal back to the Council, in which case the objecting Member State's protests are noted, but the ordinary legislative procedure may continue anyway.

The meaningfulness of Article 48(2) TFEU can be debated, not least because it has not been used to date, but also because the one Member State that really wanted it has now left the EU. However, the 'emergency brakes' are interesting from a more general constitutional perspective. In many ways, they represent the spirit of the Luxembourg Compromise or Veto that made the European project stagnate so badly in the 1970s and 1980s.[22] For every

[21] Article 82(3) and Article 83(3) TFEU respectively.

[22] As discussed in Chapter 1.

step towards a genuine supranational organization in which only *general agreement* drives policy forward, we find a few legislative provisions (or 'brakes'), which make very clear that at its core, there is a clear intergovernmental driver underpinning the EU as a whole.

Discussing the quote

Think back to Lord Lawson's claim that the UK, as a member of the EU, remained 'fully subject' to all EU legislation. Consider what you have learned about the EU's legislative procedures in Section 4.3. As a Member State, did these all make the UK 'subject to' EU legislation to an equal extent?

4.4 EU legislative competences

Having considered the possible forms of EU legislation and its process of adoption, we are left with a further big question: can the EU adopt these legislative forms in *any* policy areas it wishes to?

In general, in all policy areas, either the EU and/or the Member States will be entitled to act. The scope of the EU's legislative powers is normally referred to as a matter of legislative competence. In its dictionary definition, competence is a synonym for 'ability'; but when it is used in the context of EU law, it implies not only an *ability* to act, but a *legitimacy* when acting. In other words, when the EU has competence to legislate, its law-making is deemed valid and authoritative.

Competence is closely related to another EU law principle, namely that of conferral. It is important to remember that the EU is a creation of the Member States, and every nation is ultimately 'sovereign'—it cannot be forced to sign up to international laws that it does not wish to. As a consequence, without the Member States' willing surrender (or conferral) of powers, the EU would have no ability to act whatsoever. The notion of conferral lies at the heart of the legitimacy of the EU project: the EU is intended to be a project created *by* sovereign States, and is intended to act only within the remit set out *by* those sovereign States. If the EU overreaches on the powers it has been given, we run into serious questions about the legitimacy of its actions.

Article 5(2) TEU explicitly sets out how competences and the principle of conferral are meant to work together:

Article 5(2) TEU

Under the principal of conferral, the Union shall act only within the limits of the competences conferred upon it by the Member States in the Treaties to attain the objectives set out therein. Competences not conferred upon the Union in the Treaties remain with the Member States.

The question of when the EU can produce any of its secondary legislative forms is therefore answered by combining these two legal concepts: what competences have the Member States conferred upon the EU?

4.4.1 A history of competence

This may strike you as somewhat unbelievable, but prior to the Lisbon Treaty, the limits of the EU's competences were not plainly listed in any of the EU Treaties.

In setting up the EEC, the Member States undoubtedly conferred *some* powers to the European Economic Community back in 1957. Chapter 1 explained that, over time, they conferred *more* power with subsequent Treaties, up to and including the Lisbon Treaty. However, until Lisbon, none of the Treaties set out in a clear listed fashion what the policy areas were in which the EU institutions would be in control. As such, actually *reading* the Treaty was the only way to make clear just what powers the EEC institutions had to propose legislation, and any power not expressly stated in the Treaty was one that the then-Community did not have. For example, Article 7 EEC thus gave the Council the power to adopt legislation regarding the Community prohibition on discrimination; and Article 14 EEC made clear that border tariffs would be gradually reduced over a period of time in legislation again adopted by the Council on a Commission proposal.

In the period between 1957 and the early 1970s, a close reading of the EEC Treaty would have given a legal expert a reasonable picture of the areas of economic policy that could be legislated for by the EEC institutions. By the 1970s, however, concerns about competences emerged: namely, the EEC was no longer exclusively concerned with 'economic' policy. With the consent of the Member States, it was also moving into entirely new policy areas. The accession of the UK coincided with a new drive to expand what the European project would be about, and the Paris Intergovernmental Conference of 1972 advertised 'substantive expansion of Community jurisdiction'.[23] This announcement resulted in significant use of the Treaty's so-called 'flexible' legislative bases, enabling the EU to legislate in 'new' areas of law as long as the legislation could be linked to a stated Treaty goal, from 1973 onward.[24] The eventual culmination of this announcement was the Single European Act 1986 (SEA), which cemented European Community competences in new areas, such as the environment, regional development, and technology.

The SEA did not, however, bring about a short summary that clearly set out just *when* the EC was entitled to act in a given policy area, or what type of legislative procedures it would have to follow in that policy area. Remember from Chapter 1 that the EU eventually, prior to 2009, operated 38 different legislative procedures. The re-branded EC Treaty was a far longer document than the EEC Treaty had been, and it still had to be read very closely in order to fully grasp just what policy areas the EC institutions could and could not act in, and what procedures had to be followed. This would remain the case for all other Treaties adopted in the 1990s and 2000, to the frustration of academic commentators:[25]

[23] Ian Ward, *A Critical Introduction to European Law*, 3rd edn (CUP, 2009) 20.

[24] See Chapter 5 for more detail.

[25] See, for instance, Alan Dashwood, 'The Limits of European Community Powers' (1996) 21 ELRev 113; Udo di Fabio, 'Some Remarks on the Allocation of Competences between the European Union and its Member States' (2002) 39 CMLRev 1289; Paul Craig, 'Competence: Clarity, Conferral, Containment and Consideration' (2004) 29 ELRev 323; and for a detailed consideration, Robert Schütze, *From Dual to Cooperative Federalism: The Changing Structure of European Law* (OUP, 2009).

Stephen Weatherill, 'Competence Creep and Competence Control' (2004) 23(1) YEL 1, 4–5 (emphasis added)

[G]rasping the nature of EC competence and its effect on State competence demands analysis of Treaty provisions, secondary legislation, and judicial interpretation and **it resists simple exposition**. The whole pattern is utterly unsystematic, it is not conducive to effective monitoring and, a victim of the incremental process of Treaty revision, it is ripe for an overhaul.

However, there is a difference between observing that the EU's competences were not clearly set out—on which virtually all commentators agree—and arguing that the EU was taking *advantage* of the lack of clear limits to its powers. The 1990s and 2000s saw a number of commentators emerge who thought that the Member States had surrendered control of their own creation, and that the EU institutions were capable of stretching the EU's powers further and further.[26] Particular critical attention was directed at the Court of Justice, whose generous interpretations of EU legal provisions tended to give way to the EU institutions' legislative initiatives more often than not.[27]

Lenaerts summarized these criticisms of the competence allocation in the EU well:

Koen Lenaerts, 'Constitutionalism and the Many Faces of Federalism' (1990) 38 AJCL 205, 220 (emphasis added)

The Community may indeed exercise its specific, implied, or non-specific powers in the fullest way possible, without running into any inherent limitation set to these powers as a result of the sovereignty which the Member States retain . . . **There simply is no nucleus of sovereignty that the Member States can invoke, as such, against the Community.**

The discussions about this phenomenon of EU 'competence creep', as the idea of the EU's incremental increase of power is commonly known, were not simply ignored at the EU level. The EU Heads of State consequently attached a declaration to the Nice Treaty that made a more explicit division of competences between the EU and its Member States an area for investigation.[28] The Laeken Declaration in 2001 specified what the goals of this inquiry were to be in greater detail. First, the Heads of State wished for greater 'clarity' in the division of competences; the Treaties did not articulate the competences in a logical and transparent manner. Secondly, they also stressed for the first time the notion of 'conferral', making explicit that any actions the EU institutions could undertake were powers *granted* by the Member States. Thirdly, the notion

[26] See, for instance, Stephen Weatherill, 'Competence Creep and Competence Control' (2004) 23(1) YEL 1; and Joseph Weiler, 'The Transformation of Europe' (1991) 100 YLJ 2403—though Weiler is careful to note that he is not judging this phenomenon as 'positive' or 'negative'. He simply notes it is taking place.

[27] Weiler (n 26) 2436–47; see also Chapter 5.

[28] Treaty of Nice, Declaration 23 [2001] OJ C80/1.

of 'containment' was flagged up. In order to deal with accusations that the EU was grabbing more and more powers, clear limits to those EU powers would be set out.[29] And, finally, the Heads of State demanded 'consideration' of competence. This entailed a review of the powers the EU had been granted in the past, and whether it needed to retain these as time went on.[30]

Did this declaration or inquiry amount to any change to how the Treaties approached the competence issue? Eventually, a practical and legally relevant outcome did emerge from Brussels. The Draft Constitutional Treaty contained explicit references to the EU's competences for the first time, and these 'lists' of competences were carried over into the Lisbon Treaty.

By 2009, then, the Lisbon Treaty finally addressed this long-standing criticism of obscurity and opaqueness—insofar as it is ever genuinely possible to clearly set out *exhaustive* competences for a governance system. We will come back to the latter point in Chapter 5.

4.4.2 The Lisbon allocation

Though criticized for lacking force, the principle of conferral—now in Article 5(2) TEU—remains the starting point for the Lisbon Treaty's content on competences. In addition, the TEU now states clearly in Article 4(1) that any competence not *explicitly* conferred on the EU remains with the Member States. The legal effect of Article 4 TEU is limited, but as a political statement about limits to 'competence creep', it sends a very clear message.

The actual provisions in the Lisbon Treaty that contain the lists of EU-relevant competences are found in the TFEU, rather than the TEU. For added clarity on just when the EU institutions can legislate, the TFEU's lists are divided into various separate categories in Article 2:

- areas of competence that are **exclusive** to the EU institutions;
- areas of competence that are **shared** by the EU institutions and the Member States;
- areas of competence where the EU can only offer **supporting** or **coordinating action**.

Two particular policy areas are singled out for their own description of EU powers. One of these is economic and employment policy, where the EU only has coordinating power to 'provide arrangements' for the Member States. The other is Common Foreign and Security Policy, where the EU technically has competence, but the effects of that competence are very limited, as all decision-making is effectively intragovernmental.[31]

There is, of course, the silent 'fourth' category of competence—and that is the area of **no competence**. Any competence not explicitly stated in the EU Treaties remains with the Member States, as stressed in Article 4 TEU and implied by the principle of conferral. These are the policy areas that the Member States deem too sensitive or too nationally significant to be legislated for centrally. They include issues such as taxation, the substantive content of social security law (meaning the levels and general qualifying criteria for benefits set), the substantive content of criminal law, and nationality law. The UK's Schengen area opt-out means that it also retained its competence over its external borders and immigration policy.

[29] The idea of 'containment' is discussed in detail by Florian Mayer, 'Competences—Reloaded? The Vertical Division of Powers in the EU and the New European Constitution' (2005) 3 I-CON 493, 504–5.

[30] European Council, 14–15 December 2001, 21–2; see Chapter 10 for more on 'red tape' reduction.

[31] See Article 2(3) and 2(4) TFEU, and Chapter 16.

Article 2 TFEU spells out what the EU can do in each of the areas of competence it has:

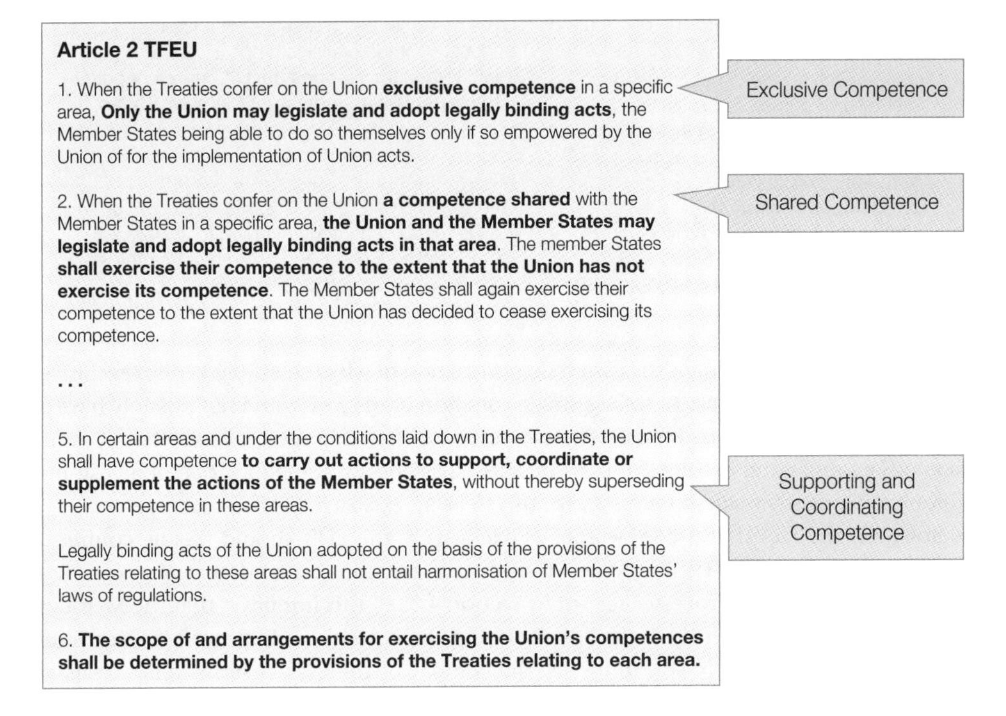

Article 2 TFEU

1. When the Treaties confer on the Union **exclusive competence** in a specific area, **Only the Union may legislate and adopt legally binding acts**, the Member States being able to do so themselves only if so empowered by the Union of for the implementation of Union acts.

2. When the Treaties confer on the Union **a competence shared** with the Member States in a specific area, **the Union and the Member States may legislate and adopt legally binding acts in that area**. The member States **shall exercise their competence to the extent that the Union has not exercise its competence**. The Member States shall again exercise their competence to the extent that the Union has decided to cease exercising its competence.

. . .

5. In certain areas and under the conditions laid down in the Treaties, the Union shall have competence **to carry out actions to support, coordinate or supplement the actions of the Member States**, without thereby superseding their competence in these areas.

Legally binding acts of the Union adopted on the basis of the provisions of the Treaties relating to these areas shall not entail harmonisation of Member States' laws of regulations.

6. **The scope of and arrangements for exercising the Union's competences shall be determined by the provisions of the Treaties relating to each area.**

4.4.3 Exclusive competences

The first competence category helpfully set out by the Lisbon Treaty is that of the EU's exclusive competences. These are policy areas where, by agreement among the EU Heads of State in the Treaties, only the EU has the power to legislate. Reasons for exclusive competence in certain policy areas are pragmatic: they are those policy areas where deviation from a single common legal standard would mean that the policy in question could not practically work. Article 3(1) TFEU sets out what policy areas those are:

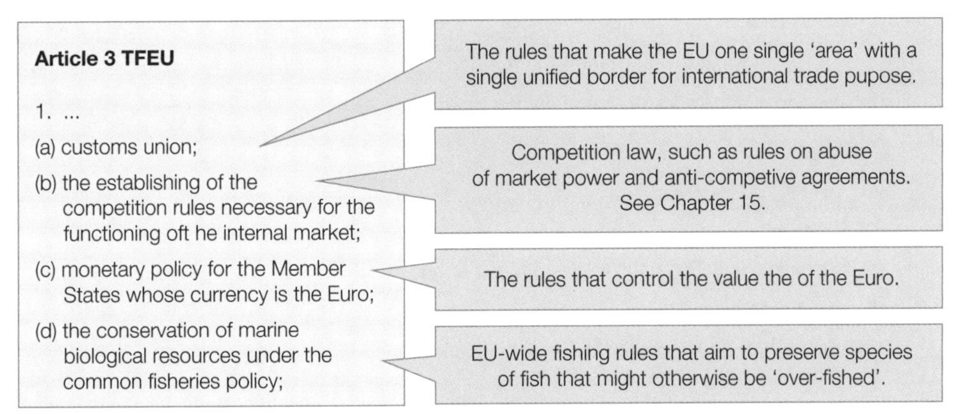

Article 3 TFEU

1. ...

(a) customs union;

(b) the establishing of the competition rules necessary for the functioning oft he internal market;

(c) monetary policy for the Member States whose currency is the Euro;

(d) the conservation of marine biological resources under the common fisheries policy;

→

→

(e) common commercial policy.

2. The Union shall also have exclusive competence for the conclusion of an international agreement when its conclusion is provided for in a legislative act of the Union or is necessary to enable the Union to exercise its internal competence, or in so faras its conclusion may affect common rules or alter their scope.

The rules that determine the EU's approach to negotiating trade deals with non-EU countries. **In 'Brexit' terms: the reasons the UK cannot negotiate trade deals with individual Member States.**

The power to sign the EU (as an institution) up to international agreements (like, for instance, the European Convention of Human Rights–see Chapters 9 and 16).

The customs union is perhaps the easiest demonstration of why the EU has certain exclusive competences. If there is meant to be a single common border, we could not possibly have a situation where each of the Member States operated different border policies when it came to goods entering and exiting the EU. The sheer existence of the policy *goal* of a customs union consequently made it necessary for this to be an exclusive EU-based competence.

However, the fact that a competence is exclusively the EU's should not be confused with the idea that the Member States do not have any input into that policy area. Remember the legislative processes set out in Section 4.3: all this implies is that the Member States cannot independently make law regarding the customs union, but Member State representatives can clearly still influence the content of the EU's customs union legislation through the Council of Ministers and the European Parliament.

Article 3(2) TFEU is of significant interest to the UK in light of Brexit, and we will consider it in more detail in Chapter 16.

4.4.4 Supporting/coordinating competences

The second relatively uncontroversial area of competence allocation is one where the EU does *not* have general legislative power. Article 2(5) makes clear that the EU can only exercise **supporting** or **coordinating competence**, or take what is called **supplementary action**, in a number of policy areas. The general areas in which the EU has this type of competence are listed in Article 6 TFEU.

Article 6 TFEU

. . .

(a) protection and improvement of human health;

(b) industry;

(c) culture;

(d) tourism;

(e) education, vocational training, youth and sport;

(f) civil protection;

(g) administrative cooperation.

What does a lack of 'general legislative ability' mean? These are policy areas where the Member States have agreed that the EU needs to be *involved* in policy-making, but cannot *control* policy. They tend to be policy areas that are, in one way or another, potentially sensitive on the national level, but are all the same policy areas that may be affected by EU-wide activity, or have EU-wide effects. The compromise the Heads of State have struck in negotiating these Treaty categories is that they have taken away the EU legislature's power to **harmonize** legislation—eg, to demand that all the EU Member States adopt *identical rules*. However, they can enact laws that do not harmonize, so to understand what the Article 6 TFEU competence limits amount to usually requires looking at other competences the EU has.

For instance, Article 152 TFEU explicitly forbids the EU to dictate to the Member States that they should organize their public health systems in any particular way, but the EU is nonetheless permitted to offer persuasive Commission guidance on 'best practice' in public health. Article 152 TFEU makes clear that the EU can offer 'incentive measures' (providing they do not harmonize) to encourage healthy behaviour. What this ultimately means is that the EU institutions may have powers in these policy areas, but they cannot dictate the direction in which Member States wish to move policy on their own. They are there as back-up regulator, and their actions at most complement existing Member State rules.[32]

4.4.5 Shared competences

The most problematic of the competence areas is **shared competence**. Sharing, especially when it is meant to take place between 27 independent nation states who very much believe in their sovereign powers to make their own laws *and* a largely independent organization that also makes laws, is not going to be easy. The bickering between the different EU Member States normally takes place in the legislative process, as discussed in Section 4.3, but the existence of shared competence between the EU and the Member States adds a second dimension of strife to the EU's policy-making. After all, shared competence suggests that *both the EU and the Member States can potentially make law*.

The TFEU clearly identifies and resolves the first stumbling block in sharing competence. In a situation where there are two potential sets of legislators—the Member States, on the one hand, and the EU on the other—it has to be determined who has the legislative 'right of way'. A situation where the EU and the Member States are simultaneously permitted to enact laws on identical subjects would result in a nonsensical legal regime; there would be at least two simultaneous, equally valid laws, and complying with all these laws would be practically impossible.

The Treaties make clear who the primary actor will be in shared competences by articulating the **principle of pre-emption**:

> **Article 2(2) TFEU**
>
> . . . The Member States shall exercise their competence to the extent that the Union has not exercised its competence. The Member States shall again exercise their competence to the extent that the Union has decided to cease exercising its competence.

Reading the final two sentences of Article 2(2) closely, you will see that pre-emption looks as if it gives the 'right of way' to the EU. The text of the provision makes clear that *once* the EU has acted, the Member States *lose* their powers to regulate, and it is only once the EU has *stopped acting* that the Member States *regain* their powers to regulate.

[32] Alan Dashwood et al (eds), *Wyatt and Dashwood's European Union Law*, 6th edn (Hart, 2011) 104.

However, a more 'Member State' focused reading of the exact same principle is possible. After all, the Member States have the power to regulate *until* the EU decides to act in a given area, and only lose their power to regulate *as long as* the EU has decided to legislate.

Neither interpretation is *wrong*; the only thing that these two valid readings of the same TFEU provision make clear is that pre-emption *alone* is not enough to clarify just *when* the EU can legislate in areas of shared competence and when it cannot. Further principles to make this determination have consequently been developed, and we will look at subsidiarity as a principle governing shared competence in Section 4.5.

In terms of the policy areas where the EU and the Member States have shared competences, they are once more very general. Article 4 TFEU sets out what is a residual list,[33] in that any competence not retained by the Member States, and not exclusive or supporting/coordinating, will be demarcated as 'shared'.

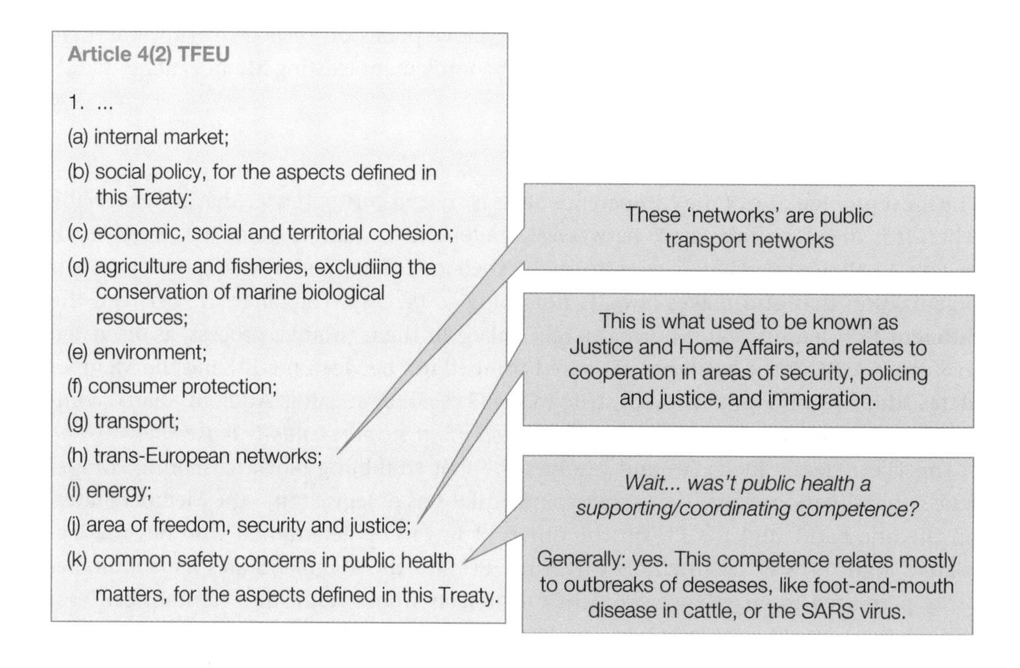

4.4.6 Has Lisbon fixed the EU's competence problem?

We can at this point make several observations about the lists of competences in the Lisbon Treaty. First of all, they are undoubtedly a significant improvement on the situation under the previous Treaties, where specific competences had to be tracked down in specific provisions in the Treaty. A quick glance at this point reveals at least the broad *policy areas* in which the EU is likely to have powers, which is much more transparent. It also enables for much more targeted searches of the remainder of the TFEU to discover specific legislative bases, as the TFEU is organized per 'policy area' much like these lists are.

Secondly, it is at this point incontestable that the EU project has indeed moved well beyond being a primarily 'economic' one, and not only because the Lisbon Treaty's preamble makes this clear. However, assessing these lists of competences, it is also clear

[33] Article 4(2) TFEU.

that the EU has no *exclusive* powers that can turn it into a 'federal' Europe: it will take more than a customs union, common trade negotiations, and a centralized policy on saving fish from extinction to fully turn the EU into the equivalent of a *country*.

The Lisbon Treaty thus bolsters the clarity of the EU's exclusive competences. Those areas where the EU has little legislative power have also been set out for the first time, presumably to the comfort of national governments, who can now point to concrete 'limits' to EU power. However, those Treaty-based allocations are only the starting point for the Member States' engagement with the EU's competences following the Lisbon Treaty.

Discussing the quote

Consider Lord Lawson's claim that the EU's law-making is driven by a desire to produce a 'full-blooded political union'. Which of the EU's competences, exclusive or shared, are most likely to result in legislation that turns the EU into such a 'full-blooded political union'?

4.5 The principle of subsidiarity

Concerns about 'competence creep', as explained in Section 4.4, have not only occupied the minds of academics, but the Member States themselves have become increasingly concerned about the level of flexibility of certain EU competences, and in particular, *shared* EU competences. The principle of pre-emption makes clear that only the EU or the Member States can legislate on a given policy, and that when the EU has legislated, the Member States can no longer do so. However, while this sets out what happens *after* the EU has acted, or when the EU *stops* acting, it does not deal with the overarching question of *when* the EU can act in areas of shared competences. Can it simply legislate whenever it chooses to in these areas, and must the Member States then step aside?

This brings us to a consideration of not only when the EU *has* competence, but when and how it is allowed to *exercise* its competence. It is important to always remember that whenever the EU can do *anything*, it is because the Member States have conferred power to the EU. Conferral does not stop at merely setting out when the EU has competence to legislate—it also covers how the EU is expected to *exercise* that competence. Over time, the EU Treaties have developed two principles in order to govern the exercise of competence: subsidiarity and proportionality. We look at subsidiarity now and will consider proportionality in Section 4.6.

4.5.1 What is the principle of subsidiarity?

Subsidiarity, as a legislative principle, was formally introduced in the Treaty of Maastricht. This explains a lot about what it is meant to preclude: you will remember from Chapter 1 that Maastricht was the Treaty where the EU truly moved from being a primarily 'economic' project to a project with significant ambitions beyond the 'economic'. Ideas such as EU citizenship, a common currency, and significant legislative powers in areas beyond the internal market may now seem relatively uncontroversial to us. However, to the

Member States negotiating the Maastricht Treaty, they were a significant change in the EU's direction and development. With this level of change came significant concerns, not least from the United Kingdom, which wanted to ensure that the EU was not getting a general power to legislate in any and all policy areas.

A particular backdrop to this was the fact that with the advent of the Single European Act, suddenly the EU legislature was actually starting to get things *done*. The stalemate that had existed between the Commission and the Council throughout the 1970s and 1980s, as discussed in Chapters 1 and 2, had disappeared with the extension of QMV in the Council. All of a sudden, the EU was starting to pump out a significant volume of legislation. Between 1984 and 1992, to make this explicit, the volume of EU secondary legislation adopted went from approximately 400 to about 2500 pieces![34]

This increase of EU activity led to symbolic statements, such as a promise in Article F TEU in Maastricht that the EU would continue to respect national identity. However, it also led to legislative intervention, in the form of the Member States wanting to ensure that the EU did not simply legislate because it *could* legislate in an area where it shared competence with the Member States. Rather, they insisted that the EU should prove that there was good reason for EU legislation as opposed to domestic legislation in these shared areas of competence. The mechanism by which the EU should justify its desire to legislate is the principle of subsidiarity, and it is set out in Article 5(3) TEU.

Article 5(3) TEU (emphasis added)

Under the principle of subsidiarity, in areas which do not fall within its exclusive competence, the Union shall act **only if and in so far as** the objectives of the proposed action cannot be **sufficiently** achieved by the Member States, either at central level or at regional and local level, but can rather, by reason of the scale or effects of the proposed action, be **better** achieved at Union level.

Article 5(3) TEU is not the best example of clear legal writing, but from it we can deduce two simultaneous conditions that the EU must 'prove' before it can 'act'—ie, legislate.

The first of these, usually termed **national insufficiency**, is that the EU will adopt legislation in shared competence areas *only if and insofar as* the Member States cannot *sufficiently* achieve the objectives underpinning that legislation. This part of Article 5(3) TEU addresses Member States' concerns about the EU legislating in all areas 'just because'—it protects against intrusion into Member State laws by setting out that where the Member States themselves are capable of achieving a legislative objective set by the EU, the EU will not intervene. This seems to give concrete meaning to a promise made in Article 10 TEU, where the EU commits to letting decisions being made as close to the citizen 'as possible'.[35]

[34] Neil Fligstein and Jason McNichol, 'The Institutional Terrain of the European Union' in Wayne Sandholtz and Alec Stone Sweet (eds), *European Integration and Supranational Governance* (OUP, 1998) 76.

[35] See Chapter 3.

The second condition, usually termed **comparative efficiency**, is that the EU will only adopt legislation in shared areas of competence when it can *better* achieve the objectives underpinning a piece of legislation. This is a matter of efficiency: where the EU, as a single legislative actor, can achieve a result 'better' than 27 separate national legislators can, it also has permission to legislate in a shared area of competence.

Pause for reflection

What do you think it would take for the EU to prove that it can achieve a legislative goal *better*? What do you think it means that the Member States cannot *sufficiently* achieve a goal?

What is confusing about the principle of subsidiarity is that *both of these conditions* must simultaneously apply. The Member States must therefore be *not sufficiently* capable of achieving a policy goal in full, *and* the EU must be able to *achieve that goal better*.

What subsidiarity seems to require is best illustrated by means of a fictive EU legislative proposal. Imagine that the EU wishes to propose legislation to improve road safety. Article 4(g) TFEU tells us that transport is a shared legislative competence, so in principle, the EU can legislate for the objective of road safety. However, any legislation proposed must satisfy the principle of subsidiarity.

Say the Commission's road safety proposal sets a default speed limit across the EU. Would that satisfy the two conditions that make up the principle of subsidiarity? If we look at national insufficiency, we need to consider to what extent the Member States are achieving the objectives of the legislation. Are the roads as safe as they can be without EU legislation? They can probably be safer—there are still accidents, and the speed limits are different in most Member States, and the Commission can show high speed as being a contributing factor to accidents. What about comparative efficiency? A single EU rule setting out an EU-wide speed limit is clearly a more efficient way of reducing speed-related car accidents than waiting for all the Member States to legislate on their own. Therefore, this proposal seems to satisfy the subsidiarity test.

Say, on the other hand, that the proposal also mandates that everyone drives on the right side of the road in all EU Member States from now on. The UK, Cyprus, Malta, and Ireland were/are outliers here: so how does this proposal fit with the principle of subsidiarity? In order to justify introducing the proposal, the Commission will need to first link driving on the right with 'road safety'. If it cannot concretely demonstrate that driving on the right is *safer*, the principle of national insufficiency would not be satisfied: left-driving would be as effective in ensuring safety as the remainder of the EU's right-driving. In other words, there is seemingly no reason here to intervene in the Member States' own legislative powers, and so decisions on which side of the road to drive on can be taken domestically, or 'as close as possible' to the EU citizen.

This fictional example makes clear that satisfying the two-part subsidiarity test is not necessarily simple. In having to prove that Member State action is *insufficient*, and prove that EU legislation is *better*, the Commission is asked to find actual evidence to *prove* that EU action is needed. This also needs to be documented, so that the Member States can in principle *challenge* the Commission's findings regarding subsidiarity.

This documentation of how a legislative proposal satisfies subsidiarity is known as an impact assessment, and is one of the ways in which the Commission altered its legislative function following the Maastricht Treaty: as of a 2002 'Better Regulation' package, all legislative proposals are now accompanied by impact assessments that attempt to justify why EU action on a given policy matter is needed.[36]

The other way in which subsidiarity has changed how the Commission behaves is indirect. The principle set out in Article 5(3) TEU requires a balancing between *self-governance* of the Member States and *efficiency* in achieving EU goals. There is one form of EU secondary legislation that seems to be underpinned by a similar balancing of Member State autonomy and EU goals—and perhaps unsurprisingly, since Maastricht, the majority of significant Commission proposals have been for directives. This precludes the kind of disproportionate interference in domestic affairs that the principle of subsidiarity also aims to prevent.

4.5.2 Monitoring compliance with subsidiarity

As of the Treaty of Amsterdam, a protocol attached to the Treaties has set out how the Commission should comply with the principle of subsidiarity when exercising its (non-exclusive) competences.[37] As of the Treaty of Lisbon, this protocol has been entirely rewritten with similar but more detailed rules.

What is now Protocol 2 on the Application of the Principles of Subsidiarity and Proportionality, which has to be considered alongside Protocol 1 on the Role of the National Parliaments in the European Union, sets out how subsidiarity is meant to apply to the Commission's behaviour in significant detail. Therefore, before proposing legislation, the Commission is required to consult a wide variety of actors on the possible implications of its legislation. This includes national parliaments, as Protocol 1 makes clear, but also includes civil society at large, regional parliaments, and anyone else clearly affected by a legislative proposal. This is in addition to the standing requirement that the Commission, in its impact assessment, provides evidence (quantitative, where possible) that Union action will produce *better* results.

In addition to these impact assessments, Protocol 2 also requires the Commission to produce an annual report on subsidiarity as part of the 'Better Regulation' toolkit, which is disseminated to all other EU institutions and, as of Lisbon, national parliaments.[38] This significant increase in transparency of the Commission's preparatory work on legislation, and the fact that all this information is (for the first time) brought to the attention of national parliaments, is a significant step towards ensuring that EU legislation is in practice developed 'as close as possible' to the citizen, especially when read in combination with Protocol 2 to the Lisbon Treaty.

[36] See its 2002 Action Plan for Better Regulation, including a Commission Communication on Impact Assessment (2002) COM(2002)276.

[37] See Protocol 30 on the application of the principles of subsidiarity and proportionality, attached to the Treaty of Amsterdam.

[38] Protocol 2, Article 9; see Chapter 10 for more on 'better regulation'.

4.5.3 Enforcing subsidiarity

While it is clear that the Commission has been expected to comply with subsidiarity since 1992, historically its compliance has only been monitored in a very piecemeal fashion. When a Member State is particularly unhappy with a piece of legislation, it has always been able to contest its compliance with the principle of subsidiarity before the Court of Justice, and occasionally, Member States have done this—resulting in a 'subsidiarity' check.

EU law in practice

A classic example of a Member State challenging a piece of EU legislation on subsidiarity grounds before the Court of Justice concerns the UK. In 1993, the EU adopted a directive limiting the number of hours that employees could be made to be at work consecutively, commonly known as the Working Time Directive.[39] For example, the Working Time Directive established that employees could not be *forced* to work more than 48 hours a week.

UK opposition to the Working Time Directive was significant. The primary ground for objection was that the UK had opted out of the EU's so-called 'Social Chapter', which produced legislation on social rights such as employment rights—but the Commission argued that the Working Time Directive dealt with matters of health and safety at work, rather than employment rights, and consequently it was made to apply to the UK as well. This motivated the challenge before the Court of Justice—but the UK government did not merely challenge the legislative basis for adoption of the Directive when in front of the Court.[40] It also argued that the proposal had violated the principle of subsidiarity.

Specifically, in paragraph 46 of the judgment, the Court recounts that the UK maintained that the Commission had not 'fully considered nor adequately demonstrated' that there was a need for EU measures on account of national insufficiency; nor that it had demonstrated that EU action would 'provide clear benefits' when compared to domestic-only action. It further argued that the principle itself did not 'allow adoption of a directive in such wide and prescriptive terms . . . given that the extent and the nature of legislative regulation of working time vary very widely between Member States'. This last argument, however, the UK did not link to the specific wording of the principle—and it is not entirely clear how it could have. Great divergence in existing national laws would seem to help the Commission's case more than the UK's case.

What do you make of the UK's argument? Do you think it was successful? [The answer will follow in Chapter 5.]

4.5.4 The Early Warning Mechanism

The Lisbon Treaty has taken steps to involve national parliaments more in EU legislative activity, and specifically, has given them a role in enforcing the principle of subsidiarity.[41]

Protocol 2 sets out a process that has become known as the **Early Warning Mechanism**. Rather than action before the Court of Justice, which can only be commenced once a piece

[39] Council Directive 93/104/EC of 23 November 1993 concerning certain aspects of the organization of working time [1993] OJ L307/18.

[40] Case C-84/94 *UK v Council (Working Time Directive)* ECLI:EU:C:1996:431.

[41] See Chapter 3 for a discussion of how this mechanism affects the EU's democratic qualities.

of EU legislation has been adopted, this is a subsidiarity check that applies *before* legislation is adopted, and thus can prevent legislation from ever arising. A further key difference between Court action and the Early Warning Mechanism is which body commences the process: only Member States (and thus Member State governments) can commence an action for annulment before the Court of Justice, whereas the Early Warning Mechanism is in the hands of national parliaments.

The Early Warning Mechanism works as follows:

- When the Commission proposes legislation, it simultaneously sends it to the Council, the European Parliament, and all national parliaments in the EU Member States.
- Each chamber of each national parliament gets a single vote (and a unicameral parliament has two votes) on whether the proposal violates the principle of subsidiarity.
- If a chamber does consider there to be a violation of subsidiarity, it can submit a reasoned opinion to the EU institutions detailing why.
- Where *one third* of national parliament chambers (so a total of 18) send such reasoned opinions, the Commission must review its proposal. This is called a **yellow card**.
- Where *one half* of national parliament chambers (so a total of 27) send such reasoned opinions, and the legislation in question is being proposed via the ordinary legislative procedure, the proposal is instead referred to the Council and European Parliament, who can then by simple majorities reject the proposal outright. This is called an **orange card**.

We have to date seen the 'yellow card' threshold be reached on three separate occasions. The first instance when an EU proposal was 'yellow carded' concerned a regulation governing the right for workers to go on strike. This piece of legislation was, following Commission review, abandoned. The second time an EU proposal was 'yellow carded' concerned a regulation establishing a European Public Prosecutor's Office. Again, following review, the proposal was abandoned by the Commission. The third 'yellow card' we have seen is perhaps the most interesting one. It concerned an EU directive on posted workers (meaning workers who remain living in one Member State, but are sent to do work in another Member State, while remaining subject to the laws of the Member State they live in), and though the proposal was yellow carded, the Commission did *not* abandon it. This highlights that while the Early Warning Mechanism is a significant improvement in terms of allowing *input* into EU legislation, its power should not be overstated. We will look in more detail into the shortcomings of the Mechanism as set up in Chapter 5.

As of the Lisbon Treaty, we thus find the principle of subsidiarity working like this:

- The Commission must conduct detailed impact assessments, consulting widely and providing quantitative evidence supporting the need for EU action where possible, to justify a piece of legislation in a shared competence area.
- Where national parliaments object to the Commission's proposal, they can use the Early Warning Mechanism to (at a minimum) request the Commission to reconsider its proposal.
- When, following adoption, a Member State government remains unconvinced that the adopted piece of legislation satisfies the principle of subsidiarity, it can start an infringement action before the Court of Justice.

Does this setup now fully assuage the concerns the Member States had when drafting the Maastricht Treaty—and so does the principle of subsidiarity work as an effective limit on the EU's exercise of competence? We will come back to this question in Chapter 5, when we apply the principle of subsidiarity to an EU legislative proposal that at least some of the Member States were unhappy with.

4.6 The principle of proportionality

Subsidiarity is the first of two Treaty-based limitations on the EU's exercise of its legislative competences. The second, the principle of proportionality, is a principle of significantly more general application: it applies not only to the EU legislative process, but also to all Member State action in those areas of law that fall within the scope of the Treaties more generally. It is consequently a general principle of law, but one that has been expressly codified as part of the checks on EU legislative powers in Article 5 TEU.

Article 5(4) TEU

Under the principle of proportionality, the content and form of Union action shall not exceed what is necessary to achieve the objectives of the Treaties.

Subsidiarity covers *when* the EU can exercise its legislative powers. Proportionality, meanwhile, covers *how* the EU can act when exercising its legislative powers, as well as how the Member States can act when they are adopting measures that fall within the scope of EU law. The following can consequently all be subjected to a proportionality review:

- Administrative actions of the EU institutions: a common example is where the Commission decides to fine companies that violate EU competition law, and those companies challenge the fines as disproportionate;[42]
- The *scope* of proposed legislation, insofar as it affects Member State powers or laws: for example, regarding the *Working Time Directive* case, the CJEU was also asked to consider if an EU-wide working week ceiling of 48 hours was proportionate;
- The acts of the Member States when acting in the field of EU law, and particularly when *deviating* from EU law: as we will see in Chapters 11 to 14, there is extensive case law considering if, for example, a 'ban' on a product, or a service, or an EU national's access to benefits in a Member State they have moved to is a proportionate measure, in light of EU free movement law.

Despite its much wider reach, proportionality is a significantly more straightforward principle than subsidiarity: what needs exploring in the definition provided in Article 5(4) TEU is the concept of 'necessary'.

The CJEU has in the course of its case law unpacked the term 'necessary' into three separate but related concepts.[43] These are clearly set out in *Fedesa*, which concerned an

[42] See Chapter 15.
[43] Case C-331/88 *Fedesa* ECLI:EU:C:1990:391, para 13.

EU directive prohibiting the use of five hormones in livestock farming. The CJEU noted that to comply with the principle of proportionality, first, the EU must demonstrate that its action is **suitable** to achieve a given objective. If it cannot demonstrate that the action it is taking will help accomplish a given goal, the legislation in question will be disproportionate. Secondly, the EU must also demonstrate that its action is the *least invasive* possible action that will achieve the objective in question. This is what makes a legislative intervention **necessary**, as opposed to excessive. Finally, the CJEU has also argued that any disadvantages caused by an adopted measure must not be **disproportionate to the aims pursued**: a sledge-hammer to crack a walnut, in other words, would not satisfy the EU's principle of proportionality.

Is this a difficult test for the EU legislature to meet? We will consider how the Court assesses whether EU legislation is proportionate in Chapter 5, as part of our examination of how the 'limits' on EU legislative powers work in practice. The EU legislature, meanwhile, appears to have taken the principle of proportionality to heart, and in a series of packages on 'Better Law-Making' have committed to not only regulate, but *deregulate* where possible.[44] This means that rather than assuming EU action is necessary, the Commission will strive to repeal 'unnecessary' legislation (which may be outdated), to co-regulate in areas of law with national authorities, and to revisit adopted legislation five years later for an assessment of how effective it has been in achieving EU goals. Much like subsidiarity, considerations of proportionality have also resulted in the directive becoming the preferred legislative form adopted by the Commission whenever possible—as it is again the least 'heavy-handed' of all EU legislative forms that have a binding effect.

4.7 Brexit and EU law

The broader issue of the EU's ability to extend the reach of the competences conferred upon it, and to what extent Brexit will alleviate such concerns, is analysed in Chapter 5. Here, instead, we will consider what will happen to 'EU law' in the UK during and after the 'transition period'.

4.7.1 The Withdrawal Agreement

As should be clear from the discussion in this chapter, there is a lot of EU law that either directly *applies* to the UK, or has actually been woven into UK domestic law either through amendments or the implementation process of directives. Over the course of the Withdrawal Agreement's transition period, this will continue to apply to the UK, so there will be no changes to the legal effects of EU law in the UK before at least 2021.[45]

[44] Interinstitutional Agreement between the European Parliament, the Council of the European Union and the European Commission on Better Law-Making [2016] OJ L123/1; see Chapter 10 for more on 'better law-making'.

[45] Possibly not until 2023, if the transition period is extended; see Withdrawal Agreement, Articles 126 and 132; note that the EU (Withdrawal Agreement) Act 2020, s 33, prohibits UK representatives from asking for an extension as a matter of domestic law—though as is true for all Acts of Parliament, this can obviously be amended if an extension is desired after all.

4.7.2 'Retained' EU law after Brexit

However, after the transition period ends, the legal *obligation* to maintain these rules will fall away for all parts of the UK bar Northern Ireland. But simply 'scrapping' it all would result in unimaginable holes in the UK legal framework, and equally undermine essential principles of the rule of law like legal certainty and legitimate expectations, if it were to happen all at once.

The European Union (Withdrawal) Act 2018 consequently does not simply wipe the legislative slate clean. Instead, it introduces a new category of domestic law called 'retained EU law'. Section 4 of the Act retains those parts of the Treaties and general principles that currently can be relied upon directly before UK domestic courts.[46] Section 3 of the Act indicates that regulations, decisions, and delegated or implementing acts that applied directly in the UK will continue to do so—but will do so as a matter of domestic law. Section 2, finally, addresses so-called 'EU-derived' domestic legislation, meaning both the domestic laws implementing EU directives and any other UK laws that are inspired by or amended on account of EU law.[47]

There are, however, key exceptions to the 'retention' of EU law. One is the Charter of Fundamental Rights; we consider the effects of this deliberate omission in Chapter 9.

Also made explicit in the Act is what will happen to CJEU case law on any 'retained' legislation. Following the adoption of the EU (Withdrawal Agreement) Act 2020, it remains generally the case that UK courts will continue to read 'retained' EU law in light of pre-Brexit CJEU rulings. However, there are exceptions to the general rule. First, final courts of appeal can diverge from CJEU readings of 'retained' EU law when they wish to: this covers the Supreme Court and the Scottish High Court of Justiciary for criminal appeals.[48] The other exception, added by the EU (Withdrawal Agreement) Act 2020, is that ministers can (by regulations adopted during the transition period) specify *when* lower courts can or must depart from previous CJEU rulings after the transition period.[49] The final appeal courts thus have a free 'choice' to depart, whereas lower courts can only follow those courts or be instructed by regulations to depart. The latter exception is highly controversial, and runs contrary to normal practice regarding the interpretation of law in the UK: as the House of Lords Constitution Committee has said, 'if the meaning of UK law, as retained EU law will become after exit day, is to be altered, it should be for Parliament to change, not for ministerial guidelines to reinterpret.'[50]

The Act is, on the other hand, ambivalent about how domestic courts apply post-exit CJEU case law to 'retained' legislation. It will no longer be binding on domestic courts, but there is no guidance on when courts may wish to be 'inspired' by CJEU interpretations of former EU law.[51] This adds a dimension of legal uncertainty to how 'retained' EU

[46] For more on directly effective EU law, see Chapter 8.

[47] Note that these would not have needed to be retained: the process of Brexit cannot actually directly 'change' domestic UK law. It is not clear why this category of law was included in the EU (Withdrawal) Act 2018.

[48] EU (Withdrawal) Act 2018, s 6(3) and s 6(4).

[49] EU (Withdrawal Agreement) Act 2020, s 26(1), amending EU (Withdrawal) Act 2018, s 6.

[50] See https://publications.parliament.uk/pa/ld5801/ldselect/ldconst/5/5.pdf, paras 105–108, where the Lords Constitution Committee argued for deleting the relevant clause from the Bill (prior to adoption).

[51] EU (Withdrawal) Act 2018, s 6(1).

law will be interpreted in practice, and it is not truly clear how it is meant to work in a system of precedent: what, then, is the authoritative interpretation of 'retained' EU law? Is it the pre-Brexit CJEU interpretation, not overruled by the Supreme Court, or is it the county court judge's new interpretation, based on post-Brexit CJEU case law, in a given case in 2023?[52]

4.7.3 The Protocol on Ireland and Northern Ireland

As will be stressed at many points in this book, the situation applicable to Northern Ireland is a little distinct from what will be happening in the remainder of the UK. It will find itself faced with a combination of 'retained' EU law, in those areas that are not addressed by the Protocol's provisions that aim to keep the border on the island of Ireland invisible, as well as *active* EU law, where the Protocol forces the application of ongoing EU internal market law.[53]

This quite obviously runs the risk of being very confusing, particularly in the early years of operation of the Protocol: businesses and individuals alike, as well as the legal teams representing them, will have to carefully investigate whether provisions applicable to them remain *active* EU law, or fall within the category of 'retained' EU law. *Active* EU law will need to be interpreted in light of ongoing CJEU jurisprudence, just as it does within EU Member States, while 'retained' EU law *can* be but does not have to be. For example, imagine a business in Northern Ireland is engaging with a business in the EU27: legal teams will find themselves needing to be aware of all current EU law as well as the 'exit day' CJEU interpretation of 'retained' EU law in Northern Ireland.

A further point worth highlighting is the commitment of the Protocol to not diminish a certain number of 'rights, safeguards and opportunities' of the people of Northern Ireland as a consequence of Brexit. This commitment, set out in Article 2(1) of the Protocol, exists in light of the 1998 Belfast/Good Friday Agreement between the UK and Ireland, which obliges both parties to ensure equivalence of specific rights, safeguards, and opportunities.[54] Those rights in Northern Ireland, then, have to in essence mirror those rights in Ireland—and as Ireland will remain a Member State, they must therefore stay in line with EU rights law, even if the UK leaves the EU.

The commitment in the Protocol is again made with regard to a fixed date: a snapshot of rights on 'exit day'. As such, the people of Northern Ireland will derive some rights from 'retained' EU law (which will, in Northern Ireland, need to be interpreted in such a way that rights are not diminished)—and will also retain rights from the ongoing EU law obligations in the Protocol, to which the Charter of Fundamental Rights will continue to apply. Again, legal teams across the EU and the UK will be faced with these differences over time, and will need a very good understanding not only of ongoing EU law and 'retained' EU law, but also *what EU law looked like on exit day*, specifically for this purpose.

[52] For a discussion, see James Lee, 'Troubling and Unnecessary: The problems of precedent in clause 26(1) in the Withdrawal Agreement Bill' (14 January 2020, LSE Brexit Blog) https://blogs.lse.ac.uk/brexit/2020/01/14/troubling-and-unnecessary-the-problems-of-precedent-in-clause-261-in-the-withdrawal-agreement-bill/.

[53] Protocol, Article 7; this dimension of the Protocol is discussed in greater detail in Chapters 10 and 11.

[54] See the 1998 Belfast/Good Friday Agreement, Part 6.

The oversight needed to ensure that 'retained' EU law does not eventually get interpreted in a way that is different, rights-wise, from how it was on 'exit day' will fall to the UK to organize, and to the courts in the UK to enforce when disputes arise: but any lasting disagreements about non-diminution of rights will have to be resolved by the Withdrawal Agreement's Joint Committee. It is an area where disputes are likely, and where domestic courts, oversight mechanisms, and the members of the Joint Committee will need to be very alert to ensure that rights are not 'accidentally' lost because of differences in interpretation after Brexit. We come back to post-Brexit fundamental rights issues in Chapter 9, once we have looked at how fundamental rights work in the EU generally in more detail.

4.8 **In conclusion**

If we look back to Section 4.1, we now have a clear picture of both *when* the EU can exercise legislative powers, and *how* it can exercise those powers when it can legislate. Competences and subsidiarity set out *when* the Member States have conferred legislative powers on the EU. The legislative forms set out in Article 288 TFEU and the general principles developed by the Court, combined with the principle of proportionality, make clear *how* EU law should look once it has been adopted.

If we think back to the two quotes at the start of the chapter, we should have more of an understanding of just how much and where the EU legislates, and why some commentators—like Lord Lawson—have concerns about this. What do the EU's legislative processes tell us about the extent to which the UK has been 'subject' to EU legislation? Has it had clear input into how the EU legislates, and when the EU *can* even propose legislation? Or has this all developed outside of the UK's powers, and will the end result be 'full-blooded political union' even with checks in place, such as competence limits, subsidiarity, and proportionality?

You should at this stage already be developing a view on the level of participation the Member States have in EU law-making, and under what limits EU law-making operates. However, we will be putting the effectiveness of limits to the EU's legislative powers to the test more explicitly in Chapter 5. If the EU pursues laws that genuinely go against the desires of a single Member State, is there any way in which that Member State can *stop* those laws from entering into force?

Key points

- EU primary law is composed of **the EU Treaties** and **general principles of EU law**.
- EU secondary law takes the form of **regulations**, **directives**, and **decisions.** Regulations are **directly applicable** and do not require domestic legislation to take effect. Directives are **binding as to their purpose**, meaning that each Member State can adopt national law to give effect to the objective of a directive as suits its own legal system.
- As of the Lisbon Treaty, most EU secondary legislation is produced via the **ordinary legislative procedure,** in which the Council of Ministers and the European Parliament have equal decision-making power.

- The division of 'power' between the Member States and the EU, in terms of who can legislate in what policy area, is set out in the EU Treaties in three categories: **exclusive (EU) competences**, **shared competences**, and **supporting/coordinating competences**. Any power the EU has, it has because that power has been **conferred** onto it by the Member States in the Treaties.
- As a limit to the EU's centralizing powers, EU legislative powers in **shared competences** are governed by the **principle of subsidiarity**, which sets conditions on when the EU can produce legislation in shared competence policy areas.
- The content of EU secondary legislation is governed by the **principle of proportionality**, demanding that EU legislative action is 'proportionate' and not overly invasive into Member State interests.
- Following Brexit, the UK will take the majority of EU law currently applicable in the UK and turn it into a new form of domestic law known as **'retained' EU law**.

Assess your learning

1. **How, and in what areas, is competence 'shared' between the EU and the Member States? (See Section 4.4.)**
2. **What is the *point* of the principle of subsidiarity? How can you tell if the principle of subsidiarity has been complied with when the EU acts? (See Section 4.5.)**
3. **When are EU legislative actions proportionate? (See Section 4.6.)**

Further reading

Armin von Bogdandy et al, 'Legal Instruments in European Union Law and Their Reform: A systematic approach on an empirical basis' (2004) 23 YEL 91.

Mette Buskjær Rasmussen and Maja Kluger Dionigi, 'National Parliaments' Use of the Political Dialogue: Institutional lobbyists, traditionalists or communicators?' (2018) 56(5) JCMS 1108.

Deirdre Curtin and Päivi Leino, 'In Search of Transparency for EU Law-Making: Trilogues on the cusp of dawn' (2017) 54(6) CMLRev 1689.

Sacha Garben and Inge Govaere (eds), *The Division of Competences between the EU and the Member States: Reflections on the Past, the Present and the Future* (Bloomsbury, 2017).

Tor-Inge Harbo, 'The Function of the Proportionality Principle in EU Law' (2010) 16(2) Eur Law J 158.

Darren Harvey, 'Towards Process-Oriented Proportionality Review in the European Union' (2017) 23(1) EPL 93.

Christilla Roederer-Rynning and Justin Greenwood, 'The Culture of Trilogues' (2015) 22(8) JEPP 1148.

Linda Senden, 'Soft Post-Legislative Rulemaking: A time for more stringent control' (2013) 19 Eur Law J 57.

Kate Sowery, 'The Nature and Scope of the Primary Law-making Powers of the European Union: The Member States as the "masters of the treaties"?' (2018) 43(2) ELRev 205.

Phil Syrpis, 'The Relationship between Primary and Secondary Law in the EU' (2015) 52(2) CMLRev 461.

Online resources

Visit www.oup.com/he/demars1e for a sample approach to discussing the quote.

5

Limits to EU legislative powers

Context for this chapter

Subsidiarity assessment: seasonal changes of time

The European Commission has proposed a Directive to end seasonal clock changes in the EU in 2019. Member States would be required to choose to apply 'permanent summer-time' or 'permanent winter-time'. Should the UK and EU reach an agreement according to the terms of the draft Withdrawal Agreement, the UK would be required to implement the proposed Directive during the transition period.

The Sub-Committee's report raises subsidiarity concerns in relation to:

- The proposal's limited subsidiarity statement, which cites increased questioning of the current summertime arrangements as a reason for action.
- Inadequate consideration of how the role of summertime arrangements varies between Member States due to the interplay between longitude, latitude, and time zone in determining daylight hours. The geographical position of the UK, for instance, means that the benefits and drawbacks of 'permanent summer-time' or 'permanent winter-time' differ significantly between its northern and southern regions. The potential implications for the UK are exacerbated by the devolution settlement with Northern Ireland, under which time is a devolved matter.
- Inadequate evaluation of alternative options, such as the possibility of allowing Member States to choose whether or not to observe seasonal clock changes but requiring coordinated arrangements for those that do.

House of Lords EU Internal Market Select Committee, 'Reasoned opinion on discontinuing seasonal changes of time recommended by Committee' (22 October 2018) https://www.parliament.uk/business/committees/committees-a-z/lords-select/eu-internal-market-subcommittee/news-parliament-2017/seasonal-change-of-time-report-published/

5.1 Introduction

Chapter 4 explored the scope of the EU's legislative powers, indicated by the answers to the following two questions:

- **_When_ can the EU make law?** (Does it have the power to legislate, or do the Member States?)
- **And, if the EU can act, _how_ can it act?** (Are there rules determining the *form* and *content* of legislation?)

The *when* questions relate to the EU's competences and the principle of subsidiarity, which governs how non-exclusive competences should be exercised by the EU (and so when the EU can act *instead* of the Member States in shared competence areas). The *how* questions relate to the forms of law the EU can produce, as well as the *content* of EU legislation. Forms of EU law range from primary sources, such as the Treaties and general principles, to secondary sources like regulations and directives. As for the content of EU legislation, it always has to be proportionate to whatever aim the EU is trying to achieve in that legislation.

Chapter 5 builds directly on Chapter 4. In Chapter 5, we will consider competences, subsidiarity, and proportionality again, with the aim of assessing if the limits set out in the Treaties actually work as concrete limits on EU legislative powers in practice. We will do this first by considering whether competences are genuinely clear and finite in how they set out limits to areas in which the EU can make law. We will then consider whether the principle of subsidiarity actually achieves what its title suggests it is meant to achieve, which is a balancing act between the interests of the Member States and the interests of the EU. Finally, we will consider whether proportionality can perhaps present a clear obstacle to excessively 'invasive' legislation.

Only with a fuller understanding of how the Treaty 'legislative limits' work once they are applied in practice can we consider what, if anything, the UK can do about the Commission legislative proposal to scrap seasonal time changes set out in the context for this chapter.

5.2 Preventing 'competence creep'

As discussed in Chapter 4, Lisbon's effort to explicitly set out a list of types of competences held by the EU is an improvement on earlier Treaties. While these competences also make it clear that the EU is definitely no longer a purely 'economic' project, the EU's exclusive competences in particular—centralized on a common trade policy, the customs union, and the common currency—obviously stop short of permitting the EU to develop all legislation needed to turn the EU into a country with a single, centralized government.

However, concerns about competence are rarely about the EU's exclusive competences. These remain of the largely 'economic' variety, where the Member States have rarely expressed reservations about conferring more power on the EU. Instead, it is in areas of **shared competence** that the Member States are the most concerned about expanding EU powers. From the perspective of federalism, this makes sense, as it is an area where they have neither given the EU *full* power to act, nor have they outright forbidden it from acting. There is thus an ongoing expectation of *some* EU action in the shared competence areas, but where the EU acts in unexpected ways in shared competence areas, the Member States can baulk at its exercise of powers.

EU law in practice

The notion of the EU 'overreaching' into domestic competences was a key factor in the 2016 referendum outcome, where the concept of 'taking back control' was central to both voter motivations and the messages of 'Leave' campaigns. The referendum, however, was not the first time that the UK had engaged actively with just how much power over UK matters the EU had been given over time.

In 2012, the UK government commenced an unprecedented (and massive) exercise in order to investigate just ***how*** many competences the EU had, and whether the balance between EU competence allocation and retained competence for the UK was struck correctly. This Balance of Competences Review produced 32 reports by the end of 2014, covering all bespoke policy areas listed in Title I of the TFEU and asking for stakeholder and expert input on whether the EU had too much, the right amount, or too little ability to legislate in these given areas, vis-à-vis the UK Parliament itself.[1]

The reports, broadly, concluded that the EU had not overreached. In each of these 32 areas, the balance of law-making power was spread approximately as desired, according to the reports' findings. This, however, was not a widely publicized outcome. The House of Lords EU Committee, in considering the Balance of Competence Review overall, regretted that it had not resulted in an executive summary (collating the findings of the 32 separate reports):[2]

> **64.** As a result, this major project, despite the good quality of its outputs, has yet to deliver an outcome, in the form of measurable benefits. It has so far made no impact on the public debate on the UK-EU relationship.

It is, of course, impossible to say if such an executive summary would have had a significant impact on the outcome of the UK referendum of 2016—but we can speculate about its effects nonetheless.

Now that you are studying EU law, and considering this issue of 'competence creep', do ***you*** think that such an executive summary would have helped inform the public debate? Do you think it would have been easy to produce—and easy to understand?

A key example of national concerns over EU 'competence creep' is the German Constitutional Court's 1993 *Brunner* judgment on the Maastricht Treaty's compatibility with the German Constitution.[3] Ultimately, the German Constitutional Court ruled in the *Brunner*

[1] See https://www.gov.uk/guidance/review-of-the-balance-of-competences.

[2] Lords EU Committee, 'The Review of the Balance of Competences between the UK and the EU' (2015) HL 140, paras 54–55.

[3] *Manfred Brunner and Others v The European Union Treaty* (Cases 2 BvR 2134/92 & 2159/92) [1994] 1 CMLR 57.

case that the German Constitution did not preclude Germany ratifying the Maastricht settlement. However, it did raise particular concerns about the extent to which the EU institutions had, over the course of time, claimed ever-increasing powers that were not *clearly* set out in the Treaty. It flagged up use of what is now Article 352 TFEU in an 'open-handed' manner, as well as usage of 'implied powers', and broad interpretation of the existing content of the Treaty so as to make EU law 'effective'. It then warned that if such usage would result in an extension of the Treaty, 'such an interpretation . . . would not produce any binding effects for Germany'.[4]

Brunner helpfully sets out the three aspects of EU law that have been deemed responsible for the EU's competence creep. First, it highlights the Treaties' so-called 'flexible provisions'; the most interesting ones are, first, Article 114 TFEU, which is a legal basis for adopting any and all harmonizing EU law for the sake of 'the establishment and functioning of the internal market'. The other is, as mentioned in *Brunner*, Article 352 TFEU, which is a safeguard clause that allows the EU to take legislative action for the sake of accomplishing Treaty objectives that otherwise would not have a needed Treaty legislative basis.

Brunner also flags up the so-called doctrine of 'implied powers', which has arisen in situations where the Treaties do not explicitly state that the EU institutions are empowered to undertake an action, but the institutions have argued that they need to undertake action A in order to attain Treaty goal B.

Underpinning all three of these areas of 'flexibility' is criticism of the manner in which the Court of Justice has interpreted the relevant treaty provisions or doctrines. Weiler observed in 1991 that the Court of Justice had at that point *never* declared Community action to be outside of Union competence.[5] The Member States' feelings about the actions of the Court of Justice are thus paramount in concerns about 'ever-closer union', in that even if the Member States agree to *limit* the EU's competences, such limits would only ever be effective if Member State *ultra vires* challenges before the Court of Justice could succeed.

In short, to those concerned about 'competence creep' in the EU, the flexibility inherent in the Treaty's provisions and the Court's interpretation of those provisions are significantly more important than explicit statements of the limits of EU powers in Articles 4 and 5 TEU.[6] We will consider to what extent those concerns are warranted in the remainder of this section.

5.2.1 Flexible treaty provisions: Article 114 TFEU

Article 114 TFEU is perhaps the most significant of the Treaties' 'safeguard' provisions. The drafters of the Treaties from the Single European Act onwards appear to have realized that completing the internal market would take a very long time—indeed, might simply prove impossible—if every action the EU undertook required a specific legal basis in the Treaties. This would require the drafters of the Treaties to anticipate exactly what specific *areas of law* would pose barriers to cross-border trade, and supply specific legislative bases

[4] Ibid, para 99. [5] Joseph Weiler, 'The Transformation of Europe' (1991) 100 YLJ 2403, 2447.

[6] See, commenting on the lasting nature of 'competence creep' even after Lisbon, Sacha Garben, 'Competence Creep Revisited' (2019) 57(2) JCMS 205.

for those areas of law (such as employment law, consumer protection, and so on). As explained in Chapter 1, the SEA was drafted with the intention of completing the internal market within *six years*. Clearly, this required an ability to take radical and fast legislative action.

In order to avoid a situation where an EU measure was clearly *needed* to act to overcome a barrier to the internal market, but such an EU measure could not be clearly connected to any other provision in the Treaties, what is now Article 114 TFEU was drafted.

Article 114 TFEU (emphasis added)

1. Save where otherwise provided in the Treaties . . . [t]he European Parliament and the Council shall, acting in accordance with the ordinary legislative procedure and after consulting the Economic and Social Committee, **adopt the measures for the approximation** of the provisions laid down by law, regulation or administrative action in Member States **which have as their object the establishment and functioning of the internal market.**

Article 114 TFEU permits the EU institutions to use the **ordinary legislative procedure** to adopt legislation that harmonizes all national law for the sake of 'establishing' and ensuring the 'functioning' of the internal market. This may have been deemed *necessary* to prevent further legislative deadlock when the SEA was drafted—but with the ever-increasing legal bases and policy areas included in the Treaties, Article 114 TFEU has become a more sensitive subject, not least because of how generously the Court of Justice has interpreted the exercise of Article 114 TFEU by the EU institutions.[7]

The classic strand of case law that highlights potential problems stemming from Article 114 TFEU pertains to a 1998 EU directive that contained market-wide rules on the advertising of tobacco products.[8] At first glance, this may seem as if it has nothing to do with the internal market; surely the most obvious reason to try to regulate whether cigarettes can be advertised will be motivated by *health* concerns rather than by *trade* concerns?

This argument was forcefully made by Germany, which protested the adoption of the EU Directive on advertising of tobacco products before the Court in *Tobacco Advertising 1*.[9] Germany stressed that the EU has no harmonizing power when it comes to *public health*. Much as it would have liked to propose and adopt legislation in order to discourage smoking for the sake of it, then, this was not something that the Treaties—either then or now—gave the EU the power to pursue.[10]

[7] See, for an example of broad interpretation by the Court, Case C-350/92 *Spain v Council* ECLI:EU:C:1995:237, where what is now Article 114 TFEU was deemed appropriate for adopting legislation that harmonized the laws on the registering of medical patents, as having different patent-registration regimes in different Member States would have negative effects on cross-border trade in medicine.

[8] Directive 98/43/EC of the European Parliament and of the Council of 6 July 1998 on the approximation of the laws, regulations and administrative provisions of the Member States relating to the advertising and sponsorship of tobacco products [1998] OJ L213/9.

[9] Case C-376/98 *Germany v Parliament and Council* (*Tobacco Advertising 1*) ECLI:EU:C:2000:544.

[10] *Tobacco Advertising 1*, paras 32–35.

Germany thus challenged the use of Article 100a EC (now Article 114 TFEU) to effectively ban the advertising of tobacco products, arguing that this was primarily about *health* and actually had only minimal impact on 'the internal market'. For one thing, a significant number of the products on which cigarettes were advertised did not actually *move* across the internal market. Ashtrays, billboards, and umbrellas, for instance, were produced and used within a single Member State, according to Germany. Even print media that contained cigarette advertisements did not travel across borders regularly: 'Considerably less than 5 per cent of magazines are exported to other Member States and daily newspapers are used to a much lesser extent than magazines for carrying tobacco advertising.'[11] Germany consequently noted that there was no 'internal market obstruction' here, and asked the Court to annul the relevant piece of EU legislation, as it could not be adopted on the basis of Article 114 TFEU.

Interestingly, the UK government agreed with the EU institutions, and argued that Article 114 TFEU was an appropriate legal basis for the adoption of the laws in question.

Case C-376/98 *Germany v Parliament and Council (Tobacco Advertising 1)* ECLI:EU:C:2000:544 (Tobacco Advertising 1) (emphasis added)

58. The United Kingdom Government challenges the applicant's assertion that the Directive is incorrectly based on Article 100a of the Treaty [*now Article 114 TFEU*] because **its principal objective is not the elimination of obstacles to trade in advertising media and associated services but the protection of human health.**

...

60. Objectively, **the Directive pursues objectives which are inseparably linked with the protection of human health and others linked with elimination of disparities in conditions of competition and liberalisation of trade.** The applicant's approach of seeking to determine which of those objectives is most important is not only contrary to the objective test propounded by the Court but also unworkable.

61. The United Kingdom Government submits that Article 100a of the Treaty confers power on the Council and the Parliament to adopt measures concerned with the establishment and functioning of the internal market and considers that **in this case the measure concerned falls into that category.**

...

65. The Court has held that a measure may be adopted with **a view to anticipating** the adoption of disparate national rules involving serious obstacles to trade. **The present situation of tolerating publications which contain tobacco advertising may change in view of the evolution of national regulations, which are becoming more strict.** There is, therefore, a risk of increased obstacles to trade which the Directive is intended to eliminate.

At the time that *Tobacco Advertising 1* was decided, it was a genuine surprise when the Court took a restrictive view of what Article 114 TFEU permitted the EU institutions to do. But, for the first time, it clearly set out that there were *limits* to Article 114 TFEU.

[11] Ibid, para 16.

While agreeing in principle with the UK arguments that the objectives of the legislature were inseparable and not to be ranked, the Court then considered to what extent the Directive actually tackled issues relating to the establishment and functioning of the *internal market*. It stressed that it had to do so on account of the principle of conferral:[12]

Case C-376/98 *Germany v Parliament and Council (Tobacco Advertising 1)* ECLI:EU:C:2000:544 (Tobacco Advertising 1) (emphasis added)

83. . . . the measures referred to in Article 100a(1) of the Treaty are intended to improve the conditions for the establishment and functioning of the internal market. **To construe that article as meaning that it vests in the Community legislature a general power to regulate the internal market would not only be contrary to the express wording of the provisions cited above but would also be incompatible with the principle . . . that the powers of the Community are limited to those specifically conferred on it.**

84. Moreover, a measure adopted on the basis of Article 100a of the Treaty must genuinely have as its object the improvement of the conditions for the establishment and functioning of the internal market. **If a mere finding of disparities between national rules and of the abstract risk of obstacles to the exercise of fundamental freedoms or of distortions of competition liable to result therefrom were sufficient to justify the choice of Article 100a as a legal basis, judicial review of compliance with the proper legal basis might be rendered nugatory.**

The Court went on to conclude that significant numbers of the products covered by the relevant directive did not actually 'cross borders', and thus did not have an effect on the establishment and functioning of the internal market; and that consequently, Article 114 TFEU was not an appropriate basis for adopting the directive in question. It annulled the first Tobacco Advertising Directive accordingly.

However, as you may have guessed from the fact that this case is now known as *Tobacco Advertising 1*, the EU institutions were not quite finished with pursuing harmonized rules on the advertising of tobacco products. A revised version of the same directive was adopted in 2003,[13] and Germany challenged some of its provisions in the Court of Justice as well.[14] However, it appeared that the Commission had learnt its lesson from *Tobacco Advertising 1*. The revised directive no longer tackled so-called 'static products', like umbrellas, billboards, and ashtrays. It *did*, however, still cover print and radio media. Germany consequently went back to the Court of Justice, and made effectively the same argument that it had made in 2000: there was not enough cross-border movement of magazines or radio programmes for it to pose an obstacle to the creation of the internal market.[15]

[12] See Chapter 4.

[13] Directive 2003/33/EC of the European Parliament and of the Council of 26 May 2003 on the approximation of the laws, regulations and administrative provisions of the Member States relating to the advertising and sponsorship of tobacco products [2003] OJ L152/16.

[14] Case C-380/03 *Germany v Parliament and Council (Tobacco Advertising 2)* ECLI:EU:C:2006:772.

[15] Ibid, paras 18–23.

This argument had succeeded in 2000, but was not to succeed in 2006:

Case C-380/03 *Germany v Parliament and Council (Tobacco Advertising 2)* ECLI:EU:C:2006:772 (emphasis added)

55. . . . on the date when the Directive was adopted, several Member States already prohibited advertising of tobacco products, as indicated in paragraph 46 of the present judgment, while others were about to do so. Consequently, **disparities existed between the Member States' national laws and, contrary to the applicant's submissions, those disparities were such as to impede the free movement of goods and the freedom to provide services.**

The Court spent significant time pointing out that legislative difference was likely to make it *less appealing* for magazine producers to try to break into the markets of other European countries, and came to similar conclusions about radio broadcasts.[16] It flagged up the internet as being a particular driver in making these forms of media less 'static' than they had been, and consequently dismissed Germany's claim.[17]

The *Tobacco Advertising* saga represents both the 'highs' and the 'lows' of judicial treatment of Article 114 TFEU. In 2000, those concerned about 'competence creep' will have been comforted by the noises the Court had made. It had limited a very open-ended provision in the Treaty, making clear that only *concrete* obstacles to the establishment and functioning of the internal market could be addressed using Article 114 TFEU as a legal basis. It explicitly recognized the market research Germany had provided, and ruled that there was simply not enough of a problem to warrant EU intervention to the extent the first Tobacco Advertising Directive had pushed for. But, within six years, it appears to have changed its mind: despite statistical evidence that, again, there was no concrete market for trade in print media and radio programmes, the Court interpreted Article 114 TFEU as permitting EU legislation for the sake of *preventing* obstacles to such a market from emerging.[18] Subsequent judgments that related to Article 114 TFEU as a legislative basis have looked more like *Tobacco Advertising 2* than like *Tobacco Advertising 1*.[19]

Questions about Article 114 TFEU thus remain to this date: is it an open invitation for the EU to stretch its competences? Or does it merely offer a necessary flexibility in the Treaties that is appropriately curtailed by the Court? It is worth here noting that Article 114 TFEU has existed—and has been complained about by various Member States—since the Single

[16] Ibid, paras 56–61. [17] Ibid, para 62.

[18] See, eg, Derek Wyatt, 'Community Competence to Regulate the Internal Market' in Michael Dougan and Samantha Currie (eds), *50 Years of the European Treaties: Looking Back and Thinking Forward* (Hart, 2009).

[19] See, eg, Case C-377/98 *Netherlands v Parliament and Council* ECLI:EU:C:2001:523 (*Biotechnology Directive*), para 15, where the Court ruled that 'recourse to [Article 114 TFEU] as a legal basis is possible if the aim is to prevent the emergence of future obstacles to trade resulting from multifarious development of national laws provided that the emergence of such obstacles is likely and the measure in question is designed to prevent them'; see also Case C-210/03 *Swedish Match* ECLI:EU:C:2004:802; Case C-301/06 *Ireland v Parliament and Council* ECLI:EU:C:2009:68; Case C-58/08 *Vodafone* ECLI:EU:C:2010:321.

European Act. What does its ongoing existence in Lisbon, without substantial amendment, suggest about the extent to which the Member States feel that the EU has 'overstepped' the limits of the competence conferred onto it?

Discussing the scenario

The scenario at the start of the chapter sets out a Commission legislative proposal to effectively end seasonal time changes—eg, the clocks going back in the winter and forward in the summer. Could this proposal be argued to fall within the Article 114 TFEU powers? Try to imagine how the Commission might attempt to use Article 114 TFEU as a legal basis for this proposal.

5.2.2 Flexible treaty provisions: Article 352 TFEU

Article 352 TFEU can be thought of as a more 'general' version of Article 114 TFEU. Article 114 TFEU deals with situations where none of the existing Treaty bases enabled action in pursuit of 'completion of the internal market'. Article 352 TFEU, on the other hand, was included in the EU Treaties to cover those situations where the EU Member States wished to create new EU legislation relating to any objective stated in the Treaties, but they found there was no existing Treaty legal basis that would cover such action.

Article 352 TFEU (emphasis added)

1. If action by the Union should prove **necessary**, within the framework of the policies defined in the Treaties, **to attain one of the objectives** set out in the Treaties, and the Treaties have not provided the necessary powers, **the Council, acting unanimously** on a proposal from the Commission and **after obtaining the consent** of the European Parliament, shall adopt the appropriate measures . . .

The wording of the provision makes clear that the Member States intended for Article 352 TFEU to be used sparingly, and only with unanimous consent from all Member States. It exists as a means of *avoiding* Treaty revision where possible. As Ian Ward has put it, 'Treaties . . . are like buses. There is always another on its way.'[20] But negotiating them is *never* a simple or speedy process, and for the sake of making the EU an effective regulator, Article 352 TFEU enables the Heads of State to respond to certain new developments without needing to re-open negotiations about the entire contents of the Treaties.

How generous is this Article? As indicated in Section 5.1, the German Constitutional Court in *Brunner* expressed some concerns, and they were rooted in experience: for a number of years, Article 352 TFEU had been used to respond to new developments that the EU Treaties simply had not considered. It consequently introduced legislation in the field of the environment *before* the EC Treaty was amended, in 1992, to create explicit EU

[20] Ian Ward, *A Critical Introduction to European Law*, 3rd edn (CUP, 2009) 49.

competences in that area.[21] However, the Court of Justice in the mid-1990s established that there are clear limits to what Article 352 TFEU can be used for. Those limits are linked to the notion of the 'objectives set out in the Treaties', as the Court stressed in its 1994 Opinion on the use of what is now Article 352 TFEU for the EU's possible accession to the European Convention on Human Rights.[22]

Opinion 2/94 *Accession by the Community to the European Convention for the Protection of Human Rights and Fundamental Freedoms* ECLI:EU:C:1996:140 (emphasis added)

29. [Article 352 TFEU] is designed to fill the gap where no specific provisions of the Treaty confer on the [EU] institutions express or implied powers to act, if such powers appear none the less to be necessary to enable the [EU] to carry out its functions with a view to attaining one of the objectives laid down by the Treaty.

30. That provision, being an integral part of an institutional system based on the principle of conferred powers, cannot serve as a basis for widening the scope of [EU] powers beyond the general framework created by the provisions of the Treaty as a whole and, in particular, by those that define the tasks and the activities of the [EU]. On any view, [Article 352 TFEU] cannot be used as a basis for the adoption of provisions whose effect would, in substance, be to amend the Treaty without following the procedure which it provides for that purpose.

The effect of this ruling on the scope of Article 352 TFEU was not insignificant; it limited concerns about 'competence creep' through excessive use of Article 352, as it was now clear that the Court of Justice would intervene if it believed the EU was going too far. Its finding in Opinion 2/94 was that there was no 'objective' in the EC Treaty to sign the then-Community up to an international human rights treaty—and if the Member States wished for this to happen, they would have to renegotiate the EC Treaty accordingly.[23]

The Lisbon Treaty has further tried to scale back the 'competence creep' inherent in Article 352 TFEU. For one thing, it has involved the European Parliament in the Article 352 TFEU procedure for the first time, diminishing the feeling of 'back-door' negotiations only by government ministers. Perhaps more importantly, Lisbon has added Article 352(3), which requires proposals to use Article 352 to be sent to national parliaments, giving them time to scrutinize these proposals and, where needed, challenge their adoption. Article 352 TFEU now also precludes harmonization in areas where the Treaty otherwise prohibits this: it consequently cannot be used to bypass Treaty-level agreements or disagreements between the Member States.

[21] See, for analysis, Robert Schütze, 'Organised Change Towards an "Ever Closer Union": Article 308 EC and the limits to the Community's legislative competence' (2003) 22 YEL 79; Alan Dashwood, 'Article 308 EC as the Outer Limit of Expressly Conferred Community Competence' in Catherine Barnard and Okeoghene Odudu (eds), *The Outer Limits of European Union Law* (Hart, 2009).

[22] Opinion 2/94 *Accession by the Community to the European Convention for the Protection of Human Rights and Fundamental Freedoms* ECLI:EU:C:1996:140; for more on the EU's accession to the ECHR, see Chapter 9.

[23] *Opinion 2/94*, paras 34–35.

Given the extent of the Lisbon amendments, and the Court's clear limits to the use of the provision, we should at this point consider whether Article 352 TFEU remains a serious 'competence creep' problem. Paul Craig does not think this very likely. He has noted that the EU's competences have grown more explicit and more detailed in every successive Treaty, and that Lisbon included many of the policy areas where Article 352 TFEU had been used historically.[24]

However, the events of the Eurozone crisis suggest this might be an overstatement. As discussed in Chapter 3, the financial crisis of 2009 had a number of Eurozone Member States on the verge of bankruptcy, and in order to rescue them from that bankruptcy, several so-called 'bail-out mechanisms' (offering very conditional loans) were established by the EU Heads of State. There was no Treaty basis for these 'bail-out mechanisms', as the drafters of the Treaties simply had not considered that an EU Member State using the common currency *could* go bankrupt and might *need* this type of rescuing. While Article 352 TFEU was not used to establish these emergency Eurozone rescue funds, it is worth noting that it potentially *could* have been. Consider the following EU objective:

Article 3 TEU

The Union shall . . . promote economic, social and territorial cohesion, and solidarity among Member States.

Can that Treaty objective be read to mean that an unprecedented financial crisis would threaten the 'economic cohesion' of certain Member States? It seems to open the door for Article 352 TFEU secondary legislation to set up a 'rescue fund', particularly as the goal of 'economic cohesion' is linked to 'solidarity among Member States'.

Ultimately, international agreements that sidestepped the EU legislative process were relied upon . . . but they did not necessarily have to be, given Article 352 TFEU's purposes.

Pause for reflection

Why do you think the Member States retained Article 352 TFEU, even if the chances of it being used are significantly smaller now that the Lisbon Treaty has once again increased the EU's competences?

5.2.3 Implied powers

The next way in which the EU institutions have been accused of 'stretching' the competences that have been granted to them is through the doctrine of 'implied powers'. In its simplest form, an 'implied power' is a power that is *necessary* in order to actually exercise a different, but expressly legislated for, power. This particular interpretation of implied

[24] Paul Craig, *EU Administrative Law*, 2nd edn (OUP, 2012) 388.

powers is not controversial. Indeed, we can see from the preceding discussion already that the drafters of the Treaty fully appreciated that there may be unintended 'holes' in the Treaty's legislative bases, and 'implied powers' are a simple way to fill those so as to ensure that the contents of the Treaties could actually be *used* by the EU institutions.

There is, however, a broader reading of when a power can be 'implied', and this broader reading links more closely to concern about 'competence creep'. Instead of looking at *powers that are necessary to exercise* **other powers**, this broad reading considers *powers that are necessary to obtain a given* **objective**. Much like Article 352 TFEU, this formulation of 'implied powers' can stretch just what areas of law the EU can move into simply by linking them to a Treaty goal. And, for critics of the EU's competence settlements, it is important to note that the Court of Justice seems to support the wider reading of 'implied powers':

Case 281/85 *Germany, France, Denmark, Netherlands, & UK v Commission* ECLI:EU:C:1987:351 (emphasis added)

28. . . . it must be emphasized that where an article of the . . . Treaty . . . confers a specific task on the Commission it must be accepted, if that provision is not to be rendered wholly ineffective, that it confers on the Commission necessarily and per se the powers which are indispensable in order to carry out that task. Accordingly, [the relevant Article] must be interpreted as conferring on the Commission all the powers which are necessary . . .

However, this type of formulation of the doctrine of 'implied powers' is the exception, rather than the rule—and it has rarely been used by the Court of Justice. A more general notion that the EU institutions have broad abilities to legislate in any area that the EU Treaties *mention*, in other words, is an exaggeration of how the Court has employed this particular 'fix' to Treaty shortcomings.

5.2.4 The Court's interpretative methods

Of greater, and more general, concern is the Court's general ability and willingness to broadly interpret the *contents* of the Treaties. Clear competences and specific legal bases in the Treaties are a prerequisite to setting out limits to the EU's ability to act. However, equally important is the ability for Member States to *enforce* such limits. It is here that the Court of Justice has, from the 1990s onwards, been accused of being very clearly on the side of the EU—and consequently, of expanding the EU's powers—purely by how it interprets the text of the Treaties.

Criticism of the Court is not entirely warranted, however; 'competence creep' through interpretation is a consequence of an accepted method of judicial interpretation, not just in the EU legal system but in most national legal systems.

When there is doubt as to the *meaning* of a particular legal provision, the most obvious recourse is to look at its literal text and deduce a meaning from its wording. However, as you will undoubtedly have found out over the course of your law studies already, the meaning of virtually all words is debatable. An alternative way of determining the meaning of a given legal provision is, consequently, to examine the *purpose* of the legislation. This is known as **teleological interpretation**, from the Greek root of *telos*, meaning 'goal'. In this type of interpretation, a court will look not only to the text of the legal provision in front of it, but will also look to the 'goal' of the legislature in adopting it, so as to try to ensure that its reading of the provision will not frustrate achievement of that goal. Clearly, in any legal system that espouses parliamentary sovereignty, this should be considered a good thing. But, in the EU context, the legislator is not a national parliament, and so teleological interpretation is likely to consider the EU's goals, rather than individual Member States' goals.

In the UK, never has the Court's interpretation of the Treaties been more controversial than in its annulment challenge to the much-protested Working Time Directive, already discussed in Chapter 4.[25] As hinted at there, this case embodies several concerns regarding 'competence creep': the UK's primary challenge was in fact about the legal basis for adopting the Working Time Directive, as it was not a legal basis that required unanimity in the Council. Consequently, the UK was unable to veto the adoption of the Directive; it was simply outvoted.

The Working Time Directive was adopted under what was then Article 118a EC, and is now Article 153(2) TFEU. The relevant Treaty Article permits the Council to adopt 'minimum requirements' relating to 'the health and safety of workers'. In addition to its protests under the principle of subsidiarity, discussed in Chapter 4, the UK protested that the Working Time Directive had little to do with the 'health and safety of workers':

Case C-84/94 *UK v Council (Working Time Directive)* ECLI:EU:C:1996:431 (emphasis added)

13. . . . the applicant argues first that that provision permits the adoption only of directives which have a genuine and objective link to the 'health and safety' of workers. **That does not apply to measures concerning, in particular, weekly working time, paid annual leave and rest periods, whose connection with the health and safety of workers is too tenuous.** That interpretation is borne out by the expression 'working environment' used in Article 118a, which implies that directives based on that provision must be concerned only with physical conditions and risks at the workplace.

The Court of Justice was not impressed by the UK's argument:

Case C-84/94 *UK v Council (Working Time Directive)* ECLI:EU:C:1996:431 (emphasis added)

15. There is **nothing** in the wording of Article 118a to indicate that **the concepts of 'working environment', 'safety' and 'health'** as used in that provision **should**, in the absence of other indications, **be interpreted restrictively**, and not as embracing all factors, physical or otherwise, capable of affecting the health and safety of the worker in his working environment, including in particular certain aspects of the organization of working time. **On the contrary, the words 'especially in the working environment' militate in favour of a broad interpretation** of the powers which Article 118a confers upon the Council for the protection of the health and safety of workers.

[25] Council Directive 93/104/EC of 23 November 1993 concerning certain aspects of the organization of working time [1993] OJ L307/18; Case C-84/94 *UK v Council (Working Time Directive)* ECLI:EU:C:1996:431.

The UK government indicated at the time that it would attempt to ensure through negotiations at intergovernmental conferences that the Directive would not apply to the UK, and that the 'social provisions could never again be imposed on the UK against its will'.[26] As discussed in Chapter 1, this was in no small part a reaction to the fact that the UK had negotiated an opt-out from the Maastricht Treaty's so-called 'Social Chapter' in 1992, and the Major government believed strongly that the Working Time Directive should have simply not have applied to the UK at all.[27]

However, the Blair government abolished the 'Social Chapter' opt-out in 1997. This ended the debate, and the Working Time Directive remains applicable to the UK to date—albeit with a great many opt-outs, which (at least in theory) place the power to work for more than 48 hours a week with employees who have opted out of their EU law rights, rather than with the employers. If the chosen pathway of 'Brexit' permits it, it is likely to be one of the first EU-originating pieces of legislation that will be axed—for the simple reason that the predominant Conservative view remains that the Court of Justice *should* have interpreted Article 118a EC in a more restrictive manner.[28]

Discussing the scenario

Consider the shared competences of 'internal market' and 'social policy, for the aspects defined in this Treaty'. Could either of these be interpreted so as to permit the 'ending' of seasonal time changes? Why or why not?

5.3 Subsidiarity as a competence limit

As explained in Section 4.5, the principle of subsidiarity aims to prevent the EU legislating in areas of shared competences where it does not *need* to, by means of forcing the Commission to prove that the Member States simultaneously cannot *sufficiently* achieve a given objective, *and* that the EU can achieve that objective *better*. However, before we conclude that it is an effective 'limit' on the EU's legislative powers, we have to consider if it actually achieves that aim.

The Lisbon Treaty's articulation of the principle sets out the following procedural safeguards to limit the possibility for the EU to 'overreach' in exercising shared competences:

- The Commission must conduct detailed impact assessments, consulting widely and providing quantitative evidence supporting the need for EU action where possible, to justify a piece of legislation in a shared competence area.

[26] Julia Lourie, *The Working Time Directive* (HoC Research Paper 96/106, 19 November 1996) 5.

[27] For a brief but accurate discussion of the Major government 'opt-out' and its effect on the Working Time Directive, see Darren Newman, 'The UK Never Had an Opt-out from the Working Time Directive' (13 July 2015) https://darrennewman.wordpress.com/2015/07/13/the-uk-never-had-an-opt-out-from-the-working-time-directive/.

[28] See, eg, http://www.huffingtonpost.co.uk/entry/michael-gove-accused-of-wanting-to-steal-holiday-days-from-workers_uk_5a368916e4b0ff955ad3d3e0.

- Where national parliaments object to the Commission's proposal, they can use the Early Warning Mechanism to (at a minimum) request the Commission to reconsider its proposal.
- When, following adoption, a Member State government remains unconvinced that the adopted piece of legislation satisfies the principle of subsidiarity, it can start an infringement action before the Court of Justice.

The limited impact of the Early Warning Mechanism was flagged up in Section 4.5, but we will explore its shortcomings here in more detail. Following that, we will consider what has historically been the primary focus of most commentators: the wording of Article 5(3) TEU itself makes it almost impossible for the principle of subsidiarity to actually achieve the goals it has set out, and that in turn results in very low-level judicial scrutiny of the principle.

5.3.1 The Early Warning Mechanism's shortcomings

The process set out in Protocol 2 to the Lisbon Treaty is intended to give national parliaments a role in the scrutiny of legislation, and in particular, aims at enabling them to prevent the EU from legislating in a way that contravenes the principle of subsidiarity.

The fact that 10 years of Early Warning Mechanism practice has resulted in only three successful 'yellow cards' suggests one of three things: either the process as designed does not work, *or* the Member States simply are not interested in engaging with it, *or* the EU actually does not propose much legislation that the national parliaments object to on subsidiarity grounds.

There are clear procedural limitations to the Early Warning Mechanism.[29] For a start, it gives very little time to national parliaments *for* the purpose of scrutinizing EU legislative proposals: a total of eight weeks from their receipt of the Commission proposal. This may sound like an adequate stretch of time, but it must be remembered that this is being added in as an *additional* function to all the work national parliaments already carry out. New parliamentary committees to engage in the Mechanism may thus be necessary—and it is unlikely that those would be set up unless the Early Warning Mechanism was seen as being a very successful limit to EU legislative overreach.[30]

The thresholds applicable to both the 'yellow' and 'orange' card systems, as well as the consequences of the issuance of these cards, are in this sense also potentially problematic. Needing 18 'votes' just to have the Commission look again at its proposal, without any obligation to change it, may deter national parliaments from engaging in the work needed to issue a reasoned opinion where they are not sure that there will be significant agreement from *other* national parliaments. The 'orange card' threshold, of 27 votes, has simply never been reached: either this suggests significant national parliamentary happiness with all Commission legislative proposals since 2010, or that something about how the Early Warning Mechanism operates is not working optimally at this point in time, and the national parliaments do not act as 'watchdogs' of subsidiarity.[31]

[29] Pieter de Wilde, 'Why the Early Warning Mechanism Does not Alleviate the Democratic Deficit' (2012) OPAL Online Paper 6/2012. Available at https://papers.ssrn.com/sol3/papers.cfm?abstract_id=2128463.

[30] Note that research suggests that particularly strong anti-European sentiment in national parliaments *is* more likely to lead to 'yellow cards': see Martijn Huysmans, 'Europscepticism and the Early Warning Mechanism' (2018) 57(3) JCMS 431.

[31] Robert Schütze, *European Constitutional Law* (CUP, 2012).

If the lack of engagement with the Early Warning Mechanism is not purely down to how much time national parliaments have *to* engage with it, what might some of the other reasons be for the lack of 'yellow cards' issued?

Parliamentary disillusionment with the process may equally be a factor. In responding to the three successful 'yellow cards', the Commission twice informed the national parliaments that they were using the Early Warning Mechanism 'incorrectly': Goldoni observes that national parliaments effectively just registered their *unhappiness* with legislative proposals like the Monti II Regulation and the European Public Prosecutor's Office, but they did not specifically address in what ways these proposals failed on subsidiarity grounds.[32] The Commission abandoned both proposals—but arguably simply because they expected similar Member State opposition in the Council of Ministers, not because the principle of subsidiarity was successfully used to defend national interests.

The Posted Worker Directive's 'yellow card' showed even more clearly what the limitations of the Early Warning Mechanism are: despite significant numbers of national parliaments protesting the legislation, the Commission simply decided to pursue it anyway. National parliaments thus experienced first-hand that they cannot effectively *veto* EU legislative efforts, and the Commission needs to consider 'yellow card' complaints, but does not have to respond to them with any legislative changes. Some have argued this is simply not enough: a true commitment to both subsidiarity and democracy would give national parliaments greater powers, such as the ability to outright reject EU legislative proposals.[33]

Of course, one possible explanation for the lack of engagement—or at least, engagement by only limited numbers of parliaments—is that most Commission proposals simply do not offend on subsidiarity grounds. There are consequently those who argue that this demonstrates the problem with the principle of subsidiarity as it is written: it does not allow national parliaments to comment on the *content* of EU legislation, but rather only to comment on whether an EU objective should be achieved by the EU or the Member States themselves, and this is not what national parliaments are interested in. We consider this argument in Section 5.3.3.

Others, however, argue that it is important to take a broader view of what the Early Warning Mechanism enables; for example, Miklin has argued that whether or not 'subsidiarity' is being addressed by the Early Warning Mechanism, the increased attention paid to EU legislative action in national parliaments is a positive development, and may in and of itself result in increased national parliamentary engagement with EU legislative processes in a more general sense.[34] Similarly, Goldoni notes that even though the first two 'yellow cards' were rejected by the Commission as they did not address subsidiarity, the end result of their receipt remains that proposals that national parliaments were unhappy with were abandoned by the Commission.[35]

[32] Marco Goldoni, 'Reconstructing the Early Warning System on Subsidiarity: The case for political judgment' (2014) 39(5) ELRev 647.

[33] Davor Jancic, 'The Game of Cards: National parliaments in the EU and the future of the early warning mechanism and the political dialogue' (2015) 52(4) CMLRev 939; Marija Bartl, 'The Way We Do Europe: Subsidiarity and the substantive democratic deficit' (2015) 21(1) Eur Law J 23; Schütze (n 31).

[34] Eric Miklin, 'Beyond Subsidiarity: The indirect effect of the Early Warning System on national parliamentary scrutiny in European Union affairs' (2017) 24(3) JEPP 366.

[35] Goldoni (n 32) 659.

In short, we can see that there are legitimate concerns about the efficacy of the Early Warning Mechanism—but all the same, there may be 'competence limiting' benefits to it in spite of its shortcomings.

Pause for reflection

Some of the alternatives to the 'yellow' and 'orange' cards that have been proposed have been:

- A 'red' card: permitting either a single Member State, or a group of Member States, to 'veto' EU legislative proposals;
- A 'late' card: asking for national parliament interventions only after the EU legislators have considered the proposal (and have amended it where needed) and are ready to adopt it;
- A 'green' card: permitting national parliaments to group together to propose, rather than object to, EU legislative initiatives.

Which of these do you think best captures the spirit of the principle of subsidiarity? Do you think there are any risks in adopting these different cards?

5.3.2 The wording of the principle: national insufficiency

One possible reason as to why the Early Warning Mechanism is of limited effect has nothing to do with Protocol 2, and everything to do with the principle of subsidiarity itself.

Let us reconsider the actual wording of Article 5(3) TEU:

Article 5(3) TEU (emphasis added):

Under the principle of subsidiarity, in areas which do not fall within its exclusive competence, the Union shall act **only if and in so far as** the objectives of the proposed action cannot be **sufficiently** achieved by the Member States, either at central level or at regional and local level, but can rather, by reason of the scale or effects of the proposed action, be **better** achieved at Union level.

The **national insufficiency** test and the **comparative efficiency** test are both clearly visible in the wording of the principle. Chapter 4 used the example of driving laws to illustrate that both of these tests are not always passed in a given scenario where the EU may want to legislate—and here, in considering if subsidiarity has flaws as a 'limiting' principle, we can delve into that issue a little bit more.

Schütze points out that there is a problem with how the simultaneous conditions apply: they both deal in extremes.[36] What if, in a given scenario, the Member States can achieve a goal perfectly fine, but the EU can still achieve it better, or more efficiently?

[36] Schütze (n 31) 177–84.

The wording of Article 5(3) TEU does not help with that scenario, and it is one that the Member States are likely to try to argue before the Court of Justice. Does Article 5(3) TEU actually reserve power to the Member States when the EU can only prove that it would be more efficient to have an EU law in a given policy area?

If not, subsidiarity becomes less helpful to the individual Member State with every accession: the more Member States the EU comprises, the easier it becomes to prove that it will be more *efficient* to have a single EU law to accomplish a given goal. To see if it is a functional limit in practice, then, we need to consider in more detail how the Court of Justice has interpreted the principle.

The *Working Time Directive* judgment is a useful case study of how the Court deals with subsidiarity challenges (as well as challenges to competence) in practice. As highlighted in Chapter 4, the UK argued that, in essence, the Commission failed to adequately demonstrate (or even consider) that the subsidiarity 'calculator' of **national insufficiency** and **comparative efficiency** had been satisfied.

The CJEU's response to these arguments was as follows:

Case C-84/94 *UK v Council* [1996] ECLI:EU:C:1996:431 (emphasis added)

47. In that respect, it should be noted that it is the responsibility of the Council, under Article 118a, to adopt minimum requirements so as to contribute, through harmonization, to achieving the objective of raising the level of health and safety protection of workers which, in terms of Article 118a(1), is primarily the responsibility of the Member States. **Once the Council has found that it is necessary to improve the existing level of protection as regards the health and safety of workers and to harmonize the conditions in this area while maintaining the improvements made, achievement of that objective through the imposition of minimum requirements necessarily presupposes Community-wide action**, which otherwise, as in this case, leaves the enactment of the detailed implementing provisions required largely to the Member States.

The Court of Justice was unmoved by the UK's arguments—but that is not the most interesting outcome of the *Working Time Directive* case in light of the subsidiarity principle. Its *reasoning* as to why EU action was needed is instrumental. The Court found that if there was a determination by the Council that to achieve an objective, harmonization was needed, the logical outcome of such a determination was that EU action was needed: only the EU can *harmonize* Member State law. In that case, how could the Member States ever 'sufficiently' achieve this?

The *Working Time Directive* case is a representative example of how the Court engages with subsidiarity complaints. It has historically undertaken a very light-touch review of the measures at hand, and seems to regularly conclude that where the EU has decided that a policy area *should* be harmonized across the EU, the principle of subsidiarity is satisfied because only EU action *can* harmonize an area of law. This, in the words of Schütze, focuses on national insufficiency (eg, the Member States *cannot* harmonize), in a way that has 'short-circuited the comparative efficiency test'.[37] There is no assessment of whether or not EU action would actually be *better*, in an empirical sense, but only a finding that the Member States simply cannot do the thing that the EU can in 'harmonizing'. This leaves unexplored whether the Member States could perhaps achieve the goal set out by the Commission in its legislative proposal in different ways.

We may, however, be slowly starting to see a change to the Court's approach, in no small part due to the Commission's increased focus on detailed impact assessments. An illustrative example is the much more recent *Vodafone* case, dealing with an EU regulation that harmonized maximum roaming charges across the EU.[38] The regulation in question, Regulation 717/2007, fixed not only maximum charges that consumers could be charged, but also put a cap on so-called 'wholesale' charges. 'Wholesale charges' are what, for instance, Vodafone in the UK pays for a UK customer to be able to use the Vodafone network in Germany. The leading UK mobile phone providers banded together to challenge the regulation on a number of fronts: first, its legal basis (which was Article 114 TFEU), and second, if fixing maximum retail charges as well as wholesale charges was a violation of the principle of subsidiarity.

Case C-58/08 *Vodafone and Others* ECLI:EU:C:2010:321 (emphasis added)

50. By the second question, the referring court asks whether Regulation No 717/2007 infringes the **principles of proportionality and subsidiarity** by reason of the fact that it **imposes not only a ceiling for wholesale charges per minute**, but **also for retail charges**, and that it imposes an obligation to provide information about those charges to roaming customers.

. . .

55. . . . it must be recalled, first, that, before it drafted the proposal for the regulation, **the Commission carried out an exhaustive study**, the result of which is summarised in the impact assessment mentioned in paragraph 5 of this judgment. It follows that the Commission examined various options including, inter alia, the option of regulating retail charges only, or wholesale charges only, or both, and that it assessed the economic impact of those various types of regulation and the effects of different charging structures.

. . .

76. . . . it must be pointed out that the **[EU] legislature**, wishing to maintain competition among mobile telephone network operators, has, in adopting Regulation No 717/2007, **introduced a common approach**, in order in particular to contribute to the smooth functioning of the internal market, allowing those operators to act within a single coherent regulatory framework.

77. As is clear from recital 14 in the preamble to the regulation, **the interdependence of retail and wholesale charges for roaming services is considerable**, so that any measure

→

[37] Schütze (n 31) 183.

[38] C-58/08 *Vodafone and Others* ECLI:EU:C:2010:321.

→

seeking to reduce retail charges alone without affecting the level of costs for the wholesale supply of [EU]-wide roaming services would have been liable to disrupt the smooth functioning of the [EU]-wide roaming market. For that reason, **the Community legislature decided that any action would require a joint approach at the level of both wholesale charges and retail charges, in order to contribute to the smooth functioning of the internal market in those services.**

78. That interdependence means that the [EU] legislature could legitimately take the view that it had to intervene at the level of retail charges as well. Thus, **by reason of the effects of the common approach laid down in Regulation No 717/2007, the objective pursued by that regulation could best be achieved at [EU] level.**

While still not a detailed consideration of the Commission's impact assessment, there is clearly more in the Court's consideration of both proportionality and subsidiarity in these paragraphs than in paragraph 47 of the *Working Time Directive* case. There are allusions not only to the *efficiency* of a centralized EU measure, but also that it achieves goals that otherwise would not be met, and that this is what justifies EU-level action.

Per the Commission's impact assessment, roaming costs were increasing rapidly (but at different rates) in all the Member States, and this was bound to have negative effects on the internal market. For example, if using mobile telephones abroad is cheaper when resident in one Member State rather than in another, this would have an impact on business and personal usage across the EU. While national regulators could fix retail roaming costs set by mobile phone providers within their territories, they could not actually tackle the 'wholesale' charges, as those were set by a separate Member State. Similarly, an EU regulation that only tackled ceilings on 'wholesale charges' would not necessarily result in those cost reductions being passed on to consumers. In light of those considerations, and not simply that a single EU harmonizing measure is all that *could* harmonize the EU roaming market, the Court concluded that the regulation complied with the principle of subsidiarity.

That said, *Vodafone* (on the facts) is a fairly straightforward example of a situation where EU action is warranted. Conferral of powers on the EU, taking the form of legal bases like Article 114 TFEU, strongly suggests that the EU *will* be in charge of taking measures that help create (or prevent distortion in) the internal market. In examples such as the roaming market, particularly considering its 'wholesale' charges, there are very clearly cross-border effects, which the EU is better placed to deal with than the Member States. It is not clear that the Court would be as willing to engage in detailed judicial review of EU legislation adopted in other shared competence fields, like the environment or social policy, where there are no wide-reaching legislative bases for a 'common market' or 'common set of rules' elsewhere in the Treaties.

Concerns about how the Court engages with subsidiarity consequently cannot be dismissed out of hand. Under its 'harmonization' approach, we very quickly find that the principle does very little to limit EU legislative action, as wherever the EU has a harmonizing power, it will then be deemed 'the appropriate actor'. *Vodafone* may be the first sign of a Court more willing and able to engage with the measuring tests implied by Article 5(3) TEU; detailed impact assessments in any event enable greater scrutiny by the Court than was possible in 1993. We will, for now, have to wait and see if the Court is willing to engage in such scrutiny when a controversial 'subsidiarity' challenge next reaches it.

Discussing the scenario

In order to propose secondary legislation that will end seasonal time changes across the EU, the EU would have to produce a detailed impact assessment arguing that this is a necessary step in order to achieve an EU policy objective:

1. Why are seasonal time changes a policy that is of interest to the EU?
2. What kinds of issues would this impact assessment need to consider?

Consider the *Working Time Directive* and *Vodafone* cases as examples, and assume here that the Commission's proposal is based on Article 114 TFEU.

5.3.3 The wording of the principle: whose objectives?

Schütze is critical of the way the principle of subsidiarity fails to offer clarity on how to combine the national insufficiency and the comparative efficiency tests, and what this results in when the Court has to assess if EU measures comply with the principle. Those concerns can, at least in theory, be ameliorated by the Court engaging in a more detailed review of the gains produced by an EU measure (in place of differing national measures). However, at least one other commentator believes the problem with subsidiarity to be a more substantial one: Davies argues strongly that the principle, as set out in Article 5(3) TEU, simply does not deal with the concerns that the Member States actually have.[39]

Key in this critique is the fact that Article 5(3) TEU discusses 'objectives of the measure' at two different points, but they are always the *same* objectives. What Davies concludes from that is that the principle of subsidiarity deals, at most, with workload allocation. Article 5(3) TEU thus sets out two alternatives that in practice are unlikely to enthuse the Member States: either *they* can legislate to achieve an EU goal, or *the EU* can legislate to achieve an EU goal. But what about Member State goals and objectives?

Fears of a 'federal' Europe are unlikely to be rooted in the fact that the EU rather than the Member States is the drafter of legislation that would otherwise be identical; they are rooted in concerns that Member States' own identity, own policy goals, and distinct national priorities are going to be overridden by EU law. This is the difference between an argument over whether the EU or the Member States draft the law that requires everyone in the EU to drive on the right side of the road, and an argument as to whether or not *driving on the left side should be possible* in those Member States who want it. Subsidiarity might, in other words, make it so that the UK writes its own detailed law changing the road rules—but given the way it is written, it cannot prevent the UK being told that 'driving on the right side of the road' is the goal that it should be trying to meet, providing the EU can connect that goal to one of its competences.

Davies, too, is critical of the Court's approach, which usually justifies EU-level legislative activity when 'harmonization' is the goal of a measure, simply because the Member States cannot harmonize legislation across the EU themselves. But, he argues, in such a literal reading of the measure at hand, the Court seemingly ignores why there are shared

[39] Gareth Davies, 'Subsidiarity: The wrong idea, in the wrong place, at the wrong time' (2006) 43 CMLRev 63.

competences in the first place: these are areas where the Member States were not conferring *all* legislative power on the EU, but rather recognized that *some* EU action might be necessary alongside national action. A proper interpretation of a principle intended to ensure appropriate balancing between EU and Member State competences, according to Davies, consequently requires an assessment of both EU and Member State interests. Until that happens, the principle merely determines *who* advances the EU's goals—but the only goals that matter, in terms of EU legislative power, are those of the EU.

In the Davies version of subsidiarity, Member States at most retain the power to implement law in areas of shared competences, but they do not have an explicit ability to stop the EU from making law altogether. Rather than being a limit to EU legislative powers, the principle of subsidiarity then at most offers to the Member States what the legal form of the 'directive' also does: it gives the Member States the ability to choose *how* to achieve an EU objective.

Pause for reflection

Consider Davies' criticism of subsidiarity. Do you agree with it? And, if Davies is right about how the Court will apply the principle of subsidiarity, what is the most the UK could accomplish in a legal challenge to a piece of EU legislation?

5.3.4 In defence of subsidiarity?

However, as with most controversial aspects of EU law, there is a different way to look at the principle. Craig advances a number of arguments as to why Davies' take on subsidiarity is too cynical, and does not realistically capture either the EU legislative process or the Court's review process of subsidiarity.[40]

The starting point for suggesting that concerns about subsidiarity are overstated is that it does not, in practice, seem to be as big an issue as academic commentary may make it appear to be. Since 1992, there have been fewer than ten challenges to EU legislation on the basis of subsidiarity.[41] Striking here is that in about half of these subsidiarity challenges to a piece of legislation, other Member States also intervened in order to defend the legislation in question. This suggests that while, occasionally, a single Member State may have a particular concern about a piece of EU legislation, the EU legislature does not seem to offend Member States generally with its approach to the principle of subsidiarity.

Craig's second point about subsidiarity is that it is, in effect, a 'back-up' measure to stop EU legislation from overly encroaching into Member State territory. This is in part evidenced by how few challenges there have been to EU legislation on the basis of subsidiarity, as nearly all of the time, Member State concerns have been dealt with via the EU's general legislative processes already. More importantly, he argues that the Treaties already balance

[40] Paul Craig, 'Subsidiarity: A Political and Legal Analysis' (2012) 50(1) JCMS 72.

[41] A search of the eur-lex.europa.eu in early 2020 suggests that there were only six cases in which the principle was specifically raised, and only five in which the parties actually based an argument on it.

Member State and EU interests. The extended negotiations about the Lisbon Treaty resulted in agreement about how competences should be defined, and this has clearly resulted in *some* policy areas being a pure EU concern and *other* policy areas being fully outside of EU legislative range. Suggesting that the principle of subsidiarity is an indication that this division of competences does not work is perhaps an overstatement: for one thing, it only applies to shared competences where there was already political agreement on power-sharing.

Furthermore, Davies' version of subsidiarity ignores how legislation is actually adopted in the EU. Consider Article 11 TEU, as discussed in Chapter 3:

Article 11 TEU (emphasis added)

1. The institutions shall, by appropriate means, give **citizens and representative associations** the opportunity to **make known and publicly exchange their views** in all areas of Union action.
2. The institutions shall maintain an **open, transparent and regular dialogue with representative associations and civil society.**
3. The European Commission shall carry out **broad consultations with parties concerned in order to ensure that the Union's actions are coherent and transparent.**

The obligations set out here mean that the Commission cannot arrive at a policy 'objective' without extensive consultation of both EU-level interest groups *and* national-level stakeholders, both on the content of a given proposal *and* the form it should take (eg, a directive or a regulation). Where something the Commission wishes to propose meets significant opposition during consultations, the Commission is unlikely to proceed—not least because that national-level opposition indicates that the Parliament and the Council are very unlikely to actually adopt the legislation in question. After all, the institutions that adopt EU legislation represent, respectively, the Member State governments and EU citizens.[42]

Craig adds together the very small number of subsidiarity challenges and the fact that the legislative process involves national interests at several points to suggest that perhaps, while the principle of subsidiarity is imperfectly drafted and difficult to judicially enforce, there simply is not much of a problem in terms of the EU treading too far into Member State territory in areas of shared competences. At that point, concerns about subsidiarity are, for lack of a better way to put it, 'academic'.

Discussing the scenario

Consider Craig's comments in light of the EU's legislative processes, as detailed in Section 4.3.

1. At which points can someone representing the UK provide input to the Commission proposal to end seasonal time changes?
2. Is input likely to have an effect (ie, will it stop the legislation from being adopted)? Why or why not?

[42] See Chapter 2.

5.4 **Proportionality as a competence limit?**

As discussed in Section 4.6, subsidiarity is only the first of two Treaty-based limitations on the EU's exercise of its legislative competences. The second, the **principle of proportionality**, sets out *how* the EU can act when exercising its legislative powers.

Article 5(4) TEU

Under the principle of proportionality, the content and form of Union action shall not exceed what is necessary to achieve the objectives of the Treaties.

The *Fedesa* case tells us what this principle requires according to the CJEU.[43] First, the EU must demonstrate that its action is **suitable** to achieve a given objective. Secondly, the EU must also demonstrate that its action is the *least invasive* possible action that will achieve the objective in question. This is what makes a legislative intervention **necessary** as opposed to excessive. Are these difficult tests to satisfy before the Court?

The Court's ruling in *Fedesa* indicates, much like the *Working Time Directive* case discussed in Sections 5.2 and 5.3, a reluctance on the part of the Court to question the EU legislature's decisions to legislate. However, while in subsidiarity assessments, it has simply pointed to 'harmonization' as being a goal only the EU can achieve, proportionality assessments of the same cases require it to come to a finding about whether or not the *way* in which the EU goes about said 'harmonization' is suitable and necessary. The Court consequently fleshed out the meaning of Article 5(4) TEU in *Fedesa* as requiring that EU action is not '**manifestly inappropriate**'.[44] That is a high bar for EU legislation to meet—and, indeed, the Court has proven to be very reluctant to strike down EU legislation because it was disproportionate.

The *Vodafone* case offers a recent example of the Court's approach to proportionality, as well as to subsidiarity. As set out in Section 5.3.2, the Court was asked to consider if setting fixed charges for both retail and wholesale charges for roaming complied with the principles of proportionality and subsidiarity.

Case C-58/08 *Vodafone and Others* ECLI:EU:C:2010:321 (emphasis added)

52. With regard to judicial review of compliance with those conditions the Court has accepted that in the exercise of the powers conferred on it the Community legislature must be allowed a broad discretion in areas in which its action involves political, economic and social choices and in which it is called upon to undertake complex assessments and evaluations. **Thus the criterion to be applied is not whether a measure adopted in such an area was the only or the best possible measure, since its legality can be affected only**

[43] Case C-331/88 *R v Minister of Agriculture, Fisheries and Food ex parte Fedesa* ECLI:EU:C:1990:391, para 13.
[44] Ibid, para 15.

if the measure is manifestly inappropriate having regard to the objective which the competent institution is seeking to pursue . . .

53. However, even though it has a broad discretion, **the Community legislature must base its choice on objective criteria.** Furthermore, in assessing the burdens associated with various possible measures, **it must examine whether objectives pursued by the measure chosen are such as to justify even substantial negative economic consequences for certain operators.**

. . .

58. . . . the average level of retail charges for a roaming call in the Community at the time of adoption of Regulation No 717/2007 was high . . . the average retail charge for a roaming call was at that time EUR 1.15 per minute, or, in other words, as explained in the summary of the impact assessment, more than five times higher than the actual cost of providing the wholesale service.

59. The Eurotariff provided for in Article 4(2) of Regulation No 717/2007 has been set at a level that is significantly below that average charge. Furthermore, the ceilings on charges introduced in that article are set, as is clear from point 3 of the explanatory memorandum to the proposal for a regulation, in relation to the ceilings for the corresponding wholesale charges, so that the retail charges reflect more accurately the costs incurred by providers.

60. In those circumstances, the introduction by that provision of ceilings for retail charges **must be considered to be appropriate for the purpose** of protecting consumers against high levels of charges.

. . .

68. In those circumstances, and particularly in the light of the broad discretion which the Community legislature has in the area at issue, which involves choices to be made of an economic nature, requiring complex assessments and evaluations, **it could legitimately take the view that regulation of the wholesale market alone would not achieve the same result as regulation such as that at issue, which covers at the same time the wholesale market and the retail market, and that the latter was therefore necessary.**

We see *Vodafone* taking a significantly more detailed look at the Commission's impact assessment than the *Fedesa* 'manifestly inappropriate' standard would suggest necessary. There is an evaluation here of quantitative data as well as argumentation made by the Commission in proposing the legislation and in the recitals to the legislation: and only on the basis of considering these factors does the Court conclude that the legislation is not 'manifestly inappropriate'.

Does proportionality then provide the check to EU legislative action that subsidiarity does not quite manage to?

Davies, in his criticism of the Court's treatment of the subsidiarity principle, notes that it proportionately has significant potential to *actually* work as a brake on EU legislative initiatives, but only under certain conditions. The Court must consider not only whether a piece of EU legislation helps achieve a goal in the least invasive way, but also whether what the EU is doing is *proportionate* to the importance of the goal itself.[45] This is the difference between, say, concluding that an EU-wide speed limit would reduce road accidents better than any other 'road safety' measures, and thus imposing an EU-wide speed limit is 'proportionate', and concluding that because driving on the left side of the road might result in one or two more accidents a year, it is proportionate to ban it altogether, regardless of how integral a cultural practice it is in four of the Member States.

Paragraph 53 of the *Vodafone* judgment seems to be acknowledging such concerns to an extent: by not only investigating if the EU measure is suitable and necessary, but also if its negative effects are disproportionate to what the measure achieves. However, it looks at negative effects on *economic operators*—not negative impact on national traditions and so it does not actually address Member State concerns so much as overarching economic concerns.

Assessing 'true proportionality', as Davies terms it, would not only stop the EU from producing legislation that is unsuitable and excessive in order to achieve a goal, but would acknowledge that not all EU goals are more important than Member State goals. The current Court approach to proportionality ignores that Member States might have those goals, which makes it difficult to see what EU action would be disproportionate *to*. As a consequence, Davies finds that neither of the limits set out in Article 5 TEU actually balances Member State interests against EU interests—and consequently shared competences are not genuinely 'shared', but rather function more like EU competences that the EU simply has not yet exercised fully.

Discussing the scenario

Would the Commission proposal to end seasonal time changes satisfy the proportionality principle as set out in *Fedesa* and *Vodafone*? Would it also satisfy Davies' 'true proportionality' test?

Craig disagrees with the notion that subsidiarity is best replaced with a stricter form of proportionality test which investigates the level of respect for Member State values and priorities an EU legislative proposal exhibits.[46] He has various grounds for opposition: the first is that what Davies proposes seems to ignore the actual text of the Treaty, which is a strange way to attempt to acknowledge Member State priorities, given that they *ratified* that text.

His more substantial concerns are about whether a switch to 'true proportionality' analysis before the Court reasoning is feasible and worthwhile. 'True proportionality' requires the Court to consider if an incursion on Member State interests is disproportionate in light of what the EU is trying to achieve. Problematically, however, it would be asked to make such an assessment in light of concerns on the part of *one* Member State, despite the fact that a *majority* of the Member States will have voted to adopt the legislation in the Council. Otherwise, it would not have been adopted. Engaging in a 'true

[45] Davies (n 39). [46] Craig (n 40).

proportionality' assessment consequently may result in the Court siding with a single Member State who was outvoted in the Council—thus effectively overruling the normal EU legislative process, and now potentially 26 other Member States' views. Is this something the Court should engage in?

Craig suggests that Member States' concerns about the EU's 'competence creep' may simply echo a discomfort with the increasing powers conferred on the EU. In any event, there is no indication that a 'true proportionality' examination would actually result in a fundamental difference in terms of its decisions in cases like *Vodafone*, the *Working Time Directive*, or *Fedesa*. Indeed, it is difficult to see how any Member State would convincingly argue that an unregulated mobile telephone market is a matter of 'national interest', or how limiting the work week out of health and safety concerns outweighs the 'national value' of permitting employers to not allow workers a reasonable rest period. As a consequence, Article 5 TEU, to Craig, seems to accomplish what it is intended to: it regulates the entire legislative process and ensures that the EU does not take action that is generally undesired by the Member States, rather than permitting a single Member State to protest a law that the other Member States wished to see adopted.

5.5 Brexit and limits to EU legislative powers

Leaving the EU is, on the surface of it, the ultimate solution to 'competence creep' concerns. Post-Brexit, further EU legislation will by and large be a non-issue in most of the UK. For business purposes, it might be interesting and worthwhile for the UK to continue to follow the EU on issues such as seasonal time changes—but such alignment will be optional, rather than obligatory, and thus control will have been taken back in a concrete manner.

However, more generally, depending on the actual relationship struck with the EU post-Brexit, portions of EU law might nonetheless have a significant impact on the UK in terms of what legislation it can produce and what policy priorities it can maintain. A close relationship to the EU's internal market will require a lot of regulatory 'similarity': whether that is in terms of outcome, and so recognition of equivalence between the EU and the UK, or in terms of content, and thus UK adoption of the EU rules, is a matter of detail.

5.5.1 The Withdrawal Agreement

We can be brief about 'competence creep' concerns and what happens to them under the October 2019 Withdrawal Agreement: they remain as described in this chapter, though the shortcomings of the principle of subsidiarity may feel amplified during the transition period because the UK will not be represented in any of the EU's law-making institutions.[47] There was significant debate in the UK during the Article 50 TEU negotiations about the extent to which *new* EU laws would apply to the UK during the transition period, during which the UK will no longer be represented in the EU's legislative institutions.[48] Depending on the length of the transition period, it is not unthinkable that *some*

[47] Withdrawal Agreement, Article 7.

[48] See https://www.independent.co.uk/news/uk/politics/brexit-transition-period-uk-britain-vet-eu-laws-theresa-may-david-davis-michel-barnier-a8183071.html.

EU law will come into force that the UK was not able to protest in the EU's institutional forums—and that does undermine Craig's defence of subsidiarity.[49]

However, this has to be considered in context: the situation that the UK will find itself in is *not that* of EU membership. In order to escape the reach of EU law more generally, a transition period to untangle the UK and EU legal orders was deemed necessary by the negotiating teams, and so this short period of less input into EU legislation was deemed acceptable. This situation does not work as a more general commentary on how well the principle of subsidiarity works to protect the Member States, but rather highlights that in *not* being a Member State, the UK will experience different problems than those the Member States themselves do. We come back to this in Section 5.5.3

5.5.2 The Protocol on Ireland/Northern Ireland

As ever, Northern Ireland is in a different situation from the remainder of the UK. The issues raised in Section 5.5.1 regarding representation in the EU institutions also apply to Northern Ireland under the Protocol on Ireland/Northern Ireland—but they apply there indefinitely. We discussed in Chapter 3 how Article 18 of the October 2019 Protocol on Ireland/Northern Ireland contains a 'democratic consent mechanism'—but that mechanism only permits the abandonment of the entire Protocol, rather than a specific bit of EU law that applies in Northern Ireland and that the UK feels is contrary to the principle of subsidiarity or otherwise *ultra vires*.

The Protocol acknowledges that the EU *may* adopt new legislation that will fall within the scope of the Protocol, and is not simply an updated version of one of the pieces of EU law already listed in the Annexes. In this case, Article 13(4) requires the EU to 'inform' the UK that such legislation is being adopted—and if the UK requests it, the Joint Committee 'shall hold an exchange of views on the implications' of that new EU measure. In a situation where the UK does not want this new EU act to apply to Northern Ireland, under the Protocol, the Joint Committee will try to find a resolution that maintains 'the good functioning' of the Protocol. If it cannot, Article 13(4) of the Protocol allows the EU to take so-called 'remedial measures'. What these are is not further specified—but the Protocol presumably is referring to an ability for the EU to apply punitive trade measures against the UK as a whole until the UK restores the 'good functioning' of the Protocol.

This is very different from what the UK could do as a Member State to object to EU legislation. Granted, it concerns a smaller volume of EU legislation—in that only internal market law affecting trade in goods, including agricultural products and live animals, is addressed by the Protocol—but that legislation will already be adopted by the time the UK gets to express an opinion on it, and they will not be able to protest its existence before the CJEU on any grounds. This is, of course, a logical consequence of not being *in* the EU—but given that parts of EU law continue to apply to parts of the UK all the same, it is very striking nonetheless.

[49] The transition period can be extended by one or two years under the Withdrawal Agreement, Article 126 and Article 132; note that the EU (Withdrawal Agreement) Act 2020, s 33, prohibits UK representatives from asking for an extension as a matter of domestic law—though as is true for all Acts of Parliament, this can obviously be amended if an extension is desired after all.

5.5.3 The future relationship

The October 2019 Political Declaration suggests that the UK will be seeking a rather 'basic' free trade agreement with the EU, in which case adoption of or alignment with EU rules will in principle not be an issue for the UK as a whole. However, this, too, is making a complex issue sound simpler than it is in reality.

Even if EU law is no longer binding automatically on the UK, it can nonetheless have a significant impact on the development of UK law. EU regulations on financial services, for instance, are likely to have a deep impact on a nationally very important UK sector—but they will no longer necessarily fit with UK priorities at all, and it is not impossible that the UK, as a non-EU Member State, will simply be left with a choice between adjusting to the new EU regulations, or not being able to trade with the EU in financial services.

A further complicating factor is, once again, Northern Ireland.

Protocol on Ireland and Northern Ireland, Article 6(2) (emphasis added)

Having regard to Northern Ireland's integral place in the United Kingdom's internal market, the Union and the United Kingdom shall use **their best endeavours to facilitate the trade between Northern Ireland and other parts of the United Kingdom**, in accordance with applicable legislation and taking into account their respective regulatory regimes as well as the implementation thereof.

Article 6(2) is a unilateral commitment made by the UK—but one that is part of the Protocol all the same. What it means is that the UK is committing to making it as *easy as possible* for goods produced in the UK to be sent to Northern Ireland. Northern Ireland, in this scenario, will be subject to EU law—and any products that are not compliant with EU law will experience more substantial checks at the border with Northern Ireland, even if they are arriving from within the United Kingdom. Making trade between Great Britain and Northern Ireland as easy as possible, in line with 'best endeavours' as Article 6(2) promises, thus seems to imply that the UK will adopt regulations as *close as possible* to those that the EU (and Northern Ireland) are upholding.

Taking back full legislative 'control' might thus be a misnomer: in many areas, national decisions can once again be taken where they cannot as a full EU member, as the EU has pre-empted national action. However, national decisions may in practice simply follow EU ones, for the sake of the continuity of business relationships as well as promises such as those made to Northern Ireland in the Protocol.

5.6 In conclusion

The competences set out in the Lisbon Treaty are perhaps not fully clear, but they are arguably as clear as any set of 'general policy areas' can be. More rigid descriptions would unduly limit EU action, and might require constant Treaty amendment. Whilst this rigidity could perhaps prevent 'competence creep', it would also prevent the EU from achieving any of its goals.

The legality principles set out in Article 5 TEU similarly have their problems, and persuasive arguments have been put forward to attempt to bolster both of them. All the same, is it genuinely the case that the Member States have no tools with which to stop the EU legislating against their fundamental interests? These concerns remain alive, but generally appear to be somewhat overstated, and reflect more on the fact that the EU has transitioned increasingly to QMV decision-making than on the fact that subsidiarity and proportionality have shortcomings as 'checks' on EU legislative action. Member States occasionally get outvoted, and generally do not like it when this happens. However, they of course ultimately retain the final 'check': they can leave the EU if they genuinely think it is moving in a direction that is wholly incompatible with national interests, values, and priorities, as we have now seen in the UK.

Discussing the scenario

Consider the EU legislative process as a whole. What could the UK have done to stop the Commission's proposal to end seasonal time changes from being adopted? And if the proposal to end seasonal time changes had been adopted by the EU legislature, would the UK have been able to have this overturned via CJEU review?

A sample approach to a response can be found online.

Key points

- The Lisbon Treaty has spelled out the competences, but concerns about 'competence creep' remain because of **flexible Treaty provisions** such as Articles 114 and 352 TFEU; the **doctrine of implied powers;** and CJEU **interpretation** of the Treaties, which uses teleology to read provisions wider than the Member States might intend.
- The **principle of subsidiarity** in theory works well to limit EU 'overreach' in areas of shared competence, but critics like Schütze note that its drafting results in a conflict between **national insufficiency** and **comparative efficiency**, particularly when the CJEU assesses EU legislative action; and Davies argues that subsidiarity fails to balance Member State and EU priorities as it promises to.
- The **principle of proportionality** has been raised as an alternative to subsidiarity—though the Court's assessments of proportionality have also been criticized. Davies thinks that 'true' proportionality assessment will result in the balancing of priorities that is missing in subsidiarity. However, Craig argues that this is untested, and that, in any event, Member State interests are appropriately represented through the existing legislative processes in the EU.
- Leaving the EU is in principle the only solution to genuinely limit the impact of EU legislation in the UK—but the **form of leaving** has significant impacts on the extent to which EU legislation nonetheless continues to impact on the UK legal order. In a **close relationship**, such as the one negotiated for Northern Ireland, the key difference with membership will be that the UK will simply no longer be able to contest the EU's use of legal bases or its compliance with subsidiarity and proportionality.

Assess your learning

1. Out of the 'grey competence areas' that the Lisbon Treaty retains, which appears the most threatening to Member State 'control' over the EU, and why? (See Section 5.2.)
2. From what you now know about the principles of subsidiarity and proportionality, do you think the CJEU should be more involved in addressing issues of subsidiarity and proportionality, or are these political concepts that the Member States and the EU should iron out during the legislative process? (Consider how engaged the CJEU is at the moment in your response—see Sections 5.3 and 5.4.)

Further reading

Marija Bartl, 'The Way We Do Europe: Subsidiarity and the substantive democratic deficit' (2015) 21(1) Eur Law J 23.

Paul Craig, 'Subsidiarity: A Political and Legal Analysis' (2012) 50(1) JCMS 72.

Gareth Davies, 'Subsidiarity: The Wrong Idea, in the Wrong Place, at the Wrong Time' (2006) 43 CMLRev 63.

Katjana Gattermann and Claudia Hefftler, 'Beyond Institutional Capacity: Political Motivation and Parliamentary Behaviour in the Early Warning System' (2015) 38(2) West Eur Polit 305.

Thomas Horsley, 'Subsidiarity and the European Court of Justice: Missing pieces in the subsidiarity jigsaw' (2012) 50(2) JCMS 267.

Martijn Huysmans, 'Euroscepticism and the Early Warning Mechanism' (2018) 57(3) JCMS 431.

Davor Jancic, 'The Game of Cards: National parliaments in the EU and the future of the early warning mechanism and the political dialogue' (2015) 52(4) CMLRev 939.

Jacob Oberg, 'The Rise of the Procedural Paradigm: Judicial review of EU legislation in vertical competence disputes' (2017) 13(2) Eur Const Law Rev 248.

Carlo Panara, 'The Enforceability of Subsidiarity in the EU and the Ethos of Cooperative Federalism: A comparative law perspective' (2016) 22(2) EPL 305.

Gerhard van der Schyff, 'The Constitutional Relationship between the European Union and its Member States: The role of national identity in article 4(2) TEU' (2012) 37(5) ELRev 563.

Online resources

Visit www.oup.com/he/demars1e for a sample approach to discussing the scenario.

6

The relationship between EU and national law

Context for this chapter

'The National Courts share responsibility for enforcing EU law with the European Court of Justice. Any person or company has a right to take the UK Government (or in some cases another person or company) to a UK court for failure to comply with EU law. Where a domestic court finds that someone has breached EU law, it will take the necessary steps to ensure EU law is given effect, which may include disapplying national legislation that conflicts with it.'

HM Government, 'Rights and obligations of European Union Membership' (April 2016) para 2.30

6.1 Introduction

The first five chapters of this book explained the history and functioning of the EU, including its law-making powers. By now, you will have a clearer picture of the EU as an international organization that creates its own laws. This chapter, as well as Chapters 7 and 8, consider how the EU legal order interacts with the pre-existing domestic legal orders in the Member States.

The Treaties, unfortunately, do not have much to say on these matters. One of the biggest questions facing the EU and its Member States when the European project commenced in 1957 was consequently what would happen when these two distinct legal systems clashed. When an EU law contradicts a domestic law, what is to be done? Who decides? And if the answer to this is 'EU law', what does this suggest about the sovereignty of EU Member States?

This final question was one that resurfaced in the 2016 referendum campaign. The context for this chapter is taken from a report that the UK government was obliged to produce under the European Union Act 2015 (which legislated for the 2016 referendum to take place).

It sets out rather plainly that there will be times when domestic courts in the UK will set aside national law, enacted by Parliament, in favour of EU law—but that is a concept that challenges the very notion of 'parliamentary sovereignty' that is so fundamental to the UK constitution. Can Parliament truly still be 'sovereign' if EU law will (and, seemingly, *must*) take precedence over UK legislation, as the April 2016 report says?

This chapter explores the answer to this question by examining the relationship between EU law and national law. Following adoption of the EEC Treaty, the Court of Justice was left to determine how EU law and national law could work together. Its case law on the hierarchical relationship between EU law and national law is fundamental to the operation of the EU, but was received with distinct discomfort in some of the Member States.

We will first explore the CJEU's jurisprudence on what is known as the doctrine of supremacy of EU law, and then spend significant time considering how supremacy has been received in Germany and the UK. While this book focuses on how EU law works in the UK, it is important to understand that the UK's relationship with aspects of EU law is not always an outlier—and, as such, we will use Germany as a case study of a different Member State that remains to date uncomfortable with the notion of the supremacy of EU law. Once we have looked at how the German and UK legal orders interact with EU law, in light of the doctrine of supremacy, we will return to the question of whether 'parliamentary sovereignty' is compatible with EU membership.

6.2 Supremacy of EU law

As noted, one of the first crucial questions the CJEU was faced with involved a logical consequence of the EU establishing its own legal order, and each Member State having a pre-existing separate legal order to boot. What happens in a situation where national law and EU law say incompatible things—say, when a national law contradicts a right or obligation set out in the EU Treaties or in EU secondary legislation?

Bizarrely, the drafters of the Treaties acted as if the EU legal order and the Member State legal orders sit 'side by side' and so such clashes would never occur. The reality is, of course, that these legal orders will interact, and the laws produced in the EU must have effects in the Member States or the EU's goals will never be achieved.

6.2.1 Clashes between legal orders

The question of how to resolve clashes between domestic and EU law came before the CJEU in the seminal case *Van Gend en Loos*.[1] A Dutch company called Van Gend en Loos imported a product from (then) West Germany to the Netherlands. The Dutch customs authorities charged them a tariff on the import. Van Gend en Loos objected, submitting that the tariff was contrary to the Treaty of Rome, which (under what is now Article 30 TFEU) forbade the introduction of customs duties between the Member States.

In order to get the product into the Netherlands, Van Gend en Loos paid the customs charge, but sought to be refunded for it in a Dutch national court. That court referred a crucial question to the CJEU: can a private party like Van Gend en Loos rely directly on the Treaties in a national court?

[1] Case 26/62 *Van Gend en Loos* ECLI:EU:C:1963:1.

We will return to the Court's answer to that question in Chapter 8—but in coming to the answer, the CJEU made a very important observation about the *nature* of the EU legal order:

Case 26/62 *Van Gend en Loos* ECLI:EU:C:1963:1 (emphasis added)

The [Union] constitutes **a new legal order of international law** for the benefit of which the states **have limited their sovereign rights . . .**

This served as the setup for the judgment in the equally seminal case of *Costa v ENEL*, in which the CJEU elaborated on the consequence of this 'limitation' of sovereign rights.[2]

In *Costa*, the CJEU was faced with an Italian national who opposed the nationalization of energy utilities in Italy, which was taking place via domestic legislation adopted after Italy joined the EEC. He had shares in a private company subject to nationalization processes—ENEL—and, to make his protest heard, refused to pay his electricity bill to them. He was sued by ENEL, but when in front of the Italian court, argued that the Italian law nationalizing ENEL was contrary to the Treaty of Rome, as it would affect competition in the internal market unfairly.

The Italian government, in protest, argued that this was not a matter that Mr Costa could raise in court. The nationalization policy was a government policy, and its compliance with Treaty obligations was for the Italian government to consider: the Treaty, after all, was addressed to the Member States and not to individuals. It also raised Italian Constitutional Court case law that suggested that the EEC Treaty did not take priority over Italian legislation—and so under the principle of *lex posterior,* the most recent law should be applied. The Italian court hearing the case referred two questions as to who was right to the CJEU. Could Mr Costa complain about the incompatibility of this Italian national law with the Treaties, and did this 'later' Italian national law override the Treaties?

The CJEU agreed in part with the Italian government, in that it found that Mr Costa could not ask the CJEU to rule on the compatibility of Italian law with the Treaties' provisions on competition and state aid, simply because the relevant part of the Treaty was directly addressed *to* the Member State and could only be enforced by the Commission. However, in rejecting that question, the CJEU revisited the idea it had introduced in *Van Gend* in far greater detail by considering what happens, generally, if there is a clash between a national law and an EU law.

Case 6/64 *Costa* ECLI:EU:C:1964:66 (emphasis added)

By contrast with ordinary international treaties, the [Treaty of Rome] has created its own legal system which . . . became an integral part of the legal systems of the Member States and which their courts are bound to apply.

By creating a [Union] of unlimited duration, having its own institutions, its own personality, its own legal capacity and capacity of representation on the international plane and, more particularly, real powers stemming from a limitation of sovereignty of a **transfer of powers from the states to the [Union], the Member States have limited their sovereign rights . . .**

→

[2] Case 6/64 *Costa v ENEL (Costa)* ECLI:EU:C:1964:66.

→

The integration into the laws of each Member State of provisions which derive from the [Treaty], and more generally the terms and spirit of the Treaty, make it impossible for the [Member] States . . . to accord precedence to a unilateral and subsequent measure over a legal system accepted by them on a basis of reciprocity.

The executive force of [Treaty] law cannot vary from one state to another in deference to subsequent domestic laws, without jeopardizing the attainment of the objectives of the Treaty.

The obligations undertaken under the Treaty establishing the [Union] would not be unconditional, but merely contingent if they could be called in question by subsequent acts of [Member States].

The precedence of [Treaty] law is confirmed by Article [288 TFEU], whereby a regulation 'shall be binding' and 'directly applicable in all Member States.' This provision, which is subject to no reservation, would be quite meaningless if a state could unilaterally nullify its effects by means of a legislative measure which could prevail over [Treaty] law.

It follows from all these observations that the law stemming from the Treaty, an independent source of law, could not, because of its special and original nature, be overridden by domestic legal provisions, however framed . . .

There are several interesting things happening in *Costa*. While it might read as the CJEU 'philosophizing' about the nature of the EU, the CJEU here actually established that if the European 'project' was ever going to work, its rules should have precedence over conflicting national law adopted at a later point in time. Not only that, but it implied that the Member States knew this when they had written the Treaty of Rome: after all, they had indicated that regulations should apply immediately within the Member States, but EU regulations would be meaningless if domestic law could just set out the exact opposite a week after the adoption of those regulations.

Opinions were divided at the time on the extent to which the CJEU 'interpreted' the Treaty or 'made new law' in *Costa*. While it was clear that there was some implied limitation of sovereignty in signing up to a Community that could create its own law, the CJEU took the concept of a regulation and applied it to *all* EU law: it found that *any* law stemming from the Treaty would in effect be 'directly applicable' and so should take precedence over national law. Article 288 TFEU, as we considered in Chapter 4, restricts that concept to regulations alone. The forceful note on which the CJEU ended its findings in *Costa* did not necessarily endear it to the Member States:

Case 6/64 *Costa* ECLI:EU:C:1964:66 (emphasis added)

The transfer by the States from their domestic legal system to the [Union] legal system of the rights and obligations arising under the Treaty carries with it a permanent limitation of their sovereign rights, against which a subsequent unilateral act incompatible with the concept of the [EU] cannot prevail.

This 'permanent limitation of sovereignty', which meant that EU law would always take precedence over 'incompatible' domestic law, is now more generally known as the principle of 'primacy' or 'supremacy'. For the sake of simplicity, we will call it supremacy in this book.

6.2.2 The principle of supremacy

We primarily find the effects of *Costa* and the doctrine of supremacy in domestic case law. When a national court observes that a national law clashes with an EU law, they must set aside that national law. The EU legal order would not work without a doctrine like supremacy: not only would domestic courts not be compelled to apply EU law instead of conflicting national law, but it is likely that different domestic courts would take different decisions as to whether to apply EU law over national law in a given scenario. The constitutions of some Member States treated international law treaties as primary legislation; but those of others did not. The end result of *not* giving precedence to EU law, in other words, was a very high probability of completely different rules applying in the Member States *precisely* in those areas where the EU was attempting to create common rules.

Since its articulation in *Costa,* the CJEU has linked supremacy to Article 4(3) TEU:

> **Article 4(3) TEU (emphasis added)**
>
> Pursuant to the **principle of sincere cooperation**, the Union and the Member States shall, in full mutual respect, **assist each other in carrying out tasks which flow from the Treaties.**
>
> The Member States shall take **any appropriate measure**, general or particular, **to ensure fulfilment of the obligations arising out of the Treaties** or resulting from the acts of the institutions of the Union.
>
> The Member States shall **facilitate the achievement of the Union's tasks** and refrain from any measure which could jeopardise the attainment of the Union's objectives.

Its argument here is straightforward: the obligation of 'sincere cooperation' would be meaningless if Member States could constantly legislate against EU laws, as this would violate both their obligation to take 'any appropriate measure' to fulfil Treaty obligations *and* their obligation to 'facilitate the achievement of the Union's tasks'. While Article 4(3) TEU is silent about the role that the national courts have to play in 'sincere cooperation' specifically, it is clear that the judiciary form part of the Member States, and thus share these obligations.

The CJEU has heard a number of further challenges in which the Member States tested the scope of the principle of supremacy after *Costa*. Effectively, they were hoping that *Costa* established a principle that only applied regarding *some* national law. The CJEU, however, remained consistent in its rulings. In *Internationale Handelsgesellschaft,* it clarified that supremacy applies regardless of the constitutional nature of the domestic law: even a (hypothetical) EU directive on postage stamps, in other words, can override a national constitution.[3] *Simmenthal* added to this that while *Costa* dealt explicitly with law adopted *after* the Treaty of Rome came into force, the principle of supremacy also applies to law that existed *before* the Treaty of Rome existed.[4] To make

[3] Case 11/70 *Internationale Handelsgesellschaft* ECLI:EU:C:1970:114, para 3.

[4] Case 106/77 *Simmenthal* ECLI:EU:C:1978:49, para 21.

supremacy even more 'effective', it added that it was not only the duty of the highest level of domestic court (eg, the supreme or constitutional court) to set aside incompatible national law:

Case 106/77 *Simmenthal* ECLI:EU:C:1978:49 (emphasis added)

21. . . . every national court must, in a case within its jurisdiction, apply [EU law] in its entirety and protect rights which the latter confers on individuals and must accordingly set aside any provision of national law which may conflict with it, whether prior or subsequent to the [EU rule].

The CJEU thus effectively turned *all* national courts into 'enforcers' of EU law, by giving them the task of considering whether *any* national law conflicts with *any* EU law in *any* case they hear. National rules that preclude lower-level courts setting aside national law are consequently contrary to the Treaties—and the CJEU has even taken the case law on supremacy *beyond* merely national courts, also obliging national administrators to 'ignore' national law where it conflicts with EU law.[5] This may sound as if it is giving a dangerous power to, in essence, civil servants who are not trained in law, let alone EU law specifically—but from the perspective of the CJEU, a broad obligation to give precedence to EU law is its best chance of ensuring that in all the policy areas where the EU has enacted measures, those measures will be the ones applied by the Member States.[6]

The consequence of a finding of conflict between EU and domestic law, however, does highlight the limitations of the reach of EU law. National courts are not legislatures, nor are they made legislatures by CJEU case law. Consequently, they can only rule that the given national law must be disapplied. The incompatible law cannot be revoked by either the CJEU or a national court, and it does not become null and void:[7]

Case C-314/08 *Filipiak* ECLI:EU:C:2009:719 (emphasis added)

83. . . . the Court has already held that the incompatibility with [EU law] of a subsequently adopted rule of national law does not have the effect of rendering that rule of national law non-existent. Faced with such a situation, the national court is obliged to disapply that rule . . .

The onus of the national legal order being made EU-compliant thus remains with the Member State generally, rather than the national court. The principle of supremacy does not change the fact that the Treaties are directed at the Member States, and, as such, they have the ultimate duty to 'sincerely cooperate' under Article 4(3) TEU.

What we thus find in the CJEU's case law from *Costa* onward is the Court navigating a blank space in Treaty law in order to, depending on your perspective, make EU law functional in the Member States, or make Member States inferior to the EU.

[5] See, eg, Case C-198/01 *CIF* ECLI:EU:C:2003:430, paras 49–58.

[6] There is a parallel here to the CJEU's interpretation of the concept of 'courts and tribunals' under Article 267 TFEU; see Chapter 7.

[7] See also Joined Cases C-10–22/97 *IN.CO.GE* ECLI:EU:C:1998:498, para 21.

It has maintained the discussed scope of the doctrine of supremacy in more recent case law: in *Melloni*, the Spanish Constitutional Court asked the CJEU if the (now binding) Charter of Fundamental Rights meant that the Spanish constitutional right to a fair trial *might* take precedence over EU law, where EU law required Spain to accept that in Italy, convictions *in absentia* could not be appealed.[8] Its question focused on Article 53 of the Charter, which states that the Charter itself cannot be interpreted as 'restricting or adversely affecting human rights and fundamental freedoms as recognised . . . by the Member States' constitutions'. The CJEU was not receptive to this argument:

Case C-399/11 *Melloni* ECLI:EU:C:2013:107 (emphasis added)

56. The interpretation envisaged by the national court at the outset is that Article 53 of the Charter gives general authorisation to a Member State to **apply the standard of protection of fundamental rights guaranteed by its constitution when that standard is higher** than that deriving from the Charter and, where necessary, **to give it priority over the application of provisions of EU law . . .**
57. Such an interpretation of Article 53 of the Charter cannot be accepted.
58. That interpretation of Article 53 of the Charter would **undermine the principle of the primacy of EU law** inasmuch as it would allow a Member State to disapply EU legal rules which are fully in compliance with the Charter where they infringe the fundamental rights guaranteed by that State's constitution.

Despite the fact that national courts appear to still be 'testing' the boundaries of the principle of supremacy, the extent of the controversy should not be overstated at this time. Efforts to embed the principle of supremacy in the Treaty as a 'binding' rule failed between the Constitutional Treaty and the Lisbon Treaty, but the Lisbon Treaty nonetheless has Declaration 17 attached to it, which states the Member States' acceptance of the supremacy of EU law as it has been developed by the CJEU.

All the same, the introduction of supremacy, and the firm establishment of EU law as a competing legal order, have resulted in some very interesting moments in the constitutional law of *some* Member States. The majority of the Member States have adopted the principle of supremacy quietly, with the domestic court challenges to the principle historically coming from Italy,[9] Germany, and France[10]—and more recently from the Czech Republic,[11] Hungary,[12] and Poland.[13] Nonetheless, looking at the UK and Germany as two example Member State legal orders that struggled with the principle of supremacy will allow us to reflect more carefully on how 'activist' the CJEU has been: has it impeded

[8] Case C-399/11 *Melloni* ECLI:EU:C:2013:107.

[9] See Raffaele Petriccione, 'Italy: Supremacy of Community Law over National Law' (1986) 11 ELRev 330.

[10] See Claudina Richards, 'The Supremacy of Community Law before the French Constitutional Court' (2006) 31 ELRev 499.

[11] See Jan Komarek, 'Czech Constitutional Court Playing with Matches: the Czech Constitutional Court declares a judgment of the Court of Justice of the EU *ultra vires*' (2012) 8 Eur Const Law Rev 323.

[12] See Gábor Halmai, 'Abuse of Constitutional Identity: The Hungarian Constitutional Court on interpretation of Article E(2) of the Fundamental Law' (2017) 43 RCEEL 23.

[13] See Adam Lazowski, 'Half Full and Half Empty Glass: The application of EU law in Poland (2004–10)' (2011) 48 CMLRev 503.

national sovereignty too much in its case law, or has it simply done what was necessary to make the EU legal order work?

Discussing the quote

On the basis of the CJEU case law as described in Section 6.2, how complete do you think the April 2016 report's summary of the role of national courts is? Does it leave anything essential out in its very short description?

6.3 National courts on supremacy

The *Costa* ruling established a doctrine of supremacy—but as is true for all international and EU law, the judgment would only have effect if complied with by the Member States. Before we can consider how Member States responded to *Costa* specifically, we need to spend a little time considering the relationship between international law and domestic law more generally.

Broadly, there are two different ways in which domestic legal systems deal with international law. Once a country has signed up to an international agreement and has ratified it as constitutionally required (eg, has obtained parliamentary approval for that agreement), the contents of that international agreement normally need to become a part of national law.

In so-called monist systems, any international law that has been ratified by a country via its constitutional processes *immediately* becomes part of domestic law—meaning that international law and national law form a single, integrated system (hence 'monist'—the prefix 'mono' means singular or one only). Once monist country A signs up to Treaty B, the obligations in Treaty B immediately form part of the national laws of country A. Any party with standing can consequently rely directly on Treaty B before a national court in country A.

Conversely, in dualist systems, international law that has been ratified by domestic constitutional processes is *not* automatically part of domestic law. Instead, international law and domestic law exist as two *separate* systems that operate side by side. Once dualist country C signs up to Treaty D, then, the government of country C is obliged to comply with the obligations in Treaty D—but nobody can rely directly on Treaty D before a national court in country C. This only becomes possible once country C adopts national legislation that implements the obligations in Treaty D in national law.

While most Member State legal systems fall somewhere between these two extremes in how they handle international law, and while many Member State constitutions now treat EU law as being distinct from 'international law' more generally,[14] these broad descriptions do help to show how different Member States have responded to the doctrine of supremacy. In a country with monist approaches to international law, the concept of supremacy of international obligations is not necessarily an awkward fit: as international law and domestic law are part of the same legal system, and the country has agreed to comply with this Treaty in signing up to it, it makes sense to avoid 'clashes' between these systems and give the right of way, so to speak, to the international obligation.

[14] See, as just one example, the German Basic Law (discussed in Section 6.3.1), which contains a bespoke provision purely on EU membership.

However, that is a very general description of how to deal with clashes between domestic and international law. What if there is a clash between an international law and something as fundamental as the *constitution* of the country at play? In examining German responses to *Costa*, we can explore that more difficult question.

Countries with dualist approaches to international law encounter separate difficulties with EU law. The UK leans 'dualist', in that without domestic legislation to give effect to international obligations, they cannot be relied upon before domestic courts: this is to give respect to the doctrine of parliamentary sovereignty, whereby only acts of Parliament can reign 'supreme'. But how do you fit a doctrine like parliamentary sovereignty with the *Costa* requirement to prefer EU law over domestic law adopted by Parliament? The UK's responses to EU case law on supremacy shed some light on this question.

Together, these two case studies of Member States responding to the CJEU's case law can be used to consider the reach of supremacy of EU law. Is it an absolute condition, or have the Member States responded to the CJEU's creation of the doctrine by making clear that they will tolerate it conditionally, rather than accept it outright in all circumstances? And what does that suggest about the relationship between sovereignty and supremacy?

Pause for reflection

Can you think of any non-EU international agreements signed by the UK that demonstrate how dualism works? Perhaps on the topic of human rights law? (If not—read Chapter 9!)

6.3.1 Germany on supremacy

As Germany was one of the original six members of the EEC, the German courts have had extensive experience with CJEU jurisprudence. However, communication between the German courts and the CJEU has not always been smooth.

As a brief primer on how EU law is given effect in Germany, we should stress that it is effectively a monist country. The German Constitution (the so-called 'Basic Law') contains specific provisions to allow Germany to transfer powers to international organizations (Article 24) and to allow Germany to participate in the 'European' project (Article 23.1). As the German Constitutional Court has observed about this provision in *Honeywell*,[15] it *implies* acceptance of the doctrine of supremacy:

Honeywell [2 BvR 2661/06, 6 July 2010] (emphasis added)

53. The primacy [of EU law] . . . corresponds to the constitutional empowerment of Article 23.1 of the Basic Law, in accordance with which sovereign powers can be transferred to the European Union . . . Article 23.1 of the Basic Law permits with the transfer of sovereign powers—if provided for and demanded by treaty—at the same time their direct exercise within the Member States' legal systems. It hence contains a promise of effectiveness and implementation corresponding to the primacy of application of Union law.

[15] *Honeywell* [2 BvR 2661/06, 6 July 2010].

However, the German Constitutional Court adds to this the following caveat:

Honeywell [2 BvR 2661/06, 6 July 2010] (emphasis added)

54. . . . Unlike the primacy of application of federal law, as provided for by Article 31 of the Basic Law for the German legal system, **the primacy of application of Union law cannot be comprehensive.**

The primacy of 'federal' law discussed in *Honeywell* refers to the fact that Germany is a federal country: laws made by its constituent parts, or *Länder*, thus cannot overrule law made by its federal government, and Article 31 of the Basic Law makes clear this is an absolute condition. But paragraph 54 of *Honeywell* suggests that the German Constitutional Court does *not* see EU law's primacy as being equally absolute. An evaluation of the dialogue between the CJEU and the German Constitutional Court about the doctrine of supremacy will make clear what, exactly, it means by this.

Phase 1: Fundamental rights

In Section 6.2, we briefly mentioned a case called *International Handelsgesellschaft* which ruled that EU law, whatever its nature, had supremacy *even* over domestic constitutional law. This response was received by the German administrative court that had referred the question with some shock: was it even possible under the Basic Law for EU law to have supremacy over the Basic Law? They requested a ruling on the matter from the ultimate authority on the Basic Law, namely, the German Constitutional Court.

In its 1974 judgment on this question, known by most as *Solange 1* for reasons that will become clear, the German Constitutional Court made several observations that suggested that it could not agree to the unconditional nature of the CJEU's findings in *Internationale Handelsgesellschaft*.[16] The dispute in *Internationale Handelsgesellschaft* concerned a clash between an EU rule regulating agricultural products and the principle of proportionality, which was a fundamental right protected by the German Basic Law. The German Constitutional Court found that the relevant EU rules did *not* actually violate this principle of proportionality—but used the opportunity presented by the reference from the administrative court to comment on its perception of the relationship between German law and EU law:

Internationale Handelgesellschaft mbH v Einfuhr- und Vorratsstelle für Getreide und Futtermittel [1974] 2 Common Market Law Reports 540 (_Solange 1_) (emphasis added)

The part of the [German] constitution dealing with fundamental rights is an inalienable essential feature of the valid Constitution . . . Article 24 [permitting Germany to transfer sovereign powers to international organisations] does not without reservation allow it to be subjected to qualifications. In this, **the present state of integration of the Community is of crucial importance.** The

→

[16] *Internationale Handelgesellschaft mbH v Einfuhr- und Vorratsstelle für Getreide und Futtermittel* [1974] 2 CMLR 540 (*Solange 1*).

→

Community still lacks a democratically legitimated Parliament directly elected by general suffrage which possesses legislative powers and to which the Community organs empowered to legislate are fully responsible on a political level. **It still lacks in particular a codified catalogue of fundamental rights the substance of which is reliably and unambiguously fixed for the future** in the same way as the substance of the Constitution . . .

Provisionally, therefore, **in the hypothetical case of a conflict between Community law and . . . [the fundamental rights in the German Constitution] . . . the Constitution prevails** as long as the competent organs of the Community have not removed the conflict of norms . . .

In summary, the German Constitutional Court found in *Solange 1* that even though in this *specific* case there was no violation of a principle in the German Basic Law, if there *were* to be such a violation, the German Constitution would prevail *as long as* (for which the German term is 'Solange', hence the case's nickname) the EU did not itself protect fundamental rights and did not enable democratic participation in its lawmaking by making the European Parliament a directly elected legislative body. In a case of conflict, the German Constitutional Court reserved the jurisdiction to decide that the German Basic Law would come first.

The German Constitutional Court effectively sent up a flare, warning the CJEU that the EU's own protection of fundamental rights was lacking and Germany would not stand for it. However, the *Solange 1* ruling cannot be seen as much more than a warning: it discusses hypothetical clashes between domestic and EU law, and the *possibility* for the German Constitutional Court to give preference to the Basic Law over EU law.

The CJEU received this warning loud and clear. Looking back on the late 1970s and early 1980s, we know that two things happened over the course of this period that addressed the issues raised in *Solange 1*: first, the European Parliament became directly elected in 1979; and second, the CJEU had started developing a body of fundamental rights jurisprudence.[17] The follow-up to *Solange 1*—appropriately known as *Solange 2*—consequently revisited, in 1987, this same question of a clash between the German Basic Law and EU law, but reached a different outcome:

Re Wünsche Handelsgesellschaft [1987] 3 Common Market Law Reports 225 (*Solange 2*) (emphasis added)

In view of [developments at the EU level, such as the establishment of EU-level fundamental rights by the CJEU, and the accession of all EU Member States to the European Convention of Human Rights], it must be held that, **so long as** the European Communities, and in particular the case law of the European Court, **generally ensure an effective protection of fundamental rights** as against the sovereign powers of the Communities which is to be regarded as substantially similar to the protection of fundamental rights required unconditionally by the Constitution, . . . **the Federal Constitutional Court will no longer exercise its jurisdiction to decide on the applicability of secondary Community legislation** . . . within the sovereign jurisdiction of the Federal Republic of Germany . . .

[17] See Chapter 9.

Solange 2 rowed back the threat made in *Solange 1*, but not unconditionally: the German Constitutional Court accepted the supremacy of EU law over German law, but only in the sense that it would not 'exercise its jurisdiction' to actually examine the compliance of EU law with the fundamental rights in the Basic Law. If any real problems were to arise, because the standard of fundamental rights at the EU level was simply not adequate, it reserved the right to set aside relevant EU law. Such real problems, however, have to date not arisen; no claimants have argued that the standard of fundamental rights protection at the EU level is inferior to the German standard.

Phase 2: *Ultra vires* review

The *Solange* jurisprudence was merely the beginning of German Constitutional Court clashes with the CJEU's development of the doctrine of supremacy. More recent case law has made it clear that the German Constitutional Court pays active attention to EU law, and intends to intervene if it ever goes 'too far'. The first example of what 'too far' could mean was found in the *Brunner* case, where a member of the German parliament named Mr Brunner challenged the constitutionality of Germany ratifying the Maastricht Treaty.[18]

In *Brunner*, the German Constitutional Court considered not only if the Maastricht Treaty was compatible with the German Basic Law, but more generally what would happen if the EU ever attempted to exercise powers that Germany had not explicitly conferred upon it (by including them in the Treaties).[19] The judgment tackles the idea of 'competence creep' and makes clear that it will intervene if such 'creep' goes too far:

Brunner v the European Union Treaty [1994] 1 Common Market Law Reports 57 (emphasis added)

99. . . . Whereas dynamic extension of the existing Treaties has so far been supported on the basis of an open-handed treatment of [Article 352 TFEU] as a 'competence to round off the Treaty' as a whole, and on the basis of considerations relating to the 'implied powers' of the Communities, and of Treaty interpretation as allowing maximum exploitation of Community powers . . . , in future it will have to be noted as regards interpretation of enabling provisions by Community institutions and agencies that **the Union Treaty as a matter of principle distinguishes between the exercise of a sovereign power conferred for limited purposes and the amending of the Treaty, so that its interpretation may not have effects that are equivalent to an extension of the Treaty. Such an interpretation of enabling rules would not produce any binding effects for Germany.**

We know German ratification of the Maastricht Treaty proceeded, and so paragraph 99 is the more interesting dimension of the *Brunner* judgment. The German Constitutional Court here makes it clear that only those powers that Germany, a sovereign state, *conferred* on the EU could be exercised by the EU, and where the EU acted in a way that was effectively *ultra vires* (or beyond its competences), the Constitutional Court would find that Germany was free to ignore the EU law in question.

[18] *Brunner v the European Union Treaty* [1994] 1 CMLR 57; for more on *Brunner*, see Chapter 5.
[19] See Chapters 4 and 5.

This *ultra vires* warning was revisited only in 2010, when the German Constitutional Court was asked to consider the constitutionality of an EU judgment that gave effect to a directive before its deadline for implementation had passed, because the directive elaborated on a general principle that did not have such an implementation deadline.[20] The claimants in *Honeywell* argued that this judgment was an example of the EU acting *ultra vires*, and as such the German Constitutional Court should declare it to be inapplicable in Germany. However, the German Constitutional Court disagreed with this argument:

Honeywell [2 BvR 2661/06, 6 July 2010] (emphasis added)

58. *Ultra vires* review may only be exercised in a manner which is **open** towards European law . . .

60. This means for the *ultra vires* review at hand that the Federal Constitutional Court must comply with the rulings of the Court of Justice in principle as a binding interpretation of Union law. Prior to the acceptance of an *ultra vires* act on the part of the European bodies and institutions, the Court of Justice is therefore to be afforded the opportunity to interpret the Treaties, as well as to rule on the validity and interpretation of the legal acts in question . . . **As long as the Court of Justice did not have an opportunity to rule on the questions of Union law which have arisen, the Federal Constitutional Court may not find any inapplicability of Union law for Germany** . . .

61. *Ultra vires* review by the Federal Constitutional Court can moreover only be considered if it is **manifest** that acts of the European bodies and institutions have taken place outside the transferred competences . . . This means that **the act of the authority of the European Union must be manifestly in violation of competences** and that the impugned act is **highly significant** in the **structure of competences** between the Member States and the Union with regard to the principle of conferral and to the binding nature of the statute under the rule of law . . .

Something very similar to *Solange 2* happens in *Honeywell*. Having established a principle that it *can* overrule EU law on set grounds (clashes with fundamental rights or *ultra vires* action), the German Constitutional Court opts to not actually overrule EU law in a case where it is claimed that one of those grounds is met. Indeed, *Honeywell* limits the possibility for *Brunner*-style *ultra vires* review to the point where it becomes very unlikely that it will review any EU law. First, the German Constitutional Court will reject an opportunity to review *unless* the CJEU has already ruled on the matter at hand; and any surpassing of allocated competences has to be 'manifest' and have a 'highly significant' competence impact, which is a high standard for any claim to satisfy.

In its 2014 *OMT* ruling on the legality of 'rescue policies' adopted by the European Central Bank during the Eurozone crisis, the German Constitutional Court found that that the relevant policy (known as 'Outright Monetary Transactions', or the OMT Policy) was indeed *ultra vires* and referred a question to the CJEU on its legality.[21] The preliminary reference sent in *OMT*, decided by the CJEU under the name *Gauweiler*,[22] concluded that the OMT policy

[20] The case—Case C-144/04 *Mangold* ECLI:EU:C:2005:709—is discussed in more detail in Chapter 8.

[21] *OMT* [2 BvR 2728/13, 14 January 2014].

[22] Case C-62/14 *Gauweiler and Others v Deutscher Bundestag* ECLI:EU:C:2015:400.

was not *ultra vires*—and the German Constitutional Court responded to this with grudging acceptance, implying that the CJEU's analysis had shortcomings but the OMT policy did not 'manifestly' breach transferred competences.[23] It reached this conclusion with a 'Solange-style' final warning, however, stressing that if in its implementation the OMT Policy did not adhere to the conditions set out for its legality in the *Gauweiler* case, it would be considered *ultra vires* by the German Constitutional Court, and the German Federal Bank would be prohibited from participating in the OMT programme.[24]

Summary: The Concept of *Kompetenz-Kompetenz*

What we learn from both the *Solange* saga and the *Brunner/Honeywell/OMT* developments is that the German Constitutional Court in *principle* is willing to accept the supremacy of EU law, but does so conditionally on the EU acting in compliance with fundamental rights and within the limitations of the competences that Germany has conferred on it. The key here is that it is not the CJEU, but rather the German Constitutional Court itself, that has the ability (or competence) to determine *if* the EU is acting within its competences . . . at least according to the German Constitutional Court. The CJEU has not challenged it on holding this power of '*kompetenz-kompetenz*', as it is known in German, and so the two courts continue to operate alongside each other peacefully, although the *OMT* case and its reference to the CJEU had commentators quite worried that the German Constitutional Court was going to be forced to ignore a CJEU ruling for the first time to save face.[25]

One German Constitutional Court judgment that we did not consider in this section, but that may hold significant implications for the relationship between the German Constitutional Court and the CJEU in future, is the so-called *Lisbon* judgment.[26] It reiterated the possibility for *ultra vires* review, but set out something further that has been described as the 'identity lock'. This 'lock' suggests that if the EU Treaties start encroaching on any of five 'essential' areas of constitutional identity, Germany will also deem the Treaties inapplicable on these points. The judgment sets out that these five essential areas are, in no particular order, criminal law, policing and military action, matters of taxation, welfare, and culture and religion. We have yet to see any case law that challenges EU action in these 'identity lock' areas, but if we do, it also remains to be seen whether the German Constitutional Court holds fast to its *Lisbon* judgment, or moves away from it so as to maintain a mostly cordial working relationship with the CJEU a little longer.

For now, Germany accepts supremacy of EU law . . . so long as it meets certain conditions, which it has set out for the CJEU since the 1970s, but never enforced when a case forced it to apply those conditions.

Discussing the quote

Consider the German Constitutional Court's case law in *Solange 2* and *Brunner*. How do the 'so long as' conditions set out in those cases fit with the April 2016 report's summary of the relationship between national courts and EU law?

[23] *OMT* [2 BvR 2728/13, 14 January 2014], paras 181–189.

[24] Ibid, para 205.

[25] See, eg, Federico Fabbrini, 'After the OMT Case: The supremacy of EU law as the guarantee of the equality of the Member States' (2015) 16 Ger Law J 1003, 1012–13.

[26] *Lisbon* [BvE 2/08, 30 June 2009].

6.3.2 The UK on supremacy

The UK, as a primarily dualist nation with an unwritten constitution, has a different relationship with the CJEU's principle of supremacy than the more monist, Basic Law-driven Germany does in some respects. However, this does not mean that supremacy was a natural fit into the UK legal order, nor does the fact that UK difficulties with supremacy do not stem from a written constitution mean they were any less substantial than Germany's.

One of the most illustrative moments of the struggles between UK constitutional principles and the supremacy of EU law was the following statement in a White Paper published by the UK government in 2017:

DExEU, *The United Kingdom's exit from and new partnership with the European Union White Paper* (February 2017) Cm 9417, para 2.1 (emphasis added)

The sovereignty of Parliament is a fundamental principle of the UK constitution. Whilst Parliament has remained sovereign throughout our membership of the EU, **it has not always felt like that.**

Parliamentary sovereignty had to be reconciled with the supremacy of EU law somehow for the UK to ever become a Member State. The idea that Parliament could do *anything*, short of binding future renditions of itself, was clearly contrary to *Costa*; but the corollary to Parliament not being able to bind itself is that it presumably could also not be bound by other institutions. The normal operation of the UK constitution would mean that any legislation that Parliament issued in the future would override EU law.

Having opted to join the EU, Parliament had to find a solution to this clash between parliamentary sovereignty and EU law supremacy. It did so by attempting to ensure that for all intents and purposes, the *reason* that EU law was supreme in the UK was because *an Act of Parliament* declared as much. The European Communities Act (ECA) 1972 in s 2(4) noted that 'any enactment passed or to be passed [by Parliament] . . . shall be construed and have effect subject to' any EU law stemming from the Treaties.

This is hardly the clearest affirmation of the doctrine of supremacy, but the UK courts opted to interpret it as such: after all, the ECA 1972 was the domestic instrument that Parliament enacted *to* join the EU, and in order to join the EU, the CJEU's case law had to be accepted (as s 3 of the ECA 1972 acknowledged).

The UK courts and supremacy

The UK courts, in early case law involving EU law, relied heavily on the part that the ECA 1972 played in *giving* EU law a role in the UK. Lord Denning, in *Bulmer v Bollinger*, was one of the first UK senior judges to have to consider what having joined the EU meant for the functioning of the UK legal system.[27] Bulmer, a UK-based beer and cider producer, claimed that it was allowed to use the name 'champagne' to market its beverages. French company Bollinger counter-claimed, noting that under EU law, 'champagne' was a protected concept that could only be applied to wine produced in the Champagne region of

[27] *HP Bulmer Ltd v J Bollinger SA (No.2)* [1974] Ch 401 (CA) 418.

France. Lord Denning used the case to explain the relationship between UK and EU law, now that the UK had joined the then-EEC:

HP Bulmer Ltd v J Bollinger SA (No.2) [1974] Ch 401 (CA) 418 (emphasis added)

The first and fundamental point is that the Treaty concerns only those matters which have a European element, that is to say, matters which affect people or property in the nine countries of the common market besides ourselves. **The Treaty does not touch any of the matters which concern solely England and the people in it.** These are still governed by English law. They are not affected by the Treaty. But **when we come to matters with a European element, the Treaty is like an incoming tide.** It flows into the estuaries and up the rivers. It cannot be held back, **Parliament has decreed that the Treaty is henceforward to be part of our law.**

Before the English judges can apply the Treaty, they have to see what it means and what is its effect. In the task of *interpreting* the Treaty, the English judges are no longer the final authority. They no longer carry the law in their breasts. They are no longer in a position to give rulings which are of binding force. **The supreme tribunal for *interpreting* the Treaty is the European Court of Justice, at Luxembourg. Our Parliament has so decreed.**

While Lord Denning does not use these exact terms, it is clear from his account of the effects of having joined the EU that supremacy of EU law was deemed to exist in the UK because Parliament willed it to exist by having adopted the ECA 1972. This is not genuinely making EU law 'supreme' at all—it is rather implying that the UK has chosen to act *as if* EU law is supreme, but it could change its mind about this at any point in time, as a sovereign Parliament can with respect to any act it has adopted.

As such, purely by means of ordinary interpretation, UK courts found it easy to conclude that *unless* it was clear from an Act of Parliament that it was intended to depart from a given provision of EU law, it was the intention of Parliament that the EU law provisions were given preference in clashes with domestic law.[28]

The UK courts' approach to supremacy was well articulated in 1991, when the House of Lords had to consider *Factortame 2*.[29] The *Factortame* saga is an infamous one in EU law, largely because it is a rare instance where one set of facts resulted in two different Court of Justice rulings on the meaning of EU law. We discuss other aspects of the *Factortame* line of case law in Chapters 7 and 8, but for now will focus on what it tells us about how the UK judiciary has responded to the principle of supremacy.

In 1988, the UK had adopted a piece of legislation, the Merchant Shipping Act 1988 (MSA 1988), which made it a requirement for companies registering ships in the UK to be, in effect, owned by UK nationals. The Spanish fishing company Factortame, which had registered its ships in the UK without problems under the previous Merchant Shipping Act, protested these rules as being contrary to the EU Treaties, which forbade discrimination on the basis of nationality.

[28] See, eg, *Felixstowe Dock and Railway Company v British Transport and Docks Board* [1976] 2 CMLR 655; *Macarthys v Smith* [1979] 3 All ER 325, 329.

[29] *Factortame Ltd v Secretary of State for Transport (No 2)* [1991] 1 AC 603.

The UK courts hearing this dispute between Factortame and the UK government asked the CJEU for an interpretation of how EU law worked on two points: first, the High Court asked the CJEU to determine if the MSA 1988 violated the Treaties.[30] Following a series of appeals regarding the High Court's award of an injunction against application of the MSA 1988, the House of Lords then also asked the CJEU if EU law required the UK to make interim relief available to Factortame while the parties awaited the other ruling.[31] In response to the question about interim relief, the CJEU confirmed that even if national law did not provide for interim relief, it should be made available in situations where it is possible that EU rights are being infringed.[32]

Lord Bridge's comments on the consequences of the CJEU's ruling on the matter of interim relief are worth citing at length, as they demonstrate general acceptance of the doctrine of supremacy:

***Factortame Ltd v Secretary of State for Transport (No 2)* [1991] 1 AC 603, 658 (emphasis added)**

Lord Bridge

Some public comments on the decision of the Court of Justice, affirming the jurisdiction of the courts of member states to override national legislation if necessary to enable interim relief to be granted in protection of rights under Community law, have suggested that this was a novel and dangerous invasion by a Community institution of the sovereignty of the United Kingdom Parliament. But such comments are based on a misconception. **If the supremacy within the Community of Community law over the national law of member states was not always inherent in the EEC Treaty it was certainly well established in the jurisprudence of the Court of Justice long before the United Kingdom joined the [EU]**. Thus, **whatever limitation of its sovereignty Parliament accepted when it enacted the European Communities Act 1972 was entirely voluntary. Under the terms of the 1972 Act it has always been clear that it was the duty of a United Kingdom court, when delivering final judgment, to override any rule of national law found to be in conflict with any directly enforceable rule of Community law** . . . Thus there is nothing in any way novel in according supremacy to rules of Community law in those areas to which they apply . . .

Resolving the clash between parliamentary sovereignty and supremacy in the UK thus took the form of making supremacy a part of UK constitutional law, by situating it in an Act of Parliament rather than in the Treaties or the CJEU's case law as such. However, to ensure that the supremacy of EU law is not at the mercy of say, unintentionally conflicting Acts of Parliament, the UK courts simultaneously developed a 'check' on the ECA 1972 by assuming that is not subject to 'implied repeal'.

The notion of 'implied repeal' was challenged forcefully in the *Thoburn* case.[33] *Thoburn*, also known as the 'Metric Martyrs' case, concerned the Weights and Measures Act 1985 and amendments to it following a variety of EU measures adopted over the course of the 1990s under the ECA 1972. Because of those amendments, as of 2000, it would be contrary to EU law for anyone to use the imperial pound as the *primary* measurement for

[30] *R v Secretary of State for Transport, ex parte Factortame Ltd and Others* [1989] 2 CMLR 353.

[31] *R v Secretary of State for Transport, ex parte Factortame Ltd* [1989] UKHL 1.

[32] Case C-213/89 *Factortame ('Factortame I')*.

[33] *Thoburn v Sunderland City Council* [2003] QB 151.

trade. Mr Thoburn, a greengrocer from Sunderland, and several other food sellers, were convicted in 2001 on account of failing to comply with this new 'parity' requirement in the 1985 Act, as they insisted on displaying their produce with imperial measurements only. They argued that, consistent with the traditional perception of parliamentary sovereignty, the 1985 Act 'implicitly repealed' the ECA 1972, and that consequently the 1990s EU measures adopted were invalid and could not apply in the UK.

In a lengthy judgment, Laws LJ argued that the doctrine of implied repeal had been changed over time—not by the EU, but rather by the common law itself. He indicated that there were now two categories of Acts of Parliament: 'ordinary statutes', which were subject to implied repeal, and 'constitutional statutes', which were not. The repeal of a 'constitutional statute' had to be express, and the ECA 1972 was found to be such a statute already in *Factortame (No 2)*, where the Merchant Shipping Act 1988 in principle would have 'implicitly overruled' the ECA 1972 if this were possible.[34] This meant the following for the UK's relationship with EU law:

Thoburn v Sunderland City Council [2003] QB 151 [69] (emphasis added)

1. **All the specific rights and obligations which EU law creates are by the 1972 Act incorporated into our domestic law and rank supreme**: that is, anything in our substantive law inconsistent with any of these rights and obligations is abrogated or must be modified to avoid the inconsistency. This is true even where the inconsistent municipal provision is contained in primary legislation.
2. **The 1972 Act is a constitutional statute: that is, it cannot be impliedly repealed.**
3. The truth of (2) is derived, not from EU law, but purely from the law of England: **the common law recognises a category of constitutional statutes.**
4. **The fundamental legal basis of the United Kingdom's relationship with the EU rests with the domestic, not the European, legal powers.** In the event, which no doubt would never happen in the real world, that a European measure was seen to be repugnant to a fundamental or constitutional right guaranteed by the law of England, a question would arise whether the general words of the 1972 Act were sufficient to incorporate the measure and give it overriding effect in domestic law. But that is very far from this case.

Laws LJ's approach was later endorsed by the UK Supreme Court in *HS2*, as well as in subsequent case law.[35]

EU law in practice

The excerpt seems to imply that Parliament would not even need to have repealed the ECA 1972 to end the effect of supremacy in the UK: it could simply adopt a separate Act declaring that EU law was no longer supreme, or even a specific Act that disapplied s 4(2) of the 1972 Act so as to end 'supremacy' in a specific policy area, for the purposes of one piece of legislation.

What do you think of that conception of parliamentary sovereignty? What do think the CJEU would make of it?

[34] Ibid, [63].

[35] *R (HS2 Action Alliance Ltd) v Secretary of State for Transport* [2014] UKSC 3, [207].

R (Miller) v Secretary of State for Exiting the European Union [2017] UKSC 5 (emphasis added)

66. . . . **The primacy of EU law means that, unlike other rules of domestic law, EU law cannot be implicitly displaced by the mere enactment of legislation which is inconsistent with it.** That is clear from the second part of section 2(4) of the 1972 Act and [*Factortame (No 2)*]. The issue was informatively discussed by Laws LJ in [*Thoburn*].

67. The 1972 Act accordingly has a constitutional character, as discussed by Laws LJ in *Thoburn* . . . **Following the coming into force of the 1972 Act, the normal rule is that any domestic legislation must be consistent with EU law.** In such cases, **EU law has primacy as a matter of domestic law**, and legislation which is inconsistent with EU law from time to time is to that extent ineffective in law. However, **legislation which alters the domestic constitutional status of EU institutions or of EU law is not constrained by the need to be consistent with EU law.** In the case of such legislation, there is no question of EU law having primacy, so that such legislation will have domestic effect even if it infringes EU law (and that would be true whether or not the 1972 Act remained in force). That is because of the **principle of Parliamentary sovereignty which is, as explained above, fundamental to the United Kingdom's constitutional arrangements**, and **EU law can only enjoy a status in domestic law which that principle allows.** It will therefore have that status only for as long as the 1972 Act continues to apply, and that, of course, can only be a matter for Parliament.

The need for express repeal of the ECA 1972 was recently stressed in the key Brexit-related case of *Miller*, where the Supreme Court was asked if an Act of Parliament was necessary for it to notify an intention to withdraw from the EU under Article 50 TEU.[36]

The judgment in *Miller* provides a complete summary of how, for the duration of its membership of the EU, the UK has made parliamentary sovereignty and the doctrine of supremacy co-exist:

Summary: Parliament and supremacy

While the doctrine of parliamentary sovereignty may have made the notion of EU law's supremacy seem difficult when the UK first joined the EEC, the UK courts have managed to reconcile these two doctrines with little difficulty. However, in the years preceding the EU referendum, Parliament has expressed some of its own reservations about the nature of the ECA 1972 and to what extent it enables any and all EU law to become automatically superior to domestic law.

The European Union Act 2011 was a direct response to dissatisfaction with the manner of ratification of the Lisbon Treaty, and set out a promise that any future changes to the EU Treaties would result in a UK referendum on those Treaties.[37] The most interesting

[36] *R (Miller) v Secretary of State for Exiting the European Union* [2017] UKSC 5, [66]–[67].
[37] See Chapter 1.

aspect of the European Union Act 2011 for the purposes of considering the UK attitude to supremacy of EU law was the inclusion of the so-called 'sovereignty clause' in s 18:

European Union Act 2011, s 18 (emphasis added)

Directly applicable or directly effective EU law (that is, the rights, powers, liabilities, obligations, restrictions, remedies and procedures referred to in section 2(1) of the **European Communities Act 1972) falls to be recognised and available in law in the United Kingdom only by virtue of that Act** or where it is required to be recognised and available in law by virtue of any other Act.

It is a very densely worded sentence, but one of no real legal effect. Section 18 merely reflects the law as it was when the UK was an EU Member State: the ECA 1972 fulfilled exactly that function, and has done since the UK joined the EEC. It is nonetheless illustrative of greater sensitivity within UK political spheres about the extent to which power had been relinquished to the EU, and to what extent the supremacy of EU law was 'imposed' upon the UK. In many ways, the adoption of the European Union Act 2011 was a portent for the 2016 referendum and its outcome, despite the fact that Parliament has always been sovereign, as the government itself acknowledges in that 2017 White Paper.

Discussing the quote

Thinking of the ECA 1972 and *Factortame* and *Thoburn*, to what extent do you think the April 2016 report accurately captured the *nature* of the relationship between the EU and the UK at that time (and during the transition period)? Is 'supremacy' forced upon the UK and its courts, or have they chosen to comply with it? Could EU law have worked in the UK without it—say, if Parliament had repealed the ECA 1972?

6.4 Brexit and supremacy

Ending the supremacy of EU law in the UK was one of the key aspects of the 'take back control' vote; it is seen as infringing upon sovereignty by those wishing to leave the EU, in the same way that CJEU judgments being binding is, and as such formed part and parcel of a set of early-announced 'red lines' by the May government.[38] We can now evaluate to what extent the Withdrawal Agreement and the Political Declaration negotiated by the Johnson government in October 2019 are delivering on this aspect of regaining sovereignty.

[38] See https://www.gov.uk/government/speeches/the-governments-negotiating-objectives-for-exiting-the-eu-pm-speech.

6.4.1 The Withdrawal Agreement

As discussed in earlier chapters, the Withdrawal Agreement preserves the 'status quo' of EU membership until at least the end of 2020—the only exception is to institutional representation, but that does not affect the ongoing supremacy of EU law in the UK during this transition period.[39]

Key here is Article 4 of the Withdrawal Agreement:

Withdrawal Agreement, Article 4 (emphasis added)

1. The provisions of this Agreement and the provisions of Union law made applicable by this Agreement shall produce in respect of and in the United Kingdom **the same legal effects** as those which **they produce within the Union and its Member States.**

   Accordingly, legal or natural persons shall in particular be able to rely directly on the provisions contained or referred to in this Agreement which meet the conditions for direct effect under Union law.

2. **The United Kingdom shall ensure compliance with paragraph 1, including as regards the required powers of its judicial and administrative authorities to disapply inconsistent or incompatible domestic provisions, through domestic primary legislation.**

In short, in order to ensure that EU law will continue to have the same effects in the UK during the transition period as it did pre-'exit day', the UK is obliged to adopt primary legislation that will have the same effect as s 2(4) of the ECA 1972 does. The ECA 1972 itself was set to be repealed under the EU (Withdrawal) Act 2018—but relevant parts of it have been 'saved' by the EU (Withdrawal Agreement) Act 2020, in order to ensure that this provision in the Withdrawal Agreement is given effect.[40] Supremacy of EU law in the UK as a whole, regardless, cannot end until the transition period does.

6.4.2 The Protocol on Ireland/Northern Ireland

Article 4 of the Withdrawal Agreement applies *to* the Protocol on Ireland/Northern Ireland. What this means in practice is that as the Protocol is made applicable by the Withdrawal Agreement, and the Protocol contains references to those parts of internal market law that will apply to Northern Ireland *after* the transition period (so as to avoid a border between Ireland and Northern Ireland), Article 4 of the Agreement ensures that all the EU legislation listed in the Annexes to the Protocol will take precedence over all other UK law.

The UK courts consequently may very possibly face situations decades from now where they have to set aside domestic law because of the lasting commitments under the Protocol. The Withdrawal Agreement auto-updates the EU law applicable to Northern Ireland:

[39] Withdrawal Agreement, Article 7. The transition period can be extended by one or two years under Withdrawal Agreement, Articles 126 and 132; note that the EU (Withdrawal Agreement) Act 2020, s 33, prohibits UK representatives from asking for an extension as a matter of domestic law—though as is true for all Acts of Parliament, this can obviously be amended if an extension is desired after all.

[40] EU (Withdrawal Agreement) Act 2020, s 1.

Article 13(3) of the Protocol makes clear that any reference to an EU act has to be interpreted as that act 'amended or replaced'. Only where the EU believes *new* EU law should form part of the Protocol is this subject to a discussion in the Joint Committee, as we examined in Chapter 5. As such, especially when we consider (as we did in Chapter 2) that there will be no UK or Northern Ireland representation at the EU institutions, it is very debatable if there is a sovereignty *gain* for Northern Ireland in the process of the UK 'taking back control'.

6.4.3 The future relationship

What the future status of EU law will become in the remainder of the UK is genuinely interesting now that the UK has formally left the EU. The May government's Political Declaration on the Future Relationship[41] suggested that the UK wished to opt into a variety of EU programmes and made it clear that any relevant EU rules would have been adopted by the UK as necessary.[42] It seems to have implicitly accepted that this would have involved what it calls the 'direct jurisdiction' of the CJEU—but had not made explicit that this, then, would also require the relevant parts of the EU legal *acquis* to remain supreme over UK law for as long as the UK participated in certain EU programmes. The version of Brexit that Theresa May's government attempted to enact would consequently only have resulted in the return of *some* sovereignty for the UK, with Parliament opting into EU programmes much in the way it once opted into the EEC.

The Johnson government's Political Declaration strikes a very different note, however. References to alignment with EU rules have been generally removed from the document, and the October 2019 Political Declaration therefore suggests a much more distant relationship. The consequence of not being directly involved in programmes run by the EU will be reduced access to those programmes, but also the absence of an external source of 'supreme' law. The October 2019 version of the Political Declaration thus seems to be proposing a deal that, in this specific sense, would be no different from 'no deal': if there are no aspects of EU law that continue to apply in Great Britain, that law also will not have supremacy over UK law.

That said, Northern Ireland once again raises interesting questions. As discussed in Chapter 5, the commitment made by the UK government to facilitate trade between Northern Ireland and Great Britain as much as possible suggests that it will attempt to stay as close to relevant EU internal market rules as possible.[43] The key distinction may be that this is a *willing* maintenance of EU rules that the UK government itself has chosen to pursue—as opposed to being 'forced' to apply EU rules because of the supremacy of EU law. Is this a genuinely meaningful distinction, or is it a primarily symbolic one? The earlier discussion on the German Constitutional Court's attitude towards the concept of supremacy may be the most appropriate parallel to the UK government's position on the EU law contained in those Annexes to the Protocol: the perception of a choice is important, even if that choice in practice is very unlikely to be exercised.

[41] See the November 2018 Political Declaration, available at https://assets.publishing.service.gov.uk/government/uploads/system/uploads/attachment_data/file/759021/25_November_Political_Declaration_setting_out_the_framework_for_the_future_relationship_between_the_European_Union_and_the_United_Kingdom__.pdf.

[42] Political Declaration, Articles 11, 25, and 83.

[43] Protocol, Article 6(2).

Finally, we have to briefly return to 'retained' EU law, as discussed in Chapters 4 and 5. The EU (Withdrawal) Act 2018 says the following about the status of 'retained' EU law after Brexit:

Section 5 Exceptions to savings and incorporation (emphasis added)

1. The principle of the supremacy of EU law does not apply to any enactment or rule of law passed or made on or after exit day.
2. Accordingly, **the principle of the supremacy of EU law continues to apply on or after exit day so far as relevant to the interpretation, disapplication or quashing of any enactment or rule of law passed or made before exit day.**
3. Subsection 1 does not prevent the principle of the supremacy of EU law from applying to a modification made on or after exit day of any enactment or rule of law passed or made before exit day if the application of the principle is consistent with the intention of the modification.

We again end up with a legislative 'timestamp' of crucial importance. Any 'retained' EU law, consequently, can under s 5(1) be effectively 'overruled' by a new piece of domestic legislation. However, when 'retained' EU law is compared back to UK law that *predates* Brexit, the principle of supremacy will apply in matters of interpretation and disapplication. What this means is that if there is a clash between a domestic law adopted in 2017 and a 'retained' EU regulation, that regulation will be able to set aside the 2017 domestic law.

What is confusing here is that a 'retained' EU law is in reality just a piece of domestic UK law after Brexit—and so what s 5(2) will actually enable is that *some* UK law will have supremacy over *some* other UK law. It does not help that s 5(2) refers to the supremacy of 'EU law' in an Act that otherwise only discusses 'retained' EU law; and it is not wholly clear what the intended effects of s 5 are on domestic legislation implementing EU directives, for example. Are they subject to this lasting pre-exit 'supremacy' condition, or will they be treated as separate domestic law?

A further point worth making is that this version of 'supremacy' does not address *all* EU law. It addresses 'retained' EU law in the form of legislation having supremacy over other legislation—but excludes general principles from this working of 'supremacy':

EU (Withdrawal) Act 2018, Schedule 1, part 3 (emphasis added)

(2) **No court or tribunal or other public authority may**, on or after exit day—

(a) **disapply** or quash **any enactment** or other rule of law, or

(b) quash any conduct or otherwise decide that it is unlawful,

because it is **incompatible with any of the general principles of EU law.**

The 2018 Act is silent on how this is to work in practice: 'retained' EU law is generally meant to be interpreted in line with CJEU jurisprudence up until the end of the transition period,[44]

[44] See the discussion about the EU (Withdrawal) Act 2018, s 6, in Chapter 4; there are two exceptions to this general rule, whereby the Supreme Court can diverge from pre-Brexit CJEU case law, and ministers can adopt regulations that enable or force other courts to also diverge.

so what happens to jurisprudence that discusses how general principles interact with EU law? Is the key there that it is CJEU jurisprudence, and the EU (Withdrawal) Act 2018 in s 6 sets out a specific rule on how courts are meant to treat CJEU case law—or is the key there that it is a *general principle* being interpreted by the CJEU?

As is generally true of the effect of Brexit on the future UK legal order, the domestic courts will likely have to determine how the new legal forms created by the EU (Withdrawal) Act 2018 all work together on a case-by-case basis.

Pause for reflection

If the UK voluntarily adopts a variety of EU legislation, and can be held to account if it does so incorrectly (resulting in clashes between the UK law and the EU original) in its 'future relationship', is the doctrine of supremacy still necessary in the UK? Why or why not? (Reflect on this again after reading Chapter 8.)

6.5 In conclusion

The Treaty of Rome tackled many different areas of cooperation, but did not set out in any great detail what was to happen if domestic and EU laws were to clash. The CJEU, in *Costa* and subsequent case law, resolved this problem from the EU side: if the EU's goals were ever to be accomplished, EU law *had* to take precedence over national law in the case of clashes.

The Member States were not unanimously happy with this finding, but seem, over time, to have come to accept it as being a 'necessary evil' of EU membership. Declaration 17 to the Lisbon Treaty suggests that by and large, the Member States agree that the CJEU's case law does what is necessary and does not go beyond it. But the threat of limitations, and the desire for greater assurances of sovereignty, remain—and the UK is a clear example of a country where some of its citizenry appear to have found that even if supremacy *is* a necessary condition for EU membership, it is simply asking too much from a sovereign country.

As such, there are further questions to be asked about supremacy: for instance, what *if* the German Constitutional Court finds that the EU has acted *ultra vires*, or if the UK Parliament adopts an Act that expressly goes against an EU law obligation over the course of the transition period? We will come back to those questions in Chapter 8, which explores how EU law can be enforced against and within the Member States (and the UK, which will continue to be treated as a Member State during the Withdrawal Agreement's transition period).

Key points

- The EU law doctrine of **supremacy** requires that any national law conflicting with any EU law is set aside by national courts in a given case.
- Originally developed in *Costa*, it has been further developed in subsequent cases such as *Simmenthal* and *Internationale Handelsgesellschaft*.
- In Germany, the doctrine of supremacy has proven slightly problematic when EU laws clash with obligations contained in the German Constitution.

- In the UK, the doctrine of supremacy has proven slightly problematic as it clashes with the notion of parliamentary sovereignty.
- Brexit means that, outside of Northern Ireland, new EU law will no longer have supremacy over UK law after the transition period ends, but the domestic legislation under which the UK will depart the EU means that **most 'retained' EU law will remain supreme to other UK law** *unless* Parliament or the Supreme Court decides otherwise.

Assess your learning

1. Is supremacy of *all* EU law over *all* national law necessary? Why or why not? (See Section 6.1.)
2. Does the German Constitutional Court genuinely set out restrictions to supremacy, or do you think it is 'all bark and no bite', given its case law over the last four decades? (See Section 6.2.)
3. Did the ECA 1972 actually declare EU law supreme, in your view, or have the UK courts interpreted it very generously to give effect to EU law obligations? Does this matter? (See Section 6.3.)

Further reading

Trevor Allan, 'Parliamentary Sovereignty: Law, politics and revolution' (1997) 113 LQR 443.

Mikolaj Barczentewicz, 'Judicial Duty not to Apply EU Law' (2017) 133 LQR 469.

Paul Craig, 'Constitutional Principle, the Rule of Law and Political Reality: The European Union (Withdrawal) Act 2018' (2019) 82(2) MLR 319.

Paul Craig, 'The ECJ and *Ultra Vires* Action: A conceptual analysis' (2011) 48 CMLRev 395.

Mark Elliot, 'United Kingdom: Parliamentary sovereignty under pressure' (2004) 2(3) I-CON 545.

Mark Elliot and Stephen Tierney, 'Political Pragmatism and Constitutional Principle: The European Union (Withdrawal) Act 2018' [2019] PL 37.

Jan Komárek, 'National Constitutional Courts in the European Constitutional Democracy' (2014) 12(3) I-CON 525.

Koen Lenaerts and Tim Corthaut, 'Of Birds and Hedges: The role of primacy in invoking norms of EU law' (2006) 31 ELRev 287.

Jo Murkens, 'Mixed Messages in Bottles: The European Union, devolution, and the future of the constitution' (2017) 80(4) MLR 685.

Daniel Thym, 'In the Name of Sovereign Statehood: A critical introduction to the *Lisbon* judgment of the German Constitutional Court' (2009) 46 CMLRev 1795.

Online resources

Visit www.oup.com/he/demars1e for a sample approach to discussing the quote.

7

Connecting EU law to domestic law: the preliminary reference procedure

Context for this chapter

Mr King worked for Sash WW on the basis of a contract where he was commissioned for work on an occasional basis from 1999 to 2012, when he retired. He was paid only when commissioned, and when he took annual leave it was unpaid.

When he retired, Mr King sought to get paid for the annual leave he took over the course of his three years of engagement. Sash WW rejected his claim, arguing that he was a self-employed worker (and so not entitled to paid annual leave).

Mr King took Sash WW to a UK Employment Tribunal. It determined that Mr King was entitled to three different kinds of holiday pay under the EU Working Time Directive, which applied to him despite the nature of his contract. He deserved a payment for annual leave he had not taken in his final year of work; a payment for leave actually taken over the entire three years; and finally, a payment for all leave that he had built up but did not take over the course of those three years, which amounted to 24 weeks of pay in total.

Sash WW appealed the Employment Tribunal's decision, and following a series of further appeals, the UK Court of Appeal is now faced with a single ground of disagreement, regarding the 24 weeks of 'pay for leave not taken between 1999 and 2012' Mr King was asking for.

Sash WW has argued that the UK implementation of the Working Time Directive—the 1998 Working Time Regulations—in regulation 13(9) precluded Mr King from 'carrying over' untaken annual leave to subsequent years. He therefore could not claim for all three years of his employment, but only for his last year; had he wanted to claim for 1999 through 2011, he should have made that claim in the relevant calendar years, per regulation 30 of the 1998 Regulations.

→

→

Mr King, on the other hand, has argued that he had the right to be paid for untaken leave for every year he worked. He cited the Working Time Directive and earlier CJEU case law on it, which had established that the right to claim payment for leave not taken only arose once a working relationship was ended—and so he had brought his claim in ample time, and regulation 13(9) was contrary to EU law.

The Court of Appeal has to decide if the time limit for claiming pay for annual leave not taken in the 1998 Regulations is compatible with the actual provisions of the Working Time Directive.

7.1 Introduction

Chapter 6 established the relationship between national law and EU law in situations where there are differences between them. Our next task, in Chapter 7, is to consider how such conflicts between national law and EU law actually *reach* the CJEU. This may seem like a technical question—but the dialogue between national courts and the CJEU has been fundamental in the development of EU law, as the remainder of this chapter will show. It is consequently as important as determining a hierarchy between EU and national law sources in ensuring that EU law works in the Member States.

The context to this chapter is not fictional. Mr King is real, as is the question that the Court of Appeal ended up having to ask about whether domestic law and EU law were compatible with each other. Note that this is a little different from simply deciding which of these two laws take precedence: *if* the Working Time Directive requires something different than what the 1998 Regulations say about carrying over untaken leave, the Working Time Directive will be applied, under the doctrine of supremacy. But the Court of Appeal is not sure if the provisions *are* incompatible.

We will be using Mr King's case—which, to be clear, is not a 'key' EU law case, but rather a deliberately average example of a domestic court facing EU law—to explore what happens when a domestic court encounters a matter of EU law it has doubts about. Can it simply decide cases involving EU law as if they were purely domestic cases, using the ordinary principles of interpretation? Or do things work differently when EU law is at play? Do national courts need to, or can they, ask for input from an EU Court? And what does such input look like? What are its consequences? All of these questions are addressed by the process set out in Article 267 TFEU: the preliminary reference procedure.

7.2 The Article 267 TFEU process

We saw in Chapter 2 that the CJEU has jurisdiction in a number of situations, including so-called enforcement actions (where the Commission challenges a Member State's compliance with EU law using its **infringement proceedings**, discussed more in Chapter 8), and annulment actions (where, for instance, a Member State challenges a piece of EU legislation as being non-compliant with a principle like subsidiarity, and requests it to be declared void as a consequence). The annulment action, discussed in detail there, applies in situations where the *validity* of an EU act is being challenged by someone.

However, the Treaties have created a distinct role for the CJEU: it can also decide cases where the validity of an EU law is not necessarily at issue, but rather its *meaning* is not entirely clear to a body that is meant to apply it. That process is set out in Article 267 TFEU, and involves two separate but related steps: first, a domestic court has to refer (or ask) a question to the CJEU about the meaning of EU law at stake in a dispute it is hearing; and secondly, the CJEU offers an interpretation of EU law to the domestic court, enabling the domestic court to decide the dispute before it. We consider both of these steps next.

7.2.1 Referring a question

Article 19 TEU stresses that the CJEU has the exclusive power to interpret EU law, meaning that it is also the only body that can declare *what* EU law means in a legally binding manner. In practice, however, the CJEU is rarely the first judicial body to actually *encounter* EU law in an ongoing dispute. Previous chapters already demonstrated that EU law is integrated into national legal orders in an increasing number of ways. The logical consequence of that development is that when a dispute takes place within a Member State, it may touch upon issues of EU law—rather than domestic law—and clarification of those issues of EU law might be needed. If that clarification can only be provided in a legally binding matter by the CJEU, there must therefore be a way for a domestic court to *ask* the CJEU a question about EU law.

That way is the so-called 'preliminary reference' or 'preliminary ruling' function, set out as one of the CJEU's powers in Article 19(3)(b) of the TEU,[1] and elaborated on in Article 267 TFEU.

Article 267 TFEU (emphasis added)

The Court of Justice of the European Union shall have jurisdiction to give preliminary rulings concerning:

(a) the interpretation of the Treaties;

(b) the validity and interpretation of acts of the institutions, bodies, offices or agencies of the Union;

Where such a question is raised before any court or tribunal of a Member State, that court or tribunal may, if it considers that a decision on the question is necessary to enable it to give judgment, request the Court to give a ruling thereon.

Where any such question is raised in a case pending before a court or tribunal of a Member State against whose decisions there is no judicial remedy under national law, that court or tribunal shall bring the matter before the Court.

. . .

[1] 'The Court of Justice of the European Union shall, in accordance with the Treaties: . . . give preliminary rulings, at the request of courts or tribunals of the Member States, on the interpretation of Union law or the validity of acts adopted by the institutions; . . .'

As is clear from the text of Article 267 TFEU, the preliminary reference procedure is there to assist national 'courts or tribunals' with both issues of *interpretation* of EU primary and secondary legislation, and *validity* of EU secondary legislation.

We can illustrate how a preliminary reference works by returning to the *Factortame* saga, first raised in Chapter 6. In *Factortame (No 1)* the Divisional Court was faced with a judicial review application from a Spanish fishing company called Factortame.[2] At the centre of the dispute was the UK's Merchant Shipping Act (MSA) 1988, which interacted with EU law obligations the UK had as a party to the Common Fisheries Policy (CFP). The CFP set out how much fishing each Member State was entitled to engage in per calendar year. As fishing was limited by these 'quotas', companies started experimenting with setting up subsidiaries or registering their own base of operations in different Member States so as to benefit from *their* quotas. The MSA 1988 restricted access to the British quota to firms with, effectively, majority British ownership, in response to this.

Factortame Ltd and similar companies had met the registration conditions under the MSA 1894 and had thus successfully fished in the UK for nearly a century, but as the MSA 1988 focused on 'British ownership', they would suddenly no longer meet the conditions to fish in UK waters under the MSA 1988. Factortame argued that preventing Spanish-owned British-registered companies from accessing British fishing quotas unless they demonstrated clear connections to the UK (via 'British ownership' conditions) violated the prohibition of nationality-based discrimination and freedom of establishment in the then-EC Treaty.

The UK government disagreed with this interpretation; it argued that the MSA 1988 was permissible under EU law, not least so as to ensure that the British fishing quota was only used by ships *genuinely* associated with the UK. A quota for the UK that could be accessed by any other EU Member State as long as it registered a subsidiary company in the UK would in practice not be a 'UK quota', as all EU Member States are permitted under the EU Treaties to set up companies anywhere else in the EU.

The Divisional Court in *Factortame (No 1)* consequently was asked to determine what the EC Treaties meant: did they permit a piece of legislation like the MSA 1988, or did they preclude it?

Discussing the scenario

Do you think a domestic court should be able to answer a question about EU law like the one it was faced with in *Factortame (No 1)*, or like the one that the Court of Appeal is faced with in the scenario involving Mr King at the start of the chapter? Why or why not?

This is the point in domestic proceedings where Article 267 TFEU becomes relevant. The text of Article 267 makes clear that the Treaty distinguishes between two types of domestic courts. If a lower domestic court decides that the meaning of the EU law at hand is debatable, it can *choose* to refer a question to the CJEU, asking for an interpretation of that EU law. If it is a national court of 'last resort'—one whose rulings cannot be judicially

[2] *Factortame (No 1)* (1989) 2 CMLR 353.

reviewed under national law, like the UK Supreme Court's rulings—it does not have a choice to refer that question; rather, it *must* refer a question of interpretation of EU law to the CJEU. We will explore the concept of 'court' and 'court of last resort', as they have been defined by the CJEU, in Section 7.3.

Why is a process like this necessary in EU law?

There are a number of reasons. First, institutionally, the CJEU is not actually a traditional court of appeal—meaning that if a national court gets the EU law 'wrong', complainants cannot simply escalate a dispute to the CJEU and get a formally binding opinion on the meaning of EU law. The EU judicial system was carefully constructed in the EEC Treaty so as to avoid implying that the CJEU was 'superior' to the national courts. Instead, the national legal system and the EU legal systems were intended to operate alongside each other. In such a situation, where courts actually operate in distinct legal spheres instead of in a clear hierarchy, one court cannot explicitly overrule another. However, when those legal spheres overlap, it is important that the courts in these respective legal spheres know what their jobs are.

The CJEU has regularly commented on the division of labour between national courts and the CJEU itself:[3]

Case 35/76 *Simmenthal* ECLI:EU:C:1976:180 (emphasis added)

4. [Article 267 TFEU] is based on a **distinct separation of functions** between **national courts** and tribunals on the one hand and **the Court of Justice** on the other hand and **it does not give the Court jurisdiction to take cognizance of the facts of the case, or to criticize the reasons for the reference.**

   The Court is entitled to pronounce on the interpretation of the Treaty and of acts of the institutions but cannot apply them to the case in question since **such application falls within the jurisdiction of the national court.**

The second reason for establishing the preliminary reference process follows from the desire to have the legal spheres not conflict with each other: if EU law is to work the same way in all Member States, it must *mean* the same thing in all Member States. The CJEU itself has forcefully made this point in many cases, such as in *ICC*, where it stressed that 'the main purpose of the powers accorded to the Court by [Article 267 TFEU] is to ensure that [EU] law is applied uniformly by national courts'.[4]

Consequently, we cannot end up in a situation where, for instance, the UK decides that it can discriminate against Spanish fishing companies who are not 'genuinely' active in the UK under EU law, but Belgium decides that this is illegal. The same rule must apply in the entirety of the EU, or many of the EU's goals cannot actually be achieved: different rules would apply in different countries, resulting in competition between the Member States rather than a 'common market'. The CJEU has made this claim forcefully, arguing that EU law is an 'autonomous legal order', and that Article 267 TFEU makes clear that the CJEU is intended to be the only court that can determine what the law *is* in this 'legal order'.[5]

[3] Case 244/80 *Pasquale Foglia v Mariella Novello* (*No 2*) ECLI:EU:C:1981:302, para 14.
[4] Case 66/80 *ICC* ECLI:EU:C:1981:102, para 11.
[5] See, eg, Case C-284/16, *Achmea* ECLI:EU:2018:158, para 37.

The uniformity of EU law is particularly important when Article 267 TFEU is used to contest the *validity* of an EU law measure, and the CJEU has been adamant that the preliminary reference process is used when a national court *believes* that an EU law may be invalid. The key case here is *Foto-Frost,* where a German court asked outright if it could declare a Commission decision invalid (as it conflicted with a Protocol to the EU Treaties that permitted duty-free trade between the-then two parts of Germany). The CJEU said no:[6]

Case 314/85 *Foto-Frost* ECLI: EU:C:1987:452 (emphasis added)

13. In enabling national courts, against those decisions where there is a judicial remedy under national law, to refer to the Court for a preliminary ruling questions on interpretation or validity, [Article 297 TFEU] did not settle the question **whether those courts themselves may declare that acts of [EU] institutions are invalid.**
14. Those courts may consider the validity of [an EU] act and, if they consider that the grounds put forward before them by the parties in support of invalidity are unfounded, they may reject them, concluding that the measure is completely valid. **By taking that action they are not calling into question the existence of the [EU] measure.**
15. On the other hand, **those courts do not have the power to declare acts of the [EU] institutions invalid.** As the Court emphasized in the [*ICC* judgment], the main purpose of the powers accorded to the Court by [Article 297 TFEU] is to **ensure that [EU] law is applied uniformly by national courts.** That requirement of uniformity is particularly imperative when the validity of [an EU] act is in question. **Divergences between courts in the Member States as to the validity of [EU] acts would be liable to place in jeopardy the very unity of the [EU] legal order and detract from the fundamental requirement of legal certainty.**

In short, where two legal orders co-exist—as they do in the EU, with the EU being one and the Member States' domestic legal orders being the other—it is important that rules that are meant to apply in *both* legal orders are understood in a common way. The preliminary reference is the EU Treaties' means of achieving that common understanding and establishes a clear communication pathway between courts of two distinct legal orders.

EU law in practice

When we say that the preliminary reference procedure can be used to 'clarify' the meaning of EU law, we rarely mean that the EU law in question is written in a way that is incomprehensible or has various meanings. While drafting errors do occur, domestic courts in practice find the meaning of EU law vague in the specific circumstance of it *interacting with national law*.

[6] And continues to say 'no' to this day: see, eg, Case C-362/14 *Schrems* ECLI:EU:C:2015:650.

If we look at some examples of other questions referred to the CJEU, it becomes clear that it is normally the interaction of a national law in a very specific policy area with an aspect of EU law that results in domestic courts having doubts about the meaning or validity of EU law. These examples stem from seminal CJEU case law on the supremacy of EU law that we considered in Chapter 6, so they are also an illustration of just how important the Article 267 TFEU process has been in the ***development*** of the EU legal order.

First, the decision in ***Costa*** that established the primacy of EU law was the result of a preliminary reference.[7] The Italian court in question asked the CJEU to clarify whether Italian Law No 1643, which nationalized the production of electricity, was compatible with the EU Treaties—and specifically, the freedom of establishment, as no other electricity companies could now enter the electricity market in Italy. In other words, it sought an interpretation of what is now Article 49 TFEU.

Internationale Handelsgesellschaft, on the other hand, was a challenge to the validity of an EU measure: the German administrative court faced with a dispute over an EU regulation on the 'common organisation of the market in cereals' asked the CJEU if certain provisions in that regulation and its subsequent implementing regulations were legal (under EU law).[8]

Finally, in ***Simmenthal***, the CJEU was asked by an Italian court to consider if Italian Law No 1239/70, setting out a series of fees for veterinary health inspection of beef, could be maintained despite its conflicting with EU law—and specifically, the free movement of goods—because it was adopted ***after*** Italy joined the European Union.[9] The Italian Constitutional Court had found in different cases that the principle of ***lex posterior*** applied to the EU Treaties in the same way it did to domestic law, and the Italian court hearing the ***Simmenthal*** dispute wanted to ask the CJEU to explain how ***lex posterior*** interacted with the EU principle of supremacy.

Can you imagine a way in which the CJEU could have established supremacy of EU law ***without*** preliminary references? Could conflicts between national laws and EU laws have reached the CJEU via any of the other direct actions before the CJEU, discussed in Chapter 2?

The *Factortame (No 1)* case offers an example of the kind of situation wherein it is very difficult for a domestic court to know what EU law requires. The EU law relevant to this case is two-pronged: first, there are the EU-established 'national fishing quotas', and then there are the EU rules on freedom of establishment, whereby companies from one Member State should not face discrimination when setting up in another Member State. Both laws are in and of themselves clear—until the MSA 1988 is added into the scenario.

The MSA 1988 seems to be attempting to make the 'national fishing quota' system work—but at the cost of freedom of establishment, as it is not letting Spanish fishermen 'establish' on the same grounds that British fishermen can. The principle of supremacy, as discussed in Chapter 6, tells us that these EU laws take priority over the MSA 1988—but as they seem to result in opposing conclusions about whether the MSA 1988 is a permissible piece of legislation under the Treaties, that only helps to some extent. As such, asking the CJEU for an interpretation of the requirements of EU law was the logical next step for the Divisional Court to take.

[7] Case 6/64 *Costa* ECLI:EU:C:1964:66.
[8] Case 11/70 *Internationale Handelsgesellschaft* ECLI:EU:C:1970:114.
[9] Case 106/77 *Simmenthal* ECLI:EU:C:1978:49.

7.2.2 Getting a response from the CJEU

Of course, *sending* a question to the CJEU is only one part of the preliminary reference process. The key to resolving disputes like *Factortame* is getting a response from the CJEU that actually helps resolve the dispute.

In light of the volume of case law it faces, over time, the CJEU has developed a series of procedural rules that determine if preliminary references are admissible. Key here is that ultimately, the decision to accept a preliminary reference is the CJEU's alone. It has the discretion to reject *any* reference, though it ordinarily tries to answer the ones that it receives—and where the problems with a question are slight, the CJEU can attempt to reformulate a question so that it becomes answerable. It made this clear as early as in *Costa*, when it stated that it held '[the] power to extract from a question imperfectly formulated by the national court those questions which alone pertain to the interpretation of the Treaty'.

That said, there are a number of established 'requirements' for preliminary references to be considered admissible. First, the domestic court must actually ask the CJEU questions that it can answer: these questions have to be regarding the meaning of an EU legal concept, and must relate to a real case. It has rejected references with questions that it found were irrelevant to the dispute the national court faced,[10] as well as hypothetical questions about what EU law *might* say in a given scenario. When the domestic court in *Meilicke* thus asked a whole series of questions about an EU directive on company law that were not actually applicable to the dispute before it, the CJEU made it clear it would not answer those.[11]

It also refuses to rule on so-called 'test cases': cases where there is no actual dispute but instead two parties who broadly agree on the meaning of the law wish to have their interpretation confirmed by the CJEU. The key case here is *Foglia*, where the CJEU found that the two parties in the case had worked together in order to force a domestic court to seek CJEU confirmation that a particular French tax was incompatible with the EU Treaties. The CJEU was not receptive to such a use of the preliminary reference procedure:

Case 244/80 *Foglia v Novello* ECLI:EU:C:1981:302 (emphasis added)

18. It must in fact be emphasized that the duty assigned to the Court by [Article 267 TFEU] is **not that of delivering advisory opinions on general or hypothetical questions** but of assisting in the administration of justice in the Member States. It accordingly does not have jurisdiction to reply to questions of interpretation which are submitted to it within the framework of procedural devices arranged by the parties in order to **induce the Court to give its views on certain problems of [EU law] which do not correspond to an objective requirement inherent in the resolution of a dispute.** A declaration by the Court that it has no jurisdiction in such circumstances **does not in any way trespass upon the prerogatives of the national court** but makes it possible to prevent the application of the procedure under [Article 267 TFEU] for purposes other than those appropriate for it.

[10] See, eg, Case 126/80 *Salonia* ECLI:EU:C:1981:136, para 6; Case C-343/90 *Dias* ECLI:EU:C:1992:327, para 18.

[11] Case C-83/91 *Meilicke* ECLI:EU:C:1992:332, para 30.

The last sentence of paragraph 18 of *Foglia* is one that has resulted in substantial debate: the CJEU seems adamant that it is not questioning the national court's decision to make a reference, but can it genuinely maintain this? And if it is questioning whether a 'real' question was submitted, what is it basing that determination on—when the facts of the case are only fully known to the national court?[12] *Foglia* may be seen as a sign that, rather than a purely cooperative relationship, the CJEU may attempt to establish a form of a hierarchy when it deems that the national court has not done *its* duty properly. We will come back to this idea in Section 7.5.

Other situations where the CJEU has declared references inadmissible are where the referring national court does not provide enough factual information for the CJEU to actually give a clear interpretation of how EU law works in a given dispute,[13] and where wholly unclear questions are being referred.[14] These, and other conditions that the CJEU's case law has established for admissibility of references, are reiterated in a set of 'recommendations' that the Court has provided to national courts when submitting references in 2018.[15] In an Annex, those 'recommendations' stress the essential elements required in a reference, and as such form a template of sorts to enable any national court to submit a reference when it wishes to.

The key to a successful preliminary reference is consequently a clearly articulated question, situated in enough factual detail to be understandable, on an issue of EU law—and an issue of EU law that is *central* to the domestic law dispute at hand. As an example of a well-written reference, we can look at some of the questions referred in *Factortame (No 1)*.

Case C-221/89 *The Queen v Secretary of State for Transport, ex parte Factortame Ltd and others* ECLI:EU:C:1991:320 ('*Factortame 1*') (emphasis added)

11. In order to resolve [the *Factortame*] dispute the High Court of Justice, Queen's Bench Division, referred the following questions to the Court for a preliminary ruling:

Question 1

Does [EU law] **affect the conditions** under which a Member State lays **down rules for determining which vessels are entitled to register in that State**, to fly its flag and carry its nationality?

→

[12] For a critical view of *Foglia,* see G Bebr, 'The Existence of a Genuine Dispute: an indispensable precondition for the jurisdiction of the Court under Article 177 EC Treaty' (1980) 17 CMLRev 525; for a supportive view, see D Wyatt, 'Foglia (No 2): The Court denies it has jurisdiction to give advisory opinions' (1982) 7 ELRev 186.

[13] Joined Cases C-320–322/90 *Telemarsicabruzzo v Circostel* ECLI:EU:C:1993:26.

[14] See *Meilicke* (n 11).

[15] CJEU, 'Recommendations to national courts and tribunals in relation to the initiation of preliminary ruling proceedings' [2018] OJ C257/01.

→

Question 2

In the light of the provisions and principles of [EU law] and in particular (but without limitation) the principle of non-discrimination on grounds of nationality, the right of establishment and the requirement of proportionality, is a Member State entitled to stipulate that in order to be registered in and entitled to fly the flag of that Member State, a fishing vessel:

. . .

(c) must be managed and its operations directed and controlled from within that Member State; and

(d) must have as its charterer, manager or operator, a citizen of that Member State, resident and domiciled therein . . .

When receiving admissible references, the CJEU will provide its interpretation of the EU law 'questions' raised in a dispute. If the dispute concerns a matter on which the CJEU has ruled before, it will simply echo its previous ruling. It does not reject the reference, but effectively 'copies and pastes' its previous findings and directs the national court to those, establishing a form of precedent.[16]

Where a provision in EU law has not been interpreted by the CJEU yet, or where the context of the domestic dispute is sufficiently different from that in previous disputes to require a new interpretation, the CJEU will provide a ruling—but only on the *meaning* of the EU law at play in the domestic dispute. It is very important to understand that the CJEU does not actually *decide* the dispute in question; the power to decide a national dispute remains exclusively that of the domestic courts. We can clearly see this in how the CJEU answered the questions referred in *Factortame (No 2)*:

Case C-221/89 *The Queen v Secretary of State for Transport, ex parte Factortame Ltd and others* ECLI:EU:C:1991:320 ('*Factortame 1*') (emphasis added)

17. Consequently, the answer to the first question must be that, as [EU law] stands at present, it is for the Member States to determine, in accordance with the general rules of international law, the conditions which must be fulfilled in order for a vessel to be registered in their registers and granted the right to fly their flag, but, in exercising that power, the Member States must comply with the rules of [EU law].

. . .

33. It follows from the foregoing that it is contrary to the provisions of [EU law] and, in particular, to [Article 49 TFEU] for a Member State to stipulate as conditions for the registration of a fishing vessel in its national register: . . . that the said legal owners and beneficial owners, charterers, managers, operators, shareholders and directors, as the case may be, must be resident and domiciled in that Member State.

[16] See the reference made in Case 28-30/62 *Da Costa* ECLI:EU:C:1963:6, which asked effectively the same questions as Case 26/62 *Van Gend en Loos*, discussed in detail in Chapter 8.

> ...
>
> **36.** Consequently, the reply to the national court must be that **it is not contrary to [EU law]** for a Member State **to stipulate as a condition for the registration of a fishing vessel in its national register** that the vessel in question must be **managed and its operations directed and controlled from within that Member State.**

These are interpretations of provisions of EU law that help the Divisional Court determine what parts of the MSA 1988 may present problems in light of EU law—but this does not conclude the domestic case at hand. The ultimate work of deciding that provisions of the MSA 1988 contravene the UK's EU law obligations is left for the Divisional Court, in line with the division of duties that is meant to exist between national courts and the CJEU.

The continuance of *Factortame (No 1)* is consequently the Divisional Court actually resolving the dispute between Factortame Ltd and the UK government. It did this by making an order giving effect to the CJEU's judgment, and directing the fishing companies to give particulars of their claims of damages. The most salient part of the CJEU's ruling in *Factortame (No 1)* was, ironically, no longer needed: the MSA 1988 had been repealed by November 1989, meaning that by the time the judgment was issued in 1991, Factortame Ltd's concrete problem in registering its ships had been resolved.

Discussing the scenario

What will the CJEU actually do in response to a preliminary reference about Mr King's dispute with Sash WW at the start of the chapter? And what will remain for the domestic court to do?

This, by means of an example, is how the CJEU and domestic courts interact: a domestic dispute encounters an EU law concept that is not 'clear', and the domestic court requests that the CJEU clarify that concept. The CJEU then provides that clarification, and using the clarification, the domestic court decides the dispute. In theory, therefore, the preliminary reference procedure sets up a communication process that should facilitate the operation of EU law in all the Member States without the CJEU actually acting as a 'court of appeal'. However, the preliminary reference procedure as set out in Article 267 TFEU is in practice not always as clearcut a process as the sketch provided by *Factortame (No 1)* would suggest.

7.3 Filling the gaps in Article 267 TFEU

There are a number of aspects to Article 267 TFEU that have required further interpretation by the CJEU in order to clarify when preliminary references can and should be submitted, and—importantly—if there are ever situations in which even a court of 'last resort' can avoid referring a question, because EU law *is* actually clear (even if the parties to a domestic dispute do not seem to think so).

7.3.1 What are 'courts and tribunals'?

Given that Article 267 TFEU is meant to coherently apply to what are now 27 different legal orders, it has to operate using general wording that can work in all the Member States—but all the same, the fact that it describes those national bodies that can refer questions merely as 'courts' or 'tribunals' is only helpful to an extent. Not all domestic bodies taking binding legal decisions are necessarily called 'courts' or 'tribunals'; and does Article 267 TFEU actually mean that *any* court can ask the CJEU a question?

The CJEU has addressed a number of these kinds of questions in its case law. It thus found in *Rheinmühlen-Düsseldorf* that the domestic hierarchy of the court system is irrelevant to the preliminary reference procedure: any court, no matter how 'low' it sits in that hierarchy for domestic purposes, has the power to refer a question about it to the CJEU.[17] This is obviously a significant ruling: it gives more concrete power to low-level courts that allows them to interact with a separate legal order themselves. They have, unsurprisingly, been rather keen on taking advantage of their distinctive position in the EU legal order—and have referred questions rather more easily than their more 'senior' counterparts have, as we discuss in Section 7.4.

The concept of a 'court' or 'tribunal' has also required significant interpretation. In some of the Member States, there are bespoke quasi-judicial bodies that are not technically *part* of the judiciary, but nonetheless take binding decisions that have legal effects. The text of Article 267 TFEU does not immediately make it clear if, for instance, an employment-related Appeals Commission in the Netherlands meets the definition of a 'court' under Article 267. The CJEU confirmed in *Broekmeulen* that it does, however.[18]

As the sole authoritative interpreter of EU law, the CJEU—and not domestic law—determines what meets the Article 267 TFEU conditions of being a 'court'. The national status of a body is consequently irrelevant in determining if it can submit a preliminary reference. However, to avoid having to make determinations on a purely case-by-case basis, the CJEU has set out the following non-exclusive conditions that it will examine in deciding if a national body is a 'court or tribunal', which it has regularly repeated in its case law from *Syfait I* onwards:[19]

- Is the body in question a body 'established by law';
- Is it permanent (or has it been established temporarily—like an arbitral panel, for instance);
- Is its jurisdiction compulsory or optional;
- Are its procedures *inter partes* (eg, between two disagreeing parties);
- Does it apply 'rules of law'; and
- Is it independent?[20]

This list may look lengthy, but the variety of bodies that exist in national legal systems that take some kind of 'formal' decision is so expansive that even with this list of

[17] Case 166/73 *Rheinmühlen-Düsseldorf* ECLI:EU:C:1974:3, para 4.

[18] Case C-246/80 *Broekmeulen* ECLI:EU:C:1981:218.

[19] Case C-53/03 *Syfait I* ECLI:EU:C:2005:333, para 29.

[20] See, most recently, Case C-175/11 *H. I. D. and B. A. v Refugee Applications Commissioner and Others* ECLI:EU:C:2013:45, para 83; and Case C-377/12 *Ascendi* ECLI:EU:C:2014:1754, para 23.

guidelines, determining if a referring body is a 'court or tribunal' is not always straightforward. Whether arbitration panels fall within the scope of Article 267 TFEU has been a particularly complex matter, with the CJEU looking on a case-by-case basis at the extent to which an arbitral panel is established by law, makes binding decisions, and has compulsory jurisdiction. Where arbitral panels are set up with the consent of the parties, outside of state control, they are deemed to fall outside of Article 267 TFEU.[21]

The status of arbitration panels sheds light on an ongoing argument about the nature of 'courts and tribunals'. It has been argued that arbitration panels, given their prevalence in modern commercial relations, should be more *clearly* covered by Article 267 TFEU, so as to ensure that EU law in those commercial relations is also consistently interpreted. Others, including one of the Court AGs, have instead expressed the view that the definition of 'courts and tribunals' has become so broad that the preliminary reference process no longer produces 'judicial dialogue' but rather involves a variety of bodies, some without formal legal training and outside of the domestic judicial hierarchies.[22] The CJEU, in any event, seems content with a broad definition of the concept—perhaps unsurprisingly so, as the more references it receives from varied sources, the more likely it will be that EU law is consistently applied across the Member States.[23]

7.3.2 What is a court of 'last resort'?

A further aspect of Article 267 TFEU that has needed some clarification is *when* a court or tribunal is one of 'last resort', and thus must submit a reference on a matter of EU law that it is uncertain about in a given dispute. The original understanding was that courts that effectively ended the 'appeals chain' in domestic law, such as supreme courts or constitutional courts, were the courts addressed by this provision. However, the CJEU's case law has made clear that it is not the legal *status* of the court that determines if it is a court of 'last resort', but rather how the legal system operates regarding the case at hand.[24] *Costa* thus established that a court is of 'last resort' if in a specific legal proceeding, no appeal from its decision is possible: as Costa's claim was for a very limited sum of money—in the form of his electricity bill—Italian law denied him the possibility of appeal.

The CJEU has been forceful about the fact that courts of 'last resort' *should* appeal, and has made it clear that there can be consequences for a national court refusing to do so. Key here is *Köbler*, which we consider in more detail in Chapter 8.[25] In short, Mr Köbler was an Austrian professor who had applied for a 'loyalty bonus' to his salary on account of lengthy service in Austrian universities, but was denied this bonus because some of his years of work had taken place in Germany, rather than in Austria. He claimed this was unjustified discrimination against him because he had exercised his EU freedom of movement.

[21] See, excluded from Article 267 TFEU, Case C-125/04 *Denuit* ECLI:EU:C:2005:69; but falling within Article 267 TFEU, *Achmea* and *Ascendi*.

[22] See the Opinion of AG Colomer on Case C-17/00 *De Coster* ECLI:EU:2001:366.

[23] See, similarly, its development of the obligation to set aside national legislation that conflicts with EU law, as discussed in Chapter 6.

[24] Case C-210/06 *Cartesio* ECLI:EU:C:2008:723.

[25] Case C-224/01 *Köbler* ECLI:EU:C:2003:513.

The Austrian Administrative Court originally referred a question to the CJEU to ask if this Austrian 'loyalty bonus' was captured by the EU non-discrimination provisions, but changed its mind about needing to refer a question to the CJEU and decided that it was not. Mr Köbler was convinced that the Administrative Court had misapplied EU law, and so brought an action for damages against the Administrative Court for a failure to apply EU law correctly that had caused him personal harm. That claim for damages *was* referred to the CJEU, which confirmed that in certain circumstances, a court could be liable for misapplying EU law, *and* for failing to refer questions to the CJEU when it should have.[26]

Discussing the scenario

Is the employment tribunal originally hearing Mr King's case a 'court or tribunal' under EU law? And was the Court of Appeal obliged to refer a question to the CJEU, or could it simply choose to do so?

7.3.3 Can the meaning of EU law be 'so clear' that there is no need to refer a question?

Köbler raises a final, and perhaps most interesting, shortcoming of the text of Article 267 TFEU, which is that it does not in any way clarify how national courts decide if an issue of EU law is in need of CJEU interpretation. What happens in a situation where a national court looks at a provision of EU law, and is presented with two different arguments as to its meaning, but thinks that one interpretation is the *obvious* correct one? If it is a lower order court, the text of Article 267 TFEU makes clear that it can choose not to refer. But what about courts of 'last resort'?

Ultimately, in *Köbler,* the CJEU determined that the national court was not liable in damages for having failed to refer a question under Article 267 TFEU, because it had withdrawn its reference in good faith: the Austrian Administrative Court had exchanged several letters with the CJEU's own registrar, and had been left with the impression that a different CJEU ruling had already given an answer to the question it had asked. This, then, is one of the two circumstances in which even courts of 'last resort' are not obliged to refer: where the CJEU has already answered the question referred in a different case, or where the same points of law have arisen in a different CJEU ruling.[27]

But what if the CJEU has not already issued a ruling that clarifies the meaning of an aspect of EU law? This is a matter that has come before the CJEU in *CILFIT*.[28] *CILFIT* involved a domestic dispute between the company CILFIT and the Italian Ministry of Health; CILFIT claimed that import duties imposed by Italian law were contrary to an EU regulation. The Italian Ministry of Health's response to this was not only that CILFIT was wrong, but that the EU regulation in question was *so clear* that there was no point in referring a question to the CJEU for an interpretation.

[26] See Chapter 8. [27] See, eg, *Da Costa* (n 16), para 38.

[28] Case 283/81 *Srl CILFIT and Lanificio di Gavardo SpA v Ministry of Health* ECLI:EU:C:1982:335.

The Italian Court of Cassation decided that this claim by the Ministry of Health was itself a matter of EU law that needed the CJEU's interpretation: is a court of 'last resort' unconditionally obliged to refer a question to the CJEU, or is that obligation premised on the existence of some *doubt* as to the correct interpretation of a provision of EU law?

The CJEU offered a response in *CILFIT*. After first noting that if it has offered an interpretation of the relevant EU law in a previous case, there is no need to refer a question on the matter, it then sets out what is known as the 'acte clair' doctrine:

Case 283/81 *Srl CILFIT and Lanificio di Gavardo SpA v Ministry of Health* ECLI:EU:C:1982:335 (emphasis added)

16. Finally, the correct application of Community law may **be so obvious as to leave no scope for any reasonable doubt** as to the manner in which the question raised is to be resolved. Before it comes to the conclusion that such is the case, the national court or tribunal must be convinced that the matter is **equally obvious to the courts of the other Member States and to the Court of Justice**. Only if those conditions are satisfied, may the national court or tribunal refrain from submitting the question to the Court of Justice and take upon itself the responsibility for resolving it.

CILFIT is an interesting compromise position. In short, it suggests that there is no duty to refer a question to a court of 'last resort' if:

- The correct application (or meaning) of EU law is so 'obvious as to leave no scope for any reasonable doubt'; and
- It is equally obvious to courts of all other Member States; and
- It is equally obvious to the CJEU.

This is asking a lot of national courts. Academic debate about what the *CILFIT* test requires has been rife, with some taking the view that the conditions set out in paragraph 16 are so limited that the national court will have no choice *but* to refer a question to the CJEU because of *CILFIT*. How can a national court ever be positive that its interpretation will be shared by all other courts in all other Member States, as well as the CJEU? Different language versions of EU law, as well as different national laws that may interact with EU law in different ways, make it nearly impossible for a national court to be sure it had satisfied the *CILFIT* test.[29]

Other issues with the *CILFIT* test are that it does not leave scope, for instance, for a national court to decline to refer a question of EU law because it is so peculiar to a specific case (in light of its facts) that waiting for a CJEU response does not make sense for the parties or the national court from a cost-benefit perspective.[30] This is not an unreasonable point: the CJEU, even when offering responses to references as a matter of priority, usually takes a few months to rule because of its general case load. While the uniform

[29] Hjalte Rasmussen, 'The European Court's Acte Clair Strategy in CILFIT' (1984) 9 ELRev 242.

[30] Niels Fenger and Morten Broberg, 'Finding Light in the Darkness: On the actual application of the *acte clair* doctrine' (2011) 30(1) YEL 180.

interpretation of EU law is undoubtedly important, in cases that are unlikely to establish a precedent because of how specific to the facts they are, it is not immediately obvious that the need for a reference outweighs the desire to speedily resolve a domestic dispute.

Critics of *CILFIT* are likely to be in favour of the recent decisions of *X and van Dijk* and *Ferreira da Silva e Brito*, which appear to have relaxed the *CILFIT* test, and thus make it less likely that courts of 'last resort' submit references to the CJEU.[31] Korzenov has interpreted the more recent case law on the *CILFIT* test as perhaps being a sign that the CJEU is looking to capture *systemic* breaches of the duty to refer by courts of 'last resort', which in light of its case load is understandable.[32]

Even though the national court might occasionally wrongly decide that a matter of EU law is 'acte clair', the time saved by the CJEU in not considering *every* interpretation of EU law made by a court of 'last resort' compensates significantly. And, as a final point, if the national court is strikingly wrong about its interpretation of EU law, it is likely that both plaintiffs and the Commission will notice—and *Köbler* has made it clear that (albeit in very limited circumstances, as we will see in Chapter 8), a domestic court that fails to refer when it should have referred a question to the CJEU can be held liable for damages.

Pause for reflection

Should national courts of 'last resort' ever be able to refuse a reference to the CJEU, in your view? And if you think they should be, are the *CILFIT* conditions the appropriate ones for the national courts to meet?

7.4 The UK courts and the preliminary reference process

A key aspect of the preliminary reference procedure that the EU Treaties cannot account for at all is that it will only work in establishing a route of communication between the EU legal order and the national legal order if *national courts and tribunals are willing to use it.*

Making a very general observation here, it seems that the less experience a domestic court has with being overruled by a different court, the less willing it is to refer a matter to the CJEU; as such, lower courts have generally made substantial use of the preliminary reference process, but constitutional courts have historically been very reluctant![33] Some of the reluctance is rooted in the jurisdiction of these constitutional courts, or even the CJEU's definition of 'court or tribunal', but an overarching reluctance may be rooted in concern for status. For a constitutional court to accept that it needs to request *help* from

[31] Joined Cases C-72/14 and C-197/14 *X and van Dijk* ECLI:EU:C:2015:564 and Case C-160/14 *Ferreira da Silva e Brito* ECLI:EU:C:2015:565; but by contrast, see Case C-379/15 *Association France Nature Environnement* ECLI:EU:C:2016:603, where the CJEU appeared to restrict the latitude on references again.

[32] Alexander Korzenov, 'The New Format of the Acte Clair Doctrine and Its Consequences' (2016) 53 CMLRev 1317.

[33] Monica Claes, 'Luxembourg, Here We Come? Constitutional Courts and the Preliminary Reference Procedure' (2015) 16 Ger Law J 1331.

a separate court is to accept that it is no longer the sole 'final authority' on all matters affecting national law. We saw in Chapter 6 that some constitutional or 'supreme' courts remain reluctant to accept this permanent limitation of their powers.

What has the UK courts' attitude towards referring cases to the CJEU been? While by no means the most prolific 'referrer' in the EU, any reluctance on the part of the UK judiciary to refer questions to the CJEU should not be overstated.

Lord Denning, adopting slightly dramatic language, set out how EU membership affected the role of the English courts in *Bulmer v Bollinger* shortly after the UK's accession:

HP Bulmer Ltd & Anor v. J. Bollinger SA & Ors [1974] EWCA Civ 14 (emphasis added)

It is important to distinguish between the task of **interpreting** the Treaty—to see what it means—and the task of **applying** it—to apply its provisions to the case in hand. Let me put on one side the task of **applying** the Treaty. **On this matter in our Courts, the English Judges have the final word.** They are the only Judges who are empowered to decide the case itself. **They have to find the facts, to state the issues, to give judgment for one side or the other, and to see that the judgment is enforced.**

Before the English Judges can apply the Treaty, they have to see what it means and what is its effect. In the task of **interpreting** the Treaty, the English Judges are no longer the final authority. They no longer carry the law in their breasts. They are no longer in a position to give rulings which are of binding force. **The supreme tribunal for interpreting the Treaty is the European Court of Justice, at Luxembourg.** Our Parliament has so decreed.

However, while this accurately captures the division of labour intended by the EU Treaties, it does not deal with some of the more practical problems of Article 267 TFEU discussed in Sections 7.2 and 7.3. Lord Denning thus spends significant time developing an explanation for *when* referring a question to the CJEU is appropriate, focusing on the fact that all courts bar the then-House of Lords have *discretion* to do so, and that in any event, no English court should refer a question to the CJEU unless an answer to that question is *necessary* to decide the dispute before it.

On the matter of discretion, he considers that other Member States' courts have considered some of the following factors when deciding whether they wish to refer a question to the CJEU or not:

HP Bulmer Ltd & Anor v. J. Bollinger SA & Ors [1974] EWCA Civ 14 (emphasis added)

Assuming that the condition about 'necessary' is fulfilled, there remains the matter of discretion. This only applies to the trial Judge or the Court of Appeal, not to the House of Lords. The English Court has a discretion either to decide the point itself or to refer it to the European Court. The national Courts of the various member countries have had to consider how to exercise this discretion. The cases show that they have taken into account such matters as the following:

→

→

(i) The **time** to get a ruling [which can be many months] . . .

(ii) **Do not overload the Court** [by sending too many references] . . .

(iii) English courts must be able to **formulate the question clearly** [and be able to **separate the facts from Treaty interpretation**] . . .

(iv) **Difficulty and importance** [of the matter raised—if not difficult, or not important, cost and time can be saved by not referring] . . .

(v) **Expense** [of referring a case to the CJEU, which falls upon the English court] . . .

(vi) **Wishes of the parties**. . . . If both parties want the point to be referred to the European Court, the English Court should have regard to their wishes, but it should not give them undue weight. **The English Court should hesitate before making a reference against the wishes of one of the parties, seeing the expense and delay which it involves.**

Using these questions as a guideline, Lord Denning ultimately concludes that the questions at play in *Bulmer*—which, as discussed in Chapter 6, related to the definition of 'champagne' under EU law—were neither 'necessary' nor warranting the exercise of 'discretion':

HP Bulmer Ltd & Anor v. J. Bollinger SA & Ors [1974] EWCA Civ 14 (emphasis added)

Even if it could be said to be necessary to decide the point, I think that an English Court (short of the House of Lords) should not, as matter of discretion, refer it to the European Court. It should decide the point itself. It would take much time and money to get a ruling from the European Court. Meanwhile, the whole action would be held up. **It is, no doubt, an important point, but not a difficult one to decide.**

Pause for reflection

Do you think all of those criteria set out by Lord Denning are equally relevant in considering when to refer a question to the CJEU? Why or why not?

The guidelines set out by Lord Denning remain of relevance, but, as a general rule, the English courts have become less reluctant to refer questions to the CJEU. The current approach taken by English courts follows Sir Thomas Bingham MR's *ratio* in *ex parte Else*:

R v International Stock Exchange of the UK and RoI, ex parte Else (1982) Ltd [1993] QB 534 (emphasis added)

I understand the correct approach in principle of a national court (other than a final court of appeal) to be quite clear: if the facts have been found and the [EU] law issue is critical to the court's final decision, the appropriate course is ordinarily to refer the issue to the Court of Justice unless the national court can with complete confidence resolve the issue itself . . . **If the national court has any real doubt, it should ordinarily refer.**

The Scottish courts have referred very few questions to the CJEU—12 in total as of 2020—but appear to be following the developments of the English courts in terms of their choices to exercise discretion. While in 1989, for instance, there were clear references to the guidelines set out by Lord Denning in *Brown*,[34] in 2006, the Inner House has applied the *ex parte Else ratio* in determining if they wished to refer a question to the CJEU.[35] Northern Ireland's courts, similarly, have referred few questions—13 in total as of 2020—but appear to follow the guidance of the English courts when they do.[36]

One of the most striking examples of a UK-originating preliminary reference is also one of the most recent, and suggests that most UK courts are comfortable with the 'division of duties' that Article 267 TFEU imagines—even when that 'division of duties' is politically extremely sensitive, as it was in the case of *Wightman*.[37]

Wightman was a judicial review application started by a number of cross-party MPs before the Scottish courts. It asked, in light of a lack of clarity in the European Union (Notification of Withdrawal) Act 2017, whether revocation of the notice to withdraw given under Article 50 TEU could be done unilaterally by the UK. While the Court of Session initially refused to refer the question, arguing it concerned a hypothetical scenario as the UK government had been clear that it would *not* revoke Article 50 TEU, on appeal the Inner House referred the question to the CJEU.

The CJEU first determined that there was a genuine dispute, in that the parties and the UK government had a genuine difference of opinion on the legal requirements for revocation. It then ruled that unilateral revocation of Article 50 TEU was an unconditional sovereign right for any Member State, providing that the decision to revoke had been taken in light of a 'democratic process' that satisfied national constitutional requirements.[38] In doing so, the CJEU thus informed Parliament that it could unilaterally enact legislation that would require a revocation of Article 50, and did not need the consent of any EU institutions to do so.

[34] *Brown v Secretary of State for Scotland* (1988) 2 CMLR 836.

[35] *Empowerment Enterprises Ltd v Customs and Excise Commissioners* [2006] CSIH 46.

[36] See, eg, *Pigs Marketing Board v Raymond Redmond* (1978) 2 CMLR 697, where the Armagh Magistrate's Court Resident Magistrate applied Lord Denning's guidelines.

[37] Case C-621/18 *Wightman* ECLI:EU:C:2018:999.

[38] Ibid, para 62.

Wightman may very well be one of the last 'key' references submitted by a UK court. Research from 2018 has suggested that the Brexit vote has already had an impact on the British judiciary even if none of the law has changed: since 2016, the UK courts have on average submitted 22 per cent fewer preliminary references per year than they did prior to the referendum.[39] As we will see in Section 7.6, eventually the number of UK-originating references will drop down close to zero—though the settlement reached for Northern Ireland means that *some* UK courts will continue to be able to make them.

7.5 **Judicial law-making?**

The historical reluctance of constitutional courts to refer questions to the CJEU brings us to a final point worth considering, which relates to the division of authority between the CJEU and national courts that Lord Denning articulates so well in *Bulmer*. Is it in reality possible to clearly distinguish between *applying* the law and *interpreting* it?

The CJEU has been accused of significant judicial activism over the years, and some of these accusations are rooted in its approach to providing 'interpretation' in preliminary references. Depending on how detailed and fact-oriented an 'interpretation' of an EU concept is, the CJEU may move on from 'interpreting', and may end up de facto deciding on the outcome of a case—or at the very least telling a national court exactly *how* to apply its interpretation, by means of very detailed guidelines. Does the CJEU consequently exercise restraint when issuing preliminary references?

Opinions differ, both per commentator and depending on the area of case law in which the CJEU is answering references. Particularly when answering questions which further develop a concept of its own creation, rather than one clearly articulated in the Treaties, the CJEU tends to give rather more specific guidance. As such, it develops its own concepts in a way that almost creates a form of precedent through successive explanations in subsequent cases. Those 'precedential' qualities are enhanced by the fact that, as discussed, there is never an obligation on national courts to refer questions to which a previous CJEU ruling has already provided an answer. As the CJEU is unlikely to overrule itself, over time these key CJEU rulings start to develop into a form of precedent that national courts are strongly encouraged to apply. If we think back to Chapter 6, the sequential development of the concept of supremacy is a good example of how the CJEU builds on its own concepts in a way that appears to give little leeway to national courts in how to apply them.

However, Davies argues that the CJEU has actually ensured that there is a lot of scope for action on the part of national courts. Where it provides very specific answers in a preliminary reference, its ruling will be easier to distinguish on the facts and thus does not establish a clear, general 'precedent'. On the other hand, where its responses to preliminary references are very general, the 'application' of its interpretations clearly still resides with the national court system.[40] As such, he would find that the fact that the CJEU refers to its own judgments on a very regular basis makes for legal certainty, rather than a strongly binding form of precedent on domestic courts.

[39] Arthur Dyevre et al, 'Uncertainty and Legal Disintegration: Evidence From Brexit' (31 October 2018). Available at SSRN: https://ssrn.com/abstract=3276189 or http://dx.doi.org/10.2139/ssrn.3276189.

[40] Gareth Davies, 'Activism Relocated: The self-restraint of the European Court of Justice in its national context' (2012) 19(1) JEPP 76.

In sum, it is likely that the CJEU's use of the preliminary reference process probably is occasionally 'activist'—but within limits. It has used the preliminary reference process to develop core aspects of EU law, but it is also cognizant of the fact that the 'division of duties' that Article 267 TFEU sets out only works when the national courts are *willing* to participate in it. The line between 'interpreting' and 'applying' is consequently fine, but one that the CJEU at the very least attempts to heed, for fear of alienating the national courts that it is hoping to engage in a dialogue.

Pause for reflection

Do you think 'application' and 'interpretation' can be separated out as cleanly as Lord Denning suggests in *Bulmer*? If not, what does this suggest about the relationship between the CJEU and the national courts? Does it remain 'horizontal', as between equals, or is it destined to become 'vertical', with the CJEU assuming a superior position?

7.6 Brexit and preliminary references

Theresa May's government was very explicit about the fact that one of its goals in achieving Brexit was ending the CJEU's jurisdiction in the UK. That jurisdiction currently includes the ability to receive preliminary references from UK courts, and so it is worth considering what happens to that aspect of CJEU jurisdiction over the course of the transition period, and beyond.

7.6.1 The Withdrawal Agreement

For the duration of the transition period, the UK's relationship with the EU will continue as if it were a Member State, with the exception of institutional representation.[41] Consequently, UK courts and tribunals will be able to refer questions to the CJEU, as made explicit in Article 86(2) of the Withdrawal Agreement, but there will be no UK judge on the CJEU when it answers these references, nor will there be a UK Advocate General to offer an opinion.

In two specific ways, however, the CJEU's jurisdiction in the UK—and so the ability for UK courts to refer questions to it—will last longer than the transition period does. The first of these is general. The Withdrawal Agreement acknowledges that not all cases pending before the CJEU will be completed prior to the end of the transition period; and furthermore, there may be cases involving the UK that factually occur during the transition period, but are registered with the CJEU after the transition period.[42] Title X of the

[41] Withdrawal Agreement, Article 7. The transition period can be extended by one or two years beyond the end of 2020 under Withdrawal Agreement, Articles 126 and 132. The EU (Withdrawal Agreement) Act 2020, s 33, prohibits UK representatives from asking for an extension as a matter of domestic law—though as is true for all Acts of Parliament, this can obviously be amended if an extension is desired after all.

[42] Withdrawal Agreement, Articles 86 and 87.

Withdrawal Agreement confirms that the CJEU will have jurisdiction to hear these cases, and that the UK (as a defendant) and UK legal representatives will have standing before the CJEU for such cases.[43]

For our purposes, the 'pending' cases could easily be preliminary references submitted by UK courts prior to December 2020 (or 2021, or 2022, if the transition period is extended[44])—and so domestic courts will receive answers to those submitted questions even after the transition period. However, cases 'involving' the UK are likely to be enforcement actions commenced by the Commission (as discussed in Chapter 8), as opposed to preliminary references: the UK as a *state* is not a party to the domestic disputes that produce Article 267 TFEU references.

The second way in which the CJEU's jurisdiction in the UK outlasts the transition period is specific to preliminary references. Part 2 of the Withdrawal Agreement, which we consider in more detail in Chapters 12 and 13, maintains many of the rights of UK nationals living in the EU and EU nationals living in the UK on 'exit day'. Part 2 of the Withdrawal Agreement effectively applies existing EU law to those groups of citizens for the duration of their lives.[45] UK courts will have to continue interpreting aspects of EU law if those EU nationals bring cases domestically—and as a consequence of this role, the Withdrawal Agreement permits them to continue to submit preliminary references to the CJEU on Part 2 of the Agreement for a period of eight years.[46]

The aim of this exception is clear: it is there to ensure legal certainty for those benefiting from EU law rights in the UK for at least eight years following the Brexit process. It is not clear why, after eight years, it is deemed unlikely that references on these EU law matters will still be necessary, however. One possible explanation is that it was simply deemed unacceptable for the CJEU's jurisdiction in the UK to last any longer than eight years, even on the limited point of citizens' rights, and this was the compromise struck between the negotiating parties.

7.6.2 The Protocol on Ireland/Northern Ireland

The Protocol on Ireland/Northern Ireland, on the other hand, does not see such a compromise. The key difference here is that under the Protocol, so as to avoid a physical border on the island of Ireland, Northern Ireland will continue to apply significant portions of EU internal market law. For as long as the Protocol remains in force, then, Article 12(4) of the Protocol emphasizes that the EU institutions will have the powers conferred upon them in respect of the EU law that applies to Northern Ireland. It stresses that 'in particular, the Court of Justice . . . shall have the jurisdiction provided for in the Treaties in this respect. The second and third paragraphs of Article 267 TFEU shall apply to and in the United Kingdom in this respect.'

Some UK courts, meaning those applying aspects of the Protocol, consequently will continue to talk to the CJEU about some aspects of EU law. But what of the others?

[43] Withdrawal Agreement, Articles 90 and 91. [44] Withdrawal Agreement, Article 132.
[45] Withdrawal Agreement, Article 39. [46] Withdrawal Agreement, Article 158.

7.6.3 The future relationship

The general position that UK courts will be in, after the transition period, is that they are permitted to take account of 'new' post-Brexit CJEU case law but are not obliged to.[47] It is at this time wholly unclear if they generally *will*. Earlier CJEU case law, already a part of the UK judiciary's canon, is unlikely to cause problems in a domestic legal system where precedent is such an important principle: the Supreme Court is unlikely to diverge from CJEU interpretations of 'retained' EU law.[48] But whether courts in the UK will find it appropriate to generally continue to track the CJEU's rulings after Brexit is something we will find out only once the transition period ends.

As discussed, courts dealing with Northern Ireland-related disputes, however, find themselves in a different situation. A hypothetical example will make the complications this creates clearer.

Imagine a piece of single market legislation like the Toy Safety Directive.[49] This directive sets out that toys need to meet certain conditions in order to be brought into EU territory. The UK has implemented the Toys Safety Directive as the Toys (Safety) Regulations 2011.

In Great Britain, following Brexit, the Toys (Safety) Regulations will be retained EU law. The European Union (Withdrawal) Act 2018 in s 6 ensures that the Toy (Safety) Regulations will generally be interpreted in line with CJEU jurisprudence on the EU Toys Safety Directive that was issued *before* Brexit.[50] Courts in the UK may pay attention to post-Brexit CJEU case law on this directive, but do not have to. Where the interaction of any domestic law with the 'retained' Toys (Safety) Regulations is unclear, the UK courts will be free to apply the ordinary rules of interpretation to decide a dispute.

In Northern Ireland, following Brexit, the EU Toys Safety Directive will continue to be binding as *EU law*, as it affects products potentially crossing the Northern Ireland-Ireland border. Presumably, Northern Ireland will need to adopt its own version of the Toys (Safety) Regulations. This version of the Regulations will need to be interpreted in line with all CJEU jurisprudence issued on the EU directive, before *and* after Brexit. Where the interaction of any domestic law with Northern Ireland's Toys (Safety) Regulations is unclear, the UK courts can or must refer a question to the CJEU, which will give them a binding interpretation of the EU directive that they *must* apply in a given case.

Over time, it is therefore entirely possible that what started in 2020 as an identical piece of legislation will be interpreted in very different ways when applied to Northern Ireland and to the remainder of the UK. And this is assuming that the 'retained' Toys (Safety) Regulations in the UK are not amended, of course.

The consequence of such differences in interpretation is more than simply adding a layer of complexity to the lives of lawyers: divergence between these two sets of

[47] EU (Withdrawal) Act 2018, s 6(1).

[48] Note here, as discussed in Chapter 4, that only the Supreme Court *can* make this choice unilaterally; lower courts can only depart from pre-Brexit CJEU case law where instructed or permitted to by regulation, or when following the Supreme Court. (See s 26(1) of the EU (Withdrawal Agreement) Act 2020, amending s 6 of the EU (Withdrawal) Act 2018.) It is unclear how lower courts' divergence via regulation would work in practice.

[49] Directive 2009/48/EC of the European Parliament and of the Council of 18 June 2009 on the safety of toys [2009] OJ L170/1.

[50] See n 48.

domestic regulations is likely to result in trade complications between Northern Ireland and Great Britain. As we discussed in Chapter 5 and 6, the UK *in* the Protocol has agreed to use its 'best endeavours' to not erect trade barriers in the Irish Sea, which suggests it has committed to avoid significantly diverging from the law applicable to Northern Ireland.[51]

We explore these issues in more detail in Chapter 11; for now, it suffices to say that the UK judiciary faces a fragmented legal order on account of the compromises struck in the Withdrawal Agreement and the desire to end the jurisdiction of the CJEU in the UK insofar as possible. UK courts will be able to resolve conflicts about the meaning of *what used to be* EU law without any references to the CJEU, but if they are faced with a situation involving Northern Ireland, they will have to resolve conflicts about the meaning of *what is* EU law through references to the CJEU—ideally without coming to entirely different readings of virtually identical pieces of legislation.

7.7 In conclusion

The preliminary reference process, as set out in Article 267 TFEU, is an essential one for ensuring that EU law works the same way in all the Member States; but more than that, it is a mechanism through which the national courts can assist the CJEU in clarifying the content of the Treaties and expanding on it where necessary to produce legal certainty. However, it is—like many things in the EU Treaties—not a flawless process, leaving substantial and somewhat vague discretion to national courts and depending entirely on their willingness to engage, and leaving similar levels of discretion to the CJEU in just how it provides *interpretation*. Even with those caveats, the dialogue between national courts and the CJEU is one of the most interesting outcomes of EU integration, and has been instrumental in the development of EU law more generally, as we have already seen and will see in the remainder of this book.

Discussing the scenario

As noted, Mr King's dispute with Sash WW is real, and so there is an actual reference and CJEU judgment that came out of the dispute.

An annotated version of the CJEU judgment in *King* can be found online, to help you identify the key parts of any CJEU judgment you may read over the course of your studies—and to allow you to consider in practice to what extent a preliminary reference *interprets* EU law or *decides* a domestic dispute.

[51] Protocol, Article 6(2).

Key points

- Any national court of tribunal **may** refer a question on the interpretation of EU law to the CJEU.
- Any national court or tribunal whose decisions (in a given judicial process) cannot be judicially reviewed **must** refer a question on the interpretation of EU law to the CJEU, where:
  - that interpretation is necessary in order to decide the dispute at hand, and;
  - the CJEU has not already interpreted the EU law in question in a previous preliminary reference; and
  - the EU law in question does not have one clear, obvious meaning that will also be obvious to all other courts in all other Member States, as well as the CJEU (per *CILFIT*).
- After Brexit, **UK courts will continue to be covered by Article 267 TFEU** in respect of those parts of EU law that make up the **Protocol on Ireland/Northern Ireland**.
- After Brexit, **UK courts will no longer be able to make preliminary references** regarding any other EU-related issues, with the exception of references regarding Part 2 of the Withdrawal Agreement, where they are permitted (or required, if courts of 'last resort') to do so for a period of eight years after Brexit.

Assess your learning

1. Did *Factortame (No 1)* need to be referred to the CJEU if we apply *CILFIT*? What about if we apply Lord Denning's guidelines from *Bulmer*? (See Sections 7.2 and 7.3.)
2. When students appeal academic decisions of any kind (like, for instance, degree classifications), the appeals process starts within their university—but the 'last resort' appeal arrives at the Office of the Independent Adjudicator, which takes a final decision on the student's appeal. Would this be a 'court or tribunal' under Article 267 TFEU? (See Section 7.3.)
3. What is the potential problem with the CJEU giving a very detailed definition of an EU law term? (See Section 7.4.)

Further reading

Matteo Bonelli, 'The *Tarrico* Saga and the Consolidation of Judicial Dialogue in the European Union' (2018) 25(3) Maastricht Journal 357.

Gareth Davies, 'Activism Relocated: the Self-Restraint of the European Court of Justice in its National Context' (2012) 19(1) JEPP 76.

Catherine Donnelly and Thomas de la Mare, 'Preliminary Rulings and EU Legal Integration: Evolution and stasis' in Paul Craig Gráinne de Búrca (eds), *The Evolution of EU Law*, 2nd edn (OUP, 2011).

Niels Fenger and Morten Broberg, 'Variations in Member States' Preliminary References to the Court of Justice—are Structural Factors (Part of) the Explanation?' (2013) 19 Eur Law J 488.

Alexander Kornezov, 'The New Format of the Acte Clair Doctrine and its Consequences' (2016) 53 CMLRev 1317.

Jasper Krommendijk, '"Open Sesame!": Improving access to the ECJ by requiring national courts to reason their refusals to refer' (2017) 42(1) ELRev 46.

Juan Mayoral, 'Judicial Empowerment Expanded: Political determinants of national courts' cooperation with the CJEU' (2019) 25(4) Eur Law J 374.

Tomasso Pavone and R Daniel Kelemen, 'The Evolving Judicial Politics of European Integration: The European Court of Justice and national courts revisited' (2019) 25(4) Eur Law J 352.

Takis Tridimas, 'Knocking on Heaven's Door: Fragmentation, efficiency and defiance in the preliminary ruling procedure' (2003) 40 CMLRev 9.

Nils Wahl and Luca Prete, 'The Gatekeepers of Article 267 TFEU: On jurisdiction and admissibility of references for preliminary rulings' (2018) 55 CMLRev 511.

Online resources

Visit www.oup.com/he/demars1e for a sample approach to discussing the quote.

8

Enforcing EU law

Context for this chapter

(Fictitious) Directive 2014/666 provides that all equipment in fitness centres should be thoroughly inspected for technical malfunctioning and other safety hazards at least once a fortnight. Directive 2014/666 set a deadline for implementation by all Member States of 1 September 2016. The Belgian government has not yet implemented the Directive.

(Fictitious) Regulation 135/2015 additionally requires that fitness centres are always staffed by trainers qualified in first aid, and that a basic first aid kit is available in the centre.

Daxina is a member of a local private gym. While doing her usual warm-up run on one of the treadmills at 8am on 31 October 2016, the treadmill spontaneously increased its speed. Daxina hit the 'slower' button repeatedly but the treadmill did not respond; when she could no longer keep up with the rapid pace, she tripped off the back of the treadmill and hit her head.

The gym trainer's shift did not start until 9am. There was a first aid kit behind the reception desk, but the receptionist did not know any first aid. As Daxina was not instructed to stay lying down following her fall, her head injury worsened while she and the receptionist awaited the paramedics. Surgery reduced swelling in her brain, but nonetheless left Daxina with a permanent speech impairment.

It later came to light that the treadmill Daxina was running on had not been inspected for technical malfunctions for over a year.

8.1 Introduction

Chapter 6 explained that in cases of conflict, EU law will take precedence over national law; and Chapter 7 introduced us to the Treaties' main means of establishing a dialogue between domestic courts and the EU's Court of Justice. By themselves, however, neither preliminary references nor the doctrine of supremacy ensure that laws produced in Brussels take proper effect in the Member States. We now need to explore how, exactly, the EU ensures that directives and regulations become not only *binding* law in the Member States, but also *effective* law in the Member States.

The Treaties only very briefly address these questions of enforcement. Chapter 2 mentioned that the Commission has an allocated job of enforcing EU law, by taking misbehaving Member States to the CJEU. However, when we explore that process in more detail, we will see that it has some significant shortcomings. It also does not address one other fundamental issue: what if private parties living in an EU Member State realize that a Member State government has not actually complied with EU law in some way? What are their options? They do not have standing before the CJEU, as Chapter 2 also made clear. So . . . do they just email the Commission, and hope it acts on their behalf?

The CJEU was presented with these questions within a few years of the Treaty of Rome's entry into force. Without clear answers in the Treaties themselves, it was forced to come up with answers more or less 'on the spot'—looking for inspiration in what the *goals* of EU law were, and how those could be realized effectively. It developed several principles that helped enforce EU law in the Member States. Daxina's fictional situation is specifically designed to allow us to explore all the main issues that arise in the enforcement of EU law domestically at once. The issues that arise when two legal orders interact are:

- Can individuals use EU law in national court proceedings, even if it has not been fully implemented as 'domestic law'?
- How do national courts interpret domestic law that appears to correspond to EU law? Who determines how they fulfil this function?
- What if a Member State is found not to comply with its EU obligations, and a private party suffers harm because of it? Can private parties sue a Member State for not complying with EU law?

After an examination of the Treaty's provisions for enforcing EU law by looking at the Commission's **infringement proceedings**, the chapter will use the scenario at the start of the chapter to explore these questions. In advising Daxina, we will need to become aware of the CJEU's development of the principles of **direct and indirect effect** and **state liability**, and we should also consider what **remedies** will be available to her.

8.2 The Treaties on enforcement: Articles 258–260 TFEU

The Treaty of Rome was designed with only a centralized (also called 'public') enforcement mechanism in place: the Commission, in its role as 'guardian of the Treaties', would be able to take action against Member States who were not 'fulfilling obligations under the Treaty'.[1] The concept of the 'Member State' is a broad one under these provisions: if the judiciary or legislature of a Member State is 'failing to fulfil a Treaty obligation', the Member State would still be held responsible for this failure.[2] Such a failure can occur in both national *legislative* practice and national *administrative* practice,[3] and covers both

[1] Paraphrased from Article 258 TFEU.

[2] See Case 77/69 *Commission v Belgium* ECLI:EU:C:1970:34 and Case C-129/00 *Commission v Italy* ECLI:EU:C:2003:656.

[3] See http://europa.eu/rapid/press-release_MEMO-07-343_en.htm?locale=en.

actions—eg, a Member State adopting a national law contrary to EU law[4]—and *omissions*—eg, a Member State failing to implement a directive on time.

The Commission's enforcement action, known as 'infringement proceedings', is set out in Article 258 TFEU.

Article 258 TFEU (emphasis added)

If the Commission considers that a Member State has failed to fulfil an obligation under the Treaties, it shall deliver a reasoned opinion on the matter after giving the State concerned the opportunity to submit its observations.

If the State concerned does not comply with the opinion within the period laid down by the Commission, the latter may bring the matter before the Court of Justice of the European Union.

Key to the working of the Article 258 TFEU process is that starting an action is entirely at the discretion of the Commission: if it *considers that* x, it *may do* y. It can choose to, or choose not to, initiate infringement proceedings against one of the Member States. Decisions on when to start proceedings are primarily about workload: 'bigger' infractions of EU law are likely to receive attention more than issues less likely to cause significant problems. However, the Commission has occasionally been accused of playing a political game in its picking and choosing of infringement actions: the UK, Ireland, and Portugal have all tried to argue that the Commission might take action specifically to make an example of a Member State, even though the actual breach of EU law obligations is fairly minor or other Member States are doing similar things.[5] The CJEU, however, refused to entertain those arguments: under the Treaties, the Commission simply has a discretionary power to act, and the CJEU considered that use of that power was not subject to judicial review.

Under the infringement proceedings, when the Commission notices a breach of EU law in a Member State and decides to take action, the first step is to start an informal discussion with that Member State's permanent representative in Brussels. Where this does not lead to a satisfactory answer—such as, for instance, a promise of change in an administrative process—the Commission will formally start infringement proceedings by issuing a letter of formal notice to the Member State. The Member State will then have 'a reasonable amount of time' to submit its observations—or, rather, a response to the Commission's accusations in the letter of formal notice.

Where the Commission is not satisfied with the Member State's response in observations, it can issue a reasoned opinion, which instructs the Member State on what to do to remedy its breach. Then, if there is no compliance with the reasoned opinion within a reasonable time, the next step the Commission can take is to refer the disagreement to the CJEU.

[4] See, eg, Case 178/84 *Commission v Germany* ECLI:EU:C:1987:126, where Germany had adopted national legislation on the quality of beer that ran contrary to the EU Treaty's provisions on the free movement of goods; we explore this more in Chapter 11.

[5] Case 416/85 *Commission v UK* ECLI:EU:C:1988:321; Case 415/85 *Commission v Ireland* ECLI:EU:C:1988:320; Case C-70/99 *Commission v Portugal* ECLI:EU:C:2001:355.

In the proceedings before the CJEU, the burden of proof lies with the Commission; it must thus prove that there is a breach of EU law occurring in the Member State. More specifically, the breaches that the Member State is accused of must be precisely those set out in the reasoned opinion—there is no opportunity for the Commission to introduce new complaints in its reference to the CJEU.[6]

Where the Commission fails to prove its case, the CJEU will declare in favour of the Member State. If it succeeds, however, the CJEU *will* declare the Member State in breach of Article 258 TFEU: it has to date refused to accept the vast majority of defences that Member States have raised in response to a finding that they failed to fulfil their Treaty obligations.[7] The only defence to a failure to fulfil obligations that it has entertained is *force majeure*, albeit in the rather extreme circumstances in *Commission v Italy* where Italy argued that it had failed to comply with statistical obligations under an EU directive because the department collecting the statistics had been bombed.[8] Even *force majeure*, then, is a very restricted defence under Article 258 TFEU.

If the Commission proves an infringement has occurred, the CJEU will issue a binding verdict that requires the Member State to rectify the breach: in other words, to amend its domestic laws and practices until they are compliant with EU law. Article 260 TFEU makes clear, however, that the CJEU can only order 'compliance'; as was explained in Chapter 7 with regards to the preliminary rulings process, the CJEU cannot rule on matters of domestic law, and potential changes to domestic legislation or domestic processes fall within this bracket. The actual steps taken to guarantee compliance thus remain a matter of Member State discretion . . . albeit with the caveat that where the Member State fails to 'comply' with the EU law it was found in breach of, Article 260 TFEU makes it possible for the Member State to be fined for non-compliance, in the form of a penalty payment and/or a lump sum.[9]

Article 259 TFEU sets out a very similar process, rarely used, for Member State v Member State infringement proceedings. The only difference is that a Member State cannot itself start sending letters of formal notice to one of its counterparts; it takes its observations to the Commission first, which then offers its reasoned opinion. However, the complaining Member State has a right to take its counterpart to the CJEU regardless of how its counterpart responds to the Commission's opinion. As noted, this process is very rarely used, as it does not help intra-EU relations for the Member States to be suing each other. Diplomatic solutions are preferred, and usually effective.

We have already observed that the absolute Commission discretion may be a shortcoming of this centralized enforcement procedure. There are, however, others. One of the primary ones is 'time': the 'reasonable time' that Member States have to respond to Commission letters, as well as the time it then takes for the Commission to respond to Member State observations, mean that enforcement actions can last several

[6] Case 51/83 *Commission v Italy* ECLI:EU:C:1984:261, paras 6–8.

[7] See, eg, Case 254/83 *Commission v Italy* ECLI:EU:C:1984:302, where Italy argued that domestic political processes were the reason for the failure; or Case 232/78 *Commission v France* ECLI:EU:C:1979:215, where France argued that the EU institutions had also failed to fulfil *their* obligations.

[8] Case 101/84 *Commission v Italy* ECLI:EU:C:1985:330, para 16.

[9] The CJEU has on occasion imposed both a lump sum and a penalty payment, where infringements were deemed particularly serious; see, eg, Case C-610/10 *Commission v Spain* CLI:EU:2012:781.

years—especially once the CJEU becomes involved. It can thus take three years from when the Commission observes a breach of EU law to when an action in light of that breach is concluded. This is far from ideal.

All the same, the administrative stage of the Article 258 TFEU action is still being used extensively, and so as to avoid excessive delays, the Commission and the Member States make a clear effort to avoid taking an investigation all the way to the CJEU. By the end of 2018, 1571 infringement proceedings were open. However, only 30 cases were referred to the CJEU in 2018, of which only one involved the UK.[10] As for the UK's involvement in Article 258 TFEU proceedings, at the end of 2018, 65 infringement proceedings involving the UK were open, of which 27 involved late transposition of EU directives. In line with the Commission success rate under Article 258 TFEU proceedings, which in 2018 was 97 per cent, the UK lost the two Article 258 TFEU proceedings that the Commission launched against it. The EU's annual statistics on Article 258 TFEU confirm that early settlement may generally be in the best interest of the Member States.[11]

In an attempt to compensate for the 'time' involved in infringement proceedings, the Commission established something called the EU Pilot in 2008, which was 'set up to quickly resolve potential breaches of EU law at an early stage in appropriate cases'.[12] However, experience has shown the Commission that many cases that are commenced through informal dialogue between the Member State and the Commission per the 'EU Pilot' nonetheless have to proceed to formal Article 258 TFEU processes; in such cases, they are not time-saving, and so the Commission has started to restrict its reliance on the EU Pilot: 2013 saw 1502 new EU Pilot dialogues, but 2018 only saw 110.[13]

Finally, while quicker infringement proceedings would undoubtedly be appreciated by the Member States, they would not resolve one of the fundamental shortcomings of what the Treaties provide: Article 258 TFEU is a public action, meaning it can only involve the Commission and Member States. The infringement proceedings do not address what happens when a private party suffers because of a breach of EU law. Where a private party is *the reason* there is a breach of EU law within a Member State, this also falls outside of the scope of Article 258 TFEU. What that means is that if you are one of a handful of EU citizens not getting a particular EU right in one of the Member States, and the Commission is not pursuing the matter, Article 258 TFEU cannot help.

Discussing the scenario

Can the Commission commence infringement proceedings against Belgium in light of what has happened to Daxina in the fitness centre? What steps would it need to take to do so? Would the infringement proceedings help Daxina?

[10] Case C-664/18 *Commission v United Kingdom*, concerning the UK's exceeding of the nitrogen dioxide limits set by the EU's Air Quality Directive (2008/50/EC).

[11] All statistics here taken from https://ec.europa.eu/info/publications/2018-commission-report-monitoring-application-eu-law_en.

[12] See https://ec.europa.eu/info/sites/info/files/report-2018-commission-staff-working-document-monitoring-application-eu-law-general-statistical-overview-part1_0.pdf, 15.

[13] Ibid.

8.3 Using EU law in national courts

The Treaties come with an enforcement mechanism that is premised on the idea that only the *Member States* obtained rights and obligations from the EU Treaties. This is simply not the reality that even the Treaty of Rome created, as various parties would start pointing out in domestic courts very shortly after it entered into force. A lack of response in the Treaties themselves left those domestic courts to figure out how EU law worked when private parties were denied their rights—and the institution they could or had to ask for help in answering these questions, via the preliminary ruling procedure set out in Chapter 7, was the CJEU.

8.3.1 Direct effect of EU law

Supremacy filled one gap in the Treaties, but did not address a closely related point: after all, knowing that EU law has supremacy over national law is only helpful if you have a right to go to a court and *make* that argument. As we discussed in Chapter 2, individuals do not have standing before the CJEU, save in very limited circumstances where they can bring an action for judicial review of an EU act. The lack of standing before the CJEU seems to leave individuals without any real recourse in situations where they are not protesting the existence of EU law, but rather are simply arguing that they are not getting their EU 'rights'. The Treaties, after all, are silent on whether or not individuals are intended to be able to go to Member State courts in order to 'claim' their Treaty rights.

Van Gend en Loos, in addition to alluding to the principle of supremacy, dealt specifically with this question.[14] As mentioned in Chapter 6, the case involved a Dutch company transporting goods across the Dutch-West German border and being charged customs duties on those goods by the Dutch authorities. One of the arguments made by the Dutch government was that Van Gend en Loos simply could not be refunded the customs duties that had been charged because the Treaty of Rome was addressed to the Dutch government, not to private companies, and so it did not in fact give Van Gend en Loos any concrete 'right' to not have customs duties levied within the European Economic Community. In a way, the Dutch government invited the national court to agree that if there was a problem with what had happened, this was for the Commission or another Member State to take up via the infringement proceedings. But, as we saw, the national court instead asked the CJEU what should happen in this scenario.

Case 26/62 *Van Gend en Loos* ECLI:EU:C:1963:1 (emphasis added)

Independently of the legislation of Member States, [Treaty] law therefore **not only imposes obligations on individuals but is also intended to confer upon them rights** which become part of their legal heritage.

The fact that [Articles 258 and 259 TFEU] . . . enable the Commission and the Member States to bring before the Court a State which has not fulfilled its obligations **does not mean that individuals cannot plead these obligations, should the occasion arise, before a national**

[14] See Chapter 6.

> court, any more than the fact that the Treaty places at the disposal of the Commission ways of ensuring that obligations imposed upon those subject to the Treaty are observed, precludes the possibility, in actions between individuals before a national court, of pleading infringements of these obligations.

In just a few sentences, the CJEU thus found that EU law did generate rights for individuals, and it stressed (in response to Member State protest) that the existence of the Commission's infringement proceedings did not mean that private enforcement of EU law was not also possible.

When creating a private enforcement mechanism, the CJEU focused on the *qualities* of EU law that necessitated this additional route to enforcing it:

> **Case 26/62 *Van Gend en Loos* ECLI:EU:C:1963:1**
>
> The wording of [Article 30 TFEU] contains a clear and unconditional prohibition which is not a positive but a negative obligation. This obligation, moreover, is not qualified by any reservation on the part of the States which would make its implementation conditional upon a positive legislative measure enacted under national law. The very nature of this prohibition makes it ideally adapted to produce direct effects in the legal relationship between Member States and their subjects.

The doctrine established by the CJEU in *Van Gend* is known as 'direct effect'. Direct effect means that when EU law has certain qualities, it can be relied upon directly in national courts by individuals. *Van Gend* set out a long list of those qualities, but subsequent CJEU case law[15] limited the qualities that EU law needs to have to be directly effective to a mere three:

- The EU provision must be *clear.*
- The EU provision must be *precise.*
- The EU provision must be *unconditional.*

Clear and precise are easier to explain: the EU provision must give a specific, enforceable right. If a provision sets out a *general policy* for the EU to pursue—eg, 'working to end all discrimination'—it is not directly effective, simply because it does not make clear what a Member State should be doing to comply with the EU law in question. It then becomes impossible for a national court to rule on whether the rule has been contradicted by national law. These types of very 'general' goals would need to be supplemented by secondary law in order to *make* a clear and precise EU law right—so, for instance, a regulation banning all gender discrimination in the workplace.

Unconditional is the term used to make clear that even if a provision is specific enough in its aim and purpose, it will not be directly effective if it is clearly addressed to either

[15] Eg, Case 43/76 *Defrenne v Sabena (No 2)* ECLI:EU:C:1976:56.

the Member States or the EU institutions for further action. A useful example of EU law being 'conditional' is *Cava*.[16] In *Cava*, a group of residents sued the region of Italy they lived in (Lombardy) after it decided that it would set up a 'waste tip' relatively close to their houses. The group of residents of Cava protested, saying this decision to set up an urban waste disposal site near their houses violated their EU law environmental rights. At play was an EU directive, which 'required the Member States to adopt appropriate measures to encourage the prevention, recycling and processing of waste'.[17] The Italian law in response to which Lombardy had set up the waste tip, meanwhile, indicated that waste disposal was to be dealt with 'almost exclusively' by means of setting up waste tips. The Italian court that heard the case referred a number of questions to the CJEU in order to determine if this national law appropriately implemented the EU directive—but first, it had to find out if that directive was directly effective.

Case C-236/92 *Cava* ECLI:EU:C:1994:60 (emphasis added)

6. The first question seeks to establish whether Article 4 of the directive confers on individuals rights which the national courts must safeguard.
7. That provision is worded as follows:

   'Member States **shall take the necessary measures** to ensure that waste is disposed of without endangering human health and without harming the environment . . .'

. . .

14. Thus, the provision at issue must be regarded as defining **the framework for the action to be taken** by the Member States regarding the treatment of waste and **not as requiring, in itself, the adoption of specific measures or a particular method of waste disposal.** It is therefore **neither unconditional nor sufficiently precise** and thus is **not capable of conferring rights on which individuals** may rely as against the State.

In short, EU law will be directly effective if it sets out a *clear* right for an individual; if the provision being relied upon is *precise*, meaning specific rather than general; and if it does not require any further action to be taken by a Member State or the EU institutions, thus making it *unconditional*.

Directions of direct effect: vertical and horizontal

A variety of Member State courts ended up sending further questions for clarification of the direct effect doctrine to the CJEU. Over the course of its jurisprudence, it has elaborated on the picture it first drew in *Van Gend*—and one of its primary clarifications has been about the so-called direction of travel of direct effect.

The cases considered so far describe so-called **vertical direct effect**. In these cases, the disputes were between an individual and (a body representative of) a state. The fact that the state had obligations stemming from EU law was not controversial; it was the

[16] Case C-236/92 *Cava* ECLI:EU:C:1994:60. [17] Ibid, para 4.

inclusion of entities *other* than Member States that made it a revolutionary doctrine. It is, as a consequence, perhaps unsurprising that the Member State courts hesitated when faced with disputes between private parties that relied on matters of EU law. Could EU law apply even in scenarios that did not involve the Member States at all—in so-called **horizontal** disputes between two private parties?

The Treaties and horizontal direct effect

The CJEU gave a clear answer in the 1975 *Defrenne* case.[18] In *Defrenne*, a Belgian stewardess sued her employer—the airline Sabena—as they forced her, but not her male colleagues, to retire at the age of 40. Ms Defrenne brought a claim, saying this rule violated what is now Article 157 TFEU, of which the first paragraph sets out that 'each Member State will ensure and maintain the principle that men and women should receive equal pay for equal work'. The CJEU concluded that this aspect of Article 157 TFEU was clear, precise, and unconditional—and while it could have concluded that *Belgium* was failing to comply with Article 157 TFEU, it instead concluded that the private employer *Sabena* failed to comply with this 'clear, precise and unconditional' obligation. Here, it established **horizontal direct effect** of Treaty provisions that met the *Van Gend* conditions.

Article 157 TFEU on discrimination is not the only Treaty provision that has since been found to have horizontal direct effect. For many decades, it was unclear if the four fundamental freedoms—free movement of goods, services, people, and capital—were directly effective both vertically and horizontally. The Treaty provisions themselves looked clear and precise—they generally simply require that there are *no restrictions* on these freedoms, as we will see in Chapters 11, 12, and 14. However, as the discussion of the history of the EU in Chapter 1 made clear, making the four freedoms work effectively required a lot of further (secondary) legislation, so could they be seen as 'unconditional'?

Clarity from the CJEU only came in 2007, when it was faced with the key *Viking* and *Laval* cases.[19] The facts of the cases are distinct but relate to an identical question about the functioning of EU law, so it makes sense to discuss them together.

Viking concerned the Finnish ferry operator Viking, which owned a ship named the Rosella that operated under a Finnish flag (eg, falling under Finnish law) between Estonia and Finland. The Rosella was running at a loss, so to cut back its expenditure, Viking opted to operate the Rosella under a so-called 'flag of convenience' in Estonia or Norway. Viking would have nothing directly to do with either jurisdiction, but in falling under the laws of Estonia or Norway, they could avoid having to comply with Finnish social security law. The Finnish Seamen's Union (FSU) realized that this would result in job and benefit losses, so it went on strike and requested via the International Transport Workers' Federation that all affiliate unions boycott Viking's activities.

Viking brought proceedings to the High Court in London, arguing that the strike action organized via Viking's request was an infringement of Viking's freedom of establishment and freedom to provide services under EU law: the strike action was making it impossible for the ferry to operate (and thus provide its service) or to set up (establish) under the Estonian or Norwegian flag.

[18] *Defrenne v Sabena (No 2)* (n 15).

[19] Case C-438/05 *Viking* ECLI:EU:C:2007:772; Case C-341/05 *Laval* ECLI:EU:C:2007:809.

Laval, meanwhile, was a Latvian company that won a public contract to build a school in Sweden. It brought along (or 'posted', in EU terms) Latvian construction workers to carry out the work. The Swedish construction unions wanted Laval to sign up to the Swedish employment agreements on employment conditions, but Laval refused. At this point, the unions set up a blockade at Laval's sites in Sweden, making it impossible for further work to be carried out at these sites. They were so successful at this that the Swedish arm of Laval was bankrupted by the action.

In both cases, the CJEU ruled that the freedom to provide services and the freedom of establishment were not only directly effective, but were horizontally directly effective, as they were clear, precise, and unconditional provisions. As for how the CJEU ruled on the conflict between the right to strike and the freedom of establishment and the freedom to provide services, we will return to this in Chapters 9 and 14, when we consider how the Court balances fundamental rights with the four freedoms.

General principles and direct effect

What of other EU primary law? The possible direct effect of general principles has been a matter debated for a long time by academics, but only recently considered by the CJEU. However, its case law does not fully settle the debate, largely because its judgments have focused on only a few specific general principles.

The first sighting of vertical direct effect of general principles took place via the Charter of Fundamental Rights, which *enshrines* the 'fundamental rights' general principles of EU law. *Åkerberg Fransson* concerned a Swedish fisherman who had a surcharge imposed for not declaring his income tax correctly in 2007.[20] Two years later, the same non-declaration of his income taxes (and their subsequent non-payment) resulted in criminal proceedings being initiated against him. Mr Åkerberg Fransson argued that this violated the 'double jeopardy' or *ne bis in idem* principle in Article 50 of the Charter of Fundamental Rights: the right not to be tried or punished a second time in criminal proceedings for an offence that has already been finally concluded.

The CJEU, against Swedish protests, determined that Article 50 CFR merely reflects an existing general principle of EU law, and that this general principle is directly effective because *ne bis in idem* is clear, precise, and unconditional. Mr Åkerberg Fransson's claim against the Swedish state consequently succeeded, and we now know that at least *some* general principles are vertically directly effective.

Similarly, only a single general principle has been declared to have horizontal direct effect by CJEU case law. However, the case law in question has been significantly more contentious, not least because the 'general principle' at stake—a prohibition on age-related discrimination—was further elaborated on in EU secondary law. Specifically, the horizontal direct effect of the non-discrimination principle was raised for the first time in the context of a directive for which the implementation deadline had not yet passed—so the commitment for the Member States to comply with it had not yet gone 'live'.

In *Mangold*—the case that eventually resulted in the *Honeywell* judgment of the German Constitutional Court, discussed in Chapter 6—the 56-year-old Mr Mangold was subject to an eight-month-long, fixed-term employment contract.[21] Mr Mangold challenged the

[20] Case C-617/10 *Åkerberg Fransson* ECLI:EU:C:2013:105.
[21] Case C-144/04 *Mangold* ECLI:EU:C:2005:709.

fixed-term nature of his employment contract, saying it ran contrary to the provisions of a directive which prohibited (employment-related) discrimination on the ground of age. This directive clashed with a German law which allowed fixed-term contracts to be offered as standard to workers over the age of 52, while they were generally prohibited for younger employees. The directive, however, had not yet entered into force. The CJEU got around the non-binding nature of the directive by focusing on the fact that the directive was only an *elaboration* on the general principle prohibiting age discrimination, which Germany was obliged to comply with even if the directive had not yet entered into force. The fact that both Mr Mangold and his employer were private parties was not considered an obstacle to this, thus suggesting that this particular general principle, at least, is horizontally directly effective. This finding has been confirmed in subsequent case law, meaning that we are aware of at least *one* general principle that can be relied on in disputes between private parties.[22]

Regulations and direct effect

Regulations operate in a very similar way to the Treaties; they, like Treaty provisions, are directly applicable, meaning that they do not have to be implemented into domestic law in order to be legally binding. However, that does not mean they are automatically directly effective. The CJEU's early case law confused the concepts of direct applicability and direct effect, but they are currently used in the following, distinct ways:

- Regulations are always **directly applicable**—they are immediately binding law on the Member States without any national legislative action being needed, unlike directives.
- Regulations *can* also be **directly effective**—where they are clear, precise, and unconditional.

Discussing the scenario

Can Daxina rely on Regulation 135/2015, which requires that all fitness centres are staffed by trainers qualified in first aid, and that a basic first aid kit needs to be available at the reception desk, before a national court?

8.3.2 The special case of directives

Direct effect of regulations and the Treaty were both implied by the *Van Gend* judgment, as we saw in Section 8.3.1: the Court's reasoning explicitly linked the idea of 'direct applicability' of EU law to its usability in domestic courts. However, as Chapter 4 discussed, not all EU secondary legislation *is* directly applicable. Directives are binding upon the Member States in terms of their *outcome*—but the method of achieving that outcome is by and large left to the Member States. Unlike regulations and the Treaties, in other words, directives are explicitly addressed *to* the Member States, with it being implicit in their design that the Member States will have to take some action—at the very least 'implementation' of the directive in domestic law—before it becomes binding.

[22] See, eg, Case C-555/07 *Kücükdeveci* ECLI:EU:C:2010:21; Case C-476/11 *HK Danmark* ECLI:EU:C:2013:590; Case C-441/14 *Dansk Industri* ECLI:EU:C:2016:278.

The key case law from the CJEU on all issues relating to the direct effect of directives has developed through UK preliminary references, and this subsection therefore takes the place of an 'EU law in practice' box.

How does the nature of directives—eg, the requirement for their implementation—fit with the idea of EU law only being directly effective if it is clear, precise, and unconditional? The CJEU was confronted with this question in *Van Duyn*, which concerned a Dutch national being prevented under UK domestic law from entering the United Kingdom because of her association with the Church of Scientology.[23] Ms van Duyn protested the UK's interpretation of a relevant EU law directive—governing restrictions on free movement of persons, and setting out that these could only be justified by clear 'public policy' or 'public security' concerns relating to an individual's particular actions. She argued that as she was only a secretary for the Church of Scientology, even if the UK felt that Scientology presented a 'public policy' concern, she herself was not doing anything that would make her a security risk. The UK disagreed, and in any event argued that Ms van Duyn could not rely on the directive before the UK courts, because the directive was not 'clear, precise and unconditional' but, rather, addressed specifically to the Member States, instructing them to take further domestic action.

The CJEU thus had to consider if directives could be directly effective.

Case 41/74 *Van Duyn v Home Office* ECLI:EU:C:1974:133 (emphasis added)

10. It emerges from the order making the reference that **the only provision of the Directive which is relevant** is that contained in Article 3 (1) which provides that **'measures taken on grounds of public policy or public security shall be based exclusively on the personal conduct of the individual concerned.'**

11. The United Kingdom observes that, since [Article 288 TFEU] distinguishes between the effects ascribed to regulations, directives and decisions, it must therefore be presumed that **the Council**, in issuing a directive rather than making a regulation, must **have intended that the directive should have an effect other than that of a regulation and accordingly that the former should not be directly [effective]**.

12. If, however, by virtue of the provisions of [Article 288 TFEU] regulations are directly applicable and, consequently, may by their very nature have direct effects, it does not follow from this that other categories of acts mentioned in that Article can never have similar effects. **It would be incompatible with the binding effect attributed to a directive by [Article 288 TFEU] to exclude, in principle, the possibility that the obligation which it imposes may be invoked by those concerned.** In particular, where the Community authorities have, by directive, imposed on Member States the obligation to pursue a particular course of conduct, **the useful effect of such an act would be weakened if individuals were prevented from relying on it before their national courts** and if the latter were prevented from taking it into consideration as an element of Community law . . .

[23] Case 41/74 *Van Duyn v Home Office* ECLI:EU:C:1974:133.

Paragraph 12 of the judgment makes clear that the CJEU's position stemmed from considerations of how to make EU law *work* within the Member States. If individuals could not claim that a Member State was violating an EU directive, this would have as a consequence that national courts could simply ignore the existence of directives—and this would hamper the general effectiveness of EU law.

Ratti added a further consideration: an estoppel principle.[24] If a Member State has not implemented a directive by its implementation deadline, or has not implemented a directive correctly, making the contents of that directive (where clear, precise, and unconditional) incapable of having direct effect would, in essence, enable the Member States to benefit from their own failures.[25]

Both *Van Duyn* and *Ratti* thus make clear that, in principle, directives can be vertically directly effective: an individual can rely on a clear, precise, and unconditional provision of a directive *against* a Member State, not least because the failure to (correctly) implement the directive will be the Member State's failure. Implicit in *Ratti*, however, is a caveat to the direct effect of directives: they will not be directly effective until *after* the implementation period has passed, simply because they are also not explicitly *binding* before this period expires.

What of **horizontal direct effect**, whereby a private party would be able to rely upon the content of a directive against another private party, where such a directive had not been successfully implemented?

The CJEU was faced with this question in *Marshall*.[26] Ms Marshall was an employee of an NHS body called the 'Area Health Authority' in Southampton, and was dismissed at the age of 62. UK law at the time operated two separate retirement ages for men and women: women normally retired at age 60, whereas men normally retired at age 65. Ms Marshall sued her employers and claimed that she was discriminated against on the basis of her gender by being dismissed, as she was happy to continue working until she was 65. Specifically, she argued that the UK law enabling her to be forced to retire earlier than her male colleagues was contrary to the EU's Equal Treatment Directive.[27]

In principle, this looks like a straightforward case. The Equal Treatment Directive, in essence, says that men and women shall be treated equally in all matters of employment. A national law that sets up different retirement ages for men and women clearly contradicts this; and the 'no discrimination' principle seems clear, precise, and unconditional. However, the Area Health Authority introduced a counter-argument that required input from the CJEU. It claimed that it was acting merely as a private employer, in compliance with the law in the country in which it was based, and so if the court found in favour of Ms Marshall, they were holding a private employer responsible for the UK government failing to do its job under the Treaties. The national court, unsurprisingly, asked the CJEU what EU law required here.

[24] Case C-148/78 *Ratti* ECLI:EU:C:1979:110. [25] *Ratti*, para 22.

[26] Case 152/84 *Marshall v Southampton Area Health Authority* ECLI:EU:C:1986:84.

[27] Then, Council Directive 76/207/EEC of 9 February 1976 on the implementation of the principle of equal treatment for men and women as regards access to employment, vocational training and promotion, and working conditions [1976] OJ 39/40; the current Equal Treatment Directive is Directive 2006/54/EC of the European Parliament and of the Council of 5 July 2006 on the implementation of the principle of equal opportunities and equal treatment of men and women in matters of employment and occupation (recast) [2006] OJ L204/23.

Case 152/84 *Marshall v Southampton Area Health Authority* ECLI:EU:C:1986:84 (emphasis added)

48. With regard to the argument that a directive may not be relied upon against an individual, **it must be emphasized that according to [Article 288 TFEU] the binding nature of a directive, which constitutes the basis for the possibility of relying on the directive before a national court, exists only in relation to 'each Member State to which it is addressed'**. It follows that **a directive may not of itself impose obligations on an individual** and that **a provision of a directive may not be relied upon as such against such a person**. It must therefore be examined whether, in this case, the respondent must be regarded as having acted as an individual.

This was a seminal judgment once more. In agreeing with the Area Health Authority's argument, the CJEU established the principle that directives do not operate equally in all cases. If you are a private party harmed by another private party, you may find that they can be held liable under obligations they have under the EU Treaties or a regulation, but they will *not* be held liable for obligations stemming from a directive.

The CJEU's jurisprudence on direct effect of directives has been criticized for creating this imbalance between beneficiaries. If your employer *happens* to be a body of the state, you can enforce EU directives against it, but if it is a private body, you cannot. Regardless of the wording of Article 288 TFEU, it is difficult to perceive this as a justified outcome. One vocal critic of the *Marshall* distinction was Advocate General Lenz, who in the later *Faccini Dori* case argued forcefully that horizontal direct effect of directives was necessary to avoid effective discrimination against those privately employed, and to provide legal certainty and uniformity to the EU legal system as a whole.[28]

Not all agreed with AG Lenz, however. Building on the Opinion of AG Slynn in *Marshall* itself, the CJEU has consistently justified its *Marshall* case law by claiming that it is necessary to distinguish between regulations and directives.[29] This is only partially persuasive: there are of course clear distinctions between how Member States are intended to *react* to those two legal forms—but those do not negate that private parties may have rights stemming from both directives and regulations, and may have an interest in enforcing those against both Member States and other private parties.[30]

Pause for reflection

Do you think the CJEU's reasoning for not giving horizontal direct effect to directives is persuasive? Why or why not? (Reconsider this point after reading the remainder of the section and Section 8.3.3!)

[28] Opinion of AG Lenz in Case C-91/92 *Faccini Dori* ECLI:EU:C:1994:45, paras 47–73.

[29] Opinion of AG Slynn in Case 152/84 *Marshall* ECLI:EU:C:1985:345: 'To give what is called "horizontal effect" to directives would totally blur the distinction between regulations and directives which the Treaty establishes . . .'

[30] For detailed commentary, see Paul Craig, 'The Legal Effect of Directives: Policy, rules and exceptions' (2009) 34 ELRev 349.

However, while the CJEU has continued to refuse horizontal direct effect of directives, it introduced a potential loophole to its position in paragraph 50 of the *Marshall* judgment. Here, it made clear that although it ultimately remains for the national court to make this determination, if an 'employer' is found to be a public body, it will be treated *as if it is the Member State*—and so its relationship to its employees will be **vertical, not horizontal.** This was a gift of hope to Ms Marshall—who did indeed return to the Court of Appeal to successfully argue that her employer was part of the 'state', and so the Equal Treatment Directive was directly effective against them.

This **broad definition of 'the state'** was further developed by the CJEU in subsequent case law. *Foster*, for many years, was the leading authority on just what qualified a body to be part of the 'state' and thus covered by a **vertical relationship** for the purposes of the direct effect of directives.[31] The facts of *Foster* are almost identical to those of *Marshall*: there were again differing retirement ages being applied for men and women by an employer, which in this case was British Gas. British Gas was historically a nationalized utility—but by the time Ms Foster complained about her required retirement at age 60, they had been privatized. British Gas thus argued that, per *Marshall*, the Equal Treatment Directive could not apply to them.

The CJEU, however, took a different view, based on the fact that even though British Gas was now a private company, it had identical 'rights and liabilities' to the former state-owned British Gas. It consequently thus operated in a position of significant privilege: it had the kinds of rights (and duties) that any arm of the government would have had.

Case C-188/89 *Foster v British Gas* ECLI:EU:C:1990:313

18. On the basis of those considerations, the Court has held in a series of cases that unconditional and sufficiently precise provisions of a directive could be relied on against organizations or bodies which were subject to the **authority or control of the State or had special powers beyond those which result from the normal rules applicable to relations between individuals**

...

20. It follows from the foregoing that a body, whatever its legal form, which has been made responsible, pursuant to a measure adopted by the State, for **providing a public service under the control of the State *and* has for that purpose special powers beyond those which result from the normal rules applicable in relations between individuals** is included in any event among the bodies against which the provisions of a directive capable of having direct effect may be relied upon.

The definitions put forward in *Foster* go beyond just 'public bodies'. Paragraphs 18–20 of the judgment make clear that any entity that is under state 'control' or has 'special powers' will be treated as a part of, or an **emanation of the state.** This in principle looks like a helpful definition, but on closer examination, it remains quite vague: what qualifies as government 'control'? Is it full ownership of a company? Or having some government officials on its management board? And when are powers 'special'? When are you, as a

[31] Case C-188/89 *Foster v British Gas* ECLI:EU:C:1990:313.

company, 'providing a public service'? And . . . how does paragraph 20 of the judgment fit with paragraph 18, when 20 suggests that state control *and* special powers are both required, but 18 treats them as separate?

The 2017 judgment in *Farrell* eventually provided an answer to the final question. It clarified that bodies against which directives can be directly effective:

Case C-413/15 *Farrell* EU:C:2017:745 (emphasis added)

34. . . . can be distinguished from individuals and must be treated as comparable to the State, **either** because they are legal persons governed by public law that are part of the State in the broad sense, **or because** they are subject to the authority or control of a public body, **or because** they have been required, by such a body, to perform a task in the public interest and have been given, for that purpose, such special powers.

However, the larger questions of 'how much control is enough to satisfy *Foster*' and 'when are powers so "special" as to satisfy *Foster*' remain ambiguous to date. Perhaps more worryingly, the consequence of *Marshall* and *Foster* taken together is that in some ways, we have unlucky EU nationals and lucky EU nationals: some, whose employers are 'close enough' to the state, will benefit from direct effect of directives . . . and others will not, simply because their employers are genuinely 'private'.

Discussing the scenario

Can Daxina derive any rights enforceable before the Belgian courts from Directive 2014/666? Would your answer change if she had had her fall in a fitness centre run by the local authority?

8.3.3 Indirect effect of EU law

Despite remaining committed to its finding in *Marshall* that directives were not to have horizontal direct effect, the CJEU has developed a number of ways in which to mitigate the consequences of *Marshall*.

We have already considered the notion of the emanation of the state, as in *Foster*, and the fact that general principles underlying a directive might be directly effective, as in *Mangold*. However, the CJEU's most advanced mitigating mechanism is its development of a further doctrine: one that enlists the national courts in trying, as best as they can, to deliver EU law rights to individuals *even where* the EU directives are perhaps not entirely clear, precise, or unconditional.

The first sight of this new doctrine was in *Von Colson*.[32] Ms von Colson had applied for a post at an all-male prison and was rejected for the post on the basis of her gender.

[32] Case 14/83 *Von Colson* ECLI:EU:C:1984:15.

This contravened the EU's Equal Treatment Directive—and this was a matter that both parties agreed upon, as the Equal Treatment Directive had been implemented into German law. Ms von Colson thus did not have to rely on EU law—she could simply rely on the national law implementing the Equal Treatment Directive in order to obtain a remedy from the court.

This, however, was where matters became problematic for Ms von Colson. Germany had implemented the Equal Treatment Directive—but its provisions on remedies were translated strangely into the German implementing law. The Equal Treatment Directive required that those who were wronged by gender discrimination in employment matters were entitled to pursue a judicial remedy. Germany's law implementing the directive, meanwhile, set out that those wronged by gender discrimination in hiring processes were entitled to get their job application fees back. Ms von Colson argued that the directive required significantly more than a travel refund—perhaps going so far as to require her to get the job she did not get on account of the discrimination—and the national court referred a question to the CJEU, asking if the directive's provision had direct effect and if so, what that direct effect amounted to.

Two things worked in favour of Ms von Colson: the first was that the timeline for implementation of the directive had passed, and the second was that her potential employer, a prison, was definitely an emanation of the state. However—was the directive's provision on remedies clear, precise, and unconditional?

Case 14/83 *Von Colson* ECLI:EU:C:1984:15 (emphasis added)

27. . . . the directive does not include any unconditional and sufficiently precise obligation as regards sanction for discrimination . . .

28. It should, however, be pointed out to the national court that although [the directive] leaves the member states free to choose between the different solutions suitable for achieving its objective, it nevertheless requires that **if a Member State chooses to penalize breaches of that prohibition by the award of compensation**, then in order to ensure that it is effective and has a deterrent effect, **that compensation must in any event be adequate in relation to the damage sustained . . . It is for the national court to interpret and apply the legislation adopted for the implementation of the directive in conformity with [EU] law, in so far as it is given discretion to do so under national law.**

The key finding of the CJEU in *Von Colson* is that when a Member State has clearly 'wrongly' implemented a directive, it is for the national court—insofar as it is legally permitted to do so—to try to interpret that national law implementing the directive so as to give effect to the *intent* of the directive. In Ms von Colson's case, that would mean a substantially higher damages award than merely her application expenses—though the final finding on what remedy Ms von Colson was to receive remained in the purview of the national court alone.

The CJEU's language makes it clear that it bases its finding of this requirement of interpretation 'in conformity with EU law' on the general obligations the Member States have under the Treaty: namely, to sincerely cooperate with the EU institutions in achieving the

EU's goals, as per Article 4(3) TEU. This doctrine, which has become known as **indirect effect**, or the duty of **consistent/harmonious interpretation**, appeared initially to apply only in those cases where a Member State wrongfully implemented a directive. However, *Von Colson* does not even directly address the lack of horizontal direct effect of directives, so it could perhaps have been foreseen that the CJEU saw this as a *general* interpretative obligation.

It confirmed this in *Marleasing*, and moved the obligations held by national courts beyond dealing with errors in implementation.[33] *Marleasing* related to an EU directive that set out an exhaustive list of grounds on which companies could be declared legally null and void; Spanish law, quite separately, permitted Spanish courts to declare companies null and void for further, separate reasons. The provision sounds directly effective—but was being relied upon by one private party in a dispute with another private party, and so the Spanish court asked what to do, in the absence of direct effect as a remedy. The CJEU set out clear directions:

Case C-106/89 *Marleasing* ECLI:EU:C:1990:395 (emphasis added)

8. . . . in applying national law, whether the provisions concerned **pre-date or post-date** the directive, the national court asked to interpret national law is bound to do so in **every way possible** in the light of the text and aims of the directive . . .

In other words, national law should be read by domestic courts in light of not only the wording but the objectives of directives—*in every way possible*. What we see here is a CJEU push for EU law having identical effects in all the Member States, even where legislation does not obviously enable this; and in the process, reinforcing the supremacy of EU law.

As such, there are only a few restrictions on the reach of indirect effect:

- it cannot apply before a directive's implementation deadline has passed;[34]
- it cannot be used to aggravate an individual's criminal liability beyond what national law specified at the time the 'crime' was committed;[35] and
- it cannot result in a *contra legem* interpretation of the national law—meaning that a law that literally says 'this never happens' cannot be interpreted to mean the complete opposite of what it says (eg, 'this sometimes happens').[36]

Discussing the scenario

Imagine that the (fictitious) Belgian Exercise Safety Regulations 2008 require that all gym equipment be inspected 'regularly'. Does this help Daxina, and if so, how?

[33] Case C-106/89 *Marleasing* ECLI:EU:C:1990:395.
[34] Case C-212/04 *Adeneler* ECLI:EU:C:2006:443, para 115.
[35] Case C-168/95 *Arcaro* ECLI:EU:C:1996:363, para 42.
[36] Case C-334/92 *Wagner-Miret v Fondo de Garantia Salarial* ECLI:EU:C:1993:945.

Advocate General Slynn, in his opinion on *Marshall*, neatly captures the kind of uncertainty that very broadly read indirect effect obligations can cause in a legal system, and what this asks of the national judiciary.

Opinion of AG Slynn in Case 152/84 *Marshall* ECLI:EU:C:1985:345 (emphasis added)

To construe a preexisting statute of 1975 or even 1875 in order to comply with a subsequent directive, **which the legislature or executive has not implemented**, in breach of its obligation, **when it has a discretion as to the form and method to be adopted**, is, in my view, **wholly different**. I am not satisfied that it is a rule of [EU law] that national courts have a duty to do so—unless it is clear that the legislation was adopted specifically with a proposed directive in mind.

Marleasing made it clear that the CJEU *did* expect the national courts to do exactly that, however.

The current scope of the doctrine of indirect effect, as well as reasons why it has been subject to criticism, is well illustrated by *Dominguez*.[37] Ms Dominguez had an accident on her way to work; as a consequence, she was on sick leave for 14 months. Upon her return to work, she asked for 22 days of paid annual leave—but was refused it, because French employment law made paid annual leave contingent on an employee having worked for at least one month in the preceding calendar year . . . unless that condition could not be satisfied because of a 'work-related illness'. Ms Dominguez relied on the currently applicable Working Time Directive to argue that she should, under EU law, have 20 days of annual leave that was not subject to any sort of 'attendance' requirement.[38] The CJEU agreed with her—and instructed the French court to do whatever was in its power to read the French employment law so as to give Ms Dominguez her 20 days of leave.

The outcome of *Dominguez* is consequently the following: under EU law, a French law that says that you are only entitled to annual leave if you have been either at work for a month, or off work because of a work-related accident, will have to be interpreted by the French courts (if at all possible!) as also covering an accident on the way *to* work . . . at least until the French parliament rewrites the relevant French law so that it is compliant with the EU's Working Time Directive.

We can see this ruling as introducing a lot of legal uncertainty. From one moment to the next, French employers were abruptly made liable for accidents that did not take place *in* the workplace, but somehow were connected to work. But how close did that connection to work need to be? If an employee stopped to grab a coffee on the way to work, were they still 'on their way' to work if they were in an accident? And what if they were on their way home? What do you *do* if you are an employer—and so a potential defendant—in this situation?

[37] Case C-282/10 *Dominguez v CICOA* ECLI:EU:C:2012:33.

[38] Directive 2003/88/EC of the European Parliament and of the Council of 4 November 2003 concerning certain aspects of the organisation of working time [2003] OJ L299/9.

The CJEU's case law has made it so that in situations where there is a difference between a directive and its national implementation, private bodies now need to start anticipating just what provisions of that national law could be made indirectly effective—and then need to decide what such a harmonious interpretation might look like, before deciding whether to comply with the exact wording of the national law or the wording of a directive. As with many other complex developments stemming from CJEU case law, indirect effects like the ones in *Dominguez* may be good news for some employees in France—but probably not for the French legal system.

Pause for reflection

Do you think the CJEU should simply overrule its ***Marshall*** jurisprudence and introduce horizontal direct effect for directives? How would ***Dominguez*** have been decided if the Working Time Directive had been horizontally directly effective?

8.3.4 Incidental effect

One final way in which the CJEU has compensated for the lack of horizontal direct effect of directives is through a doctrine called **incidental effect**. Incidental effect arises in the situation where two private parties are engaged in a dispute, and an EU directive that has not been implemented or applied (properly) has an impact on the outcome of that case *despite* not being directly effective. The doctrine was established in *CIA Security*, and a discussion of that case will make it clearer how incidental effect works.[39]

In *CIA Security*, a maker of alarm systems—CIA Security—brought a claim against competitors Signalson and Securitel before the Belgian commercial courts. It argued that they were involved in unfair trading practices, and specifically, that they had libelled CIA Security by claiming (publicly) that a CIA Security alarm system had not been approved for the market, as Belgian legislation required. CIA Security admitted they had not sought approval to market their alarm system—but argued that they had not done so because the Belgian law requiring that approval was in breach of Directive 83/19, which required any technical standards and regulations adopted in the Member States to be notified to the Commission. As Belgium had not notified the Commission of its law on alarm systems, that law could not bind CIA Security—and so Signalson and Securitel had claimed untruths about the validity of its alarm system.

The CJEU accepted CIA Security's reliance on Directive 83/19 because it did not impose a legal obligation on Signalson or Securitel, but instead simply meant that the Belgian government had failed to comply with *its* obligation. The fact that the consequence of this was ultimately that Signalson and Securitel were liable for libel was a separate matter, outside of the scope of CJEU law.

CIA Security was confirmed in *Unilever Italia*, involving a dispute over conflicting labelling requirements in Italian law.[40] Italy had adopted a national law requiring olive

[39] Case C-194/94 *CIA Security International* ECLI:EU:C:1996:172.

[40] Case C-443/98 *Unilever Italia* ECLI:EU:C:2000:496.

oil to be labelled with its geographical origin; and, under Directive 83/189, this requirement had to be notified to the Commission. Unilever supplied olive oil to Central Food without the labelling required by Italian law, and Central Food refused to pay for that olive oil, saying it was in breach of the labelling requirement. Unilever argued, however, that the Italian labelling requirement had been adopted in breach of Directive 83/189, also on account of a failure to notify the Commission. Again, the CJEU agreed, noting that Directive 83/189 did not give rights to or place obligations on private parties, but that nonetheless the Directive meant that the Italian labelling law could not be applied against Unilever.

What this strand of case law has established is that directives, while still not horizontally directly effective by *providing rights* in disputes between private parties, can work as a form of 'litigation shield' in private disputes. It is a very limited exception to the general *Marshall* rule; it has been applied only twice, and seems to only manifest when EU law requires that a Member State report domestic laws they are adopting.[41] Nonetheless, it is yet another way in which the CJEU has softened the effects of *Marshall*, by allowing directives to be used before a national court even though they are *not* horizontally directly effective.

8.4 Remedies for breaches of EU law

In the previous sections, we have seen a number of situations in which an EU law right was not extended to a private individual in a Member State, and the CJEU directed the national courts to apply EU law over domestic law, if at all possible. In all these situations, the private individuals in question had suffered some form of harm as a consequence of an infringement of EU law. Are they then entitled to a remedy of some kind? And if so, what determines what that remedy is and how to access it—EU law or national law?

8.4.1 National regulatory autonomy

For a long time, the Treaties remained quiet on the subject of remedies. We have a first statement on remedies in Article 19 TEU, which was introduced by the Lisbon Treaty.

Article 19 TEU (emphasis added)

Member States shall provide **remedies sufficient** to ensure **effective legal protection** in the fields covered by Union law.

This suggests that there are no specific remedies for breaches of EU law: the key words in Article 19 TEU indicate that the Member States *shall* provide remedies, and that those remedies must ensure *effective* legal protection. The idea of 'effectiveness' covers not only

[41] For the most recent instance of incidental effect arising before the CJEU, see Case C-390/18 *Airbnb Ireland* ECLI:EU:C:2019:1112. It once again involved a failure of a Member State (France) to inform the Commission of the application of a particular domestic law to a certain type of company.

the fact that the remedies must exist, but that they must be accessible—and so there is an expectation that there are both appropriate national *remedial* rules and national *procedural* rules for accessing these remedies. Article 47 of the Charter of Fundamental Rights similarly focuses on the *effectiveness* of a remedy—but provides no further indications of what those remedies are to look like.

Article 47 of the Charter of Fundamental Rights (emphasis added)

Everyone whose rights and freedoms guaranteed by the law of the Union are violated has the **right to an effective remedy** before a tribunal . . .

The Treaties, consequently, remain of limited help, and as with the other questions in this chapter, a more specific answer as to what remedies should be available in the Member States for breaches of EU law had to be provided by the CJEU.

In *Rewe*, the CJEU set out the basic principles that still apply today.[42] The case involved a dispute between a supermarket (Rewe) and the German government. The supermarket was charged fees for carrying out inspections of food it had imported from other Member States. The government agreed that it was entitled to a refund, but declined to pay it, because the supermarket had complained too late: there was a national time limit for contesting the validity of national administrative procedures. Rewe argued that as this time limit was not in the EU Treaties, it had no impact on its right to a remedy, and the German domestic court hearing the dispute asked the CJEU if the Treaties forbade the Member States from setting out administrative conditions for receiving remedies.

Case 33/76 *Rewe-Zentralfinanz* ECLI:EU:C:1976:188 (emphasis added)

In the absence of [EU rules], it is for the domestic legal system of each Member State to **designate the courts having jurisdiction** and to **determine the procedural conditions governing actions at law** intended to ensure the protection of the rights which citizens have from the direct effect of [EU law].

In other words, under the doctrine called **national procedural autonomy**, the Member States themselves are responsible for ensuring that breaches of EU law receive appropriate remedies—but they have to ensure that such remedies were available, and those suffering breaches of EU law have standing (where appropriate) to claim those remedies before a national court. Calling what *Rewe* established national procedural *autonomy* is thus only largely correct: while Member States have the right to determine the process to remedy breaches of EU law, there must *be* a process in place. As Article 19 TEU now confirms, it might be preferable to refer to it as national procedural *responsibility*.

[42] Case 33/76 *Rewe-Zentralfinanz* ECLI:EU:C:1976:188.

This 'responsibility' is set out in more detail in later case law. A key example is *Unibet*, involving an online gambling service that bought advertising space in a variety of different Swedish media forms to advertise its services.[43] Gambling of the variety that Unibet provided was prohibited under the Swedish 'Law on Lotteries', and so the Swedish government obtained injunctions and started criminal proceedings against the Swedish media platforms that had agreed to give Unibet advertising space.

Unibet in turn brought an action against the Swedish government; it requested (among other things) a declaration that it had a right under the EU Treaties to provide its services in Sweden. It was the application for a declaration that was dismissed: the Swedish court concluded that under Swedish law, there was no direct legal relationship between Unibet and the Swedish government, and so what Unibet was requesting was an 'abstract' or hypothetical review of a legal provision, which was inadmissible under Swedish law.

On appeal, this finding was confirmed—and the Swedish Court of Appeal found that a specific remedy did not have to be provided under EU law when national law did not provide for such an action, but made available comparable actions. It did, however, double-check this interpretation of the EU law on remedies with the CJEU, which responded in agreement:

Case C-432/05 *Unibet* ECLI:EU:C:2007:163 (emphasis added)

40. . . . [the Treaty framework] **was not intended to create new remedies in the national courts to ensure the observance of [EU law] other than those already laid down by national law.**

41. **It would be otherwise only if** it were apparent from the overall scheme of the national legal system in question that **no legal remedy existed** which made it possible to ensure, even indirectly, respect for an individual's right under [EU law].

From this observation in *Unibet*, and similar observations made by the CJEU in the later *Pelati*[44] case, we can deduce that **national procedural autonomy** exists when two requirements for remedies are met by national law:

1. The remedies and actions available are '[no] less favourable than those governing similar domestic situations'—known as the **principle of equivalence**; and
2. The remedies and actions available '[do] not render impossible in practice or excessively difficult the exercise of [EU law] rights'—known as the **principle of effectiveness.**

The CJEU's case law assessing if the national procedural rules on remedies for breaches of EU law are satisfactory has focused particularly on the principle of effectiveness: a remedy that in practice is almost unattainable because of endless administrative hurdles that have to be met is not a 'real' remedy. The CJEU's definition of effectiveness—making it 'excessively difficult' to exercise EU law rights—is deliberately broad and abstract, and thus captures a wide range of national measures that somehow make accessing remedies for breaches of EU law almost impossible in practice, as its case law demonstrates.

[43] Case C-432/05 *Unibet* ECLI:EU:C:2007:163.

[44] Case C-603/10 *Pelati* ECLI:EU:C:2012:639.

Remedies for breaches of directives, such as a failure to implement them in a timely manner, have been scrutinized in particular for their effectiveness—because, as the CJEU argued in *Emmott*,[45] of their 'particular nature'. The facts of *Emmott* illustrate why the CJEU is particularly focused on procedural rules in relation to breaches of directives. Ms Emmott sought retroactive payment for a disability benefit that she had been entitled to, but not been receiving, because her Member State of residence, Ireland, had not implemented an EU directive. She was told by the relevant Irish government department that she had to wait on filing for judicial review of her benefit decisions until an unrelated case had been decided by the CJEU, but when she then finally did file her action, the government department indicated that her action could not be heard because her delay in initiating proceedings was a bar to action. It is unsurprising the CJEU was unimpressed with the Irish 'process' in this case—though it should be stressed that *Emmott* was a 'very particular case', as the CJEU itself made clear in the subsequent case of *Johnson II*.[46]

Some less extreme examples of 'ineffectual remedies' relate to the Equal Treatment Directive we considered in Section 8.3.2. In *Von Colson,* the national implementation of a directive requiring 'judicial protection' was not 'effective' if it only guaranteed reimbursement of application fees. Compensation had to be adequate to the loss and damages suffered—so a law like Germany's, which set an upper 'limit' of compensation, could not be deemed to provide an effective remedy.

Another example of the CJEU finding a remedy 'ineffective' is *Marshall II*.[47] Following the finding in *Marshall* that the Area Health Authority was a public body, Ms Marshall pursued damages for her termination of employment on discriminatory grounds. The UK, however, operated a statutory ceiling on awards of compensation for discrimination in breach of EU law. An employment tribunal in the UK had awarded Ms Marshall damages well over that limit, including an award of interest, but then encountered the statutory restrictions. Following several appeals, the House of Lords asked the CJEU if, under EU law, Ms Marshall was entitled to full reparation for the loss sustained, regardless of what domestic law required. The CJEU ruled that the Equal Treatment Directive precluded 'caps' like the UK's statutory ceiling on damages, again suggesting that national procedural autonomy is not fully 'autonomous'.

The CJEU will thus test to see if national procedures for awarding remedies for breaches of EU law are equivalent and, most importantly, effective, considering the nature of the EU law right in question and the severity of the breach—and where national law is deemed not to have provided sufficient remedy, it is not hesitant about suggesting that a *better* and thus 'effective' remedy should be offered.

8.4.2 **State liability**

In general, therefore, EU law does not require specific remedies in domestic law for breaches of EU law. There is, however, one exception. Where a direct connection between actions of a Member State and losses suffered by a private party can be made, the CJEU has intervened to develop a specific remedy, called **state liability**.

[45] Case C-208/90 *Emmott v Minister for Social Welfare* ECLI:EU:C:1991:333, paras 21, 23.

[46] Case C-410/92 *Johnson v Chief Adjudication Officer (Johnson II)* ECLI:EU:C:1994:401, para 26.

[47] Case C-271/91 *Marshall v Southampton and South-West Hampshire Area Health Authority (Marshall II)* ECLI:EU:C:1993:335.

It applies in cases where a Member State fails to comply with its EU law obligations. Classic examples of this are, for instance, a failure to implement a directive by its deadline, or a failure to implement a directive correctly. Where this occurs, a Member State can be held liable in damages *if* a claimant's losses can be directly connected to the Member State's failure to comply with EU law. Where that causation can be proven, the case of *Francovich* tells us that the Member State will be liable for damages.[48]

Francovich related to an EU directive that harmonized EU law rules on how to protect employees if their employer went insolvent. It set out a minimum level of protection, in particular promising to pay wages that had been unpaid on account of the insolvency process. The directive was due to be implemented by October 1983, and Italy had failed to do this. Upon the insolvency of his employers, Mr Francovich went to court in Italy to attempt to retrieve his unpaid wages—and to get damages for the fact that Italy had failed to implement the directive that would have guaranteed his unpaid wages. The Italian court referred these two separate but related questions to the CJEU: did this directive on employee protection have direct effect, and did Italy owe Mr Francovich damages for failing to implement the directive?

The CJEU was succinct on the matter of direct effect: it noted that Article 5 of the directive stated that 'Member States shall lay down detailed rules for the organization, financing and operation of the guarantee institutions, complying with the following principles in particular . . .'.[49] While the 'wage guarantee' condition was precise and unconditional in terms of who was meant to *benefit* from it, the CJEU found that unfortunately, it was not clear *who* owed Mr Francovich his wages under this provision of the directive. National law was intended to set up a 'guarantee' institution, but as that had not happened, it was not clear where the money was meant to come from. Direct effect therefore was not going to help Mr Francovich—but the CJEU clearly found this a very unsatisfying result:

Joined Cases C-6/90 and C-9/90 *Francovich v Italy* ECLI:EU:C:1991:428 (emphasis added)

33. The full effectiveness of [Union] rules would be impaired and the protection of the rights which they grant would be weakened if individuals were unable to obtain compensation when their rights are infringed by a breach of [Union] Law for which a Member State can be held responsible.

34. The possibility of obtaining redress from the Member State is particularly indispensable where, as in this case, the full effectiveness of [Union] rules is subject to prior action on the part of the State and where, consequently, in the absence of such action, individuals cannot enforce before the national courts the rights conferred upon them by [Union] law.

. . .

37. It follows from all the foregoing that it is a principle of [EU] Law that the Member States are obliged to pay compensation for harm caused to individuals by a breach of [EU] Law for which they can be held responsible.

[48] Joined Cases C-6/90 and C-9/90 *Francovich v Italy* ECLI:EU:C:1991:428.

[49] *Francovich*, paras 23–25.

Paragraph 37 established what we now know as 'state liability': an obligation for the Member State to pay compensation for harm caused by their own failures to comply with EU law, *where* they can be held responsible for such harm.

The scope of the doctrine appeared to be limited to an extent by paragraph 34 of *Francovich*: it suggests that state liability is *particularly* important in those cases where there is no direct effect, and so individuals cannot simply enforce their EU law rights in national courts. The Member States attempted to rely on this as a defence in subsequent case law: if EU law was found to be directly effective, and so an individual's EU law rights could be enforced, surely there was no need for reparations to be paid?

The CJEU rejected this line of reasoning in the joined *Brasserie du Pêcheur* and *Factortame* cases.[50] These two cases are interesting because they cover completely unrelated factual scenarios, but the CJEU treated them as joined cases as they both concerned potential limits to state liability. *Brasserie* dealt with a French-German dispute regarding a German law on 'beer purity'. Brasserie, a French brewery, could no longer export beer to Germany from 1981 onwards because its beer was found to fall short of the German 'purity' law's requirements as updated in 1976. The Commission undertook infringement proceedings against Germany in light of the 'beer purity' laws, noting that the law's ban on calling an import 'beer' unless it complied with the German beer purity conventions was a violation of the EU Treaty's provisions on free movement of goods that could not be justified. In 1987, when the case was finally heard by the CJEU, the CJEU found in favour of the Commission, and thus declared the 'beer purity' law contrary to the Treaties.

This was when Brasserie used the CJEU's 1987 ruling on the beer purity law to claim for six years of reparations on account of losses suffered for its inability to sell its product in Germany between 1981 and 1987. The total sum they claimed for was almost 2 million German marks. Germany argued that as the Treaty provisions had been found to be directly effective, *Francovich* did not apply—and Brasserie was not entitled to these reparations.

The joined *Factortame* case brings us back to the lengthy chain of jurisprudence that we first visited in Chapter 6. By 1989, in *Factortame II*, the CJEU had declared the Merchant Shipping Act 1988 incompatible with the Treaties as it discriminated directly on the basis of nationality, requiring effectively British ownership. However, it was not until 1991 that a UK Divisional Court made an order that would give effect to *Factortame II* in domestic law. We here again see a lapse of time between a complaint being made about a domestic law, in light of EU law, and that law being disapplied on account of a CJEU judgment; and so Factortame brought an action for damages for losses suffered during the time its vessels could not fish in British waters. The UK, again, argued that because the Treaties had been found to confer a directly effective right on Factortame, *Francovich* did not apply.

[50] Joined Cases C-46/93 and C-48/93 *Brasserie du Pêcheur and Factortame* (*Brasserie and Factortame*) ECLI:EU:C:1996:79.

Joined Cases C-46/93 and C-48/93 *Brasserie du Pêcheur and Factortame* ECLI:EU:C:1996:79 (emphasis added)

20. The Court has consistently held that the right of individuals to rely on the **directly effective** provisions of the Treaty before national courts is only a **minimum guarantee** . . . It cannot, in every case, secure for individuals the benefit of the rights conferred on them by [Union] law and, in particular, **avoid their sustaining damage as a result of a breach of [Union] law attributable to a Member State.**

21. . . . this will be so where an **individual who is a victim of the non-transposition of a directive** and is **precluded from relying on certain of its provisions before the national** court because they are **insufficiently precise and unconditional, brings an action for damages against the defaulting Member State for breach of the . . . Treaty** . . . [T]he purpose of reparation is to redress the injurious consequences of a Member State's failure to transpose a directive . . . It is all the more so in the event of infringement of a **right directly conferred by a Union provision** upon which **individuals are entitled to rely before the national courts.**

This judgment divorced the doctrine of state liability from the doctrine of direct effect; whether a provision was directly effective had no bearing on whether a state was liable for damages where it failed to comply with its EU law obligations, and an individual suffered harm because of it.

Germany protested the CJEU's argumentation here strongly, arguing that the Treaties provided for no *general* right of reparations and it was not for the CJEU to just 'introduce' such a general right. The CJEU responded as follows:

Joined Cases C-46/93 and C-48/93 *Brasserie du Pêcheur and Factortame* ECLI:EU:C:1996:79 (emphasis added)

25. It must, however, be stressed that the **existence and extent of state liability for damage ensuing as a result of a breach of obligations incumbent on the State** by virtue of Union law are questions of **Treaty interpretation** . . .

27. **Since the Treaty contains no provisions governing [state liability]**, it is for the Court, in pursuance of the [interpretative] task conferred upon it by [Art. 19 TEU], to rule on such a question in accordance with generally accepted methods of interpretation, in particular by **reference to the fundamental principles of the [EU] legal system and, where necessary, general principles common to . . . the MS.**

Following these general statements, the CJEU raised the general legal principle of 'effectiveness', the duty of 'sincere cooperation' (as discussed in Chapter 6) that all the Member States sign up to when ratifying the EU Treaties, and Article 340 TFEU, which sets out the EU's non-contractual liability in situations where its institutions cause damage.[51] It describes the latter article as being an 'expression of the general principle familiar to . . . the Member States that an unlawful act or omission gives rise to an obligation to make good the damage caused'.[52]

Having defended the doctrine of state liability accordingly, the CJEU then proceeded to set out what conditions had to be satisfied for a state *to* be liable. A breach of EU law can thus result in state liability[53] where:

- The legal provision is intended to confer rights on individuals;
- The breach is sufficiently serious; and
- There is a direct causal link between the breach of the Member State's obligation and the damage sustained.[54]

The condition that has been subject to further significant case law is 'sufficiently serious'. It was defined in *Francovich* as covering situations where a Member State 'manifestly and gravely disregarded the limits on its discretion'.[55] Failing to amend a national law *after* the CJEU has found it to be incompatible with the Treaties, as was the case in *Brasserie and Factortame*, is an obvious example of a 'sufficiently serious' breach—Member States have no discretion in complying with CJEU judgments. Similarly, the CJEU has clarified that a failure to implement a directive by the deadline is always a 'sufficiently serious' breach, as Member States have no discretion in complying with those deadlines.[56]

However, more difficult questions arise when the facts relating to the 'breach' are not as clear-cut. In cases of *incorrect* implementation, the CJEU's assessment of the breach is in many ways dependent on just *how* wrong the implementation was. An example of wrongful implementation that resulted in state liability is *Rechberger*, in which the Austrian legislation implementing a directive on package holidays (which set out rules on compensating customers if the package holiday provider went insolvent) had a 'start date' that was four months past the directive's date of entry into force.[57] On the other hand, situations where the national law is not 'manifestly contrary to the wording of the directive or to the objective pursued by it' do not attract state liability—so, for instance, *British Telecom* found that where the provisions in a directive are themselves not entirely clearly worded, and a Member State applied a reasonable interpretation of the provision in 'good faith', it will not be liable for damages under state liability.[58]

The last substantial contribution to the doctrine of state liability that was made by *Brasserie and Factortame* is a clarification of its scope of application. The CJEU here, in paragraph 32, stressed that the right to reparation 'holds good for any case in which a Member State breaches [EU] law, whatever be the organ of the State whose act or omission was responsible for that breach'. This was not taken to be controversial . . . until the CJEU was asked to consider if state liability also applied to the judiciary.

[51] See Chapter 2. [52] *Brasserie and Factortame* (n 50), para 29.

[53] As noted in Chapter 2, a breach of EU law can now result in non-contractual liability if the same conditions are met.

[54] *Brasserie and Factortame* (n 50), para 51. [55] *Brasserie and Factortame* (n 50), para 55.

[56] Joined Cases C-178/94, C-179/94, C-188/94, C-189/94, and C-190/94 *Dillenkofer* CLI:EU:C:1996:375.

[57] Case C-140/97 *Rechberger* ECLI:EU:C:1999:306.

[58] Case C-392/93 *British Telecom* ECLI:EU:C:1996:131, para 43.

As discussed in Chapter 7, *Köbler* concerned an Austrian professor who had spent part of his career in Austria, but parts of it in other EU Member States. Austrian law made a specific salary increment (or bonus) available to university staff after 15 years of work in Austrian universities.[59] Mr Köbler was denied this increment because he had not worked for 15 years in *Austrian* universities, and challenged this as discriminatory under EU law, because it disadvantaged any Austrian professors who had exercised their EU movement rights. On hearing the case, the highest Austrian administrative court initially referred a question to the CJEU, but was told by the CJEU's registrar that an earlier CJEU case (*Schöning-Kougebetopoulou*[60]) had considered very similar questions—and had found that professional experience in another Member State should count towards totals of 'length of employment'. The Austrian court, however, considered that this earlier CJEU case was distinct from the facts before it, and thus found that Austria was justified in this form of 'discrimination' whereby the bonus was extended only to those who had worked in Austria.

Mr Köbler challenged this finding before the Austrian civil courts and claimed damages on account of the Austrian administrative courts' failure to comply with EU law. The Austrian civil court asked the CJEU if state liability also applied to judicial organs whose decisions could not be appealed—and was told in *Köbler* that in principle it did, as even those national courts are bodies of the state. Numerous Member States protested the idea of state liability for the judiciary in their pleadings in *Köbler*, and the CJEU proved sensitive to their concerns by making it clear that on account of the 'special nature of the judicial function', courts of final instance could only be liable where they 'manifestly infringed' EU law.[61]

The Austrian administrative courts were not found to have met that threshold, and Mr Köbler consequently lost the case—but the CJEU had established *potential* state liability for the judiciary. The *Köbler* liability has since been confirmed in other CJEU case law,[62] and though it operates under a very high threshold, it has been argued that the condition of 'manifest infringement' does not preclude findings of judicial state liability where serious breaches are committed by courts of final instance.[63]

Discussing the scenario

Can Daxina make a claim for damages against the Belgian government in light of the injury she has suffered?

One final point to note about state liability is that while it is a remedy that applies in all the Member States, it does not apply uniformly. The principle of national procedural autonomy applies *to* the doctrine of state liability—which sounds confusing,

[59] Case C-224/01 *Gerhard Köbler v Republik Österreich* ECLI:EU:C:2003:513.

[60] Case C-15/96 *Kalliope Schöning-Kougebetopoulou v Freie und Hansestadt Hamburg* ECLI:EU:C:1998:3.

[61] *Köbler* (n 59), para 53.

[62] See Case C-173/03 *Traghetti del Mediterraneo SpA v Italy* ECLI:EU:C:2006:391 and Case C-379/10 *Commission v Italy* ECLI:EU:C:2011:775.

[63] Björn Beutler, 'State Liability for Breaches of Community Law by National Courts: Is the requirement of a manifest infringement of the applicable law an insurmountable obstacle?' (2009) 46 CMLRev 792.

but simply means that while EU law demands that state liability is a possible remedy, its operation in terms of procedures for paying damages and amount of damages warranted are once more determined by national law. These procedures and amounts have to be equivalent and effective, like all other remedies related to EU law—but they are not determined by the CJEU.

8.5 Brexit and enforcement

What will happen to the Commission's infringement proceedings and these CJEU-developed principles on the enforcement of EU law in the UK, now that the UK has left the EU? The answer, as has been true in all other chapters so far, is very much dependent on the nature of the relationship the UK seeks to build with the EU, particularly after the transition period ends. That said, there are already a few indications of changes to principles of enforcement of former *and* future EU law that we can examine.

8.5.1 Withdrawal Agreement

Under the October 2019 Withdrawal Agreement, the CJEU-developed principles of (in)direct effect, incidental effect, and state liability will have to remain operational in the UK as they are now during the transition period. The role of the Commission also will not change, though the UK will no longer have a Commissioner: EU law can continue to be enforced against the UK as if it is a Member State until at least December 2020 under Article 4 of the Withdrawal Agreement.[64]

As was mentioned in Chapter 7, there is a possibility that infringement proceedings will be brought against the UK *after* the transition period ends. This can happen in situations where an infringement action before the CJEU is pending at the time the transition period ends, as well as on the basis of facts that took place *while* the UK was a Member State, but came to light afterwards. The latter is explicitly time-limited in Article 87 of the Withdrawal Agreement, however: the Commission effectively has four years from the end of the transition period to bring an action under Article 258 TFEU. Article 87 is explicit about this four-year time limit being to bring an action before *the CJEU*, which presumably means that all other stages of the infringement proceedings must take place within these four years—and any 'administrative' processes still ongoing after four years will be resolved in ways not specified in the Withdrawal Agreement.

8.5.2 The Protocol on Ireland/Northern Ireland

Northern Ireland, under the Protocol included with the Withdrawal Agreement, will find itself in a different situation from the remainder of the UK after Brexit, as we have seen in previous chapters. However, the difference in EU institutional involvement and national court obligation in Northern Ireland as compared to the rest of the UK becomes

[64] An extension of one or two years is accounted for in the Withdrawal Agreement, Articles 126 and 132; the EU (Withdrawal Agreement) Act 2020, s 33, prohibits UK representatives from asking for an extension as a matter of domestic law—though as is true for all Acts of Parliament, this can obviously be amended if an extension is desired after all.

particularly stark when we consider the enforcement of EU law. Not only do national courts have to set aside incompatible domestic law when it conflicts with the EU law set out the Annexes to the Protocol, as discussed in Chapter 6, but insofar as those laws are currently directly effective, they will also remain so under Article 4 of the Withdrawal Agreement—and where they are not, they may be indirectly effective under the same provision.

The EU institutions also retain 'all the powers conferred upon them by Union law' in relation to the EU law that will be applicable in Northern Ireland under the Protocol, per Article 12(4) of the Protocol. The Article stresses that this includes the jurisdiction of the CJEU—and as such, the Commission will be able to start infringement proceedings against the United Kingdom (on behalf of Northern Ireland) for any failure to comply with the relevant EU laws in the Annexes to the Protocol.

The Protocol does not make this particularly clear, and instead merely notes that insofar as Northern Ireland (or the UK, on its behalf) becomes involved in either judicial *or administrative* proceedings on account of the Protocol, legal representatives from the UK will be allowed to participate in those.[65] The infringement proceedings are, of course, primarily administrative—and so the impression generated by Article 12 of the Protocol as a whole is that the Commission will remain involved in oversight and enforcement of EU law in Northern Ireland as long as the Protocol is active.

That said, as the Protocol also establishes a 'Special Committee' made up of UK and EU representatives to oversee the functioning of the Protocol, it is likely that in practice, *minor* compliance issues will be dealt with through that political mechanism rather than Commission enforcement.[66] More generally, the Protocol in Article 12(1) stresses that UK authorities will in any event be able to work with relative autonomy in ensuring the relevant EU laws are operational in Northern Ireland:

Article 12(1) of the Protocol on Ireland/Northern Ireland (emphasis added)

Without prejudice to paragraph 4, **the authorities of the United Kingdom shall be responsible for implementing and applying the provisions of Union law** made applicable by this Protocol to and in the United Kingdom in respect of Northern Ireland.

The entirety of Article 12, as such, represents political compromises. Article 12(1) is effectively saying that the UK, which will be a non-EU country by the time the Protocol enters into force, carries the sole responsibility for ensuring that one of the EU's external borders works. Such a concession would have been impossible without lasting oversight by the EU bodies, and so Article 12(4) is also needed. The end result is much like the Protocol in general: one where the EU remains less but still visibly involved in the affairs of one part of the UK.

[65] An exception is Article 10 of the Protocol, which makes very explicit that the Commission will continue to enforce EU state aid law in the UK insofar as it affects trade between Northern Ireland and the EU. See Chapter 2.

[66] Protocol, Article 14.

8.5.3 The future relationship

The European Union (Withdrawal) Act 2018 repeals the ECA 1972, which is the means by which direct effect (and supremacy) currently operate in the UK. We discussed in Chapter 6 how the EU (Withdrawal Agreement) Act 2020 'saves' relevant sections of the ECA 1972 for the duration of the transition period—but after 2020 (or 2021, or 2022, if the transition period is extended[67]), the UK is free to do away with the CJEU's enforcement principles and remedies. It has chosen to do so; the EU (Withdrawal) Act 2018 is explicit about the ending of state liability in the UK, with a grace period of two years following 'exit' for making final claims.[68]

'Retained' EU law comes with its own interesting questions: while it does not *have* to be directly effective, or indirectly effective, it *could* be. The EU (Withdrawal) Act 2018 here establishes slightly different rules for different forms of EU-originating legislation, discussed in Chapter 4:

- 'Retained' EU law that is made up of directly applicable EU laws will be turned into domestic law.[69] It will, by that measure, no longer be 'directly effective': rather than relying directly on an EU regulation, those in the UK who want to enforce the content of such a regulation will now have to rely on the domestic law 'retaining' it. The connection between that 'retained' EU law and the original EU law is effectively severed by the 2018 Act, which does not preserve direct effect.
- 'Retained' domestic law, made up of domestic law that implemented EU law while the UK was a Member State, is in a slightly different position. As we saw in Section 8.3.2, directives can be directly effective if they are implemented incorrectly. The EU (Withdrawal) Act 2018 does not retain this form of direct effect either, however: there will thus be no comparing back to the original EU directives, unless directly effective rights in the legislation in question *have already been recognized* by either a domestic court or the CJEU.[70] This is a complex arrangement presumably aimed at limiting the reach of 'future' direct effect: it essentially means that a provision in domestic legislation implementing a directive that has already been given direct effect by a ruling maintains it, but other provisions that would qualify for direct effect under the 'clear, precise and unconditional' test would not.

Indirect effect is a bit of a mystery in the EU (Withdrawal) Act 2018. As we discussed in Chapter 4, s 6 of the 2018 Act lays down that pre-exit CJEU jurisprudence will be applied to 'retained' EU law unless conscious choices to deviate are made by either the Supreme Court or by ministerial regulation.[71] The 2018 Act is also explicit in s 5 that the principle of supremacy applies to 'retained' EU law when in conflict with other domestic law that predates Brexit—but no part of the 2018 Act discusses indirect effect directly. As it *is* part of pre-exit CJEU case law, domestic courts will be able to apply the principle broadly and be compliant with the Act. However, the fact that the 2018 Act explicitly rules out newly discovered 'direct effect' of UK legislation implementing directives makes it unlikely that

[67] See n 64.

[68] See Schedule 1 para 4 of the EU (Withdrawal) Act 2018, and for commentary: Joelle Grogan, 'Rights and Remedies at Risk: Implications of the Brexit process on the future of rights in the UK' [2019] PL 683.

[69] EU (Withdrawal) Act 2018, s 3.

[70] EU (Withdrawal) Act 2018, s 4(2).

[71] See EU (Withdrawal Agreement) Act 2020, s 26(1), amending EU (Withdrawal) Act 2018, s 6.

a broad reading of the principle is intended; indirect effect, after all, is meant to mitigate shortcomings in direct effect of directives.

The disappearance of both the 'enforcement' principles developed by the CJEU and the role of the Commission in enforcing EU law is a logical outcome of Brexit: after all, with the exception of those EU laws applicable in Northern Ireland, none of the rules retained by the UK will actually *be* EU law anymore. The effects of 'retained' EU law are unlikely, in practice, to be very different from what the effects of the relevant rules were prior to Brexit, however, in light of the general obligation to interpret 'retained' law in line with pre-exit CJEU jurisprudence. It is only in situations where the relevant law is inaccurately implemented that differences arise: references back to the EU sources will not be possible, nor will suing the UK government for a failure to implement them correctly.

We consider what role may be reserved for the CJEU more generally in Chapter 16, when we examine what is currently known about the UK's future relationship with the EU. For the purposes of this chapter, we can simply conclude that it retains a role in the enforcement of EU law in Northern Ireland indefinitely, but otherwise will not be directly involved in the development of the body of 'retained' EU law in the UK. The UK courts may wish to follow its lead—but they are no longer obliged to.[72]

8.6 In conclusion

The Treaty of Rome foresaw that EU law would need to be enforced, but failed to consider what level of enforcement would be needed to ensure that private parties and Member States alike would have their EU law rights and obligations respected. The Member States might have addressed the 'private enforcement' gap in Treaty revision—but the CJEU beat them to it, setting out several key principles that have resulted in the national courts playing a key role in making sure that EU law *works* in the Member States.

The combination of direct effect and indirect effect means that private parties can uphold most of their EU law rights whether their Member States are 'sincerely cooperating' with the EU or not; and the Commission's infringement proceedings and state liability ensure that where Member States are found to be 'uncooperative', they can be effectively 'punished' for their misbehaviour. These CJEU doctrines have resulted in one of the firmest enforcement mechanisms that exists outside of domestic law—but the fact that these *are* court-developed doctrines is also at the heart of why they have developed in sometimes unpredictable ways.

As a final point, it is worthwhile to consider the merits of the doctrines: have they merely 'filled gaps' in the Treaties, or have they gone far beyond that? Can they be criticized in their functioning? And are they all necessary? These are the questions that will help us consider to what extent accusations of the CJEU's 'activism' in the area of enforcement are justified.

Discussing the scenario

As Daxina's legal advisor, consider if she has any legally enforceable rights and remedies arising under EU law in the scenario at the start of the chapter.

A sample approach to a response can be found online.

[72] EU (Withdrawal) Act 2018, s 6(1).

Key points

- EU law can be **publicly enforced** via the Commission's 'infringement proceedings' against any of the Member States where they fail to comply with an EU law obligation.
- EU law can be **privately enforced** by individuals in national courts because of the CJEU-created doctrines of **direct effect** and **indirect effect**.
  - When EU law is **directly effective,** this means it is clear, precise, and unconditional enough to be relied upon by a private party before a national court *even* if not complied with by a Member State.
  - When EU law is not **directly effective,** the doctrine of **indirect effect** nonetheless requires that a national law is read by a domestic court to give effect to an EU law wherever possible.
  - Directives can be relied upon before domestic courts as outlined in Figure 8.1.
- Where a Member State's failure to comply with EU law causes an individual harm, that Member State is liable for damages under the doctrine of **state liability**.
- After Brexit, **direct effect** and **state liability** will no longer apply to 'retained' EU legislation. UK courts appear to be able to interpret 'retained' EU law in line with **indirect effect**, but how this is intended to work in practice is not made clear by the EU (Withdrawal) Act 2018.
- After Brexit, the **Commission's infringement proceedings** will in principle continue to apply to **Northern Ireland** in respect of the EU law that applies there on account of the Protocol.

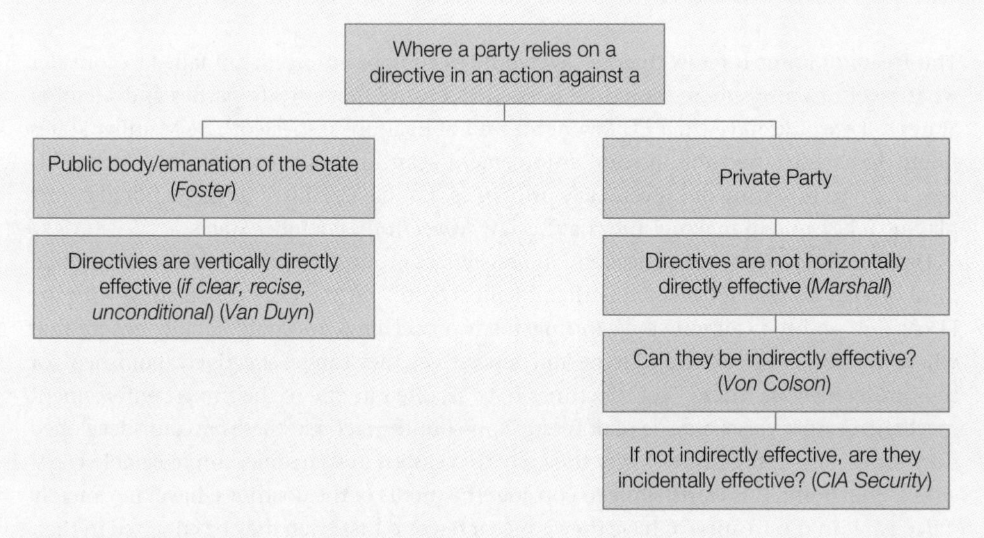

Figure 8.1 When directives can be relied upon before domestic courts

Assess your learning

1. Can direct effect work without supremacy, do you think? How do you imagine this works in practice? (See Section 8.3 and Chapter 7.)
2. Which doctrine do you think has the bigger impact on the domestic courts—direct effect or indirect effect? (See Section 8.3.)
3. Should state liability apply to directly effective EU law, in your view? Why or why not? (See Section 8.4.)

Further reading

Gerrit Betlem, 'The Doctrine of Consistent Interpretation: Managing legal uncertainty' (2002) 22(3) OJLS 397.

Damian Chalmers, 'The Positioning of EU Judicial Politics within the United Kingdom' (2000) 23 West Eur Polit 169.

Paul Craig, 'The Legal Effect of Directives: Policy, rules and exceptions' (2009) 34(3) ELRev 349.

Michael Dougan, 'Addressing Issues of Protective Scope within the Francovich Right to Reparation' (2017) 13(1) Eur Const Law Rev 124.

Gerda Faulkner, 'A Causal Loop? The Commission's new enforcement approach in the context of non-compliance with EU law even after CJEU judgments' (2018) 40(6) J Eur Integr 769.

Katri Havu, 'Full, Adequate and Commensurate Compensation for Damages under EU Law: A challenge for national courts?' (2018) 43(1) ELRev 24.

Tobias Lock, 'Is Private Enforcement of EU Law through State Liability a Myth? An assessment 20 years after Francovich' (2012) 49 CMLRev 1675.

Luca Prete and Ben Smulders, 'The Coming of Age of Infringement Proceedings' (2010) 47(1) CMLRev 9.

Stijn Smismans, 'EU Citizens' Rights post Brexit: Why direct effect beyond the EU is not enough' (2018) 14(3) Eur Const Law Rev 443.

Anna Wallerman, 'Can Two Walk Together, Except They Be Agreed? Preliminary references and (the erosion of) procedural autonomy' (2019) 44(2) ELRev 159.

Online resources

Visit www.oup.com/he/demars1e for a sample approach to discussing the quote.

9

Fundamental rights in the EU

Context for this chapter

'Under the Lisbon Treaty, the court has taken on the ability to vindicate people's rights under the 55-clause "Charter of Fundamental Human Rights", including such peculiar entitlements as the right to found a school, or the right to "pursue a freely chosen occupation" anywhere in the EU, or the right to start a business.

'These are not fundamental rights as we normally understand them, and the mind boggles as to how they will be enforced. Tony Blair told us he had an opt-out from this charter. Alas, that opt-out has not proved legally durable, and there are real fears among British jurists about the activism of the court.'

Boris Johnson, 'There is only one way to get the change we want: Vote to leave the EU' (*Telegraph*, 21 February 2016) http://web.archive.org/web/20160222022356/http://www.telegraph.co.uk/news/newstopics/eureferendum/12167643/Boris-Johnson-there-is-only-one-way-to-get-the-change-we-want-vote-to-leave-the-EU.html

9.1 Introduction

The previous three chapters considered in some detail how the CJEU has interpreted the EU Treaties over the course of the last seven decades. They highlighted what critics of the Court might describe as *procedural* and *constitutional* activism on the part of the CJEU, whereby it developed principles that governed the relationship between domestic courts and itself—but the CJEU has equally been accused of 'activism' in substantive areas of law.

One further case study of CJEU activity that is of particular interest in light of the UK's decision to pursue leaving the EU is that of fundamental rights. We saw a brief reference to fundamental rights in Chapter 6, when we considered the German courts' accusation that the EU Treaties did not respect those rights 'fundamental' to the German constitution. Since that original accusation, the EU has developed its own human rights law under the banner of 'fundamental rights'.

The contents of 'fundamental rights' were for a long time determined by the CJEU on the basis of a number of existing sources of both national and international law, and particularly the European Convention of Human Rights—but since then, the EU has codified them in a Charter of Fundamental Rights, made binding by the Lisbon Treaty. This Charter was meant to be an expression of the law, not an *extension* of the law, but the CJEU has been accused of using the Charter to develop its human rights law, to the concern of some of the Member States. At the same time, however, the Member States have all agreed to make the EU a more human rights oriented body by committing it, in the Lisbon Treaty, to joining the European Convention of Human Rights (ECHR) . . . but the CJEU has made it clear that the nature of EU law poses significant obstacles to this step.[1]

This chapter will explore the development of EU-law-based fundamental rights, from early CJEU case law to up the Charter of Fundamental Rights. The EU's relationship with the Council of Europe will also be considered, with a focus on how the CJEU and the European Court of Human Rights (ECtHR) attempt to avoid conflicting interpretations of overlapping rights, and whether the EU *can* in fact sign up to the ECHR. Finally, the UK's opt-out and the CJEU's case law on fundamental rights *after* the Charter will be discussed—enabling you to decide for yourself whether the concerns expressed by Boris Johnson about the CJEU's approach to fundamental rights in the context for this chapter are realistic ones.

Before we go any further, the most fundamental thing to remember while reading this chapter, and whenever answering any EU law exam questions, is that the ***European Court of Human Rights*** (ECtHR) and the ***European Convention on Human Rights*** (ECHR) are *not* a part of EU law.

The ECHR is an international human rights treaty administered by the Council of Europe, which is a separate international organization of which all the EU Member States are members . . . but so are many non-EU jurisdictions, including Russia. The ECHR is applied and interpreted by the ECtHR, and it is transcribed into UK law in the form of the Human Rights Act 1998.

The EU, meanwhile, has the ***Charter of Fundamental Rights*** as its human rights 'treaty'. It has also in the Lisbon Treaty committed to *joining* the ECHR, which is the easiest way to remember that the ECHR is not part of the EU.

9.2 A brief history of fundamental rights

The Treaty of Rome was an economic liberalization treaty: more ambitious provisions that might lead to a 'federal' Europe, as the Schumann Plan alluded to, were never a part of it.[2] Instead, shortly after Rome, the EU Member States proposed and debated two *further* Treaties that would have resulted in non-economic integration. When the European Defence

[1] Convention for the Protection of Human Rights and Fundamental Freedoms (European Convention on Human Rights, as amended) 1950.

[2] See Chapter 1.

Union plans were vetoed by the French Senate, the unrelated European Political Union plans, which included a lot of the civil and political rights that would soon be called 'human rights', fell by the wayside and were not revived.[3]

Instead, human rights concerns appeared before the CJEU—not because it itself was immediately determined to introduce human rights into the EU Treaties, but rather because the Member States referred questions to the CJEU about how *their* human rights law interacted with the EU legal order. All Member States were signatories of the European Convention of Human Rights, and many post-World War II constitutions also contain rights provisions, so as to ensure that atrocities like those that had been perpetuated during World War II under the guise of legality would actually be constitutionally prohibited in future.[4] Human rights were thus a firm part of the law of the Member States—but not the law of the EEC.

The first EU case law relating to human rights thus stemmed from individuals wanting their domestic human rights to effectively override aspects of EU law, or actions of the EU institutions.[5] As explained in detail when discussing the relationship between national courts and the CJEU in Chapter 6, these cases all failed: the EU principle of supremacy makes it impossible for any domestic norm, whether a human right or a constitutional principle, to override EU law. The only alternative to EU law superseding all domestic norms is that each country would have its own version of EU law, modified by its own constitutional provisions. The CJEU thus ruled out such a role for human rights in *Internationale Handelsgesellschaft*, starting an ongoing back and forth between the German Constitutional Court (wishing to prioritize the German Basic Law) and the CJEU (prioritizing EU law).

The dialogue with the German Constitutional Court, and the more general concern that the principle of supremacy would not be able to survive this kind of conflict between domestic and EU law, resulted in the CJEU finding that EU law itself contained 'fundamental rights' that it would protect. The very first example of this was *Stauder*.[6]

Mr Stauder, a German national, attacked a Commission decision that permitted distribution of butter at discount prices only where the recipient of the butter was clearly identified by name. He believed that this mandatory identification by name condition violated his right to dignity, as found in the German Basic Law. When the CJEU was referred a question on the case, it was asked if the system set up by the Commission decision was compatible with 'the *general principles* of [EU] law'.[7]

The CJEU compared various language versions of the Commission decision and found that it was not necessary for the butter recipients to be identified by name under that decision. More importantly, it concluded that 'the provision at issue contains nothing capable of prejudicing the fundamental human rights enshrined in the general principles of [EU] law . . .'.[8]

[3] For a discussion, see Gráinne de Búrca, 'The Evolution of EU Human Rights Law' in Paul Craig and Gráinne de Búrca, *The Evolution of EU Law*, 2nd edn (OUP, 2011).

[4] See, for a prime example, the German Basic Law (discussed in Chapter 6).

[5] See, eg, Case 1/58 *Stork* ECLI:EU:C:1959:4; Joined Cases 36–38/59, 40/59 *Geitling* ECLI:EU:C:1960:36; Case 40/64 *Sgarlata v Commission* ECLI:EU:C:1965:36; and Case 11/70 *Internationale Handelsgesellschaft* ECLI:EU:C:1970:114.

[6] Case 29/69 *Stauder* ECLI:EU:C:1969:57. [7] Ibid. [8] Ibid, para 7.

With this simple statement, the CJEU effectively created 'human rights' as a part of EU law. It simply stated that they existed as part of the general principles of EU law, which—as we saw in Chapter 4—were likewise 'uncovered' by the CJEU. What the specific 'fundamental rights' enshrined in the general principles were, the CJEU did not elaborate on in *Stauder*, however. For quite some time, discovering that there were fundamental rights required case law that declared their existence. *Internationale Handelsgesellschaft* and *Nold*[9] set out where 'fundamental rights' were to be derived from: a combination of Member State 'constitutional traditions', and international human right treaties, of which the most significant is the ECHR.[10]

One key facet of the CJEU's case law on fundamental rights is that the CJEU is *not* a human rights court, nor is the EU an institution that is exclusively or even primarily concerned with human rights. In all of its case law, the CJEU has always needed to strike a balance between the 'core' of the EU's legal order, which is single market law and the 'four freedoms' of movement of goods, persons, services, and capital, and those fundamental rights it recognized. Given that the Treaties were constructed specifically *to* achieve these four freedoms, it was not immediately obvious how they could be balanced with these newly 'discovered' fundamental rights. A key example of a case in which the CJEU is asked to engage in such balancing is *Schmidberger*.[11]

In *Schmidberger*, environmental protesters staged a protest on the Brenner motorway in Austria. As a result, the Austrian authorities closed the relevant road—a prominent trade route—for the duration of the protest. Schmidberger, a road transport company operating between Germany and Italy, protested the road closures as infringing the free movement of goods before the Austrian courts and sought damages for the loss of earnings over the protest period. Austria countered that the road closures had been proportionate and that, in any event, freedom of expression (Article 10 of the ECHR) and freedom of assembly (Article 11 of the ECHR) outweighed the free movement of goods in importance. The Austrian court asked the CJEU for an interpretation of this clash between 'fundamental freedoms' and free movement of goods:

Case C-112/00 *Schmidberger* ECLI:EU:C:2003:333 (emphasis added)

77. The case raises . . . the question of the **respective scope of freedom of expression and freedom of assembly**, guaranteed by Articles 10 and 11 of the ECHR, **and of the free movement of goods, where the former are relied upon as justification for a restriction of the latter.**

. . .

81. . . . **the interests involved** must be **weighed** having regard to all the circumstances of the case in order to determine whether a **fair balance was struck** between those interests.

→

[9] Case 4/73 *Nold* ECLI:EU:C:1974:51.

[10] *Nold*, paras 12–13; see also Case 36/75 *Rutili* ECLI:EU:C:1975:137; Case C-299/95 *Kremzow* ECLI:EU:C:1997:254.

[11] Case C-112/00 *Schmidberger* ECLI:EU:C:2003:333.

→

82. **The competent authorities enjoy a wide margin of discretion in that regard.** Nevertheless, it is necessary to determine whether the restrictions placed upon intra-Community trade are **proportionate** in the light of the **legitimate objective pursued, namely, in the present case, the protection of fundamental rights.**

After evaluating the length of the protest, the extent of road 'blocked', and the two competing interests over the course of several paragraphs, the CJEU concluded that blocking the road to permit the protest was proportionate in this case. However, *Schmidberger* makes clear that the CJEU will engage in a case-by-case evaluation of the proportionality of this balance between the 'four freedoms' and fundamental rights: there is no automatic hierarchy whereby either the freedoms or the rights take precedence. We will see more cases in the remainder of this chapter where, again, this 'balancing act' between the EU's economic objectives and fundamental rights falls to the CJEU, and the outcome of the case is determined by an assessment of proportionality.

Also clear from *Schmidberger* is the extent to which the EU's fundamental rights case law has been inspired by, and even made legitimate by, references to the ECHR. As all the Member States were signatories, it was uncontroversial to reference obligations in the ECHR when raising this new body of 'fundamental rights'—these were obligations held by the Member States anyway. As such, the CJEU relied heavily on the 'special significance' of the ECHR and the rulings of the ECtHR for its development of the general principles[12]—and references to the ECHR were made regularly in CJEU cases that involved manifestations of fundamental rights with ECHR equivalents, such as those to a fair trial[13] and privacy.[14]

As we saw in Chapter 6, one of the key consequences of the CJEU's 'discovery' of fundamental rights was a détente with the German Constitutional Court: it accepted that EU law contained a regime equivalent to (though separate from) domestic human rights and constitutional law, and that thus the CJEU was itself the appropriate body to rule on the validity of any EU secondary legislation. This preserved the principle of supremacy . . . but it also meant that an entirely new body of (unwritten) rules was going to be developed by the CJEU, rather than the EU legislature.

9.2.1 From the CJEU to the Charter

Given their failed pursuit of a political union treaty in the 1950s, the Member States were obviously not indifferent to the EU developing a 'human rights' face. The EU institutions consequently responded to the CJEU's case law developments with support: in 1977, the European Parliament, Commission, and Council issued a Joint Declaration

[12] See, eg, Case C-260/89 *ERT* ECLI:EU:C:1991:254, para 41.

[13] Case 222/84 *Johnston v Chief Constable of the RUC* ECLI:EU:C:1986:206, para 18; Case C-424/99 *Commission v Austria* ECLI:EU:C:2001:642, paras 45–47.

[14] Joined Cases C-465/00, C-138/01, and C-139/01 *Rechnungshof v Österreichischer Rundfunk* ECLI:EU:C:2003:294.

stating that they considered themselves bound by these 'fundamental rights' as stemming from general principles of EU law.[15] With every subsequent Treaty amendment, fundamental rights gained a more visible role in the EU legal framework: the Single European Act mentioned them in its Preamble, and the Maastricht Treaty expressly listed fundamental rights as one of the 'principles' underpinning the EU law in Article F(2). The extension of EU competences to include extremely 'people-focused' (rather than economic) areas like asylum, immigration, and criminal law under the Area of Freedom, Security and Justice umbrella meant that following Amsterdam, the Member States were keener than ever before to ensure that EU law would commit to the protection of human rights. The first tangible result of this interest was the drafting of a codification of the CJEU's case law on fundamental rights, which was achieved in 2000 in a Charter on Fundamental Rights.[16]

However, despite a consensus on fundamental rights being important, the Member States could not agree on what to do with the Charter. As discussed in Chapter 1, it consequently ended up as a non-binding declaration attached to the Nice Treaty: some Member States simply refused to countenance it becoming a part of the Treaty, out of concern that this would result in a stretch of EU competences into ever more aspects of domestic policy (as 'human rights' affect virtually all areas of policy-making). These concerns were dealt with by the time the Lisbon Treaty was ratified—in part via an opt-out for some Member States, which we will analyse in Section 9.4—and the Charter is now a binding document of equivalent value to the Treaties.

Separately, the Lisbon Treaty committed the EU to joining the ECHR—something it had already attempted to do in the 1990s, but that had failed at the time because there was no legal basis in the Treaties *for* it to join the ECHR.[17] Lisbon thus marks a 'high point' in the EU's engagement with fundamental rights.

Before we consider what fundamental rights exist and how they work, it is important to stress that the formal adoption of the Charter *does not mean* that the CJEU's pre-existing case law on fundamental rights is now meaningless, or that fundamental rights are *no longer* 'general principles' as developed by the CJEU. Article 6(3) TEU stresses that even now, fundamental rights 'constitute general principles of EU law'. What this means is that the CJEU thus can apply the Charter of Fundamental Rights as of the Lisbon Treaty . . . but it can also continue to develop separate 'fundamental rights' through the general principles, as it has always been able to do. The Charter is thus by no means a sign of 'completion' of EU fundamental rights, even if it is a very helpful snapshot of what they were at the time the Lisbon Treaty was ratified.

Pause for reflection

Do you think there is a problem with the continuance of fundamental rights as 'general principles' of EU law, now that there is a written Charter? What impact may this have on the legal certainty of the principles?

[15] See [1977] OJ C-103/1.
[16] See the Charter of Fundamental Rights [2000] OJ C-364/1.
[17] See Chapter 5.

9.3 What are the EU's fundamental rights?

The Charter is meant to be a codification of the CJEU's case law on fundamental rights—and it says very explicitly in its own Article 51 that it is not intended to *extend* the scope of EU law. Neither intention, however, is entirely lived up to in practice, as we will now see. If we consider what is in the Charter, first of all, we see some textual provisions that go beyond the CJEU's case law; and moreover, the CJEU's interpretation of the fundamental rights has *always* extended the scope of EU law to a certain extent.

9.3.1 Contents of the Charter

The Charter commences with a Preamble, explaining how the Charter fits in the framework of the EU. It commences by highlighting that the entire European project is focused on sharing a 'peaceful future' that is based on 'common values'. Next, it highlights what some of those values are—emphasizing that they include dignity, freedom, equality, and solidarity, as well as democracy and the rule of law—and stresses that EU law now directly addresses individuals. This sets the foundation for what is substantively covered within the Charter: individuals' rights that protect the relevant EU 'values'.

However, the Preamble also very carefully sets out that the EU, in adopting the Charter, does not wish to step on Member States' toes or otherwise impinge on their pre-existing obligations, whether domestic or international. It thus stresses that the Charter is there to 'strengthen' fundamental rights protection, but that it will respect 'the diversity of the cultures and the traditions of the peoples of Europe as well as the national identities of the Member States'.

The end result of this simultaneous commitment to respect national competences and international obligations in the field of human rights, but also strengthening the EU's human rights commitments, is found in the 54 Articles of the Charter.

Chapters 1–6

Following its Preamble, the Charter is made up of six bespoke categories of 'rights', as sketched out in Figure 9.1.

As the figure explains, there are a lot of 'expected' rights in the Charter, but also a few peculiarities. Some of these are EU-specific rights, such as the right to data protection; both the EU legislature and the CJEU have elaborated on this right extensively, and it is one of the areas of human rights development that the EU is best known for.[18] Big tech companies like Facebook and Google have run amok with data protection rights and the related 'right to be forgotten' in the last decade, and individuals in the EU have been able to take domestic action against their behaviour with national Data Protection Authorities and in domestic courts, where the rights are directly effective.[19]

The most controversial chapter in the Charter is undoubtedly Chapter 4. Solidarity is a common thread running throughout the welfare states operated by EU Member States,

[18] See the General Data Protection Regulation (Regulation (EU) 2016/679 [2016] OJ L119/1) and highly publicized cases like Case C-131/12 *Google Spain* ECLI:EU:C:2014:37 and Case C-362/14 *Schrems* ECLI:EU:C:2015:627.

[19] See, for coverage, https://www.bbc.co.uk/news/business-48357772.

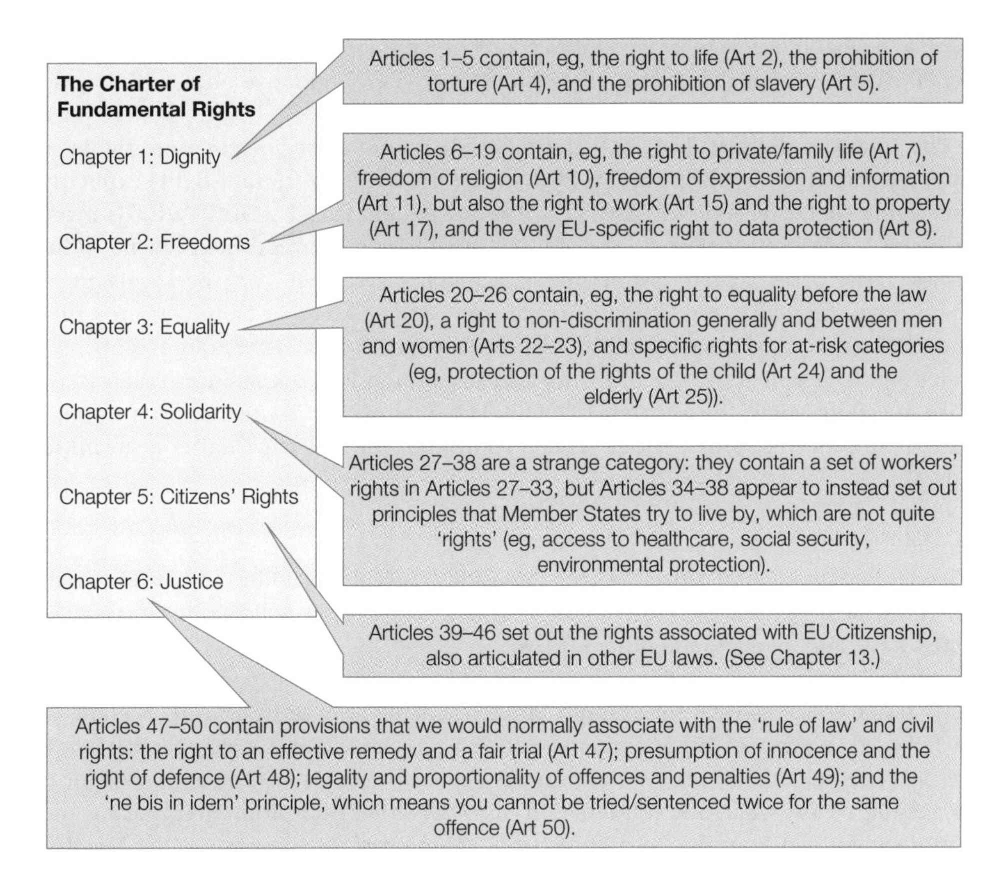

Figure 9.1 The Charter of Fundamental Rights

but there is no such thing as a 'right to solidarity' in any EU Member State constitutional tradition. What these rights reflect are what TH Marshall has referred to as the third wave of human rights development: social and economic rights, rather than civil and political rights.[20] Classic civil and political rights, like the right to own property, the right to vote, and the right to a fair trial, are easily achieved by States, because they only require a State to *not* impede them. In other words, there is no positive action needed for a 'right to property' to work: it simply states that there is such a right, and there should not be laws prohibiting anyone from owning property.

The Solidarity chapter in the Charter, however, sets out a category of 'rights' which seems to carry these kinds of positive obligations. Any right to healthcare, for example, is not something that the State can satisfy by simply 'not prohibiting healthcare'. It means the State is under a positive obligation to set up a healthcare system that its citizens can access. The same holds for a social security system. These socio-economic rights consequently depend a lot not only on the willingness of a State to comply with them, but also that State's *ability* to comply. As a consequence, in most jurisdictions, they have proven extremely difficult to enforce, because the judiciary is likely to give the State a lot of

[20] TH Marshall, *Citizenship and Social Class* (CUP, 1950) 10–27.

leeway in what it deems to be 'good' healthcare or 'appropriate' levels of unemployment benefit. These are budgetary and policy issues, not purely legislative ones, and they do not necessarily contain strict 'rights' that can be enforced.[21]

The Charter's drafters deal with the different nature of socio-economic rights as opposed to civil and political rights by limiting the nature of certain rights explicitly (by saying that 'everyone' is entitled to healthcare and social security, *as* it is made available under national law), and by declaring certain commitments to be 'principles' rather than rights.[22] Nonetheless, achieving agreement on the inclusion of socio-economic rights was difficult; there were serious Member State concerns that the CJEU would start questioning the appropriate *levels* of socio-economic rights provided by the Member States, and thus start expanding EU competences when faced with questions about the Charter.[23] The final chapter of the Charter, in order to mitigate these concerns, thus sets out general conditions for how the Charter is meant to operate.

Chapter 7

Chapter 7 of the Charter, titled 'General Provisions', specifically addresses how the Charter is intended to work both in relation to other human rights obligations the Member States have, and in relation to other EU law.

Article 51 immediately addresses the scope of the Charter, and appears to aim to directly tackle concerns that, for example, an EU 'suitable level of healthcare' is going to be imposed on the Member States. First, Article 51(1) states that the Member States will 'respect the rights [and] *observe* the principles *and promote the application thereof*'. It is not entirely clear what this combination of 'observation and promotion' means, but it is distinguished from the 'respect of rights'. That gives the impression that Member States are to *strive* to provide adequate healthcare, social security, and environmental protection—but not that there is a justiciable 'too low' level of any of these that they could be providing.

The limits of the Charter are further made explicit in Article 51(2), which states that it 'does not establish any new power or task for the Community or the Union, or modify powers and tasks defined by the Treaties'. As such, given that the EU does not currently have the competence to organize healthcare systems in the Member States, the drafters of the Charter here assert that it will not gain such a competence through enforcement of the Charter of Fundamental Rights.

Pause for reflection

Do you think the distinction between rights and principles is workable in practice? And, do you think Article 51(2) limits what the CJEU can do with fundamental rights or not?

[21] For a discussion, see Lord Goldsmith QC, 'A Charter of Rights, Freedoms and Principles' (2001) 38 CMLRev 1201, 1212–1213.

[22] Ibid. [23] Ibid.

Article 52 explains what the scope of the Charter's rights are, and how they are to be interpreted. It thus begins in Article 52(1) by setting out what the conditions are for placing limits on fundamental rights in the Charter: those limits must be 'provided for by law' and 'respect the essence of those rights and freedoms'. The Charter here notes that a proportionality test will apply to any restrictions on Charter rights, and that those restrictions must be necessary either to achieve EU objectives of general interest, or to 'protect the rights and freedoms of others'.

Article 52(2), meanwhile, makes clear that where the Charter transcribes rights existing in the EU Treaties, those rights are to be exercised in the way the Treaties set out. This is particularly relevant for Chapter V on Citizens' Rights, which are based on Article 21 TFEU of the Treaty and any legislation adopted thereunder, as we will see in Chapter 13. Finally, in order to avoid conflict between the Member States' existing human rights obligations and the 'new' Charter, Article 52(3) makes clear that where the Charter rights 'correspond' to rights in the ECHR, the 'meaning and scope' of those rights will be identical to those set out in the ECHR; and Article 52(4) similarly indicates that rights stemming from constitutional traditions in the Member States will be interpreted in 'harmony' with those traditions.

The remainder of Article 52 sets out further limitations of the Charter. First, it makes the scope of fundamental rights explicit: fundamental rights apply to *all* the acts and actions of the EU institutions, and to those of the Member States where they 'implement' or 'act within the scope of' EU law. We will consider what those last two terms mean in Section 9.3.2.

Secondly, Article 52(6) promises to take 'full account' of national laws and practices where the Charter says it will; and finally, the 'explanations' that the drafters of the Charter have drawn up as guidance for how it is to be interpreted will be given 'due regard', according to Article 52(7). All of these provisions work together to address Member State concerns that, once enacted, the Charter and its rights would be completely out of their control: their national laws, and their interpretations of the Charter's rights, should continue to have an influence on what the effects of the Charter will be.

The final provision of interest in Article 52 is paragraph (5), which expressly addresses the idea that some parts of the Charter are 'rights' and some parts are 'principles'. It states:

Article 52(5) CFR (emphasis added)

The provisions of this Charter which contain **principles** may be implemented by legislative and executive acts taken by institutions, bodies, offices and agencies of the Union, and by acts of Member States when they are implementing Union law, in the exercise of their respective powers. They shall be **judicially cognisable only in the interpretation of such acts and in the ruling on their legality.**

Article 52(5) is an acknowledgement that some rights will not be directly enforceable, but rather that the EU and the Member States (when implementing EU law) should integrate certain *principles* in the remainder of their legislation. This is a reiteration of something that is visible within some of the Charter's substantive articles—see, for example, Article 37 on environmental protection:

Article 37 CFR

A high level of environmental protection and the improvement of the quality of the environment must be integrated into the policies of the Union and ensured in accordance with the principle of sustainable development.

Article 37 sets out a principle: a 'high level of environmental protection' is something that all EU law and Member State action to implement EU law must comply with. This is not an individually enforceable right: individuals cannot start actions before national courts arguing that an EU law, or domestic law implementing an EU law, fails to meet this 'high level' of environmental protection. At most, if interpreting EU environmental law on separate grounds, national courts can take into account that it should aim for this 'high level'.

Article 53 is a general commitment to the Member States' other human rights obligations in international law and in their domestic constitutional law: it makes clear that the Charter is not to be interpreted so as to *diminish* those existing human rights. The Charter can *upgrade* human rights protections, as Article 52(3) makes explicit regarding rights also contained in the ECHR, but it will not diminish them.

What the Article 53 commitment means in practice was clarified in *Melloni*.[24] The EU, as part of the Area of Freedom, Security and Justice policies, operates the 'European Arrest Warrant' system, whereby any Member State can issue a warrant that is valid throughout the entirety of the EU.[25] Mr Melloni was subject to an extradition request from Italy, where he had been convicted of a crime *in absentia*. In Italy, it was procedurally impossible to appeal *in absentia* convictions. When Mr Melloni was eventually captured by the Spanish authorities, they hesitated to send him back to Italy as the EU rules on the European Arrest Warrant required, because the Spanish Constitution *did* permit appeals to *in absentia* convictions, and they believed that his right to an effective judicial remedy (under Article 47 of the Charter) was infringed by the Italian rules.

The CJEU stressed that where EU law is compliant with the Charter—and it found that the European Arrest Warrant system *was* compliant—it cannot be overridden by domestic constitutional rights (or, presumably, international obligations) where these give greater protection than the EU rights do. In other words, *Melloni* seems to suggest that supremacy of all EU law over domestic law (including constitutions) remains as it was before.[26]

[24] Case C-399/11 *Melloni* ECLI:EU:C:2013:107.

[25] See Council Framework Decision of 13 June 2002 on the European arrest warrant and the surrender procedures between Member States (2002/584/JHA) [2002] OJ L190/1.

[26] See *Internationale Handelsgesellschaft*; however, note that the CJEU appears to have been more willing to consider national courts' review of other Member States' fundamental rights protections where they were concerned with the prohibition of inhuman and degrading treatment—see Joined Cases C-404/15 and C-659/15 PPU *Aranyosi* and *Căldăraru* ECLI:EU:C:2016:198.

The final provision of the Charter is Article 54, which rules out the abuse of fundamental rights in a manner very similar to Article 17 ECHR. It thus precludes the use of one of the Charter rights to deprive others of a different Charter right: though clashes of rights are inevitable, one right (eg, freedom of expression) cannot be exercised for the *purpose* of 'destroying' another right (eg, freedom of religion).

Discussing the quote

Consider Boris Johnson's concerns about the vagueness of some of the contents of the Charter of Fundamental Rights, and how this might result in ever more 'CJEU activism'. In your view, does the content of Chapter 7 of the Charter address such concerns adequately, or not?

Having set out what the Charter looks like, and what rights it covers, it is now important to consider how the Charter actually in practice affects the Member States and the EU institutions when they are acting.

9.3.2 Fundamental rights before the CJEU

What does the CJEU do when faced with questions about fundamental rights? In light of the context to this chapter, it makes sense to first examine what the CJEU's case law on fundamental rights looked like before the adoption of the Charter, so that we can then clearly evaluate if the Charter has made any difference to how the CJEU interprets fundamental rights. We thus start with 'classic' CJEU fundamental rights case law, and look at Charter-era case law in Section 9.4.2.

Limits on acts of EU institutions

The most obvious and original purpose of fundamental rights, whether developed by the CJEU or now expressed in the Charter, is to stop the EU institutions from acting in a way that contravenes such rights. The Member States themselves are bound by a variety of international human rights treaties and domestic human rights commitments, but without fundamental rights, the EU institutions are in principle free to take any action they like (administrative or legal) regardless of the impact that action will have on the rights of others. Using fundamental rights, however, the CJEU can review acts of the EU institutions and declare them to be legally void; fundamental rights, like other general principles and, in the case of the Charter, like the Treaties, supersede any secondary legislation enacted by the EU legislature.

An illustrative and infamous case in which fundamental rights clashed with an EU legal act is *Kadi*.[27] Mr Kadi was one of several individuals identified by the United Nations as being connected to Osama Bin Laden, al-Qaeda, or the Taliban. The UN, in 2002, adopted a resolution that required states to freeze the assets of those individuals. There was no right for these UN resolutions to be judicially reviewed; instead, anyone identified in

[27] Joined Cases C-402/05 P and C-415/05 P *Kadi* ECLI:EU:C:2008:461.

such a resolution had to ask their Member State of residence or nationality to ask the UN Sanctions Committee for them to be delisted. This was complicated, not least because the UN Sanctions Committee did not disclose *why* individuals were included in these asset-freezing programmes.

The relevant UN resolution was implemented by the EU, rather than individual Member States. Asset-freezing in the EU was thus more or less automatic, and reasons for the assets being frozen were not clear to those subjected to this sanction. Mr Kadi, a Saudi national, contested his assets being frozen by protesting the EU act implementing the UN resolution before the EU General Court—first claiming that the EU did not have competence to freeze his assets, full stop, but secondly arguing that the freezing of his assets breached his fundamental rights to property as well as his right to be heard (eg, his right to defence).[28]

The General Court found that the EU had the competence to implement the UN resolution; however, it argued that the EU courts could not carry out a review of Mr Kadi's fundamental rights, because the EU measures were giving effect to a UN resolution rather than stand-alone EU law.[29] In the General Court's view, Mr Kadi was asking for the EU to review a UN resolution—which was outside of its jurisdiction. It thus declined to carry out this fundamental rights review, and found the EU measure to be compliant with general international law obligations.

Mr Kadi appealed this decision to the CJEU. The CJEU agreed that the EU was competent to implement the UN resolution, but disagreed with the General Court on its ability to carry out a fundamental rights review of an EU measure implementing a UN resolution:

Joined Cases C-402/05 P and C-415/05 P *Kadi* ECLI:EU:C:2008:461 (emphasis added)

285. . . . the obligations imposed by an international agreement cannot have the effect of prejudicing the constitutional principles of the [EU Treaties], which include the principle that all [EU] acts must respect fundamental rights, that respect constituting a condition of their lawfulness which it is for the Court to review in the framework of the complete system of legal remedies established by the [Treaties].

. . .

326. It follows from the foregoing that the [EU] judicature must, in accordance with the powers conferred on it by the [EU Treaties], ensure the review, in principle the full review, of the lawfulness of all [EU] acts in the light of the fundamental rights forming an integral part of the general principles of [EU] law, including review of [EU] measures which, like the contested regulation, are designed to give effect to the resolutions adopted by the Security Council under Chapter VII of the Charter of the United Nations.

[28] See Articles 17 and 48 of the Charter of Fundamental Rights.
[29] See Case T-315/01 *Kadi* ECLI:EU:T:2005:332.

Kadi makes it so that the EU institutions must comply with fundamental rights *even* when they are acting in compliance with other international law commitments the EU or its Member States might have. The CJEU thus found that Mr Kadi's right to defence had been violated, primarily by the fact that he had not been informed of why he was included on the UN sanctions list. In the absence of knowledge of what evidence the UN held against him, it was impossible for him to mount a proper defence, and, indeed, impossible for the CJEU to consider if inclusion on the list and thus freezing of his assets was proportionate. In principle, these sanctions therefore *could* be compliant with fundamental rights in EU law—but the manner in which the EU had implemented the UN resolution (and had not, for instance, insisted on further information about Mr Kadi's inclusion on the sanctions list) did violate his right to property and right to a defence.[30]

Limits on acts of the Member States when acting within the scope of EU law

The Member States are supportive of EU institutions' acts being reviewed by the CJEU for fundamental rights compliance; in a way, this simply mimics at the regional level what they themselves have all committed to (as ECHR signatories) domestically. However, the CJEU has also applied fundamental rights to situations where the Member States are *implementing* EU law or *acting within the scope* of EU law. It is particularly the latter concept that has proven controversial.

When *implementing* a directive or setting up a domestic system to give effect to a regulation, the Member States are bound by fundamental rights as they are by other general principles of EU law. This is demonstrated well by *NS*,[31] in which a UK decision under the 'Dublin II Regulation'[32]—setting up a system that allocates Member State responsibility for those seeking asylum in the EU—was challenged for violating the right not to be subjected to degrading/inhuman treatment.[33] Dublin II in principle allocates responsibility for asylum seekers to the Member State in which the asylum seeker first arrives in the EU—but the regulation grants other Member States the right to hear asylum claims even when they are not obliged to. *NS* concerned asylum seekers in the UK who were subject to a deportation order to Greece, where they had first entered the EU. They challenged this deportation order, arguing that the asylum application handling in Greece violated their Article 4 of the Charter right to not be subject to degrading treatment. The UK asked the CJEU how this fitted with the Dublin II Regulation: did fundamental rights apply to a decision to deport if the UK was aware of the conditions asylum applications were processed under in Greece?

This question is more complex than it sounds, as it challenges two principles that underpin the working of the EU's Area of Freedom, Security and Justice policies: those of **mutual recognition** and of **mutual trust**.[34] The Member States operate in these fields under

[30] Note that the CJEU's case law inspired the creation and improvement of a UN Ombudsman to consider cases like *Kadi* in future. See Juliane Kokott and Christoph Sobotta, 'The *Kadi* Case—Constitutional Core Values and International Law—Finding the Balance?' (2012) 23(4) EJIL 1015, 1020–1.

[31] Case C-411/10 *NS* ECLI:EU:C:2011:865.

[32] Regulation 343/2003/EC of 18 February 2003 establishing the criteria and mechanisms for determining the Member State responsible for examining an asylum application lodged in one of the Member States by a third-country national [2003] OJ L50/1.

[33] See Article 4 of the Charter of Fundamental Rights.

[34] Mutual recognition is made explicit in Articles 81–82 TFEU; mutual trust has been developed through CJEU case law, and has now been declared a principle of EU law by the CJEU in *Opinion 2/13*, discussed in Section 9.5.

a presumption that their counterparts adequately protect fundamental rights: EU-wide systems of judicial cooperation in areas like asylum and extradition would not work at all if Member States refused to use them because they mistrusted another Member State's justice system. That said—there is a *presumption* of mutual trust, and what the UK indicated in *NS* was that they had grounds to challenge that presumption.

The CJEU thus gave an affirmative answer: if the UK was aware of systemic deficiencies in the Greek asylum system, the principle of mutual trust was breached, and the UK *should* exercise its discretion to process NS, so as to remain compliant with fundamental rights. This stood separate from the fact that Greece had to improve its asylum application processes so that they no longer resulted in degrading treatment: both the UK *and* Greece had obligations under the Charter, and the CJEU indicated that its job was to review compliance with both of these obligations.[35]

The notion of a Member State 'acting within the scope of EU law' is even broader than this. Fundamental rights here become relevant when a Member State is attempting to limit rights guaranteed under the Treaties. In other words, any restriction to EU Treaty rights *has* to be compliant with fundamental rights as well as other general principles, such as proportionality and legality. An easy-to-grasp example of this type of 'restriction'-based fundamental rights claim is *Omega*.[36] Omega, a UK company, wanted to set up a laser-tag venue in Germany, but the local German government prohibited this, citing a German law that permitted it to 'take measures' for the sake of avoiding a risk to public order and safety. Omega claimed that Germany's law violated its right to provide a service under the EU Treaties, but the German government argued that this restriction on the right to provide services was justifiable because it aimed to protect human dignity (as protected under the German Basic Law).

The CJEU accepted the German government's argument, noting that Germany's objective of protecting human dignity was compatible with EU law, as respect for human dignity was one of the EU's fundamental rights. The fact that laser-tag games, in which people shot at each other with lasers, were legal in other Member States, which upheld a different standard of 'human dignity', was deemed irrelevant—the German decision to prohibit this sort of 'play at killing' was *not* unjustifiable in light of the EU's own fundamental rights regime.

EU law in practice

The UK has had a number of its domestic decisions on issues such as asylum and immigration subjected to fundamental rights review by the CJEU—*NS* is but one example.[37] In *Baumbast*, a UK decision to refuse a German national the right to reside in the UK (with his family) for failing to hold sickness insurance (as required by the EU Citizens' Directive, considered in detail in

→

[35] See, similarly, Joined Cases C-404/15 and C-659/15 PPU *Aranyosi* and *Căldăraru* ECLI:EU:C:2016:198, on the European Arrest Warrant.

[36] Case C-36/02 *Omega* ECLI:EU:C:2004:614.

[37] Fundamental rights were also raised in Case C-200/02 *Chen* ECLI:EU:C:2004:639, discussed in detail in Chapter 13—but not addressed by the CJEU in its judgment.

→

Chapter 13), was overruled as disproportionate in light of Mr Baumbast's right to family life.[38] In *ZZ*, a UK decision to refuse a French/Algerian dual national entry to the UK in 2006 was overruled as it failed to disclose the reasons for that refusal to Mr ZZ—and as such, violated his right to effective judicial protection disproportionately, even if there were legitimate public security grounds to deny Mr ZZ entry.[39]

Possibly the case most illustrative of the complex interaction between the EU's economic 'rights' and its fundamental rights is *Carpenter*.[40] Mr Carpenter, a UK national, married a Filipino national and applied for a UK residence permit for her. This was denied, however, because by the time the Home Office processed the application, Mrs Carpenter was overstaying her (visit) visa in the UK. She was thus told she had to leave the UK and reapply for a residency permit from the Philippines.

Mr Carpenter challenged this decision, but in an unusual way. Rather than ask if the right to family life under the Human Rights Act 1998 (and so the ECHR) was restricted in an unjustifiable way by the decision, Mr Carpenter's counsel considered to what extent the Carpenters' situation was covered by EU law, and if EU law could provide any rights protection in this case. The Immigration Tribunal thus heard that as Mr Carpenter provided services in other Member States, both online and in person from time to time, he acted as a 'service provider' under EU law. If his wife was forced to leave the UK, he would not have anyone to look after his children for him when he provided those services—and so the UK immigration decision was transformed into a restriction on his freedom to provide services under the EU Treaties. Whether such a restriction was justifiable had to be considered in light of, amongst other things, the EU fundamental rights . . . including the right to family life, which was also an ECHR right.

The CJEU heard the case on a preliminary reference from the UK court facing this argument, and decided that this was a correct interpretation of the effects of both EU free movement law and EU fundamental rights law. Mrs Carpenter, as such, should have been given permission to apply for her residence permit *within* the UK; any alternative would have been disproportionate interference with the right to family life under the ECHR and the Charter, and an unjustifiable restriction on Mr Carpenter's rights to provide services throughout the EU.

What do you make of the decision in *Carpenter*? Is this the CJEU stretching the scope of EU law unnaturally, or is this a justifiable use of fundamental rights review?

Clashes between fundamental rights and other EU law

Much of the CJEU's case law on fundamental rights concerns situations where other aspects of EU law seem to clash with fundamental rights. The free movement of goods, services, people, and capital are the foundations of the EU economic project—but prioritizing them over all other values results in the economic rights of some parties being preferred over the fundamental rights of other parties. Nowhere is this clash more visible than in the *Viking* and *Laval* cases, the facts of which we considered in Chapter 8.[41] The CJEU found in both cases that the right to provide a service and the right to establish

[38] Case C-413/99 *Baumbast* ECLI:EU:C:2002:49.
[39] Case C-300/11 *ZZ* ECLI:EU:C:2013:363.
[40] Case C-60/00 *Carpenter* ECLI:EU:C:2002:434.
[41] Case C-438/05 *Viking* ECLI:EU:C:2007:772; Case C-341/05 *Laval* ECLI:EU:C:2007:809.

in another Member State were disproportionately impeded by the unions' exercise of the right to strike, leading many commentators to consider if this was evidence that the EU will always prioritize the 'market' over 'people'.[42] *Viking* and *Laval* can be contrasted, however, with the rulings in *Schmidberger*, *Omega*, and *Carpenter*, where the CJEU clearly decided that interferences with the 'four freedoms' could be justified by fundamental rights concerns, provided those interferences were proportionate.

The other area of EU law where there are frequent clashes between fundamental rights and other EU law is in the Area of Freedom, Security and Justice. As we saw in *NS*, this area of law—usually when it comes to decisions to move humans from one Member State to another, whether they are asylum seekers or subject to extradition under a European Arrest Warrant—operates on a basis of mutual trust amongst the Member States, but in situations where Member States have doubts about the workings of another Member State's justice system on human rights grounds, they frequently ask the CJEU for input. Whereas, historically, the CJEU prioritized mutual trust and mutual recognition so as to keep the EU system on judicial cooperation working, in some recent cases (like *NS*) the CJEU has found that mutual trust does *not* outweigh fundamental rights where violations of these are significant enough.[43] Again, proportionality assessments mean that when certain rights are violated—and particularly human dignity, as an inviolable right—the CJEU will accept fundamental rights overriding other principles of EU law.

Discussing the quote

What do *Viking* and *Laval* suggest about concerns like those of Boris Johnson that the CJEU will extend the reach of fundamental rights under the Charter? What about *NS*? (Note that these cases were all decided before the Charter was adopted!)

9.4 The UK's fundamental concerns about the Charter

The UK has struggled with certain aspects of the EU's fundamental rights regime over time. Its issues have been less concerned with the CJEU's case law on these rights, heavily underpinned by the ECHR as those have been, and more with the eventual enactment into primary and secondary legislation *of* these fundamental rights. Key to the UK concerns is, unsurprisingly, the idea of sovereignty: it is not the rights themselves, but rather the further probing of domestic law for compliance with yet another set of (international) rights that was seen as problematic.

[42] See, inter alia, Niamh Nic Shuibhne, 'Settling Dust? Reflections on the Judgments in *Viking* and *Laval*' (2010) 21(5) EBLR 681; Norbert Reich, 'Free Movement v Social Rights in an Enlarged Union—the Laval and Viking Cases before the ECJ' (2008) 9(2) Ger Law J 125; Catherine Barnard, 'Social Dumping or Dumping Socialism' (2008) 67 CLJ 262.

[43] See also *Aranyosi* and *Căldăraru* (n 35).

A reluctance to adopt fully the EU rights regime was first visible in the UK opt-out from the Treaty's so-called Social Chapter of employment rights, even though this was undone by the Tony Blair Labour government when the Treaty of Amsterdam was ratified by the UK. The same reluctance appeared when, during the Lisbon negotiations, the UK (as well as Poland and the Czech Republic, eventually) pressed for and obtained what has been called an 'opt-out' from the Charter of Fundamental Rights.

9.4.1 The opt-out

The 'opt-out' is set out in Protocol 30 to the Lisbon Treaty. Article 1(1) of the Protocol stresses that the Charter does not 'extend' the ability of any courts (whether CJEU or domestic) to find that any actions or acts in the relevant Member States are inconsistent with the Charter. Article 1(2) meanwhile stresses that Title IV (Solidarity) does not create 'justiciable rights' in the UK or Poland (or the Czech Republic), unless any of these countries have provided for such rights in 'national law'. Article 2 adds that where the Charter refers to national laws and practices, this is to be interpreted strictly and on a per-country basis.

Neither of these provisions actually 'adds' anything to the text of the Charter itself. The inclusion of both 'rights and principles', as well as how Title IV 'principles' are drafted (eg, with reference to national law) reflect what is spelled out in Articles 1(2) and 2 of the Protocol. Article 51 of the Charter confirms that it does not extend the EU's competences in any way.

Protocol 30 to the Lisbon Treaty is thus, in reality, not a genuine 'opt-out'. This was not a surprise to the UK government lawyers, who were well aware that Member States cannot opt out of general principles of EU law, so it could never be a true opt-out! The probable purpose of Protocol was therefore political: it represented a Treaty-associated attempt to assure the UK public that its government was not giving up even further control to the EU. Given the Boris Johnson quote at the start of the chapter, it is very debatable if that attempt was successful.

9.4.2 CJEU rulings on the Charter

As we discussed in Section 9.3, the Charter was not intended to extend the scope of EU law; and both Article 51 of the Charter and Protocol 30 of the Lisbon Treaty reiterate this very specifically. Indeed, *prima facie*, we can conclude that it did *not* extend the scope of substantive EU law: the justiciable rights in the Charter reflect CJEU case law, and the 'principles' there are not justiciable. Nonetheless, the notion of 'implementing' EU law or acting within the scope of it, for the purposes of the Charter, remains broad—and thus potentially of concern to Member States like the UK and Poland. Has the adoption of the Charter meant that the CJEU has become 'more activist' in its usage of fundamental rights?

Åkerberg Fransson, discussed in Chapter 8, demonstrates how the CJEU approached fundamental rights post-Charter.[44] The case concerned a Swedish man who had been charged with serious tax offences—and was then charged with them for a second time.

[44] Case C-617/10 *Åkerberg Fransson* ECLI:EU:C:2013:105.

Mr Åkerberg Fransson relied on the 'double jeopardy' provision in Article 50 of the Charter and argued that he could not be subjected to criminal proceedings for the same activity twice. Sweden, and several intervening Member States, meanwhile argued that the Swedish law that permitted action to be taken against Mr Åkerberg Fransson had *nothing* to do with EU law—it was not implementing legislation. The CJEU, however, found a connection: part of what Mr Åkerberg Fransson was charged with was related to his duties to declare VAT, which *were* set out in EU secondary legislation. It thus ignored that many of the charges related to income tax, which is outside of EU competences, and found instead that the relevant Swedish legislation did give effect to or 'implement' obligations stemming to EU law.

Pause for reflection

Consider the case law we discussed in Section 9.3.2. Do you think the CJEU would have decided *Åkerberg Fransson* differently *before* the Charter was adopted? Why or why not?

However, *Åkerberg Fransson* may well be an outlier. Much of the CJEU's case law on the Charter gives no further rise to the fear that the CJEU is developing a general fundamental rights jurisdiction, able to review any piece of national legislation it wants to. We can contrast *Åkerberg Fransson* with *McB*, where the CJEU outright refused to examine Irish national law on custody rights for separated parents, and noted that the only matter of EU law raised in the case set out merely to *coordinate* the recognition of custody agreements between the Member States.[45] It then proceeded only to analyse how fundamental rights applied to the interpretation of that coordinating regulation—without specifically commenting on the Irish national provisions on custody rights.

Similarly to *McB*, cases like *Siragusa* make clear that 'implementation' of EU law cannot simply refer to any domestic law that might be *on a similar topic* to an EU law.[46] In that case, Mr Siragusa engaged in a construction project on listed buildings and then retroactively applied for planning permission, which was denied in light of Italian national law. He was thus ordered to return the buildings to their original state. The national court hearing his protest to this order asked if these Italian laws on conservation were compatible with the Article 17 Charter right to property—noting that the conservation laws were related to environmental protection, which was an area in which the EU also legislated. The CJEU did not view these Italian laws as being a form of 'implementation', however, noting that 'implementation' required a 'degree of connection above and beyond the matters covered being closely related or one of those matters having an indirect impact on one another'.[47] In other words, just because the Italian laws on conservation were arguably about environmental protection, and the EU also produces environmental protection legislation, this did not mean that the Italian laws 'implemented' EU law.

[45] Case C-400/10 PPU *McB* ECL:EU:C:2010:582, para 52.
[46] Case C-206/13 *Siragusa* ECLI:EU:C:2014:126. [47] Ibid, para 24.

We thus have some case law suggesting that the EU will use fundamental rights to examine ever more aspects of national law—but also significant case law suggesting that it applies the limitations now set out in Article 51 of the Charter, and will heed them perhaps even more carefully than it did when fundamental rights were only general principles.

Discussing the quote

You have now considered the whole EU framework of fundamental rights. What do you think about the concerns raised by Boris Johnson? Can fundamental rights be used to stretch the scope of EU law, and promote more judicial activism? And, importantly, do you think the Charter specifically enables the CJEU to do this?

9.5 The relationship between the CJEU and the ECtHR

Though both products of the Second World War, the ECHR predates cases like *Stauder* by a good 15 years. By the time the EU arrived on the 'human rights' scene, all of its Member States had already ratified this separate Treaty, and had thus committed themselves to a non-EU standard of human rights. The only way that the EU could logically compel them to also follow EU fundamental rights was if these were broadly compatible *with* ECHR rights.

Nonetheless, the very nature of the ECHR and how it is enforced by the ECtHR is distinct from anything the CJEU has done with fundamental rights. For one thing, the Council of Europe—the body that operates the ECHR—has a broader membership than the EU does. More importantly, however, the ECHR's rights can be enforced by *individuals before the ECtHR* once they have exhausted all domestic means of attaining a remedy for their wrongs. In practice, then, the CJEU and the ECtHR are likely to hear different cases—but they nonetheless will have to interpret the same rights.

9.5.1 Coherent case law

The CJEU has from its early case law onwards acknowledged the ECHR and the ECtHR as a particularly helpful source for the EU's own fundamental rights. When interpreting fundamental rights, and as now codified in the Charter, the CJEU will look to ECtHR case law and follow it as closely as possible. On the only occasions when different interpretations of the same rights have occurred, this has been largely accidental, and quickly remedied by subsequent case law. As of the Maastricht Treaty, the EU Treaties themselves explicitly acknowledge the importance of the ECHR in framing the EU's own fundamental rights.

However, the EU's respect for the ECHR does not wholly compensate for the ECHR not *applying* to the EU institutions, and cannot entirely rule out situations where it is not clear what court has jurisdiction over a factual scenario. This became clear in the

Matthews case, which brought an end to a long-standing practice of the Council of Europe of assuming that the EU acted in ways compliant with fundamental rights—and that the Member States thus did not have to check if an individual EU act was ECHR-compliant, though they were obliged to comply with the ECHR as well as EU law.[48]

Ms Matthews was a resident of Gibraltar with a UK passport, who discovered she was not permitted to vote in European Parliament elections. UK law reserved the right to vote in those elections for UK nationals on UK soil. However, Gibraltar was subject to virtually all EU law that applies in the Member States. As such, Ms Matthews argued that she found herself in a situation where she effectively had no say over the laws applying to her—and that this violated the ECHR's Protocol 1, guaranteeing a right to free elections.

The problem was that it was not entirely clear if Ms Matthews *could* take this claim to the ECtHR. The UK argued she could not: her objection was to a piece of legislation adopted by the EU that set out how European Parliament elections were to operate, and, as such, the ECtHR did not have jurisdiction over the case. It also argued its own innocence, saying it had done nothing to disenfranchise Ms Matthews personally—and could not amend this EU legislation on its own.

The ECtHR agreed that it could not scrutinize EU legislation, as the EU was not a contracting party to the ECHR. However, the relevant EU law on European Parliament elections had the status of primary legislation, of equivalent value to the Treaties. The Treaties (and other primary legislation) could not be subjected to a fundamental rights review by the CJEU, either; it was not given that power under the Treaties.[49] Consequently, the only party that could be held responsible for disenfranchising Ms Matthews was the UK, in combination with the other EU Member States.

This was the beginning of the ECtHR's development of a principle of '**collective responsibility**'. In situations where the CJEU could not ensure the protection of fundamental rights, the Member States collectively would be responsible for ensuring the ECHR was complied with, and the ECtHR would provide oversight of their 'collective responsibility'.

The ECtHR clarified that 'collective responsibility' would be the exception, not the rule, in *Bosphorus*. The case involved an aeroplane that was impounded in Ireland because of the EU implementation of a UN sanctions regime against the Former Republic of Yugoslavia (FRY). Bosphorus, a Turkish airline charter company who had leased an aeroplane to a company in the FRY, claimed that Ireland's decision to impound the plane was an infringement of its right to property and brought an action before the Irish courts. They referred the matter to the CJEU, which found that the aeroplane was covered by the relevant EU regulation, and that on balancing the right to property against the aims of the UN sanctions regime (which was to stop the FRY from conducting further aggression against neighbouring Bosnia-Herzegovina), the impounding was proportionate.[50]

Bosphorus, however, then appealed the case outcome several times in the Irish courts—and eventually went to the ECtHR to claim an infringement of their Article 1 Protocol 1 ECHR property right. The ECtHR used the case as an opportunity to once more address its relationship with the CJEU. In *Bosphorus*, it stressed that it would only exercise 'collective

[48] *Matthews v the United Kingdom* (1999) 28 EHRR 361.

[49] See Chapters 2 and 7 on the jurisdiction of the CJEU.

[50] Case C-84/95 *Bosphorus* ECLI:EU:C:1996:312.

responsibility' where it was not clear that the EU provided *equivalent protection* to the ECHR.[51] Only in situations where ECHR rights protection was found to be *manifestly deficient* in EU law would the ECtHR take a decision like it did in *Matthews*, and force collective responsibility upon the Member States to remedy this violation of rights.[52] *Bosphorus* did not meet this threshold.

Beyond that, the ECtHR has always been willing to examine the actions of Member States in implementing EU law where they have discretion in doing so—here, the ultimate 'actor' is seen as the Member State, not the EU, and so the Member State can be held to account for the manner in which it has chosen to comply with EU law. As such, in a case resembling *NS*, the ECtHR had already concluded that under the ECHR, applying the Dublin II Regulation could not result in Member States deporting asylum seekers to a country if it was clear to the authorities they would be subjected to degrading treatment there.[53]

We can consequently see that even though the ECHR and EU fundamental rights operate in different spheres, and the two courts are unlikely to be dealing with identical disputes, there will be situations in which the ECHR reaches into EU law without an express invitation to do so by the CJEU. This overlap of jurisdictions came to the fore in *Opinion 2/13*, when the CJEU had to consider just how the CJEU and the ECtHR were going to work together once the EU joined the ECHR.[54]

Pause for reflection

Does the *Bosphorus* judgment remind you of any other case law you have read about to date? (Think back to Chapter 6, and Germany.) What does this pressure from both above and below to provide 'equivalent' protection tell you about the EU's human rights role—can it ever be a *leader* in human rights, do you think?

9.5.2 EU accession to the ECHR

As discussed in detail in Chapter 5, the EU's first attempt to join the ECHR failed because the CJEU ruled in *Opinion 2/94* that the Treaties did not give the EU the power *to* join the ECHR.[55] This changed in the Lisbon Treaty, where the EU not only gained permission to join the ECHR, but is actually *ordered* to do so in Article 6(2) TEU.

We are now a decade beyond the Lisbon Treaty, and the EU is still not an ECHR signatory. This is not to say that the EU has not tried to join. Negotiations for the EU to accede to the ECHR commenced in June 2010, and resulted in an agreed 'accession agreement' text negotiated by EU and Council of Europe representatives in April 2013. Before the EU ratified this agreement, however, the CJEU was asked by the Commission to provide an

[51] *Bosphorus v Ireland* (2006) 42 EHRR 1, para 155. [52] Ibid, para 156.
[53] *MSS v Belgium and Greece* (2011) 53 EHRR 2.
[54] Opinion 2/13 *Accession of the European Union to the European Convention for the Protection of Human Rights and Fundamental Freedoms* ECLI:EU:C:2014:2454.
[55] Opinion 2/94 *Accession by the Community to the European Convention for the Protection of Human Rights and Fundamental Freedoms* ECLI:EU:C:1996:140.

opinion on its compatibility with EU law. In December 2014, the CJEU issued a now-infamous opinion, *Opinion 2/13*, which ground the accession process to a halt.

What were the CJEU's objections to the accession agreement?[56]

It highlighted various issues in *Opinion 2/13*, but, first and foremost, the nature of its own jurisdiction. Under the EU Treaties, as discussed in previous chapters, the Court of Justice is the *only* body that can interpret EU law.[57] With the EU joining the ECHR, however, the ECtHR would have to gain some sort of jurisdiction over EU law.

The proposed accession agreement designed a form of 'job-sharing' that would ensure that the CJEU was not sidelined the second the ECHR arose in a dispute.[58] It created a so-called 'co-respondent' mechanism, whereby the EU could 'join' any action directed against a Member State if it looked as if that action was going to argue that EU law was incompatible with the ECHR. It also made plain that if an action involved EU primary law (eg, the Treaties), the Member States could become 'co-respondents' alongside the EU, as they would ultimately (as per *Matthews*) be responsible for fixing any violations of the ECHR in the Treaties or other primary legislation. As such, both the EU and the Member States could be involved in cases that were addressed to one or the other, and the ECHR made clear that it would accept these cases regardless of who the application was addressed to—thus not penalizing applicants who did not understand if the EU or the Member States were responsible for a specific EU act.

The CJEU's problem with the 'co-respondent' mechanism was, simply put, that it would put the ECtHR in charge of determining how power was divided between the EU and its Member States, as 'co-respondents' could only join cases where it was conceivable that an issue of EU law was being challenged—and it would be up to the ECtHR to make that latter determination. This, the CJEU found, was problematic for the autonomy of the EU's legal order; it overrode the CJEU's exclusive jurisdiction to determine the balance of power between the EU and the Member States.[59]

It had similar problems with a further compromise set out in the accession agreement, known as the CJEU's 'prior involvement' in cases. The draft text made it possible for ECtHR proceedings involving secondary EU law (with the EU as co-respondent) to be delayed until the CJEU assessed whether the EU laws were compatible with the ECHR itself. In other words, it would enable the ECtHR to request a 'preliminary reference' of sorts from the CJEU on the EU law's compatibility with the ECHR, where the CJEU had not already issued case law that declared a piece of legislation compatible with EU fundamental rights. The CJEU's objection to this provision was that it involved the ECtHR making a determination of what the CJEU's own case law said, and thus would be giving a binding interpretation of the case law. This could be remedied, when cases were pending before the ECtHR, by asking the EU to consider, itself, if the CJEU had already issued an interpretation and otherwise commencing a 'prior involvement' process—but as drafted, it too violated the autonomy of EU law.[60]

[56] See Eleanor Spaventa, 'A Very Fearful Court? The Protection of Fundamental Rights in the European Union after Opinion 2/13' (2015) 22 Maastricht Journal 35.

[57] See Chapter 2 and Chapters 6 and 7.

[58] For the text of the draft accession agreement, see https://www.echr.coe.int/Documents/UE_Report_CDDH_ENG.pdf.

[59] See *Opinion 2/13*, paras 215–235.

[60] Ibid, paras 236–248.

The CJEU raised further objections to the accession agreement that genuinely seem insurmountable.[61] The most important of these stemmed from the fact that unlike itself, the ECtHR would have full jurisdiction over Common Foreign and Security Policy. An exception to the ECtHR's jurisdiction could not be made under the ECHR, but the ECtHR having greater jurisdiction over CFSP than the CJEU itself was clearly unacceptable to the CJEU. Short of the Member States giving the CJEU full jurisdiction as well, there does not seem to be any way to ameliorate this aspect of the association agreement.

Commentators at this point are thus sceptical as to whether EU accession to the ECHR will be possible, unless the CJEU changes its mind both about how its 'autonomy' functions and how EU law can accommodate the ECtHR and the ECHR. What this means, nobody knows: the EU *has* to accede to the ECHR . . . but nothing in the Treaties spells out what happens if it turns out it *cannot*.[62]

9.6 Brexit and fundamental rights

As a consequence of Brexit, the future role (if any) that the Charter of Fundamental Rights will play in the UK is in principle a matter of domestic law. However, as has become a recurring theme in this book, that is an oversimplification of the precise agreement struck between the UK and the EU regarding the Brexit process. We will now look at the Withdrawal Agreement, the Protocol on Ireland/Northern Ireland, and what, if anything, we can determine about post-Brexit fundamental rights.

9.6.1 The Withdrawal Agreement

As has been said in all previous chapters, beyond institutional representation for the UK, little will change over the course of the transition period: all EU law will continue to apply in the UK as it currently does, per Article 4 of the Withdrawal Agreement, and that includes the Charter of Fundamental Rights and the general principles of EU law.

Slightly more interesting in this area than in many others is the ongoing effect of CJEU jurisprudence. As discussed in Chapter 5, little new EU legislation will pass through the entirety of the EU legislative process over the course of a *short* transition period,[63] and so the UK will either have been involved in the legislative process of any new EU legislation while still a Member State—or the legislation is unlikely to enter into force before the Withdrawal Agreement's transition period ends.[64] The same is obviously not true for CJEU interpretation of EU law, which will move at the same pace it always does, and so,

[61] Ibid, paras 249–257.

[62] See Spaventa (n 56) and Adam Lazowski and Ramses A Wessel, 'When Caveats Turn into Locks: *Opinion 2/13* on accession of the European Union to the ECHR' (2015) 16(1) Ger Law J 179.

[63] Of course, the transition period can be extended by one or two years under the Withdrawal Agreement, Articles 126 and 132; note that the EU (Withdrawal Agreement) Act 2020, s 33, prohibits UK representatives from asking for an extension as a matter of domestic law—though as is true for all Acts of Parliament, this can obviously be amended if an extension is desired after all.

[64] For a useful tracker of the EU laws coming into force over the course of the transition period, see https://uk.practicallaw.thomsonreuters.com/2-631-7191?transitionType=Default&contextData=(sc.Default)#co_anchor_a276199.

in theory, further judgments developing fundamental rights—whether under the Charter or under the general principles—could be delivered between now and the end of the transition period. Depending on the nature of cases pending before the CJEU, then, we may see a few further dimensions of 'rights' being uncovered before the UK's withdrawal from the EU is complete.

9.6.2 The Protocol on Ireland/Northern Ireland

In the context of Northern Ireland, 'rights' are supremely important. The 1998 Belfast/Good Friday Agreement contains express commitments to non-diminution—meaning that the UK and Ireland are both committed to not *lowering* the standard of rights under a separate Treaty. These commitments are echoed in the Protocol on Ireland/Northern Ireland:

Article 2(1) Protocol (emphasis added)

The United Kingdom shall ensure **that no diminution of rights, safeguards or equality of opportunity, as set out in that part of the 1998 Agreement entitled Rights, Safeguards and Equality of Opportunity results from its withdrawal from the Union**, including in the area of protection against discrimination, as enshrined in the provisions of Union law listed in Annex 1 to this Protocol, and shall implement this paragraph through dedicated mechanisms.

This involves the retention of specific pieces of EU law in Northern Ireland—but also requires that insofar as the Charter of Fundamental Rights reflects the rights set out in the 'Rights, Safeguards and Equality of Opportunity', its effects do not change in Northern Ireland after Brexit. Two observations can be made about this:

- First, as the Charter's application is limited to EU acts and acts by the Member States when acting in the scope of EU law, we should remember that the Charter did not provide *general* rights protection in the UK before Brexit. Its content means that *EU-related acts and actions* have to comply with Charter rights. In the absence of EU law, then, the Charter has no genuine effects.
- Secondly, however, as has been mentioned in other chapters, the Protocol continues the application of many pieces of EU internal market law to Northern Ireland—and these will have to be interpreted in line with CJEU jurisprudence *on* EU law, under Article 4(3) of the Withdrawal Agreement. In other words, when EU law applicable in Northern Ireland is applied or interpreted, this will have to be done in light of the general principles of EU law and the Charter.[65]

As the commitment to non-diminution in Article 4 of the Protocol will be overseen by 'dedicated mechanisms', there will be domestic institutions in charge of oversight and enforcement of the commitment. If they are given adequate powers to enforce the commitment, the Charter's effects will remain as they are now—at least in relation to those parts of EU law that remain in force in Northern Ireland.

[65] See, for commentary, https://www.thebritishacademy.ac.uk/sites/default/files/europe-futures-brexit-rights-ireland-northern-ireland-protocol-withdrawal-agreement.pdf.

9.6.3 The future relationship

The Charter of Fundamental Rights is not being retained as a part of domestic UK law after Brexit. The European Union (Withdrawal) Act 2018, despite attempts to amend it in the Lords, has made this explicit:

> **European Union (Withdrawal Act) 2018, s 5**
>
> 4. The Charter of Fundamental Rights is **not part of domestic law on or after exit day.**
> 5. Subsection 4 does not affect the retention in domestic law on or after exit day in accordance with this Act of **any fundamental rights or principles which exist irrespective of the Charter** (and references to the Charter in any case law are, so far as necessary for this purpose, to be read as if they were references to any corresponding retained fundamental rights or principles).

The Political Declaration does not suggest that this position will change in the negotiations. Of course, what is set out in s 5 is qualified: the UK is not retaining the Charter itself, but appears to be retaining some 'fundamental rights or principles' that exist regardless of the Charter. This must be a reference to 'general principles' that reflect on fundamental rights—and so we have to consider what is happening to 'general principles' under the EU (Withdrawal) Act 2018. The answer to that question is provided in Schedule 1 of the 2018 Act:

> **European Union (Withdrawal) Act 2018, Schedule 1 (emphasis added)**
>
> 2. No general principle of EU law is part of domestic law on or after exit day **if it was not recognised as a general principle of EU law by the European Court in a case decided before exit day** (whether or not as an essential part of the decision in the case).
>
> 3.1 There is no **right of action in domestic law** on or after exit day based on a **failure to comply with any of the general principles of EU law.**
>
> 2 No court or tribunal or other public authority may, on or after exit day—
>
> (a) **disapply or quash** any enactment or other rule of law, . . . **because it is incompatible with any of the general principles of EU law.**

Combining s 5 and Schedule 1, we end up with the UK courts being generally obliged under s 6 to interpret 'retained' EU law in light of CJEU jurisprudence on the general principles *as it stands on the day the transition period ends*—instead of it being interpreted on the basis of the Charter itself. In a roundabout way, then, the Charter will continue to apply to retained EU law. Exceptions occur if the Supreme Court should unexpectedly choose to deviate from CJEU interpretations of a given provision of 'retained' EU law, or if the lower courts are instructed or given leave to depart from CJEU jurisprudence by regulation.[66]

The compromise struck in the 2018 Act is one that recalls the UK protests to the Charter becoming primary law, and its desire for an 'opt-out'. In enabling 'general principles' to survive, but not retaining the Charter itself, the 2018 Act effectively restores the working of fundamental rights in the UK to something close to the pre-2009 EU-wide situation. Section 6 makes clear that future CJEU case law, including on fundamental rights, will not have to be applied to 'retained' EU law—but that nonetheless means that the Charter, as it stands on 'exit' day, will—in spirit, if not in actual text—continue to influence significant portions of the UK legal order.

'Influence' is a key word, however. One of the fundamental differences between EU membership and what the EU (Withdrawal) Act 2018 establishes is the ability for individuals to bring actions on the basis of fundamental rights violations. Schedule 1 of the 2018 Act explicitly rules out a right of action based on a failure to comply with any EU law general principle (including fundamental rights), and also does not extend the limited form of supremacy it establishes in s 5 to general principles—legislation incompatible with 'retained' general principles will not be disapplied in a specific case.[67] Individuals' access *to* fundamental rights before the domestic courts is consequently curbed significantly under the 2018 Act.

Of course, it will also be possible for 'retained' EU law to be amended in ways that are not Charter-compliant in future—at least, in Great Britain. In Northern Ireland, where there is an overlap between 'retained' EU law and rights protected under Article 2(1) of the Protocol, that 'retained' EU law will also be subject to a non-diminution obligation. This may lead to situations where changes in UK law will require separate, undiminished, and Charter-compliant law in Northern Ireland, and makes it desirable for there to be clear instructions on how to apply the Charter to 'retained' EU law in Northern Ireland so as to comply with the 'non-diminution' obligation.

Post-Brexit, in an indirect way, the Charter will also continue having a different kind of influence on the UK legal order. Whether or not the EU manages to accede to the ECHR, we have seen that the CJEU and the ECtHR try to work *together* to protect human rights at a similar standard wherever possible. As such, any big developments at the EU are very likely to have an impact on how the ECHR is applied—and unless the UK also withdraws from the Council of Europe, the ECHR will (via the Human Rights Act 1998) continue to apply in the UK.

The big post-Brexit change, then, will be in enforcement of fundamental rights by private parties, and in the effects of those 'fundamental rights' that do not have an obvious ECHR corollary. The latter are rights the UK would have had to protect *as a Member State* when acting within the scope of EU law, but will not have to protect outside of the EU when doing anything regarding 'retained' EU law. There are numerous rights in the Charter that do not have ECHR equivalents: the right to data protection, the right to dignity, the rights of the child, the right to conscientious objection, and the various Title V rights on EU citizenship will 'freeze' in the UK under current legislation, but will

[66] See the discussion in Chapter 4 of the EU (Withdrawal Agreement) Act 2020, s 26(1), amending EU (Withdrawal) Act 2018, s 6.

[67] EU (Withdrawal) Act 2018, Schedule 1, part 3.

continue to develop at the EU level. It will consequently be very interesting to see what happens when the UK courts are faced with issues that would have been covered by the Charter when the UK was a Member State, but on which they are no longer *obliged* to heed CJEU case law: will they follow where the CJEU goes, or go their own way?

9.7 **In conclusion**

What can we say about the CJEU's 'activism' in the realm of fundamental rights? It should be clear by now that the Boris Johnson quote at the start of the chapter perhaps expresses genuine fears, but not legal realities: the rights he mentions in the quote are primarily related to the EU's fundamental freedoms, and so are not at all new to EU law just because they are now also mentioned in the Charter.

That said, it obviously cannot be denied that the EU's body of fundamental rights law was commenced by the CJEU, and heavily advanced by the CJEU. The fact that the CJEU's case law was historically heavily inspired by an instrument that all the Member States had ratified, in the ECHR, means that it is possible to have very mixed views about the extent of judicial law-making at work here. Is the Charter a culmination of filling *gaps* in the Treaties that should not have been there, or did the CJEU genuinely branch out into an area of EU law that the Member States ultimately opted not to pursue themselves?

The most interesting aspect of the EU's fundamental rights law is undoubtedly how the CJEU has been asked to balance 'human rights' alongside the primarily 'economic rights' that underpin the EU's single market project. This is far from its only balancing act, however. We will see, over the course of the next five chapters, that clashes between national considerations (including human rights) and the EU's internal market law are extremely common—and that much of the EU's ongoing functioning depends on how the CJEU interprets what is in the Treaties, rather than what is written there. Whether that activity is a form of 'activism' remains very much a matter of perspective.

Key points

- EU **fundamental rights** were originally developed by the CJEU as general principles of EU law, but have now been codified in the **Charter of Fundamental Rights,** which the Lisbon Treaty has made binding primary law.
- The CJEU has always heeded the work of the **European Court of Human Rights** as a source of inspiration and, following the development of fundamental rights, potential overlap; however, as of the Lisbon Treaty, the EU is mandated to **join the European Convention on Human Rights.** Due to objections by the CJEU, it has not managed to do so yet.
- The EU's fundamental rights work to review the acts and actions of EU institutions generally, and the acts of the Member States when they work within the 'scope of EU law'. The latter concept is quite broad.
- The Charter of Fundamental Rights is not being 'copied' into UK law following Brexit, meaning **where the Charter does not overlap with the ECHR**, rights may disappear.

Assess your learning

1. Are fundamental rights still general principles now that the Charter has been adopted? (See Section 9.2.)
2. Are all rights in the Charter justiciable? How can you tell if they are? (See Section 9.3.)
3. Does the CJEU *have* to heed the case law of the European Court of Human Rights, when that case law addresses an equivalent right? (See Section 9.5.)

Further reading

Catherine Barnard, 'So Long, Farewell, Auf Wiedersehen, Adieu: Brexit and the Charter of Fundamental Rights' (2019) 82(2) MLR 350.

Gráinne de Búrca, 'After the EU Charter of Fundamental Rights: The Court of Justice as a human rights adjudicator?' (2013) 20 Maastricht Journal 168.

Johan Callewaert, 'Do we still need Art. 6(2) TEU? Considerations on the absence of EU accession to the ECHR and its consequences' (2018) 55(6) CMLRev 1685.

Michael Dougan, 'Judicial Review of Member State Action under the General Principles and the Charter: Defining the "Scope of Union Law"' (2015) 52 CMLRev 1201.

Joelle Grogan, 'Rights and Remedies at Risk: Implications of the Brexit process on the future of rights in the UK' [2019] PL 683.

Andreas Hofmann, 'Resistance against the Court of Justice of the European Union' (2018) 14(2) I-CON 258.

Koen Lenaerts, 'Exploring the Limits of the EU Charter of Fundamental Rights' (2012) 8 Eur Const Law Rev 375.

Tobias Lock, 'Rights and Principles in the Charter of Fundamental Rights' (2019) 56(5) CMLRev 1201.

Paulo Pinto du Albuquerque and Hyun-Soo Lim, 'The Cross-Fertilisation between the Court of Justice of the European Union and the European Court of Human Rights: Reframing the discussion on Brexit' (2018) 6 EHRLR 567.

Daniel Sarmiento, 'Who's Afraid of the Charter? The Court of Justice, national courts and the new framework of fundamental rights protection in Europe' (2013) 50(5) CMLRev 1267.

Online resources

Visit www.oup.com/he/demars1e for a sample approach to discussing the quote.

10

The internal (or common, or single) market

Context for this chapter

'I really don't think [Brexit] would make a blind bit of difference to trade with Europe. There has been far too much scaremongering about things like jobs. I don't think we or Brussels will put up trade barriers.

'What is needed is a lot less red tape. . . . Some of it is costly for us and, quite frankly, ridiculous. Whether that means renegotiating or exiting [the EU], I don't think it can carry on as it is. It's a burden. . . . It's easier selling to North America than to Europe sometimes.'

Graeme Macdonald, CEO of JCB (a construction equipment producer), quoted in Vincenzo Scarpetta, 'Cutting red tape must be at the heart of any EU reform agenda' (18 May 2015, OpenEurope) https://openeurope.org.uk/today/blog/cutting-red-tape-must-be-at-the-heart-of-any-eu-reform-agenda/

10.1 Introduction

Chapter 1 of the book, in laying out the history of the European Union, gave an explanation of the political and economic rationale for sovereign countries to agree to work together under the banner of the Treaty of Rome. So far, the book as a whole has considered the setup and functioning of that European project—its 'constitutional' and institutional dimensions. Starting with this chapter, we will dive deeper into the economic theory underpinning the EU project since its genesis: that of the benefits of economic integration.

This chapter will set out that theory in terms that do not require a background in economics and trade, and set the scene for the means by which the EU has attempted to create what is interchangeably called the 'common market', the 'single market', or the 'internal market'. The next four chapters explore in detail those legal rules that make up the 'internal market' by looking at the free movement of goods, free movement of workers, EU citizenship, and the freedom of establishment.

One of the primary criticisms levelled at the EU by business, not only in light of the Brexit referendum but historically, is that of so-called 'red tape'. The argument goes that while trading together might have in theory been a good idea, the EU has gone so overboard in setting out rules for all its Member States that rather than make trade easier, they tend to make trade significantly more expensive. Worse is that these rules are binding on everyone in the Member States, regardless of circumstances: the local newsagent has to comply with rules that are meant to facilitate trade with France in the same way that a big supermarket or household product producer might need to, regardless of whether the newsagent ever actually exports anything.

Part of the draw of Brexit is starting from scratch on the 'red tape', and setting out simpler rules that are geared at the needs and requirements of UK industry and businesses alone, or perhaps responding to the desires of *other* trade partners, like those in North America. But are the rules coming out of the EU really as unnecessary and . . . 'frankly, ridiculous' as they have been made out to be?

The remainder of Chapter 10 will allow you to start considering this question by setting out the essential components of what makes up the 'internal market'. It will focus in on what Chapter 1 already hinted at: the lack of development of the 'internal market' before 1986, and the intended progress of the Single European Act and its completion of the 'single market' ambitions, known as the '1992 project'. What did the 1992 project concretely *change* about the way the EU pursued economic integration? And can we declare the 'single market' complete?

In the era of Brexit, and in considering criticisms of EU over-regulation that actually complicates trade, we have to consider what the differences between the internal market and *other* trade relationships are. As such, the chapter also considers what makes up different types of international trading arrangements: 'common markets', 'free trade arrangements', and 'customs unions'. That will allow us to conclude by examining what the UK's relationship with the 'internal market' will be following Brexit—and if we are likely to see any 'red tape' reduction as a consequence.

Before we do dive deeper into this, and the next few chapters, it is important to first define some key terms relating to trade inside and outside the 'internal market' that you will need to understand.

EU institutions (and particularly the CJEU) use the terms 'internal market', 'common market', and 'single market' interchangeably. They all refer to the same concept: a geographical area made up of the territories of the Member States, wherein there are (in theory) **no barriers to trade**, and which operate an identical **external trade policy**. Given that description, there are two key dimensions to the '**internal market**':

- ***Within* the internal market**, the EU operates an expansive free trade agreement, in which certain core rules in the Treaties apply: the so-called 'fundamental' or 'four freedoms'—these are **free movement of goods, services, capital, and persons**—as well as **competition law**. The core of the four freedoms is simple: there is to be **no discrimination against goods, services, capital or people from *another* Member State**, simply because they are from another Member State. The underpinning idea behind competition law (at least historically), has been that if companies do not 'compete' with each other for customers, but instead divide up the market, or abuse the fact that they are extremely powerful in terms of market share, then this would undermine the development of a 'market' as a whole.[1] To put it another way, if big

[1] See, eg, Article 3(f) of the EEC Treaty.

economic actors *in* the Member States decided to start splitting up territory between them—with a German company promising to stay in the German market, and a French company promising to stay in the French market—rather than engage in competition, then trade *between* the Member States would not happen.

- *Outside of* the internal market, the EU operates a customs union: it applies identical rules and tariffs (border charges) to all countries *not* in the EU, meaning that a television from China that is sent to Germany will undergo the same processes and pay the same charges there as it would if it were sent to France, Portugal, or Romania. We will come back to the EU customs union briefly in Section 10.4.2, and in more detail in Chapters 11 and 16.

The non-discrimination rules that apply to the 'internal market' sound as if they must be absolutes in order to work: you cannot 'sort of' treat pears from Croatia the same way as you would pears grown in the UK. But, as earlier chapters have already shown, the EU is built on compromises more than absolutes, and any sacrifices of sovereignty the Member States have made in order to achieve EU goals have been limited. As such, we find that in practice, Croatian pears must be treated the same way as UK-grown pears *unless* the UK government can clearly provide a justification for derogating from equal treatment. We will see in the next four chapters that there are broadly two sets of justifications available to the Member States: those in the Treaty, and those developed by the CJEU.

If the UK government finds an appropriate reason to mistrust Croatian pears—eg, there are genuine health concerns in eating those, which is doubtful, but let us imagine there are—it can take action to restrict their access to UK territory. But, *even* where a Member State can justify a restriction on freedom of movement, such a restriction has to be proportionate. The vast majority of CJEU case law on internal market law, as a consequence, tackles situations where a Member State has refused market access for a service, product, or person from another Member State, and the CJEU is asked if that market refusal can be justified and if it is proportionate.

These terms will surface in passing in this chapter—but are essential for the next four chapters, where we explore the building blocks of the 'internal market' in more detail. It helps to be familiar with them at this point already.

10.2 Completion of the single market

As Chapter 1 sets out, the original goal of the Treaty of Rome was general economic co-operation: the European Economic Community (EEC) was there to gradually abolish all barriers to trade between its constituent members. However, that *gradual* abolition proved to be a little *too gradual*, and by the 1970s, it appeared that not much was actually encouraging the Member States to trade with each other.

Pause for reflection

What would persuade you to, say, stop purchasing a UK brand of squash, and to switch instead to a German brand of squash? Would you need to see a significant price difference—or would you stay loyal to the product that you already know no matter what?

We should explore why in a little more detail here. The primary underpinning cause, as flagged up in Chapter 1, was shortcomings in the Treaties. Legislation relating to the internal market required unanimity in the Council; and this proved almost impossible to achieve on legislative proposals put forward by the Commission, because every encouragement of 'trade' would come at the expense of a benefit currently enjoyed by domestic industry somewhere. For example, hypothetically, if a German lightbulb manufacturer provided 80 per cent of the lightbulbs in Germany simply because its lightbulbs fitted standard German fittings, the German government would be under substantial pressure to reject EU laws that made for 'EU-wide standard lightbulb fittings'—as this would open up the German manufacturer to competition from companies in other Member States, who might be able to produce 'German-fitting' lightbulbs at a lower cost.

As such, under the EEC Treaty, discriminating *against* foreign products was already illegal—but actually seeking products from other Member States, or encouraging producers in other Member States to try to market their products abroad, remained the exception rather than the rule.

Prior to the 1980s, there was little EU law governing internal *regulations* on goods, services, and capital. A product, in other words, could probably cross a border without incurring a fee—but might incur a sales tax, or indeed a restriction on sale based on health and safety, cultural differences such as the legal age to drink, or other grounds. Member States did not have to accept products with different standards from other Member States, and there were no general Community rules setting identical standards, despite Commission efforts to introduce those rules. As Chapter 1 showed, the early EU's decision-making structures under the EEC Treaty were heavily biased towards the interests of individual Member States, who could—and did—veto just about every Commission proposal to establish common standards and regulations if it was in their 'national interest'. Domestic lobbying on matters of trade limited the extent to which the EU could establish a genuine EU-wide market in which all products were in direct competition with each other, regardless of origin.

As mentioned in Chapter 1, several things happened simultaneously in the 1970s that suddenly changed the context in which the Member States operated. The first was a global economic downturn, and less natural economic growth *within* each of their countries. The second was practical usage of the Luxembourg veto, which was used so excessively (not least by the UK) that the Member States grew exasperated and more willing to compromise. It is impossible to determine which was the predominant factor here: a desire to 'get more done' at the European level out of a belief in the European project, or a desire to 'get anything done anywhere' because growth was slowing down domestically. Either way, however, when the right proposals to bolster intra-Member State trade came along in the early 1980s, there was suddenly an appetite on the part of the Member States to engage with them.

The end product of these proposals was the 1986 Single European Act, as we saw. But for the purposes of examining the 'internal market' specifically, what is of more interest is the White Paper that *led* to the SEA 1986 being signed.

10.2.1 The 1986 White Paper

In the 1980s, Margaret Thatcher sent a UK envoy, Baron Cockfield, to the EU Commission in an attempt to revive the common market project. Cockfield's 1985 White Paper proposed 279 *positive* laws the EU would need to adopt to actually create (or 'complete') what he called the 'single market'.[2] As such, the Single European Act of 1986 built on the White Paper and promised the completion of the 'single market' by the end of 1992—not least by making it possible for those 279 pieces of legislation that were felt necessary to create the internal market to be adopted.

The SEA 1986 thus introduced an overarching power for the EU to create new legislation where this was necessary for the 'establishment and functioning of the internal market' which enabled integration to move faster. This new power, found in what is now Article 114 TFEU and considered in detail in Chapter 5, ended the practice of Member State vetoes on any and all matters they proclaimed to be of 'national interest'. It instead functioned under 'qualified majority voting', meaning that a single Member State opposing a legislative measure was no longer enough on its own to stop it from taking effect. This meant that common standards and regulations that assisted the creation of the 'single' or 'internal' market could be adopted with significantly greater speed and ease.

We discussed in Chapter 5 how Article 114 TFEU sets out a wide, but not limitless, power to **harmonize** national laws for the sake of the functioning or establishment of the EU's internal market. Now that we are considering what that 'internal market' actually looks like, it is important to remember that a very wide range of legislation *related* to the internal market can be adopted under Article 114 TFEU. As we saw, it thus clearly allows for the regulation of roaming charges in the Member States—but the CJEU's interpretation of Article 114 TFEU means that a whole lot of social policy that was *related* to the internal market could also be adopted under a provision that on paper looked as if it was geared at *economic integration* alone. Article 114 TFEU thus not only set up an internal economic market, for trade purposes, but also established common practices in a wide variety of social policy areas. Consider the discussion of the *Tobacco Advertising* cases in Chapter 5, and how adamant Germany was that regulating tobacco advertising was a matter of health policy and not *internal market policy*, and how the CJEU nonetheless found that it was appropriate to adopt directives under Article 114 TFEU as long as there was a cross-border trade effect dimension to a policy area as well.[3]

As we consider in detail in Section 10.3.2, the SEA 1986 paired legislative activity under Article 114 TFEU with a general expectation that the Member States, where EU legislation in a sector did not exist, would accept the standards being used by another Member State as 'good enough'. The combination of these two approaches—known as **harmonization** and **mutual recognition**—meant that, in practice, less legislation was needed and could be adopted more quickly, and so the 'single market' could be completed in just six years, by 1992.

10.2.2 Is the single market now 'complete'?

The EU itself estimates that, by the end of 1992, 90 per cent of all pre-existing issues plaguing the 'internal market', as identified in Baron Cockfield's White Paper, were resolved.[4] For instance, EEC regulations harmonizing customs declaration paperwork in 1987 meant that goods started moving across EU internal borders—like those travelling

[2] *Completing the Internal Market* COM(85) 310.

[3] See Chapter 5; the First Tobacco Advertising Directive was annulled only because the cross-border trade dimension was absent for some of the regulated products, as discussed.

[4] See http://www.europarl.europa.eu/aboutparliament/en/displayFtu.html?ftuId=FTU_2.1.1.html.

between Ireland and Northern Ireland, pre-Brexit—with significantly greater ease and at a reduced cost.[5]

Of course, the internal market was not just 'done' in 1992. That would suggest that the EU effectively accomplished its existential goal and further Treaties would never be necessary. The internal market in *goods*, especially prior to the internet era, looked to be in very good shape after adopting all the Baron Cockfield legislation—but other parts of the internal market are in different stages of development. Services is the usual example cited for this: even though the EU has set up the most expansive legislative framework in the world to enable and encourage cross-border trade in services, *actual* trade in services remains lagging—and obstacles to trade in services remain.[6] In practice, even fully regulated areas of activity, such as public procurement (government purchasing) and the more general trade in goods, also still encounter problems. These problems are not necessarily on account of a lacking EU legal framework, but perhaps on account of wrongful or delayed implementation and application of the EU law, as well as non-legal factors like national or 'home country' purchasing biases.[7] We thus have the *framework* for a fully operational 'internal market' as of 1992, but practical integration between the Member States' economies still remains limited.

The idea of an 'internal' or *single* market has also been challenged by the direction of travel of the EU as a whole. The larger the EU becomes, the more the different levels of economic development within different Member States start to impact on the willingness within the Council to adopt legislation that *encourages* imported business activity from those other Member States. Attempts to fully open up trade in services by strict mutual recognition—for example, 'if service providers are regulated in their country of origin, this should be good enough for every other EU member state'—were abandoned in the middle of the 2000s;[8] and while the Commission has become more active in designing internal market legislation that sets out fairly complete rules, these are once more difficult to get adopted.

Reports on whether being *in* the internal market is enabling a 'catching up' process for the newer Member States are mixed, which means it is not clear if or when the Member State economies will reach similar levels of economic development, either. Economic theory suggests that 'convergence' will take place, which means that within a free trade area or other type of shared market, the countries where average income levels are lowest will grow faster, and those with higher average income levels will grow at a steadier pace. Early signs were that this was proving true, especially regarding Eastern European enlargement, where the post-2004 Member States appeared to be 'catching up' to the economic development levels of the 15 older Member States.[9] However, the so-called EU-15 also have clear winners and losers in terms of economic development: Northern

[5] See Katy Hayward, The Origins of the Irish Border (http://ukandeu.ac.uk/explainers/the-origins-of-the-irish-border/) (The UK in a Changing EU, January 2017), citing http://eur-lex.europa.eu/legal-content/en/TXT/?uri=CELEX:31987R1062.

[6] Eg, while services represented 70 per cent of 'the EU economy' in 2014, they only represented a 20 per cent share of EU-wide trade. Even though not all services *can* be traded, the percentage that is traded remains strikingly low. See http://www.europarl.europa.eu/RegData/etudes/STUD/2014/510981/EPRS_STU%282014%29510981_REV1_EN.pdf.

[7] Ibid. [8] See Chapter 14.

[9] See https://ec.europa.eu/economy_finance/publications/pages/publication14295_en.pdf; https://ec.europa.eu/info/sites/info/files/economy-finance/anniversairy_15_years_enlargement_conference.pdf.

Member States have benefited the most from the completion of the internal market, whereas Southern European countries have become both relatively and absolutely poor. For example, the Czech Republic and Slovakia have overtaken Greece and Portugal in terms of relative prosperity, not least because of the Eurozone crisis.[10] We thus appear to remain in a situation where the 'wealthiest' EU Member States will continue to perform very well in the internal market, whereas the remainder are likely to converge around slightly lower economic performance and living standards—and producing internal market legislation that caters to both of these 'groupings' at once will continue to be a serious challenge.

The overarching criticism the 'single market' has faced, however, is that it essentially lacks a 'soul': it is seen as prioritizing economics over any other priorities that a governance system might have, such as social policy, consumer protection, employment rights, and environmental concerns. The EU has been at pains since the late 1990s to stress that its internal market project is a *social market*, not merely an *economic market*, and seeks to ensure that living conditions improve on grounds other than purely economic ones within the EU.[11] Nonetheless, when a balance has to be struck between economic priorities and social considerations, the EU is accused of usually choosing economic over social concerns. This is particularly prevalent when it comes to its activities in the field of free movement of persons and EU citizenship, as we will see in Chapters 12 and 13. At times of crisis in particular, the EU appears to genuinely struggle to operate in a way that balances economic and social concerns, given that its foundations very much remain economic, and at the core of the EU Treaties is a *market* that must be protected.

The tensions between the social dimensions of EU regulation (which would make the EU easier to 'sell' to a European citizenry concerned about the EU's impact on workers' rights and the environment, for instance) and the economic dimensions of EU regulation (for which it was established and which remain its greatest power) thus continue to this day.

10.3 What makes the single market unique?

One constant in the Brexit debate has been that *nobody* is suggesting the UK stop trading with the EU altogether. Even those most adamant about leaving the EU have insisted that the UK will indeed seek to conclude a free trade agreement with the EU, as well as with the majority of other countries in the world. The argument goes that while the UK is keen to reduce 'red tape' for businesses in the form of EU rules, it seeks to ensure that import and export to the UK will continue in a way that is as 'frictionless' as possible.

In practice, 'as frictionless *as possible*' will mean 'with significant new friction'. To understand why the EU's internal market is not simply replaceable with a free trade agreement, we have to consider the benefits and limitations of different stages of what we call 'economic integration', or reducing barriers to trade.

[10] See Chapter 3 for more on the Eurozone; https://www.ceps.eu/system/files/DG_ConvergenceEU.pdf.

[11] See, eg, The Monti Report 2010; the 1997 Action Plan COM(96) 520 final; Review of the Internal Market Strategy COM(2000) 257 final.

10.3.1 Stages of economic integration

There are a number of 'stages' that countries pass through when attempting to reduce the number of trade barriers between them.[12] The first stage in 'integrating' the economies of two countries is concluding a 'simple' free trade agreement (simple because of its coverage, not because it will be intelligible to anyone other than trade lawyers).

Free trade agreements

A 'free trade agreement' (FTA) operates where at least two countries abolish custom duties on their 'shared' border. In other words, when a shipment of a product like milk moves from country A to country B, country B does not charge any taxes on the milk being imported, and vice versa.

What of country C, which wishes to sell its milk to country A? Unless it is a part of the FTA, its milk will not move freely between country B and A; there will be an import charge when it enters country A, and another import charge when it moves from country A to country B. Only goods produced *in* countries A and B consequently benefit from the FTA and its reduced or abolished customs duties. Goods moving within the FTA between country A and B are subject to 'rules of origin', which define where the good is 'from'—where it was created or significantly modified—and so what customs duties are applicable to it.

Customs unions

The next stage in economic integration is the creation of a 'customs union'. This is an addition to the FTA. It is formed when countries A and B, already in an FTA with each other, now agree that they would like to apply a single set of rules and tariffs to their *external* borders. In other words, when country C now wishes to sell its milk to either country A or B, those countries will charge the same import taxes on that milk—and once the milk is in either country A or B, it can also freely move to the other country.

We now encounter country D. It does not have an FTA with country A or B, but wishes to form one with country A, because it produces computers that it would like to export to country A at a low tariff. Country A meanwhile produces bicycles that it would really like to export to country D at a low tariff. It makes sense for countries D and A to conclude an FTA as they clearly have something to offer each other. However, country A can no longer conclude such an FTA on its own—because its tariff on country D's computers is determined not only by itself, but also by country B. A customs union therefore must have, as a logical consequence, one **external trade policy**.

What will the group of countries inside the FTA do whenever an outside country wishes to send products into the trade area? In our example, the external trade policy would cover the negotiation of countries B and A with country D. Country B might have an interest in being able to export bananas at a lower tariff while country A is interested in lowering its bicycle export costs. As countries A and B represent a bigger market than country D does, they are likely to be able to exert some pressure on country D in negotiations. This might mean country D gets less out of the deal for its bicycle, banana, and computer industries and consumers, but ultimately still gets access to the markets of countries A and B.

[12] Bela Belassa, *The Theory of Economic Integration*, 5th edn (Routledge, 2013).

Discussing the quote

Will the UK or 'Brussels' need border controls post-Brexit if the UK is no longer in a customs union with the EU? Why? And what if they no longer have a free trade agreement? Why? Do you agree with Graeme Macdonald? Do you think that the introduction of border controls will make a significant difference to trade, or not? Why?

Stage Three . . .?

This simplified and fictional example covers the two most common stages of economic integration. While the EU has completed both these stages, it has also gone beyond them. The 1957 Treaty of Rome established Stage One: since then, the charging of duties on products from the Member States at the EU's internal borders has gradually become prohibited.[13] It also completed Stage Two in 1968, establishing a customs union—of which the UK (and its relevant overseas territories) and Ireland have been members since 1973, alongside all other Member States and Monaco.[14]

But the EU's integration project is about much more than simply having no borders for tariffs internally: it is the institutional architecture that enforces and supervises shared and mutually recognized rules within the internal market that differentiates it from a simpler FTA or customs union.

10.3.2 Key components of the EU's internal market

The use of Article 114 TFEU in order to create 'internal market legislation' as necessary has simplified cross-border trade significantly. Specifically, the use of Article 114 TFEU to set out **technical standards** for products across the EU has made it much easier for a producer in Hungary to sell products in Ireland, Spain, and Malta: there will only be one set of standards that that producer needs to comply with in order to sell, for instance, televisions, in 27 other countries. **Harmonization** of technical standards, or at least of *minimum* technical standards, is consequently one of the legal developments since 1992 that have sped up the establishment of an 'internal market' in goods.

However, harmonization is politically very sensitive. Imagine that the product at stake is a medication of some kind, and imagine that in Member State A, there are strict rules on indicating on the packaging of medication what the maximum dosage is so as to prevent accidental overdoses. Member State B, on the other hand, forbids that kind of labelling, out of concern that it will discourage consumers from actually reading the included booklet giving information about the medication. These are hypothetical examples of the kinds of rules that Member States actually have—and are very attached to, to the point where the Treaties have always been written so as to permit Member States to derogate from the trade rules where they have clear public policy reasons for doing so. In these kinds of situations, harmonizing all possible rules relating to the internal market makes

[13] Treaty Establishing the European Economic Community (1957) 298 UNTS 11, Articles 12–15.

[14] See http://ec.europa.eu/taxation_customs/40customs/customs_general_info/about/index_en.htm.

very little sense: it would be difficult, if not impossible, to achieve politically, even if voting mechanisms allowed Member States to be outvoted via Article 114 TFEU.

Concerns about harmonization in the internal market have been addressed in two ways. First, Article 114 TFEU is not limitless. We discussed in Chapter 5 that Article 114 TFEU for some time appeared to be interpreted very broadly by the CJEU, permitting legislation that was only tangentially related to the internal market to be adopted under it—but ultimately, in *Tobacco Advertising 1*, the CJEU did find that it could not be used to simply 'regulate' the internal market. The effects of *Tobacco Advertising 1* are, of course, debatable, in that the CJEU still appears to wish to give the EU legislature significant room to legislate for the internal market—but insofar as the EU produces 'red tape', it has to at least bear *a connection* to trade on the internal market.

More generally, Article 114 TFEU has always come with a number of derogations. These were introduced at the insistence of those Member States that believed they operated *higher* standards than the EU would pursue, and they wanted to ensure that they could not be forced to *lower* those standards through QMV.

Article 114(3) consequently promises a commitment to high standards, and Articles 114(4) onwards[15] permit Member States to derogate from harmonized measures in a number of situations: when their own laws already set higher standards before the EU legislated (Article 114(4)); or where scientific evidence has proven that better environmental or labour standards *can* be adopted, and a Member State wishes to act before the EU is ready to (Article 114(5)). The remainder of Article 114 sets out an onerous and strict process by which Article 114(4) and (5) exemptions can be applied for by the Member States.

When introduced, these derogations from Article 114's harmonizing power were received very reluctantly; there was fear that Article 114(4) and (5) would undo everything that Article 114(1) enabled, and consequently the 'internal market' would not actually progress at all. In practice, however, the derogations have not been relied upon, and their apparent effect has been to encourage the EU to actually aim for the desired high standards those Member States wanted.

Secondly, in light of concerns about *too much* harmonization more generally, and thus an avalanche of regulatory requirements (or red tape), the EU has sought a compromise, which it hinted at already in the 1985 White Paper. The White Paper stressed that attempts to fully harmonize all aspects of regulation would be 'over-regulatory, would take a long time to implement, would be inflexible and could stifle innovation'.[16] It noted that mutual recognition of standards may help open up markets, but that an ideal strategy for completing the 'common market' would combine 'the best' of mutual recognition and harmonization.

As such, the White Paper advocated for an approach that only harmonizes that which is 'essential'; and legislative harmonization should be limited to what it terms 'essential health and safety requirements'.[17]

When issuing harmonizing legislation, the EU can choose between **minimum harmonization** and **maximum harmonization** of standards where appropriate. Maximum harmonization is what it sounds like: the EU sets out all of the conditions that a product must comply with to be allowed into the internal market. Once such a product is on the internal market, no Member States can object to its entry, and because of the completeness of the EU legislation, national legislation in these areas is fully pre-empted.

[15] Articles 114(5), (7), and (8) were introduced by the Treaty of Amsterdam.

[16] COM(85) 310, para 64.

[17] Ibid, para 65.

The alternative, minimum harmonization, sets out a baseline for the conditions a product must satisfy, but the Member States can go above and beyond that floor if they want to . . . providing they can *justify* their stricter requirements under the Treaties, on grounds such as public policy concerns.[18]

Regardless of whether the EU is pursuing minimum or maximum harmonization, the condition to limit legislative harmonization to 'essential health and safety requirements' applies. As such, even though there are several dozen 'harmonizing' internal market directives covering specific product areas, the bulk of the internal market is regulated through the alternative identified in the White Paper: **mutual recognition**.

In establishing mutual recognition as part of the 'internal market' strategy, the Commission latched onto a seminal CJEU judgment on how discrimination against goods from another Member State works. In *Cassis de Dijon*, which we will consider in detail in Chapter 12, the CJEU determined that for the 'internal market' to function properly, products should not be subject to 'double regulation', meaning the regulatory rules in the country in which they are produced, and then different regulatory rules in the country where they are sold.[19] This prohibition on 'double regulation' has resulted in demands of mutual recognition of regulations: if German cheese has to be sold in recyclable packaging, the sale of such cheese *has* to be permitted on the Italian market as well, regardless of what the Italian rules on packaging cheese say.

The idea underpinning mutual recognition is that in an internal market that covers all the Member States, it is reasonable for all the Member States to have very similar if not identical standards for consumer protection. Regulations that were found to be good enough for German consumers, resulting in the lawful production of cheese there, should be acceptable to consumers in Italy as well. The only possible exception to this requirement for mutual recognition is where a Member State can justify its position on the basis of a particular national concern: for instance, if Italy could come up with a good public policy reason as to why cheese in recyclable packaging is problematic, it could still prevent the German cheese from entering the Italian market.

The EU's approach to economic integration after the Single European Act 1986 thus combines **harmonization** of rules and **mutual recognition** to facilitate products, goods, and services crossing borders. But, as noted, both minimum harmonization and mutual recognition come with limits at the behest of the Member States: to allow different cultural, environmental, or health and safety traditions in the different Member States to continue to exist, and to not simply permit 'a single EU law' whenever it would be convenient—which would go against both the principles of subsidiarity and proportionality—it is possible to **derogate** from these EU requirements if certain conditions are met.

We will explore how mutual recognition and derogations from the four freedoms work in much more detail in the next chapters; the main purpose of this quick overview is to demonstrate that cancelling *tariff* barriers, which a free trade area achieves, is only the very beginning of facilitating trade. If, post-Brexit, the UK has no tariffs when trading with the EU, UK producers will nonetheless find themselves needing to comply with checks to ensure that their products and services meet EU standards.

[18] For more on derogation grounds under the Treaty, see Chapters 11, 12, and 14.

[19] Case 120/78 *Rewe-Zentral AG v Bundesmonopolverwaltung für Branntwein (Cassis de Dijon)* ECLI:EU:C:1979:42.

Institutional setup

'But wait! What if we just keep the same rules as the EU does? Would the EU then not have to "mutually recognize" our rules as being the same as the EU rules, and let UK products onto the market without controls even after Brexit?'

This logical question is one that has surfaced repeatedly over the course of the Brexit debate. Unfortunately, what might hold for the UK when it is a Member State does *not* hold automatically when it is no longer a Member State.

Rules only become meaningful in complex international trade relations if there is significant mutual trust that they will be fully abided by. Country A's promise that it definitely produces milk in the same way that country B does only becomes a meaningful commitment if country B can somehow 'trust' that country A is doing that. And trust, in international trade, is heavily contingent on the ability to *check* that the rules are applied, and the ability to *ensure* that the rules are applied.

Within the EU, as Chapters 2 to 8 have shown, we can see that there is an extensive architecture in place ensuring that EU law is enforced, that there is appropriate supervision of commitments made by EU Member States, that all the Member States will 'sincerely cooperate' to ensure that the EU laws work, and that all EU law is interpreted in the same way in all Member States.[20] The EU institutions and their ability to hold each other and the Member States to account if they do not comply with the EU's laws as intended is what builds the 'trust' needed to abandon border controls altogether. Harmonized and/or mutually recognized rules, in other words, are the beginning of not needing border checks at EU internal borders; the full extent of institutional and administrative cooperation and integration that make up the EU single market is an equally essential part of it.[21]

Post-Brexit, the UK will move outside of the EU's 'control' and into a separate regulatory regime for all products, agricultural or otherwise. What this will mean in practice depends on what kind of 'new' free trade agreement the UK and the EU manage to conclude—but both the EU and the UK agree that even the very 'best', most expansive free trade agreement will not be as all-encompassing as the EU internal market is. Without CJEU and European Commission oversight of whatever product rules the UK operates, the EU will not simply accept them into EU territory. It will want to check products to make sure they meet the EU's own standards. Unless the UK and the EU either shift their negotiating positions or come up with some radical new solutions for complying with their global trade obligations, regulatory checks at the UK–EU border consequently will resurface post-Brexit . . . as they do at every other border across the world.

Discussing the quote

Following this overview, do you think that it is possible for both the UK and the EU to avoid 'putting up trade barriers', as Graeme Macdonald put it, in the absence of extensive rules that ensure that what crosses the border is acceptable to both parties?

[20] See Article 4(3) TEU and 'indirect effect', discussed in Chapter 8.

[21] See the Commission's slides at https://ec.europa.eu/commission/publications/slides-regulatory-issues_en.

10.3.3 'Overregulation' of the internal market

One of the most persistent accusations levelled at the EU is that it has not simply done what is *needed* to establish an internal market—but rather, it has gone very far beyond that, resulting in endless rules that companies in the EU and trading with the EU have to comply with, but that are absolutely not 'necessary'. The EU, in other words, is frequently accused of being guilty of 'overregulation', or of producing 'red tape', which actually stifles trade between the Member States.[22]

It is important to be specific when we talk about 'overregulation'. In practice, two different types of regulations get conflated in this discussion, but they are very much distinct. There are first of all product standards, which affect the conditions under which goods can circulate the internal market. When businesses complain about EU 'red tape', these are not normally the rules that they target: the EU operates globally recognized product standards, and compliance with the EU's standards are unlikely to be more costly than the standards operated by other countries.

'Red tape' complaints, rather, are usually geared at the EU's regulations that influence the general economic environment in which the Member States operates. Specifically, EU environmental and employment law are seen as needlessly driving up the costs of 'economic activity' and being business-unfriendly when compared to other jurisdictions, with less demanding social and environmental standards.

EU law in practice

The 'red tape' accusation does *not* solely come from the UK. All the same, the European Commission's UK Representation (which has now become a regular diplomatic 'mission' to the EU) devoted significant time to assessing and debunking a variety of myths, including ones about the EU's generation of 'red tape'. An insightful blog post from 2013 tackles the notion that the EU is 'strangling' UK firms, on account of producing 3600 new laws over a period of three years, and raises examples of both product standards and environmental and social standards:

EC in the UK, 'Are British businesses really being strangled by EU red tape?' (14 October 2013): http://web.archive.org/web/20190216115810/https://blogs.ec.europa.eu/ECintheUK/are-british-businesses-really-being-strangled-by-eu-red-tape/

Fourth, it is interesting to look at some examples quoted by, say, the *Daily Mail* as evidence of outrageous interference 'handed down from Brussels' (rather than 'negotiated and agreed by the UK', as is in fact the case in the vast majority of cases).

It turns out that, unsexy as many of the rules are, they are necessary either to prevent potentially serious harm or for the single market to work or more often than not, for both of those reasons.

→

[22] See, eg, David Oakley, 'EU Regulations Blamed for "Swamping" Business' (*FT*, 2 February 2016). Available at: https://www.ft.com/content/658bd8e0-c91d-11e5-be0b-b7ece4e953a0.

→

Yes, there do need to be rules on 'anchovy fishing in the Bay of Biscay' or there would soon be no more anchovies. Rules on the labelling of spirits ensure that drinkers know what they are buying and that exporters do not have to comply with a whole series of different national rules.

It is likely that British consumers would agree that the addition of ammonium chloride—a potentially dangerous chemical if overused—as a feed additive for animals does need to be regulated. They might also want to know in clear terms how much energy water heaters use, so they can save on gas and electricity bills. Maximum residue levels for weedkillers are necessary to ensure children do not get poisoned.

The blog post is interesting as it makes clear that the EU admittedly produces a lot of regulation in widely disparate areas. But looking at the rules raised as examples by the EC in the UK, would you say they are 'unnecessary', in the way the accusation of *red tape* suggests that they are? Do you think they would exist in the UK even outside of the EU?

Business concerns can be explained in simple economic terms: EU 'red tape' is costly for *them*, as they have to comply with EU-set standards and this might involve changes to their existing business practices. However, and especially considering that the internal market project has been accused of not being concerned enough with social considerations, it should be stressed that there are beneficiaries to both forms of 'red tape'. Individuals who are looking to be environmentally conscious, or who wish to have thorough health and safety protection at work, or who are simply looking to be *informed* in the choices they are making, will benefit from the effects of EU regulations—not least because they result in EU-wide standards, so information obtained in one country will be equally applicable to 26 others.

There are a number of other issues with the claim that the EU overregulates. For one thing, it is unclear whether the rules that it produces would actually *not otherwise exist*, in one form or another, in non-EU countries. The UK might genuinely dislike the Working Time Directive, but would it not have some other law in place that sets out working conditions and the duration of the working week for employers to comply with? And in the absence of EU air quality standards, would there simply not be any?

Finally, there is the issue of 'gold-plating'. This refers to the practice of going *beyond* the requirements set out by EU law in the process of implementing EU law into domestic law, and the UK has long had a reputation of doing this, often in response to pressure from trade unions.[23] It is particularly prevalent in social policy, which is also the area most often targeted by those complaining about 'red tape'. For example, in adopting the

[23] See the Social and Employment Policy chapter of the 2012 Balance of Competences review (2014). Available at https://assets.publishing.service.gov.uk/government/uploads/system/uploads/attachment_data/file/332524/review-of-the-balance-of-competences-between-the-united-kingdom-and-the-european-union-social-and-employment-policy.pdf, 53–4.

EU's Temporary Workers Directive,[24] the UK added conditions beyond the 'equal treatment' on issues of pay, working hours, and annual leave as required—it also added equal treatment with respect to bonuses.[25] It also offers significantly more generous maternity and parental leave than is required by EU law.[26] When such 'gold-plating' happens, it is difficult to argue that any 'overregulation' is at the request of the EU.

The 2010 Coalition government in the UK pledged to end 'gold-plating' by only implementing the 'absolute minimum regulation necessary to comply' with EU law and in 2013, then-Business Minister Michael Fallon announced that the practice had ended.[27] While it is difficult to know if the UK genuinely never 'added' to EU regulation from that point onward, by 2013 the EU's reputation as an 'overregulator' was so firmly established that the end of domestic 'gold-plating' is unlikely to have made a difference in public perception anyway.

Of course, as is true for most accusations levelled at the EU, this one is also not *wholly* baseless. Examples of EU legislation that genuinely seems to serve no purpose and benefits no one, but will cost manufacturers, *do* exist. For example, consider the Commission's 2012 proposal banning hairdressers from wearing heels or jewellery, or its 2013 proposal banning refillable jugs of olive oil in restaurants (which were accused of swapping out 'virgin olive oil' for cheaper alternatives at the expense of consumers). These clearly fit the bill of being 'red tape' . . . but they were also quickly abandoned, and certainly have not become EU law. They are the exception, rather than the rule, to the types of rules that the EU produces.

The volume of EU law is also clearly a factor in the idea that it 'overregulates'. A closer look at the EU's statistics on its legislative activity helps put this into perspective, however, as shown in Figure 10.1:

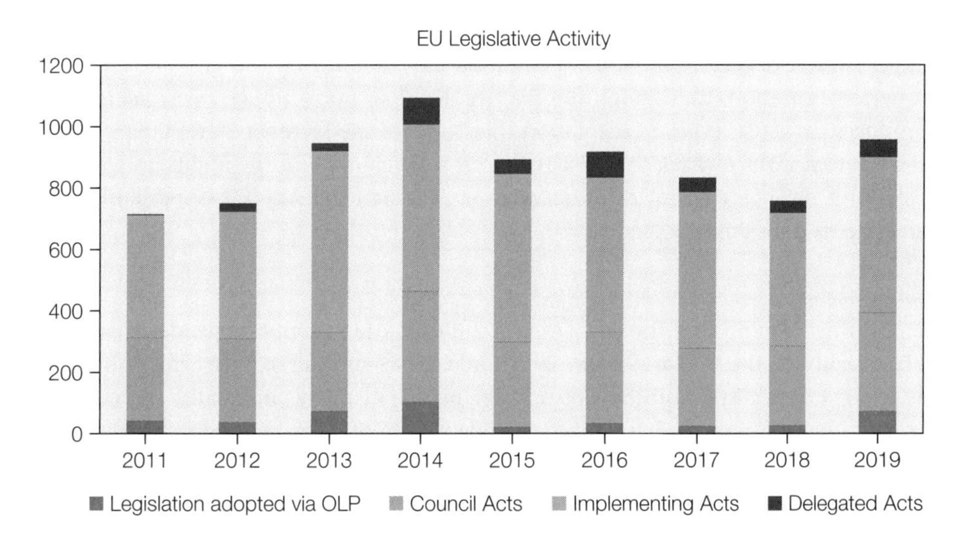

Figure 10.1 EU legislative activity 2011–2019

[24] Directive 2008/104/EC of the European Parliament and of the Council of 19 November 2008 on temporary agency work [2008] OJ L327/9.

[25] See the Agency Workers Regulations 2010.

[26] See https://www.europarl.europa.eu/RegData/etudes/ATAG/2019/635586/EPRS_ATA(2019)635586_EN.pdf.

[27] See https://www.bbc.co.uk/news/uk-politics-22277927.

The *smallest* proportion of legislative activity since 2011 has been actual legislation: the ordinary legislative procedure (OLP) has not once during this period resulted in more than 100 pieces of legislation. Instead, the vast majority of what the EU produces is implementing legislation—so, in UK terms, statutory instruments—and acts produced by the Council. The latter category rarely produces a regulatory burden on the Member States: the majority consist of Council decisions on matters such as ratifying new treaties with third countries on behalf of the EU, or admitting new Member States, or appointing new representatives to different EU bodies.

Does this amount to 'a lot' of regulation? A quick comparison to UK legislative activity would suggest otherwise. The House of Commons Library in 2017 found that 'an average of 33 UK Acts of Parliament were passed annually from 2006 to 2018', which is in line with the averages of legislation adopted under the OLP seen in Figure 10.1. It also found, however, that the UK issues an average of 3000 statutory instruments annually—which vastly outweighs the volume of implementing legislation produced in the EU.[28] The UK and the EU obviously legislate in both overlapping and distinct policy areas, so these numbers are not directly comparable. However, given the scope of activity in which the EU is active as of the Lisbon Treaty, producing approximately *one sixth* the legislation of a Member State does not on its face seem excessive.

In any event, the EU's reputation for producing *too much* regulation should not be equated to it being a bad regulator. The OECD has developed a detailed methodology for examining the 'quality' of regulations, by examining just how much effort and energy is put into scrutinizing them before, during, and after the legislative process. The UK performs very well in this analysis—but the EU performs comparably well, and significantly above the OECD average.[29] By that measure, the UK is just about *as likely* as the EU to produce unnecessary or 'low quality' legislation that is more of a burden than a necessity.

A better accusation, then, might be that the EU does not so much *overregulate* as that it produces particular types of regulation that some of the Member States are dissatisfied with. But that takes us back to a discussion on sovereignty and the ability to *prevent* EU legislation from being adopted, rather than a clear sign that the EU is legislating more than it needs to or doing so badly.[30]

Better regulation?

Even bearing in mind that the OECD research does little to support the idea that the EU is a bad regulator, the EU has not simply ignored the accusation of overregulation levelled at it. In light of persistent business protest against the quantity and quality of 'red tape' it produces, the Commission has adopted a wide variety of measures and policies that aim to achieve what it calls 'better regulation'.

Starting in 1996 with an initiative called SLIM ('Simple Legislation for the Internal Market'),[31] the Commission established a variety of taskforces whose jobs were to simplify, improve the quality, and reduce the burden of EU legislation.[32] These taskforces adopted

[28] See https://researchbriefings.parliament.uk/ResearchBriefing/Summary/CBP-7438.

[29] See http://www.oecd.org/gov/regulatory-policy/oecd-regulatory-policy-outlook-2018-9789264303072-en.htm.

[30] See Chapter 3. [31] COM(96) 204.

[32] See, eg, the Business Environment Simplification Taskforce (BEST) set up by the Commission in September 1997 at the request of the European Council.

numerous action plans to achieve improved EU legislation over the course of the 2000s in particular, under the overarching banner of the 'Better Regulation' agenda.[33] The action plans required the Commission to engage in widespread consultation and use impact assessments before producing legislative proposals.

In 2006, this was supplemented by the establishment of a so-called Impact Assessment Board, examining the Commission's impact assessments; and in 2010, this form of *ex ante* review was matched with *ex post* review of EU legislation, where the Commission engages in detailed investigations of the *effects* of its major pieces of legislation.[34] This ultimately resulted in the introduction of the Regulatory Fitness and Performance Programme (REFIT), which was tasked with evaluating the effectiveness of a *range* of policy actions in a specific area—as opposed to the effectiveness of individual pieces of legislation.

Substantial changes to the 'Better Regulation' agenda were adopted by the Juncker Commission in 2015. The Commission first of all introduced a Commission First Vice President expressly responsible for 'Better Regulation', and created a task force that investigated how subsidiarity and proportionality in legislation were working in practice. The First Vice President chaired REFIT processes, which were now open to public input and consultation as well. Also in 2015, the UK government asked for the Impact Assessment Board to be retitled to the Regulatory Scrutiny Board and to be given a new brief—and this was achieved. The members of the Regulatory Scrutiny Board are now appointed for fixed terms, divorced from any EU-related policy agenda, and as of 2017 now also conduct *ex post* evaluations.

A final big initiative proposed by the Juncker Commission was to involve the *other* parts of the EU legislature in 'Better Regulation' more expressly. In 2016, therefore, the Commission adopted an interinstitutional agreement on 'Better Law-Making', which enables the European Parliament and the Council to ask the Commission for further evidence (beyond its impact assessment) at any point in the legislative procedure. Where the Parliament and Council significantly amend Commission proposals, they have committed to carrying out their own impact assessments on these revised proposals.[35]

A constant part of the 'Better Regulation' package is a set of Commission-produced Guidelines and a 'Better Regulation' toolbox, which address civil servants in the Commission on how to apply 'Better Regulation' principles when engaged in legislative activity. The fact that much of 'Better Regulation' is focused on providing instructions to the Commission on how to draft legislation, however, is also one of its possible shortcomings. One of the criticisms of the 'Better Regulation' agenda is that by its very nature—focusing on the making of *better* rules—it pushes for more *technocratic* decision-making, rather than more *democratic* decision-making in the EU.[36] It is perhaps unhelpful to criticize that aspect of 'Better Regulation', however, given how much of the EU's legislative

[33] See COM(2002) 275; COM(2002) 276; COM(2002) 277; COM(2002) 278. [34] COM(2010) 543.

[35] To date, the Council has not actually followed through on this commitment, but the European Parliament has started to do so. See http://www.europarl.europa.eu/thinktank/en/search.html?policyAreas=EXIMAS.

[36] For this criticism, and a counterargument, see Ben Smulders and Jean-Eric Paquet, 'The European Commission and its Better Regulation Agenda' in Sacha Garben and Inge Govaere (eds), *The EU Better Regulation Agenda: A Critical Assessment* (Hart, 2018) 100–2.

activity is implementing legislation. It is of key importance that those regulations emerging from (neo)-comitology structures in the Commission are themselves of high quality, precisely *because* they continue to lack democratic oversight.[37]

Ultimately, however, the EU's action in producing 'Better Regulation' and promising to rescind policies that are either not working or no longer necessary has to be measured somehow. Have any of the initiatives since 2002 had an impact on the EU's reputation of 'overregulating'?

The Commission itself investigated to what extent the 'Better Regulation' agenda has been effective in early 2019, seeking both internal and external views and producing a report on the basis of the input from approximately 600 different stakeholders.[38] Its findings suggest that its efforts have by and large been successful, in the sense that all the EU institutions now produce more 'open, transparent and evidence-based' policy outputs.[39] It received positive feedback about the number of public consultations on legislation it has organized since 2015, and could demonstrate good commitment to both impact assessment (as in *ex ante* analysis) and evaluation (as in *ex post* analysis) of the policies that the EU's political decision-makers opted to pursue. Finally, it also responded to 90 opinions submitted through the REFIT platform, and acted in 150 cases to simplify legislation with an intention of reducing its administrative burden, especially for small and medium-sized businesses.

A detailed academic analysis of the 'Better Regulation' agenda in 2018, however, suggests that this may be overstating the successes achieved.[40] Particularly with regards to overregulation, Garben argues that the EU may unfortunately be perpetuating the myth itself: 'the crucial point is that the Better Regulation Agenda, by implicitly or explicitly formulating "EU over-regulation" as a part of the problem . . . that it is aimed at addressing, . . . feeds the existence of the very problem that it intends to solve.'[41] Rather than setting up a complex bureaucratic exercise that fights this 'problem', the EU may have been better off trying to prove to the public that the problem does not exist, by pointing at the positives of EU regulation.

Pause for reflection

What do you think? Is the very idea of 'tackling' overregulation going to lead to an impression that overregulation is a serious problem in the EU?

Even if the EU *has* regulated too much, the 'Better Regulation' agenda has proven to be ineffective at actually *getting rid* of EU legislation that is no longer relevant. The Commission has published confusing and conflicting information on how much EU law has been repealed since 'Better Regulation' started, with the statistics improving only from

[37] See Chapters 3 and 4.
[38] See https://ec.europa.eu/info/sites/info/files/better-regulation-taking-stock_en_0.pdf.
[39] Ibid.
[40] Sacha Garben and Inge Govaere (eds), *The EU Better Regulation Agenda: A Critical Assessment* (Hart, 2018)
[41] Sacha Garben, 'An "Impact Assessment" of EU Better Regulation' in Garben and Govaere (n 40).

2015.[42] Those statistics, however, reveal that startlingly little EU law has been repealed, and where it has been repealed, it is likely to have already been '"dead" legislation that was largely temporary and [did] not currently have any real impact'.[43] A specific case study carried out in 2016 with EU environmental laws that were on the Commission's 'repeal' list suggests that actually dismantling EU policy is the least likely outcome of a legislative review, but where some dismantling takes place, it *does* appear to reduce the policy burden.[44]

Views on the successes of 'Better Regulation' thus differ rather significantly between commentators in academia and the views expressed by stakeholders when the Commission asked for them in 2019. Garben suggests, not entirely facetiously, that the best way forward may be for the 'Better Regulation' agenda itself to be submitted to an impact assessment: do all these *ex ante* and *ex post* regulatory initiatives genuinely produce 'better' regulation, and regulation only where necessary, or would the EU rank highly in the OECD's regulatory practice measurements even if they were reduced? If so, the cost savings for the EU itself in scrapping 'Better Regulation' would be significant—which the Member States, as the source of the EU budget, would undoubtedly appreciate.

Discussing the quote

What does the discussion of the EU's responses to the accusation of overregulation in Section 10.3.3 suggest to you about the possibility of removing 'red tape' through a renegotiation, as Graeme Macdonald suggested in 2016?

10.4 Brexit and the internal market

While we experienced a change of government during the Article 50 TEU process, one thing about the UK approach to Brexit has been constant: the Conservative Party position has been that staying in the 'internal market' would not be respecting the outcome of the referendum. Neither the May nor the Johnson government was interested in remaining in a permanent customs union, as proposed by the Labour Party in opposition, either. The aim for the future thus appears to be a 'Stage One' free trade agreement—but, as ever, there are questions about how achievable that position is.

10.4.1 The Withdrawal Agreement

In light of the Withdrawal Agreement, it will be some time before the UK distances itself from the EU's internal market. The transition period created by the Withdrawal Agreement, as discussed in earlier chapters, effectively results in a form of ongoing 'EU membership'

[42] Robert Zribal, 'The Better Regulation Agenda and the Deactivation of EU Competences: Limits and opportunities' in Garben and Govaere (n 40).

[43] Ibid, 72.

[44] Viviane Gravey and Andrew Jordan, 'Does the European Union Have a Reverse Gear? Policy dismantling in a hyperconsensual polity' (2016) 23(3) JEPP 1466.

without institutional representation. Both the positive regulations that make up the internal market, as well as their oversight and enforcement mechanisms, *and* the EU's customs union rules will thus continue to apply to the UK until *at least* the end of 2020.[45]

10.4.2 The Protocol on Ireland/Northern Ireland

Perhaps the most interesting aspect of the Brexit negotiations has been how Northern Ireland has proven to be the key actor in shaping their outcome. Theresa May's government failed to get its version of the Withdrawal Agreement through Parliament, and at least one of the reasons for this was the arrangements contained in that Withdrawal Agreement with respect to Northern Ireland: the so-called 'backstop'.

The term 'backstop' refers to the arrangements that the 2018 Withdrawal Agreement set out in the Protocol on Ireland/Northern Ireland to ensure that no new physical infrastructure or related checks/procedures would take place between Ireland and Northern Ireland, so as to respect commitments made by both the UK and the EU and the commitments required by the 1998 Belfast/Good Friday Agreement.[46]

Throughout 2018 and 2019, the UK Parliament remained heavily divided between those who felt that a technological solution to avoiding such a hard border was possible before the end of the transition period, and those who felt that, outside of the internal market, such a border was inevitable.

Those who advocated for technological solutions effectively argued that any 'checks' needed could take place digitally or far away from the border, and so there was no need for the UK (or Northern Ireland) to continue to align with EU rules after Brexit. Such solutions are not found in full operation anywhere else in the world at this time, however, and so many others argued that the only way to ensure that there will be no new infrastructure or checks at or near the border is to ensure that there is simply no *need* for any product checks between Ireland and Northern Ireland. The only way to achieve that is to ensure that all border-related rules and processes between the UK and the EU become digital insofar as possible (which they arguably already are, for customs and certain tax purposes) . . . and to keep regulatory rules between Ireland and Northern Ireland identical, to the satisfaction of the EU, so as to ensure that checks on products are simply not necessary at that border.

The May government agreed with the sceptics, and its version of the Protocol consequently designed the following setup:

- The UK as a whole would stay in a customs union with the EU—so customs 'checks' need not take place at any Northern Ireland border, whether with Great Britain or Ireland.
- Northern Ireland would *also* remain aligned with the relevant internal market rules that make trade between Northern Ireland and Ireland frictionless. The UK would commit to ensuring Great Britain also adopted rules that would make trade between Northern Ireland and Great Britain as frictionless as possible—but there were likely to be some risk-related 'checks' on goods travelling between Northern Ireland and Great Britain post-Brexit, until a better solution to managing the Ireland/Northern Ireland border was developed.

[45] Withdrawal Agreement, Articles 126 and 132; note that the EU (Withdrawal Agreement) Act 2020, s 33, prohibits UK representatives from asking for an extension as a matter of domestic law—though as is true for all Acts of Parliament, this can obviously be amended if an extension is desired after all.

[46] For more detail, see Sylvia de Mars et al, *Bordering Two Unions: Northern Ireland and Brexit* (Policy Press, 2018).

Only when such a 'better solution' arrived would the 'backstop' disappear, and would the UK be able to both leave the EU's customs union and stop aligning regulation (in Northern Ireland) with the EU. The Withdrawal Agreement and Political Declaration agreed by the May government expressly committed both the EU and the UK to ongoing negotiations to find such a 'better solution', but in the absence of that solution, the 'backstop' was the way to preserve an invisible border on the island of Ireland.

The 'backstop' was widely seen as 'trapping' the UK in the EU's customs union—but Parliament failed to reach a consensus on how to otherwise handle the problems created by the border between Ireland and Northern Ireland. There was opposition to 'some sort of border' in the Irish Sea just as there was opposition to a return of a hard border between Northern Ireland and Ireland—but continued alignment with all internal market rules and remaining in a customs union with the EU was not genuinely 'Brexit' and so was also seen as unacceptable.

The May government eventually fell on account of an inability to make a choice between those three unappealing options. The Johnson government returned to the negotiating table and came back with a different agreement. However the UK press reported this agreement, though, the October 2019 Withdrawal Agreement simply reflects the EU's *original* proposed solution to the Northern Ireland situation, which was to have a light-touch border in the Irish Sea. Formally, Northern Ireland is in a customs union with the UK under the October 2019 Protocol. However, in practice, Northern Ireland remains in the internal market for goods and agricultural products, and will apply the EU's customs union rules to all goods travelling between Great Britain and Northern Ireland.[47] This solution might not have made it through Parliament on account of the DUP presence and the Conservative Party's dependence on it prior to the December 2019 general election, but the current Conservative Party majority has meant that it passed with ease.

The solution contained in the October 2019 Protocol, if implemented in time, will avoid the Irish land border. The UK has also committed to 'best endeavours' to keep the actual border checks between Great Britain and Northern Ireland as light-touch as possible, which suggests that it is committing to avoid significant divergence from the relevant internal market rules. In *theory*, then, it also avoids a 'hard' border in the Irish Sea. But things are not that simple: as 'Great Britain' will not be part of the customs union nor the internal market structures described in this chapter, Northern Ireland will become the EU's new 'external border'. And that means applying the EU's rules at that border, even if the UK's rules are thought to be similar.

Goods from outside of the EU coming *into* the EU simply must be proven to be compliant with the relevant EU regulations applying to them: if the EU were to relax its requirements and not 'check' anything originating from Great Britain into Northern Ireland, it would be bound as a member of the World Trade Organization to not check *any* goods from *any* other WTO member.[48] Were it to carry out those checks anyway, it would likely be brought to the WTO's dispute settlement system by other WTO members for not treating all WTO members equally. Conversely, were it not to carry out any checks on any products

[47] Protocol, Articles 4 and 5.

[48] In light of the most-favoured-nation (MFN) obligation in Article 1 of the GATT 1947; for more on WTO law, see Peter Van den Bossche and Werner Zdouc, *The Law and Policy of the World Trade Organization*, 4th edn (CUP, 2018).

from any other country in the world, those countries that the EU currently has beneficial free trade agreements with would start dispute processes—their advantages in having agreements with the EU would disappear, and so the EU would be violating its other international commitments.

This makes it sound as if the EU is exclusively responsible for the appearance of any 'border' in the Irish Sea, but the reality is that, as a WTO member, the same obligations will apply to the UK as a whole: it too must treat all other WTO members in the same way, unless it concludes separate and WTO-compliant free trade agreements with them. Beyond that, unless it plans on checking no products crossing UK borders, whether external or internal, and applying no tariffs to any imports, the only way to ensure that all those WTO members are treated the same way is to have border processes in place. Some checks, as a consequence, are inevitable—simply because outside of the internal market, it has to be *verified* that goods are compliant with the standards upheld in the country that they are being introduced to.

Discussing the quote

Will Brexit result in a trade-related 'red tape' reduction? Consider here that Northern Ireland will continue to follow a lot of the EU's rules, while Great Britain may not.

10.4.3 The future relationship

Once the transition period completes, *Great Britain*, at least, will be able to pursue trade globally with new partners, and diverge from the EU and its 'red tape' insofar as it is willing to risk creating problems in Northern Ireland. But what will that actually look like in practice?

We will end this chapter with a reference to an unexpected but regular Brexit guest: the so-called 'chlorinated chicken'. The details of what 'chlorinated chicken' is are, in many ways, a side point: what matters is that the US produces 'chlorinated chicken', and the EU will not accept 'chlorinated chicken' for import out of animal welfare concerns. Post-Brexit, the UK will find itself with a pressing question: to 'chlorinate', or not to 'chlorinate'?

A trade deal with the United States would do much to offset any economic losses stemming from Brexit, but might very well result in 'chlorinated chicken' on the UK market. If the UK decides that—as the EU is its nearest neighbour and it trades more animal products with the EU than with the US—it actually makes sense to take the EU's side and to reject 'chlorinated chicken' for import still, it may struggle to get a good trade deal out of the United States, which in many ways sees in Brexit an opportunity to get a deal with the UK that will work *for them*. However, if the UK accepts 'chlorinated chicken' for the sake of a US deal, for any chicken from the UK to be exported to the EU, then, it will be necessary to prove to the EU that the chicken in question is *not* 'chlorinated chicken'. And doing that will, undoubtedly, require compliance with a variety of different rules on how farms and factories operate, how products are transported, and what paperwork needs to be supplied when it crosses a border.

One of the benefits of the EU's internal market is that, however much regulation applies across the internal market, it enables a product produced in one country to be sold without restrictions in 26 others. Outside of the EU, either the government or individual producers are much more likely to be faced with competing regulatory demands. How to prioritize those, and whether they can be prioritized away from the EU on a purely economic level—as in, can trade with the rest of the world compensate for a loss of access to the EU market? Will producers follow the UK in going 'global' or will it not be worth it for them in light of transport costs?—will be one of the big challenges for the UK to tackle once it has formally left the internal market.

As far as domestic 'red tape' reduction goes generally, this too may be easier said than done. Parliament will be in principle free to amend or repeal any domestic legislation that is based on EU law once the UK has exited the EU, but at this point appears to still be looking for the specific 'red tape'. The Chancellor of the Exchequer, in September 2019, thus issued a so-called 'red tape challenge' that would investigate this question, in an attempt to replace 'overbearing' regulations from Brussels with business-friendly regulation that was UK-specific.

However, regulators of specific sectors have since 2016 been very sceptical that a lot of 'red tape' would actually disappear—whether on product standards or social and environmental standards.[49] Indeed, the opposite could very well be true: an HMRC assessment from October 2019 suggests that the administrative burden of making customs declarations between the EU and the UK in the absence of a trade deal following the transition period would amount to 15 billion pounds per year,[50] and even if there is a deal, goods shipped from Great Britain to Northern Ireland will at least have to fulfil a variety of administrative processes under the Protocol in order to meet the requirements of EU law.

In short, while Brexit consequently may reduce the level of EU-originating regulation of trade for some businesses in the UK, relationships with other countries will come with their own 'red tape', as will the processes established to keep the Irish border invisible.

10.5 In conclusion

It is easy to assume that the EU overregulates simply because it produces significant volumes of regulation; and, credit where due, as part of the 'Better Regulation' work, the EU has from time to time admitted itself that it has focused too much on producing rules, and less on how effective those rules are. But it is impossible to argue that the 'internal market' is not a unique and unprecedented achievement, and that however voluminous its legislation, there are distinct benefits to being *in* the internal market. We will explore those benefits in more detail in the next few chapters, when we consider how free movement of goods, workers, EU citizens, and services (as well as the freedom to establish) work.

[49] See, eg, https://www.ftadviser.com/regulation/2018/10/31/pimfa-boss-dispels-brexit-rules-bonfire/; https://www.ftadviser.com/2016/07/19/regulation/eu-legislation/regulator-rules-out-brexit-bonfire-of-regulation-k39AobCcUb9PzOkLdutvLL/article.html.

[50] See https://www.gov.uk/government/publications/hmrc-impact-assessment-for-the-movement-of-goods-if-the-uk-leaves-the-eu-without-a-deal/hmrc-impact-assessment-for-the-movement-of-goods-if-the-uk-leaves-the-eu-without-a-deal-third-edition#section-c.

Nobody can predict what the economic, let alone non-economic, consequences of leaving the 'internal market' and the EU's customs union will be at the time of writing, but everything that we know about cross-border trade suggests that barriers will arise in leaving the internal market, and doing business with the EU will not become simpler as a non-Member State. Unless the UK wishes to no longer have any domestic rules regulating products and services from other countries, and will apply no tariffs to any imports from anywhere in the world, 'red tape' will be encountered at the border; and the more it tries to trade with both its closest neighbours and its distant partners, the more voluminous that red tape is likely to become.

Key points

- Prior to 1992, EU economic integration remained limited in practice: while discriminating against foreign products violated the Treaties, there was very little in place to actually encourage trade between the Member States.
- Since 1992, the 'internal market' project has been advanced through the following combined techniques:
  - **Harmonization** of the basic health and safety standards of products;
  - **Mutual recognition** requirements which mean that products that are legally sold in one Member State should *normally* also be legally sold in any other Member State.
- The 'internal market' is not (and probably never will be!) 'complete', but remains the most advanced example of economic integration in the world despite this . . .
- . . . and in leaving it, Brexit will involve significant changes to the UK's future trade with the EU, as well as the future of UK 'internal' trade between Northern Ireland and Great Britain, as Northern Ireland will remain *in practice* in both the EU's customs union and the internal market.

Assess your learning

1. Was the 'internal market' completed in 1992? (See Sections 10.1–10.3.)
2. What are the differences between a 'free trade area', a 'customs union', and a 'single market'? (See Section 10.4.1.)
3. What is the difference between minimum and maximum harmonization? (See Section 10.4.2.)
4. What is meant by accusations that the EU produces too much 'red tape'? What is this 'red tape' trying to achieve? (See Section 10.4.3.)

Further reading

Kenneth Armstrong, 'Regulatory Alignment and Divergence after Brexit' (2018) 25(8) JEPP 1099.

Holger Hestermeyer and Federico Ortino, 'Towards a UK Trade Policy Post-Brexit: The beginning of a complex journey' (2016) 27(3) KLJ 452.

Paola Mariani and Giorgio Sacerdoti, 'Brexit and Trade Issues' (2019) 11(2) EJLS 187.

Kalypso Nicolaïdis, 'Trusting the Poles? Constructing Europe through mutual recognition' (2007) 14(5) JEPP 682.

Kalypso Nicolaïdis, 'Mutual Recognition: Promise and denial, from Sapiens to Brexit' (2017) 70(1) CLP 1.

Jacques Pelkmans, 'Why the Single Market Remains the EU's Core Business' (2016) 39(5) WEP 1095.

William Robinson, 'Time for Coherent Rules on EU Regulation' (2015) 3(3) TPLeg 257.

Richard Tauwhare, 'Brexit: Achieving near-frictionless trade' (2017) 23(3) Int TLR 89.

Stephen Weatherill, 'Maximum versus Minimum Harmonization: Choosing between unity and diversity in the search for the soul of the internal market' in Niamh Nic Shuibhne and Laurence Gormley (eds), *From Single Market to Economic Union: Essays in Memory of John A Usher* (OUP, 2012).

Stephen Weatherill, 'The Principle of Mutual Recognition: It doesn't work because it doesn't exist' (2018) 43(2) Eur Law Rev 224.

Online resources

Visit www.oup.com/he/demars1e for a sample approach to discussing the quote.

11

Free movement of goods

Context for this chapter

From: distro@belfastfizz.co.uk
To: hq@belfastfizz.co.uk; legal@belfastfizz@co.uk

Hi Seamus,

Update on what I'm sure you've heard bits and pieces of, but here it is in full. Recent shipments of Breezeblox have been stopped at several borders of EU countries. Here's what we know so far, but we obviously need Legal to investigate what is actually happening.

a) Spain: got hit with a ban by the Spanish Ministry of Health because some of the Breezeblox are shaped like spheres, and they're arguing that there's been instances of people swallowing those accidentally. We tried to argue that people don't really swallow ice-cubes spontaneously, and so Breezeblox (as a plastic ice-cube alternative) aren't likely to be swallowed either, but the law says they can't be sold—they're apparently a choking hazard.

b) Romania: stopped at the border there because a new law requires any products that may be used to consume alcohol contain a warning that drinking alcohol during pregnancy may negatively affect the pregnancy and harm the foetus. Breezeblox don't have that warning on them, so can't go on the Romanian market.

c) Italy: two different stumbling blocks here! First, the authorities made us pay for the goods to be inspected as they'd not seen anything like them and wanted to ensure they were safe for use. Then, when we delivered the shipments, we were told that they were going to be subject to a 5 per cent sales tax on 'cooling agents'—unlike ice cubes, which are excused from sales taxes altogether!

I also just got off the phone with Marketing and they've got their own issues. Apparently, in Belgium, it's now illegal to sell Breezeblox online as part of a campaign to curb excessive drinking. The theory goes that in store, someone buying a lot of hard liquor and associated Breezeblox will be warned by retailers that this may harm their health—but that kind of advice isn't going to be given through an online check-out service, and so it's more dangerous to the

→

→
public to have Breezeblox sold online. And, even more bizarrely, our advertising campaign in Slovakia has been met with an injunction because we show both adults and kids using Breezeblocks. The kids are using them to keep apple juice cool, but that doesn't matter—the Slovakian advertising regulator tells us we can't have an ad that encourages consumption of alcohol to minors, and this does that by suggesting that something they're putting in juice, Mommy and Daddy might put in a gin and tonic!

I'm Cc-ing in Legal, obviously, but thought I should keep you posted of what we're running into. Customers love what we're doing—reusable ice-cube alternatives that don't water down drinks!—but boy, are we facing a lot of issues trying to get our stuff to market in other countries.

Hope everything well,
Aoife

Aoife Loughlin
Head of Distribution
Belfast Fizz Ltd

11.1 Introduction

Free movement of goods lies at the very heart of the internal market. The idea of trade in physical items being able to happen without any barriers was the starting point that the EEC Treaty aimed for, and remains one of the greatest achievements of the EU to date. However, as with everything in EU law, there are a lot of legal rules underpinning a fairly straightforward concept—and that concept, in practice, may not be as unlimited as it sounds. The scenario at the start of this chapter sets out a number of different situations that a manufacturer of a product may encounter, and we will use it to consider in detail how the free movement of goods rules actually apply to trade between Member States in practice.

For ease of understanding, the remainder of this chapter is split into three sections.

The first part deals with what we've termed taxation issues. This section covers the Treaty rules applicable to the charging of import duties at the border, and the potential to apply taxes to imported products *once* they have entered a new Member State. The former can be called border taxation (or the application of tariffs), whereas the latter is a matter of internal taxation—so, for instance, sales taxes, or value-added taxes, being applied to goods.

The second part deals with non-taxation issues. The primary issue is quantitative restrictions: situations where a Member State either blocks a specific volume of products from entering its market, *or* outlaws/bans a product altogether. The EU rules on this encompass not only express 'product bans', but also measures that in practice make it significantly harder to sell a product in another Member State, whether they are laws, regulations, technical requirements, or administrative rules.

The final part of the chapter considers to what extent the rules on free movement of goods are absolutes: can a Member State *never* prevent a product from another Member State from being sold, or taxed, on its own territories? As you might predict at this point in the textbook, the Member States did not set up a 'Wild West' of trade, and there are times when they are able to restrict the free movement of goods—provided they do so for good reasons. We consider the possible derogations from free movement of goods and how such derogations might be justified in the final section of the chapter.

11.2 Movement of goods: taxation

The Treaty contains two separate sets of provisions that address matters of taxation when it comes to trade in products. The first of these relates to border taxation, or those tariffs charged on imports *at the border*; the rules on this are contained in Articles 28–30 TFEU. The other type of taxation that is regulated for trade purposes is so-called internal taxation, but only in situations where such taxes are discriminatory towards imports. This is regulated in Article 110 TFEU. We will consider both in turn.

11.2.1 Border taxation

At the heart of the Treaty provisions on free movement of goods lies Article 28 TFEU:

Article 28 TFEU (emphasis added)

1. The Union shall comprise a customs union which shall cover all trade in goods and which shall involve the prohibition between Member States of customs duties on imports and exports and of all charges having equivalent effect, and the adoption of a common customs tariff in their relations with third countries.
2. The provisions of Article 30 and [Article 110] shall apply to products originating in Member States and to products coming from third countries which are in free circulation in Member States.

We saw in Chapter 10 that the EU has created a customs union as well as a free trade area through its treaties, and Article 28 TFEU is an expression of that overall achievement. As such, Article 28(1) TFEU requires the adoption of a single external tariff—outward-facing—as well as the abolition of all customs duties *between* the Member States.

The definition in Article 28 TFEU is far-ranging: it covers not only express customs duties, that is, charges actually termed 'tariffs' that are collected at the border, but also so-called 'charges having equivalent effect' (CEEs). It also, per Article 28(2) TFEU, applies to *all products* that circulate the internal market: this means that once a product has crossed the EU's 'external' border, it will be treated the same as if it were created *within* a Member State.[1] Without this, the customs union would be unachievable. Article 29 TFEU adds to this that those goods manufactured outside of the EU *do* have to comply with importation formalities at the EU external border, but once this has happened, they can circulate freely. From this, we can glean that the 'origin' or 'nationality' of a good is

[1] See also Case 41/76 *Donckerwolcke* ECLI:EU:C:1976:182, paras 17–18.

effectively irrelevant for 'free movement of goods' purposes: once a good is within internal market territory, it benefits from the free movement of goods provisions.

What, then, is a 'good'?

We will see that the Treaties use a variety of different terms to describe the things that Articles 28–30 TFEU apply to: they are called imports, exports, goods, and products. All of these terms are, in effect, equivalent: according to the CJEU in *Works of Art*, they describe a tangible that 'can be valued in money and which [is] capable, as such, of forming the subject of commercial transactions'.[2] This concept of a product that can be 'bought' and the 'subject of a transaction' has been interpreted very broadly by the CJEU over time: items as far-ranging as 'waste'[3] and 'human organs'[4] have all been captured by the concept of a 'good' or a 'product' under EU law. The main exception to what constitutes a 'good' is whether it is covered by any *other* relevant part of the Treaties—in other words, if something can instead be defined as a 'service', it will not be a 'good'. For our purposes, by and large, if an item changes hands in exchange for money, it will probably be a 'good'.[5]

The prohibition on border taxes

Article 28 TFEU's prohibition on customs duties is reiterated in Article 30 TFEU in even plainer terms:

> **Article 30 TFEU**
>
> Customs duties on imports and exports and charges having equivalent effect shall be prohibited between Member States. This prohibition shall also apply to customs duties of a fiscal nature.

The stress on the abolition of customs duties or border tariffs is deliberate: they were the most obvious barrier to trade between the Member States at the time the EEC Treaty was adopted, as they are quite literally taxes charged on goods *purely* because they cross a border. Only rarely has the CJEU actually had to consider the meaning of Article 30 TFEU: *Van Gend en Loos*, discussed in detail in Chapter 8, is one of the rare instances where a Member State actually charged a border tax after the adoption of the Treaty of Rome.[6]

The concept of **charges having an equivalent effect** has been filled in a little more by the CJEU. In the *Diamonds* case, Belgium had established a Social Fund for Diamond Workers, which was funded by charging a 'contribution' to all diamond imports that would fill up this social fund with benefits to be awarded to diamond workers.[7] The CJEU here was explicit in setting out a wide scope for CEEs. The fact that the contribution charged was very small was irrelevant, as was the fact that it was not a 'customs duty' in the strict sense, and the fact that the contribution was levied for (in short) a good cause.

[2] Case 7/68 *Commission v Italy (Works of Art)* ECLI:EU:C:1968:51.

[3] Case C-2/90 *Commission v Belgium (Walloon Waste)* ECLI:EU:C:1992:310.

[4] Case C-203/99 *Veedfald* ECLI:EU:C:2001:258.

[5] One of the exceptions to 'items' being 'goods' is money: if it is legal tender, it will be 'capital' rather than a 'good'. (Case 7/78 *Thompson* ECLI:EU:C:1978:209, and Joined Cases C-358/93 and C-416/93 *Bordessa* ECLI:EU:C:1995:54).

[6] Case 26/62 *Van Gend en Loos* ECLI:EU:C:1963:1.

[7] Joined Cases 2–3/69 *Sociaal Fonds voor de Diamantarbeiders (Diamonds)* ECLI:EU:C:1969:30.

The Article 30 TFEU prohibition, in other words, is absolute, and does not come with a *de minimis* requirement, nor can a violation of Article 30 TFEU be justified. In *Works of Art*, the CJEU stressed this by noting that the general exception to free movement of goods contained in Article 36 TFEU did *not* cover taxation, and so could not 'excuse' an Article 30 TFEU violation.

Permissible border taxes?

There are, however, very limited circumstances in which a charge collected at the border will simply not be deemed to be a customs duty or a CEE.

One such situation as identified by the CJEU is that where the charge collected is specifically in exchange for a service that the importing country provides to the exporter. The CJEU has acknowledged that such a charge would not be covered by Article 30 TFEU in *theory*, but in practice, none of the Member States has successfully shown that they charged for such 'services rendered'. A good example of an attempt by a Member State is *Commission v Italy (Statistical Levies)*, where Italy imposed a small charge on both imports and exports that it was using to make available accurate statistics on imports/exports in Italy.[8] The CJEU accepted in principle the concept of charges for services rendered, but rejected the specific charge in Italy because those statistics were of benefit to all of Italy, and not exclusively the importer/exporter who was paying the charges.

The other type of 'border charge' that is not covered by Article 30 TFEU occurs in situations where EU law *itself* requires a health inspection: where such an inspection is required, Member States can recover the costs incurred for carrying out the inspection from the exporters.[9] However, the CJEU has made clear that recovery of charges can only take place where EU law *requires* an inspection—in situations where it permits an inspection, but leaves it to the Member States if they want to carry one out, no cost recovery is possible.

Remedies for Article 30 TFEU violations

The Treaties are not explicit on what happens when a Member State violates Article 30 TFEU, but *Van Gend en Loos* and other cases clearly set out what the CJEU has established as normal in practice. The first requirement is that the Member State in question eliminates the customs charge or CEE; and the second is that the exporter/importer who paid the charge has a right to repayment by the Member State imposing the charge. As we saw in Chapter 8, the specific conditions and procedures attached to how that repayment right works are a matter of domestic law under the doctrine of **national procedural autonomy**—the primary conditions attached are purely that the repayment must be effective, and equivalent to similar payment recovery claims that apply to national products.[10]

Discussing the scenario

Are any of the measures alluded to by Aoife in the scenario at the start of the chapter prohibited by Articles 28–30 TFEU?

[8] Case 24/68 *Commission v Italy (Statistical Levies)* ECLI:EU:C:1969:29.

[9] See, inter alia, Case 18/87 *Commission v Germany* (*Inspection Fees*) ECLI:EU:C:1988:453, para 8.

[10] See, eg, Case 199/82 *San Giorgio* ECLI:EU:C:1983:247, para 12.

11.2.2 Internal taxation

A very straightforward way to avoid the prohibition on border charges is to simply not tax imports *at* the border, but rather at some other point once they have entered a Member State market, by charging them more for a given tax than a domestic competing product would incur. The Treaty, unsurprisingly, thus also prohibits this kind of discriminatory taxation between imports and domestically produced products in Article 110 TFEU.

> **Article 110 TFEU (emphasis added)**
>
> No Member State shall impose, **directly or indirectly**, on the products of other Member States any **internal taxation** of any kind **in excess of** that imposed directly or indirectly on **similar domestic** products.
>
> Furthermore, no Member State shall impose on the products of other Member States any **internal taxation of such a nature as to afford indirect protection to other products.**

At first glance, the two paragraphs in Article 110 TFEU may look as if they say essentially the same thing. The first paragraph, however, relates to so-called 'similar products', whereas the second paragraph covers those products that are in a competitive relationship with each other (even if this is not explicitly stated). We will examine what the difference between those two issues—similarity and competition—is next. It is important to stress, however, that Article 110 TFEU does *not* prohibit internal taxation: governments are absolutely allowed to impose sales taxes or value-added taxes on both imported and exported products. Moreover, the taxation does not have to be on the product itself per se—taxation on the *use* of a product is consequently also captured by Article 110 TFEU, as are any charges incurred when inspecting products or complying with other internal regulatory procedures. The prohibition in Article 110 TFEU is expressly on **discriminatory** taxes that affect similar goods or **protective** taxes that affect competing goods.

Discriminatory taxes on 'similar' goods

Whether two products are 'similar' is a relatively subjective determination to make. A lot here depends not only on what the products *are*, but on how consumers relate to those products. For some people, tea and coffee might be 'similar', as they both satisfy a need for caffeine. For many others, however, there are concrete differences—and changes in the price of coffee would not result in them switching to drinking tea, or vice versa.

The CJEU originally attempted to determine if goods were 'similar' by looking at how they were classified for taxation purposes, but this soon proved to be a far too restrictive and unhelpful means of assessing similarity.[11] Instead, the CJEU now makes a determination of similarity on the basis of the characteristics, usage, and 'consumer tastes' that apply to two products.

[11] Case 27/67 *Fink-Frucht* ECLI:EU:C:1968:22.

A clear example of this is found in the *John Walker* case, which considered a Danish tax on Scotch whisky and a different spirit (fruit wine of the liqueur type).

Case 243/84 *John Walker* ECLI:EU:C:1986:100 (emphasis added)

11. In order to determine whether products are similar within the terms of the prohibition laid down in the first paragraph of Article [110] it is necessary to consider . . . **whether they have similar characteristics and meet the same needs from the point of view of consumers.** The Court endorsed a broad interpretation of the concept of similarity . . . and assessed the similarity of the products not according to whether they were strictly identical, but according to whether their use was similar and comparable. Consequently, in order to determine whether products are similar it is necessary first to **consider certain objective characteristics of both categories of beverages, such as their origin, the method of manufacture and their organoleptic properties, in particular taste and alcohol content,** and secondly to **consider whether or not both categories of beverages are capable of meeting the same needs from the point of view of consumers.**

Following this explanation of similarity, the CJEU concluded that the characteristics of the products were very distinct, both in terms of how they were made and in their alcohol content (which was 40 per cent in Scotch whisky and 20 per cent in fruit wine). This was enough to determine that the products were not similar, without needing to investigate consumer taste.[12]

It is therefore difficult to give a finite definition of 'similarity'; in practice, the CJEU will need to consider the products at hand in detail in order to form an opinion of their characteristics and how consumers respond to them.[13]

The other key aspect of the first paragraph of Article 110 TFEU is that of 'discrimination'. The text of the Treaty stresses that both *direct* and *indirect* discrimination will be caught. *Direct* discrimination takes place when the different taxes apply expressly on the basis that one product is from *abroad* (and perhaps even from a specific Member State) whereas the other is domestically produced. A tax exclusively applied to imports, for example, would be a case of direct discrimination—but so would a significantly higher tax applied to imports when compared to the equivalent tax on domestic products. The CJEU's case law has made it clear that it is not only the specific *amount* of tax that can be applied discriminatorily: the processes related to tax collection can also target imports in a discriminatory way, by for instance applying shorter deadlines for payment, or higher penalties when taxes are not paid for imported products at this deadline.[14]

Indirect discrimination is in many cases more difficult to detect. It occurs when a tax is applied not expressly on the basis that one product is 'foreign' and another is 'local', but rather where the impact of a seemingly neutral tax policy hits imports harder in practice.

[12] Case 243/84 *John Walker* ECLI:EU:C:1986:100, paras 12–14.

[13] The CJEU carries out similar analysis of product 'likeness' for the purposes of competition law; see Chapter 15.

[14] Case 55/79 *Commission v Ireland* ECLI:EU:C:1980:56; Case 299/86 *Drexl* ECLI:EU:C:1988:103.

Humblot is a very clear example of indirectly discriminatory taxation.[15] Here, the French tax code applied a seemingly 'neutral' two-tier road tax owed by car owners based on the 'horsepower' of a car's engine. This in principle is entirely permissible under the Treaties, which do not control a Member State's road tax policy. However, the threshold at which a 'higher' rate applied was set by France at 16CV, and the CJEU found that only imported cars had a higher fiscal horsepower than 16CV. As such, the *effect* of the tax was discriminatory on imports—and thus contrary to Article 110 TFEU. Similar conclusions were drawn about a French cigarette duty, where the most beneficially taxed cigarettes (with so-called 'dark' tobacco) were almost exclusively manufactured in France, and the majority of heavily taxed cigarettes (with so-called 'light' tobacco) were imported.[16]

Both *directly* and *indirectly* discriminatory internal taxes are prohibited by the first paragraph of Article 110 TFEU in the same way. However, as we will see in Section 11.4, whether taxation is *directly* or *indirectly* discriminatory has a significant impact on whether a Member State may be able to justify derogating from Article 110 TFEU.

Protective taxes on 'competing' products

As noted, the second paragraph of Article 110 TFEU looks very similar to the first. In practice, however, it is a slightly more generous version of the same principle: that imports cannot be made to suffer compared to domestic products. The second paragraph deals with products that are in a competitive relationship with each other, and the notion of a 'protective' tax, or a tax that protects a domestic product. Both the competitive relationship and the idea of a 'protective' tax are broader (and thus easier to prove the existence of) than the concepts of 'discrimination' and 'similar' goods in the first paragraph.

The key case in this area is one that involves the UK. In the UK *Wine and Beer* case, the UK applied different rates of tax to beer and wine.[17] Wine was hit with a significantly higher tax than beer was; but only beer was primarily domestically produced, with all wine at the time effectively imported. The Commission challenged the UK tax regime on the basis of Article 110's second paragraph: it did not argue that 'wine' and 'beer' were 'similar', but rather that wine and beer were in a competitive relationship with each other.

The CJEU applied similar reasoning to this case as it did in *John Walker*, in that it investigated how consumers approached wine and beer, as well as what the qualities of wine and beer are. However, as Article 110 second paragraph applies to products *in competition* with each other, rather than 'similar' products, the fact that wine and beer were made using different processes and had different flavours and alcohol contents was found to matter *less* than that they were both alcoholic beverages and that consumers may swap between them if their prices changed significantly. In light of the last point, however, the CJEU limited the 'competition' between beer and relatively cheap wine—consumers were unlikely to switch from a lager to a £70 bottle of vintage wine, after all.

Having established a competitive relationship between cheap wine and beer, the CJEU then had to consider if the UK tax regime was 'protective' of beer. It found here that cheap wines were subject to a significantly higher tax burden compared to domestic beer.

[15] Case C-112/84 *Humblot* ECLI:EU:C:1985:185.

[16] Case C-302/00 *Commission v France (Tobacco)* ECLI:EU:C:2002:123.

[17] Case 170/78 *Commission v UK (Wine and beer)* ECLI:EU:C:1980:53.

As such, even cheap wine (by the time all the taxes were paid for, and those charges were added to the retail price of the wine) ended up becoming a 'luxury' product for UK consumers, and consumers would not think of wine as a genuine alternative to beer. As such, the UK taxes on wine and beer were in violation of Article 110 second paragraph, as the tax regime in essence shielded domestically produced beer from the competition that cheap imported wine may pose.

This finding, however, was dependent on the specific application of taxes in the UK case. In a more recent Swedish case involving the same products, the CJEU ended up finding that even though wine (per bottle) suffered from significantly higher taxes, the overall taxes applied to a litre of wine and a litre of beer meant that wine was effectively twice the cost of beer both *before* the taxes were applied and *after* the taxes were applied.[18] As such, the taxation regime did *not* shield domestic Swedish beer from the competition faced by imported wine, as consumers were not urged away from wine to beer in the way they were under UK taxes in the 1980s. The 'protective effect', in other words, was absent, which meant that Article 110 TFEU was not violated.

Much like the first paragraph of Article 110 TFEU, 'protective' taxes on competing products may be justifiable under the Treaty under certain conditions. We will consider these in Section 11.4.

Remedies for Article 110 TFEU violations

Where a violation of the first paragraph of Article 110 TFEU is found, a Member State is obliged to stop discriminating against the imported product in its internal taxation policy. In other words, the taxes applied to similar imported and domestic products must be equalized.

The consequences of a violation of the second paragraph of Article 110 TFEU are slightly different. Here, it is not discrimination that must be 'removed', but rather a 'protective effect'. Cancelling out the 'protective effect' of an internal tax can be achieved without subjecting competing domestic and imported products to an identical tax regime; this is particularly true because in any tax policy, products that are merely 'competing' but not actually 'similar' are unlikely to actually be subject to identical taxes. As such, in the UK *Wine and Beer* case, the tax regime applied to wine had to be altered, but not made *equivalent* to the tax regime applied to beer, in order to satisfy the conditions of Article 110 TFEU.

In both situations, anyone who has paid tax contrary to Article 110 TFEU is entitled to a repayment of those taxes in a way that is determined by national law—provided that repayment is effective and equivalent to what wrongfully collected taxation on purely domestic products would warrant.[19]

Discussing the scenario

Are any of the situations set out by Aoife in the scenario at the start of the chapter captured by Article 110 TFEU? If so, do you think that a tax is being applied to *similar* products or products that are in *competition* with each other?

[18] Case C-167/05 *Commission v Sweden* (*Wine and beer*) ECLI:EU:C:2008:202.
[19] Case 68/79 *Hans Just* ECLI:EU:C:1980:57.

11.3 Movement of goods: quantitative restrictions

As was noted in Section 11.2, there has not been an abundance of case law on 'border taxes', for the simple reason that these are the most obvious way of undermining the working of the EU's internal market and customs union. However, more problematic than taxes—which are costly, but can be paid—are measures adopted by Member States that make it impossible for goods to be imported or exported. These are precluded by the Treaties in the directly effective (horizontally[20] and vertically) Articles 34 and 35 TFEU.[21]

Article 34 TFEU

Quantitative restrictions on imports and all measures having equivalent effect shall be prohibited between Member States.

Article 35 TFEU

Quantitative restrictions on exports, and all measures having equivalent effect, shall be prohibited between Member States.

The EU Treaties, both regarding imports and exports, thus expressly forbid both quantitative restrictions and measures having equivalent effect (MEEs) to quantitative restriction. A quantitative restriction is exactly what it sounds like: a limit on the quantity (or number) of a product that is allowed to be imported or exported. A ban is the most extreme form of a quantitative restriction, but any restriction on volume is captured by the concept—import quotas are thus also precluded by the Treaties.

In practice, few 'bans' or other forms of import/export quotas will be found; the Member States are unlikely to expressly forbid products from entering their markets *unless* they are convinced that they can justify such a restriction under the exceptions discussed in Section 11.4. A few historical examples exist, however, including a memorable UK prohibition on importing pornographic material that was declared contrary to Article 34 TFEU by the CJEU.[22]

Instead, the import and export of products is much more likely to be affected by a measure that is not an actual volume restriction, but rather has an *equivalent effect* to a volume restriction. The concept of an 'MEE' is far more flexible than the concept of a quantitative restriction, and it has been subject to significantly more case law as a consequence. The next few subsections will discuss the CJEU's case law on MEEs as applied to imported products, and the final subsection will consider how MEEs apply to exported products.

11.3.1 Stage 1: MEEs and imports

The Treaties do not define what an 'MEE' is anywhere; unpacking the term has fallen to the CJEU. Its seminal definition of the concept stems from *Dassonville*.[22]

[19] See Case C-171/11 *Fra.bo* ECLI:EU:C:2012:453, where standardization and certification measures by a private body were caught under Article 34 TFEU because national law recognized its certificates as 'compliant' with national law, and thus made market entry harder for 'uncertified' products.

[20] For more on direct effect, see Chapter 8.

[21] Case 34/79 *Henn & Darby* ECLI:EU:C:1979:295.

[22] Case 8/74 *Dassonville* ECLI:EU:C:1974:82.

Case 8/74 *Dassonville* ECLI:EU:C:1974:82 (emphasis added)

All . . . rules enacted by Member States, which are capable of hindering, **directly or indirectly, actually or potentially**, intra-[EU] trade are to be considered as measures having an effect equivalent to quantitative restrictions.

This is a *very* broad definition of what types of measures can be caught by Article 34 TFEU. Given the scope of Article 110 TFEU, it is not surprising that both direct and indirect discrimination is a violation of Article 34 TFEU—but the fact that even rules that *potentially* (as in, not currently but *may* at some point!) hinder cross-border trade are outlawed by Article 34 TFEU has meant that the consequences of Article 34 TFEU on domestic regulation have been significant. This generous definition of MEEs caught by Article 34 TFEU has resulted in very diverse and even seemingly low-impact regulatory rules being struck down in CJEU case law, such as:

- In *Foie Gras*, the CJEU determined that a French measure that limited what products could be marketed as 'foie gras' violated Article 34 TFEU *despite* the fact that most foie gras was produced in France and even where it was not, it met the French product standards anyway.[23]
- In *Buy Irish*, the CJEU determined that an advertising campaign to buy local products violated Article 34 TFEU even though in practice, since the start of the campaign, the volume of imports into Ireland had actually increased.[24]
- In *Bluhme*, the CJEU held that a Danish ban on the keeping of certain species of bees was contrary to Article 34 TFEU, even though the ban applied to less than 1 per cent of Denmark's territory.[25]

The only times when measures are *not* captured by the *Dassonville* MEE formula is when their impact on imports is too 'uncertain and indirect' to conclude that they may actively or potentially hinder trade—in which case they fall outside of Article 34 TFEU altogether.[26] Beyond that, any measure that has hindering *effects* is caught by Article 34 TFEU: the intention of the regulator is irrelevant in determining if a violation of the Article has taken place.

Discussing the scenario

Do you think any of the measures taken by Spain, Romania, Belgium, or Slovakia (as described in Aoife's email in the scenario at the start of the chapter) are quantitative restrictions? Are any of them MEEs?

[23] Case 184/96 *Commission v France (Foie Gras)* ECLI:EU:C:1998:495.
[24] Case 249/81 *Commission v Ireland (Buy Irish)* ECLI:EU:C:1982:402.
[25] Case C-67/97 *Bluhme* ECLI:EU:C:1998:584.
[26] See, eg, Case C-69/88 *Krantz* ECLI:EU:C:1990:97; Case C-379/92 *Peralta* ECLI:EU:C:1994:296.

11.3.2 Stage 2: Mutual recognition

The early CJEU cases on MEEs, with the *Dassonville* formulation of the concept applied, all involved direct discrimination against imports—meaning discrimination on the basis that they *were* products from abroad.[27] In 1979, however, the CJEU heard *Cassis de Dijon*, which would revolutionize free movement of goods in the EU.[28]

In *Cassis*, a German supermarket sought to import a French alcoholic drink called Cassis de Dijon, but found that it could not because of a German law that required alcoholic drinks to have a minimum alcohol content. Cassis contained between 15 and 20 per cent alcohol, whereas under the German law regulating spirit alcohol content, it would have had to contain 25 per cent alcohol in order to be sold on the German market.

Key to the measure in *Cassis* was that it applied to *all* products in Germany, whether imported or exported, and as such did not *target* an import. However, the CJEU found that this did not matter: the measure in place in Germany constituted an MEE all the same.

Case 120/78 *Cassis de Dijon* ECLI:EU:C:1979:42 (emphasis added)

It therefore appears that **the unilateral requirement imposed** by the rules of a Member State of a **minimum alcohol content** for the purposes of the sale of alcoholic beverages constitutes **an obstacle to trade** which is **incompatible with the provisions of Article [34 TFEU]**.

There is therefore **no valid reason why, provided that they have been lawfully produced and marketed in one of the Member States, alcoholic beverage should not be introduced into any other Member State . . .**

The underpinning motivation for the CJEU's judgment in *Cassis* is that if Germany had been allowed to maintain its domestic 'alcohol limit' laws, the French producers of Cassis would have had to manufacture a more alcoholic version of their product *specifically* for the German market. This, of course, would discourage them from sending their product to Germany—and so these kinds of rules undermine the establishment of a 'common market' in full.

The CJEU went further in *Cassis* than simply declaring the minimum alcohol content contrary to Article 34 TFEU, however. The second paragraph quoted from *Cassis* in practice takes the specific facts in that case and turns them into a far more general **mutual recognition** requirement: any product 'lawfully produced and marketed' in one Member State should be sellable in any *other* Member State, unless very specific exceptions to free movement of goods apply. Mutual recognition thus precludes a Member State, for no justifiable reason, rejecting products from another Member State if they were legally sold there: what is good enough for *one* Member State is in principle good enough for *all* the Member States.

[27] Direct discrimination in free movement of goods is sometimes referred to as 'distinctly applicable', in that it distinguishes expressly between imports/exports and domestic goods.

[28] Case 120/78 *Cassis de Dijon* ECLI:EU:C:1979:42.

The *Cassis* mutual recognition principle was applied to a wide variety of different factual scenarios by the CJEU in cases that followed. In *Rau*, a Belgian rule that required margarine butter to be sold in 'rectangular' packaging was found to be a *Cassis*-style MEE, as were German domestic *Beer Purity Laws* that required beer to be brewed with specific ingredients.[29] The CJEU consistently found that these types of national rules were in many ways just reinforcing existing consumer tastes, rather than serving genuine regulatory purposes. In other words, margarine in non-rectangular packaging would not *hurt* consumers, but rules that precluded other types of packaging being used just meant an advantage for Belgian producers, who were already producing butter in rectangular packages.

Pause for reflection

Do you think that the *Cassis* definition is too broad? What does it mean for the role of the state in setting product standards, or determining what products are appropriate to be sold within the country?

Does *Cassis* then mean that *any* national rules on product standards are contrary to Article 34 TFEU? No; there are possible justifications for national regulations that make it harder (or impossible) for products to access a Member State market—but the mere existence *of* a national rule would simply not be enough to justify hindering market access. We will look at the effect of *Cassis* on justifications for derogations from Article 34 TFEU in Section 11.4.

11.3.3 Stage 3: Selling arrangements

As mentioned in Section 11.3.2, the CJEU applied the *Cassis* mutual recognition principle to a significant number of cases following *Cassis*—and kept hearing ever-increasing volumes of references about the compatibility of national rules that governed commerce with Articles 34 and 35 TFEU. The questions went beyond product-specific regulation: a pinnacle was reached with *Torfaen v B&Q* in 1988, when a court in Wales asked the CJEU whether the UK's ban on trading on Sunday was contrary to Article 34 TFEU.[30]

The laws in question were not discriminatory, nor were they in any way designed to actually advantage or protect the domestic market: stores were simply not open on Sundays. Nonetheless, the CJEU found in *B&Q* that this regulation also fell within the *Cassis* definition of MEEs, and that B&Q therefore was experiencing a 'hindering' in free movement of goods because unlike its competitors on the continent, it could not make sales on Sundays.

This decision was heavily criticized, and marks one of the rare instances where the CJEU had a visible change of heart within a few years. An opportunity to reverse *B&Q* came before it in *Keck*, which concerned a Belgian law that prohibited the resale of products below their wholesale price.[31]

[29] Case 261/81 *Rau* ECLI:EU:C:1982:382; Case 178/84 *Commission v Germany* (*Beer Purity Laws*) ECLI:EU:C:1987:126.

[30] Case C-145/88 *Torfaen v B&Q* ECLI:EU:C:1989:593.

[31] Joined Cases C-267–268/91 *Keck* ECLI:EU:C:1993:905.

Joined Cases C-267–268/91 *Keck* ECLI:EU:C:1993:905 (emphasis added)

14. In view of the **increasing tendency of traders to invoke Article [34 TFEU] as a means of challenging any rules whose effect is to limit their commercial freedom** even where such rules are not aimed at products from other Member States, **the Court considers it necessary to re-examine and clarify its case-law on this matter.**
15. It is established by the case-law beginning with 'Cassis de Dijon' . . . that, in the absence of harmonization of legislation, obstacles to free movement of goods which are the consequence of applying, to goods coming from other Member States where they are lawfully manufactured and marketed, rules that lay down requirements to be met by such goods (such as those relating to designation, form, size, weight, composition, presentation, labelling, packaging) constitute measures of equivalent effect prohibited by Article [34]. This is so even if those rules apply without distinction to all products unless their application can be justified by a public-interest objective taking precedence over the free movement of goods.
16. By contrast, contrary to what has previously been decided, **the application to products from other Member States of national provisions restricting or prohibiting certain selling arrangements is not such as to hinder directly or indirectly, actually or potentially, trade between Member States within the meaning of the Dassonville judgment** . . . , so long as those provisions apply to all relevant traders operating within the national territory and so long as they affect in the same manner, in law and in fact, the marketing of domestic products and of those from other Member States.
17. Provided that those conditions are fulfilled, the application of such rules to the sale of products from another Member State meeting the requirements laid down by that State is not by nature such as to prevent their access to the market or to impede access any more than it impedes the access of domestic products. Such rules therefore fall outside the scope of Article [34 TFEU].

Keck thus established that, contrary to what the effect of *Cassis* had been, the prohibition in Article 34 TFEU was only directed at those rules that 'lay down requirements to be met by . . . goods', and not to how those goods were *sold*. This created a distinction between **product requirements**, which are covered by Article 34 TFEU, and **selling arrangements**, which fall outside of Article 34 TFEU and are, as of *Keck*, no longer to be considered MEEs themselves, **unless they are discriminatory**.

In subsequent case law, the CJEU clarified what counted as selling arrangements. It has made clear that any sort of generally applicable restriction on sale (so: place of sale,[32] time of sale,[33] possible seller[34]) falls outside of Article 34 TFEU, but also that advertising[35] and pricing regulations (as were at stake in *Keck* itself) are outside of Article 34 TFEU if non-discriminatory.

[32] Case C-441/04 *A-Punkt* ECLI:EU:C:2006:141. [33] Case C-69/93 *Punto Casa* ECLI:EU:C:1994:226.
[34] Joined Cases C-34-36/95 *De Agostini* ECLI:EU:C:1997:344.
[35] See, inter alia, *De Agostini*, and Case C-412/93 *Leclerc-Siplec* ECLI:EU:C:1995:26.

The treatment of advertising as a 'selling arrangement' is subject to several exceptions, however. Where a measure appears to cover both sales/advertising conditions *and* an aspect of the product itself, the CJEU tends to find that these are product requirements. As such, a German ban prohibiting the import of French Mars candy bars during a French advertising campaign that promised '10% of the bar free' *on the label* of the candy bar itself was deemed a product requirement, as it would involve changing the *packaging* of the candy bar.[36] Likewise, Austrian advertising regulations that forbade prize-winning crossword puzzles inside magazines were deemed product requirements, as forcing those to be removed from German magazines would require a change to the *content* of the magazine itself.[37]

Following *Keck*, Article 34 TFEU and national regulation thus interact with each other as demonstrated in Figure 11.1:

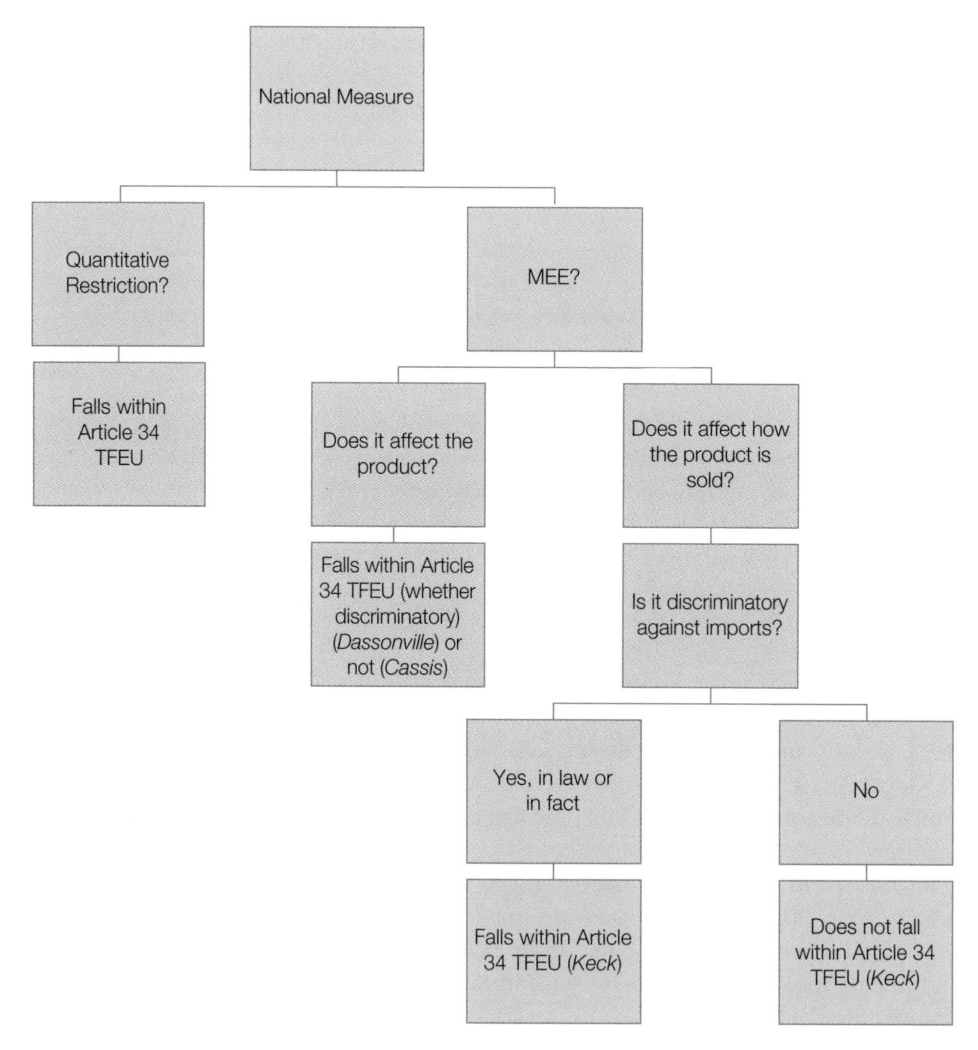

Figure 11.1 Article 34 TFEU after *Keck*

[36] Case C-470/93 *Mars* ECLI:EU:C:1995:224.

[37] Case C-368/95 *Familiapress* ECLI:EU:C:1997:325.

Discriminatory selling arrangements can be either **directly** or **indirectly** discriminatory and be caught by Article 34 TFEU. A directly discriminatory selling arrangement actually targets imports, whereas many other rules merely affect imported products more negatively than they do domestic products in practice, and thus are a form of indirect discrimination. A good example of regulatory measures that tend to be indirectly discriminatory selling arrangements are rules that require a seller's physical presence in a given local area, as this is a condition less likely to be met by suppliers from other Member States who are exclusively selling products online or via mail-order.[38]

Discussing the scenario

Reconsider the measures that you identified as MEEs before. Which of them are product requirements under *Keck*, and which of them are selling arrangements? Are the ones that are selling arrangements *discriminatory* or *not discriminatory*? Why does the distinction matter?

11.3.4 Stage 4: 'Market access'

The test in *Keck* successfully reduced the CJEU's case law, but many questions have been asked about it since its introduction. For one, the distinction between a product requirement and a selling arrangement is not always obvious, and even where it is clear, it seems to distinguish between two sets of rules for rather arbitrary reasons, given that they can both hinder market access, as *B&Q* demonstrated.

Despite many years of criticism of *Keck*, the CJEU has not outright abandoned the distinction between product requirements and selling arrangements in the way that it halted its MEE 'broadening' in *Cassis*. Nonetheless, a fourth stage of 'free movement of goods' case law appears to be underway, because the CJEU has started to employ the terminology of 'market access' in its judgments.

An early example of this happening is *Gourmet*, which concerned a complete ban in Sweden on the advertising of alcohol.[39] The CJEU determined this ban was caught by Article 34 TFEU, but rather than terming it an indirectly discriminatory selling arrangement—as the ban harmed new and 'unfamiliar' foreign alcohol more than it did Swedish alcohol that consumers were already familiar with—the CJEU simply stressed that market access would be especially impeded because of the *complete* nature of the ban.[40]

It pressed on with this new type of 'market access' reasoning in two further cases: the so-called *Italian Trailers* case and *Mickelsson*.[41] In these cases, the CJEU confirmed its earlier case law from *Dassonville* to *Keck*, but also added to the definition of an MEE that

[38] See, eg, Case C-254/98 *Heimdienst* ECLI:EU:C:2000:12 and Case C-322/01 *DocMorris* ECLI:EU:C:2003:664.

[39] Case C-405/98 *Gourmet* ECLI:EU:C:2001:135.

[40] This approach was first hinted at in *De Agostini*, where the CJEU asked the national court to investigate the effect of a Swedish ban on TV advertising directed at children under the age of 12 in order to determine if it was affecting imported products more than domestic ones.

[41] Case C-110/05 *Commission v Italy (Trailers)* ECLI:EU:C:2009:66 and Case C-142/05 *Mickelsson* ECLI:EU:C:2009:336.

any measure which hinders 'access to the market' is caught by the prohibition in Article 34 TFEU. In these two cases, the regulations that were found to be contravening Article 34 TFEU did not limit import or export of products, but rather restricted whether the relevant products (trailers that could be attached to mopeds and motorcycles, and jet skis) could be *used* in those Member States, and in that way were found to hinder 'market access'.

EU law in practice

A good recent example of the CJEU side-stepping its own earlier case law and not mentioning *Keck* is the *Scotch Whisky* case.[42] The case concerned plans by the Scottish government to introduce a minimum unit alcohol price, for the purposes of protecting human health. Whether 'protecting human health' is a goal that would permit a violation of Article 34 TFEU, we will consider in Section 11.4. For our current purposes, what matters is whether a minimum unit alcohol price is prohibited by Article 34 TFEU.

The way the Scottish unit price legislation worked, alcoholic beverages with a higher alcohol content would have to be sold at a higher price by retailers—regardless of how much it cost to produce the beverage in question. The legislation was challenged by alcohol producers from several EU countries, as they would lose the ability to sell their 'cheaper to produce' alcoholic beverages at prices which were actually 'cheaper' in Scotland.

The CJEU considered how Article 34 TFEU applied to the minimum unit alcohol price plans, and concluded that 'that legislation is capable of hindering the access to the United Kingdom market of alcoholic drinks that are lawfully marketed in Member States other than the United Kingdom . . . , and constitutes therefore a measure having an equivalent effect to a quantitative restriction within the meaning of Article 34 TFEU'.[43] This is similar to what it did in *Gourmet*, where it also avoided having to consider how Article 34 TFEU would apply to a particular 'selling arrangement' . . . by simply not declaring it a 'selling arrangement'.

What do you make of the judgment in *Scotch Whisky*? Do you think that the approach taken by the CJEU is appropriate in light of the internal market's overall functioning—or should the *Keck* test have applied, thus making it easier for the Scottish government to regulate for health concerns?

The recent twist in the case law seems to suggest that *Keck* may be 'dead': after all, selling arrangements can hinder 'market access' in the same way that product requirements can . . . depending on how *market access* is defined. Some critics have argued that rather than clarify an arbitrary distinction made in *Keck*, this 'market access' test has simply confused the operation of Article 34 TFEU further.[44] Unfortunately, we simply cannot be sure that

[42] Case C-333/14 *Scotch Whisky* ECLI:EU:C:2015:845. [43] *Scotch Whisky*, para 32.
[44] See, eg, Jukka Snell, 'The Notion of Market Access: A Concept or a Slogan?' (2010) 47 CMLRev 437; Laurence Gormley, 'Inconsistencies and Misconceptions in the Free Movement of Goods' (2015) 40 ELRev 925.

Keck is gone, and so the 'legally safe' approach to be taken at this point when considering if a national measure is contrary to Article 34 TFEU is two-tier:

1. Is it caught by *Keck*? (eg, is it a product requirement, or a discriminatory selling arrangement?)
2. If not . . . does it otherwise hinder 'market access'?

Discussing the scenario

Consider the Slovak advertising rules described in the scenario. Would these be caught by a *Keck* examination? What about by a 'market access' examination? Which is easiest to demonstrate, do you think?

11.3.5 MEEs and exports

The vast majority of the CJEU's case law on free movement of goods concerns Article 34 TFEU, not Article 35 TFEU, for the simple reason that most Member States are keen to *promote* rather than *restrict* exports. Both quantitative restrictions and measures having equivalent effects to those are thus rarely applied to exports, but a few CJEU cases have come up that clarify how Article 35 TFEU works.

A recent example showing how Article 35 TFEU operates is *Gysbrechts*.[45] In that case, a Belgian consumer protection law prohibited vendors from requesting credit card details from purchasers *before* their statutory right to withdraw from the contract had expired. This would mean that a customer who defaulted on the payment would have the goods in hand already before the payment was actually requested; and that legal proceedings would be necessary in order to either retrieve the goods or demand the payment. However, pursuing those legal proceedings against a consumer in another Member State would be highly complex and costly—and so in practice, goods that were being exported were being discriminated against, as this particular rule disadvantaged those vendors exporting to another Member State much more than those selling in Belgium itself.

The CJEU here declared that this Belgian law was indirectly discriminatory against exports, and thus qualified as an MEE under Article 35 TFEU. Both directly and indirectly discriminatory measures that negatively affect exports are consequently caught by Article 35TFEU, even if they will rarely occur. However, much as is true for all violations of Article 34 TFEU, there may be a possibility to justify a derogation from Article 35 TFEU—and, as we will now explore, the limitations set on national regulatory practice are not *as* absolute as either the CJEU or the Court's case law on MEEs and 'market access' would suggest.

[45] Case C-205/07 *Gysbrechts* ECLI:EU:C:2008:730.

11.4 Exceptions to free movement of goods

The EU rules on the free movement of goods are, not least because of the CJEU's case law, expansive—but they are not limitless. The EU does not *forbid* Member States from regulating products or taxing them; it simply requires them to have appropriate reasons *for* introducing product regulations and taxes that have an impact on trade between the Member States because they affect domestic and imported products differently. We will now explore the conditions under which Member States can *derogate* from the rules on the free movement of goods, by looking at the different justifications for restricting free movement of goods and how the CJEU assesses whether restrictions are proportionate.

11.4.1 Justifying discriminatory taxation

As discussed in Section 11.2.1, the Article 30 TFEU ban on customs charges, bar the limited exceptions set out, is absolute; there is no justification possible for the introduction of a customs charge.

The same is not true for discriminatory internal taxation, however. Article 110 TFEU does not outlaw *different* taxation, even where this has a differential impact on imports versus domestic products. What the Member States need to do, in order to justify a discriminatory internal tax, is demonstrate that the motivation underpinning that tax is a legitimate one.

We have little case law where Member States have successfully argued that their differential tax scheme is motivated by legitimate policy concerns. A rare example of a successful 'defence' of a domestic tax policy is *Chemial Farmaceutici*. Here, Italy applied different taxes to ethyl alcohol depending on how it was produced: the synthetic form, produced from oil, was taxed higher.[46] The reason for the differential tax was economic: oil, or petroleum, as a raw material, was being shielded from use for ethyl alcohol production, as Italy thought there were more important economic uses for petroleum. The CJEU here indicated that this was *in principle* permissible, provided that the design of the differential tax scheme met three conditions:

1) The tax scheme must differentiate on *objective* criteria (eg, specific qualities of the good, or its production process);
2) The differentiation must pursue legitimate objectives (whether economic or otherwise); and
3) The detailed rules under which the tax scheme operates must avoid any form of discrimination against similar imports, or any form of protection of competing domestic products.[47]

[46] Case 140/79 *Chemial Farmaceutici* ECLI:EU:C:1981:1. [47] Ibid, paras 14–15.

Chemial satisfied those criteria: a legitimate industrial policy was being pursued by Italy, and the measures impacted on Italian 'synthetic ethyl alcohol' producers in the same way as they did on non-Italian 'synthetic ethyl alcohol' producers. The fact that there were very few Italian producers did not matter; the fact that a legitimate policy goal was being pursued meant that the differential tax regime was justifiable, according to the CJEU.

A further example of how differential taxes can be justifiable if they pursue legitimate policy aims concerns environmental measures: for example, a hypothetical national regime under which cars are taxed differentially not because of their horsepower, but rather because of how polluting they are, would not find itself in violation of Article 110 TFEU, as long as the taxation scheme was not designed in such a way as to 'protect' domestic car production.[48]

While, *prima facie*, Article 110 TFEU thus seems to rule out any internal taxation that may affect more imports than it does exports, the CJEU has taken a pragmatic approach to justifying different taxation schemes, leaving slightly more national autonomy in place for the Member States than the strict wording of Article 110 TFEU would suggest.

Discussing the scenario

Consider the taxes applied by Italy in the scenario at the start of the chapter. Do you think any of these can be justified? If so, on what grounds?

11.4.2 Justifying quantitative restrictions

Unlike the Article 30 TFEU ban on customs duties, Articles 34 and 35 TFEU were not drafted to be absolutes. The TFEU itself thus contains a possibility for states to derogate from the overarching obligation to enable free movement of goods, where they can justify this, in Article 36 TFEU.

However, this is no longer the only way in which *certain* types of derogations from free movement of goods obligations can be justified. As the CJEU has further developed the concept of MEEs, and thus captured more and more national regulation with Article 34 TFEU, it has compensated for this reach into national competences by making it possible for the Member States to defend their regulatory choices on grounds *not* expressly stated in the Treaties.

We will first consider Article 36 TFEU and how it applies to Articles 34 and 35 TFEU, and then consider the CJEU-developed justifications for derogations from the free movement of goods obligations.

Article 36 TFEU

When a national regulatory measure is captured by Article 34 TFEU, it can be 'excused' if it satisfies the conditions set out in Article 36 TFEU:

[48] See, concerning actual environmental measures, Case C-132/88 *Commission v Greece* ECLI:EU:C:1990:165.

Article 36 TFEU (emphasis added)

The provisions of Articles 34 and 35 shall not preclude prohibitions or restrictions on imports, exports or goods in transit justified on grounds of **public morality, public policy** or **public security**; the protection of **health** and life of humans, animals or plants; the protection of national treasures possessing artistic, historic or archaeological value; or the protection of industrial and commercial property. **Such prohibitions or restrictions shall not, however, constitute a means of arbitrary discrimination or a disguised restriction on trade between Member States.**

The application of Article 36 TFEU is not automatic, however. The CJEU will assess whether a measure falls within the derogations listed in Article 36 TFEU, which are finite, and will also apply the general principle of proportionality to the measure in place. In short, to 'survive' having violated Article 34 or Article 35 TFEU, a national measure must be **justifiable on the grounds listed in Article 36 TFEU**, *and* it must be **proportionate**, meaning suitable to the objective stated and the least restrictive of trade possible.[49] The most regularly relied upon grounds are **public morality**, **public policy/security**, and **public health**. In all cases, the burden of proof in relying on Article 36 TFEU justifications lies with the Member State that has infringed Article 34 or Article 35 TFEU.

Article 36 TFEU can be relied upon by the Member States *regardless* of whether a national measure is directly or indirectly discriminatory. The only condition limiting its application, if a measure falls within the grounds listed in Article 36, is that any measure adopted should not constitute a means of 'arbitrary discrimination' or 'a disguised restriction' on trade. In short this means that where a national measure is in practice expressly protective of domestic goods at the expense of imports, it will fail even if it falls within the Article 36 TFEU justifications.

There are good examples of a Member State relying on **public morality** to justify product import bans, and two of these involve UK laws on importing pornographic materials. The overarching principle applied by the CJEU is that it is for the Member States themselves to determine what does and does not fit with public moral standards in their territory—but application of that standard should not affect imports more harshly than similar domestic products.

In *Henn & Darby*, the UK successfully argued that it had imposed a UK-wide ban on the import of pornography for public morality reasons—even though the possession of pornographic materials was not itself absolutely illegal in the UK. The CJEU based this finding on the fact that there was in reality no market for pornographic materials within the UK, and as such, the measure did not 'arbitrarily discriminate' against imports.[50]

Conversely, in the later *Conegate* case, a shipment of life-size inflatable dolls from Germany was seized by UK customs authorities sceptical of the claim that they were for window displays.[51] Again, the UK government relied on a public morality defence in justifying this breach of Article 34 TFEU—but here, the CJEU proved less persuaded, largely because inflatable life-size dolls were legally manufactured and marketed throughout

[49] For more on proportionality, see Chapters 4 and 5.

[50] Case 34/79 *Henn & Darby* ECLI:EU:C:1979:295.

[51] Case 121/85 *Conegate* ECLI:EU:C:1986:114.

the UK: as there *was* legal trade in such dolls, the imports were arbitrarily discriminated against, and so the UK's Article 36 TFEU defence failed.

Public policy has been interpreted with purposeful limitation by the CJEU: it has the potential to cover *anything* that a Member State wishes to pursue in a regulatory sense, but the CJEU has made clear that it would not accept such an interpretation.[52] In practice, public policy and public security tend to be argued and considered together in cases before the CJEU—with public security being the easier to argue, as it is a clearer concept. However, even public security defences have failed more often than they have succeeded: a rare example of the CJEU accepting a public security justification is *Campus Oil*, where Ireland required importers of petrol to purchase a set percentage of their requirements from an Irish state-owned oil company at fixed prices. While agreeing that this contravened Article 34 TFEU, Ireland argued that the measure was essential for maintaining Ireland's own oil-refining capacity, which was a crucial Irish security interest. The CJEU agreed that 'in light of the seriousness of the consequences that an interruption in supplies of petroleum products may have for a country's existence, the aim of ensuring a minimum supply of petroleum products at all times is . . . capable of constituting an objective covered by the concept of public security'.[53]

Public health is a little different from the other Article 36 TFEU justification grounds, in that it is easier for the CJEU to make an objective determination on whether there is a health risk justifying any regulation, and, if so, whether that regulation is then proportionate to the risk posed. Unlike public morality, which is a subjective country-specific matter, risks to health can be assessed using scientific evidence in many cases. It is for that reason that the CJEU tends to be a little stricter in considering whether measures are *genuinely* taken to protect public health, or if they are disguised restrictions on trade that have as their ultimate purpose the protection of domestic industry. As such, in *Newcastle Disease*, the CJEU determined that a UK ban on imports of chicken was in practice motivated by commercial factors more than a genuine fear that French chickens would carry 'Newcastle disease' and thus hurt public health.[54]

Where there is debate in the scientific community as to the presence of a risk to health, the CJEU tends to side with a Member State's judgement, but nonetheless will require a measure adopted for health protection to be proportionate. That said, the fact that different Member States operate different levels of public health protection has been accepted by the CJEU; measures in one Member State regarding the import of cigarettes are consequently not incapable of being justified *just because* other Member States are adopting less stringent measures.

Article 36 TFEU justifications, in large part because they can be used to excuse both *directly discriminatory* and *indirectly discriminatory* measures, are consequently construed very strictly. The CJEU interprets the main grounds listed in Article 36 TFEU narrowly, and even where measures appear to correspond to those grounds of public morality/policy/security, they nonetheless cannot represent disguised restrictions on trade or be disproportionate. They are, as such, treated as genuinely *rare* exceptions to Articles 34 and 35 TFEU, as the alternative would be that the free movement of goods could be very easily hindered by the Member States.

[52] Case 113/80 *Commission v Ireland* (*Foreign Marks*) ECLI:EU:C:1981:139; Case 229/83 *Leclerc* ECLI:EU:C:1985:1.

[53] Case 72/83 *Campus Oil* ECLI:EU;C:1984:256, para 35.

[54] Case 40/82 *Commission v UK* (*Newcastle Disease*) ECLI:EU:C:1984:33.

Discussing the scenario

Consider the actions of Spain, Romania, and Belgium as set out in Aoife's email. Do you think they can be justified under Article 36 TFEU?

CJEU-developed justifications

As we saw in Section 11.3.2, the CJEU significantly broadened the range of measures that would be caught by Article 34 TFEU when it decided *Cassis* and established the principle of mutual recognition. However, the CJEU was not oblivious to what it had done, and in the *Cassis* judgment itself recognized that a lot of trade regulation, while it might have trade-restrictive effects, served legitimate purposes.[55]

Case 4/75 *Cassis* (emphasis added)

Obstacles to movement within the [EU] resulting from disparities between the national laws relating to the marketing of . . . products . . . must be accepted in so far as those provisions may be recognised as being **necessary** in order to satisfy **mandatory requirements** relating in particular to the effectiveness of fiscal supervision, the protection of public health, the fairness of commercial transactions and the defence of the consumer.

Mandatory requirements are what the CJEU calls those justifications that are not set out in Article 36 TFEU, but instead can justify *indirectly* discriminatory derogations from Articles 34 and 35 TFEU. The key condition set by the CJEU is that the restriction of free movement of goods must be necessary, which means that in its case law it has examined both the 'requirement' stated and whether the restriction put in place in light of that mandatory requirement is proportionate. *Cassis* itself sets out several examples of mandatory requirements, including consumer protection and the protection of public health, but the list in *Cassis* is not finite, and the CJEU has accepted, for example, environmental protection as a mandatory requirement in other case law.[56]

Discussing the scenario

Which of the national measures highlighted in Aoife's email do you think are caught by Article 34 TFEU, but are *indirectly* discriminatory? Can you think of a mandatory requirement that may justify them?

[55] The 'free movement of goods' concept of 'mandatory requirements' has analogues in free movement of services, freedom of establishment, and free movement of persons. See Chapters 12 and 14.

[56] Case 302/86 *Commission v Denmark* (*Container Recycling*) ECLI:EU:C:1988:421; *Walloon Waste* (n 3).

The case law on consumer protection as a mandatory requirement is a helpful illustration of both how mandatory requirements work *and* how the CJEU applies the principle of proportionality to assessments of mandatory requirements. In the German *Beer Purity Laws* case, a domestic law laid down that beer could only be marketed as 'beer' in Germany if it was made of specific ingredients. This indirectly discriminated against foreign beer producers, whose products were most likely to contain *different* ingredients. Germany attempted to justify the law by arguing that it was necessary for the protection of German consumers, who associated 'beer' with the specific ingredients in the law. However, the CJEU found that the relevant consumer interests could be protected via less trade-restrictive means, such as compulsory labelling of beer that had *different* ingredients: this would impose a cost on those exporting beer to Germany, but would not *stop* trade, whereas the 'beer' law did.[57] The CJEU came to similar conclusions regarding *Rau* and the shape of margarine butter packaging, where labelling would have been sufficient to protect the consumer.

Pause for reflection

What do you think about the idea that consumers do not need to be protected by product bans when products can simply be labelled? Who should make that determination, in your view—the EU or the Member States?

Public health is an interesting mandatory requirement, in that it is *also* one of the grounds for a justification of directly discriminatory restrictions under Article 36 TFEU. In practice, what we find is that the CJEU is willing to consider both directly and indirectly discriminatory measures under a 'public health' justification ground, and will take a similar approach in either case. As such, in the *Beer Laws* case, German domestic law also forbade the use of additives in beer that could be marketed in Germany—and Germany attempted to justify this on public health grounds. The CJEU did not explicitly consider whether the rule was discriminatory or not before concluding that it was disproportionate and thus could not benefit from a 'public health' justification.[58]

A final interesting set of examples of mandatory requirements being raised by a Member State and being considered by the CJEU concerns the Brenner transport corridor in Austria. First, in *Schmidberger*, an environmental group organized a demonstration that resulted in the closing off of part of the A13 motorway.[59] Austria accepted that this infringed Article 34 TFEU, as it paused the movement of goods into Austria—but justified its decision to permit the demonstrations on the ground of the fundamental rights to freedom of expression and assembly. The CJEU accepted this as a justification, and found that allowing the motorway to be closed was proportionate, as the aims of the demonstration could not be met via other measures that would prove less restrictive of trade. Secondly, in *Brenner Motorway*, the Austrian government introduced a ban on

[57] *Beer Purity Laws*, para 35. [58] *Beer Laws*, para 43.

[59] Case C-112/00 *Schmidberger* ECLI:EU:C:2003:333, also discussed in Chapter 9.

lorries of a set weight using a specific part of the A12 motorway.[60] Again, this was a violation of Article 34 TFEU, but one that Austria tried to justify on environmental grounds. Here, the CJEU accepted the justification, but did not find the measure taken to be proportionate, as Austria had not considered achieving its environmental goals through 'measures less restrictive' of freedom of movement. The key to successful reliance on mandatory requirements is thus primarily adopting a truly necessary measure—there are many mandatory requirements possible, but most measures taken in light of them will be deemed disproportionate if less trade-restrictive alternatives appear possible.

Discussing the scenario

Consider all the scenarios in Aoife's email that entail violations of Article 34 TFEU, but that you think can be justified (via Article 36 TFEU or mandatory requirements). Are the measures taken by these Member States proportionate? Consider possible alternatives that could have been taken.

11.5 Brexit and free movement of goods

Finally, it is important for us to consider how Brexit may impact on the movement of goods between the UK and the EU. On 31 January 2020, the UK left the EU and entered a 'transition period', as negotiated with the EU. We will thus briefly explore what the Withdrawal Agreement sets out, both generally and specifically in the Protocol on Ireland/Northern Ireland, and then consider what may come *after* the transition period—whether it be a 'future relationship' resembling the aims set out in the Political Declaration, or something else entirely.

11.5.1 The Withdrawal Agreement

Under the terms of the October 2019 Withdrawal Agreement, free movement of goods will continue to operate across the UK as it does now[61] until the end of 2020—or possibly the end of 2021 or 2022, if the parties to the agreement opt to extend transition.[62]

11.5.2 The Protocol on Ireland/Northern Ireland

Unlike most of the Withdrawal Agreement, which represents a temporary agreement for the purposes of transitioning to the next relationship, the Protocol on Ireland/Northern Ireland as revised in October 2019 sets out a 'final' form of the relationship between the UK and the EU as it involves Northern Ireland.[63]

[60] Case C-320/03 *Commission v Austria* (*Brenner Motorway*) ECLI:EU:C:2005:684.

[61] Withdrawal Agreement, Article 4.

[62] Withdrawal Agreement, Articles 126 and 132; note that the EU (Withdrawal Agreement) Act 2020, s 33, prohibits UK representatives from asking for an extension as a matter of domestic law—though as is true for all Acts of Parliament, this can obviously be amended if an extension is desired after all.

[63] The other major exception to the temporary nature of the Withdrawal Agreement is Part 2 on Citizens' Rights, which we discuss in Chapters 12 and 13.

The remainder of the UK will be leaving the single market for goods after the transition period ends, per the intentions stated in the Political Declaration—but Northern Ireland, on account of the significant political, social, and cultural weight attached to having an open border between the Republic of Ireland and Northern Ireland, will not. Purely from the perspective of free movement of goods, this has a number of consequences for UK law as it will apply to Northern Ireland:

- Northern Ireland will *legally* be in a customs union with the UK, but *practically* will operate the same customs rules as the EU does, and as such, there will be no customs duties charged on goods travelling between Northern Ireland and Ireland. This, in effect, preserves the working of Article 30 TFEU, and thus makes it unnecessary for customs checks to take place at that border.[64]
- As for non-tariff barriers, the Protocol also ensures that goods manufactured, and cleared to enter the market, in Northern Ireland will be treated as compliant with EU standards—and thus benefit from *Cassis*-style **mutual recognition**. The way this is made to work in practice means that a lot of EU law on product standards as well as the general principle of mutual recognition will continue to apply in Northern Ireland after Brexit. The functioning of this EU law will continue to be overseen by the CJEU, as well as by the Joint Committee established by the Withdrawal Agreement for the purpose of monitoring the agreement.[65]
- However, Great Britain may *not* continue to apply the EU customs rules or the 'internal market' product standards, and will not be covered by mutual recognition the way that Northern Ireland will be. It has opted to sacrifice this kind of access to the EU, which would more or less mean staying in the single market for goods, primarily so that it is free to conclude trade agreements on its own terms with other countries.
- In order to ensure that products from Great Britain do not enter the EU in violation of EU law (either by not having the correct duty paid, or by not complying with EU manufacturing standards) once the transition period ends, they will be checked when they travel from Great Britain *to* Northern Ireland. This, in practice, will mean a functional border that separates Northern Ireland from Great Britain in the Irish Sea, albeit with the UK and EU making commitments to try to maintain as 'light-touch' a border there as possible.[66]

11.5.3 The future relationship

The end of 2020 (or 2021/2022) thus finds us with Great Britain leaving the single market, and Northern Ireland staying in it, for the purposes of goods. The Political Declaration makes it clear that the UK and the EU aim to conclude a free trade agreement during the 'transition' set up by the Withdrawal Agreement—and that the core aim of this trade agreement will be to remove all tariffs on goods between the parties.[67] That would mean that in terms of customs duties charged, little will change; but obviously there will be wholesale changes to how Great British products will be received in the EU. There will be no 'assumption' that UK goods, lawfully manufactured and produced there, comply with

[64] Protocol, Articles 4 and 5. [65] Protocol, Articles 7 and 12. [66] Protocol, Article 6(2).
[67] Political Declaration, Articles 16–18.

the standards in any Member State—and so whether or not goods travel through Northern Ireland, they will face checks of some kind, as well as significantly more paperwork. In the case where no new free trade agreement is concluded, UK goods are also likely to face customs duties when entering the EU—which means more costs, and even more paperwork.

Conversely, Great Britain will no longer have to consider whether its regulations comply with Articles 34 and 35 TFEU, and so it can change the rules on how products are manufactured and sold without considering if this might infringe the rights of one of its EU neighbours. Whether the gains to be made abroad through such regulatory changes will compensate for the loss of access to the EU markets, and whether the UK will choose to actually pursue radical product standard divergence from the EU, remains to be seen. As with everything Brexit-related, we can at most say that the access of UK goods to the EU market is likely to become more complicated after the transition period—but that the specific shape of future access is yet to be determined.

11.6 In conclusion

The free movement of goods is at the heart of the internal market project. Border taxes were always prohibited in full—without even a possibility of justifying them. Internal taxation and anything else that blocks trade is in principle *also* forbidden under the Treaties—but here, the CJEU and the Member States have managed a degree of compromise that means that certain domestic regulatory rules *can* survive because their importance and proportionality outweigh the impact that they have on free trade. The work done by the CJEU on Article 34 TFEU in particular remains of great interest: it went through a period of great liberalization and restriction of the rights of the Member States, before undergoing a U-turn of sorts in *Keck*, but now seems to be on a slow expansionary track again where the key question it asks of any measure taken by a Member State is 'how does this affect market access for competitors from other Member States?'

We will see when we explore the other 'freedoms' that the justifications highlighted in this chapter resurface elsewhere in the Treaties, whether CJEU-developed or contained in the Treaties themselves. The CJEU's case law on the justifications in particular tends to follow the same broad trends, and in a way is what ties EU 'internal market law' together. That said, the attitudes of the Member States to the movement of persons, have been rather distinct from their acceptance that mutual recognition and harmonization of product standards were necessary to create an internal market where goods flowed freely. Bear the differences in mind when you read Chapters 12 and 13, especially in light of Brexit—as it was not the EU's laws on the movement of goods that proved fundamentally problematic to the UK.

Discussing the scenario

Use the material in this chapter to write a response to Aoife on behalf of the legal department of Belfast Fizz Ltd. Treat each of the countries mentioned in her email as setting out a specific scenario, and explain how EU law applies to that scenario.

A sample approach to a response can be found online.

Key points

The CJEU's development of the Treaty rules establishing the free movement of goods has undergone various stages of development, but even now, there are a series of sequential questions that the CJEU investigates to see if a measure is prohibited under Article 34 TFEU and if it can be justified under Article 36 TFEU or the 'mandatory requirements' doctrine. The flowchart in Figure 11.2 summarizes what these questions are, and can be used by anyone to determine if a restriction on movement of goods is permissible under the Treaties:

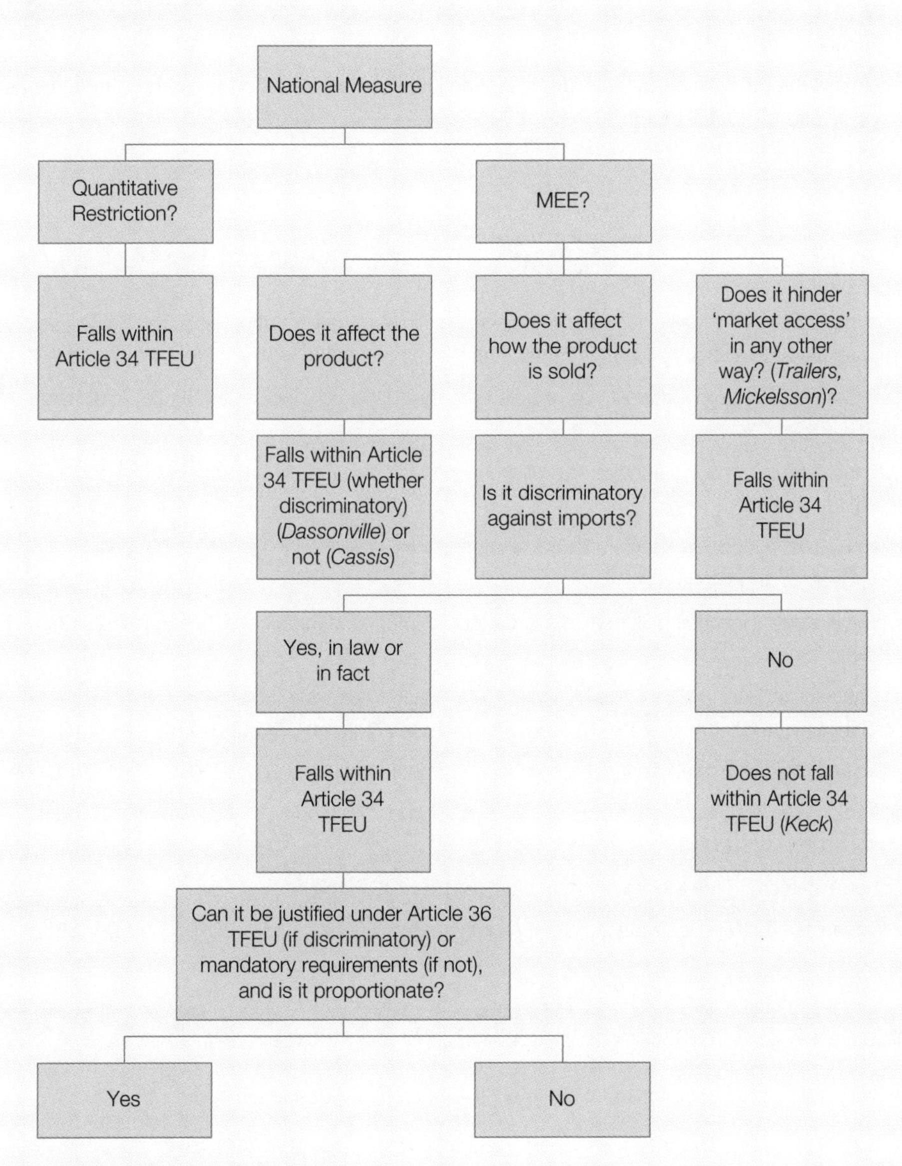

Figure 11.2 Articles 34 and 36 TFEU

Assess your learning

1. What does Article 30 TFEU cover? Are there any exceptions to it? (See Section 11.2.1.)
2. What are the differences between Article 30 TFEU and Article 110 TFEU? (See Section 11.2.)
3. What is a 'measure having an equivalent effect to a quantitative restriction'? (See Section 11.3.2.)
4. How does 'mutual recognition' in free movement of goods work? (See Section 11.3.2.)
5. What do the *Keck* test and the 'market access' test mean for Article 34 TFEU cases? (See Sections 11.3.3–11.3.4.)
6. What is the difference between Treaty-based justifications and mandatory requirements as justifications? (See Section 11.4.)

Further reading

Catherine Barnard and Niall O'Connor, 'Runners and Riders: The horsemeat scandal, EU law and multi-level enforcement' (2017) 76(1) CLJ 116.

Niamh Dunne, 'Minimum Alcohol Pricing: Balancing the "Essentially Incomparable" in Scotch Whisky' (2018) 81(5) MLR 874.

Lawrence Gormley, 'Inconsistencies and Misconceptions in the Free Movement of Goods' (2015) 40(6) ELRev 925.

Jorgen Hettne, 'Standards, Barriers to Trade and EU Internal Market Rules: Need for a new approach' (2017) 44(4) LIEI 409.

Thomas Horsley, 'Unearthing Buried Treasures: Art.34 TFEU and the exclusionary rules' (2012) 37 ELRev 734.

Max Jansson and Harri Kalimo, 'De Minimis Meets "Market Access": Transformations in the substance – and the syntax – of EU free movement law?' (2014) 51 CMLRev 523.

Barend van Leeuwen, 'Market Access, the New Approach and Private Law' (2019) 27(2) ERPL 269.

Robert Schütze, 'Re-Reading Dassonville: Meaning and Understanding in the History of European Law' (2018) 24(6) Eur Law J 376.

Stephen Weatherill, 'Free Movement of Goods' (2012) 61 ICLQ 541.

Pal Wenneras and Ketil Boe Moen, 'Selling Arrangements, Keeping Keck' (2010) 35 ELRev 387.

Online resources

Visit www.oup.com/he/demars1e for a sample approach to discussing the quote.

12

Free movement of workers

Context for this chapter

Bristol, 14 March 2019

Dear Ingrid,

So—a lot has happened since I last emailed you! Sorry it's been so long, but I think you'll get why once you read the rest of this! ☺

You know how I went on vacation to Barcelona last November? Right, so, I kind of met someone there; his name is Andreas and he's the head chef at this really posh tapas restaurant. Johnny knew him from a few years ago and introduced us and well, four months later . . . and I'm thinking very hard about moving to Spain to be with him.

Of course, figuring out how that's going to work has been a nightmare, not least of all because of Brexit, even if that hasn't happened yet. I can't speak more than about seven sentences of Spanish, and according to Andreas, Spanish law would require me to be fluent in order to teach (even if I were to teach English!) so I'm not sure what I'd be doing—probably nothing for a while, except cashing in unemployment benefit while I learn Spanish! (And no, I won't go back to protesting against private education—one time getting arrested for defacing government property as a 19-year-old was more than enough!)

Andreas has offered to move here instead but that seems stupid for any number of reasons. Sure, he has connections with restaurants in London—a friend of a friend has already told him he's got a job if he moves over, so that side of it is easy. But he's got a son (Sergio) from a previous marriage, and while he's got sole custody, I'm not sure either of us want to make a seven-year-old move to the UK if he doesn't speak English or know anyone here. Plus, Andreas has been asking me about how child benefit works and I have no idea if they would qualify for it. Maybe they can come visit me for an extended time and then we can all move to Spain once I speak some Spanish . . . ?

I thought you might be able to give me some advice, cause you've been through this with Mitchell, haven't you? You two got married in the US and then you moved to the UK from Germany for work and he came to be with you. But I remember you saying that was also an EU thing even though he's American . . . right? So was it easy to get Mitchell to the UK, and is it the same thing

→

→

as Andreas and Sergio would have to do? And what about after Jeremy was born, when you all went back to Germany? Was that an EU thing as well, even though you're German? I know that I'm basically asking for legal advice for free, haha—please don't charge me your normal hourly rate!

Anyway, I'm not looking for an urgent answer—I've got some saving to do if I am the one to give up my job here and move to Spain, and Andreas would have to sell his restaurant and there'd be some stuff to arrange with Sergio's mother, so this isn't going to happen tomorrow. Probably still a year or so away—maybe 2020 or 2021. So if you want to take six months to get back to me (sorry again it's taken me so long!) that's actually not a problem at all.

Hope you and Mitchell and Jeremy (who must be getting so big by now!) are all well, and I won't let it be this long again—pictures of A attached, just in case you're curious!

Much love,
Emma

12.1 **Introduction**

Three of the four fundamental freedoms of the EU are clearly economic in nature: capital, goods, and services. These all represent aspects of business that directly help establish a single market. The last of the four freedoms is fundamentally of a different nature, even if its origins are also rooted in 1950s ideas about what would make the internal *market* work. Free movement of persons is both the most personal and the most controversial of the four fundamental freedoms. The 2016 UK referendum showed that concerns about EU nationals being able to come without any restriction to the UK and access both British jobs and British benefits were one of the key drivers in the vote to leave the EU.[1]

This chapter will explore the 'free moment of workers', which was where free movement of persons law *began* under the Treaty of Rome. A detailed look at the rights and obligations of EU 'workers' will help us consider both whether the rules the EU has developed here are unreasonably generous, as they do not require a lot of 'actual work' in order to grant rights, and in what respects they differ from the rules for *non-workers*—which we move on to consider in Chapter 13. The CJEU's case law on the free movement of workers has been as instrumental as secondary legislation in making it a usable status in practice: the Treaty provisions set out a bar on discrimination and a bar on entry refusals, but the EU legislature and the CJEU ensured that those moving to work in another Member State would not actually *lose out*—and in some situations, actually have more rights than EU nationals who have not exercised their Treaty rights to free movement.

The scenario presented at the start of the chapter allows for an exploration of the EU's free movement of workers rules. Throughout the chapter, different dimensions of the scope of Article 45 TFEU will be raised, and you will be asked to consider Emma's situation (as well as Ingrid's situation) in light of those. This will make it possible to consider

[1] See, eg, http://lordashcroftpolls.com/2016/06/how-the-united-kingdom-voted-and-why; https://www.bsa.natcen.ac.uk/media/39149/bsa34_brexit_final.pdf; https://migrationobservatory.ox.ac.uk/resources/reports/decade-immigration-british-press/.

both if the CJEU has made the concept of the 'worker', and what rights the 'worker' has, uncomfortably broad—and what the effect of Brexit will be on the status of current and future EU 'workers'. This will prepare us for considering more generally whether EU free movement of persons law is unduly generous in Chapter 13.

It is worth understanding before we proceed further in this chapter that the terminology surrounding free movement of persons (whether workers or not) is complicated, and different countries tend to adopt different terms to mean the same thing. For the sake of clarity, the following terms will be used to discuss 'persons' throughout Chapters 12, 13, and 14:

- An **EU national** is anyone who holds the nationality of any of the Member States. They can also be referred to as an **EU citizen**—as EU citizenship is a status that is given only to EU nationals.
- Any EU national who moves from their **home** Member State (the Member State of their nationality) to a **host** Member State (any other Member State) is **exercising free movement rights.** They will be referred to as **a mobile EU national.** It is important to note that a mobile EU national will not be referred to as an **EU migrant**. You will see this alternative term used very commonly in any reading you do about EU citizenship, but this book avoids using it because, technically, **EU migration law** is the law that deals with non-EU nationals who move *into* the EU. That is a very separate area of law from **EU free movement law**.
- The term **third-country national** or **TCN** is used to refer to any family members of EU nationals who are themselves *not* an EU national—ie, where a French national is married to an Australian national, the Australian is a TCN. TCNs themselves do not have free movement rights—instead, their rights derive from their relationship to the EU national.
- Finally, it is important to remember that **UK nationals were EU nationals until 31 January 2020,** because the UK was a Member State until then. We consider what their status and rights are after 31 January 2020 in Section 12.3.

Finally: there are two pieces of secondary legislation that set out the rights and obligations held by EU nationals who engage in free movement. These are the following, and will be referred to by the bolded abridged names:

- Directive 2004/38/EC—**The Citizenship Directive**
- Regulation 492/2011—**The Workers' Regulation**

Discussing the scenario

Identify the EU nationals and third-country nationals in Emma's scenario at the start of the chapter. Who are the mobile EU nationals in each of the scenarios she sets out? (Remember she was writing in 2019!)

12.2 Free movement of workers

The free movement of *some* EU nationals was already envisaged in the Treaty of Rome. Specifically, in the 1950s, the Northern European EEC members accepted the urging from Italy to introduce free movement for those with job offers. Italy's reasoning was simple:

it suffered from significant unemployment, and was keen to send Italians with work permits to the other Member States.[2] Of course, the wording says it all: it was free movement of *workers*, not of *people*. The movement rights were consequently dependent on the existence of a job offer—but that was also *all* they required.

However, it did not take long for the Member States to realize that simply making it legal for someone to move from one Member State to another, without bureaucratic requirements like visas, did not mean that workers *would* move. In their home Member State, EU nationals were normally beneficiaries of a wide variety of public services and social security schemes; and their family members also benefited from these. Moving to a different country usually meant giving most of that safety net up—so why would anyone move, even if it was administratively *easy* to do so?

From the 1960s onwards, the EU legislature consequently attempted to eliminate as many possible deterrents from free movement of workers as possible.[3] By the 1970s, EU secondary law ensured that when an EU national moved to another Member State for the sake of employment, they would not find themselves without social security coverage. Once employed, they would become part of the social security system of their host State on equal terms with host State national workers[4]—and were they to move elsewhere, their social security build-up would move with them.[5] To encourage free movement further, the direct family members of workers were given permission to join their EU national worker family member, and became equally entitled to social security in the host State.[6] Free movement of workers, in other words, has been a priority for the EU legislature for at least five decades.

The current free movement of workers provisions are found in Articles 45–48 TFEU, with Article 45 setting out the right itself:

Article 45 TFEU (emphasis added)

1. Freedom of movement for workers shall be secured within the Union.
2. Such freedom of movement shall entail **the abolition of any discrimination based on nationality** between workers of the Member States as regards **employment, remuneration** and **other conditions of work and employment.**
3. It shall entail the right, **subject to limitations justified on grounds of public policy, public security or public health:**
   (a) to accept offers of employment actually made;
   (b) to move freely within the territory of Member States for this purpose;

→

[2] Anne-Pieter van der Mei, *Free Movement of Persons Within the European Community: Cross-Border Access to Public Benefits* (Hart, 2003) 23–4.

[3] For a critical overview, see AJ Menendez, 'European Citizenship after *Martinez Sala* and *Baumbast*: Has European law become more human but less social?' in M Maduro and L Azoulai (eds), *The Past and Future of EU Law: The Classics of EU Law Revisited on the 50th Anniversary of the Rome Treaty* (Hart, 2010) 368–72.

[4] Regulation 1612/68 of the Council of 15 October 1968 on freedom of movement for workers within the Community [1968] OJ L257/2.

[5] Regulation 1408/71 of the Council of 14 June 1971 on the application of social security schemes to employed persons and their families moving within the Community [1971] OJ L149/2.

[6] This has been the case since 1968; see Menendez (n 3) 369. These rights were also extended to the self-employed, whose position we consider in Chapter 14.

→

(c) to stay in a Member State for the purpose of employment in accordance with the provisions governing the employment of nationals of that State laid down by law, regulation or administrative action;

(d) to remain in the territory of a Member State after having been employed in that State, subject to conditions which shall be embodied in regulations to be drawn up by the Commission.

4. The provisions of this Article shall not apply to employment in the public service.

12.2.1 Personal scope of Article 45 TFEU

When mapping the scope of the 'free movement of workers', the first question we should ask is 'what is a worker'?

Unhelpfully, the Treaties do not define it; that job has largely fallen to the CJEU. It started by noting in the early 1960s that for the 'free movement of workers' to be achievable, the concept of 'worker' had to be defined in EU law rather than national law, and had to have a uniform meaning.[7] Without this, each of the EU Member States could mean something different when they described 'workers', and this would make the legal status of anyone working abroad very confusing.

Rather than providing a single definition, however, the CJEU decided to describe a 'work' relationship as having certain qualities which could apply in all Member States, regardless of whether they operate common or civil law legal systems. The first of these is **subordination**.[8] If you are a 'worker', you work *for* an employer. The alternative—where you do not work under anyone's control—is self-employment. The self-employed *also* have free movement rights, as we will see in Chapter 14, but these are covered by Article 49 TFEU.

The second is **remuneration**—if you are not getting somehow 'rewarded' or 'paid' by your employer for what you are doing, you are not a 'worker'.[9] Both of these key aspects are explained by the CJEU in *Lawrie-Blum*. Ms Lawrie-Blum, a UK national, had passed exams for a teaching qualification at a German secondary school, but the local German authorities refused to admit her to the 'preparatory service' that she needed to complete before she could sit the second batch of teaching qualification exams. The CJEU was asked if the 'preparatory service' counted as work, having been informed that in German law, those doing 'preparatory service' had the status of 'trainee teachers' and were considered civil service employees. Ms Lawrie-Blum argued that 'preparatory service' *was* work, and so she was being discriminated against on the basis of nationality in pursuing her Article 45 TFEU rights—but the German government and several lower German courts believed that an appointment to a position in a state school was not covered by the Article 45 TFEU concept of 'work'.

[7] Case 75/63 *Unger v Bedrijfsvereniging voor Detailhandel en Ambachten* ECLI:EU:C:1964:19.

[8] Case 66/85 *Lawrie-Blum v Land Baden-Württemberg* ECLI:EU:C:1986:284.

[9] Ibid.

Case 66/85 *Lawrie-Blum* ECLI:EU:C:1986:284 (emphasis added)

14. . . . Objectively defined, a 'worker' is a person who is **obliged to provide services to another in return for monetary reward** and who is **subject to the direction or control of the other person** as regards the way in which the work is done.

. . .

17. . . . The essential feature of an employment relationship . . . is that for a certain period of time **a person performs services for and under the direction of another person** in return for which he receives **remuneration**.

18. In the present case, it is clear that during the entire period of preparatory service the trainee teacher is under the direction and supervision of the school to which he is assigned. . . . The amounts which he receives may be regarded as remuneration for the services provided . . .

Trainee teachers were consequently captured by Article 45 TFEU, as they were in a subordinate relationship with their schools—and received remuneration for the teaching that they did.

The third quality that 'workers' possess requires them to satisfy a test of the *degree* of work activity engaged in. The CJEU, as such, distinguishes between, say, students who get paid to spend a single day helping out at a university open day from people who work a full (say, 36–40 hour) work-week every week. This became clear in the *Levin* case. Here, Mrs Levin—a UK national married to a non-EU national—applied for permission to reside in the Netherlands. Her request was denied, in part because she was not engaged in what Dutch law termed a 'gainful occupation'; in other words, she was not a 'worker' under EU law.

She appealed this decision, and the Dutch Council of State referred questions to the CJEU about just how much *work* was required in order for an EU national to benefit from Article 45 TFEU. The referring court noted that Mrs Levin's income from her activities fell below the Dutch minimum wage—and it asked the CJEU to clarify if this nonetheless made Mrs Levin a worker.

Case 53/81 *Levin* ECLI:EU:C:1982:105 (emphasis added)

12. . . . The meaning and scope of the terms **'worker'** and **'activity as an employed person'** should . . . be **clarified in the light of the principles of the legal order of the [EU]**.

13. In this respect it must be stressed that these concepts define the field of application of one **of the fundamental freedoms** guaranteed by the Treaty, and, as such, **may not be interpreted restrictively**.

. . .

17. It should however be stated that **whilst part-time employment is not excluded** from the field of application of the rules on freedom of movement for workers, those rules cover only the pursuit of **effective and genuine activities**, to the exclusion of **activities on such a small scale as to be regarded as purely marginal and ancillary** . . .

The CJEU consequently did not, as it could have done, declare that—for example—20 hours of work at minimum wage made someone an EU 'worker', but fewer hours, or the same hours at a lesser wage, did not. Instead, it stated that work must be '**genuine and effective**' as opposed to '**marginal and ancillary**'.[10] This is the most difficult criterion of the EU 'worker' definition, and it is where most of the case law originates. Domestic courts are the ones which, as they had to in *Levin*, make this distinction. When is part-time work genuine and effective? Does it require at least 10 hours of work a week? And what about if someone works only six hours a week, but at a high wage? The conditions set out in *Levin* mean that just about every situation of employment in which an EU national finds themselves has to be considered on a case-by-case basis.

The CJEU justified this by noting that free movement of workers is a fundamental EU right, and must be interpreted as widely as possible.[11] As a consequence, it has refused to give a definitive number of hours that is the *minimum* needed for work to be 'genuine and effective'— but it has suggested that 10 hours of employment per week would suffice.[12] Beyond this, it has also confirmed that many varieties of a-typical work result in EU worker status. Footballers are a famous example of a CJEU-confirmed worker;[13] less obvious examples are, perhaps, prostitutes (provided prostitution is legal in the relevant Member State!)[14] and trainees in a variety of contexts.[15]

The hard limits on 'genuine and effective' work are few and far between: what we know from the CJEU's case law is that in *Bettray*,[16] compulsory enrolment in a drug rehabilitation programme was not seen as 'genuine and effective' work. The key case of *Trojani*[17] is a good illustration of the difficulties in determining when work is 'genuine and effective'. Mr Trojani, a French national, resided in Belgium at a variety of camp sites and a youth hostel before being given room and board by the Salvation Army in one of their hostels—in exchange for doing a variety of odd jobs for 30 hours a week, which also resulted in him being given some pocket money. Mr Trojani applied for a Belgian 'minimum subsistence' allowance on the grounds that he in theory owed the Salvation Army 400 euros a month for his room and board. The Belgian authorities rejected his application, arguing that he was not a 'worker' under EU law, and thus not entitled to the benefit—or indeed to reside in Belgium at all. The CJEU's response is worth considering in some detail.

Case C-456/02 *Trojani* ECLI:EU:C:2004:488 (emphasis added)

20. In the present case, . . . Mr Trojani performs, for the Salvation Army and under its direction, various jobs for approximately 30 hours a week, as part of a personal reintegration programme, in return for which he receives benefits in kind and some pocket money.

21. . . . the Salvation Army has the task of receiving, accommodating and providing psycho-social assistance appropriate to the recipients in order to promote their autonomy,

→

[10] Case 53/81 *Levin v Staatssecretaris van Justitie* ECLI:EU:C:1982:105.

[11] Ibid. [12] Case C-444/93 *Megner & Scheffel* ECLI:EU:C:1995:442, para 18.

[13] Case C-415/93 *Bosman* ECLI:EU:C:1995:463.

[14] Case C-268/99 *Jany* ECLI:EU:C:2001:616.

[15] Case C-109/04 *Kranemann* ECLI:EU:C:2005:187.

[16] Case 344/87 *Bettray v Staatssecretaris van Justitie* ECLI:EU:C:1989:226.

[17] Case C-456/02 *Trojani* ECLI:EU:C:2004:488.

→

physical well-being and reintegration in society. For that purpose it must agree with each person concerned a personal reintegration programme setting out the objectives to be attained and the means to be employed to attain them.

22. Having established that the benefits in kind and money provided by the Salvation Army to Mr Trojani constitute the consideration for the services performed by him for and under the direction of the hostel, **the national court has thereby established the existence of the constituent elements of any paid employment relationship, namely subordination and the payment of remuneration.**

23. For the claimant in the main proceedings to have the status of worker, however, **the national court, in the assessment of the facts which is within its exclusive jurisdiction, would have to establish that the paid activity in question is real and genuine.**

24. The national court must in particular ascertain **whether the services actually performed by Mr Trojani are capable of being regarded as forming part of the normal labour market.** For that purpose, account may be taken of the status and practices of the hostel, the content of the social reintegration programme, and the nature and details of performance of the services.

What we see in *Trojani* is once again a very broad reading of the concept of 'worker'. As the Salvation Army instructed Mr Trojani on what 'odd jobs' he had to do for 30 hours, and gave him board and some pocket money in exchange for it, the CJEU found a relationship of subordination and remuneration in his case with ease. It then instructed the national court to examine the specific nature of the activities Mr Trojani was engaged in—only where these were 'marginal and ancillary' would Mr Trojani fall outside of the scope of Article 45 TFEU.

A final point to make about 'worker' status is that it presumes *current* employment activity that is 'genuine and effective'; but the EU legislature acknowledges that there are circumstances where employees cease being able to 'work' on a temporary basis. EU 'workers', under what is now Article 7(3) of the Citizens' Directive, retain their 'worker' status in the following situations:

- Temporary incapacity because of illness or accident (whether work-related or not);
- Involuntary unemployment after working for over a year, provided the 'worker' is registered as a job-seeker in the host Member State;
- Involuntary unemployment after working for less than a year, provided the 'worker' is registered as a job-seeker in the host Member State—'worker' status here is retained for a minimum of six months;
- Entry into vocational training, provided that training is related to the previous 'work'.

These situations are not exhaustive. In the 2012 *Saint Prix* case a pregnant French woman voluntarily quit her UK job in a nursery because when she was six months pregnant, the work became too strenuous for her.[18] She then applied for income support 11 weeks before

[18] Case C-507/12 *Saint Prix* ECLI:EU:C:2014:2007.

her due date, and was denied it because she did not meet any of the Article 7(3) criteria—she was not 'ill' (pregnancy is not an illness!) and she was not *involuntarily* unemployed. She appealed the decision until it reached the UKSC, where it was finally referred to the CJEU. The CJEU was unequivocal:

Case C-507/12 *Saint Prix* ECLI:EU:C:2014:2007 (emphasis added)

38. . . . contrary to what the United Kingdom Government contends, . . . Article 7(3) of Directive 2004/38 **[does not list] exhaustively** the circumstances in which a migrant worker who is no longer in an employment relationship may nevertheless continue to benefit from that status.

39. In the present case, it is clear from the order for reference . . . that **Ms Saint Prix was employed in the territory of the United Kingdom before giving up work**, less than three months before the birth of her child, because of the physical constraints of the late stages of pregnancy and the immediate aftermath of childbirth. **She returned to work three months after the birth of her child**, without having left the territory of that Member State during the period of interruption of her professional activity.

40. The fact that such constraints require a woman to give up work during the period needed for recovery does not, in principle, deprive her of the status of 'worker' within the meaning [of] Article 45 TFEU.

The CJEU thus continues to play a very important part in setting out the personal scope of the free movement of workers, even 60 years following the creation of the right itself.

Discussing the scenario

Consider what you have just learned. In 2019, would Emma have been a worker if she moved to Spain? What about Andreas—would he have been a worker if he had moved to the UK in 2019? Are Ingrid and Mitchell 'workers', under the Treaty definitions? Why or why not?

Job-seekers?

Initially, it would appear that the Treaty does not contemplate any protection for those trying to *become* 'workers'. Yet, the CJEU made clear in *Antonissen* in 1989 that the list of rights in Article 45(3) TFEU should not be treated as exhaustive.[19] Mr Antonissen, a Belgian national, arrived in the UK in October 1984 without a job. He was still unemployed in March 1987, when he was arrested for possession of and dealing in cocaine. When he was released on parole in December 1987, the UK moved to deport him back to Belgium. However, Mr Antonissen appealed the deportation decision, arguing that as an EU national seeking employment, he was protected by EU law from deportation on the grounds of *past* criminal behaviour.[20]

[19] Case C-292/89 *The Queen v Immigration Appeal Tribunal, ex parte Antonissen* ECLI:EU:C:1991:80.

[20] We discuss this further in section 12.2.3 and in Chapter 13.

The UK Immigration Appeal Tribunal found that he was not a worker: he had been seeking employment in the UK for a period longer than six months, and so the relevant EU provisions on the possible deportation of 'workers' did not apply to him.[21] Mr Antonissen appealed this finding before the Divisional Court, who asked the CJEU to rule on the reach of what is now Article 45 TFEU.

Case C-292/89 *The Queen v Immigration Appeal Tribunal, ex parte Antonissen* ECLI:EU:C:1991:80 (emphasis added)

12. . . . a strict interpretation of [Article 45(3) TFEU] would jeopardize the actual chances that a national of a Member State who is seeking employment will find it in another Member State, and would, as a result, make that provision ineffective.

13. It follows that [Article 45(3) TFEU]) must be interpreted as enumerating, in a non-exhaustive way, certain rights benefiting nationals of Member States in the context of the free movement of workers and that that freedom also entails the right for nationals of Member States to move freely within the territory of the other Member States and to stay there for the purposes of seeking employment.

The job-seeker has since been treated as falling within the scope of Article 45 TFEU. They do not have exactly the same benefits and rights as workers do, however. In *Antonissen*, the CJEU also found that having a *limit* on how long someone would be covered by Article 45 TFEU as a so-called 'job-seeker' was not contrary to EU law; after six months, in order to remain classed as a 'worker' under the Treaties, a job-seeker would have to 'provide evidence that [they are] continuing to seek employment and that [they have] genuine chances of being engaged'.[22]

More generally, there are limitations to the types of benefits that job-seekers are entitled to under Article 45(3) TFEU, as we will see in Section 12.2.2. They are covered by the Treaties, in other words, but are not 'equal' to workers in all ways.

12.2.2 Material scope of Article 45 TFEU

In terms of the content of the rights granted to 'workers', free movement of workers is principally concerned with two things:

- the freedom to move to engage in work;
- non-discrimination in terms of both *access to* and *exercise of* employment.

It also suggests that there are only very limited restrictions to the rights; we will consider those further in Section 12.2.3.

[21] This was, then, Directive 64/221/EC of 25 February 1964 on the co-ordination of special measures concerning the movement and residence of foreign nationals which are justified on grounds of public policy, public security or public health [1964] OJ 56/850.

[22] *Antonissen*, para 22. This has been codified in the Citizenship Directive: Article 14(4)(b) makes clear that their right to reside exists only providing they can evidence that they are 'genuinely seeking work'.

The CJEU has confirmed that Article 45(1) is both horizontally and vertically directly effective.[23] The more detailed content of Article 45(3) makes it clear that the rights of residence associated with free movement of work are unconditional. The only requirement is, indeed, that of 'work'—and even post-'work', the right to reside does not disappear. We will see in Chapter 13 that this is not how the right to reside works for all other EU nationals.

That said, the most interesting rights stemming from Article 45 TFEU are the non-discrimination rights. These require that any EU national exercising the freedom to work in another Member State must be treated *equally to* a citizen of that Member State in a comparable position. Non-discrimination applies to all hiring processes and employment conditions/benefits, but also applies to access to social security benefits and public services.

The Workers' Regulation, in Article 3, sets out several examples of discrimination in hiring processes. These include separate recruitment procedures for foreign nationals; limitations or restrictions on the advertising of vacancies; and eligibility for employment being restricted somehow (ie, by a residency requirement, such as 'you must have lived in Austria for five years', or a requirement to register with specific employment offices, like the UK's Jobcentre). Likewise, Article 7 offers examples of employment conditions and benefits that are covered by the equal treatment clause in Article 45(2) TFEU. These include conditions on pay, conditions for dismissal and reinstatement, all social and tax advantages that are linked to the employment, and access to training and re-training.[24]

Over time, the CJEU has expanded on what is meant by 'equal treatment' when it comes to both access to employment and employment conditions and benefits.

First, the CJEU has made clear that all direct discrimination is caught by Article 45(2) TFEU. Direct discrimination here means clearly separate rules for EU nationals as opposed to home nationals. An example of direct discrimination in the hiring process is *Donà*, in which an Italian national challenged an Italian law that required membership of the Italian Football Federation in order to play football professionally in Italy—but membership of the IFF was restricted to Italian nationals.[25] Another clear example is hiring quotas for foreign nationals.[26] Direct discrimination in employment conditions, meanwhile, was observed in *Marsman v Rosskamp*, where only home nationals were covered by the laws protecting disabled workers from dismissals.[27]

Indirect discrimination is sometimes harder to spot; it does not involve obvious discrimination on the basis of nationality, but rather sets out requirements that significantly disadvantage EU nationals as compared to home nationals. For example, in *Scholz*, a German law ignored employment in *other* Member States when considering job experience in a recruitment process.[28] Similarly, in *Schöning*, work in other Member States was not taken into account when considering promotions.[29] The CJEU ruled in both these cases that such

[23] Case 167/73 *Commission v France* ECLI:EU:C:1974:35 established vertical direct effect; Case C-281/98 *Angonese* ECLI:EU:C:2000:296 made clear that horizontal direct effect also applies to the non-discrimination condition in Article 45 TFEU. See Chapter 8 for more on direct effect.

[24] This has been further codified in Article 24(1) of the Citizenship Directive, which expresses that workers are entitled to equal treatment in accessing all social security and social assistance in their host Member State.

[25] Case 13/76 *Donà v Mantero* ECLI:EU:C:1976:115.

[26] *Commission v France* (n 23).

[27] Case 44/72 *Marsman v Rosskamp* ECLI:EU:C:1972:120.

[28] Case C-419/92 *Scholz v Opera Universitaria di Cagliari and Cinzia Porcedda* ECLI:EU:C:1994:62.

[29] Case C-15/96 *Schöning-Kougebetopoulou v Freie und Hansestadt Hamburg* ECLI:EU:C:1998:3.

conditions violated Article 45(2) TFEU, for the reason that ignoring activity *abroad* was significantly more likely to harm EU nationals than home nationals. Another strange but true example of indirect discrimination in employment conditions is the 1994 *O'Flynn* case, where a UK company's funeral payment plan was conditional on the funeral taking place in the UK; this again is much more likely if the person being buried is a UK national.[30]

However, the CJEU has gone further than simply looking at direct and indirect discrimination. It has interpreted Article 45(2) TFEU as also covering restrictions on free movement of workers that do not quite amount of discrimination. *Kraus*, for instance, concerned a German student who was told he could not use his UK LLM title in Germany without prior authorization. He alleged discrimination based on the fact that he had exercised his free movement rights and thus held a 'foreign' qualification. The CJEU agreed with Kraus, stating here that a measure such as requiring permission for the use of a foreign academic title is liable to *hamper or to render less attractive* the exercise by EU nationals of fundamental freedoms guaranteed by the Treaty.[31]

Bosman is perhaps the most infamous example of the CJEU's generous reading of restrictions on Article 45(2).[32] Mr Bosman was a professional footballer from Belgium who played for a Belgian club but wished to transfer to a French club. The European football transfer system at the time required that all clubs that bought players paid a transfer fee to the club the player was bought from, regardless of whether that club was in the same country or in a different European country. Mr Bosman's transfer fell through because the French club, in a lower division, was thought by the Belgian club to be insolvent, and so they did not formally process the transfer documentation. Mr Bosman brought an action against his (former) Belgian club arguing that this transfer system was contrary to the EU's rules on free movement of workers.

The transfer system was clearly *not* concerned with footballer nationality or cross-border movement per se: had Bosman wished to transfer to another Belgian club, it also applied. All the same, at Mr Bosman's insistence, the CJEU was asked to consider if the transfer system was compatible with Article 45 TFEU. It first ruled that sportspersons counted as 'workers', even if their transfers to and from clubs were arranged *between the clubs* rather than in direct contracts with the players themselves. It also confirmed that footballing federations like the FA, UEFA, and FIFA were subject to the Treaties, and the free movement of workers provisions in particular, in that they set rules that had similar effects to laws.

Case C-415/93 *Bosman* ECLI:EU:C:1995:463 (emphasis added)

96. Provisions which **preclude or deter a national of a Member State from leaving his country of origin** in order to exercise his right to freedom of movement therefore **constitute an obstacle to that freedom even if they apply without regard to the nationality of the workers concerned** . . .

103. . . . although **the rules in issue** in the main proceedings **apply also to transfers between clubs** belonging to different national associations **within the same Member State** and are similar to those governing transfers between clubs belonging to the same national association, **they still directly affect players' access to the employment market in other Member States and are thus capable of impeding freedom of movement for workers** . . .

[30] Case C-237/94 *O'Flynn v Adjudication Officer* ECLI:EU:C:1996:206.
[31] Case C-19/92 *Kraus v Land Baden-Württemberg* ECLI:EU:C:1993:125, para 32.
[32] Case C-415/93 *Bosman* ECLI:EU:C:1995:463.

The *Bosman* judgment, involving an altogether unremarkable footballer, fundamentally changed the manner in which transfers in European football took place. The CJEU's ruling made clear, more than anything, that any measure that made it *more difficult* for EU nationals to exercise free movement for the purpose of work would be subject to CJEU scrutiny, and would be difficult to justify.

Nonetheless, there are some limitations to the generosity of Article 45(2) TFEU. For a measure to be deemed to discourage inappropriately the free movement of workers, it must have a measurable effect. Where the effect of a measure is 'too uncertain and indirect', as the CJEU noted in *Graf*, it fails a 'remoteness' test and will not be deemed to be a violation of Article 45(2) TFEU.[33] *Graf* concerned an Austrian rule whereby compensation on termination of employment only applied in cases of involuntary termination of employment (and therefore not when the worker resigned to take a job elsewhere). Mr Graf challenged the rule because he quit his job to go and work in Germany, and felt that this was impeding his freedom of movement—but the CJEU here concluded that the rule in question did not seem to affect other EU nationals more than home nationals, not least because it also would not apply to all Austrians who quit their jobs in order to take up another position in Austria.

Bosman considered a situation where it was impossible for someone to go and work in another Member State *unless* a specific action took place, whereas *Graf* looked at a situation where a person could work in another Member State and was treated no better or worse than someone in the same situation who did not leave the home State. The scope of Article 45(2) TFEU finds its limit between these two cases: it covers situations where there is a clear and specific effect on someone's ability to exercise free movement (even if identical rules apply to non-movers), but not those situations where there are rules in place that affect movers and non-movers in identical ways.

Discussing the scenario

Consider the (fictional) Spanish law Emma mentions that requires teachers in Spain to speak Spanish, regardless of what they teach. Do you think this violates Article 45 TFEU? Why? And what about child benefit for Sergio if Andreas had come to work in the UK before Brexit—do you think a benefit such as child benefit is covered by Article 45 TFEU? What makes you think that?

Job-seekers?

What of the rights of job-seekers? In Section 12.2.1, we saw that the CJEU determined in *Antonissen* that they are covered by Article 45 TFEU—but their rights are not identical to those of workers. Job-seekers do not have unconditional rights to reside in a host Member State, nor do they have unconditional access to benefits in the host State. The latter point was made clear in *Collins*[34]—a peculiar case that resulted in a significant clarification of the limits to job-seekers' rights.

Mr Collins was a dual Irish-American citizen, born in the United States, who had spent a total of approximately 16 months working and studying in the United Kingdom between 1978 and 1981. He then returned to the United Kingdom in 1998 in order to find work there, and claimed job-seeker's allowance (JSA) upon his arrival. This was rejected,

[33] Case C-190/98 *Graf* ECLI:EU:C:2000:49.

[34] Case C-138/02 *Collins* ECLI:EU:C:2004:172.

as Mr Collins was found to not be 'habitually resident' in the United Kingdom—he had not lived in the UK for a very long time (so could not have retained worker status), and did not currently qualify as a worker, as he was not yet employed. Mr Collins appealed this decision to the UK Social Security Commissioner, who referred several questions to the CJEU in order to determine if Mr Collins had a right to reside *despite* not being a worker, and if he had a right to JSA on some other grounds *beyond* being a worker.

Case C-138/02 *Collins* ECLI:EU:C:2004:172 (emphasis added)

63. In view of the establishment of citizenship of the Union and the interpretation in the case-law of the right to equal treatment enjoyed by citizens of the Union, . . . **it is no longer possible to exclude from the scope of [Article 45(2) TFEU]**—which expresses the fundamental principle of equal treatment . . . —**a benefit of a financial nature intended to facilitate access to employment** in the labour market of a Member State.

64. The interpretation of the scope of the principle of equal treatment in relation to access to employment must reflect this development . . .

65. The 1996 [UK Social Security Regulations] introduce a difference in treatment according to whether the person involved is habitually resident in the United Kingdom. Since that requirement is capable of being met more easily by the State's own nationals, the 1996 Regulations place at a disadvantage Member State nationals who have exercised their right of movement in order to seek employment in the territory of another Member State . . .

66. A residence requirement of that kind can be justified only if it is based on objective considerations that are independent of the nationality of the persons concerned and proportionate to the legitimate aim of the national provisions . . .

68. The jobseeker's allowance . . . is a social security benefit which replaced unemployment benefit and income support, and requires in particular the claimant to be available for and actively seeking employment and not to have income exceeding the applicable amount or capital exceeding a specified amount.

69. It may be regarded as legitimate for a Member State to grant such an allowance only after it has been possible to establish that **a genuine link exists between the person seeking work** and the **employment market of that State**.

70. The existence of such a link may be determined, in particular, by **establishing that the person concerned has, for a reasonable period, in fact genuinely sought work** in the Member State in question.

. . .

72. However, while a residence requirement is, in principle, appropriate for the purpose of ensuring such a connection, if it is to be proportionate it cannot go beyond what is necessary in order to attain that objective. More specifically, its application by the national authorities must rest on clear criteria known in advance and provision must be made for the possibility of a means of redress of a judicial nature. In any event, if compliance with the requirement demands a period of residence, the period must not exceed what is necessary in order for the national authorities to be able to satisfy themselves that the person concerned is genuinely seeking work in the employment market of the host Member State.

Collins was decided after the status of EU citizenship was established in the Maastricht Treaty, and the CJEU's reasoning reflects on how that status might have changed the rights possessed by job-seekers. Job-seekers were in principle subject to the 'equal treatment' obligations in Article 45(2) TFEU—but Member States were found to have the right to decline job-seekers' applications for benefits if they could not demonstrate a 'real link' to the host State employment market. This is where job-seekers have significantly fewer rights than workers do: a worker is entitled to all benefits from day one of arriving in a host State to start work, whereas a job-seeker has to demonstrate a 'real link' to that State in order to access only *limited* benefits.

All the same, *Collins* also makes clear that assessing a job-seeker's 'real link' with the employment market is an EU-compatible measure in principle, but such a 'real link' must be measured in a way that is *proportionate*. The implication of the *Collins* judgment is that the UK demanded *too long* a period of residence before considering there to be a 'real link' between job-seekers and the UK employment market, and this length of time needed to be reconsidered.

As will become clearer after we consider the scope of EU citizenship in Chapter 13, when it comes to equal treatment in access to benefits in the host State, job-seekers resemble the economically inactive EU citizen more than they do the EU worker.

Discussing the scenario

Say Emma had learned to speak Spanish by September 2019 and moved to Spain but did not have a job lined up when she first arrived there. Would she have been a job-seeker, and if so, what rights would she have had?

12.2.3 Justifying derogations from Article 45 TFEU rights

The Treaty-based grounds for derogating from free movement of workers are indicated in Article 45(3) TFEU. There are a total of three grounds: public policy, public health, and public security. As is the case for the other 'freedoms', they can be used to justify direct and indirect discrimination, as well as measures that hinder free movement but are not discriminatory.[35] The Treaty does not clarify these grounds to any particular extent.

Public policy has been only rarely been separately invoked as a justification for restricting the free movement of persons; one seminal case in which it has come up is *Groener*, in which a Dutch national was declined a full-time post as a lecturer in art in Dublin because she failed a test on the Irish language.[36] Ireland required all those employed in public education to either hold a certificate testifying to their competence in the Irish language, or to qualify for an exemption as there were no alternative candidates for the post; this policy was rooted in the Irish constitution, which declares Irish the first national language and English the second national language, and permits further legislation that requires the use of either of these languages. Mrs Groener did not qualify for an exemption as there were other qualified applicants for the lectureship in art, and

[35] See also Chapters 12 and 14.

[36] Case 379/87 *Groener v Minister for Education and City of Dublin Vocational Education Committee* ECLI:EU:C:1989:599.

so instead was given the option of sitting a test to demonstrate competent knowledge of Irish, but unfortunately failed that test. Mrs Groener subsequently challenged the Irish laws in question—stating they were contrary to Article 45 TFEU, as in practice they were indirectly discriminatory, and she did not need to speak Irish in order to teach art (which was predominantly taught in English).

The CJEU recognized the policy as being potentially indirectly discriminatory, but indicated it could be justified as 'part of a policy for the promotion of the national language', provided it is applied proportionately and in a non-discriminatory manner. The fact that the requirement was for a *competent* rather than *fluent* level of Irish meant that it was not disproportionate, and while the requirement was obviously more easily satisfied by Irish nationals than other nationals, the fact that competence could be established with tests taken outside of Ireland and that a failed test could be re-taken meant that—in light of importance of preservation of the Irish language—the policy was non-discriminatory.[37] The case itself was decided on the basis of the detailed workers' rights set out in the Workers' Regulation, and the Irish court's third referred question as to whether or not a language requirement could be treated as an Article 45(3) public policy exemption was not expressly answered—but the CJEU's response makes it seem likely that language preservation would have been an accepted public policy justification in 1989.

More commonly, the CJEU treats 'public policy' and 'public security' as a combined, single justification.[38] Key to a restriction on an EU worker's rights of movement on these grounds is their *personal* and *current* behaviour, according to the CJEU's case law. General preventative measures cannot result in a refusal of entry or residence to an EU worker,[39] nor can their past association with a particular organization of concern to national security agencies.[40] However, current membership of a group that is deemed to be harmful to society in one way or another *can* be grounds for excluding an EU citizen from the host State, as *Van Duyn* made clear: while the ruling is best known for establishing that directives have vertical direct effect, the CJEU's actual finding in the case was that the UK *was* permitted to refuse entry to a Dutch woman who was intending to work as a secretary for the Church of Scientology, a 'dangerous' organization according to the UK.[41]

One further condition attached to the exercise of derogations on the grounds of public policy or security is implied in the non-discrimination requirement of Article 45(3) TFEU: a restrictive measure cannot be taken against an EU citizen if identical conduct would not have consequences of some kind for a home national.[42] In other words, as *Adoui* made clear, if prostitution is legal within the host State, EU citizens from another Member State cannot be deported if engaging in prostitution in the host State.

There is no case law on the public health derogation—but we will revisit it in Chapter 13 when considering derogations from the free movement rights of all EU citizens, as the EU legislature has clarified what kind of health concerns would qualify for this derogation in the Citizenship Directive.

Beyond the Treaty-based derogations, the CJEU has developed a further set of grounds on which free movement of workers can be restricted. Indirectly discriminatory measures

[37] Ibid, paras 21–23.
[38] Chapter 13 will show that the legislature has also done this in the Citizenship Directive.
[39] Case 67/74 *Bonsignore v Oberstadtdirektor der Stadt Köln* ECLI:EU:C:1975:34.
[40] Case 41/74 *Van Duyn v Home Office* ECLI:EU:C:1974:133, para 17.
[41] See Chapter 8.
[42] Case 115/81 *Adoui and Cornuaille v Belgian State* ECLI:EU:C:1982:183; see also *Jany* (n 14).

and non-discriminatory measures that restrict the free movement of workers can consequently be justified by what the CJEU has varyingly called **imperative** or **overriding requirements** in the **general** or **public interest**.

The language requirements in *Groener*, if not satisfying the Article 45(3) 'public policy' justification, would potentially be considered 'imperative requirements of the public interest'—namely, preservation of a key component of Irish culture. *Kraus* and *Bosman* can also be used as examples of how 'imperative requirements' work in restricting free movement of workers. Unlike the Treaty-based derogations, they are subject to significant judicial review via the proportionality test. Defensible restrictive measures thus have to meet the following test, clearly articulated in *Gebhard*:[43]

- The measure must be applied in a non-discriminatory manner;
- The measure must be justified by imperative requirements in the general interest;
- The measure in place must be suitable for securing the attainment of the objective which they pursue;
- And the measure in place must not go beyond what is necessary to attain the objective.

Kraus concerned a German process whereby authorization had to be requested and granted before a German national could use an academic title obtained abroad in Germany. This was indirectly discriminatory—as it was more likely to affect EU nationals than German nationals—but applied in a non-discriminatory manner. The German government's justification was that this was a matter of quality control: the public had to be protected from 'abuse of academic titles' that were not granted according to rules laid down in Germany. The CJEU recognized this as a legitimate 'imperative requirement', and recognized the authorization process as being suitable for achieving this 'imperative requirement'—but attached conditions of proportionality to its exercise. Consequently, the authorization procedure had to be simple, inexpensive, and any decisions taken on the validity of these academic titles had to be reasoned and subject to judicial review. Only if these conditions were upheld would the 'imperative requirement' of protecting the public from abuse of academic titles be proportionate.

In *Bosman*, meanwhile, we saw the CJEU consider Belgian transfer rules for footballers, which required the club *buying* a player to pay a transfer fee directly to the club *selling* the player. The measure was non-discriminatory, but nonetheless found to be restrictive of the movement of EU national football players. The Belgian Football Federation attempted to justify the measure on two separate 'imperative requirements'. The first of these was the need to maintain a financial and competitive balance between clubs. Did the rules on transfer fees achieve this goal? The CJEU found that they did not, as the richest clubs would remain in the best position to buy players; nor would it restore financial balance between clubs, thus improving competitive balance. The second justification was that there was a need to support the search for and to train young players. The CJEU also did not think that the transfer fee rules accomplished better youth football in Belgium: it was impossible to predict how *good* a young player would become, and the fees were not matched particularly to the actual cost of training players. Consequently, the transfer fee

[43] Case C-55/94 *Gebhard* ECLI:EU:C:1995:411; note that *Gebhard* is a case on freedom of establishment but the same four-part test applies to all freedoms involving the movement of persons.

regime was deemed to be inappropriate in achieving either of these 'overriding requirements'. The CJEU did not need to look further, but also examined whether less restrictive measures could not be used to achieve these goals—and found that balancing the income of football clubs could be accomplished in a number of ways that would not restrict player movement. The football transfer rules consequently failed all parts of the proportionality test, and had to be scrapped in their entirety.

Discussing the scenario

Think back to your answer to the (fictional) restriction on employing teachers in Spain—did you think it violated Article 45 TFEU? Now consider if you think the requirement for teachers in Spain to speak Spanish, even if they teach English, can be justified. Does such a requirement meet the *Gebhard* test? What would make such a requirement proportionate?

The public service exemption (Article 45(4) TFEU)

One final aspect of the material scope of Article 45 TFEU is found in Article 45(4) TFEU, which makes clear that not *all* employment is covered by the equal treatment provision in Article 45(2) TFEU. The so-called **public service exemption** explicitly allows discrimination in access to public service employment.

Again, the CJEU here declared that the meaning of 'public service' must be EU-wide, rather than domestic.[44] When setting out the qualities of Article 45(4) TFEU 'public service' employment, the Court furthermore made it clear that this is not just every job in a host Member State government. In *Commission v Belgium*, the CJEU specified that a job would count as being in the 'public service' for Article 45(4) TFEU purposes if it involved 'direct or indirect participation in the exercise of powers conferred by public law and duties designed to safeguard the general interest of the State or other public authorities'.[45] It added that jobs that qualified for the discrimination exemption in Article 45(4) TFEU presumed 'a special relationship of allegiance to the State and reciprocity of right and duties which form the foundation of the bond of nationality'.[46]

What does this mouthful actually mean? The CJEU has only rarely given examples of the *types* of employment that fall within the scope of Article 45(4) TFEU. One such example is that of masters and chief mates on merchant ships.[47] Beyond that, the Commission believes that Article 45(4) TFEU also covers a significant volume of employment with the police, tax office, judiciary, and the diplomatic service.[48]

It is perhaps easier to illustrate the limits of Article 45(4) TFEU by considering what type of employment is not EU 'public service'. Most city council positions would not qualify—especially not where there is no connection to 'allegiance to the State', for example in jobs such as gardener, plumber, and refuse collector.[49] Nurses, again, do not meet the criteria set out in *Commission v Belgium*; nor do teachers, trainee lawyers, or those working

[44] Case 152/73 *Sotgiu v Deutsche Bundespost* ECLI:EU:C:1974:13.

[45] Case 149/79 *Commission v Belgium (Public Services)* ECLI:EU:C:1982:195, para 10.

[46] Ibid.

[47] Case C-405/01 *Colegio de Oficiales de la Marina Mercante Española* ECLI:EU:C:2003:515.

[48] See Commission, *Free movement of workers in the public sector* SEC(2010)1609 final, 13.

[49] See, eg, Case C-290/94 *Commission v Greece* ECLI:EU:C:1996:265.

for public utility companies, regardless of how state-owned those companies are.[50] These are the kinds of professions that do not require any particular relationship or allegiance to the host State, and consequently cannot reasonably be reserved for home nationals.

Conversely, the professions that are covered by Article 45(4) TFEU may result in exposure to state secrets or other nationally sensitive information. As a topical example, there were a variety of positions within the Department for Exiting the EU that were reserved for British nationals, out of a fear that the loyalty of non-UK nationals to the UK in the Article 50 TEU negotiations might not have been absolute. This may have been paranoid—but it is entirely permissible under Article 45(4) TFEU.[51]

12.2.4 Geographical scope of Article 45 TFEU

A third aspect of Article 45 TFEU is that it is not a general grant of *workers' rights*. Instead, Article 45(3) makes clear that Article 45 rights only apply where there is *movement* of some kind between two Member States. The most obvious example of this is an EU national who moves across the EU to work and live in another Member State: a Belgian national moving to and working in Spain, for instance, is covered by Article 45 TFEU. However, that is not the only situation in which an EU national can rely on Article 45 TFEU. Free movement of workers applies to all EU nationals who find themselves in some kind of 'cross-border situation'. This means that a Belgian national who lives in Belgium and works in Belgium is not covered by Article 45 TFEU; however, a Belgian national who lives in Belgium and works in the Netherlands—a so-called 'frontier worker'—will be.[52]

The final type of 'cross-border situation' covered by Article 45 TFEU is the most controversial one: it relates to EU nationals who move *back* to their home Member State after having worked in a host Member State. In *Surinder Singh*,[53] a UK national and her Indian spouse, who had lived and worked in Germany for two years, moved back to the UK in 1985. They subsequently separated; and following the start of divorce proceedings, Mr Singh's right to reside—under UK immigration law, as spouse of a UK national—was cut short. Mr Singh appealed a decision to deport him, stating that he had a right to reside in the UK under EU law. His wife had, before they returned to the UK, been exercising her free movement rights; and those extended to him. The UK argued that the EU rules did not apply here: a UK national moving back to the UK would only be covered by UK immigration law, which was significantly more demanding than the EU free movement rules are.[54] The CJEU, however, disagreed:

Case C-370/90 *Surinder Singh* ECLI:EU:C:1992:296 (emphasis added)

19. A national of a Member State **might be deterred from leaving his country of origin** in order to pursue an activity as an employed or self-employed person as envisaged

→

[50] See, eg, Case 307/84 *Commission v France* ECLI:EU:C:1986:222; Case C-4/91 *Bleis* ECLI:EU:C:1991:448; Case C-173/94 *Commission v Belgium* ECLI:EU:C:1996:264.

[51] See https://www.thetimes.co.uk/article/europeans-blocked-from-jobs-in-department-running-brexit-nk6hltpfd.

[52] Case C-457/12 *S. and G.* ECLI:EU:C:2014:136.

[53] Case C-370/90 *Surinder Singh* ECLI:EU:C:1992:296.

[54] Ibid, para 14.

→

by the Treaty in the territory of another Member State if, on returning to the Member State of which he is a national in order to pursue an activity there as an employed or self-employed person, the conditions of his entry and residence were not at least equivalent to those which he would enjoy under the Treaty or secondary law in the territory of another Member State.

20. He would in particular be deterred from so doing if his spouse and children were not also permitted to enter and reside in the territory of his Member State of origin under conditions at least equivalent to those granted them by Community law in the territory of another Member State.

Surinder Singh means that when an EU national has legitimately exercised free movement rights to another EU Member State, and then again is engaging in an economic activity once returning to their home country, their return to their home country is covered by free movement law. In practice, this will not be of interest to EU nationals who move by themselves—but it will be of interest to family members of EU nationals who are third-country nationals. The *Surinder Singh* 'route' has become a means by which binational couples (one an EU national, the other not an EU national) can try to avoid restrictive national immigration laws.

EU law in practice

At the time of writing, the UK immigration rules require that UK nationals earn at least £18,600 a year in order to bring a non-EU national family member into the UK to live with them, and that is only the start of the 'red tape' involved. This is a standard that many cannot meet—either because they make less money, or because they have unpredictable income streams (ie, they free-lance) and thus cannot prove that they have a steady income amounting to that sum per year.

For these families—say, one American and one British—the two options are either 'not living together' or 'finding a way around the UK immigration rules'. Option two is where the *Surinder Singh* 'route' came in while the UK was a Member State—and became increasingly popular over time, arguably bolstering negative perceptions of EU free movement law in the UK. The BBC reported in 2013 that approximately 20,000 non-European family members were brought into the UK via *Surinder Singh*, whereby the UK national in question spent a period of three months working in another EU Member State, and their non-EU family members joined them in that State before they all moved back to the UK.[55] For those UK nationals, such a temporary 'stay' abroad represented the only way they could live with their family in their home country—but the *Surinder Singh* route does require that temporary 'stay' to be or have been a genuine *stay* abroad, involving living and working there for a period of time. Following Brexit, as we will discuss in Section 12.3, the *Surinder Singh* route will no longer be available to UK nationals.

Do you think the *Surinder Singh* route counts as an 'abuse' of EU law, the way the UK government has argued? Or is it simply a facet of EU law that offers benefits to some and not to others?

[55] See http://www.bbc.co.uk/news/uk-23029195.

The judgment made it clear that only in cases where such a relationship was clearly a 'sham' could this right be curtailed—to the dissatisfaction of a number of Member States, who felt that this was a case of the EU facilitating their own nationals dodging their own immigration laws. We return to this issue in Chapter 13, when we consider further 'family movement' rights granted by CJEU case law.

Purely internal situations

A final question worth asking is: what of EU national workers who do *not* move across a border in any way? Do they get any rights or protection out of Article 45 TFEU?

The CJEU has considered this question, usually in circumstances where home nationals suddenly find themselves with fewer concrete rights than free moving EU nationals and *other* home nationals. This is usually described in the literature as a '**purely internal situation**', and we can use the case of *Walloon Government* to see how these are treated in EU law.[56] *Walloon Government* concerned an insurance scheme in the Flanders region of Belgium that was only available to residents of that region of Belgium. Following a Commission infringement procedure in 2002, access was also extended to residents of other EU Member States who worked in Flanders. The other region in Belgium, Wallonia, did not have such a care insurance scheme; Wallonian residents who worked in Flanders were excluded from the care insurance scheme. The Wallonian government contested this, ultimately resulting in a referred question about whether residents of Wallonia *could* be denied access without violating Article 45(2) TFEU as it applies to employment benefits.

Case C-212/06 *Walloon Government* ECLI:EU:C:2008:178 (emphasis added)

37. First, application of the legislation at issue in the main proceedings leads, inter alia, **to the exclusion from the care insurance scheme of Belgian nationals working in the territory of the Dutch-speaking region or in that of the bilingual region of Brussels-Capital but who live in the French- or German-speaking region and have never exercised their freedom to move within the European Community.**

38. **[EU] law clearly cannot be applied to such purely internal situations.**

. . .

41. Second, the legislation at issue in the main proceedings may also exclude from the care insurance scheme employed or self-employed workers falling within the ambit of Community law, that is to say, **both nationals of Member States other than the Kingdom of Belgium working in the Dutch-speaking region or in the bilingual region of Brussels-Capital but who live in another part of the national territory, and Belgian nationals in the same situation who have made use of their right to freedom of movement.**

. . .

45. **[Article 45 TFEU] militates against any national measure which**, even though applicable without discrimination on grounds of nationality, **is capable of hindering or rendering less attractive the exercise by Community nationals of the fundamental freedoms guaranteed by the Treaty . . .**

→

[56] Case C-212/06 *Walloon Government* ECLI:EU:C:2008:178.

→

46. In the light of those principles, measures which have the effect of causing workers to lose, as a consequence of the exercise of their right to freedom of movement, social security advantages guaranteed them by the legislation of a Member State have in particular been classed as obstacles . . .

47. Legislation such as that as issue in the main proceedings is such as to produce those restrictive effects, inasmuch as it makes affiliation to the care insurance scheme dependent on the condition of residence in either a limited part of national territory, viz., the Dutch-speaking region and the bilingual region of Brussels-Capital, or in another Member State.

. . .

54. It follows that domestic legislation such as that at issue in the main proceedings entails an obstacle to freedom of movement for workers . . . prohibited in principle by [Article 45 TFEU].

Workers are thus *only* protected by Article 45 TFEU if they are 'moving'. In the case of the Flemish care insurance scheme, this meant that residents of Flanders who also worked there, regardless of nationality, were covered; and EU national residents of Wallonia working in Flanders should also be covered. But Belgian residents of Wallonia who worked in Flanders do not fall within the scope of EU free movement law; their lack of movement outside of Belgium simply means that EU law is not engaged for them.

Is the outcome of *Walloon Government* a satisfying one? Perhaps not—but it is also a consequence of limitations of competence that the Member States themselves have placed upon the EU. We will revisit the CJEU's approach to 'purely internal situations' in Chapter 13, as it has been particularly under fire since the development of EU citizenship as a status.

Discussing the scenario

In 2019, were all of Emma's suggested ways of being with Andreas 'cross-border situations' under EU law? As Ingrid is a German national, what conditions would she have needed to meet to ensure her move back to Germany with Mitchell and Jeremy was covered by EU law?

12.3 Brexit and free movement of workers

Undoubtedly, the movement of EU nationals to the UK played a key role in the 2016 referendum debate. However, the debate rarely focused in on precisely which *type* of EU national benefiting from free movement was perceived to be problematic: was it the economically active EU nationals, benefiting from the rights described in this chapter, or the economically inactive EU nationals, who are covered by different provisions that we consider in Chapter 13?

The debate did not at any point clarify this: it merely resulted in a post-referendum commitment to 'end free movement' of Europeans. We will consider how the Article 50

TEU negotiations have played out in ending the free movement of 'workers' in this chapter and look at the remainder of EU citizens in the next chapter.

12.3.1 The Withdrawal Agreement

The rights set out in Article 45 TFEU will be unchanged during the transition period that the Withdrawal Agreement establishes. What this means is that while the UK will in a 'formal' sense have left the EU when this agreement entered into force, the rights of EU nationals to come and work in the UK, and the rights of UK nationals to go and work in the EU, do not actually cease until the transition period *ends*. A long transition period, consequently, will mean several more years of 'free movement of workers' under the rules established in the TFEU and elaborated on by the CJEU.

Beyond that, the Withdrawal Agreement, in Part 2, establishes provisions on 'Citizens' Rights'. These are of key importance for those who are, *at the time the transition period ends*, exercising their EU free movement rights—whether as EU nationals in the UK, or as UK nationals in the EU.[57] The Withdrawal Agreement sets out in Part 2 that for the duration of their lives, these qualifying EU and UK nationals will continue to benefit from their Article 45 TFEU rights *in the country they reside in at that time*.[58] This includes not only all general equal treatment rights,[59] but also rights to be joined by non-EU family members under EU law.[60] In the UK, such EU nationals will have to apply for a new form of residence permit, titled 'settled status'. The UK courts will continue to be able to refer questions about Part 2 of the Withdrawal Agreement to the CJEU for a period of up to eight years after the transition period,[61] and the UK will establish an Independent Monitoring Authority that takes over the Commission's work in overseeing and enforcing the free movement rights maintained in Part 2 of the Withdrawal Agreement.[62] These rights, consequently, are well-protected, in a way that lasts significantly beyond Brexit.[63]

However, that is not to say that *all* rights that EU national workers currently hold will survive Brexit. While EU nationals in the UK will, on account of still being EU nationals, be able to exercise their freedom of movement to go and work in another EU Member State at any time in the future as well, UK nationals living and working in an EU Member State at the end of the transition period will be able to continue to live in *that* Member State and hold the rights that EU national workers hold in *that* Member State. They will not have onward rights of movement, because they will not be EU nationals anymore.[64]

[57] For workers specifically, see Withdrawal Agreement, Article 24.

[58] Withdrawal Agreement, Articles 13 and 39.

[59] Withdrawal Agreement, Article 12 and 23.

[60] Withdrawal Agreement, Article 10(1)(e). See the discussion in Section 12.2.4.

[61] Withdrawal Agreement, Article 158.

[62] Withdrawal Agreement, Article 159.

[63] Note, however, that the EU (Withdrawal Agreement) Act 2020, implementing the Withdrawal Agreement in the UK, appears to foresee that the Independent Monitoring Authority's functions can be delegated to or transferred to another institution by regulation—which the Lords Constitution Committee has criticized, noting that it makes the Independent Monitoring Authority appear far less 'independent' from government than if only primary legislation can adjust what the Authority is responsible for. See https://publications.parliament.uk/pa/ld5801/ldselect/ldconst/5/5.pdf, paras 61–63.

[64] This is left implicit in the text of the Agreement, which discusses only rights pertaining to the one 'host State' that the UK national is living in.

EU nationals are thus treated much more generously than are UK nationals by the Withdrawal Agreement—but even for them there are limits. Generally, an EU national can move back and forth between different Member States and benefit from Article 45 TFEU rights as long as they are working (or seeking employment under the conditions established by the CJEU). But EU nationals benefiting from the Withdrawal Agreement in the UK can only come *back* to the UK on Article 45 TFEU conditions if they do not leave the UK for longer than five years. After five years of living abroad, their right to enter the UK under those EU rules preserved by the Withdrawal Agreement disappears, and cannot be regained.[65]

Many will consequently benefit from the Withdrawal Agreement by having their status, as it stands at the end of the transition period, preserved—but all the same, even for those workers covered by Part 2 of the Agreement, their movement will be less 'free' than it is now.

12.3.2 The Protocol on Ireland/Northern Ireland

In many previous chapters, we saw that Northern Ireland found itself in a different position from the remainder of the UK on account of the Protocol on Ireland/Northern Ireland attached to the Withdrawal Agreement. However, there is no exceptional treatment in the Withdrawal Agreement for EU nationals working in Northern Ireland, or UK nationals from Northern Ireland who have exercised their freedom to work in other Member States.

That said, because the Part 2 rights first of all require that the 'free movement' is being exercised specifically at the end of the transition period, there are some issues specific to 'Northern Ireland' that the Protocol perhaps should have addressed. The first of these is that those with Irish nationality who are born in Northern Ireland[66] are not automatically captured by Part 2 of the Withdrawal Agreement. While they hold an 'EU nationality', in that they are Irish, they are caught by the 'purely internal situation' doctrine if they are still living in their 'home' Member State (the UK, in this case) at the end of the transition period. Their position needs to be contrasted with Irish nationals from the Republic of Ireland who have moved *to* the UK before the end of the transition period: they *are* covered by Part 2 of the Withdrawal Agreement, because they have moved from one Member State (Ireland) to a state treated as another (the UK). We will return to this in Chapter 13, when we consider what the problems are with having two different categories of 'Irish nationals' in the UK, one of which is protected by Part 2 of the Withdrawal Agreement and one which is not.

In terms of EU and UK nationals who *are* exercising their free movement rights, frontier workers, meaning those who live close to the border and work across it in another Member State, are covered by the Part 2 provisions—but only if they are frontier workers specifically when the transition period ends.[67] An Irish national worker resident in Ireland who takes up a job for a business in Northern Ireland *after* the transition period will be in a different position altogether, and their position will not be covered by EU law.

[65] Withdrawal Agreement, Article 15(3).

[66] See Article 1 of the 1998 Belfast/Good Friday Agreement, in which the UK and Irish governments commit to recognizing '. . . the birthright of all the people of Northern Ireland to identify themselves and be accepted as Irish or British, or both, as they may so choose, . . .'

[67] https://www.nihrc.org/publication/detail/continuing-eu-citizenship-rights-opportunities-and-benefits-in-northern-ireland-after-brexit.

Because the UK and Ireland are part of a so-called Common Travel Area that also enables free movement of people, and because the UK and Irish governments have recently adopted a bilateral agreement that continues social security arrangements between the UK and Ireland after Brexit, this type of 'frontier' work will nonetheless be able to take place in much the same way it does while EU law applies in the UK. However, those who become 'frontier workers' after the transition period will not be protected in the way that those covered by Part 2 of the Withdrawal Agreement are. Their situations will be covered purely by domestic laws, without the possibility for references to the CJEU, and while there will be a mechanism in place to ensure that their rights under the 1998 Belfast/ Good Friday Agreement are not diminished under Brexit, this does not address all the rights that frontier workers hold under EU law.[68]

The fact that these future frontier workers fall outside the scope of the Withdrawal Agreement may, on the one hand, come with limited practical consequences: the frontier work will be able to take place. However, if those future frontier workers encounter any legal difficulties, or if they find themselves temporarily unable to engage in their work, they will be less protected under the Common Travel Area's arrangements than they are now under EU law, or they would be if covered by Part 2 of the Withdrawal Agreement.[69]

12.3.3 The future relationship

The position of the frontier worker in Northern Ireland and Ireland is the same position as the one that the remainder of the post-Brexit UK workforce will find itself in. The Political Declaration of October 2019 makes it very explicit that 'free movement' will end when the transition period does. As such, UK nationals who *after the transition period* want to work in an EU Member State (with the exception of Ireland, as described in Section 12.3.2) will have to do so on the basis of whatever immigration rules exist in those Member States for third-country nationals to take up employment.

The EU has a directive in place covering what it terms 'third country high-skilled workers'. These workers qualify for something called an EU Blue Card, provided they hold a firm job offer (a work contract), the required professional qualifications, and are working at a minimum salary level.[70] Of course, the difference between an EU national exercising free movement and a 'Blue Card holder' is immediately clear: *some* UK nationals will qualify for this status. It is not a 'right' in the way that free movement of workers is.

There are similar EU directives for so-called 'seasonal workers', who are usually active in agricultural industries; and on intra-company transfers, meaning for those non-EU national workers employed by a multinational company that has branches both in and outside of the EU.[71] Beyond that, the EU has also adopted a 'Single Permit Directive',

[68] For a very detailed analysis, see Sylvia de Mars, Colin Murray, Aoife O'Donoghue, and Ben Warwick, *Continuing EU Citizenship 'Rights, Opportunities and Benefits' in Northern Ireland after Brexit* (2020), Available at https://www.nihrc.org/publication/detail/continuing-eu-citizenship-rights-opportunities-and-benefits-in-northern-ireland-after-brexit. [69] Ibid.

[70] Council Directive 2009/50/EC of 25 May 2009 on the conditions of entry and residence of third-country nationals for the purposes of highly qualified employment [2009] OJ L155/17.

[71] Directive 2014/36/EU of the European Parliament and of the Council of 26 February 2014 on the conditions of entry and stay of third-country nationals for the purpose of employment as seasonal workers [2014] OJ L94/375.
Directive 2014/66/EU of the European Parliament and of the Council of 15 May 2014 on the conditions of entry and residence of third-country nationals in the framework of an intra-corporate transfer [2014] OJ L157/1.

which establishes a single permit that entitles a holder to both live and work in the EU. However, while it creates a single document that can *demonstrate* that right to reside and work, the actual conditions for the vast majority of third-country nationals to work in any EU Member State are set by national law, and not EU law.[72]

The same will be true for the UK with respect to EU nationals after Brexit. The UK immigration rules at this time require non-EU nationals to either be highly skilled, as they would be for the 'Blue Card', or in demand for a particular job, and in any event, earning over set thresholds in order to be allowed to live in the UK. Whatever these rules require in detail, the key point after Brexit is that they will apply to both non-EU nationals *and* EU nationals.[73]

Working in each other's jurisdictions after Brexit, in other words, will not become wholly impossible. It will, however, become less than a right. The part-time worker making minimum wage is unlikely to qualify for the visa or permit they need to engage in work in either the UK or the EU after Brexit, whereas the highly-skilled probably will continue to, unless the 'future relationship' negotiations result in a more generous outcome than set out in the Political Declaration.

Discussing the scenario

Imagine you are receiving this letter from Emma in early 2020. If you were advising in early 2020, what rights do she and Andreas have now that they may lose if she or Andreas move after the transition period?

12.4 In conclusion

It is striking that the right to free movement of so many economically active people across the EU is established by but a single provision in the TFEU. Of course, that provision is supplemented by a lot of secondary law and a lot of generous interpretation by the CJEU—but all the same, Article 45 TFEU has changed many lives since 1957, by enabling those who would not qualify for a work visa in another Member State to be able to avoid that process altogether, simply take up a job, and experience equal treatment to host State nationals.

The CJEU's case law has not always been well received by the Member States, and there are aspects of the 'simplicity' of the free movement of workers that do not always correspond to the reality of how that movement works. To put it very simply: most EU nationals speak English, but few outside of the Czech Republic speak Czech. Finding a job in a country where you do *not* speak the primary language is, of course, more of a challenge. While movement of workers has thus in theory been 'free' in all directions, in practice, there are more and less common directions of travel for employment purposes. This has meant differing popularity for the EU's free movement of workers in different Member States.

[72] Directive 2011/98/EU of the European Parliament and of the Council of 13 December 2011 on a single application procedure for a single permit for third-country nationals to reside and work in the territory of a Member State and on a common set of rights for third-country workers legally residing in a Member State [2011] OJ L343/1.

[73] See https://www.gov.uk/government/organisations/uk-visas-and-immigration.

Nonetheless, on the basic right of free movement of workers, the CJEU and the EU institutions have remained steadfast: it is *as core* to the internal market as the movement of goods, capital, services, and the freedom of establishment are.[74] In making 'freedom of movement of people' a red line in the Brexit negotiations, the UK distanced itself from the EU in a way that the EU never seemed likely to compromise on.

Discussing the scenario

Use the material in this chapter in order to write a response to Emma on Ingrid's behalf. Treat each paragraph as setting out a specific scenario, and explain how EU law applies to that scenario. Take care to distinguish between the rights Emma and Andreas held in 2019, the rights they hold in 2020, and the rights they will hold after the end of the transition period.

A sample approach to a response can be found online.

Key points

Table 12.1 summarizes the rights of different types of 'movers'.

TABLE 12.1 Summary of free movement of workers

Type of Mover	Source of Rights	Rights	Derogations from Rights
EU National Worker	Article 45 TFEU The Worker's Regulation The Citizenship Directive	• Right to enter and reside (unconditional) • Right to permanent residence after 5 years • Right to equal treatment in access to all benefits (unconditional, from day of arrival)	Article 45(3) TFEU—public policy, public security, public health 'Overriding Requirements'—if proportionate

[74] The same is not per se true for their rights to benefits: David Cameron, when Prime Minister and attempting to renegotiate the UK's relationship with the EU prior to the 2016 referendum, managed to negotiate for an 'emergency break' to limit the access of benefits to new EU national workers if a Member State experienced an inflow of workers of an 'exceptional magnitude'. For a quick discussion, see: https://fullfact.org/europe/explaining-eu-deal-emergency-brake/. (The 'emergency break' was abandoned when the 2016 referendum vote turned out in favour of leaving the EU.)

Type of Mover	Source of Rights	Rights	Derogations from Rights
EU National Job-Seeker	Article 45 TFEU The Citizenship Directive	• Right to enter and reside for up to 3 months (and up to 6 months, if genuine chance of employment) • Right to equal treatment to benefits that facilitate access to the labour market	Article 45(3) TFEU—public policy, public security, public health 'Objective Justifications'—such as 'real link' requirement—if proportionate

Assess your learning

1. What is a 'worker' under EU law? If you lose your job, do you stop being a 'worker'? And what about if you are looking for work—does that make you a 'worker' under EU law? (See Section 12.2.1.)
2. Are EU national 'workers' in a host Member State entitled to equal treatment in *all* circumstances? Are national rules on employment that are not discriminatory (in law or in fact) permitted under Article 45 TFEU? (See Section 12.2.2.)
3. When can an EU national 'worker' be deported from their host State? (See Section 12.2.3.)
4. Can EU nationals ever benefit from Article 45 TFEU in their home State? (See Section 12.2.4.)
5. What will happen to EU nationals currently working in the UK, and UK nationals working in the EU, after the transition period? (See Section 12.3.)

Further reading

Catherine Barnard and Amy Ludlow, '"Undeserving" EU Migrants "Milking Britain's Benefits"? EU citizens before social security tribunals' [2019] PL 260.

Catherine Barnard and Sarah Fraser Butlin, 'Free Movement vs Fair Movement: Brexit and managed migration' (2018) 55(2/3) CMLRev 203.

Paul Downward, 'An Assessment of the Compatibility of UEFA's Home Grown Player Rule with Article 45 TFEU' (2014) 39(4) ELRev 493.

Nicola Kountouris, 'The Concept of "Worker" in European Labour Law: Fragmentation, autonomy and scope' (2018) 47(2) ILJ 192.

Dion Kramer, 'From Worker to Self-Entrepreneur: The transformation of homo economicus and the freedom of movement in the European Union' (2017) 23(3/4) Eur Law J 172.

Niam Nic Shuibhne, 'Reconnecting Free Movement of Workers and Equal Treatment in an Unequal Europe' (2018) 43(4) ELRev 477.

Karen Perry and Madison Steenson, 'A Post-Brexit Impact: A case study on the English Premier League' (2019) 10(1) JSEL 1.

Suvi Sankari and Sabine Frerichs, 'From Resource to Burden: Rescaling solidarity with strangers in the single market' (2016) 22(6) Eur Law J 806.

Eleanor Spaventa, 'Mice or Horses? British citizens in the EU 27 after Brexit as "former EU citizens"' (2019) 44(5) ELRev 589.

Online resources

Visit www.oup.com/he/demars1e for a sample approach to discussing the quote.

13

EU citizenship

Context for this chapter

Guillermo, an Italian thirty-five-year-old, moved to Germany with his Algerian wife and Italian fourteen-year-old son, with the intention of finding a job in civil engineering there. The job offer he had when he moved his family to Germany fell through, and though he applied for many more jobs, he struggled to get past the interview stage. However, he had ample savings, and the family was able to live on those in Germany for a period of six months.

Guillermo decided he would pursue a Master's degree at a German university, as this would both add to his CV and help him learn the German language better. He was given a place at the (fictional) University of Franken, and decided he would apply to the German government for a student loan. His application was denied, and the authorities responded by saying that as he did not have a genuine link with Germany, he was not entitled to government financial support for his studies.

Meanwhile, Guillermo's son Antonio is arrested alongside some of his friends for spray-painting anti-capitalist slogans on an overpass. He is sentenced to a community service programme for 100 hours, and otherwise released back into his parents' care.

After a long conversation with his wife, Guillermo decided that he would continue looking for a job for another few months, but that as his money was running low, they would have to return to Italy by the end of the year. Guillermo at this point applied for unemployment benefit and child benefit at the Franken local council, in the hopes of making his savings last longer.

That application was also declined, and two days later, Guillermo received a letter from the German immigration authorities calling him in for an interview. At the interview, they asked after his personal finances as well as what his family members were doing. He explained his son was in school, and his wife managed the household, while he looked for work. When asked, he had to admit that his wife and son spoke no German, and his own was improving but not fluent.

Three days later, he received a letter informing him that he had no right to reside in Germany under EU law, nor did his wife and son, as he did not hold sufficient finances to support himself. Additionally, his son was subject to deportation proceedings as the German immigration authorities believed him to be a threat to public security.

13.1 Introduction

In Chapter 12, we examined the origins of the EU's free movement of persons by looking in detail at the EU's rules on the free movement of workers. Chapter 13 will consider how free movement of persons *developed*, culminating into a constitutional identity for EU nationals that extends rights to economically inactive free movers as well.

The controversy surrounding the development of 'citizenship rights' is of particular interest given the Brexit referendum; limitless immigration from the EU was found to be one of the primary reasons why the UK voted to leave the EU.[1] However, as Chapter 12 also noted, too much of the public debate about free movement does not delve into the detailed functioning of free movement, and conflates the rights held by those who are in work, or economically active, with those who are not.

Reading this chapter alongside Chapter 12 should make it clear that there is no such thing as a single, absolute right of 'free movement'. Economic activity in particular is a core determinant of just how many rights those exercising free movement under the EU Treaties have, and whether or not those rights can be easily restricted by the Member States. However, it is equally clear that the introduction of EU citizenship, while originally thought of as a fairly empty concept, has introduced significant changes precisely for those *not* economically active. Exploring the scenario at the start of the chapter will highlight to what extent EU citizenship has meant a convergence of 'free movement rights' for the economically active and inactive, and whether any differences or shortcomings are still justifiable.

13.2 Citizenship in the EU Treaties

EU citizenship was formally established in 1992, and can be used as a marker to separate two distinct eras of CJEU case law on free movement of persons.[2] However, citizenship did not come out of thin air in the Maastricht Treaty. Expansions in free movement of persons' rights were underway on a number of fronts from the 1970s onwards, even if the establishment of a citizenship itself was seen as too radical a proposal in 1975, when an EC report called the Tindemans Report first suggested it might be created.[3]

For economically inactive EU nationals, the Treaties did not offer a basis of legal rights in the 1980s and 1990s. However, the EU legislature was willing to extend them free movement rights as well—albeit under certain conditions. Three separate directives in the 1990s consequently made it so that students, pensioners, and the independently wealthy could exercise free movement to another Member State as well, providing they would not become an 'unreasonable burden' on that Member State.[4]

[1] See, eg, http://lordashcroftpolls.com/2016/06/how-the-united-kingdom-voted-and-why; https://www.bsa.natcen.ac.uk/media/39149/bsa34_brexit_final.pdf; https://migrationobservatory.ox.ac.uk/resources/reports/decade-immigration-british-press/.

[2] For the first era, see Chapter 12.

[3] Report by Mr Leo Tindemans, Prime Minister of Belgium, to the European Council. Bulletin of the European Communities, Supplement 1/76 (See https://www.cvce.eu/en/education/unit-content/-/unit/02bb76df-d066-4c08-a58a-d4686a3e68ff/63f5fca7-54ec-4792-8723-1e626324f9e3.)

[4] See Directive 90/364/EEC of the Council of 28 June 1990 on the right of residence [1990] OJ L180/26, Art 1; Directive 90/365/EEC of 28 June 1990 on the right of residence for employees and self-employed persons who have ceased their occupational activity [1990] OJ L180/28, Art 1; and Directive 93/96/EEC of the Council of 29 October 1993 on the right of residence for students [1993] OJ L317/59, Art 1.

By the 1990s, virtually all EU nationals consequently had *some* movement rights. However, these were not all rooted in a Treaty provision—and non-moving EU nationals had no rights whatsoever in EU primary law. The establishment of EU citizenship changed this. As a consequence of EU citizenship, both static and 'moving' EU nationals now had certain rights stemming from EU law; and it was not only economically active EU nationals who were protected by the Treaty, but students, pensioners, and the independently wealthy also were protected by a primary law provision.

The rights and duties linked to EU citizenship are now set out in Articles 20–25 TFEU, with Article 20 TFEU outlining them all:

Article 20 TFEU (emphasis added)

1. Citizenship of the Union is hereby established. **Every person holding the nationality of a Member State** shall be a citizen of the Union. Citizenship of the Union shall be **additional to and not replace national citizenship**.
2. Citizens of the Union shall enjoy the rights and be subject to the duties provided for in the Treaties. They shall have, inter alia:
   (a) **the right to move and reside freely** within the territory of the Member States;
   (b) **the right to vote and to stand as candidates in elections to the European Parliament** and in **municipal elections in their Member State of residence**, under the same conditions as nationals of that State;
   (c) **the right to enjoy**, in the territory of a third country in which the Member State of which they are nationals is not represented, **the protection of the diplomatic and consular authorities of any Member State** on the same conditions as the nationals of that State;
   (d) **the right to petition the European Parliament**, to apply to the European Ombudsman, and to address the institutions and advisory bodies of the Union in any of the Treaty languages and to obtain a reply in the same language.

These rights shall be exercised in accordance with the conditions and limits defined by the Treaties and by the measures adopted thereunder.

13.2.1 Personal scope of EU citizenship

The personal scope of EU citizenship is set out very explicitly in Article 20(1) TFEU. First, being an EU citizen is conditional on being an *EU national*. It is not a status open to anyone who does not hold the nationality of an EU Member State. As a consequence of Brexit, UK nationals will consequently all lose their EU citizenship, unless they hold *another* EU nationality. We are likely to end up with a Northern Ireland full of EU citizens, in other words, while in Scotland, Wales, and England, they will be few and far between.

The other key aspect of the personal scope of EU citizenship is the last sentence of Article 20(1) TFEU. It makes it clear that the drafters of the Treaties envisioned EU citizenship as providing perhaps something of a *bonus* to national citizenships, but definitely considered it to be a secondary status to national citizenship. This suggests that EU citizenship was not meant to come with *expansive* rights—bear that in mind when we consider how the CJEU has treated EU citizenship in its case law, in Section 14.4.

The CJEU has been asked if the conditions for obtaining one of those national citizenships are within the scope of EU law. Its answer has consistently been that this is a matter for national law alone, albeit with the caveat that nationality law in the Member States must have 'due regard' for EU law.[5] For several decades, this seemed to mean purely that nationality was a matter for national law—and the introduction of EU citizenship did not seem to have changed this position. Then, in 2010, *Rottmann* was decided, and changed the notion of 'due regard to EU law' in a dramatic way.[6]

Mr Rottmann was an Austrian national who gave up his nationality to become a national of the Member State he resided in: Germany. However, the German government subsequently discovered that he had not disclosed a prior criminal conviction in his German citizenship application—and revoked his German nationality as a consequence. This left Mr Rottmann stateless, and as he wished to remain a German national, he contested this revocation on the basis of EU law: namely, he would lose his *EU citizenship* as a consequence of losing his German nationality. Germany, on the other hand, contested his claim, noting that the CJEU had always agreed that German nationality law was a matter for German law. What did the CJEU do?

Case C-135/08 *Rottmann* ECLI:EU:C:2010:104 (emphasis added)

39. . . . according to established case-law, it is for each Member State, having due regard to [EU] law, to lay down the conditions for the acquisition and loss of nationality . . .

41. Nevertheless, the fact that a matter falls within the competence of the Member States does not alter the fact that, in situations covered by European Union law, the national rules concerned must have due regard to the latter . . .

42. It is clear that the situation of a citizen of the Union who, like the applicant in the main proceedings, is faced with a decision withdrawing his naturalisation, adopted by the authorities of one Member State, and placing him, after he has lost the nationality of another Member State that he originally possessed, in a position capable of causing him to lose the status conferred by [Article 20 TFEU] and the rights attaching thereto falls, by reason of its nature and its consequences, within the ambit of European Union law.

. . .

56. Having regard to the importance which primary law attaches to the status of citizen of the Union, when examining a decision withdrawing naturalisation it is necessary, therefore, to take into account the consequences that the decision entails for the person concerned and, if relevant, for the members of his family with regard to the loss of the rights enjoyed by every citizen of the Union. In this respect it is necessary to establish, in particular, whether that loss is justified in relation to the gravity of the offence committed by that person, to the lapse of time between the naturalisation decision and the withdrawal decision and to whether it is possible for that person to recover his original nationality.

→

[5] Case C-369/90 *Micheletti* ECLI:EU:C:1992:295.
[6] Case C-135/08 *Rottmann* ECLI:EU:C:2010:104.

→

. . .

58. It is . . . for the national court to determine whether, before such a decision withdrawing naturalisation takes effect, having regard to all the relevant circumstances, observance of the principle of proportionality requires the person concerned to be afforded a reasonable period of time in order to try to recover the nationality of his Member State of origin.

The outcome of *Rottmann* is significant. The CJEU walks a careful line between crossing into a purely *national* competence—namely, the conditions for earning and losing nationality—and ensuring that EU citizenship is a meaningful status. Neither Mr Rottmann nor the complaining Member States will be overly satisfied with the outcome: the Member States have lost *some* control over their nationality laws, and must ensure those are proportionate when exercised on EU citizens, but at the same time, if they are found proportionate, Mr Rottmann nonetheless loses both his German and EU citizenships.

Is this invasion into nationality law justifiable? The academic community was divided on it. Some, like Shaw, consider it a 'hollowing out [of] national competences' that has not been matched by a fleshing out of EU citizenship into a more meaningful status.[7] However, Kochenov and Plender have instead argued that *Rottmann* is a prime example of EU citizenship reaching its full potential: it is, after all, an example of there not needing to be 'cross-border movement' in order for an EU national to obtain a clear right from the Treaties, and this is an important step away from the 'purely internal situations' doctrine we discussed in Chapter 12.[8]

Pause for reflection

What do you make of *Rottmann?* Could it have been decided another way? *Should* it have been decided another way? Why or why not?

13.2.2 Material scope of EU citizenship

The Treaty provisions on EU citizenship need to be read in combination with a separate Treaty provision: namely, Article 18 TFEU.

Article 18 TFEU (emphasis added)

Within the scope of application of the Treaties, and without prejudice to any special provisions contained therein, any discrimination on grounds of nationality shall be prohibited.

The European Parliament and the Council, acting in accordance with the ordinary legislative procedure, may adopt rules designed to prohibit such discrimination.

[7] Jo Shaw, 'Citizenship: Contrasting dynamics at the interface of integration and constitutionalism' in Paul Craig and Gráinne de Búrca (eds), *The Evolution of EU Law*, 2nd edn (OUP, 2011) 608.

[8] Dimitry Kochenov and Richard Plender, 'EU Citizenship: From an incipient form to an incipient substance? The discovery of the treaty text' (2012) 37 ELRev 369.

While Article 20 TFEU does not contain its own non-discrimination clause in the way that Article 45 TFEU does, Article 18 TFEU is applicable to the *entirety* of the Treaty, and thus also attaches a right of non-discrimination on the basis of nationality to EU citizenship.

Rights stemming from Article 20 TFEU

Article 20(2) TFEU sets out a list of 'rights and duties' that come with EU citizenship; these are then further elaborated on in Articles 21–25 TFEU. It is important, first of all, to note the final sentence in the provision, which makes it clear that even though certain EU citizenship rights may *seem* unconditional, they are all potentially subject to limitations set out in *other* parts of the Treaties and EU secondary legislation.

The first of the EU citizenship rights is a general right of movement and residence. Article 20(2)(a), however, does not expand upon the rights that EU nationals already had under Article 45 TFEU and the 1990s residence directives for students, pensioners, and the independently wealthy; instead, Article 21 TFEU makes clear that the EU has the power to adopt further secondary legislation to make the free movement of EU citizens effective. It is on the basis of Article 21 TFEU that the EU legislature adopted the Citizenship Directive and its detailed rules on the exercise of free movement by EU citizens.

More novel are the rights set out in Articles 20(2)(b), (c), and (d) TFEU (and detailed in Articles 22, 23, and 24). They grant certain political rights to EU nationals who live outside of their home countries or countries of nationality, which is unprecedented in other international agreements. These rights are, in turn, the right to vote *and* stand in both European Parliament elections *and* municipal elections in the Member State they live in; consular protection from *any* Member State embassy to EU nationals if their country of citizenship does not have an embassy where they are; and finally, the right to make use of the EU institutions in whatever language they are most comfortable with.

The electoral rights are particularly interesting, as they set out only a basic framework. Certain Member States allow non-EU nationals to vote in European Parliament elections, and this has been deemed fine by the CJEU.[9] Simultaneously, Member States cannot treat their own nationals living outside the EU in different ways depending on *where* they live.[10] The CJEU has consequently turned the voting right into one that is neither purely territorial—residing in the EU—nor nationality-based—having EU nationality.

The right to vote in what the Treaties call 'municipal' elections is also interesting. Ordinarily, when a word in the Treaties can have different meanings, the CJEU will develop an EU-specific meaning that is then applicable across the Member States—but that has not happened here. It has left the Member States the freedom to determine what 'municipal' signifies, meaning that in Member States with several levels of below-parliamentary elections, EU nationals might have the right to vote in all of those. In the UK, EU nationals could not vote in parliamentary elections, but they could vote in local elections.

[9] Case C-145/04 *Spain v United Kingdom* ECLI:EU:C:2006:543.

[10] Case C-300/04 *Eman and Sevinger* ECLI:EU:C:2006:545, where the Netherlands permitted Dutch nationals to vote in EP elections anywhere in the world, but those with Dutch nationality born in the Netherlands' overseas territories were not permitted to vote in them.

13.3 The CJEU on free movement of EU citizens between 1992 and 2004

The Treaty provisions on EU citizenship are sparse—but they make clear that they were intended to be supplemented by detailed secondary legislation, setting out all conditions attached to and rights stemming from Articles 20 and 21 TFEU. The substance of EU citizenship has consequently come from two sources other than the Treaty: the first of these is CJEU case law, as we will see in this section.

Eventually, in 2004, the EU legislature responded to the CJEU's case law with the kind of secondary legislation that the Treaty envisages in Article 21 TFEU: this is the Citizenship Directive, and we will explore it in Section 13.4.

13.3.1 The economically active (workers, job-seekers)

As discussed in Chapter 12, the free movement rights of workers were *always* clearly set out in EU primary law. As a consequence, they are the category of EU nationals on which EU citizenship had the least impact.

13.3.2 The economically inactive (students, the retired, and the independently wealthy)

A compromise on the movement rights of students, the retired, and the independently wealthy was already reached in 1990 after 10 years of stalled negotiations by the EU legislature; however, these EU nationals were not granted unconditional free movement rights. Key to their ability to move was the condition that they had 'sufficient resources' to not pose an 'unreasonable burden' on the finances of the host Member State, and that they had sickness insurance.[11] Here, then, the EU legislature spelled out the limits of its cross-border solidarity: host Member States were willing to *host* these economically inactive EU migrants, but were not willing to *support* them.

Did the development of EU citizenship make a significant difference to the rights of the economically inactive? The combination of Article 18 TFEU, which generally precludes non-discrimination on the basis of nationality, and Article 21 TFEU, which establishes rights of movement and residence for all EU citizens, could be read to grant equal access to welfare even for the economically inactive. Article 21 TFEU, furthermore, makes it sound as if the 'EU citizen' has a right to reside that is not dependent on secondary legislation, though it could be influenced by that. Was this the intention of the creation of EU citizenship?

In the absence of a quick response from the EU legislature, the CJEU pounced upon these questions.

First, the CJEU has been consistent in finding that any national legislation which disadvantaged anyone who had exercised free movement rights was to be deemed a restriction

[11] See Directive 90/364/EEC of the Council of 28 June 1990 on the right of residence [1990] OJ L180/26, Art 1; Directive 90/365/EEC of 28 June 1990 on the right of residence for employees and self-employed persons who have ceased their occupational activity [1990] OJ L180/28, Art 1; and Directive 93/96/EEC of the Council of 29 October 1993 on the right of residence for students [1993] OJ L317/59, Art 1.

of Article 21 TFEU, which granted the freedom to move to *all* EU nationals.[12] Similarly, any rules in the home State that would *deter* an EU citizen from moving elsewhere were contrary to Article 21 TFEU—this included not only barriers to *leaving* the country outright, but also the introduction of obstacles or lost rights upon that EU citizen's *return* to the home State.[13] What these two general findings mean is that, according to the CJEU, all EU nationals are in principle entitled to equal treatment when either living in the host State, or returning to the home State—even economically inactive EU nationals.

The first case in which the CJEU made this explicit was *Martínez Sala*.[14] In this case, the CJEU concluded that any mobile EU nationals would be entitled to equal treatment in relation to benefits in the host State, providing they were *lawfully resident* in the host State. The conditions for 'lawful residence' were those in the 1990s residence directives in the case of Ms Martínez Sala—but Germany had granted her a residence permit despite the fact that she did not meet those conditions. At that point, the CJEU said, EU citizenship entitled her to equal treatment.

A grander statement of the effect of EU citizenship was made in *Grzelczyk*.[15] Here, the CJEU declared that 'Union citizenship is destined to be the fundamental status of nationals of the Member States'.[16] It used that statement to start eroding the limitations set out in the 1990s residence directives. In *Grzelczyk*, a French student requested a benefit in his final years of studies in Belgium and was declined the benefit because students were only permitted to reside in the host State if they had sufficient resources to not burden the host State. However, the CJEU held that conditions such as 'unreasonable burden' had to be read in light of a 'certain degree of financial solidarity' towards fellow EU citizens.[17] Because Mr Grzelczyk's financial difficulties were of very short duration, Belgium should consider granting him the benefit on account of his EU citizenship status—and in any event, he should not automatically lose his legal right to reside because he claimed a benefit in the host State.[18]

Discussing the scenario

What does *Grzelczyk* suggest about Guillermo's rights to unemployment benefit or child benefit? In what circumstances can Germany deny his application?

13.3.3 Justifying derogations from Article 18, 20, and 21 TFEU rights

While Article 21 TFEU makes it clear that the EU legislature *can* impose limits on the free movement of EU citizens, the CJEU has applied a proportionality test to all national measures that implement such limits. The 1990s residency directives already applied the Treaty-based derogations of public security, public policy, and public health to economically inactive EU nationals—but the CJEU made it clear that these are not the only possible

[12] Case C-192/05 *Tas-Hagen and Tas* ECLI:EU:C:2006:676.
[13] Case C-244/98 *D'Hoop* ECLI:EU:C:2002:432.
[14] Case C-85/96 *Martínez Sala v Freistaat Bayern* ECLI:EU:C:1998:217.
[15] Case C-184/99 *Grzelczyk* ECLI:EU:C:2001:458.
[16] Ibid, para 31. [17] Ibid, para 44. [18] Ibid, paras 43–44.

derogations from the free movement of EU citizens. Where a Member State cannot *justify* a limitation of the free movement of an EU citizen, or where that limitation is not deemed proportionate, the CJEU will declare it to be in violation of Articles 18, 20, and 21 TFEU, as applicable.

What makes a difference in treatment justifiable? The CJEU has made it clear that only those differences rooted in *objective* rather than *subjective* grounds are Treaty-compatible. This is very similar to the CJEU's case law on derogations from the four freedoms on account of 'imperative' or 'overriding' requirements in the general interest, as we have seen in Chapters 11 and 12.[19] Again, justifiable measures cannot be *directly* discriminatory. On the other hand, rules that differentiate between those who have lived in the host State for *some time* versus those who have *just arrived* have been generally approved as long as they are proportionate.[20]

The CJEU-approved limitations are usually identified as being requirements for the existence of a **'real link'** with the host Member State's employment market, or a **'certain degree of integration'** into host Member State society. These are then subject to the *Gebhard* test set out in Chapter 12:

- The measure must be applied in a non-discriminatory manner;
- The measure must be justified by imperative requirements in the general interest;
- The measure in place must be suitable for securing the attainment of the objective which they pursue;
- And the measure in place must not go beyond what is necessary to attain the objective.

A clear example of how the CJEU engaged with restrictions on free movement of persons following EU citizenship is found in *D'Hoop*.[21] Ms D'Hoop was a Belgian national who went to secondary school in France, rather than in Belgium. Her French diploma was recognized as equivalent to Belgian diplomas—and she used it to study at a Belgian university. Following her graduation, she applied for an unemployment benefit called a 'tideover allowance'. Belgian legislation required that anyone applying for tideover allowance had either undergone secondary education *in* Belgium, or was the child of an EU national worker in Belgium who had undergone secondary education in *another* Member State. Neither scenario covered Ms D'Hoop, in that she was a Belgian national who had exercised free movement to go to secondary school in France, and so her application for tideover allowance was rejected. She challenged that decision, and a Belgian court asked the CJEU if the relevant Belgian law was precluded by the EU Treaties.

Case C-244/98 *D'Hoop* ECLI:EU:C:2002:432 (emphasis added)

33. In situations such as that in the main proceedings, national legislation introduces a difference in treatment between Belgian nationals who have had all their secondary education in Belgium and those who, having availed themselves of their freedom to move, have obtained their diploma of completion of secondary education in another Member State.

→

[19] And as we will see in Chapter 14.

[20] Case C-138/02 *Collins* ECLI:EU:C:2004:172.

[21] Case C-244/98 *D'Hoop* ECLI:EU:C:2002:432.

→

34. By linking the grant of tideover allowances to the condition of having obtained the required diploma in Belgium, the national legislation thus places at a disadvantage certain of its nationals simply because they have exercised their freedom to move in order to pursue education in another Member State.

35. Such inequality of treatment is contrary to the principles which underpin the status of citizen of the Union, that is, the guarantee of the same treatment in law in the exercise of the citizen's freedom to move.

36. The condition at issue could be justified only if it were based on objective considerations independent of the nationality of the persons concerned and were proportionate to the legitimate aim of the national provisions . . .

38. The tideover allowance provided for by Belgian legislation, which gives its recipients access to special employment programmes, aims to facilitate for young people the transition from education to the employment market. In such a context it is legitimate for the national legislature to wish to ensure that there is a real link between the applicant for that allowance and the geographic employment market concerned.

39. However, a single condition concerning the place where the diploma of completion of secondary education was obtained is too general and exclusive in nature. It unduly favours an element which is not necessarily representative of the real and effective degree of connection between the applicant for the tideover allowance and the geographic employment market, to the exclusion of all other representative elements. It therefore goes beyond what is necessary to attain the objective pursued.

D'Hoop demonstrates that EU citizenship had a significant impact on the free movement rights of EU nationals who were not economically active. Their rights to equal treatment and to move and reside in a host Member State are now *also* rooted in the Treaty, per the CJEU. Derogations from these rights had to satisfy the same test as applicable to derogations from all other Treaty 'freedoms': an objectively justifiable reason of the general interest had to be at stake, and the measures the Member State adopted had to be effective for protecting that interest, as well as proportionate.

Discussing the scenario

Is the German authorities' refusal of Guillermo's application for benefits justifiable? If so, on what grounds?

13.3.4 The geographic scope of free movement post-Maastricht

What of the requirement for a 'cross-border situation' in order for the free movement provisions to apply, as we discussed in Chapter 12? We would struggle to think of national citizenship as a meaningful status if all rights stemming from it required citizens to move abroad—and so many were hopeful that EU citizenship would fundamentally revisit this limitation on the scope of EU free movement rights. However, the Member States were adamant that the status of EU citizenship was not intended to be an expansion of the scope of EU law to internal situations—or indeed, any expansion of the scope of EU law at all.

The CJEU, by and large, echoed this sentiment, and a number of its cases repeated this point about the scope of EU law. However, then along came several cases in the early 2000s where the CJEU appeared to have done away with the 'cross-border situation' as it had been understood for several decades.

In both *Chen*[22] and in *Garcia Avello*,[23] the CJEU was faced with situations of EU nationals who had *not* actively crossed a border, but held a nationality of a Member State which was not the one they lived in. In the case of Chen, this was the Irish nationality (obtained by having been born in Northern Ireland) of a baby who now lived in the United Kingdom (as all Irish nationals can do on account of an agreement between the Republic of Ireland and the UK). In the case of *Garcia Avello*, these were dual Belgian and Spanish national children who were born and raised in Belgium, to a Spanish national father and a Belgian national mother.

None of the children in these cases had left the Member States they had been born in; but their EU nationality was found to trigger EU law all the same.

Garcia Avello involved a Belgian law that made it impossible for the Garcia Avello children to have a surname that would be a combination of the parents' surnames, as would have been the normal naming practice in Spain. The CJEU granted them the right to have such a surname—and thus declared the Belgian 'same surname as father' law incompatible with EU law—as they were *Spanish* nationals who resided in *Belgium*, and despite the fact that the same rules applied to all Belgian nationals living in Belgium. They were found to not be in the same circumstances as Belgian nationals resident in Belgium; the fact was that these children would have different surnames in different EU Member States, and this might cause them a number of difficulties in future legal relationships—ie, contracts, diplomas, and so on. The combination of Articles 18 and 20 TFEU consequently meant that the children in this case *were* entitled to have the surname they were registered with in Spain as well, and any restriction of this would be contrary to the Treaty.

Garcia Avello may strike most as a reasonable outcome over a relatively minor and very procedural issue—it seems appropriate for people to have the same name in all the countries they are nationals of, particularly when those countries have extensive free movement and mutual recognition rules, as EU Member States do. However, *Chen* involved a rather more controversial set of circumstances that was also deemed to be covered by the Treaty.

As noted, baby Catherine Chen was born in Northern Ireland, and then she and her Chinese national mother moved to Wales. The mother did not qualify for a UK visa in her own right, but attempted to claim a right to reside as caretaker of an EU national (in this case, Irish) baby. The UK authorities rejected her claim because the EU national here was a baby, and was not exercising any Treaty rights—but Mrs Chen appealed, and the UK

[22] Case C-200/02 *Zhu and Chen* ECLI:EU:C:2004:639.

[23] Case C-148/02 *Garcia Avello* ECLI:EU:C:2003:539.

Immigration Appellate Authority referred questions to the CJEU about Mrs Chen's right to reside as a *caretaker* of an EU national who was not exercising Treaty rights.

Case C-200/02 *Zhu and Chen* ECLI:EU:C:2004:639 (emphasis added)

18. The Irish and United Kingdom Governments' contention that **a person in Catherine's situation cannot claim the benefit of the provisions of [EU] law on free movement of persons and residence simply because that person has never moved from one Member State to another Member State** must be **rejected** at the outset.

19. The situation of **a national of a Member State who was born in the host Member State** and **has not made use of the right to freedom of movement cannot, for that reason alone, be assimilated to a purely internal situation**, thereby depriving that national of the benefit in the host Member State of the provisions of Community law on freedom of movement and of residence . . .

26. As regards the right to reside in the territory of the Member States provided for in [Article 20 TFEU], it must be observed that that right is granted directly to every citizen of the Union by a clear and precise provision of the Treaty. **Purely as a national of a Member State, and therefore as a citizen of the Union, Catherine is entitled to rely on [Article 20 TFEU].** That right of citizens of the Union to reside in another Member State is recognised subject to the limitations and conditions imposed by the Treaty and by the measures adopted to give it effect . . .

27. With regard to those limitations and conditions, [the 1990s residence directives] provide that the Member States may require that the nationals of a Member State who wish to benefit from the right to reside in their territory and the members of their families be covered by sickness insurance in respect of all risks in the host Member State and have sufficient resources to avoid becoming a burden on the social assistance system of the host Member State during their period of residence.

28. It is clear from the order for reference that **Catherine has both sickness insurance and sufficient resources, provided by her mother, for her not to become a burden on the social assistance system of the host Member State.**

29. The objection raised by the Irish and United Kingdom Governments that the condition concerning the availability of sufficient resources means that the person concerned must, in contrast to Catherine's case, possess those resources personally and may not use for that purpose those of an accompanying family member, such as Mrs Chen, is unfounded.

. . .

45. **. . . a refusal to allow the parent, whether a national of a Member State or a national of a non-member country, who is the carer of a child to whom [EU law grants] a right of residence, to reside with that child in the host Member State would deprive the child's right of residence of any useful effect.** It is clear that enjoyment by a young child of a right of residence necessarily implies that the child is entitled to be accompanied by the person who is his or her primary carer and accordingly that the carer must be in a position to reside with the child in the host Member State for the duration of such residence . . .

Catherine Chen and her mother were consequently both deemed to have residency rights in the United Kingdom, despite neither being a UK national and Catherine not having exercised any free movement rights of her own.

Pause for reflection

Do you think the decision in *Chen* was the right decision for the CJEU to take? Why or why not? Say the CJEU had decided that Mrs Chen had 'taken advantage' of baby Chen's EU nationality, and this was not the purpose of EU law. What would the consequences of that decision have been for baby Chen, and for the rights stemming from EU citizenship?

Chen is perhaps the most obvious case of the CJEU moving beyond what the EU legislature had intended EU citizenship to be in its case law, though we have seen the CJEU also using EU citizenship to 'soften' the other conditions the legislature had attached to the free movement of economically inactive EU nationals.

EU law in practice

The outrage following *Chen*, which was seen as a major incursion into UK immigration law—a reserved, purely national competence, particularly for those Member States who did not sign up to the Schengen Agreement—was significant, and not only in the UK. Nobody disputed that Mrs Chen had deliberately given birth in Northern Ireland to *give* Catherine Irish nationality, but the CJEU made very clear that this had no bearing on the validity of Catherine's EU nationality.

Under significant pressure from the UK, Ireland amended its Constitution in 2004.[24] Prior to 2004, anyone born on Irish soil (including in Northern Ireland) was entitled to Irish nationality. As a consequence of ***Chen***, however, the Irish Constitution now says the following on nationality:[25]

Irish Constitution, Article 9.2 (emphasis added)

1. Notwithstanding any other provision of this Constitution, **a person born in the island of Ireland**, which includes its islands and seas, **who does not have, at the time of the birth of that person, at least one parent who is an Irish citizen** or entitled to be an Irish citizen **is not entitled to Irish citizenship or nationality**, unless provided for by law.
2. This section shall not apply to persons born before the date of the enactment of this section.

The consequences of *Chen* were thus significant well beyond the status of Catherine Chen herself. As of 2004, nobody born on the island of Ireland is entitled to Irish nationality *unless* at least one of their parents is entitled to Irish nationality.

[24] For a discussion, see Sylvia de Mars and Colin Murray, 'With or Without EU: The Common Travel Area after Brexit', forthcoming in (2020) 21(5) Ger Law J.

[25] Introduced by the Twenty-seventh Amendment of the Constitution Act 2004 (previously Bill no. 15 of 2004).

What do you make of the fact that a CJEU ruling on EU citizenship ultimately had this kind of effect on the Irish Constitution, even though nationality acquisition is not an EU competence?

13.4 Impact of the Citizenship Directive in 2004

How did the EU legislature respond to all of this case law? Its answer came in the form of secondary legislation in 2004: a revision of the 1990s residency directives that aimed to set out, very clearly, in a single document, the operation and nature of free movement rights for *all* EU citizens. This was the Citizenship Directive.

13.4.1 Clarifying the Treaty-based derogations from free movement

The Treaty-based grounds for derogating from free movement of persons rights are repeated in Articles 27–33 of the Citizenship Directive. There are a total of three grounds: public policy, public health, and public security. These can be grounds to restrict both *entry* and *residence* of an EU citizen—but the CJEU has stressed that they have to be interpreted in a way that is 'particularly restrictive' given the fundamental nature of EU citizenship.[26]

Public policy and public security

The contents of the Citizenship Directive on these points is a codification of long-standing CJEU case law, and is one of the few areas of EU citizenship where the legislature appears to have fully endorsed the Court's approach.

Article 29(2) is very clear on the limits that apply to public policy and security derogations, which are considered to be of the same variety:

Article 29(2) CD (emphasis added)

Measures taken on grounds of public policy or public security shall comply with the **principle of proportionality** and shall be **based exclusively on the personal conduct of the individual concerned**. Previous criminal convictions shall not in themselves constitute grounds for taking such measures.

The personal conduct of the individual concerned must represent a genuine, present and sufficiently serious threat affecting one of the fundamental interests of society. Justifications that are isolated from the particulars of the case or that rely on considerations of general prevention shall not be accepted.

A further step taken by the Citizenship Directive is in offering EU nationals and their family members a certain degree of protection against Member States liberally applying derogations on the grounds of public policy or security. Article 28 of the Directive

[26] C-482/01 *Orfanopoulos and Oliveri* ECLI:EU:C:2004:262.

consequently sets out a number of factors the host Member State must take into account before expelling an EU national or their family member:

Article 28 CD (emphasis added)

1. Before taking an expulsion decision on grounds of public policy or public security, **the host Member State shall take account of considerations** such as how long the individual concerned has resided on its territory, his/her age, state of health, family and economic situation, social and cultural integration into the host Member State and **the extent of his/her links with the country of origin.**
2. The host Member State may **not take an expulsion decision against Union citizens or their family members**, irrespective of nationality, **who have the right of permanent residence** on its territory, **except on serious grounds of public policy or public security.**
3. **An expulsion decision may not be taken against Union citizens, except if the decision is based on imperative grounds of public security**, as defined by Member States, if they: (a) **have resided in the host Member State for the previous 10 years**; or (b) **are a minor**, except if the expulsion is necessary for the best interests of the child . . .

In short, this means that the longer an EU citizen has lived in the host State, the more difficult it is to expel them from that host State—and after 10 years, this can only be done exceptionally. Examples of what the CJEU has considered to be 'imperative' grounds of public security are indeed quite extreme: dealing of narcotics as part of organized crime,[27] the sexual exploitation of children,[28] and terrorism[29] have been found to meet the 'imperative' threshold, but most criminal activity would not. In line with the general development of the case law on EU citizenship, the degree of integration is thus instrumental in restricting an EU citizen's right to reside in the host Member State.

Discussing the scenario

Can Antonio be deported from Germany after having been arrested for spray-painting graffiti on an overpass? If so, on what grounds?

Public health

As noted in Chapter 12, there is no case law on the public health restriction, and it is designed to apply only in the case of infectious and contagious diseases. Where there is a risk of an epidemic identified by the World Health Organization, any Member State can restrict entry to all EU citizens; and similarly, when there is a domestic epidemic that has resulted in quarantining of home State nationals, a Member State can also close its borders to EU citizens. However, restrictions on the ground of public health can *only* take place if the EU citizen has not already resided in the host State for more than three

[27] Case C-145/09 *Tsakouridis* ECLI:EU:C:2010:708.
[28] Case C-348/09 *PI* ECLI:EU:C:2012:300.
[29] Case C-300/11 *ZZ* ECLI:EU:C:2013:363.

months—after that time, they must be treated or quarantined, as relevant, *within* the host State, as opposed to be turned around for treatment in their home State.

13.4.2 On all EU citizens

The Citizenship Directive introduced a few innovations that will benefit all EU citizens.

First of these is the clarification that free movement of all EU nationals must be made as administratively simple as possible. All EU nationals must be permitted to enter and exit a Member State simply on showing they have a passport or ID card with the nationality of a Member State; further formalities are precluded by the Citizenship Directive.

Secondly, under Article 16 of the Citizenship Directive, five years of residence in accordance with the Citizenship Directive results in an EU national obtaining a status of permanent residence in that Member State. For workers, this does not come with explicit further rights—but should they become unemployed and no longer qualify for worker status once they are permanent residents, this new status means they have integrated enough to still be entitled to benefits in their host State. In the UK, having evidence of permanent residence status is a pre-condition of applying for UK nationality; it is consequently a definitive signpost of having *settled* in the host State, rather than simply temporarily working or living there.

13.4.3 On the economically inactive

The Citizenship Directive reiterates the restrictions set out in the 1990s residence directives: Article 7(1) thus makes clear that economically inactive EU citizens need to have sufficient resources and sickness insurance in order to have a right to reside in the host State *beyond* three months. The rights of the economically inactive thus have remained conditional, albeit tempered by very generous CJEU case law.[30] What the Citizenship Directive does do is introduce an incremental approach to the residency rights of EU citizens, regardless of their economic activity.

First, as implied by Article 7(1), host State residence of *all* EU citizens is unconditional for three months. The conditions of 'sufficient resources' and sickness insurance only start to apply *after* three months, though Article 24(2) makes clear that during those three months, economically inactive citizens are not entitled to benefits. The Article 7(1) conditions then do apply between three months and five years; at this stage, economically inactive EU citizens are entitled to equal treatment but are also expected to not be 'unreasonable burdens' on the host welfare State. As we will see, this apparent contradiction has become a very hot issue in CJEU case law, as the Directive itself does not make clear when a burden is 'unreasonable'. Finally, at five years of residence compliant with the Citizenship Directive, economically inactive EU citizens can apply for permanent residence under Article 16, as described in Section 13.4.2. Once they are permanent residents, their economic inactivity no longer matters; they are at that point entitled to benefits in the host State on equal terms with home state

[30] See, inter alia, Herwig Verschueren, 'Free Movement of EU Citizens: Including for the Poor?' (2015) 22(1) Maastricht Journal 10; Floris de Witte, 'The End of EU Citizenship and the Means of Non-Discrimination' (2011) 18(1) Maastricht Journal 86; Charlotte O'Brien, 'I Trade, Therefore I am: Legal personhood in the European Union' (2013) 50(6) CMLRev 1643.

nationals under Article 24(1) CD, and cannot have their right of residence revoked if they have insufficient resources or no sickness insurance.

The Citizenship Directive has one very particular caveat when it comes to equal treatment for students: it is that they are *not* entitled to student grants and loans in the host State, per Article 24(2) CD. This was clearly a political compromise: Member States feared that access to student finance would result in mass applications to the country with the most generous student loan/grant regime, and that this would be unaffordable for that Member State, not least because there was no guarantee that the EU national student benefiting from studying abroad would stay *working* abroad and thus repay this public investment by contributing taxes to the host State. The compromise has one exception to it: students who are family members of *workers* in the host State are entitled to equal treatment in student grants and loans. We can thus once again see that EU citizenship is a hierarchy, and the worker is at the pinnacle of it.

Discussing the scenario

Can Guillermo appeal the decision not to give him a loan for a Master's degree? If so, on what grounds?

13.4.4 On family members of EU citizens

At the other end of the hierarchy, we find those who are not themselves EU citizens, but instead are given rights because of their *relationship* to EU citizens. We discussed in Chapter 12 how workers have had the right for their families to move with them and also benefit from equal treatment since the 1970s, and with several limitations in place, similar rights were extended to family members of economically inactive EU nationals in the 1990s. The Citizenship Directive consolidates these rules and sets out *two* categories of 'family' members which benefit from different rules under the Directive.

First, Article 2(2) defines **direct family members**. This includes spouses, children, and any other directly dependent relatives in 'the ascending line'—so grandparents. Where a Member State recognizes same-sex relationships, those 'partners' are also covered by the direct family member rules; and as of *Coman*, even those host States that do not permit same-sex marriage are required to recognize same-sex marriages concluded elsewhere for the purposes of the Citizenship Directive's rules.[31] These are the family members that *must* be admitted by the host State according to Article 3(1). Their rights are parasitic on the EU national, meaning that as long as the EU national qualifies for the right to reside in the host State, their family members will as well.

However, the Citizenship Directive also sets out rules for a second category in Article 3(2): that of **extended family members**. This is anyone *else* in the family tree who is dependent on an EU national, or anyone in a partnership that is not formally registered—a so-called 'durable relationship'. Under Article 3(2) of the Citizenship Directive, the Member States only have a *duty to facilitate* entry and residence for the 'family' of the EU national—which suggests that while the Member State must make it *possible* for these extended family members to move with the EU national, the exact rules dictating

[31] Case C-673/16 *Coman* ECLI:EU:C:2018:385.

their movement can be set out in national law, and are not themselves EU law rights. What does this mean in practice? The CJEU has indicated in *Rahman and Others*[32] that this places extended family members somewhere *between* direct family members and third-country nationals in their ease of 'movement' to a host State:

Case C-83/11 *Rahman and Others* ECLI:EU:C:2012:519 (emphasis added)

21. Whilst it is therefore apparent that Article 3(2) of Directive 2004/38 does not oblige the Member States to accord a right of entry and residence to persons who are family members, in the broad sense, dependent on a Union citizen, the fact remains, as is clear from the use of the words 'shall facilitate' in Article 3(2), that **that provision imposes an obligation on the Member States to confer a certain advantage**, compared with applications for entry and residence of other nationals of third States, **on applications submitted by persons who have a relationship of particular dependence with a Union citizen**.

The most interesting aspect of this interpretation of Article 3(2) is the distinction it draws between *family members of EU nationals*, whether direct or extended, and *other third country nationals*. The implication is that whereas ordinarily, *third-country nationals* are subject to national immigration rules entirely, when those third-country nationals are in a relationship of some kind with an EU national, they are subject to something *easier* than national immigration rules. At the time when *Rahman and Others* was decided, this was indeed the CJEU's position—but it has not always been.

Prior to the adoption of the Citizenship Directive, the CJEU applied two distinct sets of rules when it came to the free movement of EU family members. Where those family members were *themselves* EU nationals, or where they were third-country nationals who were already legally living in another Member State (via national immigration law), they could benefit from the EU free movement rules: they could *accompany* or *join* the EU national in the intended host Member State. However, in *Akrich*,[33] the CJEU ruled that those EU nationals who had third-country national family members who did *not* already have 'prior lawful residence' in one of the Member States could not rely on EU law in order to have their third-country national family member *enter* the EU.

In other words, an Irish national in a relationship with an American who both lived in Belgium and then moved to Bulgaria could benefit from EU law—but an Irish national in a relationship with an American who still lived in America could *not* rely on EU law in order to move to Bulgaria *with* that American.

What caused the *Akrich* ruling? Some of it was undoubtedly Member State outrage at the consequence of competence limitation of the EU: as we saw in Chapter 12, UK immigration law, for example, is much stricter on family reunification for UK nationals than EU law is on family reunification for EU nationals who move to the UK. While a UK national with an American partner thus would have to demonstrate a minimum income and pay significant fees to bring their American partner to the UK, a Greek national could simply bring their American partner to the UK on the display of a passport and evidence

[32] Case C-83/11 *Rahman and Others* ECLI:EU:C:2012:519.
[33] Case C-109/01 *Akrich* ECLI:EU:C:2003:491.

of their relationship. This is the consequence of the '**purely internal situation**' rule, in that, how UK law treats UK nationals with foreign partners is simply outside of the scope of what the EU can legislate on. However, it is a consequence that makes many people very resentful either of their government, *or* of the EU nationals who benefit from much simpler immigration rules. The *Akrich* limitation ameliorated the difference in treatment by ensuring that *all* EU nationals, regardless of where in the EU they live or are moving to, will have had to deal with restrictive national immigration rules at *some point* in order to be joined by their third-country-national partners.

However, the CJEU revisited *Akrich* in its 2010 *Metock*[34] judgment. It reconsidered the importance of EU citizenship as a status, and considered the impact of restrictive immigration rules on 'family life' for EU nationals and their families in the host State. It also highlighted that the EU legislature's own Citizenship Directive did not actually require 'prior lawful residence' for third-country nationals—so this was a restriction that had to be considered in light of the Treaty rights to free movement, and was deemed both unjustifiable and disproportionate. The 'purely internal situation' doctrine first raised in Chapter 12 thus bites significantly harder again—and as a consequence, many EU citizens who reside in their home State have considered 'doing a *Surinder Singh*' in order to gain EU residency rights for their third-country-national family members. Criticism of the ongoing application of the 'purely internal situation' despite the advent of EU citizenship has been substantial, and we consider it further in the next section.

Discussing the scenario

Consider Guillermo's wife and son. Is their move covered by EU free movement of persons law? If so, what rights do they have? What are those rights dependent on?

13.5 Current concerns about EU citizenship

The EU legislature and the CJEU are, at this stage, broadly on the same page when it comes to the free movement of persons—and significant progress has been made since 1957, and even since 1992, when 'citizenship' as a status was introduced. The key difference upheld by both the CJEU and the legislature is that economically active EU nationals can move relatively unrestrictedly, while economically inactive EU nationals continue to have to satisfy certain conditions.

However, and perhaps unsurprisingly given that so much of what makes up EU citizenship rights is determined first by the CJEU and only legislated for secondly, there remain controversial issues that the CJEU has not addressed to the satisfaction of all on-lookers. The first of these is an 'old' issue: the fact that EU citizenship has not done away with the inapplicability of EU law to 'purely internal situations'. The other is a 'new' issue, in that in recent years, the CJEU appears to be limiting the generosity of its earlier 'citizenship' case law by implying *duties* to the status of EU citizenship, and in the process seemingly restricting the rights it comes with. We will look at each of these contentious aspects of EU citizenship law in turn.

[34] Case C-127/08 *Metock and Others* ECLI:EU:C:2008:449.

13.5.1 Purely internal situations

As discussed in Chapter 12 and in Section 13.3.4, accessing the majority of EU citizenship rights still requires a 'cross-border' element. The ongoing existence of 'purely internal situations' remains one of the most contentious aspects of the EU's handling of EU citizenship and free movement of persons. AG Sharpston, in her opinion in *Walloon Government*, came out sharply against the traditional distinction between 'cross-border' and 'purely internal' situations, maintaining that Treaty provisions on EU citizenship 'challenge the sustainability in its present form of the doctrine'.[35]

However, the CJEU has generally continued to apply the doctrine, in large part in deference to the Member States. It repeated in *Walloon Government* that '[c]itizenship of the Union is not intended to extend the material scope of the Treaty to internal situations which have no link with Union law'.[36] However, Article 20 TFEU itself does not actually mention *cross-border* movement as being a condition for rights stemming from EU citizenship—and some authors, like Kochenov and Plender, have criticized the fact that the CJEU is sticking to an 'internal market logic' when being presented with what they call 'the logic of citizenship'.[37]

Are there any signs of a change in the CJEU's approach? Some might argue that *Garcia Avello* and *Chen* were the first examples of 'movement' becoming less integral to EU citizenship rights—but both cases concerned very distinct circumstances, and do not establish a broader principle of rights that are not contingent on 'cross-border situations'.

2011, however, saw a case that shook up all preconceptions of EU law's lack of effect on 'purely internal situations'. In *Ruiz Zambrano*,[38] the CJEU had to consider the EU residence rights of a family in Belgium. The children had both been born in Belgium, and as a consequence had Belgian nationality. However, Mr Ruiz Zambrano was a failed Columbian asylum seeker, who had been awaiting an asylum decision for several years—during which he had started a family—but now had been told he had no right to reside or work in Belgium. His children, and indeed, Mr Ruiz Zambrano himself, had never left Belgium since arriving there. He attempted to rely on the precedent set in *Chen*, and a Belgian court referred questions as to whether Mr Ruiz Zambrano could have any rights stemming from EU law to the CJEU.

Unlike in *Chen*, the Ruiz Zambrano family did not have sufficient resources or private health insurance. The CJEU thus had to consider if there was a direct right stemming from Article 20(2) TFEU that could grant Mr Ruiz Zambrano the right to remain in Belgium.

Case C-34/09 *Ruiz Zambrano* ECLI:EU:C:2011:124 (emphasis added)

41. As the Court has stated several times, citizenship of the Union is intended to be the fundamental status of nationals of the Member States . . .

42. In those circumstances, **Article 20 TFEU precludes national measures which have the effect of depriving citizens of the Union of the genuine enjoyment of the substance of the rights conferred by virtue of their status as citizens of the Union** . . .

→

[35] Opinion of AG Sharpston in *Walloon Government* ECLI:EU:C:2007:398, para 140.
[36] *Walloon Government*, para 39.
[37] Kochenov and Plender (n 8) 371.
[38] Case C-34/09 *Ruiz Zambrano* ECLI:EU:C:2011:124.

→

43. A refusal to grant a right of residence to a third country national with dependent minor children in the Member State where those children are nationals and reside, and also a refusal to grant such a person a work permit, has such an effect.

44. It must be assumed that such a refusal would lead to a situation where those children, citizens of the Union, would have to leave the territory of the Union in order to accompany their parents. Similarly, if a work permit were not granted to such a person, he would risk not having sufficient resources to provide for himself and his family, which would also result in the children, citizens of the Union, having to leave the territory of the Union. In those circumstances, those citizens of the Union would, in fact, be unable to exercise the substance of the rights conferred on them by virtue of their status as citizens of the Union.

In this amazingly short judgment, the CJEU appeared to have done away with 50 years of precedent on 'purely internal situations'; instead, it brings the facts of the case within the scope of EU law by stating that without a right to reside in the Member State that the Ruiz Zambrano family had never left, the Ruiz Zambrano children would be deprived of the 'genuine enjoyment of the substance' of EU citizenship rights.

In subsequent case law, the CJEU has clarified what this 'genuine enjoyment' amounts to—and has made it clear that *Ruiz Zambrano* is a very narrow exception to the 'purely internal situations' doctrine, rather than its end. The only reason that EU citizenship applied in the *Ruiz Zambrano* case is that the entire family, including the EU national children, would have had to leave the territory of the EU *as a whole* if the parents could not reside and work in Belgium.

McCarthy[39] was the first test of the *Zambrano* doctrine, and immediately carved it out as an exception, rather than a precedent. Mrs McCarthy was a UK national who had always lived in the UK, but, through her ancestry, had rights to an Irish passport. She married a third-country national and attempted to apply for an EU right to reside for her husband as a family member of an EU citizen, under the Citizenship Directive. This was rejected by UK officials, and the McCarthys did not qualify for a visa for the third-country national husband under UK immigration rules. Mr McCarthy consequently was told to leave the UK, and Mrs McCarthy appealed the UK's determination that she could not rely on EU law.

When asked to comment, the CJEU here noted that this *was* a 'purely internal situation'—primarily because Mrs McCarthy was not under pressure to leave the EU as a whole, unlike the Ruiz Zambrano family. To the CJEU, Mrs McCarthy being in a position where she could live *within* the EU but only *without* her partner did not mean that she was deprived of the 'genuine enjoyment' of her EU citizenship rights. The CJEU further felt the need to emphasize that Mrs McCarthy was not economically active and thus was not actually exercising any Treaty rights, regardless of her non-movement—but failed to note that she was a permanent carer of her handicapped child, and thus not in a position to 'work' or otherwise exercise Treaty rights. The outcome of the case was described as 'despicable' by Kochenov and Plender, and already it was clear that *Ruiz Zambrano* was going to be the exception rather than the new rule.[40]

[39] C-434/09 *McCarthy* ECLI:EU:C:2011:277.

[40] Kochenov and Plender (n 8) 390.

Dereci[41] furthered this impression, making it clear that *Zambrano* offered rights only in situations where an EU citizen was forced to leave the territory of the Union—not where families were going to be split up because an EU citizen and a third-country national could not live together in any particular EU Member State. The next 'purely internal situation' case that the CJEU decided in fact reemphasized the particularity of both *Zambrano* and *Chen*: in *Alokpa*,[42] French national children were born in Luxembourg to a third-country national mother who had no resources, and she was informed that neither *Chen* (where the parent *did* have sufficient resources) nor *Zambrano* (where the family had to leave the entire EU) applied in this situation, as the family could move to France.

The exceptionalism of *Zambrano* has become clear in other ways as well. *Home Secretary v CS*[43] involved a third-country-national parent in the UK, who was married to a UK national and was the sole carer of a UK national child. The third-country-national parent was found guilty of a criminal offence and sentenced to 12 months' imprisonment, and the UK subsequently wished to expel her; however, a deportation order against her would lead to her child being forced to leave not only the UK, but the EU as a whole. She claimed *Zambrano* rights as a consequence of this, but the CJEU made it clear that an expulsion order could be possible in these circumstances—which would then also result in the expulsion of the UK national child, even though it was the child's *parent's* personal behaviour that was deemed adverse to public policy and security.

Zambrano thus initially looked as if it was setting up new rules, and made the 'cross-border situation' requirement for free movement rights a thing of the past. However, it has now been proven to be a very narrow exception to a general EU citizenship regime that still does not cover 'purely internal situations'. The *Surinder Singh* route discussed in Chapter 12 thus remains as relevant as it ever has been, and indeed, has itself been reinforced by the CJEU in the last few years.

In *O and B*,[44] the CJEU stressed that providing the EU nationals had actually genuinely established 'family life' in the host Member State, they would be able to bring their third-country-national family members with them to the home Member State once they returned there, as they would have exercised Article 21 TFEU rights. Of course, *O and B* remains contingent on the EU citizen in question actually satisfying the conditions set out in the Citizenship Directive for those not *working* abroad: the conditions of sufficient resources and health insurance, in other words, would have to be satisfied in both the host State *and* upon the return to the home State, unless the EU citizen started working there.

Pause for reflection

What do *you* think should happen with 'purely internal situations' in the EU? Is the *Zambrano* exception too limited, or should it be expanded further? Should the CJEU further pursue the end of the 'purely internal situation' or should this be left to the EU legislature?

[41] Case C-256/11 *Dereci and Others* ECLI:EU:C:2011:734.
[42] Case C-86/12 *Alokpa and Moudoulou* ECLI:EU:C:2013:645.
[43] Case C-304/14 *Home Secretary v CS* ECLI:EU:C:2016:674.
[44] Case C-456/12 *O and B* ECLI:EU:C:2014:135.

13.5.2 Citizenship duties: unreasonably burdensome EU nationals

One of the other points of contention about the status of EU citizenship is the allusion in Article 20 TFEU to 'duties' of citizenship. There do not appear to be any of those . . . at least, there are none set out in the Treaties.

However, the most recent case law on the free movement of EU citizens does seem to suggest that there *is* some sort of duty, or at least an *expectation*, of EU citizens who exercise their free movement rights. This has been described by Azoulai as the 'duty to integrate in the host society'.[45] Azoulai argues that this has been implied in all the CJEU's case law surrounding EU citizenship: from *Grzelczyk* onwards, the CJEU has made it clear that while EU citizens have a 'duty' not to become an *unreasonable burden*, the host Member State owes a *certain degree of solidarity* to that EU citizen. This is a trade-off of rights (to equal treatment) and duties (to 'not be an unreasonable burden').

The Citizenship Directive appears to reflect similar thinking; after all, the longer an EU citizen resides in the host Member State, the more fixed and independent from their economic activity their rights become, and the harder it becomes to expel them from the host State territory. But is this not merely a measure of 'time spent abroad'? And is 'time spent abroad' truly the same thing as *integration* in the host State?

Azoulai suggests that there is also a qualitative element of a *degree* of integration that looks beyond time spent in the host State.[46] Article 28 of the Citizenship Directive again supports this: it refers to 'social and cultural integration into the host [S]tate' as being a relevant consideration before taking an expulsion decision. The CJEU has also more recently referred to the 'level of integration' in the host State as being part of the 'integration objective' underpinning permanent residency in its case law.[47]

What we see there is the CJEU taking a slightly different approach over time, and in more recent case law, it actively considers to what extent the EU citizen has *become a part of* the host State in its case law. 'Good' EU citizens, to put it very simply, are those who 'integrate', and they are entitled to the full scope of EU citizenship rights; whereas 'bad' EU citizens do not 'integrate' and consequently are not entitled to the full scope of EU citizenship rights.

Does this sound extreme? Perhaps—but there is evidence of it in the CJEU's most recent judgments. On expulsion orders, the CJEU has negatively commented on the values demonstrated by those in prison: in *Onuekwere*, it noted that a prison sentence shows 'the non-compliance by the person concerned with the *values* expressed by the society of the host Member State',[48] and in *M.G.*, it strongly implied that imprisonment might break the 'integrating links previously forged with the host Member State'.[49] In *M.G.*, it ultimately found that any time spent in prison cannot count towards the 'ten year residence' period that grants EU citizens enhanced protection from expulsion.[50]

The fact that the CJEU has declared those in prison not to be 'ideal' EU citizens is perhaps understandable; the deportation of criminals of foreign origin is an extremely

[45] Loic Azoulai, 'The (Mis)construction of the European Individual: Two essays on EU citizenship law' (2014) EUI Working Paper 14.

[46] Ibid.

[47] Case C-325/09 *Dias* ECLI:EU:C:2011:498, para 64.

[48] Case C-378/12 *Onuekwere* ECLI:EU:C:2014:13, para 26.

[49] Case C-400/12 *M.G.* ECLI:EU:C:2014:9, paras 36, 38.

[50] Ibid, para 33.

controversial subject in many of the Member States, as it was in the UK prior to Brexit. But the CJEU has gone further than that, as exemplified by the *Dano* case.[51] Ms Dano was a Romanian national who lived in Germany, where her son was born, since 2010. She there resided in her sister's apartment, and her sister provided for them. Ms Dano was in receipt of child benefit for her child, Florin, but these payments were cut off when German authorities determined Ms Dano did not herself have a right to reside in Germany. She appealed this decision, and the CJEU was asked to comment on whether or not she had residency rights.

Case C-333/13 *Dano* ECLI:EU:C:2014:2358 (emphasis added)

39. Ms Dano attended school for three years in Romania, but did not obtain any leaving certificate. She understands German orally and can express herself simply in German. On the other hand, she cannot write in German and her ability to read texts in that language is only limited. She has not been trained in a profession and, to date, has not worked in Germany or Romania. Although her ability to work is not in dispute, there is nothing to indicate that she has looked for a job.

. . .

73. In order to determine whether economically inactive Union citizens, in the situation of the applicants in the main proceedings, whose period of residence in the host Member State has been longer than three months but shorter than five years, can claim equal treatment with nationals of that Member State so far as concerns entitlement to social benefits, it must therefore be examined whether the residence of those citizens complies with the conditions in Article 7(1)(b) of Directive 2004/38. Those conditions include the requirement that the economically inactive Union citizen must have sufficient resources for himself and his family members.

74. To accept that persons who do not have a right of residence under Directive 2004/38 may claim entitlement to social benefits under the same conditions as those applicable to nationals of the host Member State would run counter to an objective of the directive, set out in recital 10 in its preamble, namely preventing Union citizens who are nationals of other Member States from becoming an unreasonable burden on the social assistance system of the host Member State.

. . .

76. . . . Article 7(1)(b) of Directive 2004/38 seeks to prevent economically inactive Union citizens from using the host Member State's welfare system to fund their means of subsistence.

. . .

78. A Member State must therefore have the possibility, pursuant to Article 7 of Directive 2004/38, of refusing to grant social benefits to economically inactive Union citizens who exercise their right to freedom of movement solely in order to obtain another Member State's social assistance although they do not have sufficient resources to claim a right of residence.

[51] Case C-333/13 *Dano* ECLI:EU:C:2014:2358.

Discussing the scenario

Consider what you thought about Guillermo's entitlement to unemployment benefit and child benefit in Germany under *Grzelczyk*. Does your answer change in response to *Dano*? Why or why not?

Dano appears to be the start of a new era of CJEU case law; it distances itself in significant ways from *Grzelczyk* and *Martinez Sala*, where individual circumstances of EU citizens applying for benefits had to be carefully considered—and all rejections of equal treatment had to be proportionate. In *Dano*, meanwhile, the CJEU appears to emphasize the rights of the host Member State to *deny* these benefits, providing they do so in a manner that takes individual circumstances into account. There is no mention here of a 'certain degree of solidarity', as there was in *Grzelczyk*; indeed, the implication of *Dano* seems to be that that degree of 'solidarity' only exists for those EU citizens who have appropriately *integrated* into the host State.

What is the context for this change of heart in the CJEU? Some, like Spaventa, suggest it is the economic crisis of 2008 and 2009, and what it meant for Member State public finances; others, like Verschueren, have linked it to political temperatures in many of the Member States, where concerns about 'benefit tourism' continue to rage.[52] The CJEU's approach in the last few years has been one that not only requires demonstrable 'integration' before benefits must be extended to EU nationals by the host State, but one that might even challenge the notion that 'worker' status automatically signifies a suitable degree of integration.[53] It has furthermore found recently in the *Brey* ruling that if an economically inactive EU migrant qualifies for a *need*-based benefit, this is likely to be sufficient evidence that they do not possess 'sufficient resources' to have a right to reside under the Citizenship Directive.[54] This means a scaling back of the requirement for the Member States to consider individual circumstances of EU citizens, and brings about significant questions about just how 'fundamental' a status EU citizenship is in the current political climate in the EU.

Pause for reflection

Do you think the CJEU should be responsive to political concerns about free movement in the Member States? Why or why not?

[52] Eleanor Spaventa, 'Seeing the Wood Despite the Trees? On the scope of union citizenship and its constitutional effects' (2008) 45 CMLRev 13; Herwig Verschueren, 'Preventing "Benefit Tourism" in the EU: A narrow or broad interpretation of the possibilities offered by the ECJ in Dano?' (2015) 52 CMLRev 363.

[53] Case C-20/12 *Giersch and Others* ECLI:EU:C:2013:411, paras 64–65.

[54] Case C-140/12 *Brey* ECLI:EU:C:2013:565, para 63.

13.6 Brexit and EU citizenship

The observations in Chapter 12 about ending the free movement of persons are equally applicable here: the UK electorate's concerns did not appear to have been per se about EU citizenship as a *status*, but rather with the free movement and equal treatment rights that were its substance. Of course, EU citizenship does exist as a separate status, and we should consider what is happening to that status over the course of the 'transition' and 'future relationship' process, as well as to the many ways in which freedom of movement for economically inactive EU nationals—while still not unconditional—has been made possible *by* the existence of that status.

13.6.1 Withdrawal Agreement

As of 31 January 2020, UK nationals are no longer EU citizens. Under the Withdrawal Agreement, however, the majority of the EU citizenship rights outlined in this chapter will continue during the transition period as if the UK were still a Member State. The exceptions are those rights which relate to the make-up of the EU institutions: consequently, UK nationals resident in the UK will not be able to vote in European Parliament elections any longer, as there will be no MEPs representing the UK during this time.[55]

As discussed in Chapter 12 with reference to workers, we can now generally stress that EU citizens in the UK and UK nationals in the EU who are exercising free movement of persons rights at the end of the transition period will be covered by Part 2 of the Withdrawal Agreement, which preserves the majority of those rights for the duration of their lives.

13.6.2 The Protocol on Ireland/Northern Ireland

The Protocol on Ireland/Northern Ireland in this respect is not very different from the remainder of the Withdrawal Agreement: EU 'citizenship' rights relating to representation in EU institutions will disappear upon the entry into the force of the Withdrawal Agreement, whereas all other rights will last for the duration of the transition period.

That said, there is a particular dimension to citizenship in Northern Ireland, and it is that under the 1998 Belfast/Good Friday Agreement, those born there can choose to be British, Irish, or both.[56] This means that there will be people born and raised in a part of the UK who nonetheless are entitled to be EU citizens not simply because their parents are EU nationals—but because they were born in Northern Ireland. They are in a distinct position from other EU nationals in the UK: they have not *moved* to another Member State, and consequently are not captured by Part 2 of the Withdrawal Agreement.

As discussed in Chapter 12, the EU rules on bringing non-EU national family members into an EU Member State are significantly more generous than the UK domestic ones. The exclusion of those born in Northern Ireland from Part 2 means that, effectively, there will be *some* Irish nationals in the UK who continue to benefit from EU 'family reunion' rights

[55] Withdrawal Agreement, Article 7(a).

[56] Whether anyone born in Northern Ireland can 'opt out' of UK citizenship has recently been brought before the UK courts; see *De Souza* [2019] UKUT 355.

under the Withdrawal Agreement, and *other* Irish nationals in the UK (specifically, born and raised in Northern Ireland) who will not.

On 10 January 2020, the UK government appeared to recognize that this runs contrary to the commitments of equal treatment of all Irish and UK nationals in the 1998 Belfast/ Good Friday Agreement.[57] It therefore committed to amending domestic law so as to ensure that those born in Northern Ireland will be able to benefit from the same 'family reunion' rights that are available to Irish nationals in the UK, even if under EU law they technically find themselves in a 'purely internal situation'.

As Irish nationals not born in Northern Ireland will have exercised free movement in order to be in the UK, this means that *as a matter of domestic law* the UK will grant the family reunion rights in Part 2 to the 'people of Northern Ireland'. This sidesteps the *McCarthy* ruling to the benefit of the people of Northern Ireland, but appears to do so only for the limited time during which Irish nationals moving to the UK will be a matter of EU law—so, until the end of the transition period. The position of Irish nationals moving to the UK *after* the transition period is no longer a matter of EU law, just as no other EU nationals will be moving to the UK under EU law after 2020 (or 2021 or 2022): those Irish nationals will be benefiting from the Common Travel Area, but the Common Travel Area arrangements do not cover third-country family immigration rules at this time. This is thus a concession to the particular situation those in Northern Ireland find themselves in—but a time-limited one all the same.

The Protocol addresses the more general position of those with Irish nationality in Northern Ireland in its preamble:

Preamble of the Protocol on Ireland/Northern Ireland

RECOGNISING that Irish citizens in Northern Ireland, by virtue of their Union citizenship, will continue to enjoy, exercise and have access to rights, opportunities and benefits, and that this Protocol should respect and be without prejudice to the rights, opportunities and identity that come with citizenship of the Union for the people of Northern Ireland who choose to assert their right to Irish citizenship . . .

The UK and the EU appear to pledge here (in the preamble, and so in non-binding terms) that Irish citizens in Northern Ireland will 'continue to enjoy, exercise and have access to rights, opportunities and benefits' on account of their EU citizenship. The remainder of the Protocol, however, does not elaborate on this. So what does it mean?

From what we can tell at this stage, it means simply that Irish citizens living in the UK (much like any other EU citizen living in the UK) will be able to continue to exercise their free movement rights *to other Member States*. They will also benefit from the few non-mobile rights that EU citizens have, such as the ability to access consular services of other Member States in foreign countries where Ireland does not have an embassy. But they are not covered by Part 2 of the Withdrawal Agreement, and consequently do not continue to benefit from the ongoing application of relevant rules of EU law *unless* they have previously lived and/or worked in another Member State, with now possibly the exception of 'family reunion' rights.

[57] See https://assets.publishing.service.gov.uk/government/uploads/system/uploads/attachment_data/file/856998/2020-01-08_a_new_decade__a_new_approach.pdf, 48.

The key factor here, in addition to the fact that, by and large, they have not exercised free movement rights, is that they are not themselves *living* in an EU Member State—and this in practice means that many rights that are associated with EU citizenship are not accessible to them, much as a German national in New York City also *has* EU citizenship rights but cannot *do* much of anything with them. A clear example is the voting rights established in Article 20 TFEU: as a matter of domestic UK law, Irish nationals are already allowed to vote in both local and Westminster elections, but UK law cannot give these Irish nationals a right to vote in European Parliament elections. Such a right, effectively for 'Irish nationals abroad', would have to be granted under Irish law—but is not obligatory under EU law in the way that Article 20 TFEU makes voting rights in European Parliament elections obligatory for EU nationals living *in* another Member State. What this means is that Brexit cannot strip these Irish citizens born in the UK from their EU citizenship—but that is very distinct from suggesting that their 'access' to rights, opportunities, and benefits is not impacted by the fact that they will shortly no longer live in an EU Member State.

13.6.3 The future relationship

The Political Declaration is succinct about the future of 'EU citizenship' and the movement rights for economically inactive EU and UK nationals after Brexit: UK nationals will not be EU citizens as they simply will not hold the nationality of a Member State any longer, and the free movement of persons will end.

October 2019 Political Declaration (emphasis added)

48. Noting that **the United Kingdom has decided that the principle of free movement of persons between the Union and the United Kingdom will no longer apply**, the Parties should establish mobility arrangements, as set out below.
49. The mobility arrangements will be based on non-discrimination between the Union's Member States and full reciprocity.
50. In this context, the Parties aim to provide, through their domestic laws, **for visa-free travel for short-term visits.**
51. The Parties **agree to consider conditions for entry and stay for purposes such as research, study, training and youth exchanges.**
52. The Parties also **agree to consider addressing social security coordination** in the light of future movement of persons.

If we use the Citizenship Directive as a benchmark of what is possible, the parties will aim to preserve the rights of persons to travel (without visas) for a period of what will probably be approximately three months between the UK and the EU27. Discussions will take place about movement of students, researchers, and trainees—and will also cover social security coordination, so as to encourage any covered movement.

For most not involved in business relationships with the EU, Brexit will not come with such tangible effects—but the loss of EU citizenship means that study exchanges, or moves abroad to retire there, will go from being fairly automatic to being issues that 'may be negotiated' as part of the future relationship.

There were discussions for some time in the European Parliament of an amendment to the Treaties to establish a category of 'associate citizenship', for those like UK nationals who (unwillingly) cease to be EU citizens, but they did not make it into the Withdrawal Agreement.[58] As such, UK nationals will only be *former* EU citizens, who may or may not benefit from the legacy rights set out in the Withdrawal Agreement, depending on how much they have exercised their EU citizen rights before the transition period ends.

13.7 In conclusion

Chapter 1 of this book pointed out that when it was first introduced in Maastricht, reactions to EU citizenship as a status were at best muted—it did not appear to contain any 'new' rights, and as a consequence felt rather empty. Over time, however, the CJEU and the EU legislature, as well as the drafters of subsequent Treaties, have ensured that 'citizenship' of the EU has become a rights-bearing status—albeit not one that is genuinely comparable to citizenship of a *country*.

The primary beneficiaries of EU citizenship to date have been the economically inactive holders of EU nationalities: the possibility of moving to another country for them opened up after 1992, even if more recent CJEU case law suggests it might be closing again, quite separately from Brexit. And Brexit, of course, had as a natural consequence the end of EU citizenship for many who held it until 31 January 2020. Whether that is a symbolic loss or a genuine one is very much dependent on what a given UK national was planning on doing with their life: if they had or have concrete plans to go and live abroad, the lack of EU citizenship status makes that more complicated for both those who work and those who do not, as Chapter 12 and Chapter 13 together have demonstrated.

Discussing the scenario

Use the material in this chapter to address whether the actions of the German authorities against Guillermo and his family are justifiable. Treat each paragraph as setting out a specific scenario, and explain how EU law applies to that scenario.

A sample approach to a response can be found online.

[58] For a discussion, see: https://researchbriefings.parliament.uk/ResearchBriefing/Summary/CDP-2018-0061.

Key points

The key points of EU citizenship rights are summarized for you in Table 13.1.

TABLE 13.1 EU citizenship rights

Type of Mover	Source of Rights	Rights	Derogations from Rights
EU National in their Home State	Article 20 TFEU	• Voting in European Parliament elections • Access to other Member States' consular services if temporarily abroad (eg, on holiday) • Right to petition EU institutions	n/a (*there is no derogation from the status of EU citizenship*)
EU National Worker Exercising Free Movement	Article 45 TFEU The Worker's Regulation The Citizenship Directive	• Right to enter and reside (unconditional) • Right to permanent residence after five years • Right to equal treatment in access to all benefits (unconditional, from day of arrival) • Right to vote in European Parliament and local elections • Access to other Member States' consular services if temporarily abroad (eg, on holiday) • Right to petition EU institutions	Article 45(3) TFEU—public policy, public security, public health 'Overriding Requirements'—if proportionate
EU National Job-Seeker Exercising Free Movement	Article 45 TFEU The Citizenship Directive	• Right to enter and reside for up to three months (and up to six months, if genuine chance of employment) • Right to equal treatment to benefits that facilitate access to the labour market • If holding a right to reside: right to vote in European Parliament and local elections • Access to other Member States' consular services if temporarily abroad (eg, on holiday) • Right to petition EU institutions	Article 45(3) TFEU—public policy, public security, public health 'Objective Justifications'—such as 'real link' requirement—if proportionate

Type of Mover	Source of Rights	Rights	Derogations from Rights
Economically Inactive EU National Exercising Free Movement	Article 18 TFEU Article 20 TFEU Article 21 TFEU The Citizenship Directive	• Right to enter and reside for up to 3 months • Right to enter and reside for between three months and five years if *self-sufficient* and possessing *sickness insurance* (and not an 'unreasonable burden' on the host State) • Right to permanent residence after five years • Right to equal treatment in access to benefits (limited) • If holding a right to reside: right to vote in European Parliament and local elections • Access to other Member States' consular services if temporarily abroad (eg, on holiday) • Right to petition EU institutions	Article 29 Citizenship Directive—public policy, public security, public health 'Objective justifications'—such as a 'real link' or 'genuine integration' requirement—if proportionate *More recently:* prevention of 'unreasonable burden' on the host State, where all requests for need-based benefits imply such a burden—and proportionality of measure restricting right to reside here assumed

Assess your learning

1. **Did economically inactive EU nationals have movement rights before 1992? (See Section 13.2.)**
2. **In what ways did the movement rights of economically inactive EU nationals change after 1992? (See Sections 13.3 and 13.5.2.)**
3. **Are the rights of economically active and economically inactive EU citizens the same as of the introduction of the Citizenship Directive? (See Section 13.4.)**
4. **Do EU citizens who have not moved out of their home country benefit from EU citizenship? (See Sections 13.2.2 and 13.5.1.)**

Further reading

Loic Azoulai, 'The (Mis)construction of the European Individual: Two essays on EU citizenship law' (2014) EUI Working Paper 14 *[note: the second essay is in French—read the first one!]*

Richard Bellamy, 'A Duty Free Europe? What's wrong with Kochenov's account of EU citizenship rights' (2015) 21 Eur Law J 558.

Stephen Coutts, 'Citizens of Elsewhere, Everywhere and . . . Nowhere? Rethinking Union citizenship in light of Brexit' (2018) 69(3) NILQ 231.

Camille Dautricourt and Sébastien Thomas, 'Reverse Discrimination and Free Movement of Persons under Community Law: All for Ulysses, nothing for Penelope?' (2009) 34 ELRev 433.

Kai Hailbronner, 'EU Citizenship and Access to Social Benefits' (2005) 43 CMLRev 1245

Dimitry Kochenov, 'EU Citizenship Without Duties' (2014) 20 Eur Law J 482.

Niamh Nic Shuibhne, 'Limits Rising, Duties Ascending: The changing legal shape of Union citizenship' (2015) 52 CMLRev 889.

Volker Roeben et al, 'Revisiting Union Citizenship from a Fundamental Rights Perspective in the Time of Brexit' (2018) 5 EHRLR 450.

Eleanor Spaventa, 'Earned Citizenship—Understanding Union Citizenship through its Scope' in Dimitry Kochenov (ed), *EU Citizenship and Federalism: the Role of Rights* (CUP, 2017).

Daniel Thym, 'The Elusive Limits of Solidarity: Residence rights and social benefits for economically inactive Union citizens' (2015) 52 CMLRev 17.

Online resources

Visit www.oup.com/he/demars1e for a sample approach to discussing the quote.

14

Freedom of establishment and free movement of services

Context for this chapter

UP A GREEK CREEK

Evan Cooper, *The Reporter Online*, 19 January 2018

Sitting behind the desk in her home office, she looks calm—but that's only because months of ridiculous treatment by the Greek administration has made her almost unflappable.

'Of course, when the rejection letters first came in, I was outraged, and dejected. But there's something about an administrative process that manages to just wear you out,' Allison Mead tells me, pointing at a stack of letters on her desk that would make an onlooker think she was very behind on her taxes.

Nothing could be further from the truth. Allison is a chef from Milton Keynes who was looking for a change, and when her partner Mina got a job offer in Greece, she thought that opportunity for change had presented itself.

'It's true we're not exactly internationally recognised for our cooking—but I've run a food stall here for the better part of six years now where I combine Mina's Portuguese heritage with some English classics, and I think there's a market for that abroad. There's nothing quite like it anywhere, including in Greece.'

It's said with a small smile, but that smile quickly fades.

'So . . . I tried to open up a bistro in Athens. Which was easier said than done. The first thing they stopped was me using my title. I've got several diplomas from the British Culinary Institute, which allow me to say that I'm a Professional Chef in the UK. They've got a similar title in Greece, but the Greek Food Institute told me that my diplomas are too different and won't be recognised here. So I had to find another way to draw crowds to my restaurant, if it couldn't be my expertise.'

→

→

And she had another way in mind, in offering a unique dining experience in Greece: not just food, but food and live entertainment, all organised around a theme celebrating Portugal.

'It took a lot of planning, and a lot of reaching out, but I'd say it went smoothly until I had to start applying for the licenses for the key element of what I had planned: live music.' She fishes the first letter from the stack. 'Here's the original rejection of the live entertainment request. When they read that I was planning on having Portuguese artists over for tasting menu events, they wrote back citing . . . what is it, the (fictional) Greek Public Order Regulations 1996, which allow local councils to reject applications for any licenses on "cultural" grounds.'

. . . what does *that* mean?

'Basically, the council told me that unless I played music that really showed off Greek culture, I was not getting this license. When I objected to that, they told me in person that were also refusing my license application because I was asking for too many live entertainment events, and so my venue and its planned activities were going to cause public disorder, which was also banned under the Public Order Regulations.'

Public disorder? What kind of music events was she planning on having?

'Tasting menus accompanied by thematic *Fado*,' Allison says, rolling her eyes. The traditional Portuguese music style, on acoustic guitar, may be *passionate* but is hardly known for instigating mosh pits and violence. 'Yeah. In Greece, *Fado* apparently is a threat to public safety.'

But that wasn't the end of Allison's dream. Failing to get permission for live music, she investigated installing a large screen in the bistro that would allow her to stream concerts from Portugal instead. She *then* found out that streaming was also illegal without a license, under the Greek Audio-Visual Services Regulations 2013.

'Yep, and I didn't apply for a license beforehand, because I didn't know. So they took away the screen and the projector, and disconnected my internet for a month as well. When I then did apply for the license, they said that they would respond to my application within 12 months, as they need to thoroughly investigate the source of the stream and what kind of content may be played in Greece if it is permitted. Until then, I am not allowed to stream anything.'

She looks out the window, out on the city where she's chosen to make a life for herself, but that seems to want to stop her at every turn.

'It just isn't going to be the same, you know, without the music. The atmosphere is missing, and the whole affair with closures and equipment being seized has made the locals kind of wary of the restaurant, so . . . I'm really struggling to get it off the ground, at this point.' She takes a deep breath and shrugs. 'Surely the whole point of the EU is that we *can* just move abroad and start a business and do things like this? But apparently that's not how it actually works.'

The Athens City Council and the Greek Food Institute were not available for comment.

14.1 **Introduction**

We have seen how *workers* have benefited from progressive EU Treaty and secondary law over the course of the EU's existence—and now it is time to consider their self-employed peers as well as companies. This chapter analyses the rights of the **self-employed** and **companies** to conduct their business in another Member State insofar as they are subject to *specific* separate rules. Self-employed people are, of course, also EU citizens, and so it is in general worth bearing in mind that the provisions of the Citizenship Directive and the Treaty's non-discrimination provision discussed in Chapter 13 are equally applicable to them.

Freedom of movement for self-employed people and companies has always been possible under the Treaties based on the two fundamental freedoms of 'establishment' and 'movement of services'. That said, a combination of CJEU case law and secondary legislation has taken what appeared to be straightforward prohibitions on *restricting* the movement of the self-employed and companies, and transformed them into a far more detailed legal landscape. The scenario at the start of this chapter sets out several different situations that self-employed EU citizens (or companies) may encounter, and we will use it to consider how the Treaty rules work for self-employed people in the Member States in practice.

For ease of understanding, the remainder of this chapter is split into three sections.

The first part deals with the action of *permanently* settling abroad in order to engage in an economic activity. This is known as establishment in EU law.

The second part deals with the action of *temporarily* being abroad in order to engage in an economic activity. Anything that is not free movement of workers or freedom of establishment falls into this category and is known as services provision.

The final part of this chapter will consider to what extent the rules on freedom of establishment and provision of services are absolutes: can a Member State ever refuse someone or a company wishing to provide services or establish in their territory? The answer is that they can, and we will consider the possible derogations from freedom of establishment and services provision and how such derogations might be justified in the final section of the chapter.

It is necessary at this stage, before we progress into the chapter discussion, to distinguish between free movement of workers, freedom of establishment, and the freedom to provide services. The Treaties leave all these concepts open, which means that definitions have come from the CJEU. We saw in Chapter 12 that in EU law 'work' means engaging in an activity under the direction of another person, in a way that is not marginal or ancillary. 'Establishment', in many ways, means the opposite: the CJEU has described activity as 'established' if there is no relationship of subordination, if the activity is carried out under the person's own responsibility, and if it is carried out in return for remuneration.[1] This separates 'establishment' from 'work'.

However, the CJEU has further specified that to be 'establishment', an activity has to be also carried out on a stable and continuous basis, in the economic life of another Member State.[2] This temporal dimension is what separates 'establishment' from the freedom to provide services, which is business activity in exchange for remuneration that takes place on a cross-border and a temporary basis.

Pause for reflection

Do you think the dividing line between 'temporary' and 'stable' activity is always clear? Why or why not?

[1] Case C-268/99 *Jany* ECLI:EU:C:2001:616.

[2] Case C-55/94 *Gebhard* ECLI:EU:C:1995:411.

14.2 Establishment

The Treaty provisions on freedom of establishment are found in Articles 49 to 55 TFEU. Beyond that, there is also significant secondary legislation adopted on the basis of Article 53 TFEU, including the Directive on mutual recognition of professional qualifications, which is essential in making the Article 49 'right' to establishment workable in practice. We will consider both in turn.

14.2.1 Establishment under the Treaty provisions

The basic right to 'establishment' is set out in Article 49 TFEU:

> **Article 49 TFEU (emphasis added)**
>
> Within the framework of the provisions set out below, restrictions on the freedom of establishment of nationals of a Member State in the territory of another Member State shall be prohibited. Such prohibition shall also apply to restrictions on the setting-up of agencies, branches or subsidiaries by nationals of any Member State established in the territory of any Member State.
>
> Freedom of establishment shall include the right to take up and pursue activities as self-employed persons and to set up and manage undertakings, in particular companies or firms within the meaning of the second paragraph of Article 54, under the conditions laid down for its own nationals by the law of the country where such establishment is effected, . . .

Article 49 TFEU makes a few aspects of freedom of establishment explicit. First, it definitely applies to any person or company (as detailed further in Article 54)[3] from *one* Member State who wishes to set up a business (ie, 'establish') in *another* Member State. That is the first sentence of Article 49 TFEU, and can be described as **primary establishment**. The second sentence adds to this that 'establishment' also captures anyone setting up subsidiaries or branches in a Member State *other than* the one in which their primary business is established—also known as **secondary establishment**.

EU law in practice

A classic example of a case involving secondary establishment is *Stanton*.[4] Mr Stanton operated a company in Belgium, *and* was employed in the United Kingdom. As a UK employee, he paid contributions for UK social security automatically (as part of his salary). He asked the Belgian authorities to exempt him from having to pay the Belgian self-employment social security contributions, on the basis that under Belgian law itself, self-employed people in Belgium did not owe social security contributions if they 'habitually pursued' a different principal or primary occupation.

→

[3] Article 54 TFEU and EU company law are not discussed specifically in this chapter.

[4] Case 143/87 *Stanton* ECLI:EU:C:1988:378.

→

According to the Belgian social security institution, this Belgian law only covered those who had a primary occupation *in Belgium*, because such a person would already be paying into the Belgian social security system. Someone like Mr Stanton, who was instead contributing to the UK social security system, would end up practising a profession in Belgium without paying any social security there at all if this law was applied to him.

The Belgian employment tribunal asked the CJEU to consider what the freedom of establishment under the Treaties meant for someone in Mr Stanton's situation. Their first observation was that the Belgian law in question was not nationality-specific: as such, there was no direct discrimination at play. However, the freedom of establishment provided for in the Treaty was there to enable those like Mr Stanton who were 'employed in one Member State and [wished], in addition, to work in another Member State in a self-employed capacity'.[5] National legislation that puts those like Mr Stanton at a disadvantage when they wish to secondary establish in another Member State was, as such, precluded by the Treaty. Belgium, therefore, was obliged to exempt Mr Stanton from paying social security in Belgium, as anyone in his position employed in Belgium as opposed to another Member State *would* be exempted.

What do you think about this ruling? Should someone who has jobs, or is self-employed, in two different Member States, pay taxes (and/or social security contributions) in both these Member States, at all times? Would such a requirement make people more or less likely to set up businesses in other Member States while maintaining a job in their home State?

Next, the second paragraph of Article 49 TFEU makes clear that as part of this 'right to establish', those establishing in another Member State also have a right to equal treatment with the nationals *of* their host Member State. The actual wording of the second paragraph also highlights that Article 49 TFEU covers both access to establishment in another Member State, *and* exercise of establishment in another Member State: equal treatment is required under Article 49 TFEU in both cases.

Over time, it has become clear that there are further aspects to Article 49 TFEU. One of the earliest cases on Article 49 TFEU thus held that the provision had vertical direct effect. In *Reyners*, a Dutch national who had attended law school in Belgium, found he could not join the Belgian Bar because he was not a Belgian national.[6] The CJEU, examining Belgium's argument that giving full effect to Article 49 TFEU required further legislation, concluded that the non-discrimination obligation in Article 49 TFEU was itself specific enough to be directly effective. Beyond that, the CJEU has also captured under 'vertical direct effect' those rules of private bodies that are 'designed to *regulate*, collectively, self-employment'.[7]

It was much later that the CJEU found that Article 49 TFEU was also, at least *sometimes*, horizontally directly effective. We considered this briefly in Chapter 8, but in the *Viking* and *Laval* judgments, the CJEU effectively held that the activities of trade unions could form a restriction to Article 49 TFEU establishment rights.[8] It noted that Article 49 TFEU did not only apply to those private bodies that carried out a 'regulatory' task, despite

[5] *Stanton* (n 4), para 12.
[6] Case 2/74 *Reyners* ECLI:EU:C:1974:68.
[7] Case C-309/99 *Wouters* ECLI:EU:C:2002:98.
[8] See Case C-438/05 *Viking* ECLI:EU:C:2007:772 and Case C-341/05 *Laval* ECLI:EU:C:2007:809.

what its own earlier case law had suggested—and stressed that trade unions themselves had a very particular power and ability to impede in freedom of establishment. Whether Article 49 TFEU could be horizontally directly effective in situations where the private parties involved are less 'powerful', or perhaps are just single private persons, remains to be seen.

Article 49 TFEU also applies to nationals of a Member State who have been abroad, but return to 'establish' in their home Member State, possibly with qualifications obtained abroad. Additionally, rather than just precluding discrimination between host State nationals and EU nationals 'establishing' in that Member State, it also precludes any and all measures that make establishing in a host State less attractive. As we will see next when examining CJEU case law on Article 49 TFEU, over time the Court has become more concerned with 'market access' than with discrimination in establishment, much as it appears to have done in its case law on free movement of goods.[9]

Discussing the scenario

Is Allison wanting to set up a bistro a form of 'establishment'? Why or why not?

Article 49 TFEU and discrimination

Reyners is a fairly typical example of a directly discriminatory measure restricting access to a profession: there is express discrimination on the basis of nationality in refusing to let a Dutch national (even trained in Belgium!) join the Belgian Bar because they are not Belgian. A further example is the *Factortame* saga, in which the Merchant Shipping Act 1988 made it illegal for Spanish owners to operate a shipping business in the UK.[10] However, the CJEU quickly determined that indirect discrimination would also be caught by Article 49 TFEU.

Thieffry once more concerned legal professionals, but this time, the Belgian national who wanted to train at the French bar was refused not on the basis of his nationality but rather on the basis of his Belgian qualifications. While French *universities* recognized his Belgian doctorate and admission to the bar, the Paris Bar association did not—they found he lacked a degree in French law. The CJEU did not accept this: as the French universities found his qualifications to be equivalent, and he had satisfied the practical training that was required for French lawyers to join the Paris Bar, the French state could *not* justify refusing Mr Thieffry admission purely on the basis that his equivalent qualification was not from France.

The *Thieffry* example is illustrative of a lot of CJEU establishment case law: it concerned qualifications, and the fact that qualifications from one Member State were not recognized in another Member State. The CJEU came down hard on any national regulatory requirements of professions that meant that *equivalent* foreign qualifications were not accepted. There were thus positive obligations set out for the Member States to ensure that processes were in place to check the equivalence of foreign qualifications, and *where*

[9] See Chapter 11.
[10] Case C-221/89 *Factortame* ECLI:EU:C:1991:320; see Chapters 7 and 8 for more discussion of the case.

qualifications were equivalent, to admit those holding them to a relevant profession in the same way that those holding domestic qualifications would be.[11]

Vlassopoulou is a helpful illustration of the requirements that the CJEU holds the Member States to.[12] It is yet another case involving a lawyer wishing to work with foreign qualifications in a host Member State: here, Ms Vlassopoulou was told by the German authorities that she could not join the German Bar with her Greek degree and several years of legal practice in Germany, as she had not sat the relevant German examinations that permitted entry to the German Bar.

Case C-340/89 *Vlassopoulou* ECLI:EU:C:1991:193 (emphasis added)

16. Consequently, a Member State which receives a request to admit a person to a profession to which access, under national law, depends upon the possession of a diploma or a professional qualification must take into consideration the diplomas, certificates and other evidence of qualifications which the person concerned has acquired in order to exercise the same profession in another Member State by making a comparison between the specialized knowledge and abilities certified by those diplomas and the knowledge and qualifications required by the national rules.
17. That examination procedure must enable the authorities of the host Member State to assure themselves, on an objective basis, that the foreign diploma certifies that its holder has knowledge and qualifications which are, if not identical, at least equivalent to those certified by the national diploma. That assessment of the equivalence of the foreign diploma must be carried out exclusively in the light of the level of knowledge and qualifications which its holder can be assumed to possess in the light of that diploma, having regard to the nature and duration of the studies and practical training to which the diploma relates . . .
18. In the course of that examination, a Member State may, however, take into consideration objective differences relating to both the legal framework of the profession in question in the Member State of origin and to its field of activity. In the case of the profession of lawyer, a Member State may therefore carry out a comparative examination of diplomas, taking account of the differences identified between the national legal systems concerned.
19. If that comparative examination of diplomas results in the finding that the knowledge and qualifications certified by the foreign diploma correspond to those required by the national provisions, the Member State must recognize that diploma as fulfilling the requirements laid down by its national provisions. If, on the other hand, the comparison reveals that the knowledge and qualifications certified by the foreign diploma and those required by the national provisions correspond only partially, the host Member State is entitled to require the person concerned to show that he has acquired the knowledge and qualifications which are lacking.

[11] See, eg, Case 222/86 *Heylens* ECLI:EU:C:1987:442.
[12] Case C-340/89 *Vlassopoulou* ECLI:EU:C:1991:193.

In other words, the CJEU obliged mutual recognition of *equivalent* qualifications, and this was to be carried out by host State institutions. The host State could still set its own standards, but could not demand they were met in situations where *equivalent* standards were already met.[13] Conversely, where the home State standards had not been met in full—because, for example, the legal curriculum in one Member State covered different things than in another Member State—it could require 'topping up' so as to supplement the existing knowledge with further knowledge—but the host State could not simply refuse to acknowledge any qualifications already obtained.

We will see that the approach set out in *Vlassopoulou* is the one that the EU legislature by and large adopted when drafting Directive 2005/36/EC—but once again, the big 'moves' in opening up freedom of establishment and precluding indirect discrimination via national regulation were made by the CJEU first.

In terms of direct discrimination regarding *exercise* of establishment in another State, the CJEU has also been unequivocal. In *Commission v Belgium*, a Belgian rule that required only *non-Belgians* to have lived in Belgium for over one year before they could register an aircraft was caught by Article 49 TFEU.[14] Indirect discriminatory measures affecting the *exercise* of establishment are also captured, and usually relate to social security legislation that makes benefits more difficult to obtain for non-national EU citizens. For instance, in *Commission v Luxembourg*, the CJEU declared a Luxembourgian rule that required those eligible for child benefit to be resident in Luxembourg to have more of an impact on non-Luxembourgian EU nationals: they may operate businesses in Luxembourg, but can just as easily live across the border in Germany, France, or Belgium.[15]

Discussing the scenario

Consider the CJEU's case law on mutual recognition of qualifications. Can you think of some reasons why it might have been possible for the Greek Food Institute to reject the British Culinary Institute qualification?

Article 49 TFEU and non-discrimination

As is true for the free movement of goods and persons, the early CJEU case law concerned directly and indirectly discriminatory measures alone. However, as we also saw in Chapters 11 and 12, the CJEU slowly moved beyond the notion that only *unequal treatment* between host and home State nationals would engage Article 49 TFEU. Non-discriminatory measures that nonetheless made life significantly harder for those *trying* to exercise their freedom of establishment were consequently also tackled by the CJEU.

The clearest indication of the scope that the CJEU assigns to Article 49 TFEU came in *Gebhard*.[16] In yet another case involving the legal profession, *Gebhard* concerned a German national who faced disciplinary proceedings before the Milan Bar Council for using the title *avvocato* for the legal practice he had permanently set up in Italy. The Milan Bar

[13] This is akin to the doctrine of mutual recognition established by *Cassis de Dijon* regarding the free movement of goods; see Chapter 11.

[14] Case C-203/98 *Commission v Belgium* ECLI:EU:C:1999:380.

[15] Case C-111/91 *Commission v Luxembourg* ECLI:EU:C:1993:92.

[16] *Gebhard* (n 2).

Council argued that his qualifications had not been formally recognized in Italy, and so he could not use this title, nor open up a practice on a permanent basis. The 'recognition' of qualifications to practise as *avvocato* applied to both Italian and non-Italian nationals. The CJEU accepted that such a qualification rule could be upheld by Italy . . . providing that it met certain conditions:

Case C-55/94 *Gebhard* ECLI:EU:C:1995:411 (emphasis added)

36. Where the taking-up or pursuit of a specific activity is subject to such conditions in the host Member State, a national of another Member State intending to pursue that activity must in principle comply with them . . .

37. It follows, however, from the Court' s case-law that **national measures liable to hinder or make less attractive the exercise of fundamental freedoms guaranteed by the Treaty must fulfil four conditions**: they must be applied in a **non-discriminatory** manner; they must be **justified by imperative requirements** in the general interest; they must be **suitable** for securing the attainment of the objective which they pursue; and they must **not go beyond what is necessary** in order to attain it.

Paragraph 37 establishes a more general 'market access' test for freedom of establishment, which is very similar to the test applied for free movement of goods the CJEU introduced in the *Italian Trailers* and *Mickelsson* cases.[17] The CJEU could have found that the Italian measure was indirectly discriminatory—but chose to avoid the idea of discrimination altogether, and instead focused on whether the measure was an *obstacle* to market access.

Following *Gebhard,* the CJEU has consistently held that any measure that might make market access more difficult for anyone hoping to establish in a host Member State will be caught by Article 49 TFEU, unless justifiable.[18] As just one example (and not involving lawyers), in *Commission v Spain*, a Spanish retail law that meant that larger retail stores were subject to far more stringent regulation than smaller retail stores was found to restrict access to the market, and thus hinder trade across the internal market, and fall foul of Article 49 TFEU.[19]

The CJEU has effectively copied over its case law on 'market access' from free movement of goods to freedom of establishment, though it has not made this explicit. Nonetheless, the principles that apply to 'market access' tests in goods have been reflected in CJEU judgments involving services and establishment: a recent example of this is *Pelckmans*, which concerned Belgian legislation that prohibited stores from being open seven days a week.[20] Pelckmans' competitors brought an action before the Belgian courts to force the Pelckmans garden centre to comply with this ban. The CJEU confirmed that as far as free movement of goods under the Treaty is concerned, this type of measure is not covered by Article 34 TFEU.[21] However, it also considered if the Belgian rule impeded freedom of

[17] See Chapter 11 for a discussion.

[18] See, eg, C-442/02 *CaixaBank* ECLI:EU:C:2004:586; Case C-346/04 *Conijn* ECLI:EU:C:2006:445; Case C-212/97 *Centros* ECLI:EU:C:1999:126.

[19] Case C-400/08 *Commission v Spain* ECLI:EU:C:2011:172.

[20] Case C-483/12 *Pelckmans* ECLI:EU:C:2014:304.

[21] See the discussion surrounding *Keck* in Chapter 11.

establishment, and here found that 'any restrictive effects [the measure] might have on freedom of establishment are too uncertain and indirect for the obligation laid down to be regarded as being capable of hindering that freedom'.[22] In other words, it ensured that measures falling outside of *one* 'fundamental freedom' because of their limited impact on the internal market would not then be caught by *another* 'fundamental freedom'.

Whether rulings like *Pelckmans* are a sign that the CJEU is trying to unify how it approaches the 'four freedoms' remains unclear;[23] for our purposes, it suffices to say that in principle any 'certain' and 'direct' obstructions to market access are likely to be found to be violations of Article 49 TFEU and will need to be justified somehow. We come back to justifications in Section 14.4.

Discussing the scenario

For each of the following aspects of the scenario at the start of the chapter, decide if they are: a) directly discriminatory; b) indirectly discriminatory; or c) non-discriminatory.

- Rejecting Allison's qualification from the BCI.
- Refusing her the licence for live music on the 'culture' ground.
- Refusing her the licence for live music on the public disorder ground.

Article 49 TFEU and purely internal situations

The similarities between free movement of goods and freedom of establishment have been flagged up so far, but there are other areas where freedom of establishment works more similarly to free movement of persons. This is unsurprising in many ways: both of these freedoms involve actual EU nationals crossing borders, and as such are always subject to the Citizenship Directive.

A more interesting way in which there is an overlap between free movement of persons and freedom of establishment lies in the area of reverse discrimination. As we discussed in Chapter 12, in the absence of movement, EU law does very little to help EU nationals, *prima facie* because the EU simply does not have the competence to tell Member States how to treat their own nationals without there being an 'EU dimension' to a situation. The only way in which an EU national can invoke EU law against their home Member State is by *having* moved, as is demonstrated by cases such as *Surinder Singh* regarding the free movement of workers.[24]

The CJEU has upheld a similar 'red line' with regards to freedom of establishment. A French national who has never left France consequently cannot rely on any of the EU establishment rules for setting up or running a business in France. A prime example of the 'purely internal situation' doctrine biting with respect to freedom of establishment is the *Walloon Government* case, where Belgium operated a 'care' (as in sickness) insurance regime that was only available to those living in the Flanders region of Belgium

[22] *Pelckmans* (n 20), para 25.

[23] For a good discussion of the 'convergence' of the market freedoms, see Alina Tryfanidou, 'Further Steps on the Road to Convergence Among the Market Freedoms' (2010) 35(1) ELRev 36, and Alina Tryfanidou, *The Impact of Union Citizenship on the EU's Market Freedoms* (Hart, 2016).

[24] See Chapter 12 for a discussion.

or in Brussels.[25] The CJEU declared this to be a restriction on both free movement of workers and freedom of establishment as it would deter migrant EU workers or self-employed persons from exercising their right to leave their Member State and move to, say, Wallonia, where such care insurance was not available. It thus found that any EU nationals working or established in either Wallonia or Flanders should be eligible for the scheme—but stressed emphatically that this would not apply to non-mobile Belgian nationals, as their treatment was outside of the EU's competence.

However, there are various situations where even EU nationals established or establishing in their home Member State will have experienced enough of a 'cross-border' situation to invoke EU law. For example:

- A national of Member State X obtains qualifications in Member State Y; wishes to use those qualifications in Member State X; and Member State X does not recognize the Member State Y qualifications.[26]
- A Member State X national who operates businesses or is self-employed in both Member State X and Member State Y; lives in Member State Y but has earnings in both Member State Y and X; and is therefore subjected to a higher 'non-resident' tax in Member State X, *only* because he operates an establishment in Member State Y as well.[27]

The latter situation is rare, and the former used to be significantly more regular, but has been ameliorated by the fact that the EU has adopted secondary legislation to facilitate the mutual recognition of qualifications, as we will now briefly consider.

14.2.2 **Making establishment practically possible: Directive 2005/36/EC**

Having a right to legally set up or operate a business, or be self-employed, is only one half of what is necessary in order to actually exercise a right to establishment. Article 53 TFEU recognizes this, and thus obliges the EU to take appropriate measures to ensure that exercise is *in practice* also possible for those EU nationals moving between Member States for establishment:

Article 53 TFEU (emphasis added)

1. In order to make it easier for persons to take up and pursue activities as self-employed persons, the European Parliament and the Council shall, acting in accordance with the ordinary legislative procedure, issue **directives for the mutual recognition of diplomas, certificates and other evidence of formal qualifications** and for the coordination of the provisions laid down by law, regulation or administrative action in Member States concerning the taking-up and pursuit of activities as self-employed persons.

[25] Case C-212/06 *Walloon Government* ECLI:EU:C:2008:178; the case is discussed in detail in Chapter 12.
[26] Case 115/78 *Knoors* ECLI:EU:C:1979:31.
[27] Case C-107/94 *Asscher* ECLI:EU:C:1996:251.

The mutual recognition of qualifications is an obvious barrier that the EU has eradicated over time. Following decades of sector-specific directives on the recognition of qualifications, 2005 saw the adoption of the 'general' mutual recognition directive, Directive 2005/36/EC,[28] which now applies to the majority of medical professionals as well as to all professions for which specific regulatory rules were not retained. An EU database allows any self-employed person to quickly check if their profession falls under the Directive 2005/36/EC rules, or more specific ones.[29]

Specific legislation remains for the mutual recognition of the qualifications of, for example, lawyers, sailors, insurance intermediaries, and 'some professions handling toxic products'. Lawyers are in an interesting position here, in that under the EU directive regulating their profession, they can establish in any other country and carry out their profession permanently *as long as* they operate on whatever their home country title is: so, for example, a UK solicitor can become a solicitor in Italy by having their qualifications registered. Only after three years of practice in that host country can they apply to acquire a 'host country title'.[30]

In broad terms, Directive 2005/36/EC reflects the approach of the CJEU in cases like *Vlassopoulou*. It thus formalizes the obligations for host Member States to verify equivalence in qualifications, and to only impose further obligations on EU nationals wishing to establish in their State where there is an actual difference in knowledge and practical training absent in those qualifications. There are, however, also 'automatic recognition' provisions codified in the Directive: as such, nurses, midwives, doctors, dentists, pharmacists, architects, and veterinary surgeons have had their basic training standards in each EU Member State coordinated, and this means that they can simply apply for confirmation of their ability to establish in another Member State once they hold that training.[31]

In general, under the Directive's rules, the 'equivalence' test of qualifications is applied in the first instance. Where in the country of origin, a profession is not regulated and so there is no 'qualification' to present, the Directive indicates that two years of practical experience will grant recognition.[32] If there is doubt as to the level of knowledge and experience of a candidate, an 'adaptation period' of up to three years before recognition of a profession or an aptitude test can be set up by the host Member State so as to determine and make up any shortfall in qualification.[33]

The overall effects of the 'mutual recognition' regime in place in the EU is well demonstrated by *Koller*.[34] Koller, an Austrian national, obtained a law degree in Austria, but then moved to Spain for the remainder of his 'qualifying'. He thus took a number of courses and exams and had his Austrian degree declared as 'equivalent' under the relevant EU directives. When he then returned to Austria as a licensed Spanish lawyer, the Austrian authorities refused his application to take the aptitude test that would admit him to the Austrian legal profession, claiming that he had not satisfied the practical experience requirement of

[28] Directive 2005/36/EC of the European Parliament and of the Council of 7 September 2005 on the recognition of professional qualifications [2005] OJ L255/22.

[29] See https://ec.europa.eu/growth/tools-databases/regprof/index.cfm?newlang=en.

[30] Directive 98/5/EC of the European Parliament and of the Council of 16 February 1998 to facilitate practice of the profession of lawyer on a permanent basis in a Member State other than that in which the qualification was obtained [1998] OJ L77/36.

[31] Directive 2005/36/EC, Chapter III.

[32] Ibid, Article 5(1)(b). [33] Ibid, Article 14.

[34] Case C-118-09 *Koller* ECLI:EU:C:2010:805.

Austrian qualification—and had in fact moved to Spain to *avoid* the five years of practical experience that lawyers must have before they can register as qualified in Austria.

The CJEU declared his situation to fall within the scope of the predecessor of Directive 2005/36 as well as the directive specific to the legal profession, and overruled the Austrian decision, noting that the whole purpose of the aptitude test was to *test* whether the applicant met the Austrian required standards. If he was equivalently qualified, he would pass—and if not, he would not.

The detailed legislative regime on mutual recognition of qualifications has thus made cross-border establishment significantly simpler than it was before, and is an essential aspect of the freedom of establishment working in practice.

Discussing the scenario

Can Directive 2005/36/EC help Allison? If so, how?

14.3 Services

The rules on the free movement of services are contained in Articles 56 to 62 TFEU. Where 'services' are provided by self-employed people, the Citizenship Directive (as discussed in Chapter 12) also applies to them, particularly on issues like entry into another Member State and the possibility of them being expelled from another Member State. For companies, on the other hand, the rules in Articles 56 to 62 TFEU set out both the rules on the freedom and on derogating from the freedom. Beyond that, there is further secondary legislation that *also* affects the free movement of services: Directive 2005/36/EC also regulates the provision of services abroad,[35] and the so-called Services Directive of 2006 sets out a further general programme for eliminating discrimination against service providers (as well as those established) from other Member States.

14.3.1 Services under the Treaty provisions

Articles 56 and 57 set out the basic terms under which 'free movement of services' operates.

Article 56 TFEU (emphasis added)

Within the framework of the provisions set out below, **restrictions on freedom to provide services within the Union** shall be **prohibited** in respect of **nationals of Member States** who are **established in a Member State other than that of the person for whom the services are intended.**

The European Parliament and the Council, acting in accordance with the ordinary legislative procedure, may extend the provisions of the Chapter to nationals of a third country who provide services and who are established within the Union.

→

[35] A key exception to this is the legal profession, which has separate directives regulating lawyer services (Council Directive 77/249/EEC of 22 March 1977 to facilitate the effective exercise by lawyers of freedom to provide services [1977] OJ L78/17) and lawyer establishment (Directive 98/5/EC).

→

Article 57 TFEU (emphasis added)

Services shall be considered to be 'services' within the meaning of the Treaties where they are **normally provided for remuneration**, in so far as they are not governed by the provisions relating to freedom of movement for goods, capital and persons.

...

Without prejudice to the provisions of the Chapter relating to the right of establishment, **the person providing a service may, in order to do so, temporarily pursue his activity in the Member State where the service is provided, under the same conditions as are imposed by that State on its own nationals.**

Articles 56 and 57 TFEU indicate that a 'service' is effectively any activity that is carried out in a cross-border fashion on a temporary basis for remuneration. A service provider consequently has to be established in *one* Member State (say, Germany) and be providing a service in *another* Member State (say, France), and this service has to be 'temporary'—otherwise, they would be establishing in that Member State. The line between 'temporary' service provision and 'establishment' is not always entirely clear: for example, having an 'office' abroad does not necessarily mean 'establishment' there.[36] The CJEU is thus forced to make a lot of factual determinations about just how 'temporary' an activity abroad is in order to determine if it is caught by Article 49 TFEU or Article 56 TFEU.

One further key condition made clear by Article 56 TFEU is that the free movement of services is dependent on Member State nationality. Foreign nationals cannot, as a matter of EU law, benefit from the free movement of services; but as per Article 57 TFEU, EU nationals are entitled to equal treatment with host State nationals carrying out equivalent activity in the host State.

Several aspects of this general description of 'services' are worth unpacking further in light of CJEU case law. As is the case for freedom of establishment, the CJEU has broadened what the Treaties say about services in Articles 56 and 57 TFEU significantly.

The Treaty provisions only speak about services provision: eg, a Germany lawyer going to see a client in France. The CJEU's case law, however, has made it clear that services reception is also covered by Article 56 TFEU.[37] A seminal illustration of this is *Cowan*, in which a British tourist who had been attacked while on holiday in Paris should have had access to a French criminal compensation scheme—'tourism' apparently being the service that he was receiving abroad.[38] Finally, the CJEU has found that where neither the provider nor the recipient leaves their Member State of origin, but the service itself crosses borders, this too is captured by Article 56 TFEU. This became clear in *Alpine Investments*, where a Dutch law on cold-calling was found to impede a 'cold-calling' service set up in Belgium from exercising its Article 56 TFEU rights in the Netherlands.[39] The service itself was cross-border, as many advertising, broadcasting, and 'internet'-related services will be found to be.

[36] As was discussed in *Gebhard* (n 2).
[37] Joined Cases 286/82 and 26/83 *Luisi and Carbone* ECLI:EU:C:1984:35.
[38] Case 186/87 *Cowan* ECLI:EU:C:1989:47.
[39] Case C-384/93 *Alpine Investments* ECLI:EU:C:1995:126.

Also worth noting is that the CJEU's case law places no conditions on how regularly a service is provided or received: a one-off tourist incident, as in *Cowan,* is captured by Article 56 TFEU, as is occasional service provision abroad, which was found to be present in the *Carpenter* case on account of Mr Carpenter's occasional work on the continent.[40] Indeed, the *Gourmet* case—involving an advertising campaign in Sweden launched by a company *not* in Sweden—resulted in the CJEU ruling that the *potential* of service provision or reception abroad would establish a cross-border element.[41] In *Gourmet,* the advertising ban for alcohol products in Sweden was absolute, meaning there were no 'service recipients' in Sweden to find—but the CJEU noted that there *could* have been, had the advertising campaign been launched.

The concept of '**remuneration**' has also been subject to much case law, primarily on account of Member States arguing that the receipt of public services abroad could not be captured by Article 56 TFEU, because by and large they were not offered for 'payment'. The CJEU has clarified that some form of 'consideration' for the activity in question is expected, but that that consideration does not have to be paid directly by the person receiving the service.[42]

Situations where 'remuneration' is absent include public education, where the activity being provided for the State is 'fulfilling its duties towards its own population' and where nobody pays directly for the activity itself (but rather, taxation covers it).[43] Conversely, private for-profit education establishments *are* covered by Article 56 TFEU.[44] The CJEU has also found that healthcare paid for and received in another Member State is a service under Article 56 TFEU, even where the treatment is paid for by a sickness insurance fund[45] or, controversially, the general taxpayer, as the NHS is.[46] The latter case law has resulted in an intervention by the EU legislature so as to try to shape the development of cross-border healthcare more directly and to prevent the CJEU from overly 'liberalizing' what they appear to view as a clear state activity.[47]

Pause for reflection

Do you think public services like public healthcare and public education (eg, primary schools) should be covered by the rules on free movement of services? Why or why not? Do you think there is a clear distinction between 'public healthcare' and 'public education' as a service?

[40] Case C-60/00 *Carpenter* ECLI:EU:C:2002:434; see Chapter 9 for more discussion.

[41] Case C-405/98 *Gourmet* ECLI:EU:C:2001:135, para 38. Note that *Gourmet* also involved the free movement of goods; this dimension is discussed in Chapter 11.

[42] Case 263/86 *Humbel* ECLI:EU:C:1988:451 and Case 352/85 *Bond van Adverteerders* ECLI:EU:C:1988:196.

[43] *Humbel*, para 18.

[44] Case C-76/05 *Schwarz* ECLI:EU:C:2007:492 and Case C-56/09 *Zanotti* ECLI:EU:C:2010:288.

[45] Case C-157/99 *Geraets-Smits* ECLI:EU:C:2001:404.

[46] Case C-372/04 *Watts* ECLI:EU:C:2006:325; note that the CJEU was careful not to declare treatment *by* the NHS a 'service', but instead just concluded that treatment abroad *funded* by the NHS was.

[47] See, inter alia, the overview provided by Stephane de la Rosa, 'The Directive on Cross-Border Healthcare or the Art of Codifying Complex Case Law' (2012) 49 CMLRev 15.

A further interesting aspect of the case law relates to the nature of services. Arguments have been made by the Member States that activities that are illegal under their domestic law should not benefit from free movement of services under EU law, but these attempts—ranging from gambling[48] to prostitution[49] and abortion[50] as services obtained abroad—have been by and large unsuccessful. The CJEU's case law can be summarized as having found that as long as a 'service' is legal in *one* Member State, it is free to be provided in *all* Member States—unless, of course, a Member State can justify restricting provision of a service.

Article 56 TFEU is vertically directly effective, as confirmed by the CJEU in a case that looks like a 'services' equivalent of the *Reyners* establishment case. In *Van Binsbergen*, a Dutch lawyer who had moved to Belgium in the middle of court proceedings in the Netherlands was told he could no longer represent his client, as under Dutch law, only those established in the Netherlands could act as legal counsel.[51] The CJEU found that Article 56 TFEU was directly effective despite the Article 59 TFEU obligation to legislate so as to liberalize services, and that the Dutch law in question was a discriminatory restriction on the freedom to provide (in this case, legal) services.

The horizontal direct effect of Article 56 TFEU was confirmed significantly later, but in a very similar fashion to how it was confirmed under Article 49 TFEU in CJEU case law. As such, the CJEU ruled that any measures 'aimed at collectively regulating' services would be caught by Article 56 TFEU in *Walrave*,[52] and made explicit in *Laval* that it was irrelevant if those measures were public or private.

As we will see, the 'purely internal situation' doctrine observed with regards to people and establishment also bites vis-à-vis services, and the CJEU here, too, has slowly moved from considering only discriminatory measures in light of Article 56 TFEU to also capturing non-discriminatory measures that make market access more difficult as being restrictions of the free movement of services.

Discussing the scenario

Which, if any, of the activities Allison discusses in the interview fall under the free movement of services? What makes you think so?

Article 56 TFEU and discrimination?

The CJEU case law on Article 56 TFEU is in many ways similar to the case law on Article 49 TFEU. Measures that discriminate against service providers or recipients from other Member States, on the basis of their nationality, are thus contrary to Article 56 TFEU.[53] An example of this kind of direct discrimination is *FDC*, where a Spanish law that granted a licence for the 'dubbing' (voice-overing in Spanish) of foreign films only on the condition that those distributing those films *also* distributed a Spanish film.[54] Here, the 'foreign film' distribution service was treated worse than a film distribution service that specialized in Spanish films, specifically on account of their 'foreign' status.

[48] Case C-275/92 *Schindler* ECLI:EU:C:1994:119.
[49] Case C-268/99 *Jany* ECLI:EU:C:2001:616.
[50] Case C-159/90 *Grogan* ECLI:EU:C:1991:378.
[51] Case 33/74 *Van Binsbergen* ECLI:EU:C:1974:131.
[52] Case 36/74 *Walrave and Koch* ECLI:EU:C:1974:140.
[53] See, eg, *Case C-76/90 Säger* ECLI:EU:C:1991:331.
[54] Case C-17/92 *FDC* ECLI:EU:C:1993:172.

In free movement of services, indirect discrimination tends to take the form of conditions being attached to where a service provider is *established*—eg, where the service originates from. *Van Binsbergen* is thus an example of indirect discrimination, as is *Commission v Germany*, in which the CJEU declared a German law that required insurance companies that wanted to provide insurance to German customers to be established and authorized in Germany to be caught by Article 56 TFEU.[55] The consequence of the latter rule not being precluded by Article 56 TFEU would effectively mean that all service provision had to be 'establishment', and so it is unsurprising that the CJEU declared it to be incompatible with the free movement of services.

Article 56 TFEU and non-discrimination

However, the majority of recent CJEU case law has concerned measures that were not discriminatory—whether directly, or by affecting foreign nationals worse—but nonetheless were found to make the exercise of free movement of services significantly more complicated. *Säger* made this explicit with respect to services for the first time. In the case, concerning German legislation that precluded those involved in the maintenance of industrial property rights being patent renewal services, the CJEU ruled that all measures that were 'liable to prohibit or otherwise impede the activities of a provider of services established in another Member State where he lawfully provides similar services' in principle violated Article 56 TFEU. This is very similar to the wording that the CJEU employed in *Cassis de Dijon* to enable mutual recognition of regulation in free movement of goods, as we saw in Chapter 11.

In *Schindler*, the CJEU added that any national regulations that prohibited service delivery (gambling, in this case) were caught by Article 56 TFEU even if they were not discriminatory at all; and shortly thereafter, in *Alpine Investments*, it said outright that any measure that was 'liable to affect market access' for service providers or recipients was caught by Article 56 TFEU. The Dutch prohibition on cold-calling potential clients applied both to those cold calls being made domestically *and* those cold calls being made to other Member States, and while the former was outside of the scope of Article 56 TFEU as it involved a 'purely internal situation', the latter meant that potential clients in other Member States could not be reached via the 'cold-calling' marketing service.

Only those non-discriminatory measures that cannot demonstrably impede market access fall outside of Article 56 TFEU. The most relevant example of the CJEU making such a determination is *Grogan*. *Grogan* concerns the former Irish constitutional ban on abortion. In light of that ban, Irish student associations made information available on campus about the fact that abortions were legally available in the UK, and provided contact information for UK abortion clinics. An activist company dedicated to preventing the decriminalization of abortion, called the Society for the Protection of Unborn Children (SPUC), started proceedings against these students in light of the abortion ban in Ireland. The Irish courts had declared it to be also prohibited under the Irish Constitution for anyone to 'assist pregnant women in Ireland' to obtain abortions abroad, 'inter alia by informing them of the identity and location of a specific clinic . . . '.

The referring court asked the CJEU to first of all consider if providing abortions could be considered a 'service' under Article 56 TFEU, and then asked if the Irish ban on distribution of information about abortion was precluded under the EU Treaties.

[55] Case 205/84 *Commission v Germany* ECLI:EU:C:1986:463.

The CJEU was quick to rule that 'medical termination of pregnancy', if legal in the Member State where it is performed, was definitely a service; the SPUC argument that it was an 'immoral' activity was simply not for the CJEU to address. As for whether the information distribution *about* the service—'advertising' abortion services, in a way—could be banned under the Treaties:

Case C-159/90 *Grogan* ECLI:EU:C:1991:378 (emphasis added)

24. As regards, first, the provisions of [Article 56 TFEU], which prohibit any restriction on the freedom to supply services, it is apparent from the facts of the case that **the link between** the activity of the students associations of which Mr Grogan and the other defendants are officers and medical terminations of pregnancies carried out in clinics in another Member State **is too tenuous** for the prohibition on the distribution of information to be capable of being regarded as a restriction within the meaning of [Article 56 TFEU].
25. The situation in which students associations distributing the information at issue in the main proceedings are not in cooperation with the clinics whose addresses they publish can be distinguished from [earlier case law which held that] a prohibition on the distribution of advertising was capable of constituting a barrier to the free movement of goods . . .
26. The information to which the national court's questions refer is **not distributed on behalf of an economic operator established in another Member State**. On the contrary, the information constitutes a manifestation of freedom of expression and of the freedom to impart and receive information which is **independent of the economic activity** carried on by clinics established in another Member State.
27. It follows that, in any event, a prohibition on the distribution of information in circumstances such as those which are the subject of the main proceedings cannot be regarded as a restriction within the meaning of [Article 56 TFEU].

In other words, the fact that the students were themselves not engaged in an activity 'for remuneration' meant that they were not providing information *services* under Article 56 TFEU. The voluntary nature of the distribution of information meant that in spite of the finding that abortion services were services under the EU Treaties, the Irish constitutional ban on disseminating abortion clinic contact information fell outside of the scope of EU free movement of services law.

Finally, as is true for the other 'freedoms' discussed in Chapters 11 and 12, these non-discriminatory restrictions on market access *can* in principle be justified; we will revisit the CJEU's case law on justifications for non-discriminatory restrictions of the freedom to provide services in Section 14.4.

Discussing the scenario

Is the refusal to let Allison stream live concerts from Portugal a directly discriminatory, indirectly discriminatory, or non-discriminatory measure?

Article 56 TFEU and purely internal situations

The emphasis on the cross-border element of free movement of services makes it clear that 'purely internal situations' are also not caught by Article 56 TFEU. However, as with the other freedoms considered in Chapters 11–13, the CJEU has found cross-border elements in situations that involve only one Member State and its nationals.

A good example of this is *Deliège,* which involved a Belgian judoka who brought an action against the Belgium judo federation (LBJ) for refusing to select her for an international judo competition in Paris that she felt she was the best qualified for.[56] Ms Deliège argued that she was a service provider, as she temporarily and in exchange for pay performed 'judo' abroad, and the LBJ's operation of a selection quota was a barrier to her exercising her free movement of services on subjective grounds. The Belgian, Greek, and Italian governments intervened to argue that the case fell outside of CJEU jurisdiction as there was no cross-border element to a Belgian athlete's registration with a Belgian sports federation. The CJEU disagreed, however—as athletic competitions take place all over the EU, the situation was not 'wholly internal' to Belgium, and so her freedom to provide her professional services in these tournaments was impeded.[57]

14.3.2 **The Services Directive: Directive 2006/123/EC**

The name of the 'Services Directive'[58] is slightly misleading, as it does not deal solely with free movement of services; it also covers establishment in other Member States, and as such attempts to regulate the free movement of the self-employed and companies generally.

The general right for services to cross borders, whether temporarily or permanently, is once again only a starting point for achieving genuine free movement in the internal market: the legal *right* does not also make it a practical *possibility*. The Services Directive in its current form effectively coordinates the administrative processes applied by the Member States to the operation of services and establishment. It has helped to make information more readily available in all the Member States, and for relevant processes to be carried out electronically where possible. The rights of service recipients are also set out, as are a variety of consumer protection measures relating to the 'quality of services' (including information and possible dispute settlement). It thus takes up a similar role to Directive 2005/36/EC, but aims to eradicate different kinds of 'obstacles'.

An original goal for the Services Directive was to give full effect to the type of *Cassis* mutual recognition that was in principle introduced for services in the *Säger* judgment—but *in reverse*. The Directive thus proposed that all service providers should be only regulated by their 'country of origin'.[59] This goes quite a way beyond the CJEU's case law, which obliges the host State to consider the regulation of the home State so as to avoid a double regulatory burden: under this proposal for a 'country-of-origin' regulatory system, the home State's rules would be applicable in the host State no matter what.

Member State backlash against the proposal for 'country-of-origin' regulation was substantial, and the revised draft of the long-negotiated Services Directive removed it.

[56] Joined Cases C-51/96 and C-191/97 *Deliège* ECLI:EU:C:2000:199. [57] Ibid, para 58.

[58] Directive 2006/123/EC of the European Parliament and of the Council of 12 December 2006 on services in the internal market [2006] OJ L376/36.

[59] See the discussion in Chapter 3 on the adoption of this Directive.

The current formulation of mutual recognition principles in the Services Directive is not far removed from the CJEU's case law, and consequently those principles have significantly less of an effect on opening up services markets than the 'country of origin' principle would have done: mutual recognition of services regulation remains subject to the exemptions we will discuss in the next section.

The final Services Directive has been considered something of a disappointment.[60] Its original ambitions were significantly greater than its final text suggests: not only does it not radically open up the internal services market by setting up a more forceful mutual recognition principle, but it does not even cover all *services*. In addition to sectors that have been historically excluded, amongst which is the legal profession, there are also now exclusions for social services, healthcare, and so-called 'services of general interest' (or public services). The majority of these exclusions came about in the European Parliament, where there was extreme Member State concern about the effects of a widely liberalizing Services Directive on their public and social services provision—and the end result is, at best, a set of administrative improvements and greater cooperation amongst the Member States.

14.4 Exceptions to free movement of services and establishment

As we saw for free movement of goods and workers in Chapters 11 and 12, for services and establishment there are once again two sets of justifications available for any national measures that restrict these 'fundamental freedoms'. There are those found in the Treaty, which can be relied upon to justify both discriminatory and non-discriminatory measures; and then there are those developed by the CJEU, which can only be relied upon to justify indirectly discriminatory and non-discriminatory measures.

The rules on justifying exceptions to free movement of services and freedom of establishment under the Treaty and CJEU derogations are *very* similar to the law on justifying exceptions to Article 34 TFEU on the free movement of goods. There is, however, one particular element to stress: where a measure restricts the freedom of a self-employed person, rather than a company, the Treaty exceptions have to be read in correlation with the Citizenship Directive discussed in Chapter 13. Expulsion of a self-employed person thus cannot be an automatic consequence of a valid restriction on free movement of services provision, and will in practice only rarely occur, with 'acceptable discrimination' being the more likely consequence of a justified breach of Article 49 TFEU and Article 56 TFEU.

14.4.1 Justifying directly discriminatory measures

When a national regulatory measure is caught by either Article 49 TFEU or Article 56 TFEU, it can be 'excused' if it satisfies the conditions set out in Article 52 TFEU (establishment), which is also applied to services under Article 62 TFEU:

[60] See, eg, Catherine Barnard, 'Unravelling the Services Directive' (2008) 45 CMLRev 323.

Article 52 TFEU (emphasis added)

1. The provisions of this Chapter and measures taken in pursuance thereof shall not prejudice the applicability of provisions laid down by law, regulation or administrative action providing for **special treatment for foreign nationals on grounds of public policy, public security or public health.**

Article 62 TFEU

The provisions of Articles 51 to 54 shall apply to the matters covered by this Chapter.

As discussed in Chapter 11 in relation to Article 36 TFEU, to 'survive' having violated Article 49 or Article 56 TFEU, a national measure must be **justifiable on the grounds listed in Article 52 TFEU**, *and* it must be **proportionate**, meaning suitable to the objective stated and the least restrictive of trade possible.[61] In all cases, the burden of proof in relying on Article 52 TFEU justifications lies with the Member State that has infringed either Article 49 TFEU or Article 56 TFEU.

Article 52 TFEU can be relied upon by the Member States *regardless* of whether a national measure is directly or indirectly discriminatory, or even not discriminatory at all. Most examples of Member States' Article 52 TFEU justifications for measures restricting either freedom of establishment or free movement of services fall in the **public policy** category. In *Bond van Adverteerders*, the Netherlands attempted to justify a ban on foreign TV broadcasts that contained advertising directed at those living in the Netherlands, whereas Dutch broadcasters were subjected to a regulated but separate regime that did permit some advertising towards the Dutch public. The measure was found to be directly discriminatory, and so the CJEU stressed that only an Article 52 TFEU justification could be relied upon.

The general rules applicable to Article 52 TFEU are neatly set out by the CJEU in this case, and can be summarized as follows:

- Purely economic aims cannot constitute grounds for public policy justifications (or other justifications).[62]
- Where a measure is justifiable on public policy grounds, it nonetheless has to be proportionate.[63]
- As the freedom of establishment and free movement of services are 'fundamental principles' of the Treaty, derogations to those fundamental principles have to be interpreted strictly.[64]

The measure at hand in *Bond van Adverteerders* was found to not be justifiable on public policy grounds because it was disproportionate and discriminatory, as foreign broadcasters could be subjected to a similar regime to that applicable to Dutch TV broadcasters.

[61] For more on proportionality, see Chapter 4.
[62] *Bond van Adverteerders* (n 42), para 34.
[63] Ibid, para 36.
[64] Ibid, para 36.

The goal of maintaining a 'non-commercial' broadcasting system in the Netherlands, however, appears to have been accepted as a valid public policy ground by the CJEU.

The CJEU came to a slightly different conclusion in *FDC*, where an obligation to *also* distribute Spanish films in order to receive a licence to dub foreign films was found to be discriminatory. Here, the CJEU concluded that the aim pursued by Spain was undoubtedly economic: it wished to 'guarantee the distribution of a larger number of national films'. Spain's argument that there was a 'cultural' aim to the measure, namely protecting the national film industry, was rejected on two grounds: first, 'cultural policy' is not a ground in Article 52 TFEU; and secondly, as there were no particular restrictions on quality or content of the Spanish films that had to be distributed, the cultural policy goal was also unconvincing.[65] The CJEU thus rejected this as falling within the scope of a public policy justification.

Two particular cases serve as particularly interesting demonstrations of the amount of leeway that the Member States have when attempting to justify discriminatory measures under Article 52 TFEU. *Omega* is an interesting example of a case that seems to contain both public morality and public policy defences, even if the CJEU explicitly considered public policy alone.[66] It concerned Omega, a German company that operated so-called 'laserdromes' that hosted games of laser-tag. Laser-tag effectively involves two teams shooting at set targets (whether in the form of jackets they are wearing, or static targets) with a form of 'toy gun' that emits lasers, with the last person standing being declared victor. The introduction of a 'laserdrome' in Germany proved controversial with the German public, with protesters including the Bonn police making clear that they were intending to prohibit any games that played at 'killing' people. Omega responded by stressing that the laser-tag targets in their Bonn 'laserdrome' would be attached to the walls, not to people. The Bonn police, however, discovered that jackets *were* also targets, and so it issued a prohibition that would be accompanied with a fine if games were played that were 'playing at killing' people. The prohibition was based on a German regional law that permitted the police to take measures that were necessary to 'avert a risk to public order or safety'.

The equipment used in the Omega 'laserdromes' was made by the British company Pulsar, and so Omega argued that the prohibition was an infringement on the free movement of services, where the service that Pulsar was providing was shipping Omega equipment and technology which was legally being used in the UK. The German courts referred the matter to the CJEU, which quickly determined that this prohibition on 'playing at killing' *was* captured by Article 56 TFEU, and then considered if it could be justified.

Case C-36/02 *Omega* ECLI:EU:C:2004:614 (emphasis added)

28. . . . In this case, the documents before the Court show that the grounds relied on by the Bonn police authority in adopting the prohibition order expressly mention the fact that the activity concerned constitutes a danger to public policy. . . .

30. . . . public policy may be relied on only if there is a genuine and sufficiently serious threat to a fundamental interest of society . . .

→

[65] *FDC* (n 54), paras 17–21.

[66] Case C-36/02 *Omega* ECLI:EU:C:2004:614; the case is also discussed in Chapter 9.

→

31. The fact remains, however, that the specific circumstances which may justify recourse to the concept of public policy may vary from one country to another and from one era to another. The competent national authorities must therefore be allowed a margin of discretion within the limits imposed by the [Treaties].

32. In this case, the competent authorities took the view that the activity concerned by the prohibition order was a threat to public policy by reason of the fact that, in accordance with the conception prevailing in public opinion, the commercial exploitation of games involving the simulated killing of human beings infringed a fundamental value enshrined in the national constitution, namely human dignity.

34. . . . the [EU] legal order undeniably strives to ensure respect for human dignity as a general principle of law. There can therefore be no doubt that the objective of protecting human dignity is compatible with [EU] law . . .

35. **Since both the [EU] and its Member States are required to respect fundamental rights, the protection of those rights is a legitimate interest which, in principle, justifies a restriction of the obligations imposed by [EU] law, even under a fundamental freedom guaranteed by the Treaty such as the freedom to provide services.**

Omega thus stressed that the Member States have a significant margin of discretion in determining when a matter is of 'public policy' concern for them, and any matter that relates to fundamental rights is very likely to fall within that margin. The CJEU went on to consider if the prohibition on 'playing at killing' was proportionate, and here again stressed that it was irrelevant that *other* Member States may be more tolerant of laser-tag games: it was for Germany to determine if it wished to ban 'playing at killing' outright.[67] As the prohibition was clearly aimed at stopping 'commercial exploitation' of violence against people, and only applied to laser-tag games that involved human targets, the CJEU concluded the prohibition was justified under Article 52 TFEU.

A very different example of an Article 52 TFEU defence is found in *Laval*. As discussed in Chapter 8, Laval was a Latvian company that won a public contract to build a school in Sweden. It brought along (or 'posted', in EU terms) Latvian construction workers to carry out the work. The Swedish construction unions wanted Laval to sign up to the Swedish employment agreements on employment conditions (the so-called 'collective agreements'), but Laval refused, arguing that the Latvian workers were signed up to a Latvian 'collective agreement'. At this point, the unions set up a blockade at Laval's sites in Sweden—making it impossible for further work to be carried out at these sites. They were so successful at this that the Swedish arm of Laval was bankrupted by the action.

The CJEU concluded that the actions of the trade unions were a restriction on Laval's freedom to establish and provide services in Sweden. One particular aspect of the applicable Swedish laws on trade union action was that they prohibited trade union action that aimed to ignore or undermine collective agreements signed by third parties . . . but only in relation to work activity to which the Swedish collective agreement would apply. The prohibition on trade union action thus did not apply to Laval, or any other foreign

[67] Ibid, paras 37–38.

company that was temporarily engaged in an activity in Sweden, and was bringing its own workforce. In practice, the way that the Swedish law on trade unions worked would mean that *either* Laval applied the Swedish collective agreement, *or* it could legally face a trade union blockade.

The CJEU determined swiftly that this particular aspect of Swedish trade union law was directly discriminatory, as it specifically targeted foreign companies and their collective agreements. As such, only an Article 52 TFEU defence for the measure would be possible—but could Sweden provide one?

Case C-341/05 *Laval* ECLI:EU:C:2007:809 (emphasis added)

118. It is clear from the order for reference that the application of those rules to foreign undertakings which are bound by collective agreements to which Swedish law does not directly apply is intended, first, **to allow trade unions to take action to ensure that all employers active on the Swedish labour market pay wages and apply other terms and conditions of employment in line with those usual in Sweden**, and secondly, **to create a climate of fair competition, on an equal basis, between Swedish employers and entrepreneurs from other Member States.**

119. Since **none of the considerations referred to in the previous paragraph constitute grounds of public policy, public security or public health** within the meaning of [Article 52 TFEU], applied in conjunction with [Article 62 TFEU], it must be held that discrimination such as that in the case in the main proceedings cannot be justified.

This stood in contrast with the remainder of the *Laval* judgment, where the CJEU ended up determining that strike action by trade unions *in general* served as an overriding reason of public interest. We thus see once again that the CJEU takes a very firm line on measures that appear to be directly discriminatory against foreign nationals, and will not easily take a broad reading of what 'public policy' means. *Omega* remains the exception, more than the rule, in the application of Article 52 TFEU.

Discussing the scenario

Do you think any of the measures taken by the Athens City Council can be justified under Article 52 TFEU? On what ground? And do you think they would be found to be proportionate?

Article 51 TFEU: the official authority exception

One specific Treaty derogation applicable to services and establishment is found in Article 51 TFEU on establishment (and is extended to services by Article 62 TFEU): the general requirements of free movement do not apply to any activity that results in the 'exercise of official authority'. This is, in many ways, a proxy for the Article 45(4) exception applicable to free movement of workers, and the CJEU has again taken a narrow view on what 'the exercise of official authority' encompasses. *Reyners* thus limited it to activities that had a 'direct and specific connection' with official authority,[68] and the activities of any

[68] *Reyners* (n 6), para 45.

private parties will never qualify for this derogation if there is, for example, a supervisory entity in place that takes 'final decisions' on matters of official authority.[69] This derogation, not unlike Article 45 TFEU, thus fails more often than it applies.

14.4.2 Justifying indirectly or non-discriminatory measures

We saw in Chapter 11 that the CJEU has developed a second set of justifications that can only be applied to indirectly discriminatory or non-discriminatory measures. In free movement of goods, these are called **mandatory requirements.**

The CJEU has developed a similar additional set of justifications for use regarding indirectly discriminatory and non-discriminatory barriers to free movement of services and freedom of establishment. However, they are normally termed **imperative requirements** in services/establishment case law, or otherwise referred to simply as **objective justifications.**

Van Binsbergen gives a good overview of how imperative requirements work in relation to the free movement of services and freedom of establishment. Any measure adopted by a Member State must be pursuing a legitimate public interest objective. The case law on cross-border healthcare is interesting here in demonstrating what counts as 'legitimate': the CJEU has held that purely financial or economic motivations are not public interest objectives, but ensuring the financial sustainability of a public healthcare system *is*.[70] In other words, where a social objective is combined with a financial one, the CJEU is likely to accept a justification. Other examples of accepted imperative requirements include protecting the public from the abuse of academic titles not gained through normal processes,[71] the public interest and public safety that immigration rules aim to protect,[72] and the protection of the standards of quality of postgraduate education.[73]

Most attempts to raise imperative requirements fail at the next hurdle, which is that the measures taken to protect them must apply equally to everyone in the Member State, regardless of nationality. Any measures that are discriminatory will therefore not be deemed appropriate to protect a relevant interest. A lot of the case law on broadcasting has resulted in the CJEU finding that while the aims of protecting national culture through mandating a variety of programming and setting up a few programming restrictions were in principle imperative requirements, the rules in practice were protectionist in that they significantly advantaged domestic broadcasters, and as such could not be justified.

The final generally applicable test for an imperative requirement defence is whether the Member State measure adopted is proportionate: both 'appropriate' and 'the least restrictive measure' possible.[74] The *Viking* case is of interest here. The CJEU stressed quickly in both *Viking* and *Laval* that collective action by trade unions, so as to protect workers, was a fundamental right—and as such an imperative requirement capable of justifying a

[69] See, eg, Case C-438/08 *Commission v Portugal* (*Vehicle Inspection*), para 37.

[70] See, eg, *Geraets-Smits* (n 45) and *Watts* (n 46).

[71] Case C-19/92 *Kraus* ECLI:EU:C:1993:125.

[72] *Carpenter* (n 40).

[73] Case C-523/12 *Dirextra Alta Formazione* ECLI:EU:C:2013:831.

[74] See the general discussion of proportionality in Chapter 4.

derogation from the Treaties. Where the actions undertaken by the trade unions in *Viking* became contentious was in their detail:

Case C-438/05 *Viking* ECLI:EU:C:2007:772 (emphasis added)

81. First, as regards the collective action taken by FSU, even if that action—aimed at protecting the jobs and conditions of employment of the members of that union liable to be adversely affected by the reflagging of the *Rosella*—could reasonably be considered to fall, at first sight, within the objective of protecting workers, **such a view would no longer be tenable if it were established that the jobs or conditions of employment at issue were not jeopardised or under serious threat.**

...

84. If, following [an] examination, the national court came to the conclusion that, in the case before it, the jobs or conditions of employment of the FSU's members liable to be adversely affected by the reflagging of the *Rosella* are in fact jeopardised or under serious threat, it would then have to ascertain whether the collective action initiated by FSU is suitable for ensuring the achievement of the objective pursued and does not go beyond what is necessary to attain that objective.

...

86. As regards the **appropriateness** of the action taken by FSU for attaining the objectives pursued in the case in the main proceedings, it should be borne in mind that it is common ground that **collective action**, like collective negotiations and collective agreements, **may**, in the particular circumstances of a case, **be one of the main ways in which trade unions protect the interests of their members.**

87. As regards the question of whether or not the collective action at issue in the main proceedings **goes beyond what is necessary to achieve the objective pursued**, it is for the national court to examine, in particular, on the one hand, whether, under the national rules and collective agreement law applicable to that action, FSU did not have other means at its disposal which were less restrictive of freedom of establishment in order to bring to a successful conclusion the collective negotiations entered into with Viking, and, on the other, whether that trade union had exhausted those means before initiating such action.

While *Viking* recognizes that 'collective action by trade unions' is a fundamental right, it is not treated as a 'limitless' right that will always override the freedom of establishment. The CJEU asks the national court to evaluate how serious the risk to the protection of workers posed by Viking's actions is—and only if sufficiently serious would the trade unions' actions *to* protect their fundamental rights be proportionate.

We see a similar balancing exercise in *Carpenter*, which involved the UK attempting to deport an UK national service provider's non-EU spouse for a violation of her visa conditions. Here, the CJEU held that while applying immigration law for reasons of public order and safety was a legitimate aim, those state concerns had to be balanced with the rights of the Carpenters to family life.[75] As overstaying a visa was not a *serious* risk to

[75] *Carpenter* (n 40), paras 43–45.

public order and safety, deporting Mrs Carpenter was thus declared to be a disproportionate means of ensuring public order and safety were maintained.

In summary, the functioning of imperative requirements is the same as that of mandatory requirements we assessed in Chapter 11: objective justifications to restrictions of the free movement of services or freedom of establishment must be non-discriminatory as well as necessary, the latter of which results in case law examinations of both the 'requirement' stated and whether the restriction put in place in light of that mandatory requirement is proportionate.

Discussing the scenario

Consider the Athens City Council's decision to not grant the live music licence because it may incite public disorder, and the 12-month 'investigation period' for the applications for licences to stream concerts. Can they be justified using imperative requirements? If so, which ones? And are they proportionate?

14.5 Brexit and free movement of the self-employed

Finally in this chapter we will consider how Brexit will impact on the free movement of services and the freedom of establishment. We will thus briefly explore what the Withdrawal Agreement sets out, both generally and specifically in the Protocol on Ireland/ Northern Ireland, and then consider what may come *after* the Withdrawal Agreement.

14.5.1 The Withdrawal Agreement

Under the terms of the October 2019 Withdrawal Agreement, free movement of services and freedom of establishment will continue to apply to the UK and its nationals as they do now[76] until the end of 2020—or possibly the end of 2021 or 2022, if the parties to the agreement opt to extend the transition period.[77] The Withdrawal Agreement explicitly continues the application of the current provisions on mutual recognition of qualifications found in Directive 2005/36/EC.[78]

14.5.2 The Protocol on Ireland/Northern Ireland

Unlike most of the Withdrawal Agreement, which represents a 'temporary' agreement for the purposes of transitioning to the next relationship, the Protocol on Ireland/Northern Ireland as revised in October 2019 sets out a 'final' form of the relationship between the UK and the EU as it involves Northern Ireland.[79]

[76] Withdrawal Agreement, Article 4.

[77] Withdrawal Agreement, Articles 126 and 132; note that the EU (Withdrawal Agreement) Act 2020, s 33, prohibits UK representatives from asking for an extension as a matter of domestic law—though as is true for all Acts of Parliament, this can obviously be amended if an extension is desired after all.

[78] Withdrawal Agreement, Article 27.

[79] The other major exception to the 'temporary' nature of the Withdrawal Agreement is Part 2 on Citizens' Rights, discussed in Chapters 12 and 13.

However, the Protocol does not address freedom of establishment or free movement of services at all. As discussed in Chapter 13, the Protocol notes in its preamble that Irish citizens from Northern Ireland will continue to benefit from their rights as EU citizens, which of course enables them—like any other holder of an EU nationality—to provide and receive services or establish in *any other Member State* as they always have. However, following the transition period, businesses established in Northern Ireland will no longer be covered by the EU rules on free movement of services, much as businesses in the remainder of the UK will not, as they will not be based in Member State territory. Additionally, UK nationals (whether from Northern Ireland or Great Britain) will also not be able to exercise the freedom to establish in any of the other EU Member States. Indeed, the current government information suggests that even the mutual recognition of professional qualifications, which currently exists in EU law, has not been bilaterally recreated so as to enable those from the UK to practise their profession in Ireland after Brexit, and vice versa.[80]

14.5.3 The future relationship

The section on the Protocol on Ireland/Northern Ireland should make clear that both in the situation of the transition period ending without a 'new' agreement in place, and according to the aims set out in the Political Declaration, free movement of services and freedom of establishment as we knew them as an EU Member State will effectively end across the UK.[81] Those already 'established' before the end of the transition period will continue to benefit from the relevant rights under EU law—but future establishment, and ongoing services provision, will be subject to new rules.

Establishment has been completely unaddressed in the Political Declaration: it is not clear what the Parties are intending, whether it be largely the continuance of the current establishment regime, or the application of far stricter rules. On services, the Political Declaration alludes to the conclusion of 'ambitious, comprehensive and balanced arrangements on trade in services'.[82] It is not clear what this would look like in the details, though the Political Declaration stresses non-discrimination and an allowance for 'temporary entry and stay of natural persons for business purposes'—but in defined areas of services.[83] Additionally, the Political Declaration suggests that 'appropriate arrangements' should be made regarding regulated professions and the mutual recognition of qualifications, 'where in the Parties' mutual interest'.[84] The remainder of the provisions on services stress regulatory autonomy and close co-operation, and so the picture sketched by the Political Declaration is one that is far removed from the effective mutual recognition of services regulation and general freedom to provide and receive services that operates in the internal market.

Should the transition period come to an end without agreement on the 'future relationship' in place, the lack of a replacement for the mutual recognition of professional qualifications legislation means that the practice of exercising a profession abroad—temporarily or otherwise—will face either an absence of clear rules, or significantly more restrictive national immigration rules. Companies establishing abroad (and EU companies establishing

[80] At the time of writing, relevant UK government information can be found here: https://www.gov.uk/guidance/ireland-providing-services-after-eu-exit.

[81] For an analysis of the UK approach to 'retaining' relevant EU law—which in practice means it will not be retained—see https://publiclawproject.org.uk/wp-content/uploads/2019/10/191017-Freedom-of-Establishment-Regulations-briefing.pdf.

[82] Political Declaration, para 27.

[83] Political Declaration, para 30.

[84] Political Declaration, para 34.

in the UK) as of the end of the transition period may be subject to domestic company law, or may face additional regulatory burdens before being permitted to trade.[85] Both services and establishment will experience new regulatory barriers—ones that the EU will be reluctant to scrap altogether, as it cannot remove them for the UK without being obliged to also remove them for many of its other trading partners.[86] Self-employment, or the running of businesses, across the EU and UK border is thus likely to become significantly more difficult than it is for many currently engaged in either activity.[87]

14.6 In conclusion

The rules on services and establishment in many ways mirror each other, and the primary thing to understand is how to differentiate between them. Both enable business to move across borders, but for different durations of time. This, too, is an essential part of operating an internal market successfully: it is one thing to be able to send *products* to other Member States, but with global supply chains and ever-more interlinked corporate structures, the chances are that instead of goods simply being shipped abroad, they will be part-produced there—or come with a 'service', like installation or maintenance, attached.

Having now considered the free movement of goods, workers, services, and establishment, we can see that there are broad similarities between how the CJEU has developed the 'fundamental freedoms'—but that each also has unique qualities, highlighted by slight differences in the case law as to what is required behaviour on the part of the Member States. A drift towards 'market access' considerations is visible in case law for all 'freedoms' considered here, perhaps as a sign that while the internal market project will never be finished, it is now at so advanced a stage that the kinds of rules that are hampering 'free movement' are no longer generally concerned with where a product, service, or person is *from*—they are simply making cross-border activity difficult in some way.

Leaving this environment will be a substantial change for the UK, particularly in areas like movement of services across borders, where the internal market far exceeds what any other international agreement (including others signed by the EU has achieved to date.

Discussing the scenario

Use the material in this chapter in order to explain to Allison whether she had any rights under EU law that have been violated by the Athens City Council and the Greek Food Institute. Treat each of the decisions taken as setting out a specific scenario, and explain how EU law applies to that scenario.

A sample approach to a response can be found online.

[85] For a helpful overview of the various possibilities, see https://warwick.ac.uk/fac/soc/law/research/centres/globe/policybriefs/web_pb3_final_s_connelly_by_research_retold_-_22_may_2018.pdf.

[86] This is beyond the scope of the current chapter, but most EU Treaties contain so-called 'Most Favoured Nation' clauses on services—meaning that when the EU opens up the services market to one of its trading partners, it has agreed to also open them up to *all other* trading partners. For a discussion, see http://blogs.sussex.ac.uk/uktpo/publications/most-favoured-nation-clauses-in-eu-trade-agreements-one-more-hurdle-for-uk-negotiators/.

[87] For an interesting overview in light of Brexit, see https://www.cer.eu/sites/default/files/brexit_trade_sl_pbrief_6.12.18.pdf.

Key points

- Under Article 49 TFEU, EU nationals and companies have the right to establish in another Member State, and to equal treatment with nationals in the process of establishing. **Establishment** refers to a stable and continuous presence in another Member State.
- Under 56 TFEU, EU nationals and companies have the right to provide and receive services in another Member State, and to be treated equally with national service providers/receivers. **Services** refer to a temporary activity across borders, in exchange for remuneration.
- Where restrictions on movement of services or establishment are **directly discriminatory**, they can only be justified under Article 52 TFEU derogations (which is referred to in Article 62 TFEU, for services), where they are proportionate.
- Where they are **indirectly discriminatory or non-discriminatory**, they can be justified under Article 52 TFEU as well as **imperative requirements**, where they are proportionate.
- The current 'Brexit' landscape, in the form of the Withdrawal Agreement and the Political Declaration, makes **no clear arrangements for the free movement of services or the freedom of establishment** for either Northern Ireland or the UK as a whole once the **transition period** ends.

Assess your learning

1. What is the difference between free movement of services and freedom of establishment? (See Section 14.1.)
2. Does it matter if measures that restrict the freedom of establishment or the free movement of services are discriminatory or not? Why? (See Sections 14.2–14.3.)
3. How can restrictions on the free movement of services and freedom of establishment be justified under the Treaties? Are there other justifications possible? (Section 14.4.)
4. *Bonus question if you also studied Chapters 11–13*: What are the key similarities and differences between the 'freedoms' discussed in this book? (See Chapters 11–14.)

Further reading

Diamond Ashiagbor, 'Unravelling the Embedded Liberal Bargain: Labour and social welfare law in the context of EU market integration' (2013) 19 Eur Law J 303.

Stefan Enchelmaier, 'Always at Your Service (Within Limits): The ECJ's case law on Article 56 TFEU (2006–11)' (2011) 36(5) ELRev 615.

Elisa Faustinelli, 'Purely Internal Situations and the Freedom of Establishment Within the Context of the Services Directive' (2017) 44(1) LIEI 77.

Vassilis Hatzopoulos, 'The Court's Approach to Services (2006–2012): From case law to case load?' (2013) 50 CMLRev 459.

Dion Kramer, 'From Worker to Self-Entrepreneur: The transformation of homo economicus and the freedom of movement in the European Union' (2017) 23 Eur Law J 172.

Barend van Leeuwen, 'Euthanasia and the Ethics of Free Movement Law: The principle of recognition in the internal market' (2018) 19(6) Ger Law J 1417.

Niamh Nic Shuibhne, 'The Social Market Economy and Restriction of Free Movement Rights: Plus c'est la même chose' (2019) 57(1) JCMS 111.

Dagmar Schiek, 'Towards more resilience for a social EU—the constitutionally conditioned internal market' (2017) 13(4) Eur Const Law Rev 611.

Alina Tryfonidou, 'Further Steps on the Road to Convergence Among the Market Freedoms' (2010) 35(1) ELRev 35.

Floris de Witte, 'The Constitutional Quality of the Free Movement Provisions: Looking for context in the case law on Article 56 TFEU' (2017) 42(3) ELRev 313.

Online resources

Visit www.oup.com/he/demars1e for a sample approach to discussing the quote.

15

Competition law

Context for this chapter

Ilektrikí Enérgeia (IE) is a (fictional) energy company from Greece, specializing in the provision of electricity to commercial and residential customers. Its primary focus has historically been on providing electricity in Greece and Bulgaria, but in the last decade, IE has expanded its activities to other European countries.

At the start of 2018, IE supplied electricity to 60 per cent of the households in Greece and Bulgaria. In mid-2018, IE adopted a new pricing strategy, with the aim of consolidating and expanding its market share. The strategy entailed setting different pricing rates for residential customers depending on where they lived. In regions in Greece and Bulgaria where IE faced significant competition, residential customers paid on average 40 per cent less for their electricity supply than residential customers did in regions in Greece and Bulgaria where IE was the only operating electricity utility. IE argues that its strategy is sensible, as it needs to respond to competition where it exists.

Separately, also in the summer of 2018, IE announced that it would shortly expand into the commercial utility sector in Romania. Magyar Hatalom (MH) is the largest electricity provider in Hungary and Romania, and has been quickly expanding its business southward into northern Bulgaria, with a particular focus on the non-residential market: it has found that commercial enterprises are more likely to switch energy providers than homeowners are.

Suddenly, in early 2019, MH announced that it was withdrawing from the commercial energy sector in Bulgaria. The company's press release indicated it was consolidating its activity and 'refocusing on its traditional Romanian and Hungarian business customers'.

Three weeks later, IE sent around a memo to its shareholders noting that it was suspending its efforts to expand to the southern Romanian commercial utility sector, as the costs of doing so were higher than anticipated.

In March 2019, MH raised its prices for existing commercial customers in Romania by 10 per cent.

15.1 Introduction

The last five chapters considered both the intention behind creating a single market in the EU, and the primary means by which the EU has progressively integrated the European market: the development of the law on the fundamental freedoms. However, one key dimension of ensuring that there is fair trade within the single market is still missing from the discussion, and that is how the EU has responded to potential anti-competitive behaviour by enterprises in the EU.

This chapter considers the foundations of EU competition law, or those rules applied by the EU in an attempt to ensure that business practices within the single market remain 'fair'. As we will see, competition law is an attempt to regulate the behaviour of private companies when active in the internal market so as to ensure that competition between different entities remains 'fair'. The rules of competition law aim to assist the completion of the internal market *as well as* to address consumer welfare in more general terms. A further particularly interesting dimension is that unlike most internal market law, competition law applies *regardless* of the nationality of the companies or businesses active in the internal market. As such, UK companies active on the continent after Brexit will have to know these rules, regardless of whether they continue to apply in the UK.

In detail, the chapter addresses the two Treaty provisions that address anti-competitive behaviour: Articles 101 and 102 TFEU.[1] The scenario at the start of the chapter covers the potential effect of these two provisions, and will help you understand both *why* the EU wishes to regulate competition and *how* it attempts to do so. The chapter concludes with an assessment of what will change in this area following the end of the transition period: will the UK be able to adopt a separate competition law policy, or will it remain bound up in the EU rules? And if so, why?

Before we go into answering this question, it will help to set out a few preliminary definitions, as like many other specialist areas of law, EU competition law comes with its own terminology.

First of all, while competition law aims to regulate the practices of what we would normally call 'companies' or 'businesses', the EU's competition regime actually applies to what is known as an **undertaking**. The term 'undertaking' is used because the EU competition laws apply to *all* Member States, and rather than trying to extensively regulate company law in all the Member States, the EU has opted to use an 'umbrella' term.

The key case here is *Höfner v Macrotron*, where the CJEU defined an undertaking as '[encompassing] every legal entity engaged in an economic activity, regardless of the legal status of the entity and the way in which it is financed'.[2] With this focus on economic activity, the CJEU has found that opera singers,[3] individual inventors,[4] as well as more traditional 'businesses' are all captured by the concept of the undertaking. Even state-run entities will be classed as undertakings if they are engaged in economic activity: the only potential economic actors who are *not* undertakings are government-run entities (so, for

[1] As this is a general introduction, the chapter does not discuss more specialist aspects of EU competition policy, such as the regulation on mergers or the EU's state aid provisions.

[2] Case C-41/90 *Höfner v Macrotron* ECLI:EU:C:1991:161, para 21 (emphasis added).

[3] UNITEL Re [1978] OJ L157/39.

[4] Reuter/BASF [1976] OJ L254/40.

instance, public authorities) when they are acting for what the CJEU has termed *social purposes*, rather than *commercial purposes*.[5]

As such, a single entity may be classified as not an undertaking when it exercises public powers, but may be acting as an undertaking when engaged in other activities—in the sense of offering goods or services, and thus participating in the market.[6]

A final preliminary point about an undertaking is that it does not necessarily refer to a *single* company, or business, or entity. Regardless of what domestic law says about the relationship between a parent company and a subsidiary company, under the EU's competition rules these can be treated as a 'single economic entity', and thus a single undertaking, if the subsidiary has no concrete 'economic independence' or other freedom to act in the market.[7] Determining whether or not a subsidiary entity *has* that freedom to act is an investigation of fact, and not without controversy, not least because the CJEU's case law has made parent entities liable for their subsidiary company's behaviour *unless* a presumption of their involvement can be rebutted.

The other key term that will come up frequently in EU competition law is that of the **relevant market**. We will explore what makes up a relevant market in much more detail later, but for now, it suffices to say that undertakings are not engaged in abstract economic activities: they make or sell a specific good or service, and perhaps do so in *specific parts* of the European Union. Before any decision can be made about whether or not an undertaking is behaving anti-competitively, there is a need to look both at *what* it is doing and *in what market*, so as to determine whether it is having actual anti-competitive impacts in the internal market.

15.2 What is competition law?

Before we consider the core EU rules on competition law, it is worthwhile to first spend a little time considering *why* the EU has rules on competition law. The need for the four freedoms is easy to explain in terms of trade and the establishment of the internal market, but the connection between the EU's economic goals and competition law is a little less straightforward. Competition law may also have *more* than simply internal market-related objectives. We will therefore first consider what the probable purposes of EU competition law are, and at the end of this section, we will quickly sketch out how the EU institutions are involved in enforcing competition law.

15.2.1 The objectives of competition law

The very general aims of competition (or antitrust, as it is known in the US) law are easy to summarize: it is there to prevent anti-competitive behaviour, and where any is found to take place, it is there to stop and penalize anti-competitive behaviour. The basic idea underpinning the regulation of business practices is that while in a free market, *ideally*, trade happens on a level playing field, the reality of economic actors of any kind is that they may try to 'cheat' the system for personal gain—and this would ultimately harm the

[5] Case T-319/99 *FENIN v Commission* ECLI:EU:T:2003:50.

[6] Case C-49/07 *MOTOE* ECLI:EU:C:2008:376, para 25 onwards.

[7] Case T-102/92 *Viho Europe BV v Commission* ECLI:EU:T:1995:3, paras 50–51.

natural, market-driven competitive process. This cheating can take multiple forms, but the ones the EU Treaties have been concerned with since the Treaty of Rome are captured by two primary forms of behaviour:

- Restrictive or anti-competitive agreements (under Article 101 TFEU);
- Abuse of dominant status (under Article 102 TFEU).

Anti-competitive agreements, in short, are agreements that distort natural competition on a market. A clear-cut example is when undertakings form a cartel: they sign agreements whereby they agree to only serve customers in specific parts of a market (and, in our case, the internal market), thus effectively carving up that market and making it so that customers have no choice but to do business with one specific undertaking. Once the market is carved up like that, the undertakings in a cartel are free to charge higher than normal prices in those parts of the market where they are active—again because the consumers will not be able to switch to other suppliers.

Abuse of a dominant status involves undertakings that are in a dominant position in the market. There are market-leaders in most industries, and being successful is not against the law—but where a market leader takes advantage of being in a position where most customers prefer or require their product, this, too, harms competition on a market, and will normally result in far higher prices and perhaps even lower quality products for consumers. For example, a market leader could operate at a loss for a limited period of time by dropping prices so low that new competitors could not possibly match them without going bankrupt. At that point, the market leader could very well end up a **monopoly**, or a single undertaking so powerful that in practice it is the only supplier of a good or service on the market—at which point it would undoubtedly raise its prices. A dominant undertaking could also make it impossible for businesses in other parts of the supply chain to use its competitors, by introducing contractual commitments that demand loyalty, and punishing them by refusing to supply them if they *do* source products or services from competitors. Or, it could do what Microsoft has done . . .

EU law in practice

While Microsoft may slowly be losing part of its absolute dominance in computing to Google and Apple, the vast majority of desktop and laptop computers still use Windows, and Microsoft has not hesitated to strategically take advantage of that over the years.

In the mid-2000s, it had been on the Commission's radar for several practices starting in the late 1990s, like 'bundling' Windows Media Player with Windows installations, and refusing to supply the information that would enable competing software companies to design office network systems that were compatible with Windows computers.[8] Both practices were seen as Microsoft taking advantage of its dominant position in the operating systems market: most people would use Windows, and were then forced to also use Windows Media Player, despite not having chosen to 'buy' Windows Media Player; and nobody would buy a server product that could not connect well with Windows computers in the office, either, when the Microsoft server software did so just fine.

[8] In technical terms: it refused interoperability information that competing software producing companies, like Sun Microsystems, needed to design work group server operating systems that would integrate well with Windows-running computers.

A binding 2004 Commission Decision first found Microsoft guilty of abuse of dominance in the market to the sum of nearly 500 million euros, but this was followed up by penalty payments of nearly 300 million euros in 2006 when Microsoft continued to refuse to supply interoperability information,[9] and a further penalty payment of nearly 900 million euros in 2008, when it still had not complied with the Commission Decision.[10] Microsoft appealed the Commission's infringement decision of 2004, but it was broadly upheld by the EU Courts, as were the penalty payments when Microsoft appealed those.[11]

Given that the total penalty sum was well over a billion euros, one would think that Microsoft would not attempt the practices at hand again, but Windows Media Player was not the last product to be 'bundled' to Windows computers.

When anyone installed a copy of Windows in the 2000s, or started up a newly bought computer with a pre-installed copy of Windows, they were not offered a choice of what browser they would use; Internet Explorer simply installed and acted as the default browser, even though consumers had only opted to use *Microsoft Windows*, not *Microsoft Internet Explorer.* This 'bundling' or 'tying' of Internet Explorer with Windows was seen by the Commission as having very negative effects on competing browsers, like Google Chrome and Mozilla Firefox: adept computer users will have had a browser preference and will have known how to circumvent the Internet Explorer 'default' settings, but the average computer user would simply use Internet Explorer because it was there.

The Commission determined that this closed off the competitive market for browser software, and let Microsoft know that this was deemed to be anti-competitive practice.[12] Microsoft responded by volunteering to offer both computer manufacturers and users a choice of browser when they first ran Windows, thus enabling them to opt out of the Internet Explorer default.[13]

When Microsoft updated Windows 7 with a so-called 'Service Pack', or a collection of important security and functionality updates, in 2011, it failed to include the 'Select your web browser(s)' screen in that update, however, and so from May 2011 until July 2012, Internet Explorer was once again the default for anyone running a new computer or new Windows installation with Windows 7 Service Pack 1. When confronted about this by the Commission, Microsoft acknowledged that Service Pack 1 was missing the browser choice screen, but all the same, the Commission fined Microsoft 516 million euros, which was 1.02 per cent of its annual turnover in 2012.[14]

In sum, Microsoft's business practices—bundling non-Windows products *to* Windows to take advantage of its near-**monopoly** in operating systems, and trying to freeze out competition by not giving them technical information that would let their products work with Windows computers—cost them well over 2 billion euros between 2004 and 2013, as all of these practices were found to be contrary to EU competition law.

Do you think that chasing down abuse of dominance as the Commission did with Microsoft is an important aspect of creating an internal market? What would happen if the EU did not pursue anti-competitive behaviour, but instead this was left to the Member States, do you think?

[9] Summary of Commission Decision of 12 July 2006 [2008] OJ C138/10.

[10] Summary of Commission Decision of 27 February 2008 [2009] OJ C166/20.

[11] See Case T-201/04 *Microsoft v Commission* [2007] ECLI:EU:T:2007:289 and Case T-167/08 *Microsoft v Commission* ECLI:EU:T:2012:323.

[12] See http://europa.eu/rapid/press-release_MEMO-09-15_en.htm?locale=en.

[13] See https://web.archive.org/web/20090618132052/http://microsoftontheissues.com/cs/blogs/mscorp/archive/2009/06/11/working-to-fulfill-our-legal-obligations-in-europe-for-windows-7.aspx and http://news.bbc.co.uk/1/hi/technology/8537763.stm.

[14] Case COMP/C-3/39.530 *Microsoft (tying)* [2010] OJ C36/7.

The Treaty of Rome tied competition law to the internal market by arguing that there was very little benefit in creating an 'internal market' in Europe if that market was going to be full of anti-competitive behaviour.[15] Trade between the Member States would not happen if big economic actors *in* the Member States decided to start splitting up territory between them rather than engaging in competition—by, for instance, declaring that a French provider would 'have' the French market, whereas a German provider would stay in the German market. This is well-illustrated by *Consten v Grundig*.[16] Grundig, a German undertaking, manufactured a variety of electronic goods. They appointed Consten in France as their exclusive distributor in France, and promised that no other retailer would be permitted to sell Grundig products in France. A third undertaking, UNEF, purchased Grundig products in Germany and brought them to France for sale there, without permission from Grundig. This undertaking was sued by Grundig and Consten for an abuse of copyright.

However, the Commission viewed the agreement concluded between Grundig and Consten as being itself contrary to EU law. When the CJEU was asked for its opinion, it agreed:

Joined Cases 56 and 58/64 *Consten and Grundig* ECLI:EU:C:1966:41 (emphasis added)

8. . . . an agreement between producer and distributor which **might tend to restore the national divisions in trade between Member States** might be such as to frustrate the most fundamental objections of the [EU]. **The Treaty,** whose preamble and content aim at abolishing the barriers between States, and which in several provisions gives evidence of a stern attitude with regard to their reappearance, **could not allow undertakings to reconstruct such barriers.**

Completing the internal market also would not happen at all if there was a big economic actor—say, a Google or an Apple—in the market that acted in such a way as to make it almost impossible for other companies in the same industry to survive: there is no 'trade' happening if there is only one undertaking in a market, and it makes the survival or setting up of other companies impossible by its behaviour.

To prevent these kinds of anti-competitive practices from obstructing the internal market, the Treaty of Rome introduced what are now Articles 101 and 102 TFEU, and these continue to be essential 'weapons' in ensuring competition in the internal market is as clean as it can be today. The CJEU regularly points out that without competition law, the internal market would not function.[17]

However, since the early 2000s the Commission has also stressed that the goal of Articles 101 and 102 TFEU is to 'protect competition on the market as a means of enhancing consumer welfare . . .'.[18] Competitive markets are seen as being greatly beneficial to

[15] See Article 3(f) of the Treaty of Rome.

[16] Joined Cases 56 and 58/64 *Consten and Grundig* ECLI:EU:C:1966:41. See also Case COMP/C-3/37.792 *Microsoft* [2007] OJ L32/23.

[17] See, eg, Case C-126/97 *Eco Swiss* ECLI:EU:C:1999:269.

[18] See, for instance, http://europa.eu/rapid/press-release_SPEECH-05-512_en.htm.

consumers: firms having to compete with each other will result in lower prices, greater innovation, more choice, and more efficiency because of specialization. The ultimate winner in all of these scenarios is the average consumer; and as such, the Commission focuses on eradicating anti-competitive behaviour for the *sake* of the consumer.

While an intuitively attractive justification for competition law, it has never been entirely clear if the Treaties themselves actually conceive of the objectives of Articles 101 and 102 TFEU as being related to issues of consumer welfare. However, to the Commission, it is definitely one of the big justifications and aims of the EU's competition law regime, along with establishing the internal market.[19]

Pause for reflection

From the perspective of competition law, are really powerful companies (like Microsoft) always problematic? Would it make sense to just 'outlaw' companies that are that dominant? Why or why not?

15.2.2 Enforcing competition law

Out of all the areas of 'internal market law', competition law is the most delegated one. Whereas the 'four freedoms' are only enforceable domestically because of CJEU case law establishing those rights before the courts, competition law has actually required the Member States to set up their own authorities to enforce competition law directly.

We end up with a two-strand enforcement regime in the EU:

1. Public enforcement of competition law takes place through the European Competition Network. This is the collective name for the Commission's Directorate-General on Competition Law (known as DG Comp) and the National Competition Authorities in the Member States (NCAs).
2. Private enforcement of competition law, via the domestic courts, in the same way that the four freedoms are also enforceable.[20]

Enforcement by the Commission is unsurprising, given its general role as enforcer of EU law, but there are certain unique powers the Commission has in the area of competition law. These are set out in Council Regulation 1/2003, and grant the Commission powers not only to find undertakings guilty of breaches of competition law, but to carry out investigations into their activities *and* to fine them.[21] The fines in particular are nothing to sneeze at: they reach maximums of 10 per cent of total turnover for the preceding year for

[19] See, eg, Margrethe Vestager, 'The values of competition policy', Speech to the CEPS Corporate breakfast, 13 October 2015, Brussels, available at https://ec.europa.eu/commission/commissioners/2014-2019/vestager/announcements/values-competition-policy_en.

[20] For more detail on how this works, see Chapter 8 on direct effect; Articles 101 and 102 TFEU are directly effective. For an example of how this works, see Frederick Abbott, 'The UK Competition Appeal Tribunal's Misguided Reprieve for Pfizer's Excessive Pricing Abuse' (2018) 49(7) IIC 845.

[21] Council Regulation (EC) No 1/2003 of 16 December 2002 on the implementation of the rules on competition laid down in Articles 81 and 82 of the Treaty [2004] OJ L1/1.

violations of Articles 101 and 102, and these can even be supplemented by period penalty payments for repeat infringers not changing their behaviour.[22]

This seems like excessive power to the Commission, which essentially gets to act as both police and judge in its competition law role—but the Commission's findings do not come without appeal rights. The vast majority of EU case law on competition law is actually made up of appeals to Commission infringement decisions, which can be challenged first before the EU's General Court—and the General Court's decisions can then be appealed on points of law (or legal interpretation of the facts) to the CJEU.

Furthermore, the 2003 Regulation in some ways reduced the Commission's overall role in enforcement of Articles 101 and 102 TFEU. National Competition Authorities (NCAs) have been granted full enforcement powers as well under this Regulation, and those new powers and significantly greater cooperation and coordination between NCAs and the Commission have resulted in less of a 'monopoly' for the Commission in enforcing competition law, as well as a significantly reduced workload. NCA decisions can also be 'challenged', albeit in an indirect way: via the preliminary reference process, discussed in Chapter 7.

However, even with this reduced role, criticism of the Commission's enforcement powers has been substantial. One set of complaints focuses on the lack of separation of powers the system contains.[23] Other criticism has been made about the absence of criminal-level due process in Commission proceedings which result in quasi-criminal types of fines being applied.[24] Forrester has consequently proposed that a quasi-judicial stage be introduced into the Commission's investigations, where the fact-finding and legal proceedings are conducted by one or three qualified persons ('judges', if you will) who will come to a recommendation for the College of Commissioners.[25] Neither criticism has to date been responded to by the Commission or the drafters of the Treaties, however.

Pause for reflection

What do you think of Forrester's suggestions? Why might the Commission be hesitant to change its approach to competition law enforcement proceedings?

15.3 Article 101 TFEU

Articles 101 and 102 TFEU both set out what the Commission investigates when it suspects anti-competitive behaviour, as well as what an undertaking needs to prove in order to escape the Commission's fines. We will begin with Article 101.

[22] Regulation 1/2003, arts 23(2) and 24.

[23] Donald Slater, Sebastien Thomas, and Denis Waelbroeck, 'Competition Law Proceedings Before the European Commission and the Right to a Fair Trial: No need for reform?' (2009) 5(1) ECJ 97.

[24] Ian Forrester, 'Due Process in EC Competition Cases: A distinguished institution with flawed procedures' (2009) 34(6) ELRev 817.

[25] Forrester (n 24).

Article 101 TFEU (emphasis added)

1. The following shall be prohibited as incompatible with the internal market: all **agreements** between undertakings, **decisions** by associations of undertakings and **concerted practices** which **may affect trade between Member States** and which have as their **object or effect** the prevention, restriction or distortion of competition **within the internal market**, and in particular those which:
   (a) directly or indirectly fix purchase or selling prices or any other trading conditions;
   (b) limit or control production, markets, technical development, or investment;
   (c) share markets or sources of supply;
   (d) apply dissimilar conditions to equivalent transactions with other trading parties, thereby placing them at a competitive disadvantage;
   (e) make the conclusion of contracts subject to acceptance by the other parties of supplementary obligations which, by their nature or according to commercial usage, have no connection with the subject of such contracts.
2. Any agreements or decisions prohibited pursuant to this Article shall be automatically **void**.
3. The provisions of paragraph 1 may, however, be declared inapplicable in the case of:
   - any agreement or category of agreements between undertakings,
   - any decision or category of decisions by associations of undertakings,
   - any concerted practice or category of concerted practices,

which **contributes to improving the production or distribution of goods or to promoting technical or economic progress**, while allowing **consumers a fair share of the resulting benefit**, and which does not:

   (a) impose on the undertakings concerned **restrictions which are not indispensable** to the attainment of these objectives;
   (b) afford such undertakings the possibility of **eliminating competition in respect of a substantial part of the products** in question.

Article 101 deals with so-called 'anti-competitive agreements', concluded between two or more undertakings with either the *object* or the *effect* of hindering competition on the relevant market. Article 101(1) prohibits these kinds of agreements, and Article 101(2) declares that any agreement struck in violation of Article 101(1) is void. Article 101(3) provides that certain types of agreement are excluded from the prohibition as a very limited exception, provided they meet strict requirements that mean that they are generally 'beneficial' agreements.

Assessing whether or not anything is happening that violates Article 101 TFEU can be set out as a five-step 'checklist' against which the behaviour of a company must be measured. The following steps provide a general structure for investigating Article 101 problems:

1. Does the scenario involve *undertakings*? (And at least two of them—you cannot have an anti-competitive agreement with yourself!)
2. If so, does it involve an *agreement, decision of an association, or concerted practice* by undertakings?
3. If so, does that agreement (or decision/concerted practice) have the object or effect of preventing, restricting, or distorting competition?
4. And if it has the *effect* of harming competition, is this an *appreciable* effect? (Or a de minimis one?)
5. If so, does the agreement have an *effect* on the *trade between Member States*?

   If yes: the scenario violates Article 101(1), and Article 101(2) makes the relevant agreement/decision/concerted practice void . . .
6. . . . unless Article 101(3) applies, and the agreement/decision/concerted practice:
   a. Improves the production or distribution of goods or promote technical or economic progress AND
   b. Ensures that consumers receive a fair share of the resulting benefits AND
   c. Does contain indispensable restrictions; AND
   d. Does not substantially eliminate competition.

We will now explore each of the above six steps in turn, with the exception of the definition of an undertaking, which we considered at the start of the chapter. Once you have determined that you are dealing with at least *two entities* that are engaged in an economic activity, it is time to consider what that entity is doing.

15.3.1 What is an 'agreement'?

Article 101 TFEU captures 'anti-competitive agreements', but like all legal terms, the concept of an agreement has a very specific definition—and a far wider one than it implies, which is that of a 'written contract'. Unsurprisingly, undertakings interested in violating competition law do not always leave so obvious an evidence trail.

To cover this, Article 101 TFEU applies not only to 'agreements between undertakings', but also 'decisions of an association of undertakings' and 'concerted practice by undertakings'. Agreements between undertakings are commonplace: for instance, in order for a bottle of soft drink to arrive in a supermarket, there will be agreements in place between those who *produce* the soft drink, those who *distribute* the soft drink to different parts of the world, those who sell it on to supermarkets (wholesalers), and the actual supermarket itself (retailer). These kinds of agreements are known as **vertical agreements**, as they cover different levels of the supply chain. They can be anti-competitive, but usually are not: the undertakings do not tend to be in direct competition with each other. As a hypothetical example to illustrate this point, Coca-Cola is not competing with a supermarket that sells Coca-Cola in the way that it is competing with Pepsi.[26] However, if their behaviour is captured by the rest of Article 101(1) TFEU, they will nonetheless be declared void.

Significantly more likely to be problematic from a competition law standpoint are **horizontal agreements**. Continuing with our hypothetical example, a horizontal agreement might be between two producers of *different* soft drinks, or two supermarkets wishing to each specialize in selling only *one* of those soft drinks. Consumers are likely to be harmed by those types of agreements: if Coca-Cola and Pepsi concluded an agreement, this is unlikely to mean lower prices for the consumer, or more availability of different soft drinks in different supermarkets. Instead, in this imaginary scenario, the consumer might end up with each product's price going up by the same amount, or might be stuck only being able to buy Coca-Cola in London and Pepsi in Edinburgh and Birmingham, for example.

We will explore the contents of anti-competitive agreements more in the next sections; for now, we need to consider the concept of an 'agreement' in more detail. First, the Commission and the CJEU agree that an 'agreement' does not need to be a *single* formal agreement to fall foul of Article 101(1).[27] The fact that 'decisions of associations of undertakings' are also included makes it clear that the agreement does not even have to be binding: if a trade union, for instance, issues a recommendation for a certain type of anti-competitive behaviour, this can also be caught by Article 101(1) if the members of the trade union follow through on it.

Finally, 'concerted practice' makes it clear that there does not even need to be anything written down at all: if a number of undertakings are all behaving in a way that seems suspiciously coordinated, and not something that would spontaneously happen in a market, the Commission is likely to start an Article 101(1) investigation. *Suiker Unie*, concerning a cartel of sugar producers, considered this concept in detail: there was no formal agreement between the relevant sugar producers, but they nonetheless appeared to be engaged in behaviour together that fixed prices of sugar artificially high.[28] In its ruling in *Suiker Unie*, the CJEU described 'concerted practice' as:

Joined Cases 40–48, 50, 54–56, 111, 113–114/73 *Suiker Unie* ECLI:EU:C:1975:174 (emphasis added)

26. . . . **a form of coordination between undertakings** which, without having been taken to the stage where an agreement properly so-called has been concluded, **knowingly substitutes** for the risks of competition **cooperation in practice between** them which leads to conditions of competition which do not correspond to the normal conditions of the market . . .

However, just because the Commission *thinks* market behaviour is unusual, it cannot issue a decision against a set of undertakings unless it can actively prove 'concerted practice'. The burden of proof in all Article 101 TFEU investigations is on the Commission.

[26] Richard Whish and David Bailey, *Competition Law*, 8th edn (OUP, 2015) 661.
[27] Case T-8/89 *DSM NV v Commission (Polypropylene)* ECLI:EU:T:1992:107.
[28] Joined Cases 40–48, 50, 54–56, 111, 113–114/73 *Suiker Unie* ECLI:EU:C:1975:174.

Finally, the concepts of 'agreement', 'decisions of associations', and 'concerted practice' are not mutually exclusive—a genuine cartel, meaning an ongoing operation between several independent undertakings that aims to engage in anti-competitive practices, is likely to be operating under a combination of agreements, decisions, and concerted practices.

Discussing the scenario

In the scenario at the start of the chapter, has IE engaged in any activity that might constitute an 'agreement', a 'decision of associations of undertakings', or 'concerted practice' with any other parties?

15.3.2 The object or effect of harming competition

Provided we have found more than one undertaking as well as an 'agreement' or 'concerted practice', our next step is to consider what that 'agreement' or 'concerted practice' actually does. As noted, it is entirely normal for undertakings to have agreements with undertakings, and Article 101 TFEU is only concerned with those agreements that are 'anti-competitive'.

Step 3 above makes clear that the definition of 'anti-competitive' is intended to be broad: it is meant to capture all activity that has either as its **object** or as its **effect** the 'prevention, restriction or distortion' of competition. The word 'or' is operative in Article 101(1) TFEU, as the CJEU confirmed in *STM*:[29]

Case 56/65 *STM* ECLI:EU:C:1966:38 (emphasis added)

These . . . are **not cumulative but alternative conditions** . . . suggest[ing] **first the need to consider the very object of the agreement**, in the light of the economic context in which it is to be applied. . . . Where, however, an analysis of the said clauses does not reveal a sufficient degree of harmfulness with regard to competition, **examination should then be made of the effects of the agreement.**

In *Beef Industry*, the CJEU confirmed that in considering if an agreement is prohibited by Article 101(1) TFEU, 'there is . . . no need to take account of its actual effects once it appears that its object is to prevent, restrict or distort competition within the [internal] market.'[30]

Infringement by object

How does the CJEU determine that the **objective** (or **object**) of an aspect of an agreement is to harm competition? It does not do a detailed market analysis; instead, as the CJEU has put it, certain types of behaviour can be seen as 'by their very nature . . . being injurious to the proper functioning of . . . competition'.[31]

[29] Case 56/65 *STM* ECLI:EU:C:1966:38.

[30] Case C-209/07 *Beef Industry Development and Barry Brothers* ECLI:EU:C:2008:643, para 16.

[31] Ibid, para 17.

The non-exhaustive list of examples of behaviour listed in Article 101(1) TFEU are all such serious restrictions of competition that they all restrict competition by their very nature; they are also called 'hardcore' restrictions of competition, primarily because their effect does not need to be examined. The consequences of agreements of these types will, invariably, be higher prices—and so harmed consumer welfare.

Infringement by effect

Finding a **restriction by object** is, in many ways, the easier finding. If the agreement at play does not contain a hardcore restriction of competition, it then has to be examined whether the effect of the agreement is anti-competitive—eg, if it results in higher prices for the consumer. This requires extensive market analysis, and again, the burden of proof in showing this **anti-competitive effect** lies with the Commission.

The CJEU has made clear that there is a clear sequence of questions it will investigate when trying to determine if the effect of a restriction is anti-competitive. This has become known as the *Delimitis* test, named after the key case in which the CJEU set it out.[32] *Delimitis* concerned a beer supply agreement between a brewery and the licence-holder of a pub owned by the brewery; the agreement came with a condition that required the licence-holder to purchase a set minimum volume of beer from the brewery. This was seen as not restrictive by object, largely because it enabled both the licence-holder and the brewery to carry out their respective trades on beneficial terms.[33]

The CJEU evaluated the following questions after determining this was not anti-competitive by object, as both parties in principle benefited from the agreement:

1. First, what is the relevant market to this scenario?
2. Secondly, what are the possibilities for competitors to enter the market?
3. Finally, does the agreement appreciably make it *harder* for competitors to enter the market (and thus contribute to foreclosing the market)?

The relevant market in *Delimitis* was the market for beer being sold for consumption in pubs. Whether the agreement had a restrictive effect was not immediately obvious, however: if this was an agreement that applied to a *single pub*, would it genuinely distort or restrict competition in the internal market? The CJEU found that much depended on whether or not these agreements were commonplace; how many beer breweries there were, and how big a market share the current brewery held; how many pubs there were, and how many of those were linked to this brewery; the brand loyalty of customers more generally; and possible other factors, for example, if it was easy to set up new pubs, how long these minimum buying clauses lasted, etc.[34]

Hence, in order for the agreement and the minimum buying obligation to be contrary to Article 101(1) TFEU, the Commission had to prove that this type of agreement was common, and made it significantly more difficult for other breweries to access the 'beer sold for consumption in pubs' market. If the Commission could not prove this—and it failed to, in *Delimitis*—a minimum purchase obligation would not have demonstrable anti-competitive effects, and so would not be precluded by Article 101 TFEU.

[32] C-234/89 *Delimitis v Henninger Bräu* ECLI:EU:C:1991:91.
[33] Ibid, paras 11–13.
[34] Ibid, para 27.

We can see the Commission effectively arguing a restriction by effect in *Van den Bergh*.[35] Van den Bergh Foods Ltd, called HB in the judgment, was Ireland's primary manufacturer of ice-cream products—especially the single-wrapped ice creams that you can buy from a freezer display in a supermarket, which the General Court termed 'impulse ice-creams'. The company supplied ice-cream retailers with these freezer display cabinets for a number of years on a 'loan' basis, at nominal rent, but on the condition that *only* HB ice-cream was stocked in them.

In 1989, Masterfoods, a Mars subsidiary, tried to enter the Irish ice-cream market. When retailers started stocking Mars ice-cream in their freezer cabinets, HB started demanding that they comply with the exclusivity clause in their loan agreements. Following a long stretch of litigation and negotiation with the Commission, in 1998 the Commission issued a decision declaring the HB exclusivity clauses to be contrary to Article 101 (and Article 102) of the TFEU.

The key difference between *Delimitis* and *Van den Bergh* is what the Commission found in its investigation of market effects. When HB challenged the decision before the General Court, the Commission was able to demonstrate that the collective sum of the retailer agreements concluded by HB had made a real impact on competition in the market:

Case T-65/98 *Van den Bergh Foods Ltd v Commission* ECLI:EU:T:2003:281 (emphasis added)

18. **The Commission states that only a small proportion of retail outlets in Ireland**, 17 per cent according to the Lansdowne survey, **have freezer cabinets which are not subject to an exclusivity clause**. It maintains that those outlets may be referred to as 'open' outlets, in the sense that retailers are free to stock in them the impulse ice-cream of any supplier . . . **As regards the other outlets**, 83 per cent according to the Lansdowne survey, in which the suppliers have installed freezer cabinets, **the Commission considers that other suppliers cannot have direct access to them for sale of their products without first overcoming substantial barriers**. It submits that 'newcomers to the outlet are foreclosed' from them and that 'although this foreclosure is not absolute, in the sense that the retailer is not contractually precluded from selling other suppliers' products, the outlet can be said to be foreclosed in so far as entry thereto by competing suppliers is rendered very difficult' . . .

19. **The Commission finds that in some 40 per cent of all outlets in Ireland the only freezer cabinet/s for the storage of impulse ice-cream in place in the outlet has or have been provided by HB** . . . It observes that 'a supplier who wishes to gain access for the sale of his impulse ice-cream products to a retail outlet (that is, **a new entrant to the outlet**) in which at least one supplier-exclusive freezer cabinet is in place **can only do so if that outlet has a non-exclusive cabinet** . . . or if he can persuade the retailer **either to replace an *in situ* supplier-exclusive freezer cabinet or to install an additional freezer cabinet** alongside the *in situ* supplier-exclusive cabinet/s' . . . It considers . . . , on the basis of the Lansdowne survey, that **it is unlikely that retailers will adopt one or other of those measures** if they have one (or more) freezers supplied by HB and concludes that 40 per cent of the outlets in question are de facto tied to HB (recital 184). **Other suppliers are therefore foreclosed from access to those outlets, contrary to Article [101(1) TFEU].**

[35] Case T-65/98 *Van den Bergh Foods Ltd v Commission* ECLI:EU:T:2003:281.

The General Court found that the Commission had demonstrated that the *effect* of the measures at play was thus significantly more notable than it was in *Delimitis*, as it spread far beyond a single retailer and these agreements were commonplace, and so in *Van den Bergh*, a violation of Article 101 TFEU *was* found.

15.3.3 **Appreciable or *de minimis* effects?**

Delimitis and *Van den Bergh* raise interesting examples of the next relevant question that the CJEU has asked of anti-competitive agreements in violation of Article 101(1) TFEU. Agreements that restrict competition by their **effect**, according to *Delimitis*, appear to need to have an actually *noticeable* effect on competition in order for a violation of Article 101(1) TFEU to be found. This was not a concept that was newly introduced in *Delimitis*, but rather has been a standing aspect of CJEU interpretations of Article 101 TFEU from 1960 onwards: the prohibition in Article 101(1) TFEU applies only where anti-competitive agreements have an effect on the **internal market**, rather than say, a single producer. As such, the CJEU has been consistent in finding that agreements that do not have an **appreciable** effect on competition in the internal market are *not covered* by the Article 101(1) prohibition.

This notion of appreciable effects is also described by noting that there is a ***de minimis*** aspect to Article 101(1) TFEU: a certain minimum 'effect' on the internal market is a pre-condition for finding a violation of Article 101(1) TFEU. This was first established by the CJEU in *Völk*, and has been further elaborated on in Commission Notices that make clear what kind of 'market effect' the Commission considers appreciable.[36] These notices (with the current one being published in 2014)[37] determine the threshold for Article 101(1) TFEU applying by means of looking at the **market share** of the relevant undertakings involved in the agreements or practices: if their aggregate (combined) market share is **at least 10 per cent** and they are on the same level of the supply chain so have concluded a **horizontal agreement**, the agreement will be found anti-competitive. Where undertakings are at different levels of the supply chain, and thus in a **vertical agreement**, their aggregate market share has to be **at least 15 per cent** for the effect of the agreement to be deemed appreciable.

Finally, it is key to remember that **this further test of appreciability only applies to restrictions of competition by *effect***. Hardcore infringements, meaning restrictions of competition by object, are always deemed to be appreciable.

Discussing the scenario

Consider what IE and MH appear to be doing. Are their practices likely to be restrictions of competition by object or by effect? Try to explain the difference—and make clear what the Commission would need to prove in order for a restriction of competition by effect to be established.

If you think they are restricting competition by effect, do you think the effect is appreciable—does it satisfy the *de minimis* test?

[36] Case 5/69 *Völk* ECLI:EU:C:1969:35.

[37] *De Minimis* 2014 Notice [2014] OJ C291/1.

15.3.4 An effect on trade between Member States

The final part of an assessment of a violation of Article 101(1) TFEU reflects the roots of the provision: competition law was originally included in the EU Treaties first and foremost because anti-competitive behaviour would hinder the establishment of the internal market, as we discussed in Section 15.2.

Given those origins of Article 101(1) TFEU, it is unsurprising that its wording also directly references the idea of the internal market: Article 101(1) TFEU has particular problems *only* with those agreements that will negatively **affect trade between Member States**. This is a jurisdictional test, and one not dissimilar to the concept of the 'purely internal situation' that we saw when looking at the four freedoms in the previous chapters:[38] EU law does *not* apply to situations where they are fully internal to a Member State, and there is no cross-border dimension to them. Consequently, anti-competitive behaviour that does not have any impact on cross-border trade within the internal market *cannot* be contrary to EU law.

The CJEU has offered clarification of just how the idea of an effect on trade between the Member States should be interpreted, and in doing so, has made it a requirement that is very easy to satisfy—presumably so as to not exclude the application of EU competition law from behaviour that the Commission *wishes* to prohibit, but cannot explicitly link to 'trade' at the time it discovers it.

The current definition of an effect on trade is found in the *STM* case:

Case 56/65 *STM* ECLI:EU:C:1966:38 (emphasis added)

> . . . it must be possible to foresee with a sufficient degree of probability on the basis of an objective set of factors of law or fact that the **agreement in question may have an influence, direct or indirect, actual or potential, on the pattern of trade between Member States.**

Given that all that is needed is a *potential indirect influence* on trade, the Commission has an easy time demonstrating that there are likely to be cross-border consequences of anti-competitive behaviour *even* where all the anti-competitive behaviour takes place within a single Member State's territory. *Delimitis* gives us a clear example of that: the CJEU there reasoned that even if beer from other Member States was allowed to be sold in the pub under the agreement with the brewery, there would nonetheless be a notable effect on trade between Member States if the exclusivity clause meant that the pub was not in *need* of any beer from other Member States.[39]

The test set out in Step 5 above, then, is an easy one to satisfy for the Commission—but it must nonetheless be satisfied.

Discussing the scenario

Do the practices of IE and MH have an effect on trade in electricity between Member States? (What kind of effect? Consider the *STM* definition.)

[38] See Chapters 11–14.

[39] *Delimitis* (n 32), paras 30–32.

15.3.5 Consequences of a violation of Article 101(1) TFEU

If all the first 'five' steps are satisfied, and we have found either an anti-competitive agreement or practice that has an effect on trade between the Member States and is restrictive by object, or has an appreciable restrictive effect on competition, we have found a violation of Article 101(1) TFEU. What then?

Article 101(2) declares these types of agreements automatically void, where they are formalized; informal practices cannot as such be declared void, but must also be stopped as a consequence of finding a violation of Article 101(1) TFEU.

It is worth noting that Article 101(2) TFEU has direct effect, and consequently national courts can declare agreements in violation of Article 101(1) TFEU void—there is no need to refer a finding of a violation of Article 101(1) TFEU to either the Commission or the CJEU.

The ultimate consequence of a finding of a violation of Article 101(1) TFEU, and thus a 'void' agreement under Article 101(2) TFEU, is likely to be a claim for damages: the CJEU has explicitly confirmed that the harm suffered by competitors in light of the anti-competitive agreement can result in a private claim for damages.[40] The Commission can fine violators of Article 101(1) TFEU, but those fines go to the *Commission*, not the undertakings harmed by the anti-competitive behaviour—so a private claim for damages is likely if the harm sustained was significant. As with all other aspects of remedies, EU law does not determine what the remedies for breaches of competition law should be in domestic law—merely that they should be effective and equivalent.[41]

15.3.6 Exemptions from Article 101(1) TFEU

Other than the *de minimis* rule set out earlier, there are two other situations in which a violation of Article 101(1) TFEU is not unlawful, and does not result in the relevant agreement being automatically rendered void under Article 101(2) TFEU.

The first situation is where the relevant agreement qualifies for the exception set out in Article 101(3) TFEU. That Article sets out four *cumulative* conditions, which all have to be satisfied in order for an agreement to be considered lawful under EU law *despite* its anti-competitive effects or nature.[42] As set out in Step 6 above, to qualify for an Article 101(3) TFEU exemption, an agreement must:

a. Improve the production or distribution of goods or promote technical or economic progress; AND
b. Ensure that consumers receive a fair share of the resulting benefits; AND
c. Not contain indispensable restrictions; AND
d. Not substantially eliminate competition.

Few agreements qualify, not least because most anti-competitive agreements do not result in a benefit to consumers. However, the other reason that Article 101(3) TFEU is relied on very little is because of the second situation that results in a violation of Article 101(1) TFEU not being unlawful: the so-called block exemptions, set out in a number of EU regulations.

[40] Case C-453/99 *Courage Ltd v Crehan* ECLI:EU:C:2001:465. [41] See Chapter 8.
[42] Case T-395/94 *Atlantic Container Line and Others v Commission* ECLI:EU:T:2002:49.

Block exemptions cover certain categories of agreements and operate under strict conditions. Where these conditions are satisfied, the relevant agreements are automatically exempt from Article 101(1) TFEU. The types of conditions included in 'block exemption' regulations include specific market share thresholds (ie, meaning that undertakings that hold a very significant market share will never qualify for a block exemption); additionally, 'hardcore' competition restrictions will automatically disqualify an agreement from being exempted from Article 101(1) TFEU. These 'hardcore' restrictions are by and large the same as the restrictions by object discussed earlier: the block exemption for vertical agreements, for instance, mentions price fixing, market sharing or splitting, and output limitations.

Vertical agreements covering less than an aggregate 30 per cent market share are covered by a block exemption,[43] as are technology transfer agreements (covering product licensing)[44] and specific sectoral agreements, covering, for instance, motor vehicles.[45]

Discussing the scenario

Consider the behaviour of IE and MH. Do they qualify for an exemption under Article 101(3) TFEU, do you think? If not—what happens?

15.4 Article 102 TFEU

As we saw in Section 15.3, one half of the Treaty provisions on competition law deal with the behaviour of at least *two* undertakings, acting together in anti-competitive ways. However, as the example of Microsoft demonstrated, it is perfectly possible for a single undertaking to behave in an anti-competitive way all by itself—and for that anti-competitive behaviour to have a big effect on the internal market. This is what Article 102 TFEU tackles: anti-competitive behaviour by **dominant undertakings**.

Article 102 TFEU (emphasis added)

Any **abuse** by one or more **undertakings** of a **dominant position within the internal market** or **in a substantial part of it** shall be prohibited as incompatible with the internal market **in so far as it may affect trade between Member States**.

Such abuse may, in particular, consist in:

(a) directly or indirectly imposing unfair purchase or selling prices or other unfair trading conditions;

(b) limiting production, markets or technical development to the prejudice of consumers;

(c) applying dissimilar conditions to equivalent transactions with other trading parties, thereby placing them at a competitive disadvantage;

(d) making the conclusion of contracts subject to acceptance by the other parties of supplementary obligations which, by their nature or according to commercial usage, have no connection with the subject of such contracts.

[43] Regulation 330/2010 [2010] OJ L102/1.
[44] Regulation 316/2014 [2014] OJ L93/17.
[45] Regulation 461/2010 [2010] OJ L129/52.

Key to Article 102 TFEU is the second word in the provision: it tackles abuse of dominant positions, not their *existence*. It is very important to understand that the existence of a monopoly is not contrary to EU law. Companies like Microsoft and Google are perfectly fine to exist under EU law! However, EU competition law takes a closer look at how such monopolies behave, for the very simple reason that their behaviour can have disproportionate impacts on the levels of competition in the market. The CJEU summarizes the EU's attitude clearly in *Michelin*:

Case 322/81 *Michelin* ECLI:EU:C:1983:313 (emphasis added)

57. A finding that an undertaking has a dominant position is not in itself a recrimination but simply means that, irrespective of the reasons for which it has such a dominant position, the **undertaking concerned has a special responsibility not to allow its conduct to impair genuine undistorted competition on the [Internal] Market.**

Abuse of a dominant position can also be carried out in a market where, say, there are *two* or *three* main actors, rather than just the one. We would call this an oligopoly; a classic example of an oligopolistic market is that of aeroplanes, where Boeing and Airbus are effectively the only two suppliers.

In order to see if Article 102 TFEU has been violated, we again can follow a number of steps in order to assess whether we are looking at a situation both of market dominance and of abusive behaviour by a dominant undertaking:

Tackling Article 102

1. Does the scenario involve at least one undertaking?
2. Is that undertaking dominant in what we will call the relevant market?
   a. First, what is the relevant market?
   b. Second, what is the undertaking's market strength?
   c. Third, what are the barriers to entry in the relevant market like?
3. If the undertaking is dominant in the relevant market, does that market cover (in geographical terms) at least a substantial part of the internal market?
4. If so, is the dominant undertaking engaging in abusive practices?
5. And finally, does the abuse affect trade between Member States?

If yes, the undertaking has violated Article 102 TFEU, unless it can provide a justification for its practices.

Steps 1 and 5 here should look familiar: we considered the definition of an undertaking in the introduction earlier, and considered the concept of measures that have an effect on trade between Member States in Section 15.3. The definition set out there, courtesy of the *STM* case, *also* applies to Article 102 TFEU, according to the CJEU's case law.[46] Consequently, when the Commission can prove that abusive behaviour by a dominant undertaking has an actual/potential direct/indirect effect or influence on trade, it will be caught by Article 102 TFEU.

The first Article 102 TFEU-specific question to assess, then, is what dominance means for the purposes of EU competition law.

15.4.1 What is a 'dominant position'?

As Step 2 makes clear, there are several questions we need to ask in order to form a picture of whether or not a given undertaking is in a position that we could call **dominant**. Primarily, we have to give the idea of dominance context: an undertaking is not just generically dominant, but it is likely to be dominant in *something, somewhere*. In the case of Microsoft, for instance, its dominance is in computer-operating software—probably worldwide.

We can use the key case of *United Brands* to explore dominance further.[47] United Brands Company was, at the time of the case, the primary supplier of bananas in Europe (under the brand Chiquita). The Commission found that it abused that position in a number of ways. First of all, it forbade other entities in the supply chain, such as its distributors, to sell bananas that were not supplied by United Brands. Second of all, it operated different prices in different Member States that were fixed on a weekly basis, and the prices that it charged in Denmark, Belgium, Luxembourg, and the Netherlands were deemed 'unfair'. In considering just what made the behaviour of United Brands of interest to Article 102 TFEU, the CJEU stressed that it found itself in a dominant position, meaning:

Case 27/76 *United Brands v Commission* ECLI:EU:C:1978:22 (emphasis added)

65. . . . a **position of economic strength** enjoyed by an undertaking which enables it **to prevent effective competition being maintained on the relevant market** by affording it the power to behave to **an appreciable extent independently of its competitors, customers and ultimately of its consumers** . . .

In every instance where the Commission wants to argue an Article 102 TFEU breach, it therefore has to consider what the **relevant market** of operation is. It has to then prove that the undertaking it is pursuing is actually in a **dominant position in the relevant market**, by assessing its **market share**, and by seeing how difficult it would be for competing undertakings to enter that market by considering if there are **barriers to entry**. We will assess each of these issues in turn, using *United Brands* as a key example of an examination of dominance.

[46] Cases 6–7/73 *Commercial Solvents v Commission* ECLI:EU:C:1974:18, paras 31–32.
[47] Case 27/76 *United Brands v Commission* ECLI:EU:C:1978:22.

The relevant market

Defining the relevant market correctly is crucial to the Commission's case in proving a breach of Article 102 TFEU. It has to demonstrate that the undertaking in question is a dominant supplier in a given product in a specific region, and it will attempt to make both the product and the region as 'narrow' a concept as possible. The undertaking being accused of abusive behaviour will want to attempt to prove that the market at hand is very large, so as to show that it is only a minor actor in that market: Microsoft, in other words, will want to argue that its relevant market is 'computer software', where the Commission wants to argue that its relevant market is the far more specific 'operating system software'.

The relevant market is specific to each case, and requires an assessment of three distinct markets so as to draw a clear picture of just where, and in what, the undertaking is dominant. These three markets are:

- The product market
- The geographical market
- And, where relevant, the temporal market.

The product market sounds like the simplest one to prove, but it is very often the source of appeals to competition authority (whether the Commission or NCAs) decisions. Determining what the product market in a given case is requires an examination of what we call 'substitutability', or how much the price has to change before consumers will switch to a different product. By that test, we can see how Microsoft would fail to argue it is acting in just the general *software* market: you need an operating system to run a computer, and cannot replace it with just *any* software if Windows' prices go up, not least because if you did make a switch, you would probably also have to replace all your *other* software. The relevant product market that Microsoft acts in is thus the operating system software market, and substitutability there is low.

A contrasting example might be the soft drinks market we referenced earlier: if consumers happily switched to soft drink B when the price of soft drink A went up by even a few pence, there would be high substitutability in that market, and it would be unlikely that the producer of soft drink A or B was in a dominant position there.

The geographic market is effectively the market where the undertaking conducts its business on identical terms. Undertakings will conduct business on very different terms if there are barriers between different regions or countries, such as language barriers, cultural/lifestyle barriers, regulatory barriers, or even transport costs that rise the further away from the site of production a product has to travel. The fact that business is being done somewhere in the EU, in other words, does not automatically mean that the relevant geographic market is the *whole* of the EU: transport costs and cultural differences are very likely to mean that we will not see Irn Bru stocked in many supermarkets in Spain.

Finally, for some products, a temporal market (meaning the market of 'time') is also a factor. Particularly in agricultural products, there are likely to be periods in which some producers are very active, and then entire periods where there is basically no activity. In a season in which oranges are not being sold, and demand for them is low because they are out of season, it is unlikely that anyone is in a dominant position in the orange market. Note, however, that there is not necessarily a temporal market for all products—and if a given product is available and used year-long, this is not a necessary component of assessing the relevant market.

We can use *United Brands* to set out how the CJEU has evaluated relevant markets. First, on the product market, it considered the substitutability of the banana as a fruit. If the price of bananas went up, how quickly would consumers switch to other fruits? It concluded that they would not:

Case 27/76 *United Brands v Commission* ECLI:EU:C:1978:22 (emphasis added)

31. The banana has **certain characteristics**, appearance, taste, softness, seedlessness, easy handling, a constant level of production **which enable it to satisfy the constant needs of an important section of the population** consisting of the very young, the old and the sick.

United Brands, which had tried to argue it was merely active on the 'fruit' market, thus failed in that argument, and the CJEU found that the banana market was 'sufficiently distinct' from other fruit markets.[48]

Discussing the scenario

What is the product market that IE is active in? Consider what the Commission will want to argue, and what IE might argue in order to prove it is *not* dominant in a product market. Applying the substitutability test, who do you think will succeed in their argument?

The geographic market was also considered in *United Brands*. The Commission argued that the Benelux, Denmark, Germany, and Ireland were the relevant geographic market, because it was in these Member States that bananas were sold on more or less equivalent terms. In the other Member States at this time (namely, France, Italy, and the UK), regulations that gave advantages to bananas produced in former colonies applied, and so they were not comparable 'markets'. United Brands agreed on this latter point, but argued that its business activities in all the other Member States were also subject to very different regulatory regimes and consumer habits—noting, for instance, that the Germans ate 2.5 times as much fresh fruit as the Irish did.

The CJEU considered these arguments and first stressed that the geographic market had to be defined as an area 'where the objective conditions of competition applying to the product in question [are] the same for all traders'.[49] It argued that while transport costs and tariffs differed across the Member States, these differences were not discriminatory in the Benelux, Denmark, Germany, and Ireland, and the area was thus 'sufficiently homogeneous' for the purposes of Article 102 TFEU to be considered as a single market.[50]

[48] Ibid, para 35. [49] Ibid, para 44.

[50] For context, the differences in tariffs can be accounted for by the fact that the EU Customs Union did not apply to bananas until 1993 (in a very particular exception to what is set out in Chapter 10). Those particularly curious can find more detail here: http://www.mag.go.cr/rev_agr/v30n02_111.pdf.

Discussing the scenario

From the facts given in the scenario, what do you think IE's geographic market is? And do you think a temporal market applies to the scenario?

Combine your answers to these questions with your definition of the product market and you have arrived at the relevant market.

Market share

In deciding if an undertaking is in a dominant position, we have to know in *what* and *where* it is operating—hence determining what the relevant market is—but we also very much have to know *how much* it is doing. An undertaking that sells only a few of any product in any given year is not going to be 'dominant' in a market, however specifically defined. The Commission therefore needs to be able to prove conclusively that the market share or market strength of the undertaking is substantial enough for that undertaking to be dominant.

To measure strength, and to consider if it is substantial, the Commission has to consider the pure *volume of sales*—eg, how many products—or to look at its *profit*—eg, where fewer sales at great value also indicate dominance. This will result in statistics that can be compared to others operating on the relevant market, and a percentage of market share held by the undertaking under investigation can be calculated accordingly.

The CJEU observed in *Hoffmann-La Roche*, a case involving a dominant producer in the vitamins market, that 'although the importance of the market shares may vary from one market to another, the view may legitimately be taken that very large market shares are in themselves, and save in exceptional circumstances, evidence of the existence of a dominant position'.[51] In further case law, it has given us useful guidance on what very large market shares may look like, and the Commission has also made clear how it conducts investigations into market share and what it is looking for when it does:

- The *Virgin/British Airways* case found that 39.7 per cent market share resulted in dominance.[52]
- *Hoffmann-La Roche* found dominance at 43 per cent market share.
- *United Brands* found dominance at 40–45 per cent market share.
- *Akzo* made clear that a presumption of dominance operates at market shares over 50 per cent.[53]
- The Commission's 10th Annual Report on Competition Policy suggests that a market share of anywhere between 20 per cent and 40 per cent suggests dominance.

Key to a successful investigation into market share is that the Commission is thorough: it cannot selectively consider a *part* of the market and use the sales volume it finds there to prove a very large market share. However, the CJEU's rulings make clear that the Article

[51] Case 85/76 *Hoffmann-La Roche v Commission* ECLI:EU:C:1979:36, para 41.

[52] *Virgin/British Airways* [2000] OJ L30/1.

[53] Case C-62/86 *AKZO* ECLI:EU:C:1991:286.

102 TFEU version of a monopoly does *not* mean that the market has to be controlled *exclusively* by a single undertaking. Microsoft, in other words, with its 'quasi-monopoly' in the operating systems market, is most definitely in a dominant position—but undertakings that hold a smaller but nonetheless substantial portion of a market share can also be.

Barriers to entry

Using market share to arrive at a presumption that an undertaking is in a dominant position is exactly that: a presumption. Undertakings with a market share over 50 per cent can be *presumed* to be dominant, but the Commission has to nonetheless investigate the specific market and conclude that this market share is stable. If a new competitor could enter tomorrow and take 40 per cent of a 50 per cent market share away, there will be no dominance in a given market. In other words, the Commission also has to consider what the barriers to entry in a relevant market are—only where these are high, in combination with a substantial market share, can it 'prove' that an entity is in a dominant position.

The types of barriers to entry that the Commission will have to account for can be anything from regulatory provisions that restrict the number of operators in a sector—eg, licences—to the use of intellectual property rights that make it impossible for new entrants to produce a substitutable product,[54] or the combination of experience and technological expertise.[55] The latter is defined very broadly by the Court and the Commission: even 'simple' products can operate in markets with very high barriers to entry. *United Brands* once more provides an instructive example.

Case 27/76 *United Brands v Commission* ECLI:EU:C:1978:22 (emphasis added)

122. The particular barriers to competitors entering the market are the exceptionally large capital investments required for the creation and running of banana plantations, the need to increase sources of supply in order to avoid the effects of fruit diseases and bad weather (hurricanes, floods), the introduction of an essential system of logistics which the distribution of a very perishable product makes necessary, economies of scale from which newcomers to the market cannot derive any immediate benefit and the actual cost of entry made up inter alia of all the general expenses incurred in penetrating the market such as the setting up of an adequate commercial network, the mounting of very large-scale advertising campaigns, all those financial risks, the costs of which are irrecoverable if the attempt fails.

123. Thus, although, as [United Brands] has pointed out, it is true that competitors are able to use the same methods of production and distribution as the applicant, they come up against almost insuperable practical and financial obstacles.

[54] See the *Microsoft* example earlier, where the refusal to supply interoperability information was based on Microsoft's intellectual property rights.

[55] See *United Brands* (n 47) and *Hoffmann-La Roche* (n 51).

As such, in *United Brands* the CJEU ultimately found that United Brands was in a dominant position in the relevant market, namely the banana market in the Benelux, Ireland, Denmark, and Germany, as it held a 40–45 per cent market share and there were 'almost insuperable' practical and financial barriers to market entry.

Discussing the scenario

What is IE's market share? Can we presume it is dominant, or not? And do you think there are significant barriers to entry to the relevant market that IE operates in? Try to guess what these might be—we appreciate you are not an expert in the field of energy.

Then, complete the following:

IE is/is not in a dominant position in the relevant market, namely __________, as it holds a ____ market share and there are/are not substantial barriers to entry into that market.

15.4.2 Dominance in (a substantial part of) the single market?

Step 3 sets out an obvious check that nonetheless has to be satisfied. In order for EU competition law to have any bearing on what an undertaking is doing, it has to be dominant *in the internal market*. The most dominant car manufacturer in China who also has a 3 per cent market share in the EU cannot possibly be declared to be contravening Article 102 TFEU, simply because its market share in the EU does not put it in a position where its activities would affect competition in the internal market substantially.

However, Article 102 TFEU also makes clear that dominance for EU purposes does not have to take place in the *entire* internal market. The Microsofts of the world will obviously satisfy a dominance test in all Member States, and so be responsible under Article 102 TFEU for their activities anywhere in the EU, but they are the exception—not the rule. Many undertakings will be active in only a portion of the internal market, but their activities may nonetheless have effects beyond that portion of the internal market. Take, for example, a bakery like Greggs. It is not active outside of the UK, but is undoubtedly one of the UK's leading bakery chains. Were it to engage in some sort of uncompetitive behaviour, this would affect the bakery market in the UK—and not only for UK-based competitors.

As such, Article 102 TFEU requires that an undertaking is dominant in at least a *substantial part* of the single market. The CJEU has defined this very broadly: in the *Suiker Unie* cases, several of the applicants tried to argue that they were not dominant in a *substantial part* of the single market. The CJEU set out the following test:

Joined Cases 40–48, 50, 54–56, 111, 113–114/73 *Suiker Unie* ECLI:EU:C:1975:174 (emphasis added)

371. For the purpose of determining **whether a specific territory is large enough to amount to a 'substantial part of the [Internal] Market'** within the meaning of [Article 102] of the Treaty **the pattern and volume of the production and consumption of**

→

→

the said product as well as the habits and economic opportunities of vendors and purchasers must be considered.

372. Insofar as sugar in particular is concerned it is advisable to take into consideration in addition to the high freight rates in relation to the price of the product and the habits of the processing industries and consumers the fact that Community rules have consolidated most of the special features of the former national markets.

373. From 1968/69 to 1971/72 Belgian production and total Community production increased respectively from 530 000 to 770 000 metric tons and from 6 800 000 000 to 8 100 000 000 metric tons. . . .

374. During these marketing years Belgian consumption was approximately 350 000 metric tons whereas Community consumption increased from 5 900 000 000 to 6 500 000 000 metric tons. . . .

375. If the other criteria mentioned above are taken into account these market shares are sufficiently large for the area covered by Belgium and Luxembourg to be considered, so far as sugar is concerned, as substantial part of the [Internal] Market in this product.

We can see from this test that the *volumes of production* and *consumption* determine whether or not an 'area' is a substantial part of the single market. The CJEU applied this same test to a different sugar producer, active in the 'southern part of Germany', later in the case—and found that based on consumption and production, even just the 'southern part of Germany' satisfies the 'substantial part' test.[56] This is, as such, not a difficult condition to satisfy in the Commission's process of proving a violation of Article 102 TFEU—but it is an essential one.

15.4.3 Abuse of dominance?

Finally, under Step 4, we consider *what* the undertaking is doing. Remember, being 'dominant' is not a violation of EU law: the EU is not interested in punishing successful businesses for those successes, but rather wishes to ensure that those undertakings whose activities will have a substantial impact on the internal market are not taking *advantage* of their market power by trying to edge out competition in the internal market. There are no Article 102 TFEU violations, in other words, unless an undertaking in a dominant position is *abusing* their dominant position.

What does 'abuse' look like? Article 102 TFEU gives us a first indication, setting out a non-exhaustive list of activities that are seen as abusive when engaged in by a dominant undertaking. The CJEU's decision in *Hoffmann-La Roche* also provides a definition:

[56] *Suiker Unie* (n 28), paras 444–448.

Case 85/76 *Hoffmann-La Roche v Commission* ECLI:EU:C: 1979:36 (emphasis added)

91. The concept of abuse is an objective concept relating to the behaviour of an undertaking in a dominant position which is such as to influence the structure of the market where, as a result of the very presence of the undertaking in question, the degree of competition is weakened and which, through recourse to methods different from those which condition normal competition . . . has the effect of hindering the maintenance of the degree of competition still existing in the market . . .

It is important to note that the Commission is not obliged to prove that the dominant undertaking's behaviour is having a particular effect *at this time*. The General Court in the 2001 *Michelin* case stressed that 'for the purposes of establishing an infringement of Article [102 TFEU], it is sufficient to show that the abusive conduct of the undertaking in a dominant position tends to restrict competition or, in other words, that *the conduct is capable of having that effect*' (emphasis added).[57]

In investigating abuse of dominance, the Commission is therefore primarily focused on demonstrating that certain types of behaviour are taking place—rather than proving that that behaviour is currently having an effect on the internal market. 'Abusive behaviour' is generally split into two broad categories of action: so-called pricing behaviour, and non-pricing behaviour. We will look at some examples of each in turn.

Abusive pricing behaviour

Abusive pricing behaviour is what it sounds like: a situation where a dominant undertaking is charging prices that in one way or another have as an objective *restricting* or *eliminating* competition in the relevant market.

One example of abusive pricing behaviour is **predatory pricing**, or **predation**. When an undertaking engages in predatory pricing, it sets prices for its products that are impossible for competitors with lower market shares to meet—with the objective of driving those competitors out of business, and *then* raising prices for their own benefit. This is not to mean that Article 102 TFEU has a problem with undertakings charging *low* prices for their products and services—but rather when the prices charged are almost unbelievably low, and not in line with normal market expectations.

An extreme example of predatory pricing is so-called pricing 'below cost'. Seen in *AKZO* and *Tetra Pak (No. 2)*,[58] pricing below cost involves a very dominant entity setting prices for their products where they are actually selling them at a loss—but because of their market position, they can afford to do this for a short period of time, and in that time hope to eliminate all competition (which probably will not be able to mimic this behaviour, as a smaller market share will also mean smaller financial reserves).

[57] Case T-203/01 *Michelin* ECLI:EU:T:2003:250, para 239.
[58] Case C-333/94P *Tetra Pak (No. 2)* ECLI:EU:C:1996:436.

AKZO, a company dominant in the organic peroxides market, makes for an illustrative example. Organic peroxides are used in two forms: in the plastics industry, and in food additives. AKZO had always been active in both the 'plastics' and the 'food additive' markets, but its competitor ECS had focused on the 'food additive' market. When it started becoming active in the 'plastics' market, AKZO offered ECS customers flour additives below the cost of their production. The strategy would not hurt AKZO, as the predominant part of its business came from the 'plastics' market—but ECS would suffer significantly if it tried to compete with AKZO at those prices in the 'food additive' market.

The CJEU found that this was not normal business strategy, and that there was no reason for AKZO to be interested in selling each unit of these flour additives at a loss unless it was interested in 'eliminating competitors so as to enable it subsequently to raise its prices by taking advantage of its monopolistic position'.[59] Where an undertaking is selling at a loss generally, but not explicitly selling each unit of a product below the price it costs to *make* that unit, the Commission has to go through a little more effort to prove that there is an *intention* to eliminate competition, however; there may also be other reasons for selling at those kinds of discounts, such as a desire to sell perishable goods for *any* money rather than letting them expire.

Two other categories of abusive pricing behaviour are **excessive pricing** and **discriminatory pricing**. Both of these were taking place in *United Brands*. Excessive pricing involves a dominant undertaking that sets prices that appear to have nothing at all to do with the market value of a product, and are increased by a dominant undertaking simply because it can get away with charging more (as it has little competition). Discriminatory pricing is what it sounds like: charging different consumers or other undertakings different prices for reasons that cannot be objectively justified (eg, production costs are different in different Member States).[60] In *United Brands*, distributors in different Member States were charged different prices for bananas on the basis of what United Brands thought they would pay—not what the actual value of the bananas was. In some Member States, this was well above the market value of bananas. The Commission succeeded in proving that there was no connection between the different prices charged and the market value of bananas in the relevant Member States by means of detailed economic evidence; in the absence of such evidence, a claim of excessive pricing is unlikely to succeed. The lack of objective justification for the different prices was easier to prove: despite identical banana production costs, Danish distributors were charged almost 2.5 times what Irish distributors were.

An alternative to simply overcharging customers and other undertakings on the supply chain is effectively 'bribing' them by means of **loyalty rebates**. Where these are issued, an undertaking effectively limits competition on the market by giving discounts only where virtually *all* of a product is bought from that undertaking—and so, once more, competitors will find themselves struggling to actually offer competitive prices in comparison, as they will be selling much less product.

Historically, loyalty rebates were treated as being anti-competitive by their very nature—but the 2017 *Intel* case has brought nuance to the CJEU's position on this.[61] It did not formally overrule its own position in *Hoffmann-La Roche*, which determined that loyalty

[59] *AKZO* (n 53), para 77. [60] See also, eg, Case T-228/97 *Irish Sugar* ECLI:EU:T:1999:246.
[61] Case C-413/14 P *Intel* ECLI:EU:C:2017:632.

rebates were per se anti-competitive, but 'clarified' it by making clear that an undertaking could rebut a presumption that its loyalty rebate restricts competition.[62] Between the *Intel* ruling and the CJEU's finding that pricing that is not *fully* predatory needs a demonstration of 'anti-competitive intent', some academics have started to question if abusive pricing behaviour is still actually to be treated as anti-competitive by object.[63] For now, we will have to await further case law that may make a changed CJEU position on pricing behaviour more explicit.

Abusive non-pricing behaviour

As Article 102 TFEU itself makes clear, pricing strategies are not the only ones that a dominant undertaking can adopt in order to frustrate competition in its market. The natural consequence of an undertaking holding a particularly large market share is that many other undertakings will be dependent on it for supplies or services they themselves need. *AKZO* demonstrates this: it sold peroxides that were used in two separate industries. It was guilty of giving anti-competitive discounts to suppliers—but imagine that it had simply refused to supply anyone who was doing business with its competitor, ECS. The impacts of such demands would also have clearly anti-competitive effects: ECS would struggle to find customers, or those undertakings needing the peroxides in the plastics industry (where ECS was less active) would struggle to obtain them.

A **refusal to supply** thus *can* be abusive behaviour under Article 102 TFEU . . . but it is not automatically so. As a general rule, all undertakings are free to contract with whomever they wish to. A refusal to enter into such a contract and thus supply is only abusive where the Commission can prove that the *intent* of the dominant undertaking is to exclude others from the market. A classic example of the Commission successfully doing this is *Commercial Solvents*. Zoja, an Italian producer of a drug, needed a raw material (aminobutanol) produced by Commercial Solvents in order to produce a drug called ethambutol. Commercial Solvents, however, intended to expand into the ethambutol market itself—and in order to eliminate competition in the ethambutol market, it refused to supply Zoja with the raw materials it needed. The CJEU found that the refusal to supply was abusive in this instance because it would 'eliminate one of the principal manufacturers in the [internal market]' of the drugs in question.[64]

One particular type of refusal to supply that is abusive is the 'vengeful' variety, which was seen in *United Brands*. United Brands, on top of its other anti-competitive behaviour, ceased supplying one of its distributors with bananas because they had violated United Brand's **exclusivity clause**, discussed under Article 101 TFEU above. The CJEU also deemed this to be abuse: it was effectively punishing 'a long standing customer who abides by regular commercial practice' and was ordering supply as normal, which would ultimately harm consumers.[65]

What we can glean from the CJEU's case law on refusal to supply is that while freedom to contract in principle applies to all undertakings in the internal market, those who are

[62] Ibid, paras 137–138.

[63] See, eg, Pablo Ibáñez Colomo, 'The Future of Article 102 TFEU after *Intel*' (2018) 9(5) JECL & Pract 293.

[64] *Commercial Solvents*, para 25. See also Cases T-69/89 *RTE v Commission* ('*Magill*') ECLI:EU:T:1991:39, paras 73–75.

[65] *United Brands* (n 47), paras 182–183.

in dominant positions in their relevant market will have any refusals to supply scrutinized by the Commission. Where the effects of a refusal to supply harm competition, it will be found contrary to Article 102 TFEU.

Meanwhile, *United Brand's* exclusivity clause was itself an abuse of dominance of the non-price variety. Exclusivity clauses are frequently tied in with loyalty rebates, but not always, as *Hoffmann-La Roche* demonstrates. Here, Hoffmann-La Roche concluded agreements with 22 vitamin purchasers which either obliged them to purchase, or offered them a rebate if they did purchase, all or most of their vitamins from Hoffmann-La Roche. The CJEU found that both were abusive of Hoffmann-La Roche's dominant position in the vitamins market: whether the producers were offered an incentive or merely pressured into exclusivity was irrelevant.[66]

As a final example of abusive non-pricing behaviour, similar in effect to exclusivity clauses, are the practices of **tying** and/or **bundling**. This is what we saw Microsoft engaging in earlier in the chapter: an undertaking dominant in product market A ties a separate product B to all purchases of product A, resulting in customers having no choice but to obtain both products. The effect of this is that the dominance in market A will result in foreclosure of the market for product B, as consumers will automatically end up with product B and thus not be looking for competing products.

Discussing the scenario

Is IE engaged in any abusive pricing or non-pricing behaviour in the above scenario?

15.4.4 Justifying abuse of dominance

At this point, the Commission will have found that an undertaking is dominant in a relevant market that covers a substantial part of the internal market, and that it is abusing that dominance in some way. Is there any defence for the undertaking?

Unlike Article 101 TFEU, Article 102 TFEU does not come with an explicit exemption clause. However, in a mirror to its jurisprudence on the fundamental freedoms, the CJEU has developed a practice of trying to discern if abuse of dominance by an undertaking can in some way be **objectively justified**. As in its other internal market case law, there are two components to such a justification under Article 102 TFEU:

1. There must be a legitimate reason for the behaviour; and
2. The abusive practices must be proportionate to the reason.[67]

Examples of justifications attempted under Article 102 TFEU include that the undertaking argues that its behaviour has been objectively necessary;[68] or that it is successfully

[66] *Hoffmann-La Roche*, para 90.

[67] See Commission, *Commission Guidance on the Commission's enforcement priorities in applying Article 92 of the EC Treaty to abusive exclusionary conduct by dominant undertakings* [2009] OJ C45/7, para 29.

[68] Case 311/84 *CBEM v CLT and IPB* ECLI:EU:C:1985:394, paras 26 and 27.

increasing efficiency, to the point where consumers are benefiting from its anti-competitive activities.[69] Neither of these grounds is easy to satisfy: behaviour is only objectively necessary where it is required for reasons beyond the undertaking's control that somehow justify the behaviour. Examples are, for example, setting terms on the purchasing of a product for health and safety reasons, or refusing to supply a business because they had failed to pay for their previous purchases. The 'trade-off' defence, whereby anti-competitive behaviour is justified because of efficiencies gained by it that will be transferred to the consumer, requires that the undertaking meet a test very similar to the one set out in Article 101(3) TFEU: the behaviour must be *necessary* to gain the relevant efficiency, and it cannot eliminate competition altogether.[70]

Discussing the scenario

Consider in what ways IE has abused its dominance on the relevant market. Can this abuse be justified on any grounds, in your view?

15.5 Brexit and competition law

Competition law is an interesting area of law in terms of Brexit, largely because it is an area where the obvious fact that the UK is not geographically leaving *Europe* has a very significant impact. UK businesses that are active in the internal market will continue to be subject to EU competition law—and even those businesses that are not yet active in the internal market, but look to become active, will wish to be aware of the competition rules that bind their continental competitors.

Beyond that, what we know of the plans for the 'future relationship' at this point allows us to comment more expressly on the future of EU competition law *in* the UK.

15.5.1 The Withdrawal Agreement

Under the October 2019 Withdrawal Agreement, EU competition law will remain applicable to the UK until the transition period ends. This includes Commission and CJEU oversight and enforcement insofar as necessary regarding activity taking place within the UK—though, of course, this chapter will have made it clear that competition law enforcement is not so much against the *Member State* as against undertakings operating in that Member State.

Any administrative proceedings commenced by the Commission *before* the end of the transition period will also be concluded under Commission jurisdiction, as set out in Article 91(1)(b) of the Withdrawal Agreement. Unless the UK Competition and Markets Authority (the CMA) and the Commission agree otherwise, the application of any decisions taken under Commission proceedings will also be overseen by the Commission.[71] The effects of EU competition law will consequently be felt across the UK for some time regardless of Brexit.

[69] Case 209/10 *Post Danmark* ECLI:EU:C:2012:172, paras 41–43.
[70] Case C-95/04 P *British Airways* ECLI:EU:C:2007:166, para 86.
[71] Withdrawal Agreement, Article 95(2).

15.5.2 The Protocol on Ireland/Northern Ireland

The original 'backstop' negotiated between the May government and the EU had called for a 'level playing field' between the UK and the EU on a variety of issues, including competition law. The concern here was that the UK would be in the customs union, and so it would benefit from EU trade agreements, but might be able to undercut the EU with 'looser regulation' that would attract greater inward investment. This was seen as offering too many potential benefits to a country that was trying to leave the EU—and so the condition for having a single customs territory between the EU and the UK was to promise not to undercut in regulatory areas like competition law.

However, the October 2019 Protocol no longer contains a 'backstop', and, crucially, no longer has the UK as a whole inside the EU's customs territory. Northern Ireland will now apply the EU customs code at its borders for goods travelling from Great Britain to Ireland—but otherwise, the UK as a whole is no longer 'benefiting' from EU trade policy. In these circumstances, the UK negotiators successfully argued that a 'level playing field' commitment was unreasonable: other countries *near* the EU but not actually in its customs territory are not required to apply EU-level competition law rules or (for example) employment laws, either.

As such, where the Protocol used to contain provisions requiring the UK to continue to follow EU-level competition law standards, these were removed as of October 2019. But are things really that simple?

15.5.3 The future relationship

Brexit, in principle, can mean freedom from EU competition law—not for UK business, as it will continue to apply to them if they are active in the EU, but for UK authorities enforcing competition law. In the summer of 2019, the UK authorities continued to stress that at the end of the transition period, the CMA would assume the Commission's responsibilities in overseeing competition law in the UK.[72] The bigger question, of course, is what rules the CMA will be asked to apply.

On this front, a 2019 statutory instrument creates a new s 60A in the Competition Act which requires all domestic regulators and courts involved in competition law to apply UK competition rules consistently with pre-Brexit CJEU case law, albeit with scope for flexibility where the UK and EU markets are wholly distinct or economics no longer makes 'similar treatment' rational.[73] As such, despite the absence of an express commitment to a 'level playing field' in the Withdrawal Agreement, as a matter of domestic law, it appears that UK competition law will not 'regress' from EU standards quickly.

Of course, in a global economy, anti-competitive behaviour is very rarely centred on a single country. For the purposes of enabling effective investigations, the Commission and the CMA will want to conclude an agreement for future cooperation as quickly as possible—but this is likely to be dependent on the direction of travel of the 'future relationship' negotiations.

[72] See https://www.gov.uk/government/speeches/uk-competition-law-enforcement-the-post-brexit-future.

[73] The Competition (Amendment etc.) (EU Exit) Regulations 2019 (SI 2019/93).

On that point, the Political Declaration continues to reference the idea of a 'level playing field':

Political Declaration, para 77 (emphasis added)

Given the Union and the United Kingdom's geographic proximity and economic interdependence, the future relationship must ensure open and fair competition, encompassing robust commitments to ensure a level playing field. The precise nature of commitments should be commensurate with the scope and depth of the future relationship and the economic connectedness of the Parties. **These commitments should prevent distortions of trade and unfair competitive advantages.** To that end, **the Parties should uphold the common high standards applicable in the Union and the United Kingdom at the end of the transition period in the areas** of state aid, **competition**, social and employment standards, environment, climate change, and relevant tax **matters. The Parties should in particular maintain a robust and comprehensive framework for competition** and state aid **control that prevents undue distortion of trade and competition**; . . . In so doing, **they should rely on appropriate and relevant Union and international standards, and include appropriate mechanisms to ensure effective implementation domestically, enforcement and dispute settlement.**

It seems clear, then, that the EU continues to expect non-regression if anything but a shallow trade agreement is concluded between the UK and the EU after Brexit. The EU has continually stressed that the UK cannot be treated as just any other neighbouring country, and that the combination of the UK and EU's 'geographic proximity' and 'economic interdependence' means that any policy adopted by the UK will have an impact on the EU, *and* vice versa.

At the time of writing, the relevant negotiations remain in their early stages, and so we can at most speculate on just 'how close' the UK and the EU are willing to get. Early indications on the part of the UK have been that it is unwilling to engage in *any* regulatory alignment with the EU—but this may change over the course of the negotiations.[74] Ultimately, the future of UK competition law may simply be a matter of pragmatism: are there *significant* gains for the UK in diverging from the EU standards? And if not, is it really worth diverging when that means subjecting multinational businesses across Europe to two separate competition law regimes? We will have to wait and see.

15.6 In conclusion

This chapter has provided an introduction to the EU rules on competition law. There is significantly more to them than was presented here, and many more examples of anti-competitive behaviour across the EU can be found, even by simply reading newspapers. It is nonetheless already clear from the examples raised in this chapter that competition law

[74] See https://www.parliament.uk/business/publications/written-questions-answers-statements/written-statement/Commons/2020-02-03/HCWS86/.

is a 'core' element of internal market law, and one where the Commission is genuinely a driving force, both in terms of policy development and enforcement.

Following the transition period, the UK's CMA will be in a position where it *may* wish to develop a UK-specific competition policy—or it may find that Articles 101 and 102 TFEU effectively govern the UK market as well outside the EU as they did inside the EU. The EU has concerns about the UK policing anti-competitive behaviour differently (and potentially 'less') in a bid to make the UK a welcoming business environment, and has tried to leverage the depth of the 'future relationship' on a significant alignment with EU policy standards in areas like competition law. Whether it will succeed is still a matter of negotiation; and so the future of Articles 101 and 102 TFEU in the UK itself is yet to be determined.

Discussing the scenario

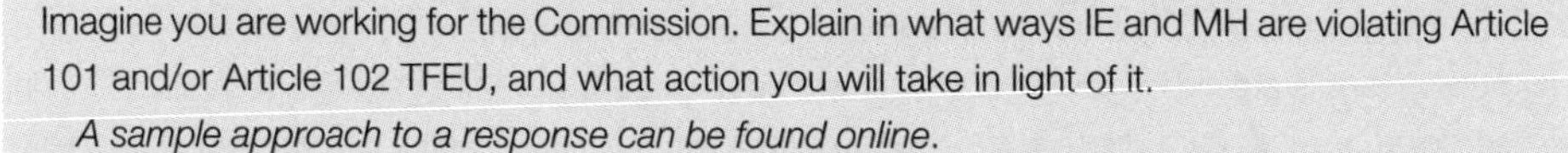

Imagine you are working for the Commission. Explain in what ways IE and MH are violating Article 101 and/or Article 102 TFEU, and what action you will take in light of it.

A sample approach to a response can be found online.

Key points

- EU competition law, enforced by the Commission (which has very broad investigative powers in this area), has two principal objectives: **supporting the internal market**, and **protecting consumer welfare.**
- **Article 101(1) TFEU** prohibits **anti-competitive agreements** or 'concerted practices' between two or more undertakings that (will) have an **effect on trade in the internal market.**
- **A violation of Article 101(1) TFEU** results in those agreements being **declared void under Article 101(2) TFEU** . . . unless they can be exempted following the cumulative test set out in Article 101(3) TFEU.
- **Article 102 TFEU** prohibits an undertaking that is **dominant** in at least **a substantial part of the internal market** from **abusing its dominant position**, where this may affect **trade in the internal market.**
- A violation of Article 102 TFEU can only be justified by **objective necessity** or **consumer-benefiting efficiency gains**. Both these conditions are subject to **proportionality**.
- After Brexit, domestic law suggests that the **UK will not diverge from EU competition law quickly**; and **the EU would like the UK to continue applying very similar rules.**

Assess your learning

1. What do you think about the European Commission's enforcement powers in competition law? Are they excessive, or just right? (See Section 15.2.2.)
2. What is an anti-competitive agreement? What is the difference between horizontal and vertical agreements from an EU competition law perspective? (See Section 15.3.1.)

3. What is the difference between an infringement by **object** and an infringement by **effect**? Which is EU competition law most concerned about, and why? (See Section 15.3.2.)
4. How do competition authorities determine the **relevant market**, and why is this important for Article 102 TFEU? (See Section 15.4.1.)
5. When is an undertaking **dominant**, and why does this matter? Is it always a problem? (See Sections 15.4.2–15.4.4.)

Further reading

Frederick Abbott, 'The UK Competition Appeal Tribunal's Misguided Reprieve for Pfizer's Excessive Pricing Abuse' (2018) 49(7) IIC 845.

Pinar Akman, 'The Role of Intent in the EU Case Law on Abuse of Dominance' (2014) 39(3) ELRev 316.

Ian S Forrester, 'Due Process in EC Competition Cases: A distinguished institution with flawed procedures' (2009) 34(6) ELRev 817.

Joe Gaffney, '"Competition is a Sin": Can super-dominant undertakings compete on the merits?' (2019) 40(12) ECLR 559.

Julia Heit, 'The Justifiability of the ECJ's Wide Approach to the Concept of Barriers to Entry' (2006) 27(3) ECLR 117.

Belinda Hollway and Cian Mansfield, 'Follow the Sectoral Leader: Follow-on actions from UK concurrent regulators' decisions' (2019) 12(4) GCLR 137.

Saskia King, 'The Object Box: Law, Policy or Myth?' (2011) 7(2) ECJ 269.

Ronit Kreisberger and Conor McCarthy, 'Competition Damages Litigation in the United Kingdom: The impact of Brexit' (2018) 4(4) CLPD 48.

Okeoghene Ododu, 'Interpreting Article 81(1): Demonstrating Restrictive Effect' (2001) 26(3) ELRev 261.

Chris Townley, 'Which Goals Count in Article 101 TFEU? Public Policy and Its Discontents' (2011) 32(9) ECLR 441.

Online resources

Visit www.oup.com/he/demars1e for a sample approach to discussing the quote.

16

Negotiating a 'future relationship': EU external relations law

Context for this chapter

'Our relationship with the EU is already very well developed. It doesn't seem to me to be very hard . . . to do a free trade deal very rapidly indeed.'

Boris Johnson, Treasury Select Committee (March 2016)
https://parliamentlive.tv/event/index/66ab01e2-3d9b-4eb9-9186-2a669355c082?in=10:09:15

16.1 **Introduction**

At the time of writing, the political wrangling that accompanied the first stage of Brexit is finally over; the Withdrawal Agreement negotiated in October 2019 has entered into force, and the UK is in the process of negotiating its future relationship with the EU.

This is not a politics text, and so much of the last three years of constant parliamentary tension has been a side-issue for us: perhaps interesting, but not particularly clarifying. What matters for those of us who are looking at law is purely that, as of 31 January 2020, the first steps in the Brexit process have been completed. Now that we have adopted the Withdrawal Agreement, the UK will be looking to conclude what the EU terms a 'future relationship' agreement with the EU over the course of the transition period. That 'future relationship' will address both the conditions under which the UK trades with the EU in the future—or, if you will, what replaces the internal market—*and* how the UK and the EU relate to each other diplomatically—or, if you will, what replaces 'membership' of the EU as an institution. The aim is to have reached an agreed deal covering as much of the 'future relationship' as possible by December 2020.

As with almost everything else that happens in the EU, the EU Treaties set out clear processes for the conclusion of international agreements between the EU and other countries. This chapter explores what those processes are. It first considers what powers the EU has to conclude international agreements, and then considers how decision-making relating to those international agreements takes place within the EU institutions. We may now have left the EU, but we will continue to have to engage with the EU, its institutions, and its laws for the foreseeable future—and it is now important to understand how the EU will approach the 'future relationship' negotiations. The chapter will conclude with a few observations about what those UK–EU 'future relationship' negotiations will involve, and why the transition period may not be long enough to actually work out what that 'future relationship' is.

Before we go into detail in considering the processes the EU set out for the conclusion of international agreements, it is helpful to remind yourself of several key terms that will appear regularly in this chapter. **International agreements**, or **treaties**, are concluded *between* countries—and regional bodies like the EU. If they are concerned with trade, they are normally known as **free trade agreements**. A **customs union** is an advanced free trade agreement. However, the EU's international agreements are not all about trade, and it also has capacity to conclude agreements in other areas, such as **human rights**, **judicial cooperation (and recognition of judgments from other jurisdictions)**, and **environmental policy**.

16.2 Goals for the 'future relationship'

In October 2019, the UK and the EU negotiated a new Withdrawal Agreement and Political Declaration with the EU. The Political Declaration sets out what both sides will pursue when, over the course of the transition period, negotiating what has been called the 'future relationship' agreement(s) that will apply between the UK and the EU. They give a general idea of the policy areas in which the UK and the EU will want to cooperate in the future, and, as such, an indication of what *kinds* of international agreements may come into existence to govern the UK–EU relationship after the transition period.

Broadly, the Political Declaration sets out future cooperation in two distinct areas, both called 'partnerships'. The first indicated 'partnership' to be pursued is an **economic** partnership. Here, the Political Declaration indicates that the UK and the EU will seek to conclude at the very least a free trade agreement following Brexit. The clearest indication of the shape of that trade agreement makes clear that the UK and the EU are both seeking to keep tariffs and barriers as low as possible, but accept that some barriers will arise from regulatory differences between the two countries following Brexit.

A further 'partnership' that is flagged up in the Political Declaration is a **security** partnership. The themes that are raised in the Political Declaration under this banner cover areas such as judicial cooperation in criminal matters, foreign policy, security and defence, and a range of more specific areas in which cooperation will be sought. These specific areas include cyber security strategy, judicial cooperation in civil matters, illegal migration, counter-terrorism, and the exchanges of classified information.

The final provisions of interest in the Political Declaration are those on **governance** of the future UK–EU relationship. They are not very detailed, but make clear that the EU institutions will by and large not be involved in the management of the EU–UK relationship. They allude to mediation as well as arbitration as a means of dispute settlement between the UK and the EU, and refer to the CJEU very explicitly as only having jurisdiction over the interpretation of provisions of EU law that will then be binding *on* arbitration tribunals.

In the remainder of this chapter, we will firstly consider what powers the EU has to adopt international agreements in the areas indicated in the Political Declaration. Secondly, we will consider how those powers are to be exercised by the EU. This will allow us to assess just how 'rapid' and simple it will be for the UK to conclude a future relationship agreement with the EU in the fields flagged up by the Political Declaration, as well as providing a clearer picture of just how the EU and the UK will manage their external relations vis-à-vis each other after Brexit.

16.3 **The EU's external powers: Rome to Lisbon**

The EU Treaties have always made provision for the EU to engage in international relations. They first did this by clearly establishing that the EU as an institution would have legal personality, which is a condition now reflected in Article 47 TFEU. While the Treaties have never stressed that the EU has *international* legal personality, this is the obvious interpretation of the provision, as the Treaties have given the EU specific legal bases through which to conclude international agreements and conduct international relations.

The first legal basis through which the EU could take international action concerned the so-called Common Commercial Policy, which is the collection of rules that make up the EU's customs union and trading policy. What is now Article 207 TFEU has existed since 1957, and enables the EU to conclude trade agreements with third countries. A separate provision, now found in Article 217 TFEU, similarly permitted the EU to conclude so-called 'association agreements'. As we will see, these are agreements that allowed third countries to 'associate' with the EU in a broader way than simply by striking a trade agreement with it.

As has been the case with the EU's internal competences, its external competences have grown over time. This is both because of Treaty revision, and because of CJEU interpretation of just what the then-Community was capable of doing. In cases such as *ERTA*[1] and *Kramer*,[2] the CJEU interpreted the EU Treaties as meaning that in a policy area where the EU had the competence to organize internal policies, this also gave the EU the power to adopt external policy. As a consequence, the EU would avoid the Member States adopting individual external positions on a matter that was an 'EU' matter within the internal market.[3] This doctrine, known as *implied* powers—where the internal competences *imply* that the EU as a whole will have a common policy, both internally and externally—has been codified in the Lisbon Treaty.[4] EU external relations law is thus made up of a combination of *express* competences for the EU to act in the Treaties, and *implied* competences to act.

Under the Lisbon Treaty, we have already seen that the EU's competences—whether exclusive or shared with the Member States—have been made explicit for the first time.[5] It is worth stressing that, because of the doctrine of *implied powers*, these competences describe not only the EU's internal powers but also its external competences.

[1] Case 22/70 *Commission v Council* (ERTA) ECLI:EU:C:1971:32.

[2] Joined Cases 3, 4, and 6/76 *Kramer* ECLI:EU:C:1976:96.

[3] Ibid, paras 19–20.

[4] See Article 3 TFEU, on the 'implied' exclusive competences of the Union.

[5] See Chapter 4.

The TEU also contains an 'umbrella' provision that applies to all EU international activity, including the signing of international agreements:

Article 21 TEU (emphasis added)

1. The Union's action on the international scene shall be guided by the principles which have inspired its own creation, development and enlargement, and which it seeks to advance in the wider world: **democracy, the rule of law, the universality and indivisibility of human rights and fundamental freedoms, respect for human dignity, the principles of equality and solidarity, and respect for the principles of the United Nations Charter and international law.**

   The Union shall seek to develop relations and build partnerships with third countries, and international, regional or global organisations which share the principles referred to in the first subparagraph. It shall promote multilateral solutions to common problems, in particular in the framework of the United Nations.

2. The Union shall define and pursue common policies and actions, and shall work for a high degree of cooperation in all fields of international relations, in order to:
   (a) safeguard its values, fundamental interests, security, independence and integrity;
   (b) consolidate and support democracy, the rule of law, human rights and the principles of international law;
   (c) preserve peace, prevent conflicts and strengthen international security, in accordance with the purposes and principles of the United Nations Charter, with the principles of the Helsinki Final Act and with the aims of the Charter of Paris, including those relating to external borders;
   (d) foster the sustainable economic, social and environmental development of developing countries, with the primary aim of eradicating poverty;
   (e) encourage the integration of all countries into the world economy, including through the progressive abolition of restrictions on international trade;
   (f) help develop international measures to preserve and improve the quality of the environment and the sustainable management of global natural resources, in order to ensure sustainable development;
   (g) assist populations, countries and regions confronting natural or man-made disasters; and
   (h) promote an international system based on stronger multilateral cooperation and good global governance.

3. **The Union shall respect the principles and pursue the objectives set out in paragraphs 1 and 2 in the development and implementation of the different areas of the Union's external action covered by this Title and by Part Five of the Treaty on the Functioning of the European Union**, and of the external aspects of its other policies.

As such, there are key principles that the EU has identified as underpinning its own tion that it is obliged to also take into account and respect when engaging in intern relations. Article 21(2) TEU makes clear that these range from values such as resp democracy and the rule of law to the abolition of barriers to trade and to sustainable development. Any international activity the EU engages in, in other words, should be compatible with its *other* international activities, as well as with the EU's internal policies and principles.

As set out in Section 16.2, this chapter will focus on the types of agreements that the UK may be looking to conclude with the EU following the transition period, insofar as indicated in the Political Declaration. This means evaluating the following EU external competences, and how the EU can act in those:

- the EU's powers under the Common Commercial Policy;
- the provision on 'Association Agreements';
- the international dimension of Area of Security, Freedom and Justice powers;
- and the Common Foreign and Security Policy.

16.3.1 External competences in the Treaties

Part V TFEU sets out the Treaty rules on the EU's exercise of external competences, with the exception of the EU's Common Foreign and Security Policy, which is detailed in Title V of the TEU instead. A general comment on the EU's treaty-making powers is set out in Article 216(1) TFEU:

Article 216 TFEU (emphasis added)

1. **The Union may conclude an agreement with one or more third countries or international organisations where the Treaties so provide** or where the conclusion of an agreement is necessary in order to achieve, within the framework of the Union's policies, one of the objectives referred to in the Treaties, or is provided for in a legally binding Union act or is likely to affect common rules or alter their scope.
2. **Agreements concluded by the Union are binding upon the institutions of the Union and on its Member States.**

This summarizes decades of the CJEU's case law on both 'implied' and 'express' EU external competences, and makes it clear that in any area where the EU has an *internal* competence, it could very well also have an external competence. However, there are several key policy areas in which Title V makes the EU's external face more explicit. We will look at these in turn.

16.3.2 Exclusive competence: the Common Commercial Policy

The first clear area in which the UK will want to have a 'future relationship' with the EU is in trade. In EU terms, that means that it will engage with the EU's competence regarding the so-called 'Common Commercial Policy'.

As mentioned in Section 16.3, the EU has always had a very explicit external competence in trade. The EU's powers to conclude trade agreements are found in Article 207

TFEU. More generally, the ability for the EU to shape any sort of commercial or trade policy is known by the term 'Common Commercial Policy' (CCP). What makes up the CCP is alluded to in Article 207 TFEU:

Article 207 TFEU (emphasis added)

The common commercial policy shall be based on uniform principles, **particularly with regard to** changes in tariff rates, the conclusion of tariff and trade agreements relating to trade in goods and services, **and the commercial aspects of intellectual property, foreign direct investment, the achievement of uniformity in measures of liberalisation, export policy and measures to protect trade such as those to be taken in the event of dumping or subsidies.** The common commercial policy shall be conducted in the context of the principles and objectives of the Union's external action.

The measures listed in Article 207 are in essence all aspects of 'trade'. The article describes the conclusion of trade agreements, but also trade defence measures—such as anti-dumping measures—that can be adopted by the EU if its economic activity is threatened by the actions of a third country. The scope of the CCP is consequently broad: the CJEU has commented on the CCP by comparing it to the external trade policy of a *state*, and has noted that it therefore needs to be considered progressively—as trade opens up, it starts involving more and more areas of law—as opposed to statically.[6]

The CJEU made clear in the 1970s that the CCP is an area of exclusive competence. In *Opinion 1/75*, it stressed that, for the Common Commercial Policy to be effective, Member States could not operate their own 'commercial and trade policy'.[7] Member States taking separate action from the EU on trade-related matters run the risk of the EU and its Member States treating third countries inconsistently for trade purposes.

As of the Lisbon Treaty, Article 3 TFEU makes the EU's exclusive competence in the Common Commercial Policy explicit, and sets out how that exclusive competence relates to other *implied* competences that the EU can exercise:

Article 3 TFEU (emphasis added)

1. **The Union shall have exclusive competence in the following areas:**

   . . .

   (e) common commercial policy.

2. **The Union shall also have exclusive** competence for the conclusion of an international agreement when its conclusion is provided for in a legislative act of the Union **or is** necessary to enable the Union to exercise its internal competence, **or in so far as its conclusion** may affect common rules or alter their scope.

[6] *Opinion 1/75* ECLI:EU:C:1975:145; for more information about 'opinions', see Section 16.4.5.
[7] Ibid.

The CJEU has interpreted Article 3 TFEU broadly, stressing in particular that the EU has exclusive external competences where 'common rules' can be affected.[8] For example, in 2011, the Council adopted a decision alongside the 'representatives of the governments of the Member States' to participate in negotiations for a Council of Europe Convention that would protect certain rights of broadcasting organizations. The Commission started an action for annulment of the decision on the basis that the negotiations fell within the EU's exclusive competences via Article 3(2) TFEU, and so could not have been started by a 'hybrid decision' agreed alongside Member State government representatives. Its evidence was that the EU had already adopted substantial law on the rights of broadcasting organizations for the sake of the internal market.

On the other hand, the Council, supported by several Member States, argued that the proposed Council of Europe Convention fell in an area of shared competences. The CJEU considered whether the proposed negotiations could affect the existing EU rules on rights of broadcasting organizations in detail, and finally concluded that:

Case C-114/12 *Commission v Council* ECLI:EU:C:2014:2151 (emphasis added)

102. It is apparent from the above analysis that the content of the negotiations for a Convention of the Council of Europe on the protection of neighbouring rights of broadcasting organisations . . . **falls within an area covered to a large extent by common EU rules and that those negotiations may affect common EU rules or alter their scope.** Therefore, **those negotiations fall within the exclusive competence of the European Union.**

A further way in which the Lisbon Treaty has expanded the EU's ability to conclude international trade agreements is in its redrafting of Article 207 TFEU itself. Historically, that article as a legal basis covered trade agreements in goods alone. As such, trade agreements covering services or intellectual property or investment were deemed to fall within shared competences. Much as the internal market's focus switched from movement of goods to movement of services after the 1980s, international trade agreements no longer primarily focus on goods. Consequently, the Lisbon Treaty has given the EU the exclusive competence to also conclude trade agreements that cover issues *beyond* goods.[9]

The exceptions to this exclusive competence are in areas that are deemed of national 'sensitivity', such as cultural or audio-visual services. Any Treaties covering those types of services or, for example, health services, are treated as 'shared' and therefore operate under different decision-making processes.[10] We will see in Section 16.4, when we consider the EU's treaty negotiation process in detail, that the expansion of the exclusivity of Article 207 TFEU has a significant impact on the extent to which the Member States can 'block' EU trade policy.

[8] See, eg, Case C-114/12 *Commission v Council* ECLI:EU:C:2014:2151; *Opinion 1/13 on the Hague Convention on Child Abduction* ECLI:EU:C:2014:2292.

[9] As confirmed by the CJEU in Case C-414/11 *Daiichi Sankyo* ECLI:EU:C:2013:520, para 55.

[10] Article 207(4) TFEU.

Examples of recently concluded Article 207 TFEU agreements are the EU–South Korea free trade agreement and the EU–Canada 'CETA' agreement.[11] While both are expansive, in that they address trade in goods, services, intellectual property, investment, and a number of other issues such as mutual recognition of standards, they nonetheless deal exclusively with matters of *trade*, and do not—for example—facilitate the movement of people outside of employees, or cover any political matters.

16.3.3 Shared competence: 'association agreements'

One interesting aspect of the Political Declaration is that it appears to foresee not one, but rather a *set* of agreements or 'relationships', covering different policy areas. The EU has a particular external relations competence for concluding agreements that go beyond 'trade' and touch upon other areas of cooperation.

Article 217 TFEU, on the conclusion of 'association agreements', has existed as long as the Article 207 TFEU competence to conclude trade agreements has, perhaps as a sign that the EU's internal and international ambitions were never *wholly* economic.

The difference between the type of agreements that the EU can conclude under Article 207 and Article 217 is best explained by reference to Article 217 itself:

Article 217 TFEU (emphasis added)

The Union may conclude with one or more third countries or international organisations agreements **establishing an association involving reciprocal rights and obligations**, common action and special procedure.

The concept of 'agreements establishing an association' may give an initial impression that what is being discussed in Article 217 is something that is *less* binding than a formal trade treaty, but this is deceptive. The term 'association' is used to describe a relationship between the EU and a third party (whether a country or an international organization) that is 'closer' than a purely economic relationship. Key, albeit vague, is the notion that such an 'association' involves 'reciprocal rights and obligations, common action and special procedure'. These allusions to working together and being bound in terms of both 'rights and obligations' make it clear that where the EU seeks to form an 'association', something of a more political nature is happening than can happen under the CCP under Article 207 TFEU.

There is no real further clarity in the Treaties on what an 'association' may look like, so it is best addressed by example. Early EU 'association agreements' were concluded with Greece, Turkey, and a variety of African, Caribbean and Pacific (ACP) countries in the 1960s, and more recent association agreements were concluded with former Soviet satellite states in Eastern Europe.[12] These agreements are not all alike: the latter were drafted as

[11] Free Trade Agreement between the European Union and its Member States, of the one part, and the Republic of Korea, of the other part [2011] OJ L127/6; and Comprehensive Economic and Trade Agreement between Canada, of the one part, and the European Union and its Member States, of the other part [2017] OJ L11/23 (CETA).

[12] See, eg, [1963] OJ L/26/296; [1964] OJ L27/3865; [1964] OJ L93/1430.

a precursor to a formal application for EU membership, whereas others (such as the ACP ones) appear to form an 'end state'.

The most recent high profile 'association agreement' concluded by the EU was with Ukraine; it proved politically very sensitive to Russia, difficult to ratify because of unanticipated Dutch opposition, and has resulted in substantial unrest in Ukraine from the 2013 negotiations onward.[13] Worth noting about the EU–Ukraine Agreement is exactly where it positions itself between a 'trade agreement' and 'EU membership'. Where it is inconceivable, for example, that the CJEU would have an explicit role in most trade agreements the EU concludes, the EU institutions are given express roles under the Ukraine agreement, and the CJEU has jurisdiction over the interpretation of all EU law as it is applied in the Ukraine. We will consider this in more detail in Section 16.5.

As the UK will be seeking a 'relationship' with the EU that goes beyond a pure 'trade' agreement, its final form may very well be that of an 'association agreement', simply because that designation offers the EU significant flexibility in terms of policy areas in which agreements can be struck.

16.3.4 Shared *and* exclusive competence: agreements in the Area of Security, Freedom and Justice

As noted in Section 16.2, the UK and the EU have agreed in principle to pursue a 'security' partnership as part of their 'future relationship'. The term is used in the Political Declaration to discuss cooperation in foreign policy and security, but also a wide variety of other areas covered by the EU Treaties. Some of the policy areas alluded to in the Political Declaration concern criminal and civil law, where EU law in the Area of Freedom, Security and Justice currently regulates the cross-border recognition of judgments, the mutual admissibility of evidence between the Member States, police and judicial cooperation, and a variety of other aspects of both criminal and civil law across the internal market.[14] We will use this desire for cooperation in these areas as a case study of how the EU and the UK can strike agreements for ongoing cooperation in areas that are *neither* purely economic *nor* purely related to Common Foreign and Security Policy.

The EU does not have explicit external competences in civil and criminal law, but it has been exercising 'implied' ones since the early 2000s, based on the 'internal' powers set out in Articles 81–83 TFEU. As an example of the CJEU condoning the use of these powers, it ruled in *Opinion 1/03* that the EU had the exclusive competence to conclude the Lugano Convention, which addresses recognition and enforcement of civil law judgments, as the conclusion of such a convention would affect 'common rules'.[15] Since the adoption of the Lisbon Treaty, a number of international agreements addressing

[13] Association Agreement between the European Union and the European Atomic Energy Community and their Member States, of the one part, and Ukraine, of the other part [2014] OJ L161/3 ('EU–Ukraine Association Agreement').

[14] See Section 4.4.5. We discuss aspects of Area of Freedom, Security and Justice policies in Chapter 9.

[15] *Opinion 1/03 on the Competence of the Community to conclude the new Lugano Convention on jurisdiction and the recognition and enforcement of judgments in civil and commercial matters* ECLI:EU:C:2006:81.

policing and data protection matters have been negotiated by the EU and the US, and these also have been determined to fall in the EU's Area of Security, Freedom and Justice competences.[16]

The institutional roles played by the EU in the conclusion of non-economic agreements in both these areas and other 'shared competence' areas are set out in Article 218 TFEU, which covers EU treaty conclusion very generally, and which we will consider in Section 16.4. Were the UK to want to provide continuity, among other things, regarding the recognition of UK judgments in criminal and civil matters in the EU, and vice versa, it would need to conclude an agreement (whether stand-alone, or as part of an 'association agreement') using the Article 218 TFEU procedure to make this happen. The same holds for any desire it might have for ongoing collaboration in areas such as education[17] and environmental policy.[18]

16.3.5 Exclusive competence: agreements in Common Foreign and Security Policy

As noted, the UK and the EU have agreed to pursue a 'future relationship' in 'security', which is the term used to describe both judicial and legal cooperation across the internal market—as discussed in Section 16.3.4—and matters of defence policy, foreign policy regarding international developments, and any 'security' or counter-terrorist actions the EU takes (both independently, and as a member of the United Nations). These defence and security-related aspects of the EU's external relations are covered by the so-called Common Foreign and Security Policy (CFSP). Under EU law, foreign policy and security are treated as wholly distinct from all other policy areas where the EU may take action. The rules on the CFSP competences are not set out in Title V of the TFEU, but rather are found in the TEU. The reasons for this are a combination of historic and ongoing, and relate primarily to the sensitivity of foreign and security policy. Even where the Member States have by now in principle agreed that EU-level action may be of interest when it comes to foreign and security policies, these are not areas in which they wish to give the EU the ability to overrule their interests. As such, there are key differences between the scope of CFSP powers set out in the Treaty, and how the EU institutions operate when acting in the area of CFSP, that will have significant effects on how easy it will be for the UK to conclude an agreement with the EU that touches upon these competences. We will consider the first point now, and move on to the second in Section 16.4.

In Article 24 TEU, the scope of the EU's CFSP competence is described as covering 'all areas of foreign policy and all questions relating to the Union's security, including the progressive framing of a common defence policy that might lead to a common defence'. Beyond the express mention of a future possible 'common defence policy', the concepts of 'foreign policy' and 'security' are not set out in more detail. CFSP activity

[16] See, eg, the SWIFT Agreement [2010] OJ L195/5, and the Agreement between the United States and the EU on the use and transfer of passenger name records to the US Department of Homeland Security [2012] OJ L215/5.

[17] Article 165(3) TFEU, which falls within the area of 'supporting' competences, but nonetheless permits international action.

[18] Article 191(4) TFEU, which is a shared competence.

is, of course, subject to the Article 21 TEU principles—but beyond that its scope appears very open-ended.

The open-ended nature of CFSP activity is also reflected in the *types* of measures that the EU can take under the CFSP banner. Article 25 TEU thus makes explicit:

- a power for the European Council to adopt 'general guidelines';
- a power for the Council to adopt decisions regarding 'specific operational action' where necessary;
- a power for the Council to adopt decisions that set out 'positions' defining an EU approach to a specific international area;
- and a power for the Council to adopt decisions that establish 'arrangements' to implement 'action' decisions and 'position' decisions.

These are EU instruments that are largely distinct from the instruments that the EU generally can adopt under Article 288 TFEU. Last but not least, it is implied in Title V of the TEU that the EU can also conclude international agreements on CFSP matters.

CFSP has been isolated from other EU external action to the extent possible, but in the increasingly integrated world, it is often very difficult to separate economic matters fully from 'foreign policy' or 'security' matters. As Title V of the TEU and Title V of the TFEU set out entirely different procedures for 'external action' decision-making, as of the adoption of the Lisbon Treaty, the CJEU has tended to side with the Council when it argues that a matter is a CFSP matter and thus not subject to the TFEU 'external action' Articles that were discussed earlier in this chapter.[19]

One particularly difficult area of overlap between the 'economic' and the 'CFSP' dimensions of measures is where the EU, on account of international obligations, is required to apply sanctions to other international actors. These are clearly economic 'restrictive measures', as the Lisbon Treaty calls them—but at the same time, they are usually adopted for 'foreign policy' purposes, rather than economic ones. As such, they do not intuitively fall within either the CFSP regime or the more general 'external action' regime exclusively.

The Lisbon Treaty's solution to this overlap is to require the engagement of both the CFSP process *and* the more general 'external relations' processes set out in Title V of the TFEU. Article 215 TFEU thus establishes that first, a *decision* to interrupt 'economic and financial relations' with a third country or a legal person has to be taken using the CFSP processes—but once that has happened, the Commission and the High Representative together draft a proposal to actually apply 'restrictive measures', which is then adopted by the Council through qualified majority voting. In other words, a CFSP 'decision' has to be taken, but a 'TFEU' process applies the actual sanctions.

EU 'CFSP' action thus remains unique in the Treaties, but not fully separate from its other external actions, despite best efforts to insulate it. For the UK, this means that the negotiations on the future 'security' relationship are going to involve discussions with the EU in policy areas where the EU has variable competences, and so agreements will be more difficult to conclude, as we will see in the next sections.

Table 16.1 summarizes the different policy areas in which the EU has 'external' powers that are relevant to the future relationship between the EU and the UK.

[19] See Case C-658/11 *Parliament v Council* (EU–Mauritius Agreement) ECLI:EU:C:2014:2025 and Case C-130/10 *Parliament v Council* (Al-Qaeda Sanctions) ECLI:EU:C:2012:472.

TABLE 16.1 EU external powers relevant to the future relationship

Type of Agreement	EU Policy Area	Shared or Exclusive EU Competence?	Treaty Basis
Free Trade Agreement (goods, services)	Common Commercial Policy	Exclusive, with limited 'national sensitivity' sector exceptions (see Section 16.3.1)	**Article 207 TFEU**
Association Agreement	Varied—'agreements establishing an association involving reciprocal rights and obligations, common action and special procedure'	Shared (see Section 16.3.2)	**Article 217 TFEU**
Agreements on aspects of civil and criminal law (eg, judicial cooperation, recognition of judgments)	Area of Freedom, Security and Justice	Shared internal competences, but exclusive external ones where 'common rules' are affected under Article 3(2) TFEU (see Section 16.3.3)	**Articles 81–83 TFEU**
Agreements on security and defence matters	Common Foreign and Security Policy	Shared (see Section 16.3.4)	**Article 25 TEU**

Pause For Reflection

Consider the discussion in Section 16.3 about the different policy areas in which the EU has 'external' powers. What will be missing from the UK–EU future relationship if the UK focuses on a 'free trade agreement' alone? How important do you think these other policy areas will be to the UK?

16.4 EU institutions' roles in external relations

Having set out that the EU has the capacity to conclude both simple and complex 'free trade agreements', as well as any number of more expansive international agreements that cover non-economic issues (such as judicial cooperation, education, or the environment) in the shape of 'association agreements', it is now important that we consider what roles are played by the EU institutions when the EU negotiates these types of international agreements. The roles of some institutions have been hinted at in Section 16.3

already, but it is imperative to understand what institutions will play the key roles in determining the shape and feasibility of the UK–EU future relationship. The UK will be negotiating with the EU—and probably the Commission, as EU negotiator—but the EU's actions will be steered to differing extents by the Council, the European Parliament, and the Member States separately, and awareness of *whose* agreement is ultimately needed will help the UK achieve success in very difficult and time-pressured negotiations over the course of the transition period.

16.4.1 Negotiating agreements generally

The general rules applying to the EU institutions when negotiating international agreements are contained in Article 218 TFEU. Concluding new agreements between the UK and the EU on AFSJ matters and on 'other areas' of cooperation, such as participation in research networks or student exchanges, will have to follow the process set out in Article 218 TFEU; trade agreements, and agreements addressing CFSP, on the other hand, follow slightly distinct processes, discussed in the next two sections.

Article 218 TFEU sets out the division of tasks between the different EU institutions over the course of the negotiating process, as well as the organization of 'votes' to adopt international agreements once they have a 'draft' shape that the negotiators agree to.

The Article 218 TFEU process is as follows:[20]

1. The Commission, in most cases, will 'recommend' starting negotiations to the Council (Article 218(3) TFEU).
2. The first formal step, called the 'opening' of treaty negotiations, is taken by the Council of Ministers. Article 218(2) TFEU gives the Council the job of starting the negotiating process as well as setting out negotiating 'directives', which are the general *goals* and *limits* the actual negotiators will have to try to achieve and comply with.
3. The actual negotiating of an international agreement will take place with representatives from the third country, and a Council-nominated EU delegation. Article 218(3) TFEU thus lets the Council nominate the 'Union negotiator' or the head of a 'Union negotiation team'. Ordinarily, the negotiators chosen will work for the Commission.
4. Then, though the Commission 'team' is formally in charge of the negotiations themselves, Article 218(4) TFEU makes clear that it is bound by the Council's negotiating directives, and can also be made to work cooperatively (or in consultation) with a special Council committee during the negotiations.
5. When a draft agreement has been negotiated, it is to be formally adopted by a Council decision under Article 218(6). As of the Lisbon Treaty, the Council can only take such a decision after obtaining the consent of the European Parliament when negotiating the vast majority of types of treaties. This effectively gives the European Parliament a 'veto' over the signing and adoption of a treaty.

This process is illustrated in Figure 16.1.

[20] See also this helpful summary of the process in relation to trade agreements by the Commission: https://trade.ec.europa.eu/doclib/docs/2012/june/tradoc_149616.pdf.

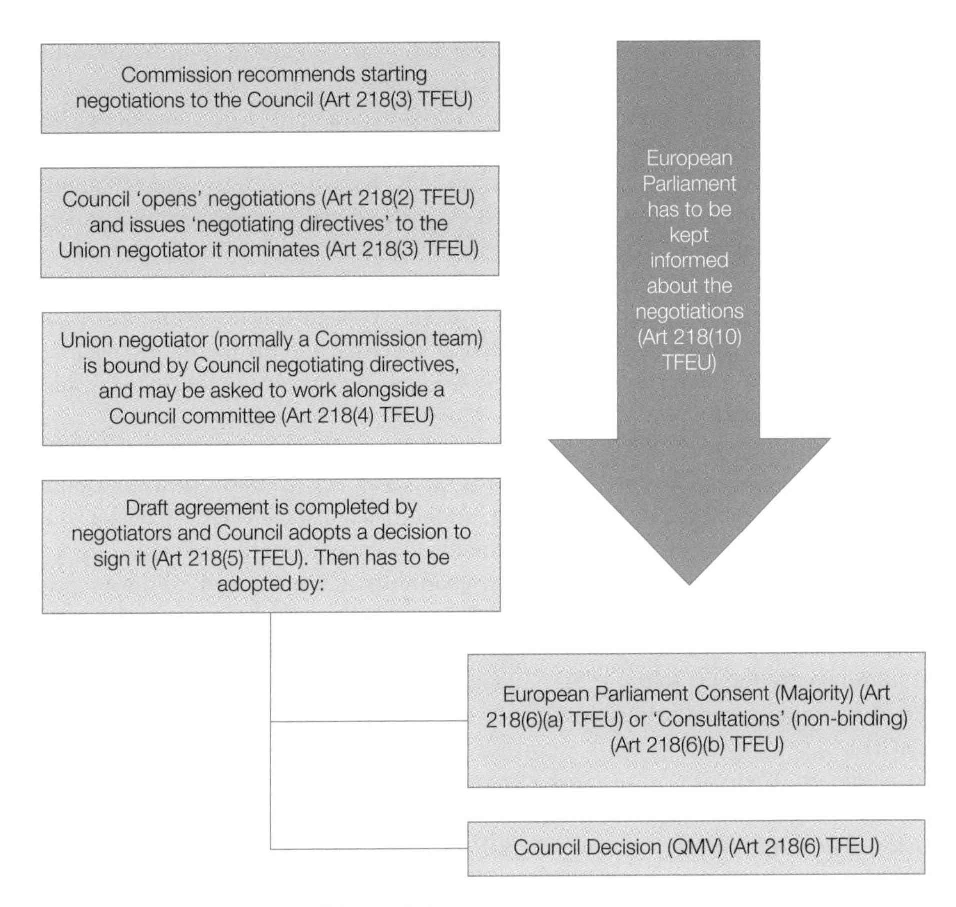

Figure 16.1 The Article 218 TFEU negotiating process

As is the case with internal legislating, the bulk of the 'treaty drafting' work is in practice conducted by the Commission. However, Article 218 TFEU is very explicit about the actual decision-making power and direction of travel of these negotiations being down to the Council—thus leaving the overall shape of the EU's external relations in the hands of Member State representatives.

The Treaty itself is not explicit about whom the Council can choose to send as a negotiating team. As was the case for the Article 50 TEU process,[21] it is ordinarily the Commission that engages in the negotiations—but the European Parliament has pushed for inclusion of MEPs as observers of the negotiations, so as to further bolster its oversight role in international relations.[22] This role is given teeth by the fact that, as of the Lisbon Treaty, Article 218(6) TFEU gives the European Parliament a veto over already-negotiated

[21] See Chapter 2.

[22] See Framework Agreement on relations between the European Parliament and the European Commission [2010] OJ L304/47, as amended.

treaties; and those teeth have been used by the European Parliament to push for further involvement in the treaty-negotiating process over time.[23]

As such, Article 218(10) TFEU also gives the Parliament a right to be 'immediately and fully informed' at all stages of the negotiation. These 'information rights' have been contentious, particularly between the Council and the Parliament, with the Council arguing that many confidential matters are discussed over the course of treaty negotiations, and the Parliament demanding insight into these regardless. The current inter-institutional agreement that sets out how the European Parliament and the Commission cooperate—known as a 'framework agreement'[24]—makes it very explicit that the European Parliament's 'information rights' also cover confidential material, and the European Parliament has successfully enforced its rights against the Council a number of times since the adoption of the Lisbon Treaty.

As for the voting procedures for adopting international agreements, the general rule is that the European Parliament has to offer simple majority 'consent', and the Council takes decisions by qualified majority voting, under Article 218(8) TFEU. There are, however, exceptions; where international agreements are concluded in areas where internal legislation would require Council unanimity, unanimity is also required for the adoption of international agreements. Key examples of 'unanimity' agreements identified in Article 218(8) TFEU are accession agreements, for countries wishing to join the EU, and the eventual joining up of the EU to the ECHR. The latter is treated as so sensitive by Article 218 TFEU that it *also* requires ratification by all the Member States before the EU can 'join' the ECHR.

In summary, therefore, prior to the Lisbon Treaty there were two 'formal' actors involved in international agreement negotiations in the EU: the Council and the Commission. The European Parliament has pushed for a greater role, and has exercised its veto over international agreements repeatedly since the adoption of the Lisbon Treaty, changing the balance of power between the EU institutions substantially in external relations as a consequence.[25] Now, the Commission and the Council will seek out European Parliament opinion as early as possible, and attempt to incorporate it, so as to avoid a veto of an already 'agreed' text after several years of negotiating with a third party.[26] External relations, in short, are starting to look more and more like the internal relations between the EU institutions: this is particularly emphasized by the fact that European Parliament 'consent' is required for *all* agreements adopted in fields of EU competence that are internally covered by the ordinary legislative procedure.[27] Any detailed agreement concluded between the UK and the EU, in other words, is likely to be subject to a European Parliament 'veto'; and as such, awareness of the European Parliament's positions on key issues in the negotiations will be essential for the UK to adopt a realistic negotiating position.

[23] For a detailed discussion, see Christina Eckes, 'How the European Parliament's Participation in International Relations Affects the Deep Tissue of the EU's Power Structures' (2015) 12(4) I-CON 904.

[24] Framework Agreement (n 22). [25] See Eckes (n 23). [26] Ibid.

[27] Article 218(6)(v) TFEU.

Discussing the quote

Consider the number of steps and EU actors involved in the Article 218 TFEU procedure. What does this suggest about how 'rapidly' trade or other international agreements can be concluded?

16.4.2 Negotiating CCP Agreements

When commentators discuss the 'future relationship', they are by and large referring to the fact that the UK and the EU will need a free trade agreement to replace internal market membership. If this free trade agreement is negotiated as a separate agreement from say, the 'security' relationship alluded to in the Political Declaration, the EU will be following the Common Commercial Policy agreement process set out in Article 207 TFEU.

As Article 207(3) TFEU makes clear, trade agreements are concluded by and large according to the process set out in Article 218 TFEU. However, the remainder of Article 207 TFEU sets out a few special rules for those agreements that touch upon CCP. The third paragraph of Article 207(3) TFEU thus stresses that there *will* be a special committee appointed by the Council to oversee CCP negotiations, where such a committee is optional under Article 218 TFEU.

The Council voting rules for CCP agreements are generally qualified majority, but there are again exceptions, set out in Article 207(4) TFEU. These cover the 'latest' additions to exclusive CCP competences, and so agreements that cover trade in services and intellectual property require Council unanimity insofar as internal voting procedures would do so as well. Further singled out for Council unanimity are agreements covering 'cultural and audiovisual services' where there is a risk that these hamper 'cultural and linguistic diversity'. Unanimity is also required for those agreements that risk disrupting national social, educational, and health services. These two latter policy areas are ones where the EU internally only has a 'supporting' competence, and so it makes sense that they are singled out for more rigorous Council control.

16.4.3 Negotiating CFSP agreements

Of course, the 'future relationship' between the UK and the EU is intended to also encompass a 'security' agreement that touches upon foreign policy and defence—and here, the EU is bound by the rules set out in the Treaties on the CFSP.

We saw in Section 16.3 that CFSP remains a policy area treated 'differently' under EU law, and this is also reflected in the process relating to the negotiation and conclusion of CFSP agreements. First, here, the High Representative rather than the Commission has the exclusive power to recommend the opening of negotiations. A consequence of this distinction is that it is also unlikely that the Commission will be 'in charge' of EU negotiations in the CFSP domain, with such a role more likely to be reserved for the High Commissioner as well.

CFSP agreements are also the agreements where the power of the European Parliament remains the most limited. As the Parliament has no role in the adoption of internal CFSP decisions, it also has no power of 'consent' over CFSP external agreements.[28] Article 218(6) TFEU further makes clear that European Parliament does not even have to be *consulted* on CFSP agreements—which is the 'backup' to the 'consent' power it has regarding international agreements in all other policy areas. CFSP decision-making thus remains firmly in the hands of the Council, with the role of the Commission and the European Parliament very much minimized throughout the process.

Pause for reflection

Which of the 'partnerships' the UK wishes to pursue do you think will be most difficult to find agreement on, in light of the EU's institutional organization during the negotiations?

16.4.4 On competences: negotiating 'mixed' agreements

The Political Declaration sets out a number of goals, covering an agreement in free trade but also a variety of 'other' agreements. Section 16.3 showed that while CCP is an EU exclusive competence, many other policy areas flagged up in the Political Declaration are ones that fall within the 'shared' competence category. This, as a consequence, means that many treaties are concluded in policy areas where both the EU and the Member States have treaty-making powers. Such treaties are likely to have both the EU (as an institution) *and* the Member States as signatories—they cover issues where neither the Member States nor the EU have exclusive powers, and so participation of both the Member States and the EU (as legal actors) is required. These types of agreements are known as 'mixed' agreements.

The determination of whether an agreement is 'mixed' is not an easy matter, and is regularly contested by the Member States and the European Parliament in situations where the EU believes it has an exclusive competence.[29] The consequence of a finding of 'mixity' is not generally felt until the negotiating process has been concluded. In any event, for the purposes of negotiating mixed agreements, Member States do not normally alter the general process set out by Article 218 TFEU. Negotiations will be carried out by EU institutions, with the Member States providing oversight and steer via the Council and any special committees set up.

However, in terms of ratifying an agreement, 'mixity' presents a rather distinct problem, in that the EU *alone* cannot adopt a mixed agreement. Any agreement with 'mixed' content, therefore, needs both to follow the Article 218 TFEU process of ratification, and also be ratified in line with national constitutional practices in every single one of the Member States. It is through this latter requirement that years of negotiations over a free trade agreement with Canada almost fell apart: Wallonia, as one of the two federal

[28] Article 218(6) TFEU.

[29] See, eg, the pushback against the Commission's intention to declare CETA an EU-exclusive agreement; for a useful summary, see Tobias Dolle and Bruno G. Simões, 'Mixed Feelings about "Mixed Agreements" and CETA's Provisional Application' (2013) 7(3) EJRR 617.

components of Belgium, voted against the adoption of the Comprehensive Economic and Trade Agreement (CETA) in the first instance, until certain concessions were negotiated.[30] There are as such even more hurdles to overcome in signing a 'mixed agreement' than in any other type of agreement, and negotiations are likely to take longer as a consequence. Given that the transition period under the Withdrawal Agreement is intended to finish by December 2020, and the EU and the UK embarked on the 'future relationship' negotiations only in March 2020, the prospect of any agreements negotiating being 'mixed' is consequently a worrying one.

Pause for reflection

How likely do you think it is that either the economic or security partnership sought by the UK and the EU will result in a 'mixed' agreement? Does this change your answer as to which agreement will be most difficult to conclude?

16.4.5 The role of the CJEU

This heading is not meant to suggest that the Court of Justice plays an active role in Treaty negotiations, as it does not. Instead, Article 218 TFEU expressly acknowledges its role as the sole interpreter of the Treaties, and gives it a very specific and binding 'advisory' function in external relations. Article 218(11) TFEU consequently makes clear that a Member State or any of the three EU legislating institutions can request a so-called 'opinion' from the CJEU on whether an international agreement is compatible with the Treaties.

We encountered two such opinions already when we considered fundamental rights in Chapter 9—and both, in fact, were 'adverse' opinions that resulted in the EU being precluded from signing up to the ECHR. In 1994, they found in *Opinion 2/94* that the EU did not have the competence to sign up to the ECHR; whereas in 2013, in *Opinion 2/13*, the CJEU found that the overlapping jurisdictions between the ECtHR and the CJEU were incompatible with the EU Treaties and legal order.[31]

The 'accession to the ECHR' agreements are not the only international agreements that the CJEU has declared incompatible with EU law on that latter ground, however. Back in 1991, the original EEA Agreement proposed the establishment of an 'EEA Court' to oversee disputes about the EU law that would apply to EEA signatories who were not EU Member States. This may seem logical, but the CJEU rejected the formation of a 'competing' Court with a similar jurisdiction to itself on the grounds of the 'autonomy of EU law' in *Opinion 1/91*.[32] Autonomy, it ruled, meant that only *it* could offer binding interpretations of EU law, and the EU legal system would cease to work if alternative bodies had similar powers. A more limited role without such binding powers to interpret provisions of EU law for the 'EFTA Court' was required for the CJEU to offer a positive opinion of the EEA Agreement, which it then did issue in *Opinion 1/92*.[33] It has held steadfast to this

[30] See https://www.bbc.co.uk/news/world-europe-37749236.

[31] *Opinion 2/94* ECLI:EU:C:1996:140 and *Opinion 2/13* ECLI:EU:C:2014:2454.

[32] *Opinion 1/91* ECLI:EU:C:1991:490, paras 35–36.

[33] *Opinion 1/92* ECLI:EU:C:1992:189.

requirement for the 'autonomy' of the EU legal system, making the conclusion of other international agreements and their dispute settlement systems rather more complicated, as we shall see in the next section.[34]

Discussing the quote

Do you think it is likely that any agreement between the UK and the EU that reflects the goals set out in the Political Declaration will be concluded 'very rapidly indeed'? Why or why not?

16.5 Governance of the EU's international agreements

The Treaties are fairly silent on how the EU is meant to manage and enforce the international agreements it concludes. Short of the requirement that they be compatible with EU law, and how the CJEU has interpreted such 'compatibility', the EU and its negotiating third-country (or organization) partner are free to set up both the overall 'governance' (as in management) of an international agreement and its 'dispute settlement' (as in enforcement) how they see fit.

This section will offer a few examples of what the governance provisions in concluded EU agreements look like, so as to consider to what extent the proposals in the Political Declaration are distinct or 'standard'.

16.5.1 'Management' of concluded agreements

The majority of international agreements, no matter how expansive in scope, will be governed by a combination of political high-level oversight bodies *and* 'day to day' management bodies. The Political Declaration makes clear that the UK and the EU anticipate those types of bodies: Part IV sketches out that both parties seek to enable dialogue at a number of political 'levels', and that a so-called 'Joint Committee' will manage and supervise the 'implementation and operation of the future relationship'.[35] However, it does not include any particular detail on how either the high-level 'political' meetings or the Joint Committee are intended to work. It is therefore instructive to look at how existing EU agreements are institutionally managed; we will consider the EEA Agreement, the Ukraine–EU Association Agreement, and Canada's CETA as relevant examples that might, in some way, reflect aspects of the future UK–EU relationship.

The EEA

An example of a very expansive international agreement is the EEA Agreement concluded between the European Free Trade Association (EFTA) countries and the EU in 1991.[36] As discussed in Chapter 1, the EEA Agreement is a compromise struck between the EU and

[34] See, very recently, Case C-284/16 *Achmea* ECLI:EU:C:2018:158, discussed later.

[35] Political Declaration, paras 122–127.

[36] Agreement on the European Economic Area [1994] OJ L1/3.

those European countries that were not interested in a 'political' union, but did seek very deep trade integration. In short, then, the EEA provides for single market membership, but does not cover external trade policy of any of the EEA non-EU States that are signatories.

Several institutions are set up under the EEA Agreement. In terms of overall political 'steer' for the EEA Agreement, it establishes the EEA Council, which meets biannually and sets down guidelines for the 'day to day' management body, the Joint Committee.[37]

The Joint Committee is made up of 'representatives of the Contracting Parties', which in practice means the Commission and representatives from the EFTA states.[38] Article 92 EEA makes it responsible for securing the 'effective operation and implementation of the Agreement', and gives it a specific power to ensure that EEA law stays 'in line' with its EU equivalent where EU law is amended. Decisions on these issues of amending EEA law are to be taken with 'one voice', meaning unanimity—but in practice, this is unlikely to amount to a 'veto power' for any of the EFTA states, as a lack of agreement is more likely to lead to a suspension of the EEA Agreement within a period of six months.[39] Political pressure consequently results in generally swift and unanimous decision-making before the Joint Council.

A final body set up by the EEA Agreement is the EEA Joint Parliamentary Committee.[40] It facilitates exchanges between MEPs and parliamentarians from the EFTA states. It can make non-binding resolutions and issue reports so as to indicate parliamentary opinion of the EEA Agreement's functioning—but it has no binding decision-making or oversight powers.

The EU–Ukraine Association Agreement

As discussed in Section 16.3, the possibility of concluding association agreements has existed under the Treaties for a long time. The most recent and perhaps most expansive example of the association agreement 'structure' being used dates from 2014, when the EU signed an association agreement with Ukraine. The EU–Ukraine Association Agreement, which will be used as the example of an association agreement, is thus composed of a so-called 'Deep and Comprehensive Free Trade Agreement' (DCFTA), but also contains provisions on 'political dialogue' and 'cooperation in fields of mutual interest'. The latter two areas go beyond economic policy.

The EU–Ukraine Association Agreement is governed through four bodies:

- the Summit
- the Association Council
- the Association Committee
- a Parliamentary Association Committee.

The 'Summit' is a high-level political meeting that takes place once a year, and much in the way the European Council does for the EU, it sets general guidance on the implementation of the association agreement.[41] One level lower, more similar to the EEA Joint Committee, the Association Council meets more regularly; it is comprised of ministers of both Ukraine and the EU Member States, as well as members of the Commission, and supervises and monitors the application and implementation of the agreement.[42] The Association

[37] Article 90(1) EEA. [38] Article 89(1) EEA. [39] Articles 93(2) and 102(3) EEA.
[40] Article 95(4) EEA. [41] EU–Ukraine Association Agreement, Article 460.
[42] Ibid, Articles 461(2) and 462(1).

Committee, composed of civil servants from both the EU and Ukraine, assists the Council with these supervisory and monitoring duties.[43] Finally, the Parliamentary Association Committee formally arranges for the European Parliament and the Ukrainian Parliament to meet and exchange views, and, uniquely, can also request information from the Association Council on the functioning of the association agreement.[44]

The Association Council and Committee have decision-making powers under the Agreement, where the other two bodies do not. The Association Council can thus both take binding decisions and make recommendations relating to the agreement, and can amend the annexes (citing EU law) where necessary, much as the EEA Joint Committee can.[45] The Association Committee does not have distinct stand-alone powers, but *any* of the Association Council's powers can be delegated to it.[46]

CETA

The EU–Canada Free Trade Agreement, known as the 'Comprehensive Economic and Trade Agreement' (CETA), was concluded in 2017 and marked one of the EU's most ambitious 'free trade agreements' concluded to date.

In terms of its coverage, it deals with trade matters, and substantially liberalizes trade in goods, but makes only limited commitments regarding the more sensitive area of services. It also addresses issues of competition, protection of intellectual property, and the conditions under which government contracts are concluded within either jurisdiction. Finally, and moving slightly beyond the area of pure 'trade', it also contains provisions that work as 'level playing field' safeguards on labour and environmental law issues, committing both signatories to maintaining a certain standard of labour and environmental protections.

Compared to the EU–Ukraine Association Agreement and the EEA, the CETA institutional structure looks very limited. The agreement establishes a Joint Committee, but no further bodies to deal with either management or enforcement.[47] The Joint Committee takes its decisions by agreement (so unanimously) and can take binding decisions where CETA sets out that it can—but these instances are very limited. The most interesting power held by the Joint Committee is its power to adopt binding interpretations of the provisions of CETA. These interpretations are then binding on any of the bodies involved in dispute settlement under CETA, which is considered in Section 16.5.2.

16.5.2 'Enforcement' of concluded agreements

In light of the fact that all State parties to international agreements are sovereign, it is not immediately obvious that they *can* be taken to any type of 'court' if disputes about those agreements arise and they do not wish to go to court. As a matter of practice, in fact, most states reject involvement of 'courts' when it comes to dispute resolution regarding international agreements—and instead make specific provisions *in* the agreements themselves to set up how disputes are to be resolved, and what happens when a party simply refuses to fall back in line, having been found to breach the agreement. Bodies like the Commission, as a standing 'monitor' of compliance, are unusual in international agreements; instead, the 'policing' tends to be done by the representatives of the states party to the agreement.

[43] Ibid, Article 464. [44] Ibid, Articles 467(1) and 468. [45] Ibid, Article 436(1).
[46] Ibid, Article 466(4). [47] CETA, Article 26.

The Political Declaration sketches out a two-strand dispute resolution system in very general terms: first, the parties are to attempt to resolve disputes through consultation via the Joint Committee. If that fails, either party can refer a disagreement or a dispute to an independent arbitral panel, which will take a binding decision. If a concept of EU law arises in the dispute, the parties agreed in the Political Declaration that the arbitration panels have to refer questions about that concept to the CJEU—as a form of 'international preliminary reference'. The CJEU will offer an interpretation that is binding on the arbitration panel, which will then proceed to decide the dispute. Where an arbitration panel's decision is ignored, the Political Declaration makes clear that 'the future relationship will . . . set out the conditions under which temporary remedies in case of non-compliance can be taken', but again, does not contain any particular detail on how these remedies are to operate.[48] It is therefore helpful to consider what precedents exist for the enforcement of the EU's international agreements, as the UK and the EU may wish to copy aspects of these 'models' as an example.

The EEA

The primary enforcers of the EEA Agreement are the EFTA Surveillance Authority and the EFTA Court. In many ways, these act as 'mirrors' of the Commission and the EU Court of Justice, albeit with more limited powers.[49]

The Surveillance Authority effectively polices the EFTA states in the EEA on their compliance with EU law, and also enforces EEA competition law against them. Its most important role is referring non-compliant EFTA states to the EFTA Court of Justice, especially as (unlike the Commission) it has no further powers that are unrelated to enforcement.[50]

The EFTA Court has powers *similar* to the Court of Justice, but within the constraints of *Opinion 1/91*. It thus deals with infringement proceedings brought by the EFTA Surveillance Authority, as well as actions brought by one EFTA state in the EEA regarding another EFTA state in the EEA.[51] It does not, however, have the power to fine EFTA states for non-compliance with their EEA obligations. The EEA Agreement also enables national courts in the EFTA states to seek preliminary references from the EFTA Court, but unlike in the case of the CJEU, these are not binding on the Member States—largely because binding interpretations from another court would infringe upon the CJEU's autonomy, as discussed in Section 16.4.5.[52]

In practice, EFTA Court decisions are normally followed much in the way that CJEU judgments are, and so the more 'limited' role of the EEA institutions in terms of how much they impose on the EFTA States is perhaps more symbolic than practically significant.[53]

The Ukraine–EU Association Agreement

The Ukraine–EU Association Agreement establishes a more or less 'standard' two-tier dispute resolution mechanism, but also contains unique enforcement powers.

[48] Political Declaration, paras 129–132.

[49] See the Agreement between the EFTA States on the establishment of a Surveillance Authority and Court of Justice [1994] L344/3.

[50] Ibid, Articles 7–9, 31. [51] Ibid, Articles 31–32. [52] Ibid, Article 34.

[53] See Thomas Burri and Benedikt Pirker, 'Constitutionalization by Association? The Doubtful Case of the European Economic Area' (2013) 32 YEL 207.

On enforcement, Article 475 effectively gives the Association Council substantial power to monitor the extent to which Ukraine is complying with its obligations under the Association Agreement. These powers are so far-reaching that, under Article 475(2), they even permit 'missions' onto Ukrainian territory to police the extent to which Ukraine is meeting the goals set out under the association agreement. This is unprecedented, and has not to date been exercised, not least of all because, despite its legal possibility, this would be a politically *very* sensitive move for the EU to insist on making.

The Association Agreement's provisions on dispute settlement make clear that any disputes about the agreement in *general* are to be resolved within the Association Council.[54] Where agreement cannot be reached there, a suspension of obligations under any part of the Agreement except the DCFTA is the recourse permitted by the agreement.[55]

Where there is a dispute regarding either party's compliance with the DCFTA, the normal procedure to be followed has two distinct steps. The first step to dispute resolution is consultations (or meetings) between the parties, seeking a resolution through conversation. Where consultation fails, binding arbitration is the second level of dispute settlement arranged for in the Association Agreement.[56] The arbitrators are to be independent of both parties, and where the 'losing' party fails to comply with an arbitral panel's ruling, a further arbitration panel can be set up to permit temporary suspensions of obligations under the DCFTA or the payment of compensation for non-compliance with the arbitral decision.

An alternative to this two-step process is mediation, which the DCFTA also permits as a separate problem-solving mechanism.[57]

None of the enforcement or dispute resolution mechanisms described here involve the EU bodies, or indeed, any other type of formal 'court'. However, in order to comply with the CJEU's demands for the 'autonomy of EU law', the arbitral panels are required to request CJEU interpretations of any EU law provisions that arise in disputes between the parties.[58] This *interpretation* of the meaning of the relevant EU law at stake in the dispute is as binding on the arbitration panel as a preliminary reference ruling is on a Member State.[59] As such, while EU institutional involvement in dispute management under the EU–Ukraine Association Agreement is minimal, there is nonetheless a mechanism at work that ensures that EU law will remain consistently interpreted throughout the EU's internal and external relations.

CETA

There are no specific provisions in CETA that discuss enforcement. Where there are enforcement issues, the parties are almost inevitably going to end up in dispute resolution, rather than there being a separate body to oversee and remedy enforcement issues.

CETA's general dispute settlement mechanisms are not dissimilar from those of the EU–Ukraine Association Agreement. Consultation is the first step suggested by the Treaty.[60] Where it fails regarding disputes on trade and investment, the parties may seek out mediation; or, otherwise, the complainant can pursue binding arbitration, which works in an

[54] EU–Ukraine Association Agreement, Article 477. [55] Ibid, Article 478.
[56] Ibid, Articles 303–321. [57] Ibid, Articles 327–336. [58] Ibid, Article 322(2).
[59] See Chapter 7. [60] CETA, Article 29.4.

identical fashion to EU–Ukraine arbitration.[61] A failure to comply with an arbitral ruling justifies countermeasures taken by the complainant, until compliance is achieved.

A separate dispute settlement process is set out regarding the commitments in CETA to protect labour and environmental standards and laws. Here, consultation is once again the first step of dispute resolution, but instead of it leading to mediation or arbitration, it instead leads to the convening of a Panel of Experts. Such a panel will be composed of either labour lawyers or environmental lawyers, and it will provide a report on the dispute.[62] While this report is not binding, it will be made public and as such will exert significant pressure on the parties to seek resolution according to its recommendations.

Finally, and controversially, CETA contains provisions that permit foreign investors from either the EU or Canada to sue the other signatory party for compensation on the grounds that it has failed to comply with its CETA obligations.[63] These claims are to be first addressed through consultations, but where this fails, within six months they can be brought before a CETA-created Investment Tribunal. Any Investment Tribunal decision can be appealed before an Appellate Tribunal.

The investor-state dispute settlement (ISDS) mechanism included in CETA has been widely criticized, largely because its inclusion in CETA gives significantly more rights to foreign investors than to any other (and non-foreign) party affected by state decisions in the realm of CETA. Canadian companies who are investing in Canada have to instead pursue their claims in domestic courts, which may or may not offer the same remedies as the Investment Tribunal would regarding a claim. More generally, and less a criticism of the CETA system itself, the very idea of a foreign investor being able to sue a state for taking decisions in their own territory that somehow harm this investor is likely to have repercussions on the types of policies states are willing to adopt. As such, ISDS in general has come under significant criticism since its inception, and it is not immediately obvious that future EU agreements will provide the same scope for it as CETA does.[64]

CETA, unlike the other two international agreements discussed here, contains absolutely no role for any of the EU institutions, including the CJEU. This is because as an agreement, CETA does not refer to concepts of EU law. The general observation we can therefore make about the EU's external relations is that the closer the relationship a third country is seeking with the EU, and the more aspects of EU law it involves, the more likely that third country is to run into the EU institutions (or, at least, institutions that act very much *like* the EU institutions).

Table 16.2 summarizes the existing governance structures in EU international agreements.

[61] Ibid, Articles 29.5–29.6.

[62] Ibid, Articles 23–24. [63] Ibid, Articles 8.18–8.23.

[64] Of note here is the CJEU's Case C-284/16 *Achmea* ECLI:EU:C:2018:158 judgment, which declared investor-state arbitration *between* EU Member States and investors from other Member States as contrary to the Treaties. In response to the judgment, 22 of the 28 Member States signed a political declaration that committed to terminating all bilateral investment treaties by the end of 2019, thus eliminating the possibility for further intra-EU ISDS. See https://ec.europa.eu/info/sites/info/files/business_economy_euro/banking_and_finance/documents/190117-bilateral-investment-treaties_en.pdf.

TABLE 16.2 Existing governance structures in EU international agreements

	The EEA Agreement	**EU–Ukraine Association Agreement**	**CETA**
Institutions: High-Level	EEA Council (general policy direction, no binding decision-making powers)	The Summit (general policy direction, no binding decision-making powers)	n/a
Institutions: Day-to-Day Management	Joint Committee (takes binding decisions unanimously)	Association Council (takes binding decisions); Association Committee (assists Association Council)	Joint Committee (takes binding decisions unanimously in limited circumstances)
Institutions: Inter-Parliamentary Cooperation	Joint Parliamentary Committee (no binding decision-making powers)	Parliamentary Association Committee (no binding decision-making powers)	n/a
Dispute Settlement Processes: Stage 1	EFTA Surveillance Authority (administrative process/investigation)	Consultations in the Association Council	Consultation in the Joint Committee
Dispute Settlement Processes: Stage 2	EFTA Court Rulings (enforcing the EEA Agreement against EFTA Member States, formally non-binding but in practice followed)	Under the DCFTA: Arbitration (binding) or Mediation (binding) Where disputes involve EU law, **arbitrators are required to ask for CJEU interpretations of that EU law.**	Arbitration (binding) *Or* Panel of Experts Report on social and environmental 'level playing field' standards (non-binding) *Or* Investment Tribunal (and Appellate Tribunal) for ISDS (binding)

Pause for reflection

Bearing in mind the Political Declaration, which of the three models set out in Table 16.2 do you think will be most acceptable to the UK, in light of its desire to regain sovereignty after Brexit? Which do you think will be least acceptable? And what does your answer suggest about the nature of the future relationship between the UK and the EU: will it be rather shallow, or very deep?

16.6 In conclusion

We are in full speculation mode when we consider the shape and content of the future EU–UK agreement; the Political Declaration says very little about the specifics that will be pursued. However, just on the basis of examining what the EU can and cannot do, and how it can do it, regarding international agreements, we can come to several observations about the direction of travel of these next Brexit negotiations.

The October 2019 Political Declaration seems to take a step back from desiring an 'association agreement', though it of course remains a possible framework in which the two separate aspirational partnerships are concluded.[65] What is clear is that the UK will want to conclude a free trade agreement, and, as such, the Article 218 TFEU process (as amended by Article 207 TFEU) will be seen again. What is also highly likely, given the number of 'non-economic' cooperation areas that are flagged up under the security partnership, is that the UK and the EU will be negotiating separately in the area of the CFSP, and that that 'security' relationship in particular is likely to cross over into the territory of a 'mixed' agreement.

What, then, is the UK facing? It will need agreement to its proposals by the Council; the Commission negotiators and the High Representative; the European Parliament, especially where the economic dimension is negotiated, but also regarding certain aspects of justice cooperation; and, where any demands do not touch *only* upon EU competences, all 27 of the Member States, including their federal parliaments where necessary.

In general terms, at the time of writing, this seems impossible by the end of 2020, which is the default 'end date' of the Withdrawal Agreement's transition period.[66] Should the negotiations have to continue *after* the transition period ends, they will not be swifter, and finding agreement amongst so many different stakeholders is likely to take years, not months, however identical the rules applying in the UK and the EU at the time of 'Brexit' are.

Indeed, some of the most contentious decision-making will be about how this future relationship will be managed and enforced, which can only be determined when a clearer picture develops of just how 'close' the UK and the EU will be in the future. The May government's Political Declaration made it clear that the UK, at the time, sought to 'join' a number of existing EU programmes, and was willing to adopt EU law as necessary to

[65] All references to a 'free trade area' have been replaced with 'free trade agreement', for example.

[66] Withdrawal Agreement, Articles 126 and 132; note that the EU (Withdrawal Agreement) Act 2020, s 33, prohibits UK representatives from asking for an extension as a matter of domestic law—though as is true for all Acts of Parliament, this can obviously be amended if an extension is desired after all.

participate in those—but the final Political Declaration does not make this nearly as clear. All the same, the Johnson government has expressed an interest in the continuance of certain EU programmes, such as the Erasmus student exchange; will it be willing to have the UK follow aspects of EU law in order to make participation in the programmes feasible, or not? Will future CJEU involvement in the interpretation of relevant EU law in a future relationship agreement actually be acceptable to the UK when the extent of that relationship becomes clearer, or not?

If the oversight and management of the desired 'security partnership' set out in the Political Declaration become contentious in this way, its successful and swift conclusion looks hazier than the conclusion of a trade agreement does. But even the conclusion of a trade agreement may run into a great number of hurdles in light of the EU's demands.

On the subject of the EU's demands, a particular aspect of the Political Declaration to draw attention to is the provision contained in paragraph 77:

October 2019 Political Declaration, para 77 (emphasis added)

Given the Union and the United Kingdom's geographic proximity and economic interdependence, **the future relationship must ensure open and fair competition, encompassing robust commitments to ensure a level playing field**. The precise nature of commitments should be commensurate with the scope and depth of the future relationship and the economic connectedness of the Parties. **These commitments should prevent distortions of trade and unfair competitive advantages**. To that end, **the Parties should uphold the common high standards applicable in the Union and the United Kingdom at the end of the transition period** in the areas of **state aid, competition, social and employment standards, environment, climate change, and relevant tax matters**. The Parties should in particular maintain a robust and comprehensive framework for competition and state aid control that prevents undue distortion of trade and competition; commit to the principles of good governance in the area of taxation and to the curbing of harmful tax practices; and maintain environmental, social and employment standards at the current high levels provided by the existing common standards. **In so doing, they should rely on appropriate and relevant Union and international standards, and include appropriate mechanisms to ensure effective implementation domestically, enforcement and dispute settlement**. The future relationship should also promote adherence to and effective implementation of relevant internationally agreed principles and rules in these domains, including the Paris Agreement.

Paragraph 77, on the 'level playing field', is not new to the October 2019 Political Declaration—but its importance there *has* been amplified. Under the November 2018 Withdrawal Agreement negotiated by the May government, there were commitments to a 'level playing field' both in the Withdrawal Agreement (and particularly the 'backstop' designed for Northern Ireland) and in the Political Declaration. The changes to the Protocol discussed in Chapters 10 and 11, whereby the UK as a whole is no longer in the EU's customs union under the Protocol, have meant that the 'level playing field' is now solely committed to as a 'goal for the future relationship'.

Nonetheless, it is a *key* part of the otherwise very general commitments made in the Political Declaration. The EU will do what it can to leverage closeness of relationship, in whatever area the UK seeks it, with commitments to non-regression in policy areas like competition law, employment law, environmental law, and even taxation. The UK, simultaneously, will want to avoid those commitments where it feels that it will gain an advantage out of 'lowering' standards—for the sake of lowering 'red tape', as discussed in Chapter 10. If the EU remains firm on the 'level playing field', divergence from key areas of EU law will become impossible if a deal is achieved; and that then raises questions as to whether any of the assumed benefits of Brexit can actually materialize.

Arguably, the outcome furthest away from what the UK is looking for would be to lose representation in the EU institutions without actually 'taking back control' and developing an independent economic and trade policy out of new, UK-specific regulations.[67] So, if neither party moves on the 'level playing field' during the negotiations, we may find ourselves facing yet another 'cliff edge' at the end of the transition period. In this scenario, Citizens' Rights will be mostly preserved, as we saw in Chapters 12 and 13, and Northern Ireland will avoid a land border—but it is difficult to anticipate the situation the remainder of the UK will be in.

So as to not end on too pessimistic a note, the UK can and should take some comfort from the fact that—as this chapter has shown—the EU has concluded many international agreements spanning very many fields over the course of its existence, and so where political compromise proves possible, legal agreement absolutely is. Whether that political compromise and legal agreement will be found 'very rapidly indeed' between the UK and the EU, however, is much harder to state with any certainty at all.

Key points

- The EU's **external competences** by and large mirror the EU's **internal competences**, and as such are a mixture of **shared** and **exclusive.** Negotiations between the UK and the EU on the 'future relationship' will thus touch upon both shared and exclusive competences.
- The primary actors in concluding international agreements on behalf of the EU are the **Council** and the **Commission,** though the **European Parliament's** role is now substantial in agreements that cover policy areas such as trade. To successfully conclude a 'future relationship', both the UK and the EU will need to keep the European Parliament 'on side' during the negotiations, which will limit the room to manoeuvre the negotiators have.
- The 'closer' a relationship the EU forms with an external actor, the more likely it will be that both **EU law** and **EU institutions** play a role in overseeing that relationship once it is formalized in an agreement. That said, the Political Declaration suggests that the UK and the EU have agreed that the CJEU will retain its ***interpretative*** role over EU law, but will hold no other role in the 'future relationship'. If this remains the case, the UK's 'future relationship' with the EU will by default be distant—more akin to 'Canada' than to what the Ukraine or the EEA countries have agreed.
- Given the likelihood of the **mixed** nature of the future relationship agreements between the UK and the EU, **it is likely they will need to be ratified by the Council, the European Parliament, and all of the EU Member States**.

[67] Indeed, in January 2020 the Chancellor, Sajid Javid, promised that the UK would diverge from EU regulatory standards, albeit in very general terms that did not distinguish between product standards and social and environmental standards or state aid/competition rules, as discussed in Chapter 10. See https://www.ft.com/content/18ddc610-3940-11ea-a6d3-9a26f8c3cba4.

Assess your learning

1. **What are the EU's exclusive competences in external relations? (See Section 16.3.)**
2. **Will the European Parliament be able to 'veto' the future relationship negotiated by the UK? (See Section 16.4.)**
3. **When does it become necessary for the CJEU to be involved in the enforcement and supervision of EU international agreements? (See Sections 16.4–16.5.)**

Further reading

Mark Clough, 'Potential Changes to the UK's International Trade Law Framework if it Leaves the EU' (2019) 25(3) Int TLR 141.

Christina Eckes, 'How the European Parliament's Participation in International Relations Affects the Deep Tissue of the EU's Power Structures' (2015) 12(4) I-CON 904.

Mauro Gatti and Pietro Manzini, 'External Representation of the European Union in the Conclusion of International Agreements' (2012) 49(5) CMLRev 1703.

Panos Koutrakos, 'Institutional Balance and Sincere Cooperation in Treaty-Making under EU Law' (2019) 68(1) ICLQ 1.

Adam Lazowski, 'Withdrawal from the European Union and Alternatives to Membership' (2012) 37(5) ELRev 523.

Emily Lydgate and Alan Winters, 'Deep and Not Comprehensive? What the WTO rules permit for a UK-EU FTA' (2019) 18(3) World TR 451.

Billy Melo Araujo, 'UK Post-Brexit Trade Agreements and Devolution' (2019) 39(4) Legal Studies 555.

Christian Riffel, 'Squaring the Circle: High-quality, deep FTAs with Australia and New Zealand without the EU Member States' approval?' (2019) 44(5) ELRev 694.

Fiona Smith, 'Brexit as Trade Governance' (2019) 20(5) JWIT 654.

Christopher Vajda, 'The EU and Beyond: Dispute resolution in international economic agreements' (2018) 29(1) EJIL 205.

Online resources

Visit www.oup.com/he/demars1e for a sample approach to discussing the quote.

Index